Fire and Blood

MEXICO
Revolutionary Period: 1910–1920

Los Angeles
San Diego
Tijuana
Mexicali
Santa Fe
UNITED
El Paso
Ciudad Juarez
Nogales
SONORA
CHIHUAHUA
COAH
Hermosillo
Chihuahua
BAJA CALIFORNIA NORTE
GULF OF CALIFORNIA
BAJA CALIFORNIA SUR
La Paz
Culiacan
SINALOA
DURANGO
Durango
Torreon
Mazatlan
ZACATECAS
Zacatecas
NAYARIT
AGUASCALIENT
Aguascalientes
San Blas
Tepic
Guadalajara
JALISCO
Colima
Apat
Manzanillo
COLIMA
MICH

N

PACIFIC OCEAN

0   Miles   300

palacios

STATES

San Antonio

Galveston

New Orleans

RIO GRANDE

Nuevo Laredo

GULF OF MEXICO

NUEVO
LEON

Monterrey

Matamoros

Ciudad
Victoria

TAMAULIPAS

Tampico

YUCATAN

AN
UIS
TOSI

San Luis Potosi
lores Hidalgo

PANUCO R.

VERACRUZ

El Tajín

BAY OF
CAMPECHE

Merida

Chichen Itza

uajuato

QUERETARO
HIDALGO

Campeche

CAMPECHE

QUINTANA
ROO

Queretaro

Pachuca

Tlaxcala

Jalapa

Chetumal

zcuaro

Mexico City

MEXICO D.F.

TLAXCALA

Cordoba

Veracruz

TABASCO

relia
ladolid)

luch)

Puebla

Orizaba

La Venta

Cuernavaca

PUEBLA

VERACRUZ

Villahermosa

CARIBBEAN SEA

S R.

Taxco
Iguala

MORELOS

Huajuapan

Coatzalcoalcos

Palenque

Chilpancingo

Monte
Alban

Oaxaca

CHIAPAS

Bonampak

Acapulco

GUERRERO

OAXACA

Tuxtla
Gutierrez

San Cristobal
de las Casas

USUMACINTA

GRIJALVA

R.

FIRE
and
BLOOD

A History of Mexico

T. R. Fehrenbach

DA CAPO PRESS

For My Mother

Library of Congress Cataloging in Publication Data

Fehrenbach, T. R.
  Fire and blood: a history of Mexico / T. R. Fehrenbach.—1st Da Capo
Press ed.
    p.   cm.
  Includes bibliographical references and index.
  ISBN 0-306-80628-2 (pbk.: alk. paper)
  1. Mexico—History. I. Title.
F1226.F43   1995
972—dc20   94-45811
                                                                  CIP

First Da Capo Press edition 1995

This Da Capo Press paperback edition of *Fire and Blood* is a
republication of the edition first published in New York in 1973,
here updated with a new foreword and new text. It is reprinted by
arrangement with the author.

5 6 7 8 9 10

Published by Da Capo Press, Inc.
A member of the Perseus Books Group

CONTENTS

FOREWORD

Much about Mexico that has recently come to the world's attention is actually old: Modernization, reform, social turmoil, one-party rule, and the struggle to break free from an oppressive past are all themes that have been carried out for generations.

Mexico's present makes no sense without Mexico's past. There have always been "many Mexicos," the Mexico of varied terrain, the Mexico of the Amerindian heritage, of the Spanish Conquest, of the Revolution, and of the era when elections and bankers rule. These are all part of modern Mexico, creating not only colorful diversity and vast historic pageantry but also great confusion.

However, through all this diversity and change runs a powerful historic continuity. Mexico has always been a potentially explosive society that, despite upheavals, rests on an inherently stable base. It has always been easier for outsiders to see the color and cruelty, the violent potential, and the suffering of the people than to understand this essential continuity.

This book, written for English-speaking readers, is an attempt both to bring Mexican history to life and to make it intelligible to North Americans. The people of the United States like to believe that political will and good intentions can solve most human dilemmas. They often find it hard to understand Mexicans, who know better. And Mexicans are baffled by people who lack a timeless, tragic view of life. Yet both peoples have something to learn from each other.

Most Mexicans are aware, North Americans less so, that fate has placed both nations upon the same continent, interacting, intermingling, coming constantly closer while remaining strangers divided by their pasts. Yet both heritages are vital parts of the American whole.

And together they will forge its future.

T.R. FEHRENBACH
San Antonio, Texas
September 1994

PART ONE

The Tyranny of Circumstance: The Amerindians

1

THE OLD ONES

The forces of the past still live on and exert their influence on us, though we may not be consciously aware of this. It is frightening to realize in full depth what it means to be a human being: that is, to realize that we are all imbedded in the flux of generations, whose legacy of thought and feeling we irrevocably carry along with us.
Kurt W. Marek (C. W. Ceram) *Gods, Graves, and Scholars.*

The rise of man in ancient Mexico is shrouded in mystery.

For that matter, no one knows for certain where or when the human race began, or how it became differentiated and scattered across the globe. Scientists have deduced from the study of skeletal fragments that the genus *Homo* appeared in Africa during the late Pleistocene era some hundred thousand years ago, with perhaps a half million or more years of cultural evolution already in his past. Bones also indicate that *Homo sapiens*, true man, the symbol-drawer and weapon-maker, the hunter and killer, began forging into a still subarctic Europe out of Asia about 30,000 B.C. And about the same time, as prehistory goes, human beings also entered the Americas.

The old bones of possible human ancestors—larger apes, pithecanthropi, or hominids such as Neanderthal men have never been found in the Western Hemisphere. The first Americans, tall, erect, gregarious, using fire, wearing animal skins, and armed with flint-tipped spears, arrived from the Eastern Hemisphere.

Thirty to forty thousand years ago, during the last great Ice Age, from which the earth is still emerging, huge areas of the northern hemisphere were covered with glaciers. Ice gripped much of what is now the United

States. Southwestern North America, however, was fertile. The high plateaus of these southlands were rich savannahs of waving grasses, dotted with trees and sweetwater lakes. They teemed with mammalian life, and these regions, if not man's cradle, were certainly vast nurseries for the species.

When much of the earth's water supply was locked in glacial ice, the oceans shrank and land bridges rose. One of these connected Asia and Alaska across the Bering Strait. Even during the last Ice Age ice-free valleys and corridors led north and south through Siberia and Alaska. It was through these valleys and across the ephemeral land bridge that the first Americans almost certainly came. They were adventurous and incredibly tough, enduring enormous hardships and traveling thousands of miles.

In relatively recent times ancient human campsites have been found over much of the southwestern United States and the country that is now Mexico. These campsites, the remains of ages-extinct fires, have revealed the bones of Pleistocene animals, artifacts, and tools. The modern carbon-14 dating process exploded many theories by proving that some of these firesites are much, much older than previously believed—some dating back approximately thirty thousand years. The animal bones found come from species like the American camel and the wooly mammoth, which have been extinct for thousands of years.

In central Mexico, on the banks of the Rio Atoyac, a mastodon bone has been found that bears unmistakably human carvings—symbols from the brain and hand of man. Nearby, the skulls of other vanished animals have been uncovered, some imbedded with flint points. This same region has revealed hundreds of stone and bone artifacts, abandoned or buried beside the bones of mastodons, elephants, and the small Pleistocene ancestor of the horse. A rock showing the impression of a human hand and containing the skull of a saber-toothed tiger and the femur from a human skeleton which must have stood eight feet tall has been unearthed.

Who were these people? It is impossible to answer dogmatically, because their skeletal characteristics do not seem to resemble any surviving human stock. They had massive teeth set in strong jaws, and curved, flat leg bones. The bones they left behind in limestone and calcified rock are as different from those of later American Indians as the skeletons of modern Frenchmen are from Chinese. This ancient, longheaded people may have been a precursor of the Mongoloid branch of mankind, or they may have been a Caucasoid ancestor.

The few relics these old Americans left tell a great deal: that they were true *Homo sapiens*, not half-men, that they made weapons and knew fire and used symbols, and that they were the most formidable predators the world had yet evolved.

At that time huge beasts roamed over the high plains of the American

Southwest and Mexico. There was the enormous imperial mammoth, and the awe-inspiring American elephant. Mastodons, ground sloths, giant armadillos, and a bison four times the weight of the modern North American buffalo grazed the lush meadows. There were antelope, camels, miniature horses, various cats, snakes, wolves, birds, and bears. Modern men would feel immensely courageous hunting most of these beasts with high-powered rifles; the first Americans killed all of them with flimsy, flint-tipped spears.

The large, curving horn of Middle America was rich, varied, mysterious, and geologically new, with two great mountain ranges thrown up no more than fifty million years before. The mountain chains, or cordilleras, generally rose from north to south, one on the east facing the green Gulf, the other sloping westward to the blue Pacific. Between these mountain ranges a broad, high central plateau, called the *meseta*, also rose from north to south, tapering with the horn of Mexico. The center of this plateau, eons ago, was crossed with a smoking volcanic strike, leaving it cut up into countless jumbled valleys.

The rugged cordilleras and the rising volcanoes left Mexico one vast mountain, rising from the surrounding seas, pocked with valleys at varying altitudes. The eastern coastal plains, extending inward about sixty miles—though covering the whole peninsula of Yucatán—were humid, tropical, or subtropical, sometimes lush jungles, sometimes miasmic swamps. The western mountains went down precipitously to the Pacific; their bones baked dry under the tropic sun. But the central plateau, with its valleys, green forests, and brimming lakes, had a climate of eternal spring and was eminently fit for man.

This great plateau was very different then. It had not been despoiled. The air was much more humid then than now. Vast stands of pine, oak, fir, and alder trees covered the mountainsides. Rich volcanic, alluvial soils were washed down to surround the numerous lakes; broad, wet meadows of sedge and grass grew around the water. Millions upon millions of birds flocked about the lakes, and their waters teemed with freshwater fish; the forests and meadows were filled with grazing herbivores.

Like the animals, men sought the lakes and marshes where there was water, grass, and salt. In these places, also, the gigantic, dangerous beasts could be more easily trapped and killed. The first Americans lived on fresh meat; they knew the sharp thrills of the chase, the fierce joy of the kill, the exultation of the triumphant hunters' safe return, and the satiety of the communal feast.

They roasted their bloody meat in huge kitchen middens in the rock. They flaked keen flints around glowing coals. They must have shivered in the ice-age night-wind, and roared songs of worship or defiance at the cold, high moon. They took shelter in caves, and they may have chanted paeans

of thanksgiving to the returning sun. Like most primitive men, they probably prayed to the spirits of the animals they killed. They may have had
drums and flutes and made music. They surely wondered about the meaning of life and worried about the future of the dead, because they were
men, with the conscious and subconscious minds of men.

They lived short, strenuous, terrible, brutal, and exhilarating lives, but
for all their nakedness and crude techniques they had the brains, sensibilities, and perceptions of modern men.

How many millennia this race wandered over the southwestern United
States and parts of Mexico is unknown. These people never became separated or culturally varied; the relics they left are always identical. Over
thousands of miles and thousands of years, this people made their spear
points and artifacts in exactly the same way.

They lived together in small hunting societies ranging from about twenty
to sixty members. Everyone had kinship and a place. Territorial arrangements were probably carved out with neighboring bands, and very early,
man learned the necessity of exogamous mating relationships. At any one
time the total population of these people was probably no more than a few
thousand. They had a precarious dominion over the beasts, but none over
nature, and for thousands of years they failed to progress or change.

But the earth changed and warmed. The glaciers shrank northward, the
oceans rose, the land bridges sank, the sun burned away the mists and fresh
inland seas. The winds blew more fiercely, drying the earth. In Middle
America, the rivers dug deeper into the ground, now slicing down mountainsides; the broad waters of the *meseta* shrank into still wide, but more
marshy, lakes. To the north of the central highlands, where the plateau
widened and flattened out between the cordilleras, the trees died and the
landscape dried into semideserts. And though the inner valley between the
southern mountains remained still fresh and green, the great Pleistocene
mammals began to disappear.

Climatic change probably killed off the mammoth, the camel, the mas-
todon, and the elephant, but their extinction may have been hastened by
Paleolithic spears. And when the Pleistocene animals were gone, the first
Americans had vanished with them.

The race may have simply died out, unable to adapt, it may have been
exterminated by a newer race; or the stock may have changed or interbred
with fresh waves of invaders so much over generations as to become un-
recognizable. At any rate, after some millennia, the old ones vanished.

But a second invasion had already taken the land; these new people
must have crossed the northern land bridge before it finally disappeared,
sometime before 7000 B.C. Later peoples, however, could have passed
through the Aleutian island chain. This later immigration, however, apparently either spanned many centuries, possibly millennia, or else the invad-

ers arrived in small, fragmented streams. Unlike the earliest American culture, the newcomers were or became extremely varied culturally.

As the small bands spread across the cold northlands, reaching each ocean, they must have become isolated and inbred. These people made their Stone Age artifacts in countless distinctive styles; within a broad genetic Mongoloid framework, they also differentiated widely in skin color, bone structure, and height. The most important indicator of long periods of relative isolation was their linguistic development which grew amazingly complex: 140 different stocks, divided into about 1200 mutually incomprehensible languages and dialects.

Although some Negroid characteristics appeared occasionally among these people, their mainstream was definitely Asian. They were Mongoloid in skin shade, ranging from yellowish to copper to dark brown, in head shape, and in hair-color and form. Some had the characteristic Asian eye fold.

Spreading across all North America and Middle America, some invaders did not stop until they climbed the Andean peaks of the southern continent. They made their homes in the highlands, on the coastlines, and on the islands of the Caribbean. They deposited small numbers of people all across the hemisphere. Some folk never left the far northwest, but there was a general pattern of restless migration from north to south.

Columbus, thinking he had reached India in 1492, called the people he found in the New World *indios*. The descendents of this race, including modern Mexicans, prefer to think of themselves as "indigenous" rather than wanderers out of prehistoric Asia. Anthropologists assigned them to the Mongoloid branch of human stock and called them Amerindians, or American Indians.

Like all men of the eighth millennium B.C. the Amerindians were Stone Age hunters and gatherers. They ate wild fruits, seeds, and berries, but the staple of their diet was meat and fish. They hunted bear, rabbits, and a variety of deer, as well as a smaller bison and a great proliferation of native birds. Depending on their habitat, Amerinds ate insects, shellfish, turkey, and even snakes.

Many Amerinds, especially in the uplands, followed the game herds across the plains and high plateaus. The best hunting was still around the waterholes in the forested country; here men could more easily trap or kill elusive animals on foot. Many Amerindians congregated in the hospitable region of the *meseta*.

As the kinship bands grew larger, they developed into clans, phratries of clans, and tribes, which were no longer united by direct blood ties, but which retained a common spirit due to territoriality, common language, and common ways. But blood and community was always more important to the Amerindian than ties of place; his organization remained social rather than territorial in concept and scope.

The Amerinds brought with them out of Asia a great bag of Stone Age flint, obsidian, or bone artifacts and tools: knives, scrapers, drills, axes, picks. They wore skin garments and wove crude baskets out of reeds. Their principal weapon was the ubiquitous spear, but they soon discovered the throwing stick, or *atlatl*, which gave their darts more range. They also brought domesticated dogs from Asia.

Soon after the Amerind migrations began, the earth assumed its present form. The rising oceans now completely isolated the Amerindians from further human currents from the Old World.

The Amerindians were racially similar, though not identical, but they were fantastically varied culturally. Every kinship band spoke a different dialect and made its artifacts in different styles. These nomadic, hunting bands and clans constantly impinged on each other as the land became more populated. They followed what seems to have the oldest collective human logic: they made war on everyone outside the immediate tribe or clan. Whether such conflict arose from the instinctive desire to seize or hold good hunting lands or from the early-realized need for exogamous mating, which led to raiding and counter-raiding for females between bands; or whether warfare arises from some other instinct or need is so far undetermined. What is inarguable is that warfare became deeply imbedded in the Amerind heart and mind. All Amerindians were warlike, though some were vastly more aggressive than others. War was not just practiced; it was socialized. In most Amerindian tongues the words "male" and "warrior" became synonymous.

In a pattern that was generally true everywhere, the more successful tribes also tended to be most warlike. Which came first is immaterial; the peoples who succeeded in holding the best ground grew in numbers, and also became more adept and powerful. The clans who were reduced to marginal territories tended to appear more peaceful; that is, they acted as fearful skulkers rather than imperious warriors. The actual practice of war varied enormously. Some Amerind violence was carried to the point of dispersion or extermination of enemies; more often, however, violence took on a ceremonial tone. It was beyond the capacity, and perhaps the vision, of primitive peoples to destroy an enemy; raids and expeditions were carried out more to seize loot, women, or to prove manhood, leadership, or skill at war.

The powerful or lucky warrior came to be the most respected member of the tribe. He was the best provider for his immediate clan, and also their best defender in constant peril from outside. It was inevitable that the warrior-male became utterly dominant within the family group. Women did his bidding, as well as all menial work; the social specialization biology required between the sexes in a hunting society made any other course impossible. The male who was not aggressive in hunt or war was not just a personal failure; he was a social disaster. But except on mass hunts, or in war, the only genuinely socializing acts, in which leadership devolved upon exceptionally capable men, all warriors lived within their tribes as peers. This was logical, also: the duties, and therefore the rights, of all warrior males were identical.

There was no place for the man who could not kill animals or fight. Probably, the widespread custom of torturing captive males that arose among many Amerind tribes (women and children when captured were normally adopted without prejudice within the clan) orginated as a courage rite, merely reinforced by a primordial human love of inflicting pain. Such torture was also ritualized and socialized. The victim had to prove his manhood to the last; the tormentors had to assert their moral superiority by breaking the victim's courage and will. It was considered very bad luck to fail. The manner of a man's dying, in most Amerindian eyes, came to be as important, in fact more important, than the way in which he lived.

There was no real notion of social purpose beyond holding the clan together through the hunt or war. The rudiments of government—as everywhere on the globe—rose from the concept of chieftainship in war. Since all Amerinds were originally nomadic, and many peoples never ceased to be so, they never developed a strong sense of property beyond the communal concept of a tribal hunting ground.

The ties within the social organization were and had to be immensely close. Widows or young orphans were immediately adopted into an existing family. Responsibility—and power—went from brother to brother, rather than directly from father to son. But if the warrior was the most important and dominant person within the family and tribe, there was no person without function or place. Everyone had important duties, to hunt, to fight, to skin and cook meat, to make garments and chip flints, to bear burdens, to instruct the young. So long as they could function, all people were caught up in an endless chain of circumstance and duty. The concept of the autonomous individual did not and could not exist. No clan member could be free from sexual, communal, and kinship ties. Outcasts and renegades faced early death.

The majority of Amerind peoples never rose above this primitive hunting/warrior culture. They made only one technical innovation, the bow and arrow. This weapon may have been brought in from Asia, but its use diffused into Middle America so late that it probably was reinvented in North America. The bow made no real change except to give both hunting and warfare greater scope.

These Amerindian cultures were ingenious and valiant in their struggles against the environment. Hunters learned to use almost everything from the animals they killed: meat, eating the whole animal for a vital diet; hides for garments and shelter; horn and bone for tools. But men's powers over the environment were very small. They had no control over food supply, nor any way to store it. Animal life waxed and waned in cycles; there were good years and lean. In bad times children died; in fact, most tribes regularly practiced infanticide. Population remained sparse and thin.

These nomads did not make permanent shelters nor were they able to accumulate burdensome artifacts. The only beast of burden in North or Middle America was the dog.

The hunting cultures were successful, because they survived. Men passed on their courage and their customs with their seed. The short, sturdy, dark-eyed peoples of the Americas were engaged in an endless fight for life in which individuals rarely lived beyond thirty years, but they rarely despaired. They were children of the sun and wind, as much a part of nature as the animals they killed. They grew up attuned to their world; they knew how it had been, was now, and always would be.

2

FARMERS AND MAGICIANS

*The two-edged nature of power is nothing new in human affairs.
All important new inventions have both freed men from former
weakness and deficiency and enslaved them to a new regimen. The
hardy hunter surely despised the first farmers, bowed down by the
heavy labor of the fields; and through subsequent centuries barbarian freemen regularly scorned the servile habits of their civilized
neighbors. Yet these repugnances never for long arrested the spread
of agriculture or of civilization. Civilized history . . . may be understood as a series of breakthroughs toward the realization of greater
and greater power—including . . . the delicate but altogether real
power in art and thought as well as power's cruder, ruder forms.*
William H. McNeill, *The Rise of the West.*

Nine thousand years ago there was no essential difference in the way men
lived anywhere in the world, although they had long begun culturally to
differentiate. But during the seventh millennium B.C., somewhere in the
Middle East, people learned to plant and harvest hoarded seeds from wild
cereal grains. Agriculture was a simple invention, but it marked the most
fundamental revolution in human history, changing man from a highly
successful predator of other animal life to a manipulator and shaper of the
earth, and life itself.

Previous technologies, such as weapons, did not change life styles; agriculture did. It assured a vastly increased, dependable food supply and
brought about a population explosion and the concentration of large num-

bers of people in a single area. This in turn led to social specialization and leisure, which in turn led some men to learning, rational philosophy, organized religion, and high art. All human civilization rests on the cultivation of cereal grains.

The inhabitants of the naturally watered uplands of the eastern Mediterranean region domesticated wild wheat and barley seeds sometime during the seventh millennium. Agricultural villages have been discovered in this area which can be radiocarbon-dated to plus-or-minus 6250 B.C. Once learned, the technique spread rapidly. Rice agriculture seems to have been discovered independently in monsoon Asia not long afterward. By about 4000 B.C. farming technology and village life styles had diffused over most of Eurasia.

This chronology is important to the history of the New World, where the breakthrough came much later. Although some authorities have claimed that squash was planted in Middle America by 6000 B.C. and that farming began two thousand years later, there is no hard evidence of this. The oldest carbon-dated grain seeds found in Middle America go back only to about 2500 B.C., and the oldest village sites, to the second millennium. Beans and squash were no doubt harvested before maize, or Indian corn, was developed from the wild plant later Amerindians called *teocintli*. The evidence suggests a development gap of four thousand years between American and Eurasian agriculture—a time gulf with enormous repercussions.

The first native corn sprouted in Middle America between the Rio Pánuco and the borders of Costa Rica, the area where teocintli was found. Wild corn may have first been domesticated in the tangled vegetation of the hot, humid eastern coastal plain, on the lower slopes of the great cordillera, or even on the high, cool, sunny central plateau. Corn had reached its geographical limits in North America when white men arrived.

There is no evidence that agriculture was in any way diffused into the Americas. The Amerinds probably invented agriculture twice in the New World, just as the technique was developed more than once in Eurasia.

The peoples of the coast and thick southern jungles practiced a slash-and-burn type of maize farming, and maize also grew well up in the highlands, even up to ten thousand feet, but it did best of all in the temperate valleys of the *meseta* where the altitude ranged from about thirty-five hundred to eight thousand feet above sea level and the soils were the most well watered and arable in Middle America. The ancient Valley of Mexico was still extremely hospitable to man. The old Pleistocene forests still stood, as they would stand until men cut them down and denuded the earth; the lakes were yet blue and broad; rain fell steadily from May into October.

Only a small percentage of Mexico however, was really suitable for natural farming, and this geographic fact was always to limit man's advance.

Amerind peoples began to congregate in the *meseta* valleys by at least 8000 B.C. Large concentrations of them settled to farm between the Rio Pánuco and Sinaloa on the north southward into the isthmus of Tehuantepec. Clusters of people filtered through the valleys in the modern state of Veracruz, and all across the immense, cut-up Oaxaca plateau. These regions, with the Valley of Mexico, were soon dotted with scattered, greening *milpas* or cornfields, which the Amerinds cleared by burning, then scratched out with digging sticks.

These *milpas* were the nuclei of farming villages. People with food ripening on the earth became affixed to the spot. They erected permanent shelters out of mud, thatch, reeds, and wattle and made clay or stone pottery in order to store, prepare, and cook their corn and beans.

More infants lived or were allowed to live; older people lived longer, perhaps by several years. Within a short time, villages numbered up to several hundred souls, and more and more villages sprouted across the land.

The new numbers could not be supported by hunting alone; men now had to shape the earth and vegetable life for survival. Thus the new powers of environment that came with a steady food supply were very much a two-edged blade. Men had gained one sort of power only by surrendering another. When both men and women took up incessant toil in the fields, it marked a fundamental change in human affairs: men were no longer quite so much a part of nature as they had been.

Life in these ugly, growing, mud-walled villages was a blend of old forms and new. The houses were haphazardly scattered about without design or plan, but the people in them were still kin; farming populations lost none of their old concern with consanguinity and descent. But a small, increasingly important territorial factor undoubtedly was added. Men saw the earth they were manipulating in a slightly different light; the vicinity, or place where the village clan or tribe lived took on new meaning.

The farming way of life also caused a radical decline, at least at first, in warfare. Diggers in the soil were by necessity more peaceable than nomadic hunters or gatherers; longer-settled agricultural folk seem to have been less warlike than tribes still on the move. But violence was continually infused or reinfused into the farmers by nomadic invaders; when warlike societies settled down into older communities, they revived the spirit of conflict throughout the whole community.

There remained no basis for social differentiation beyond the demands of age and sex. Every family head was a farming peasant; every man duplicated every other man's toil. All adult males were equals in an association of peers. The norm—which was the pattern for mankind almost everywhere in this stage—was a communal, tribal democracy of working farmers, each of whom had no social purpose except to feed his family.

The decline of warfare actually caused a decline in the practice of government. There were civil elders, but chieftainship was a part-time job. Such men were more arbiters in disputes than rulers. Without social purpose, and without socializing acts, men had no need for government.

Organization revolved around kinship instead of property or office. Farm land was held in common by the tribe, just as the hunting grounds had been. Since the society was really an extended family, the concept of individual ownership could not easily arise. Further, in kinship societies, as in families, individualism was and had to be subdued. The individual was important only through what he contributed. The margin of survival, within the family and without, within the clan, was very thin. There was no surplus to support any kind of life outside the family circle.

The ancient Middle American villages, crude, unsanitary, with a constant high death rate, were much like similar agricultural villages everywhere as they have survived today. They were cribbed, communal, caked by custom, circumscribed by circumstance. Men were tyrannized by the eternal agricultural cycle. Life was hard, but not unbearable within its limited horizons. The material and psychic needs of people were satisfied—and actually, the vast majority of men who have ever lived on earth have followed this life style.

Farming man had more time, and perhaps more need, to sophisticate his primordial religious concepts. Human beings were never able to conceive of nonexistence easily; though their constant awareness of physical death was real enough. The oldest grave sites reveal artifacts and offerings buried with the dead and burial rites that strongly indicate a belief in afterlife. Farmers remade the earlier, animal-centered cults of their ancestors. They were subject to cosmic forces—rain, hail, sun, fertility—which they saw daily influence their lives, but could not understand. They began to deify the powerful elements and to express anthropomorphic conceptions of these gods in art. The highland farmers of Mexico made clay figurines, which they often buried with the dead. Many of these figurines, fecund, peaceful, and with exaggerated female characteristics, seem to represent an earth-mother, the universal deity among primitive farming man.

They also indicate what the farming folk of ancient Mexico looked like: they went naked, with tatooed or painted bodies, but they wore a sort of turban made of maguey fibers, and also an assortment of necklaces and ornaments of stone and seeds. They daubed their hair with crimson substances, and plugged their ear lobes, and nasal septums with stone jewelry.

This culture exploded over the highlands about 1500 B.C. and lasted about five centuries, during which many of the fundamental folkways of Amerindian Middle America were established. The people of the small, scattered, communal kinship villages throughout the remote mountain valleys turned the earth with digging sticks, planting corn seeds when the rains came; they watched the plants sprout and grow tasseled ears under the broiling sun. They gathered the ripened grain in baskets, singing. Wives and mothers ground the maize to make a pasty dough, which was patted into cakes and baked over charcoal fires.

About 1000 B.C., a new, strange, and ultimately terrible people pushed in among the highland farmer folk. These invaders may have originated,—or at least their culture germinated—in the eastern coastal jungle plains. Some historians once called them Olmecs, from a later Amerindian term meaning, "from where rubber grows." Olmec, however, came to be applied so indiscriminately for so long that as a cultural term it became meaningless. A more modern, better name for the people who brought a new culture into Mexico is the Magicians.

These people were shamans, or dominated by shamans, and their entire life-view was based on magic.

There were cogent reasons why magic was to take such an enormous hold on the Meso-American heart and soul. When the farming populations began to explode, latent disaster always lay over the land and people. Even the deep and sheltered valleys of central Mexico were subject to sudden killing frosts, unseasonal snows, and prolonged, disastrous droughts. These freakish events came at irregular times. And the ancient volcanoes erupted without warning, darkening the skies and destroying whole mountainsides with spectacular lava flows.

The primitive mind could not accept such events as random, accidental, without human meaning. History shows that in areas of irregular weather or rainfall natural forces have made men more concerned with invisible, omnipotent cosmic powers than with the reality they perceived on earth. Meso-American man devoted tremendous effort to trying to understand why some years it failed to rain on schedule, withering his cornfields and threatening him with starvation and extinction.

Like most primitive agriculturists, the highland farmers had come to venerate fire, water, the sun, and the concept of fertility. They were already making these forces into gods when the Magicians arrived with strange new ideas and practices.

The Magicians claimed they could control the rainfall by rituals. They carried a jaguar-toothed rain god with them and gave it orders through magical ceremonies and ritual dances. It should be understood that the Magicians did not practice "magic" in the modern sense—their "magic" was entirely practical in their eyes, confused with methodology.

The masks and carved figurines the Magicians left behind give some notion of their rituals. Shamans or witch doctors daubed their faces in black or white. They put on masks made out of clay or green stone, some representing deformed men, the jaguar god, or carniverous beasts with birds' heads. They wore high, triple-tiered hats and long ocelot-skin robes. The Magicians carried rattles and made faces; their masks are usually shown with snarling mouths. They performed mystic dances, making noise and shrieking commands to the rain god.

This magic, which was merely a variant of a common manifestation among many primitive peoples, was convincing. The Magicians grew in numbers, created whole new communities, and apparently even dominated the separate farming culture of the highlands for many years. Magician congregations and influence spread from southern Veracruz into Puebla, Morelos, Tabasco, the Oaxaca valley, and even southwest into Guerrero. Over all this area the shamans brought the fang-mouthed rain god and inculcated a belief in mystic-magical rites to manipulate natural phenomena.

Magician artifacts and artwork show that their vision was strangely distorted. They were obsessed with monsters in human form. Their figurines portray men with genital or glandular deformities, with pointed Mongoloid heads, with cleft skulls, and with animal mouths. They appear to have believed such persons holy. The skeletal remains of the Magician folk perhaps indicate an origin for such visions. These people had a congenital adenoidism of the mouth, low, squat, obese frames with short legs. The male skeletons show surprising feminine characteristics. And if the Magicians derived, possibly as mutations, from the generic Amerind stock, they were divergent in several puzzling ways. Their bones reveal Negroid characteristics. This has led some anthropologists to insist that there must have been African immigration into Middle America at one time.

The Magicians also practiced self-mutilation, possibly in emulation of some historic deformed births. Children's heads were deformed by elongating the soft skull backward to a point, and Magicians mutilated their teeth.

But the Magician vision was also dual. Some of their figurines were of lovely young girls, with almond eyes and wasp waists, exquisitely carved.

This strange people were something much more than a race of fat-faced, squatty shamans who terrorized the south-central highlands. For all their preoccupation with magic—or perhaps because of it—they were also the developers and transmitters of a remarkable cultural advance. They were expert at carving and shaping stone. Their work was incomparably more sophisticated than the crude farmer art, and also the best of it was charming, judged by any taste or style.

Magicians made axes out of green jadeite and mirrors from polished pyrites; they fashioned necklaces and ornaments from several varieties of polished stones. They especially valued green substances, such as the native jade and serpentine. Magicians left artifacts made from these materials hundreds of miles from where they were naturally found, indicating that they initiated or practiced long-range trade.

The Magicians developed rubber-making and learned to weave cotton fiber into thread for cloth. They shaped rubber into balls and, wearing knee-pads and gloves, played a sort of ritual game in a ball court. Magicians smoked tobacco in stone pipes.

The Magician era was a time of progress and expansion; villages grew, some to several hundred people. The Magician centers themselves became semiurban enclaves. The largest of these were clustered on the semitropical cordillera slopes. In these centers, Magicians left a number of carved stone bench-thrones. They also left representations of these thrones, on which sit fat, helmeted, Buddha-like shamans, or possibly, gods.

The magician shamanate also infused something terrible into Meso-America. The burial sites dating from this time have yielded up countless mutilated skeletons: decapitated, with smashed skulls, amputated arms or legs, and the remains of children put to a violent death. At some period the Magicians came to believe that dances and imprecations and rituals did not command or placate the powerful cosmic forces, and they instituted ceremonies considered far more potent: human sacrifice.

Near the middle of the first millennium B.C. the Magicians either became absorbed into the surrounding populations, or were destroyed when their magic failed during a period of prolonged drought. But the notion that men could and must control the cosmic forces of nature through magical rites was too pervasive to die completely. The Magicians' work lived after them.

It is difficult to make direct links with the prehistoric Magician-Olmec age and the Meso-American culture that came afterward. But it seems certain that the Magicians developed much, if not all, of the cultural patina that overlaid the basic maize-culture. This era was a great turning point for Meso-American man.

Magical influences continued in Meso-American civilization; green jade was valued above all other substances, including gold; its peoples played ceremonial handball games; they carved stone with exquisite skill; they all practiced human sacrifice. They all suffered from a surrealistic rather than natural vision in art, and, until the Spanish toppled the last idols, all the rain gods of the highlands were portrayed with jaguar teeth.

The Magicians, migrants or mutants, vanished, but they had laid the groundwork for and started the stirrings toward a colorful civilization whose fallen splendors, and whose overtones of psychic horror, haunt men yet.

3

BUILDERS
AND PRIESTS

*I have seen him that is beaten, him that is beaten . . . and I have
seen him that is set free from forced labor. Every artisan that
wieldeth the chisel, he is wearier than him who delveth. The stone-
mason seeketh for work in all manner of hard stone; when he has
finished his arms are destroyed and he is weary. The field worker,
his reckoning endureth forever. The weaver in his workshop, he
fareth more ill than any woman; his thighs are upon his belly and
he breatheth no air . . . I tell thee, the fisherman's work is upon the
river, where it is mixed with crocodiles. Behold, there is no calling
that is without a director, except the scribe, and he is the director
. . . Thou art to set thine heart on learning.*

From the Egyptiac *Instruction of Duauf, Son of Khety.*

There has been, and always will be barring some definitive discovery, a
dispute over the origins of Meso- or Middle American civilization. The
Amerindian civilizations of both South and Middle America resembled
certain cultures in the Old World in striking ways: art work, seals, tombs,
pyramids, and corbelled arches. Amerindian calendars, social organization,
symbols such as the swastika, and zodiacal signs were startlingly similar to
those once used in the Eurasian Middle East. The art of the ancient Egyptians and the Mayas, particularly, was much alike, and some Amerindian
pottery decoration resembles the Chinese. All this evidence—and it is
impressive—has made perhaps a majority of archeologists and historians,

above all those of the Old World, think there must have been a diffusion of civilization into America out of Eurasia in prehistoric times.

It is now known that it was possible for men to have crossed the Pacific thousands of years ago, following the trade winds from the Orient. Despite its greater length, such a Pacific passage was far more feasible than a crossing of the rougher, contrary-winded Atlantic. Some plant life probably reached South America in this way, though not necessarily on boats or rafts manned by early sailors. But there is no evidence of an actual voyage at any time.

There is no evidence that any civilized techniques crossed over the Bering Strait. The only high cultures in America appeared near the Tropic of Cancer and again on the Andean plateau, a long way from the far northwest. Also, Amerindian civilizations rose millennia after the land bridges sank, far too many years afterward for a landborne diffusion to have effect.

The enormous time gulf between the Old World civilizations the American cultures resemble and their counterparts in the Western Hemisphere, more than anything else, severely questions the diffusion theory. While culture-bearing Mesopotamian or Egyptian seamen could have strayed across the Pacific, there is no way such men could possibly have sailed across a time gap of at least three thousand years. When the Mayas did their "Egyptiac" artwork, and Amerindians erected new pyramids, the ancient civilizations of the Middle East had long been dust.

However popular, the diffusion theory is, it has to fall back on speculations or fantasies: strayed sailors from the Persian Gulf, sunken Atlantis, wandering Phoenicians, Scandinavian giants, brave Irish missionaries with more zeal than geographic sense, or lost tribes of Israel. All of these hypotheses have been proposed, but no direct link has ever been proved.

Dominant American opinion, unlike European, holds that the growth of civilization was spontaneous on American soil. Modern Mexicans believe this, not so much as a scientific hypothesis as a xenophobic dogma.

While there is no demonstrated psychic unity among civilized men, human invention has tended to follow a common path, indicating that there must once have been a certain psychic unity among primitive man. Most primitive art shows a vital unity, wherever it is found. The evidence seems to indicate, not that ancient Sumerians visited the Americas, but that the first temple builders in Mesopotamia and along the Nile saw the world with very similar eyes. Modern archeology is tending to reinforce this view.

What is clear, however, is that a distinctive, separate civilization did rise in Middle America in the first millennium B.C. Attempts to date this civilization earlier—and until recently, it was dated much later—are still speculative. This high culture did not spring up overnight; it was the work of many generations of men. The cornfields were its base; the Magician cults gave it a certain orientation. In fact, it began to coalesce rapidly about the time the Magicians disappeared. It seems to have begun first on the lower mountain slopes, perhaps in the state of Veracruz, sometime after 650 B.C. But it spread very widely until it covered the entire region known today as Middle America, from Costa Rica in Central America to the Pánuco River in Mexico. It was halted by rain forests on the south, deserts to the north.

The barbaric, agricultural Meso-Americans were quite varied culturally. Villagers spoke different languages, had different legends, and different physical shapes. To lump all these people together as "Amerindians" is ethnically correct, but it is also as definitive as describing as "Europeans" Frenchmen, Britons, Prussians, and Danes. But with the growth of an indigenous civilization something occurred that was like the growth of the "Western" civilization in medieval Europe. All the differentiated peoples within one broad geographic area by a process of diffusion came to have one single basic culture, though there were distinct regional styles.

There was never really a separate "Mexic," "Yucatec," "Aztec," or "Maya" civilization in Middle America; there was simply a unitary civilization developing local variations on a common theme. The common thread of this civilization ran from the Pánuco River to Guatemala, and from the state of Sinaloa to Costa Rica, through many peoples who continued to speak distinct languages and to differ in countless minor ways.

Nor was this Meso- or Middle American civilization made by the proprietors Europeans found in the sixteenth century. The Mexica or Aztecs, the Maya, Tarasca, Tlaxcalteca, Mixteca, and Zapotec peoples were all inheritors rather than creators.

The great pyramids Cortés passed north of the City of Mexico were not built by the contemporary "Aztecs," but by some vanished race. A great series of peoples rose and fell over many centuries in south-central Mexico.

The origins and formative years of this civilization have always been frustrating to explore, because while it left some five thousand archeological sites behind it passed down no records. The earliest civilized Amerindians drew pictographs on pressed figbark, quickly destroyed; or else, like the Maya culture, they carved on stone walls and stelae in hieroglyphs whose Rosetta Stone has not yet been found. This civilization can be approached only through architecture and art, and reconstructed from its fallen walls and idols, which fortunately, by their size, styles, and profusion, tell a great deal about the men who made them.

The phases of this civilization can, then, only be given a complex, bewildering, and—for anyone except specialists—a totally unsatisfactory breakdown into periods of different building styles. Inevitably, because most archeologists came from a Western background, these periods became defined in Western terms. Further, the excavation work has always been uneven, with some minor sites exhaustively uncovered and more important ones scarcely touched. Far too little correlation between sites and periods has been done. All of this has made Mexican archeology a jumble.

Historians have tended to avoid the archeological mazes and to divide the whole vanished civilization into three broad archeological-historic phases: the Preclassic, the Classic, and the Historic. Certain subclassifications are needed within these; the Classic period is usually divided into Transitional, Classic, Baroque, and Terminal. These terms always refer to art and architectural styles, but such styles tend to show the true course of events.

With the Preclassic era, beginning about 650 B.C., a recognizably common culture had spread from the borders of Costa Rica northward as far as the Pánuco River, westward along the fringes of Sinaloa, and southward across the central highlands to the Pacific. This culture had a large number of distinctive common characteristics before anything that might be called a genuine civilization began.

The agriculture of all Meso-American peoples, who never invented the plow, was laborious and small-scale, carried out on countless tiny plots, often reclaimed from marshes or lakes. During this period a prolonged drought shrank or dried up the mountain lakes.

All Meso-Americans fermented juice from the maguey plant and they used its leaves for fiber. They all valued cacao beans, both as chocolate and as counters—a sort of money surrogate. They learned to polish obsidian and other stones, and used obsidian chips to provide a cutting edge for their flat wooden clubs and swords. They all grew cotton and made cotton-padded body armor. They wore turban-type headdresses and heeled sandals.

Though at different times and places, every people erected temple-pyramids with steps, laid stucco floors, and built ball courts. They all did fresco work and painted colored murals. This architecture and art varied enormously in size, perfection, and style, but all of it is immediately unmistakable as Meso-American.

All the different peoples gradually developed a form of writing, usually a combination of hieroglyphs and stylized drawings, or pictographs. The written language, like the spoken, varied greatly from place to place, and one people could not decipher another's markings. All drew maps and kept historical accounts and chronicles, although they could not reduce their poetry, without phonetics, to writing. The common form of written record was a sort of folding picture book made of bark and now called a codex.

The Meso-Americans' single greatest achievement was their superb calendar which featured a year of eighteen months, each divided into twenty days. Five "useless" days were left over, and these were considered dangerously unlucky. The entire calendar recycled every fifty-two years; and although the Meso-Americans thought of time as cyclical rather than linear, with the universe repeating endless cycles, the end of a cycle was considered a portentous or ominous time. The calendar was more in consonance with the true movement of the earth against the stars than either the Julian or the modern Gregorian. But because each separate subculture began its calendar at a different time, it has been almost impossible for archeologists to correlate the whole.

All Middle Americans developed naming rites and pole dancing, and they all began to use the specialized marketplace for barter.

By 650 B.C. every people also employed human sacrifice to propitiate a growing pantheon of demon-forces, which had different names in different areas.

Finally, all the people were warlike. Though bellicosity receded as tribes developed permanent agriculture, there was invariably a later resurgence, either through the infusion of new, savage, nomadic stock, or the development of new quarrels between more civilized men. The old idea that the Maya subculture was pacifistic, or at least more peaceable than the Mexic, is a fiction. The Maya peoples were as hostile toward each other as the highland tribes; in fact, they carried on their conflicts more tenaciously and bitterly than other Amerindians, especially in the subculture's declining years. However, at certain periods the Maya cities employed Mexic mercenaries, and this may have given root to the rumor. Maya wars may have had ideological causes, but back of them lay the eternal reason—the struggle for power.

The influence of Meso-American civilization seems to have radiated far beyond Middle America. Farming, irrigation techniques, building with stone, metallurgy, and some military techniques spread far north of the Pánuco. The Caddoan tribes of the Mississippi basin and the Pueblo peoples of the North American Southwest reflected certain traits of the southern culture.

The Preclassic era is sometimes called the Age of the First Builders, or the Age of the First Priests. Between 650 B.C. and 150 B.C. on the Christian calendar, certain trends coalesced to transform the face of ancient Mexico.

The burgeoning populations of Middle America did not shed the vanished magicians' mystical-magical visions and practices; instead, they formalized them into a ceremonial religion. Now, the amorphous forces of fire, sun, rain, earth, and fertility appeared as distinct personalities, each with its peculiar form, idiosyncrasies, and demands. Each form collected its devotees, priests, and rituals. The surrealistic vision of gods as monsters, nourished by human blood, was retained. It was, however, this syncretism of a series of random superstitions into a powerful, ritualized, awesome mass cult that spurred the Amerindians to civilization.

The peoples began to erect cult centers across the land. From these came the first Meso-American cities—the creators and sustainers of a civilized life style.

Unlike Greco-Roman and Western European cities which grew from a political and commercial base, the isolated Meso-American were founded on religious mysticism, much like the first temple communities of the Middle East. It has been said that the fuel of this civilization was maize or Indian corn. But its spark was the Amerindians' fear of the unknown and uncertain forces which made corn grow—the still unexplained miracle of regenerative life on earth.

The more populated the inhospitable regions of Mexico became, the more vulnerable men became to their ecology. The original hunting nomads could always migrate in bad years—but for large, settled populations life was now a constant battle for sufficient food. Any kind of natural accident, any freakish weather, wreaked enormous tragedy on men and women who were no longer used to going hungry, slaying their infants, or dying young. In fact, the evidence is strong that every major turning point in human development in Middle America was closely connected with a natural disaster of some sort.

This concern with and dependency upon natural forces like the sun and rain surely led to the culture's finest accomplishment, the calendar, and its finest efforts, expressed in enormous, decorated edifices. But it also brought on the Meso-American civilization's ineradicable gangrene of the soul: sacrificial bloodshed. Fear of the gods led men to erect great temple pyramids in their cult centers, but it also caused them to substitute magic, savage rituals, and symbolic destruction for a more rational philosophy or the beginnings of natural science.

The great problem was the cyclical climate; rains fell across the highlands only part of the year, and sometimes they did not fall at all. Arrival of the rainy period was often erratic; a premature shower might easily cause hungry farmers to plant too soon, only to see their precious hoarded seeds sprout and die in the burning ground. When this happened whole villages died off. The farmers had to have some way to measure the moons between the rains; they could tell the seasons accurately only by measuring the movements of the earth against the constant stars.

At a very early period some unknown genius devised such a calendar, and it was perfected gradually over many years.

Thus, the Meso-Americans came to have a haunting sense of being ruled inexorably by time. They were engaged in a desperate race against its passage, and came to have a profound feeling that time was circular. They lived in endless cycles, always judging the future against the past. They developed an enormous historical sense, but they also lived in a captive universe, with no real concept of linear progress. Their calendar only measured centuries, endlessly repeated. Some peoples even believed in destroying their possessions and starting anew, at a cycle's end.

The calendar's invention created an order of priests and gave them enormous power. The calendar could only be kept by a specialized, preferably hereditary elite, which acquired, husbanded, and transmitted knowledge beyond the understanding of any toiling villager. The calendar began and sustained specialization and social differentiation. The creation of a skilled elite, freed from all primary labor, was a necessary first step toward what we call civilization—city life, organized around the performance of specialized tasks, and the enhancement of powers over nature from such organization. Only a skilled, intelligent elite, relieved from food production, could have the leisure to create craftsmanship, philosophy, architecture, or high art.

By the time a calendar was in use, some men, possibly the same priests, had grasped the principles of erecting stone on stone. Now the knowledge gap between a calendar-keeper, who must measure and keep records, and a priest-engineer or architect, and an ordinary farmer or laborer was as great as that between a nuclear physicist and a workingman today. It was inevitable that such men, possessing skills essential to society, and with no other counterbalancing aristocracy or elite, should begin to direct society.

The technical perfection of the calendar and the massive engineering accomplishments of the first center-builders show clearly that the early priests and engineers could grasp much of their environment empirically. Such people must have determined a great deal about the world from rational, pragmatic observation and experimentation. But this original creativity and empiricism only reached a certain level of expertise and never afterward advanced. The directing classes developed a peculiar dualism of mind and vision that they could never destroy.

Out of their past, and out of the mysterious subconscious, the autochthons of Meso-America made a universe that was both impressive and appalling. The priests and builders could not really distinguish between the physical forces they shaped and measured and the apparently supernatural events that ruled their lives. The real world of the grass, the maize, the rain, the moon, and the sun was mixed inextricably with the mystic dreads and visions that lie close to all human consciousness. All primitive peoples have tended to see natural forces as gods, or like more sophisticated folk, ruled by gods. But the great peculiarity of the Meso-American mind, so great a difference that it was almost one of kind, was that the precariousness of life caused these men to see their gods mostly as monsters.

The Mexic gods were capricious, willful, cruel, lustful and in need of human blood to sustain them. Other gods have been similarly characterized —but probably never to such an extreme degree. The Greeks also carved out mutated demons and things part-beast, part-men, things that never were. The oldest Egyptians suffered from a somewhat similar vision, but these cultures never chose the path of symbolic destruction to assuage their monsters.

Virtually all cultures have believed their gods or God could be affronted and propitiated. Most cultures have devoted at least part of their energies and substance to discovering what their gods desired, by supporting interpretive priests, or in other ways. And sacrifice is obviously an ancient instinct that lies very close to the human heart. The surrender of something of value, real or symbolic, is part of all great religions and philosophies.

But the Meso-American vision failed to see the general in the particular and carried its worship to extremes. The main manifestation was not just the institutionalization of human sacrifice in the Preclassic period—human sacrifice had been widely practiced by Mesopotamians, Phoenicians, Indo-Europeans. But the ancient Meso-Americans were not really religious in the Judaic, Hellenic, Christian, or Islamic sense of the term. Their practice of human sacrifice was a perversion of practical methodology. Like other peoples, the Meso-Americans hit upon the use of magical and mystical means rather than mechanical or philosophical ways of coping with fundamental human fears and problems, but unlike other peoples, they never relinquished such ideas. Their magic was a surrogate for science.

The spilling of blood on stone altars, or the hurling of virgins into deep wells, was more than a perversion of the symbology of water and the seed. These acts were seen as entirely practical. Because the gods had made man from their own bodies, they were nourished by human blood; in fact, they required it as corn required periodic waterings. A regular harvest of human flayings, burnings, beheadings, and cardiectomies was necessary to make the sun rise and the plants bear fruit. Taught by the first priests, who derived the vision from vanished shamans, the Meso-Americans made this methodology into a vast, driving force, which brought them together, put them to work erecting cult centers, allowed priest-engineers to direct their lives and labor, and permeated every segment of their culture.

During the first millennium B.C. the most advanced Meso-Americans formed theocratic societies, dominated by religious elites. They were deeply fatalistic, since disaster, despite magic, was really beyond human control at times. Society was also grotesquely moral, in modern terms, because the monster-gods were too fearful to be defied. Meanwhile, society remained tribal and communal in organization.

During these centuries people came to believe their collective duty was to understand and honor and propitiate their god-visions. This infused the whole developing society with exotic ideals. And in this service, the tribes began to expend what might be called their gross national product on massive pyramids, huge temples, and increasingly more fantastic art.

The new cult centers that rose at Cuicuilco, Tlapacoya, and Cholula were built by thousands of straining men, but they were not for the use of men. They were intended to be religious foci—monuments to the gods where magic rites would take place. But since such centers inevitably became the focal points of human congregation and activity—every tribesman had to help erect them, and sustain the priesthood, and to come regularly to worship—they inevitably performed the role of the *poleis* in Meso-American culture, drawing skilled elites and artisan-engineers who gradually became the sustainers of a genuinely civilized way of life.

This peculiar origin also assured that the Meso-American civilization would rise along two entirely separate planes. In the service of the demonic deities, men crafted manifestations of higher culture and mechanical skill, raised immense temples and carved brilliant artwork—while the purpose of all this civilized effort remained bloody-minded and mystical at the core.

When the first cult centers rose in the Preclassic age, from Veracruz northwestward to Guanajuato and Nayarit, and south down the highlands into Oaxaca and beyond, the village farmers had obviously come under the disciplined direction of a ruling class—the priestly elite, which had become largely hereditary. It was established and reverenced for its knowledge, and above all for its supposed ability to interpret the will of the gods. It was the priesthood that ordered the stone cult centers built, by commanding the labor of thousands of men.

And though the priesthood may have driven men to enormous efforts and sacrifices through superstition and fear, as a body it was entirely creative in these dawn years. Priests formed a creative, as well as a dominant, elite. They not only discovered principles of building with stone, but they also experimented successfully with irrigation techniques. The breakthrough to irrigation was enormously beneficial: it increased the small area of arable land in south-central Mexico, and, as a result, agricultural wealth and population. Thousands of farmers now lived where there had only been hundreds in the centuries before.

Those who lived around Cuicuilco put together a crude, but distinctive stepped pyramid, with a vast, flat, altar-temple at the top. The Preclassic pyramid-temple at Cholula was even more impressive; it was one of the largest structures built on any continent in any age by the hand of man. The sweat and sacrifice that went into these edifices is still incalculable— but it was not wasted, despite the fear-driven population's exotic goals. The cult centers were essential in the drive toward civilization, and probably such a concerted, disciplined, communal effort would never have been undertaken with a ruling elite, and without and ultrarational spur.

The great centers were devoted to the gods. But the men who serviced the gods lived in and around them, and lesser temples, palaces, and houses were erected for their use. While most people still lived in their crude, primitive, wattle-walled villages, god-worship lent a great cultural thrust: the walls of buildings began to be decorated with murals and carvings, and the interiors of palaces were improved with inlaid woods and stucco floors.

The cult centers also quickly developed a secular function; they became marketplaces. All farmers, apparently, either by command or custom, came to live within a day's walk, some fifteen miles, of a religious center. They journeyed regularly to participate in ceremonies, their one great socializing act, and they brought food and artifacts as tribute, which was rendered to the gods, but used by the center-dwelling priests and artisan-engineers. In time, the farmers also brought other surplus products for exchange, with artisans, and with other farmers from different valleys. Religious days became also barter days in fields and squares around the temples, and this civilizing practice became a lasting feature.

Concentration and specialization inevitably produced other effects. Ceremony in the late Preclassic age became much more refined. Priests no longer pranced and shrieked or shook rattles; they developed impressive rituals. They went robed; they burned incense in the temples. The construction of complex tombs in many places shows that the people had adopted intricate burial rites. And along with ritual and complex ceremony, forms of deference between the priesthood and the common man came into use.

The vision of the priests now created the god-forces into definite, stylized forms. The representations of the old gods, fire, rain, earth-mother, were depicted as universally recognizable shapes. The idols carried forward the grotesque concepts of the earlier age, but now they were carved with exquisite skill. And as the major gods took on stylized forms, they began to receive service from a specialized corps of priests and acolytes.

Men had begun to see life through religious or ideological filters. However distorted these might be, the Mexic Amerindians were no longer merely creatures who were part of nature, feeling themselves part of nature. They had laid the foundations for a unique civilization, which in the next millennium would entirely change the face of Mexico.

4

WHERE MEN BECAME LORDS

> *. . . Nothing ever impressed me more forcibly than the spectacle of this once great and lovely city overturned, desolate, and lost; discovered by accident overgrown with trees for miles around, and without even a name . . .*
> John L. Stephens: *Incidents of Travel in Central America, Chiapas, and Yucatan (1841–1843).*

The era of the first priests and builders ended abruptly about 150 B.C. There seems to have been a series of droughts and violent volcanic eruptions, and there is also evidence of warfare between communities in the highlands, which were now heavily populated. Some peoples migrated or were driven out; others were overrun and enslaved. Many centers and villages were abandoned suddenly. Great confusion swept through the Valley of Mexico, and correlation of the archeology of the many scattered sites throughout Middle America has recently indicated that this disruption occurred throughout most of Mexico; despite the compartmentalization of geography, the Meso-American culture was remarkably integrated, and disasters and sudden advances spread rapidly throughout the entire region.

This era of confusion was brief. By the first century B.C. new centers were rising in the same regions, but usually on new sites and were to become the nuclei of a colorful, luxurious, and quite amazing civilization. Because of the splendor, by any standard, of its monuments, this period is called the Classic era. It was the Golden Age of ancient Mexico, producing mind-stopping sculpture, temples, pyramids, and cities—almost all of the architectural grandeur that still lies strewn across the face of Middle America, from great Teotihuacán in the north to Monte Albán outside Oaxaca to Palenque on the borders of Chiapas, which was the Athens of the Maya world. During a few centuries, men erected the Pyramids of the Sun and Moon that rise so starkly from the devastated Mexic plateau, and built the exquisite, haunting centers that, in modern times, were found tumbled and overgrown with weeds and trees. Ironically, perhaps, so much of this ancient grandeur survived because all these sites were abandoned and forgotten centuries before Cortés came.

In this age, Meso-American civilization made great technical and cultural advances, which it was unable to repeat, or even sustain.

About the first century B.C. identifiable regional cultural styles developed: Maya, Tarasca, Totonac, Huaxtec, Zapotec, Teotihuacán. Although these separate peoples created distinctive art styles, they remained a single civilization, following the same life patterns, worshipping the same gods, and holding the same world view. They rose and fell together, from the mountains of the north to the jungles of the south.

This civilization had three great focal points: Teotihuacán in the Valley of Mexico, Monte Albán in the region of the Zapotecs, and a splendid series of Maya cities in the south, from Palenque to Copán. Some of these Maya centers were located in present-day Mexico, some in Guatemala; but they were part of a common culture that ran from Costa Rica to the Pánuco.

The great centers of Classic Mexico were continuations and refinements of what had gone before, built by labor of thousands upon thousands of men using—incredibly—Stone Age tools and sustained by the produce of thousands of *milpas*. Nothing, really, is known about the societies that built them, except from the evidence of the ancient stones themselves. Such vast cities, permeated with religious symbology and built primarily for the worship of the gods, could only have been erected by a powerfully motivated, disciplined, and organized population ruled by theocrats. Seeing the Egyptian pyramids, which were raised by a similarly technically primitive society, Lewis Mumford, the urbanologist, remarked that in Egypt began a monstrous perversion of human goals, the pouring of wealth and labor and lives into monuments of no use to man. The Egyptian pyramids were ordered by god-kings for their own, ultrarational reasons, and built by laborers, whether native or foreign, who were no better than slaves.

But whether the great pyramids of both worlds should be regarded as perversions or accomplishments, they prove that men united and driven by ultrarational goals can do almost anything. The American pyramids at Cholula and Teotihuacán were the largest structures in the Western Hemisphere until a greater building was erected at Cape Kennedy to support the landings on the moon.

It is not known for certain whether the greatest centers, like those at Palenque and Monte Albán, were merely the foci of religious ceremonies or the hearts of genuine local empires. The question is probably moot: the temple complexes, though built as ceremonial centers, had to draw upon a wide, populated region for construction and support. There was no separation between "church" and "state" in Amerindian Mexico. The centers or cities came about because priests ordered them built, and the priesthood had ultimate power over all mens' bodies and minds. The great centers drew enormous tribute and therefore ruled.

The surviving ruins of Teotihuacán, thirty-three miles northeast of the modern capital of Mexico, extend for miles. Yet much, if not most, of the actual original center is still buried beneath cornfields. The present observer gets a poor conception of Teotihuacán's real extent and size. The original sacred city was at least four miles long and two miles wide, a solid array of temples, palaces, schools, plazas, courtyards, and towering stone monuments.

Teotihuacán was built in several stages, over an extended period, and its design was apparently thought out in detail from first to last by master architects, who all worked according to a central plan; thus, it seems that Teotihuacán did not grow up as people came to live there, but was constructed solely in honor of the gods.

The entire complex was connected by a long, broad, central avenue, which ran between enormous temple-pyramids, wide plazas, and massive houses or palaces. One single plaza, called the Citadel by archeologists although it was never a fortress, measured four hundred yards on each side, and was enclosed by thick stone walls, on which pyramidal temples were subsequently built.

Mile after mile of the walls of Teotihuacán were carved with plumed serpents and covered by brilliant frescoes. The huge façades of certain temples projected gigantic representations of monstrous snake and jaguar gods. Other walls were laboriously carved with violent bas-reliefs, mostly of serpents—fitted with polished obsidian eyes, which have since disappeared—and decorated with sea shells or stuccoed. Some were painted in polychromatic colors.

Almost all archeologists feel the whole complex was laid out according to some intricate astronomical scheme. At certain times of day light strikes certain structures; there is a haunting suggestion that once they were all correlated according to sun, moon, and stars.

But here, where the priesthood believed that the sun and moon were born, generations of docile workers sweated to raise mighty pyramids to honor them. The so-called Pyramid of the Sun, which next to the Preclassic pyramid at Cholula, is the greatest monument ever built in Mexico, contained a million cubic yards of earth and stone. It was over two hundred feet high and once measured seven hundred feet at its base. A huge, squat temple decorated its top. This enormous edifice was damaged disastrously by the errors of early excavators, who tore much of it apart, but even in its reconstructed ruins it strikes awe in the modern visitor seeing it for the first time. But the modern visitor who climbs the ancient steps under the violent tropic sun, or the cold highlands moon, also instinctively feels a wrongness, a certain terror. All Teotihuacán represents something far removed from the Westerner's heart and mind. The massive imagery evokes a feeling of totally inhuman ideals. This city was made by men, but not for men, and few men feel comfortable there.

The language, race, and origin of the people who built and worshipped at Teotihuacán are all obscure. They never called their center "Teotihuacán"; this is a Nahuatl name, applied by later invaders of Mexico, which means "City of the Gods," or "The Place Where Men Became Lords." And the rulers of Teotihuacán must have been lords indeed of central Mexico.

When the city rose, about the first century A.D., the plain surrounding it was heavily forested and well-watered, totally unlike the arid, blasted landscape it is today. Priest-engineers probably directed the laying out of irrigation canals and fields even before the great walls were built. The palaces and houses could have contained some thirty thousand people during the city's prime, but it could not have been a self-contained city. Like Athens or Rome, it must have extended its lordship over vast expanses of adjacent territory—at least ten thousand square miles. And the subtle influences of Teotihuacán's civilization spread even further than that—imitations of its pottery and art styles appeared as far away as Guerrero state.

After the center was laid out, the theoracy of Teotihuacán seems to have flourished steadily in peace and prosperity for some three centuries. The exuberant art created there grew increasingly refined and graceful. The calendar was brought to its final, exquisite, astronomical perfection.

Teotihuacán was one of these rare dawn-societies with the ability to create new forms. Plazas and concourses were paved with lime cement. A network of drains beneath the sacred city carried away its excess water and wastes. Causeways and aqueducts, roads and bridges, drainage canals and dikes crisscrossed the surrounding verdant countryside. Architectural engineering, though it never completely matured in the techniques of arch-building and laying courses, rose to and remained at a very high order—some of the most magnificent buildings the world would ever see, work which was accomplished without iron tools or explosives and which has, in fact, remained beyond the abilities of the modern Mexican successor state.

During these centuries, as men piled tradition upon tradition into a genuine cultural heritage, the more intellectual arts evolved. The Classic Age developed a genuine form of writing, which, in the absence of a true alphabet or calligraphy, combined drawings or pictographs with glyphs to represent concepts, words, or sounds. Mathematics—so necessary for astronomy—reached the level of a fine art. The priests invented the concepts of the zero—which had eluded the Indo-Europeans—and of positioning numbers. These achievements prove the existence of an educated elite with the time and inclination to pursue intellectual research.

Teotihuacán's fourth century bloomed out of the Transitional into the truly Classic stage of building and art. Now Mexic civilization reached its highest level of grace and elegance. The themes of Teotihuacán were still religious, cult-devoted, but they had become more muted and refined. In men's minds and on the wall, the old monster deities persisted, but they came to be rendered with a certain simplicity and even charm—even so, their essential savagery remained.

These same Classic styles, in considerable variation, pervaded most of Middle America, though at different times, throughout the first millennium A.D.

At Monte Albán, looming on its mountain above the present-day city of Oaxaca, the Zapotec race built their great center. Stupendous effort obviously went into the tunneling and carving out of this mountain-peak complex. With obsidian tools and enormous patience, thousands of workers remade an entire mountain top, creating a splendid temple-fortress with temples, palaces, tombs, and ball courts high in the thin air.

At Xochicalco, near modern Cuernavaca, another people erected their ceremonial center on a mountain with perhaps the finest pyramid in all Mexico. This race tooled enormous slabs of rock along the mountainsides into awesome serpents and enthroned lords and covered their temples with weird hieroglyphs painted boldly in red, blue, green, vermilion, and black.

Far to the east, other peoples created splendid basalt structures along the coast. The subcultures of the Veracruz region still showed strong Magician influences. Men in the tropic regions chiselled gigantic heads with thick lips from stone and jaguar-masks from green serpentine. At this time the coastal tribes, unlike the inland peoples, excelled in carving quartz, jadeite, crystal, obsidian, and gems of pale amethyst. These various coastal cultures have been called Olmec, Totonac, and Huaxtec. "The "Olmec" was almost certainly a continuation of the earlier, probably the earliest almost-civilized culture of Mexico fostered by the Magicians. The Totonac tribes were apparently later invaders of the region. The Huaxtecs, however, spoke a language related to the Maya root stock of the far south; they were probably a Maya people somehow separated from the main body a thousand years earlier.

The great center of the Totonacs was Tajín, devoted to their rain god. Tajín, whose original extent was tremendous, was greatly influenced by—or perhaps influenced—Teotihuacán and had plazas, ball courts, and massive dirt pyramids covered with outer rocks.

The Maya subculture built the most remarkable, and most lovely, Classic structures in Mexico. The most beautiful of these was Palenque, in Chiapas state, where Meso-American sculpture achieved what is generally considered its epitome. All the buildings of Palenque were constructed on stepped pyramids; they were decorated with fantastic bas-reliefs, stucco ornaments, hieroglyphs, and representations of human forms, who seem to be variously gods, rulers, and slaves. The stucco-modeling on Palenque's walls had convincing realism and ranks among the best in the world.

All these great cities or centers, though not exactly contemporaneous with one another, flourished across the face of south-central Mexico for a period between three and five hundred years.

Both the great cult centers and the smaller ones that rose in many valleys and on several mountaintops reached the apex of their creativity and power about 500 A.D. For several centuries the priest-rulers had extended their sway over the countryside, entrenching their order not through military or economic power but through their sovereignty over the hearts and minds of the population. The primordial faith and fear that began the cults continued, once the cults were formalized, as religious enthusiasm. And, strikingly, during these centuries of building, the culture was remarkably unwarlike.

The educated groups developed colorful and gripping rituals to impress the people and performed vital services. The rulers alone kept the calendar and calculated the time of planting from the stars. They knew closely-guarded mathematical and engineering secrets. Above all, they had the ear of the gods. The hereditary center-dwellers ordered and supervised the immense public projects like road and canal building and the raising of temple-pyramids. They commanded and assigned labor, and they collected a share of all crops in taxes or tithes. Yet they did not rule the countryside of swarming villages in a temporal way—the villagers continued to cultivate their myriad small plots in peace and to live their ancient communal life as always.

The masses of farmers did not participate in this civilization, except with their sweat and straining backs, and as religious worshippers. Despite the vast gulf that opened between the average man and the educated elite, this was still a collective society, ruled by religious ideology. In such societies, sharp hierarchy does not necessarily bring class conflict. Everyone was caught up in the vast, communal enterprises; the great temples and massive artwork must have elevated the minds of all men, and the secular knowledge of the priests, particularly in irrigation, must have improved the quality of life for everyone.

Life in these centuries must have been exhilarating for the builders of civilization. They acquired traditional knowledge and went on to experiment with new things. Some of them planned and supervised the monumental projects; others enjoyed the leisure to calculate the stars and measure time. And still others created a high order of art, and this obviously was a labor of love. And if the hard, meager life of the peasant was still not splendid, it was no worse than it had been, and at least all farmers lived amid or near splendid things, and were surely impressed.

The intense religious feeling that built the pyramids continued to decorate walls and buildings with sculpture and art.

But soon after about 500 A.D. this admirable beginning apparently stabilized. The causes of creativity are unknown, and so are the exact reasons for its decline or loss. It is probable that the tiny creative minority, after an immense burst of sustained energy and elán, came to believe the Mexic world was made; that they had found the basic answers to all things, and that now mere continuity of this civilization was more desirable than unsettling advances. Historically, except for the rare periods of intense creativity when new cultures are made, men have usually resisted change unless they found their world intolerable.

The continuing artwork shows that the Classic civilization grew increasingly sensual, lazy, complicated, gross, and fat. The pristine simplicity of the best years was replaced by uninspired complexity and over-elaborate adornment. Religious symbolism in art had been so well-defined and formalized that now artists merely repeated and repeated the traditional forms in more and more stylized and elaborate ways, but with considerably less sophistication. Now, every inch of walls or tablets was smothered in an excess of thick carvings, and pottery was buried under a mass of appliqué. Symbolism ran wild, until everything was cluttered and complex. The civilization had entered its Baroque stage.

Art reflects life, and the whole culture must have gradually entered into a baroque frame of mind. Doubtless the elite grew sensual and fat, at least of mind, and thought more in symbolic than in sophisticated terms.

Now, nothing was invented or extemporized.

There is some evidence that all high orders of human civilization may be finally unhealthy to the human psyche, because historically the elán of all superior cultures has been almost impossible to maintain. The world of Palenque and Teotihuacán reached floodtide just as the Greco-Roman world was disintegrating. The Mexic civilization was younger than the Hellenic, and it survived it by some centuries, but these were centuries of unmistakable decay.

Then, in the ninth century, the entire civilization suddenly degenerated into a short period archeologists have called Terminal. When it ended, Classic civilization in Amerindian Mexico was dead.

In the absence of written records it is difficult to piece together the real story of what happened. The records of Teotihuacán are lost, and the stelae of the Maya cities are undecipherable. The reasons for the disaster are still speculative—but then, even with written records and a certain continuity, historians still disagree on the causes of the decline and fall of Rome. Perhaps the evidence of Baroque building and art styles, ending in tumbled walls and abandoned cities left to sun and rot and wind, is better evidence of despair than any confused contemporary accounts could be. Social conflicts involving class war, changes in religious beliefs, crop failure, soil exhaustion, climate changes, insect plagues, mass epidemics, and warfare have all been given as reasons by modern scholars. And in fact, perhaps all of these things occurred.

When the collapse of the ninth century is put in perspective with the decline of other, similar civilizations in other parts of the world and with events that occurred in Mexico before and after the catastrophe, a certain pattern does take shape.

Impressive as the courts and plazas and temples of this civilization were, they had always rested on a pitifully fragile base. The people were kept alive by corn, which was grown by very primitive agriculture on small fields, in a region where nature and geography combined to limit sharply the amount of arable soil. These tender cornfields were terribly vulnerable to freakish weather or natural disaster, and the very religion that had sparked the growth of the brilliant civilization came from the efforts of men, through magic, to assure the corn's growth. And while the magic seemed to have worked over many centuries, the primitive farming never produced much surplus. Neither the villages nor the cities supported by the villages could survive a succession of bad crop years; if the food supply failed, both the physical and psychic supports of the entire civilization were severely threatened.

There is botanical evidence that a serious drought began in the ninth century and lasted until about 1000 A.D. These dry cycles had come before and would appear again; each time they wrought enormous physical and psychological havoc on Amerindian Mexico.

The Mexic civilization was vulnerable in other ways. The ordinary people lived outside the centers in small, dirty, crowded shelters very much like the *jacales* the majority of Mexican peasants live in today. Their life, though little is really known about it, certainly cannot have been attractive. They were bound to the great stone cities only by a sense of collective enthusiasm, or the tentacles of a communal religious fear, and were patient, primitive, and highly ceremonial. And they were becoming human ants, taking orders and employing principles they did not fully understand to build splendid monuments and palaces amid general ignorance and, perhaps, misery. The farmers were certainly alienated in real terms from the priest-lords. Mexic civilization, as opposed to Amerindian culture, was an exotic growth imposed upon a people who neither fully understood it nor shared fully in it. If anything happened to the prestige or the authority of the ruling elite, with little to sustain the higher culture among the people, the civilization could easily melt away, while the people carried on as always.

Almost certainly crop failures and attendant calamities struck the Meso-American world after the year 800, and while great attention has been paid to the disappearance of the Maya subculture in Chiapas and Guatemala, all of Mexico was affected.

The withering of the corn brought hunger, and hunger unhinged the social order. Without a surplus, the great centers could not be fed. Further, the failure of the priestly magic to avert the wrath of the gods probably destroyed the religious order, at least temporarily. There is some evidence in the Maya country of the revival of simplistic earth or fertility cults, which obviated the need for elaborate cult centers and a costly priesthood to ensure the growing of corn. Even if such revived cults were ephemeral, they could have delivered death blows to Copán, Tikal, and Palenque.

Furthermore demoralization must have been inherent in a culture that had grown brittle and static, lacking creativity and hardihood.

The drought encompassed the arid and semiarid regions of the north, beyond the Valley of Mexico, and since, in such period, drought is rarely equally severe at the same time in all areas, whole populations were set on the move. The disaster would have hurt the tribes north of the fringes of the civilization as badly as the settled peoples; their corn and beans also withered, and animal life grew scarce. But these northern tribes, who were nomadic and semi-nomadic folk in whom the ancient warrior traditions had never died, streamed southward, toward the still-green valleys and cool lakes of the central highlands.

Between 800 and 900, archeology shows, vast migrations and disruptions, the beginnings of bitter fratricidal wars, and the disappearance of whole peoples from the earth occurred. In this age all of the greatest cult centers, north and south, were either destroyed or abandoned.

Large numbers of people migrated out of the far south into Mexico's Pacific northwest at the same time northern tribes climbed the south-central volcanic strike. Others went from the highlands toward the coasts. The Maya vanished quietly, probably all at one time. Some remained in the southern jungles, but a segment of this race later reappeared on the barren limestone plains of Yucatán.

Civilization in the central highlands died hard. The people of Monte Albán were pushed out of their mountain fortress by northern invaders. Other centers were abandoned, or they regressed. But many of the minor centers in and around the Valley of Mexico somehow survived, although the culture retrogressed almost to barbarism.

In the north, great Teotihuacán did not go gently from this world. This fact was of far greater importance to the Mexic universe than the mysterious disappearance of the Maya—because the death struggles of Teotihuacán were to have deep influences upon the coming Historic Age.

Hunger created violent social tensions; surpluses and authority disappeared. The universe of priest and common man alike was brought into serious question; magic failed, causing apathy and deep despair. In such an age, rulers could continue to make the peasants of the countryside work or deliver up their tithes only by force and fear. The peasants no longer feared the gods, or rather, no longer believed the priesthood could command them, and so the rulers of Teotihuacán began for the first time to employ soldiers and bureaucrats in the failing Classic civilization; they oppressed the countryside to make sure the great center lived.

In any case, the authority of the priest-lords vanished as the gods no longer heeded their despairing sacrifices and prayers. The elite had probably become intellectually sterile by this time—the art and architecture of the century shrieks the implication—too bound by old ideas and ideology to grasp brutal reality. Warriors and a sort of secular bureaucracy soon shunted the priests aside and dwelt in their palaces. Teotihuacán now sought relief and plunder from foreign wars. A vast conflict broke out in the ninth century between the central highlands and the Totonac peoples of the Gulf coast. The evidence of militarism is not entirely clear, but it exists, and some historians trace the causes of all that followed in the Historic age to events that took place at Teotihuacán, the model and the education of the Mexic world, rather than to the fierce, starving nomads of the north who poured into central Mexico. They arrived in the midst of this terminal era to find disorder and dissension.

The fate of Teotihuacán is clear; its ruins tell an old and simple story. About the year 850 the vast complex was overrun, sacked, and burned. Its huge warehouses were looted and set afire. Its people, rulers and ruled, may have been killed or enslaved; probably, most of them were dispersed. They disappeared as an identifiable race. All Mexic legends agree that the city was destroyed by Amerindians from the north.

Like Nineveh of the Assyrians, the once-splendid city was made desolate and left for grass to grow in its blood-spattered streets. Earth covered the giant pyramids; the long concourse crumbled slowly. Teotihuacán became a ghostly ruin, avoided by men.

But great Teotihuacán, like imperial Rome, was not that easy to kill. Human effort can fail, but tradition is not so easily lost. The lords of Teotihuacán vanished from history, but the memory of what they had done remained. The once-promising and brilliant civilization of the Classic Age was dead. The ghost of that tradition, however, would haunt Amerindian Mexico for half a thousand years.

5

THE WAR EAGLE

O Lord of Battles, under whose Empire we live . . .
O! Our Lord! Let those nobles who die in war
Be gently received by the Sun and Earth.
We know Thou hast sent them to this world,
So they might die in battle . . .
O Lord of Battles, allow them to be seated
Among the famous valiants who precede them!

From a Nahua War Prayer.

The so-called Historic period of Amerind Mexico begins with the *Völker-wanderung* and interregnum that followed the sack and fall of Teotihua-cán. During the ninth and tenth centuries, Otomí, Pame, and Nahua-speaking barbarians poured out of the north over the central highlands, settling in pockets throughout the valleys of the high plateau and dominat-ing or dispersing the older villagers. During the turmoil, a general popula-tion decline probably occurred, making it easier for the barbarians to seize new homes.

Meanwhile, the Mayas had moved eastward, into Yucatán. Around Oaxaca, where the splendid Monte Albán culture was dead, Mixteca tribesmen appeared and drove the older Zapotecs south and southwest. The former Zapotec state, which had extended into Puebla, was pushed into southern Oaxaca and Guerrero, beginning an interminable Mixtec-Zapotec conflict whose overtones have not yet entirely disappeared.

The Tarasca invaded Michoacán, possibly coming from the far south, while Nahuas and Otomís filtered through the central plateau, impinging on the Huaxteca and older peoples of the eastern coast. This era marks the beginning of the ethnic face of modern Amerindian Mexico.

But the term "Historic" is optimistic. Although the major peoples—Nahua, Maya, and Mixtec—all reduced their spoken languages to a form of writing, only about a dozen genuine pre-Conquest records or documents, which all stem from the last centuries of pre-Cortesian Mexico and which are random documents rather than histories have survived the years. The Mayan hieroglyphs have not been deciphered. About all that students have been able to gather from the ephemeral Maya reflowering in Yucatán is a list of rulers.

The Mexic peoples all had a profound sense of history, however; the cyclical nature of their calendar and seasons made them look to the past in order to read the future. They duly recorded all great events, or at least those that seemed important to the educated groups, on figbark scrolls. Although there is much more documentation on Historic Amerind Mexico than was once supposed—some forty verified and probably two hundred old accounts, some transcribed in Nahua pictographs, Latinized Nahuatl script, or sixteenth-century Spanish from documents that later disappeared—all this evidence poses problems for historians.

The old Nahuatl writing is extremely difficult to translate. Nahuatl was never reduced to a true phonetic or ideographic alphabet, like Latin or Chinese. It was transitional, a combination of pictographs, ideographs, and glyphs—partially-phonetic symbols—all run together, which worked quite well for calendar-keeping, astronomical records, and numerical accounts, such as tribute rolls, but which failed to express concepts or poetry adequately. As Philip II's court historian, Don Antonio de Mendoza, put it in the sixteenth century: "In the Province of Mexico they had libraries of histories and calendars, painted in pictures . . . because their characters were not sufficient, like our own writing, they could not set things down exactly; they could only give the substance of their ideas."

The Spanish conquerors destroyed these vast libraries, leaving only a dozen manuscripts saved at random. A handful of Spanish priests, who were not only curious and well-meaning men but excellent historians and ethnologists, preserved almost all that remains of Mexican antiquity. Diego de Landa and Bernardo de Sahagún studied the native past in order to understand the indigenous "superstitions and lies of the Devil" the better to root them out. Since all Mexic writing was suffused with the Mexic religion, it was impossible in Spanish minds to separate Nahua literature from idolatry. But some priests preserved, or were responsible for the creation of, about thirty post-Cortesian accounts in which the conquered Amerindians related their former glories and the agonies of the Conquest. Sahagún also rendered spoken Nahuatl into the Latin alphabet and saw to it that much information was preserved in this script. These transliterations probably afforded more knowledge than intact libraries would have, for two reasons. One was, as Herrera, a Spanish historian, wrote: "The Indians learned many speeches, songs, and orations in chorus; they taught them to the young by memory in special schools, and in this manner the texts were preserved . . . when the Castilians entered that country and taught the natives the art of writing, the Indians then wrote out their speeches and songs as they had known them from memory. . . ." Nahua poetry and orations could not be transcribed in their limited form of writing, which was why they were passed down orally.

Second, the pictographic writing of the folded, painted figbark picture books—called codices—is so symbolic that accurate translation is impossible even for Nahuatl scholars. The scribes constantly used symbols that must have been clear enough to contemporary readers, but which escape modern interpretation. Since the writing was only partially phonetic, using glyphs for common expressions, correlation with spoken Nahuatl as it has survived is of minor use. Much of what the ancient scribes put down can only be rendered as guesswork, though some such "guesses" are confidently advanced and adamantly defended.

Another problem is that the Nahua scribes either deliberately used legends for fact when it suited them or were unable to distinguish fact from myth. This problem is made acute because all written Mexic history comes down through later Nahua, or Mexica, minds and eyes. The Mexica of Tenochtitlán, or even the Acolhua of Texcoco, wrote as the last of a succession of lords of Mexico. Their view of history is colored, and to absorb it uncritically would be much like taking for granted a history of Western Europe written entirely by the Nazi leadership of Germany in 1945, as one historian has stated.

The Nahua legends, like the letters Hernando Cortés wrote his king from Mexico, should not be taken at face value for fact. They contain self-serving propaganda. In fact, the Mexica themselves were great destroyers of old histories, especially those that did not confirm Mexica greatness in the past. And the Mexica understanding of the past was not too clear; they were inheritors of a culture whose origins they only dimly understood. The people Cortés conquered knew less about their ancient history, probably, than modern archeologists now know. But history does not consist of written or rewritten accounts so much as actual changes upon the face of the earth: the movement of peoples, their rise and fall, their deeds, and the effect these produce on posterity. Mexic history, therefore, is not really important in detail, only in its lasting influences.

A final problem in Mexic history is a confusion of chronology. During the Historic epoch more than a dozen calendars were used in the highlands alone; none of these calendars is easily correlated with another, or with the Maya calendar in Yucatán. Nor can the Mexic calendar be correlated with the Christian, as the Hebrew, Roman, and Mohammedan have been. On the Christian calendar, Mexican Amerindian dates are conjectural.

But still, through this confusion of legends, symbolism, and mythology, leading to many variant histories, some Mexican historians, such as Wigberto Jiménez Moreno, have traced a significant framework of events.

The barbarians who demolished—or later claimed to have demolished—Teotihuacán were Nahua-speaking tribesmen from the north of Mexico. Nahuatl was a language of the great Uto-Aztekan linguistic stock which reached high into Utah and Colorado and which penetrated into Central America in historic times. The breeding ground of the Nahuas ("People of the Vicinity"), may have been in the present-day United States. All Nahuas, early and late, carried the traditions of desert warrior clans into the Valley of Mexico; they entered a highly civilized region with the approximate cultural equipment of Apaches. They had learned at least rudimentary agriculture, but they had not forsaken unremitting war.

The first Nahuas, who were in on the destruction of Teotihuacán, are called Tolteca or Toltecs. This was not their own name for themselves; in fact, all the Nahua-speaking invaders, of which there were at least seven major divisions or tribes, called themselves by band names, usually derived in Amerind fashion from some original warchief or tribal Abraham. "Tolteca" seems to be an older term for glutton, that is, barbarian or vandal, which the Nahuas probably richly earned in their ravages of central Mexico and which they soon lost, or rather, turned into a glorious name. These warriors were not to serve history purely as destroyers. When a barbarian culture clashes with a superior one, the result, quite often, is the barbarian conquest of the civilized one, particularly if the civilization is static or decaying. But almost invariably, superior organization forms and life styles are too attractive to the conquerors to be utterly erased. Like the Germanic tribes who sundered the Roman Empire, the Nahuas were impressed by certain advantages of the older culture. And the culture of the highlands had, even in confusion, obvious organizational advantages over the communal, warlike democracy of the hunting bands. The disciplines, deference, learning, and social order of the conquered populations would be and was immediately attractive to the barbaric war chiefs, who were and had to be capable and intelligent men. Such elected or chosen war leaders found the concept of hereditary lordship over a docile population much too attractive to be spurned and were the first to adopt civilized ways and to try to enforce an organizational revolution on their barbaric followers.

All the Nahua tribes brought their own especial totems or tribal deities south into Mexico, and these tribal deities were merely added to the burgeoning pantheon. More important was the transmission of the ancient mysticism and surrealistic vision to each primitive-minded people from the north. The triumph of the monster-gods actually was the most important factor in the renewal of Mexic civilization; once the barbarians succumbed to a belief in ceremony and the placating of the pantheon, they fell into the pattern a millennium of peoples of south-central Mexico had already developed and were forced to recreate a priestly elite and, through civilized irrigation techniques, produce a tribute surplus.

One thing only could have shattered this pattern, and that would have been the arrival of a superior religion or an entirely new vision of human purpose. The Nahua tribesmen brought neither, and so they accepted the old visions, revitalized them, and continued them almost intact.

Another civilizing process was also at work. The great centers had been religious or magical in inspiration, but over the centuries they had come to provide the millions of peasants in the valleys with a genuine marketplace. Everywhere, specialized Amerindian marketplaces had evolved, large, colorful, vibrant plazas of exchange around the temples and pyramids where the people could trade what was left of their surplus crops after tithes and tribute. These markets were a fixture, and perhaps the most pleasant, socializing aspect of Meso-American life. They did not lead toward a mercantile society, because there was no permanent mercantile class; the marketplaces were sites of ephemeral bargaining during the assemblage of people for ceremonial rites. Neither a truly mercantile ethos emerged nor even a concept of money. But the flourishing, transient markets did cement a lasting bond between hill farmers and center artisans. The bulk of the population had come to live within fifteen miles of a center with its market plaza; religion compelled it, and the commerce made the long walk on certain days attractive to all.

Thus both religion and marketplaces gave Meso-American culture a peculiarly urban focus, which could survive even the destruction of the organized state. The Roman world, conversely, had no such cement; when the Roman state and long range trade collapsed during the later empire, villas and rural estates easily turned into the self-sufficient, stagnating medieval manors of the European Dark Ages. But Mexic civilization, like that of much of the Orient, had created an enduring relationship between farmer and townsman that made the whole culture almost indestructible.

What began to occur after the catastrophes of the ninth century was this: the invading Nahua, Tarasca, Mixteca, and other warlike tribes who seized new territories in the highlands dispersed rather than destroyed the old civilization. Some of the priesthood and the artisans survived, keeping their knowledge and techniques alive. Meanwhile, the warlike tribesmen, under their chiefs, supplanted the former ruling groups, and after a period of stabilization, new centers began to rise, which, like the old, supported a civilized way of life.

There were changes in the culture, but no great advances. The fallen Classic civilization seems to have inspired everything that followed: religion, architecture, social orders. The basic changes were the rise of a lay,

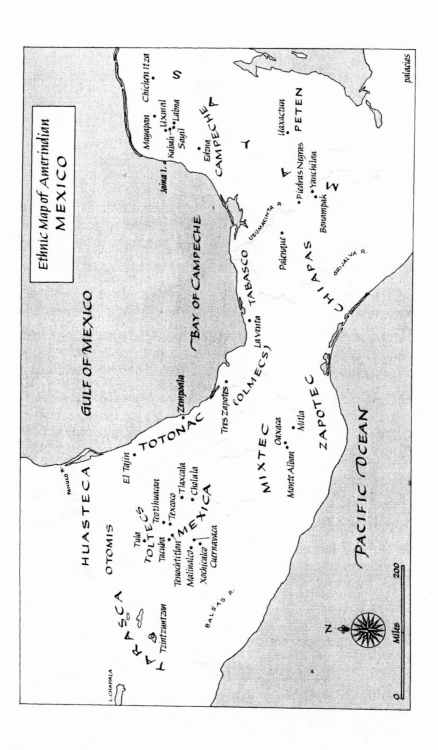

Ethnic Map of Amerindian
MEXICO

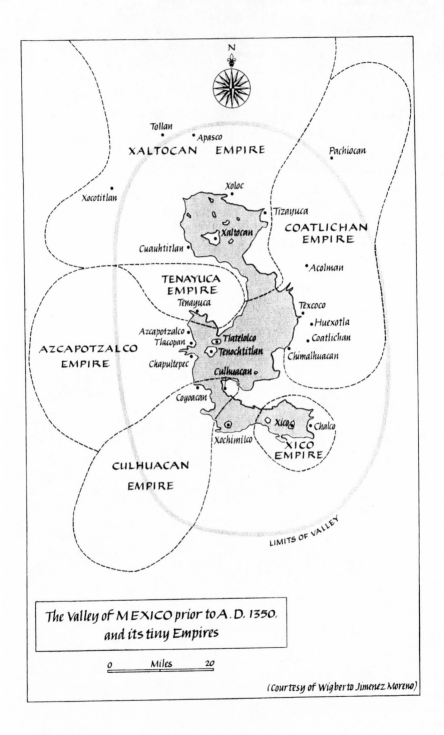

N

Tollan
• Apasco
XALTOCAN EMPIRE
Pachiocan

Xoloc
• Tizayuca
Xocotitlan
COATLICHAN
EMPIRE
Xaltocan
Cuauhtitlan
• Acolman
TENAYUCA
EMPIRE
Tenayuca
Texcoco
• Huexotla
Azcapotzalco
• Coatlichan
Tlacopan
Tlatelolco
AZCAPOTZALCO
Tenochtitlan
EMPIRE
Chimalhuacan
Chapultepec
Culhuacan
Coyoacan
Xico
Chalco
CULHUACAN
Xochimilco
XICO
EMPIRE
EMPIRE

LIMITS OF VALLEY

The Valley of MEXICO prior to A.D. 1350,
and its tiny Empires

0   Miles   20

(Courtesy of Wigberto Jimenez Moreno)

war-oriented aristocracy deriving from the conquering bands, and the infusion of a warlike spirit through the entire culture. Between 1000 and 1519 there were several cycles of regeneration and retreat. The retreats never returned to sheer barbarism—but the renascences never surpassed the Classic age. Most historians look upon the whole Historic period, which lasted some five hundred years, as regressive overall.

The rise of the Tolteca hegemony in Tula illustrates the pattern of these years. During the *Völkerwanderung* of the tenth century, Nahua influence or dominance spread over the present-day Mexican states of Hidalgo, Mexico, Tlaxcala, Querétaro, and into parts of Guerrero and Veracruz. Many invaders gathered particularly around the triple, connected lakes in the Valley of Mexico. In this region, which they called Anáhuac ("Near the Water"), Nahua-speaking or dominated cities arose; since it had been heavily settled for a long time, the urban instincts of the population were strong.

About this time the first historic personages of Amerindian Mexico appeared. The walls and stelae of the past ages may record names and lineages. But while these cannot be deciphered, many Nahua legends have been preserved. The tales of rulers and great men were always highly symbolic, filled with details that had a rich meaning to the Nahua if not the modern mind, and mixed fantasy and magic with a hard core of fact. These accounts and legends, however, do trace a record across the years.

Mixcóatl (Nahuatl: "Cloud Snake," symbolic for hurricane) was an important chieftain of the tenth century. He founded a capital at Culhuacán ("Crooked Hill") near the narrows between lakes Texcoco and Xochimilco, near where the University of Mexico now stands. According to a very colorful account Mixcóatl found a bride and fathered a son, but was slain by his brother Atecpanecatl (Nahuatl: "Lord of the Water Palace") before the child was born.

The brother then ruled in Culhuacán, while Mixcóatl's pregnant wife fled to her own kinfolk, probably in Tepoztlan, gave birth about the year 947 to Ce Acatl Topiltzin ("Our Prince, Born in the Year 1-Reed" [a designation of the cyclic Mexic calendar]), and died doing so. The young prince was sent to the ancient center at Xochicalco, where he was trained into the priesthood, and because of his lineage and piety became the high priest of Quetzalcóatl ("Snake of Precious Feathers," or "Plumed Serpent"). According to custom, the high priest of this ancient god took the deity's name as an added title, a fact which certainly caused much later confusion among chroniclers.

Ce Acatl Topiltzin Quetzalcóatl, now a grown man, went to Culhuacán and slew his uncle, revenging his father and in Nahua eyes committing a holy act. Mixcóatl now passed into the Mexic pantheon as a minor deity, a hunting god; many great or heroic leaders were so deified. Topiltzin then assumed the lordship of Culhuacán.

For unexplained, possibly pragmatic and perhaps symbolic reasons, Topiltzin took his tribesmen first to another city, and then founded Tula, about fifty-five miles north of the present capital of Mexico, in Hidalgo state. This city, Tula, was to become the second Rome of Amerindian Mexico. Its roots and religion, however, lay deep in the heritage of Teotihuacán.

Topiltzin was a rare man and rarer prince. He was chief of a dominant tribe, but his personal qualities made him the most important single figure in legendary Mexico. The old accounts say that he worshipped the ancient arts and revered artists, gathering hundreds of highlands artisans and craftsmen into Tula. Some also came to Tula from great distances out of the south. They were not Nahua, and Topiltzin's kinsmen derisively called them Nonoalca, or "those who cannot speak properly." But the foreigners brought with them the traditions and skills of ancient times. Topiltzin, during his youthful exile, had been introduced to this older culture; he had acquired insights and tastes he would not have had if his upbringing had been that of the normal Nahua lordling. At Tula he began what can only be called a revolution from the top.

Tula began to rise in barbaric magnificence; the artisans drew inspiration from Teotihuacán, but the new architecture was less refined and sensual than the old. Topiltzin saw to it that agriculture was improved, probably through vast irrigation projects. Meanwhile, the Nonoalca introduced the art of working metals, and the Tolteca culture grew skilled working with gold and silver, the sweat of the sun and tears of the moon, and copper as well, but metals were used only for artwork and ornamentation. Topiltzin was respectful of the inheritors of the older civilization and gave them patronage, which was incomprehensible to his own people and which apparently aroused no little hostility among the pure Nahua warrior clans and priesthood. Even more incomprehensible to them was Topiltzin's earnest desire to abolish death and war.

With Topiltzin, the one great Mexic struggle toward a newer humanism began. Topiltzin was loyal to his particular deity, the Snake of Precious Feathers, the giver of fertility and life, bringer of corn to men, the most humane of the monster-pantheon. Quetzalcóatl was a great god of the older civilization, worshipped along with the even older deities of fire and water. Representations of plumed serpents had covered Teotihuacán's walls. The principal god of the Tolteca, however, was the dark deity, of the moon, night, and monsters, represented by a shining mirror and called Tezcatlipoca (Nahua: "Smoking Mirror"). It is believed that the Nahuas brought Tezcatlipoca with them out of the northlands. Like the fire and rain gods, Tezcatlipoca demanded human sacrifice.

Topiltzin tried to end these bloody rituals, urging that the gods be rendered only offerings of bread, flowers, snakes, incense, or butterflies. The orthodox, who feared that Tezcatlipoca would desert the Toltecs, and that the other gods, fed such pale sustenance, would take away the rain, were affronted. More important, Topiltzin-Quetzalcóatl's espousal of the "light" against the "dark" god, and his patronage of the Nonoalca, plunged Tula into a great power struggle with religious, cultural, and ethnic overtones. On one side stood the revolutionary princeling; on the other, the conservative warlords and priests, and probably the mass of Tolteca clansmen.

It is possible that Topiltzin was a fanatic, obsessed only with the supremacy of his chosen god. The modern reader of these ancient chronicles can hardly fail to think otherwise.

According to the legends, a vast warfare broke out among the gods, in which Tezcatlipoca overcame his feathered rival. In actuality Topiltzin was deposed and forced to flee from Tula. Pictured as weeping and wailing, Prince Topiltzin went to Cholula, the city of the massive pyramid. Here Quetzalcóatl was especially revered. When Cortés came, Quetzalcóatl was still the principal god of the Cholulteca, which had important consequences.

Now, the career of Topiltzin-Quetzalcóatl became absolutely inseparable from legend. Apparently, he ruled in Cholula for twenty years. But he also appears in Maya legends, from the coasts of Yucatán. A Maya account states that about the year 987 the Cholulteca were led on a great invasion of Yucatán by their god-king, Kukulcan, who has been positively identified with the Mexic Quetzalcóatl; but by now it was no longer really possible to separate the man from the god, either in the symbolic pictographs or, probably, in the chroniclers' minds. Between 987 and 1000 Quetzalcóatl either ruled or lived among the Maya, also—but myths and legends concerning Topiltzin-Quetzalcóatl-Kukulcan sprouted all over south-central Mexico as well. No personage ever created a deeper impression on the Meso-American mind, although the doctrines Topiltzin taught were everywhere abortive.

The stones of Yucatán record more definite evidence, however, that Kukulcan lived: Maya centers began to rise and flourish at this time, from Chichén Itzá to Mayapán. Chichén's ruins show unmistakable signs of Toltec influence. Reflections of Tula are visible in Mayapán, though on a more barbaric scale. The renascence of the highlands sparked the great Maya revival in Yucatán.

Inevitably a barbaric culture could not accept the death of a man like Quetzalcóatl-Kukulcan. There were many legends telling how he disappeared from earth—on a great pyre, or on a raft, sailing out to sea toward the east. But all legends stated that Our Prince Plumed Serpent assured his followers that he would come again to overthrow his enemies. His second coming would occur in some indeterminate year in the future, but when the cyclical calendar again stood at the year 1-Reed. Thus a threat of ultimate destruction hung over the rulers of Mexico and their monster gods.

The failure of Topiltzin's vision at Tula did not destroy the city's greatness. In fact, a sort of humanism did enter the highlands with the Nahua tribes, but it was suffused with violence.

Yet this was humanistic compared with what had gone before. The peaceable art of Teotihuacán was monstrous in conception and inhuman in representation, with its friezes of glorified snakes. The motifs on Tula's wall were dominated by warriors, men of the Coyote (*Cóyotl*) and Jaguar (*Ocelotl*) societies who waged relentless warfare on the peoples of the lowlands and coast. Although the knights of the Cóyotl and Ocelotl may have infused a potentially disastrous militarism into Mexic society, they were still men, and they are depicted as human beings. Teotihuacán was built for the gods, but Toltec Tula was built for warriors.

The Tolteca lived like the people of Homeric legends. Their world was filled with miracles and magic, drenched with the smell and symbology of blood. But there was a new realism and humanity amid the martial harshness of the heroic age, and the warrior dominance of central Mexico did spark a genuine cultural renascence. The new building and the new art, which had obvious roots in the craft and religion of Teotihuacán but which lacked the baroque sensuality and decayed spirit of the last centuries of the Classic age spread out widely from the Valley, generating rebirths elsewhere, as in Yucatán. Ironically, the Toltec name lost its original connotation of barbarian, and in later times was synonymous with artist. The age when Tula threw its warriors and its hegemony over much of central Mexico saw a rekindling of civilization.

This renascence did not go very far. Except for metalworking, nothing new arose. The old vision and the old gods still lived on amid the greater military furor. Over the emblems of the Coyote and Jaguar orders spread the mighty War Eagle, now the totem of the highland warrior clans. The old gods lived, but the War Eagle ruled men's minds.

South-central Mexico had a heavy human population by this time. The jumbled valleys were in close proximity and, at the same time, remote. They remained split up among separate peoples, clans, and tribes, some culturally differentiated in minor ways, others differing in nothing except direct descent from separate Nahua ancestors. These heavily-populated, connected regions, all enjoying the same basic cultural cement, desperately needed new concepts of political or territorial organization.

They found none; in fact, they were not able to conceive of any. The Nahua people were a case in point: divided up into almost identical but jealously intact tribes, they made a fetish of consanguinity and descent. They trusted only kinsmen, regarding everyone else as aliens. Between clans within a tribe there could be cooperation, but it was almost impossible to extend friendship, trust, or organization beyond the tribal group. The result was that the Nahuas made internecine as well as foreign wars against the lowlands; the more numerous and powerful tribes dominated the weaker, and learning from the ancient ritual centers, exacted tribute. There was no approach toward any sort of territorial, or supratribal state, even among the Nahua-speaking conquerors. The politics of Toltec Mexico remained volatile and precarious, therefore, as one ephemeral tribal hegemony followed another.

Tula gained supremacy over a wide area, perhaps as great an empire as Teotihuacán, but Tula could never organize this lordship into any kind of permanent state. Lordship was imposed by war or threat of war; subordination was expressed by taxes or tribute. Subordinated tribes and cities were otherwise independent, smouldering centers of resentment against their present lords.

In this period following 1000 A.D., as new cities rose and old ones went through renascence, the Nahua language and culture both seeped down deep into the highlands surrounding the Valley of Mexico. Nahuatl must originally have been a quite primitive tongue, but in civilized surroundings it developed exotic growths. It was highly inflected, like Greek, Latin, and other basically primitive languages; it now grew new idioms and forms of expression. Nahuatl was flowery, symbolic, given to poetic forms. But it revealed Mexic culture in a more basic way—Nahuatl developed more deferentials than feudal Japanese or any other Asiatic tongue. Deference and lordship, as well as courtesy, could be expressed profusely; there were countless ways of saying *the honorable, venerable, highborn, noble, revered,* or *lord.*

At the same time, language and culture retained all their older, tribal, communal forms. Individualism was difficult to express even in language, let alone in life. The tribe or group was everything; the person—unless a true lord—nothing. Men said, instinctively, *us* or *our,* not *me* or *mine.* Mexic society was thus ant-like, with all persons in their allotted, natural, place, sex, or rank—but it was a vast series of small ant-tribes scattered throughout one great hill, none of which could really think beyond its own community.

The hegemony of Tula crumbled in the second half of the twelfth century, leading to the second interregnum in civilized Mexico. The ancient Nahua picture books give a symbolic, but possiby quite accurate account of the events leading to Tula's decline and fall.

By about the middle of the twelfth century A.D., Tula had enforced its hegemony over more than twenty cities in the central highlands. Tolteca wielding atlatl, or throwing sticks, held sway over large sections of Veracruz, Hidalgo, Mexico, Morelos, Querétaro, Tlaxcala, and parts of northern Guerrero state. They did not conquer Huexotzingo or Cholula to the east. Tula could not have impinged on Yucatán, but Toltec culture, whether spread by Topiltzin or from some other source, left large influences in Tabasco, Campeche, and along the peninsular coast.

For all the fierceness of the highlands military orders, Toltec civilization was no more secure than that of its predecessor, Teotihuacán: it depended on constantly ripening fields of corn. And in the decade of 1150, rain stopped falling over large areas of the plateau. A written codex placed the blame on Ce Cóatl Huemac Quetzalcóatl ("Huge Hand, Born in the Year 1-Snake, High Priest of the Plumed Serpent"), the last lord of Tula. Huemac played a dramatic game of sacred ball with Tláloc ("Lord of Waters") the rain god. The Tolteca won the game, and Tláloc offered him corn. But Huemac scornfully refused this gift, demanding valuable feathers and green jade, which the god gave him angrily remarking that the lord Huemac would find corn leaves more precious than fine feathers, and corn grain easier to eat than cold stone. And thus it came to pass that the palace of Huemac was filled with treasures while his people starved.

The drought brought panic and public crisis. Huemac tried to solve this problem by making war against the Huaxteca people to his east. But the war against the coast did not succeed. Then, the priests and people tried another traditional gambit. They spurned their old gods, who had denied them rain, and took up the worship of the Huaxtec goddess Tlazolteotl, the Eater of Filth.

They also began an orgy of sacrifice to placate the gods. This ritual murder, like the worship of the Dung Goddess, was alien, a custom of the tribes of the coast. The victim was tied on a rack above the cornfields, his heart was painted and then pierced in a ritual dance. The blood was dripped into the parched earth.

In the end, however, Huemac and the Tolteca were destroyed by the Nonoalca, the alien artisans who had dwelled in Tula since Topiltzin's time.

If the accounts are to be believed, Huemac ordered the Nonoalca to give him a woman measuring four hands across the buttocks. When they presented one, Huemac found her wanting—his name, Huge Hand, gives a logical reason for his displeasure. The Nonoalca became furious, and began to ravage the Toltec lands.

The Nonoalca were driven out, or else left voluntarily, moving into the state of Oaxaca and Puebla and toward the coast. But by now Huemac's subjects had had enough; there was a general uprising among the Tolteca clans, and about 1168, Huge Hand fled to Lake Texcoco, to a cave on a hill called Chapultepec ("Hill of the Grasshoppers"), where he died a few years later.

The Toltec empire then disintegrated. Along with civil war and Nonoalca uprisings, new barbarian invasions, which always occurred in a period of general drought, gave the Tula hegemony its coup de grace. Into the Valley poured waves of so-called Chichimeca ("Of the Lineage of the Dog") savages, who ate meat raw, wore the skins of beasts instead of civilized woven loin cloths, and, most important, used the bow and arrow, a weapon incomparably superior to the Toltec throwing stick. Tula was completely destroyed, living on only in Nahua legend; some historians thought the city was synonymous with Teotihuacán until modern archeology uncovered Tula's ruins and found conclusive evidence that Topiltzin and Huemac lived.

The people of Tula were dispersed, most fleeing southward into Anáhuac, where they settled at Culhuacán, Chapultepec, and Xico and now called themselves Culhua, from Culhuacán. Other refugees went further south, to Cholula, where the Olmeca-Xicallanca people of the Puebla region enslaved them and made them suffer many indignities until these Toltecs revolted and, with considerable cunning, sent messengers inviting the Chichimeca tribesmen who had inherited the valley of Tula to come to their aid. By this time grass had long grown between Tula's stones.

Seven bands of barbarians marched to the rescue, certainly not to help Toltecs but in search of lands and loot. Still, an alliance was made and Cholula fell. The barbarians settled down in this area, building cities of their own, and Cholula itself finally became part of the Nahua-highland world. The Olmec culture which had held the region for centuries was at last dispersed.

Following the destruction of Tula, successive hordes descended upon the vale of Anáhuac, dispersing some peoples and subordinating others. By the close of the twelfth century a second Mexic interregnum had begun.

Early in the thirteenth century, a large mixed horde of Chichimeca led by the war chief Xolotl, or "Monster," came down into the northern reaches of the Valley. These peoples spoke Pame and Otomí, indicating they came from somewhere in Hidalgo, though possibly they could have derived from as far north as the banks of the Río Pánuco, possibly the valley of Metztitlán. All the semiarid regions west of the Huaxteca country were a barbarian reservoir, a cultural fount of tribes that continually shocked and reinvigorated the civilization to the south.

These people first encamped just north of the great, interconnected lakes that formed the heart of Anáhuac. After Xolotl sent warriors under his son Nopal ("Prickly Pear," or "Cactus Fruit") to scout the northern Valley, the barbarians moved around the northern lake, Xaltocan, to a place called Tenayuca, and made their homes in caves.

Xolotl the Monster, who is said to have ordered a count made of his followers, was no mere savage Otomí or Pame brave; he had long-range plans. He seized all of the northern Valley, began to make a permanent little empire, and cement alliances with other tribes who flocked to his totem by giving each leader one of his daughters—of which he apparently had many—and assigning them lands. About 1230 Xolotl gave Acolna-huacatzin of the Tepaneca the area around Azcapotzalco, west of Lake Texcoco. To Chicocuauhtli ("Seven Eagle") of the Otomí he assigned the northern part of the lake, including the marshy island of Xaltocan. Tzon-tecomatl of the Acolhua (there were several tribes of this lineage) received a region across the lake from Azcapotzalco some years later. These place names and tribal names are given in Nahuatl, because they were only preserved in Nahua codices and legends.

Xolotl's domains impinged upon the Culhua-Tolteca peoples who had settled at Culhuacán, Chalco, Xico, and Coyoacán around the southern finger of the great lake. Around the year 1246 Xolotl's barbarians fought with the civilized Nahua of Culhuacán and defeated them.

The lances and clubs of the highland warriors were no match for the flint-tipped arrows of the northerners. Xolotl imposed his own man, Huetzin, as lord of Culhuacán, and Nopal took a Culhua princess as his wife.

When Xolotl died, he was succeeded by Nopaltzin (the *tzin* suffix, fre-quently added to proper names by the Nahua-speaking, was a deferential signifying high birth or exalted station; later chroniclers used it widely in referring to these barbarian chiefs), who from a permanent throne, taught his braves how to plant corn, ordered them to erect houses like most of the Toltec-Culhua, and had a pyramid built. He also extended his overlordship beyond the Valley into Morelos, Puebla, and the valley of Toluca.

But meanwhile, if the *atlatl* of the Culhua had been no match for the barbarian arrows, the barbarian ethos was no match for the comforts and arts of civilization. At Azcapotzalco, Acolnahuaca ("Great Man") at-tracted large numbers of the Tolteca and Nonoalca, who built an impres-sive center; the Otomí also built one at Xaltocan, out on the lake; and Coatlichan and Texcoco of the Acolhua peoples across the middle lake coalesced into important centers. All around the lake, the rude conquerors, now in contact with peoples who practiced writing, metalwork, engineering, architecture, and the fine arts, began to disappear into the civilized popula-tion, leaving only the ruling lineages.

The chroniclers related the conversion of Nopaltzin's son Tlotzin ("the Lord Hawk") from barbarism to civilization in pictographs. The account has a striking humorous quality even after hundreds of years. Tlotzin gov-erned a sector of the Chichimec domain in the far southeast of Anáhuac, close by the Nahuatl-speaking cultural centers of Xico and Chalco. He became friendly with a local high priest and took him deer-hunting—the royal Chichimeca sport. The city-bred priest, however, introduced Tlotzin to *tamalli* (Sp: *tamales*) and got him drunk on *octli* (Sp: *pulque*), the fermented juice of the maguey plant. These blandishments convinced the wild Hawk of the superiority of civilized life, and he commanded his warriors to leave their caves and study the ways of the Toltecs.

Tlotzin's son, Quinatzin, moved the center of the Chichimeca hegemony from Tenayuca to Texcoco. Tenayuca was now being surpassed in size and elegance by the originally-subject cities to its south, including Xaltocan out on the water. And the old barbarian dialects were vanishing; Otomí and Pame were being supplanted by Nahua dialects, which Tlotzin's grandchildren spoke as their native tongue. Inevitably, some barbarians assimilated faster than others, causing a split in their ranks. Finally, a civil war broke out between the conservative, cruder Chichimecs who remained in the north and those who had been seduced by civilization. The savage holdouts were defeated and driven from the Valley.

And by this time, the middle of the fourteenth century, A.D. the original Chichimec empire had dissolved. As each chief or lordling who ruled a subject city inevitably founded a new lineage—and thus not only a dynasty but a new tribe—each center tended to separate and become the seat of a miniature Chichimec-ruled empire. The lords or chiefs were closely related by blood, but as they founded different "tribes" the cities began to become independent and separate in fact.

Each vigorous center bordering the triple lake of Anáhuac carved out a small territorial hegemony, creating a confused and impinging series of city-sovereignties. The island-city of Xico dominated the southeast, Culhuacán controlled a large area of the southwest, and Tenayuca held sway over a small region to the north. But the three greatest centers and empires were those of Azcapotzalco, Coatlichan-Texcoco, and Xaltocán. In each of these, Chichimec dynasty and the older Mexic civilization had fused, and a new vigor was the result.

The Valley was thus divided into six major sovereignties, with several minor towns still independent. Political fragmentation was complete.

All of these centers were inordinately jealous of one another, like Greek or Italian city-states. Yet this very hostility, perhaps, engendered a genuine cultural renascence, just as it had in the Old World. The tribes vied with one another to raise pyramids, palaces, and temples. Azcapotzalco, which was populated by a very mixed race and had a powerful ruling house, laid out great plazas and fine parks. But while Azcapotzalco was politically and militarily more powerful, the most important cultural center was still Culhuacán, whose Tolteca-lineage dynasty enjoyed immense prestige; wars were sometimes waged among the Chichimeca-descended lordlings for the hands of Culhua princesses.

Each prince or lord was suspicious of all the others; each city, although most spoke the same language and followed the same civilization, was hostile to the rest. They soon began to make war.

One prince, Tezozómoc of Azcapotzalco, the Tepaneca grandson of Xolotl, assumed predominance over all the others. Tezozómoc ("Angry Stone Mask") wanted personal and dynastic dominion of the whole Valley, and to achieve his goal he employed treachery, murder, terrorism, espionage, arson, and invasion. He was helped immensely by his longevity; he grew in shrewdness and wisdom as his body withered, outlived many of his rivals, and was able to manipulate inexperienced princes and divided enemies.

Also, according to the custom, he took many women and had many sons, who became his loyal deputies, army commanders, and governors in his conquered lands.

Tezozómoc conquered Culhuacán about 1367, enlarging his holdings both to the south and across the lake. The genius of Tezozómoc did not lay in armed campaigns, however, and many of his greatest gains came through diplomacy, shifting alliances, and the playing off of one rival against another. He was a phenomenon with whom the other princelings could not cope. He took over the Tenayuca hegemony and moved against the large and quite powerful empire of Xaltocan. But first he immobilized rival Texcoco, ruled by Xolotl's great-great grandson Techolatlallatzin ("Mud Dropping from a Stone") through an alliance.

Tezozómoc seized Xaltocan about 1380, destroying it forever as a flourishing independent state. The allied Texcoca derived nothing from this war, and eventually gave some Xaltocan survivors refuge at Otumba. Meanwhile, the lord of Texcoco committed the serious political mistake of giving parts of his holdings to several petty chieftains who conspired with Tezozómoc against Texcoco. They in turn became the victims of Tezozómoc.

One by one, Tezozómoc conquered Coatlichan, Amecameca, Cuauhnauac or Cuernavaca, Xochimilco, Cuitláhuac, Mizquic, and Huexotla. His troops marched as far north as the valley where the ruins of Tula weathered in sun and grass, into Morelos state, to Toluca, and through the Tetela region around Puebla.

By the close of the fourteenth century he had control of everything around the Valley except the shrunken empire of his kinsman, Techolatlallatzin, who died in 1409 and left a son, Ixtlilxóchitl ("Black Flower"), a young and inexperienced prince at Texcoco. Tezozómoc immediately claimed his throne, because of his closer lineage to Xolotl and because the new prince was unfit to rule.

The ruler of Azcapotzalco made demands, including tribute, by sending baled cotton to Texcoco to be spun. Ixtlilxóchitl tried to avoid war by acceding to some of these demands. Finally, the two cities went to war; by ruses and stratagems Tezozómoc seems to have destroyed the morale of the Texcoca army, lifted a siege of his own city, and advanced upon Texcoco.

The accounts, always favorable to Ixtlilxóchitl, claim that the prince fled his capital to prevent slaughter, taking with him his ten-year-old son. The warriors of Tezozómoc followed, determined to kill both heirs to the throne. Finally run to earth, Ixtlilxóchitl ordered his son Nezahualcóyotl ("Fasting Coyote") to climb a great tree, while he made a last stand, obsidian-toothed sword in hand.

After a brave fight he died, the enemy stripped his body of clothing and jade and left it for the beasts, and little Nezahualcóyotl climbed down and stood watch over his sire's body throughout the night.

The next morning, refugees from Texcoco arrived; one was the young prince's tutor. This man led Nezahualcóyotl eastward into the mountains.

In rage, Tezozómoc ordered several thousand Texcoca children killed. Each child was asked who his lord was, and unless the answer was "Tezozómoc," he was killed.

Nezahualcóyotl found sanctuary in Huexotzingo, and in the Nahua city of Tlaxcala. There was a price on his head, and he lived in constant peril for many years. According to legends, he had several narrow escapes and was saved now and again by men loyal to the ideal of Acolhua liberty. As a symbol of opposition to the tyranny of Tezozómoc, he became a great hero throughout the highlands.

Beyond Anáhuac, over the southern mountains, the course of events was roughly similar to that of the Valley of Mexico. The Mixteca, a great people with roots in the Preclassic past, continued a high culture in Oaxaca, but battled with the older Zapotecs. The Zapoteca created a new empire that reached to Tehuantepec. The far southern valleys were geographically divided and their human populations were complex. Mazateca, Cuicateca, Mixe, Huave, Zoque, Chinanteca, and other peoples lived scattered throughout these secluded valleys. All these tribes were urban-oriented and observed the same calendar and gods, but the southern tribes were more isolated from each other in habitat and mind than the peoples to the north, or those to the southeast, in Yucatán. Here minor empires rose and fell; men were subordinated and forced to pay tribute, but the region was never really unified, nor the separate tribes destroyed. Isolated peoples clung to their deep valleys and steep cliffs, maintaining their own parochial worlds; they would continue this pattern into modern times.

Yucatán was also culturally part of the Mexic world, but the renascent Maya peoples here went through a steep degeneration throughout the historic period. They never regained the glories of the Classic era, when great cities flourished in Chiapas and Guatemala. The Toltec influence apparently sparked a brief revival of civilization about 1000 A.D., but the Maya peoples were totally unable either to form a lasting political organization, or, on the lowlands, to leave each other in peace. What happened to the

Maya is reasonably well known, though the details, for lack of a written
documentation, are obscure.

Under an ephemeral alliance, the new cities, Mayapán, Chichén Itzá,
and Uxmal dominated the peninsula. But this alliance cracked about the
year 1200, and Hunac Ceel of the Cocom family of Mayapán established
hegemony over the other centers, using Mexic mercenaries armed with
bows and throwing sticks. But the militaristic theocracy of the Cocom
dynasty was short: eventually, the Xiu rulers of Uxmal and the Itzá of
Chichén rebelled against Mayapán. There was bitter internecine warfare.
Mayapán was destroyed about 1441, and Uxmal was abandoned by its
people a decade later.

The Xiu and Itzá, however, could not resolve their rivalry. It spread
through the eighteen smaller, less civilized city-states that replaced the
great centers. These cities engaged in civil war, while the whole culture
degenerated rapidly. A series of natural disasters, including hurricanes,
brought pestilence and depopulation. Finally, only the city of Tulum,
perched on cliffs in Quintana Roo, overlooking the blue Caribbean, remained. This city survived into the sixteenth century, but was degenerate.

The remnants of the Itzá peoples retreated out of Yucatán into Guatemala. They left no cities—there was no civilization in the Maya region
when the Spaniards came and subdued the last Itzá, living deep in Guatemala as savages in the seventeenth century.

The written history of the Maya, carved on stone, is not readable, although certain dates and lists of dynastic rulers have been deciphered. The
fate of the Maya, however, is to be understood from their deserted pyramids and tree-tumbled stones. Maya farmers continued to wrest a wretched
living from the jungles, but the Maya civilization destroyed itself without
outside help.

6

THE MEXICA

*When the Mexica erected a temple to Huitzilopochtli, the Culhua
came and asked them: What will you put in such a great temple?
The Mexica told them, fresh hearts and warm blood. Then the
Culhua were angry, and threw foul things into the temple.*

From the *Tira de la Peregrinación*.

Where the Mexica, who gave Mexico its name, came from they themselves
did not know. Their legends told of an ancestral home, Aztatlán, supposed
to lie somewhere in the northwest of Mexico. The Mexica spoke Nahuatl in
historic times, but this may not have been their original language; like the
descendents of Xolotl they may have adopted Nahuatl, one of the tongues
of the great Amerindian Uto-Aztecan linguistic stock, after they entered
central Mexico as Chichimeca wanderers in the thirteenth century. However, William H. Prescott, the historian, called the Mexica "Aztecs" from
their language, and they have been popularly called Aztecs ever since
although the term in Nahuatl did not exist. As members of this linguistic
stock, their way station on the trek out of Asia could have been anywhere
from Colorado to the Mexican state of Nayarit. The Mexica had a strong
historic sense and developed a need to create a usable past, but they were
never able to trace their ancestors beyond the destruction of Tula, in which
they claimed a part. Whatever its origins, this tribe made its history in the
Valley of Mexico.

The Mexica or Aztecs left many accounts and records, but most of these
were written down after the Spanish Conquest. And even the pre-Conquest
legends that were recorded were highly colored, even invented. This was
not unusual; all peoples in all times have had their peculiar national myths.

Other legends about the Mexica have derived from modern misinterpretations of ancient scripts. The strong tendency of many later Mexicans to identify emotionally with the Mexica or Aztecs has created historical problems and popular myths which are almost impossible to eradicate.

The Mexica appeared in the era following Tula's fall; they were one of the many migrant peoples who harassed the civilized central plateau. But unlike the other barbarian Pame and Otomí tribes who quickly settled into the urban Tolteca culture, the Mexica were peculiarly bellicose and unruly, and they clung to their identity and traditions.

One Mexica custom was their worship of Huitzilopochtli (literally, "Left-handed Hummingbird"). Huitzilopochtli was their especial tribal deity—every Meso-American people and locality possessed one—and may have once been a tribal chieftain who was deified. Mexica legends stated that Huitzilopochtli first commanded them to call themselves "Mexica" and to leave Aztatlán. Huitzilopochtli was above all the god of a warrior clan: the sun god, god of war and hunting, and later, of the tribal aristocracy. His symbol was the eagle—the same War Eagle that figured so prominently in the Nahua culture—and, as essentially another Tezcatlipoca, he was inserted into the highlands pantheon in the same manner. The Mexica accepted Tezcatlipoca, as they eventually accepted Tlazolteotl the filth goddess and Xipe, Lord of the Flayed, who, like the fire god Huehueteotl ("Most Revered Ancient God") and Quetzalcóatl were of very ancient, non-Nahua origin.

Huitzilopochtli appeared in the twelfth century. When he was a man, he led his people from place to place; when he became a god, he spoke to the people through the mouths of priests. Mexica accounts state that their god continually ordered them to move on, and for many years the tribe did not stay long in one place. This was probably due less to the orders of Huitzilopochtli than to the fact that no other tribe found them comfortable neighbors. There are a number of legends or accounts detailing events of these years; interestingly, they all indicate that the Mexica were peculiarly detested and abhorred because of their incorrigible woman-stealing and love of human sacrifice.

In the thirteenth century, the Mexica begged Lord Acolnahuacatzin of Azcapotzalco for permission to inhabit the hill of Chapultepec, from which they drove away another Chichimeca squatter band. The Mexica lived around Chapultepec until about the end of the century, making many enemies and no friends; on one occasion the rulers of Culhuacán and Chalco across the lake, and Azcapotzalco and Xaltocan sent an expedition against them. The Mexica were routed, and their war chief and his daughters were captured and sacrificed at Culhuacán. The codex, *Tira de la Peregrinación,* a Mexica Exodus, shows that the survivors of this raid hid weeping in the reeds and cattail rushes along the lake.

At a later time Coxcox, Lord of Culhuacán, permitted the tribe to hold some useless, snake-infested territory. But the Mexica apparently thrived on eating rattlesnakes, grew stronger, and erected a temple to Huitzilopochtli. The same accounts state that the cultured Culhua, however, were disgusted at peculiarly bloody Mexic sacrificial practices, and on one occasion threw ordure into this temple.

But the Mexica were fierce, and thus useful, if disgusting neighbors. Culhuacán frequently warred with Xochimilco ("Country of Flowery Fields") and Coxcox enlisted the Mexica tribesmen as mercenaries, promising them freedom from Culhuacán if they would capture eight thousand Xochimilca.

The tribe did so, and brought large bags of Xochimilca ears, cut from these captives, to Coxcox's throne. The pictographs showed Coxcox registering horror at these bloody trophies, but he kept his promise. Now the Mexica asked for a favorite daughter of Coxcox, that they might pay her a great honor. The ruler of Culhuacán was invited to attend the ceremony.

When Coxcox arrived in the Mexica temple, he found a Mexica priest prancing about in his daughter's skin; the girl had been sacrificed and flayed. Coxcox bellowed for his warriors, and once again the bewildered Mexica had to flee into the marshes and reeds. When the Culhua ceased hunting them, the bedraggled tribesmen sullenly took refuge on two low-lying, swampy islands out in the lake, called Zoquitlán, or Place of Mud.

These barren, offshore islands were a sort of no-man's land, outside the declared hegemonies of Culhuacán, Azcapotzalco, and Texcoco. Here the Mexica were able to eke out a miserable existence, mostly from lake products like fish and duck eggs, for several generations. They held these mud flats by sufferance of powerful neighbors, who were probably restrained more by the balance of power than by respect for the inhabitants. All accounts agree that the Mexica were despised and humiliated because of their ferocious practices. The clans on the islands were ostracized and driven in upon themselves. Some historians believe this experience led to the later characteristics of the race: the extraordinary unity of the Mexica nation, its belligerence, and its merciless aggression against all outsiders. The Mexica shared these traits to an almost unbelievable degree.

The tribe built up two towns on the muddy isles, Tlatelolco and Tenochtitlan. Tlatelolco ("The Mound") was apparently settled first, on the smaller island to the north. Its people, separated from Tenochtitlan by a short stretch of dirty water, split off from the main body of the Mexica.

The founding of the larger town is surrounded by numerous legends; the best known apparently derives from a later misinterpretation of a Nahua codex (the old Nahua codices were and are extremely difficult to read, and their pictographic representations, reduced to small or stylized form, were often given rather fanciful interpretations by later chroniclers). According to this legend, the Mexica wandered from place to place seeking a sacred spot where, according to prophecies, they would see an eagle perched on a cactus growing out of a stone. They discovered this phenomenon, with a serpent in the eagle's beak, at Tenochtitlan ("Place of the Cactus on a Stone"). New light was thrown on this legend when in modern times, a stone carving was unearthed on the site of the present-day National Palace of Mexico. This original carving, which the symbolic pictographs undoubtedly were meant to represent, is, in full scale, quite different from the stylized Eagle on the Cactus on the Stone. In this sculpture the pears of the cactus are not pears at all, but stylized human hearts, and the "cactus" itself is a mass of hearts emerging from the opened chest of a sacrificial victim. The eagle, representative of the sun and war-god, does not have a serpent in its beak but rather a curlicue which is the Nahua glyph symbolizing *atlachinolli*, or war. This whole symbology is much more characteristic of the Mexica ethos than the romanticized myth invented out of the misinterpretation of a pictograph. Logic has not, however, prevented the mythical version of the founding of Tenochtitlan, the Mexica capital, from being institutionalized in the national seal of the Mexican Republic.

The people of Tenochtitlan called themselves Tenochca or Mexica and their country either Tenochtitlan or Mexico. Later the Tenochca preferred to be known as Culhua-Mexica, denoting their descent from Toltec-Culhua bloodlines. "Mexico" may mean "in the navel of the moon" according to some authorities, or may have been a tribal term which became literally meaningless over the years.

Most Nahua place names, along with proper names and a vast number of indigenous words for animals, earth-objects, and the like, survived through a Spanish filter, just as earlier Amerindian dialects filtered into Spanish through Nahuatl. The Spaniards naturally reduced Nahuatl to their Latin alphabet and pronounced it like Spanish, just as most Europeans pronounce ancient Latin like their spoken tongue. But Nahuatl was and is a very different language, highly inflected, with different stresses and rhythms and with sounds that do not occur in Spanish at all. Like certain Oriental languages, Nahuatl has no "r" sound. The Spaniards tended to elide the almost unpronounceable gutterals, and they changed the "gobbled" sound of Nahua word-endings by dropping the "l" and adding a vowel. Above all, the Spanish had trouble with the pervasive Nahuatl sound similar to "sh" (as in the English "mush"), which does not occur in Spanish.

Most words that modern Mexicans think of as "Indian" have been transmuted into Mexican-Spanish. Thus *cóyotl*, the indigenous wild dog, became coyote: *tzópilotl* (buzzard) zopilote, and *'tómatl*, tomate, all softened with Latin endings and changed stress. The bothersome "sh" sound was arbitrarily written down as "s," "j," or "x" and given the Spanish values for these consonants. The Nahua *Mexico* (English pronounciation approximately: may-SHEE-koh) became Méjico or México (MEH-hee-koh). The "x" spelling became de rigeur only after independence, because Mexicans believed this was more indigenous than the Spanish "j." The native language of all but an ineffective, illiterate minority of Mexicans became Spanish, however, and it was impossible to change Spanish pronunciations. Spanish rules of accentation were also applied to Nahuatl.

Most modern Mexican usage tends to be a compromise. TenochTITlan, except for Nahua purists, became TenochtitLAN. The name Motecuhzoma, which sounded exactly like "Montezuma" to Cortés, is spelled Moctezuma in Mexican Spanish. The ubiquitous "x," pronounced as an "s" in Xochimilco, as a Spanish "j" in Oaxaca, and indigenously when applied to the archeological ruins at Uxmal, actually confuses all Spanish-speaking peoples except born Mexicans.

During the fourteenth century the Mexica came under the suzerainty of Tezozómoc of Azcapotzalco, when he conquered Culhuacán and annexed that city's territories to his own. Because the Mexica and Tlatelolca submitted peacefully, Tezozómoc permitted them to choose their own chiefs or governors. Tlatelolco, the northern isle, chose a son of Tezozómoc and thus began an Azcapotzalcan dynasty, while Tenochtitlan selected a grandson of the former lord of Culhuacán about the year 1376 for governor, beginning a Culhua line.

This chief, Acamapichtli ("Handful of Reeds"), was to be immortalized by Republican Mexico and his name taught to school children as the first ruler of the "Mexican nation." But Acamapichtli was no sovereign prince, rather the Toltec-Culhua spokesman for a tributary tribe. The Mexica chose such a chief because of the prestige of Culhuacán in the Mexic world. Because his wife was apparently sterile, Acamapichtli was presented with many nubile daughters by the families of Tenochtitlan. The Mexica were puritanical and possessive of their women like most nomadic warrior peoples, but the impregnation of as many women as possible had become a Tolteca warlord custom, and Tenochtitlan accepted its new prince's ways. Acamapichtli now preceeded to found not only a Culhua dynasty, but a numerous mixed Culhua-Mexica aristocracy with his offspring.

This had profound social effects among the Mexica barbarians. Since Acamapichtli was of royal blood all his children, even those born of slave girls like his son Itzcóatl, were greatly respected. These children were called *pipiltin* and freed from onerous tribal duties and even taxes. They became an elite.

The Mexica had lived in Anáhuac in a primitive society of kinship bands and clans. As they gradually had become agrarian, a warrior-peasant community, the clan structure had survived. Each *calpulli* had its own totem, quarter or locality, and held lands and even houses in common. Even as the people became urbanized the clans remained as great extended families. The clan feeling was so strong that the individual Mexica developed no sense of individuality or personal autonomy. Intensely parochial, the clan's great strength was that it stood as one body in work and war.

Within the loose association of the tribe, each clan practiced simple self-government, in a sort of communal democracy in which all family heads were peers. The clan elected certain offcers at large: the *teachcuatin*—"eldest kin"—who acted as civil chiefs, and a war leader, the *techutli*. Such elections were usually for life, though military command was rotated. There were also many minor officials, who apportioned living space and fields, and decided minor disputes among the clan's human cells. No family owned its fields, but fields were by custom assigned in perpetuity and taken away only for crimes or a failure to work. In effect, the clansmen were more ruled by the conventional wisdom of custom than by formal laws or chiefs. And because the families were so closely-knit and connected by blood, few if any Mexica thought of their society as oppressive. If no one had a private life, everyone did have a recognized place and role.

The several clans were drawn into the tribe by ties of common language, custom, and history, which gave all Mexica a common spirit. Clan elders came together in the tribal *tlatocan*, or council, in which each served as a *tlatoani* or spokesman. This council made the great decisions for the tribe and elected tribal officers, such as the *hueytlatoani*, the "revered speaker" who though originally only what his title implied—he who spoke for the tribe—gradually became supreme general, supreme priest, and supreme judge. When the Mexica chose Acamapichtli as their governor, he became revered speaker for the tribe.

But the Culhua princeling brought Toltec ways and instituted an elite revolution. Tolteca practices were dynastic and founded on military aristocracy. Acamapichtli's sons received a Toltec education: literacy, astronomy, theology, and all the millennia-old arts. Thus the new governor infused the apex of society with civilized Culhua notions and practices and learning, including concepts of exalted lineages. This was outside of and foreign to the communal clan structures and began to undermine them, especially in the selection of high officers. Acamapichtli's line, called that of the Eagle, was revered and held a special place, so much so that when he died about 1396, his son Huitzilihuitl ("Hummingbird Feathers") became revered speaker. Apparently, a compromise between old tribal customs and Toltec aristocracy came about. The speakership remained elective—but the electors were restricted now to the four greatest officers of the tribal council, at least one of whom had to be of Eagle lineage. While Huitzilihuitl's election probably was still the result of natural selection, forces had been set in motion that would implant an immutable custom of choosing chiefs only from Eagle blood. Thus Acamapichtli's descendents were able to become a small, respected, powerful *pipiltin* elite, and more important, perpetuated themselves through electing one of their number the Mexica ruler.

The people accepted this. The Culhua lineage was prestigious but also capable, and it was well-equipped to deal with the prickly, continual problem of handling relations between Tenochtitlan and the overlords at Azcapotzalco, whom the sophisticated Culhua dynasty could handle more effectively than simple clan chiefs.

During his tenure Acamapichtli carefully avoided trouble with the ruling Tepaneca, and the twin island cities prospered in peace, even while Tezozómoc continued to ravage Anáhuac. But this very prosperity had perils. The Azcapotzalca overlords resented it and raised their demands for tribute. Acamapichtli urged his people to comply, which they did resentfully; their old drawings show them weeping as they delivered up ducks and fish and eggs and forced labor to build the fine parks of Azcapotzalco.

Huitzilihuitl, however, secured a daughter of Tezozómoc in marriage, a dynastic coup, and the tyrant reduced tribute to token levels. Both the islands now furnished Tezozómoc with warriors for his aggressive wars. Huitzilihuitl and the lord of Tlatelolco helped Tezozómoc conquer the Valley between 1396 and 1416, doubtless learning much about both the practice and the rewards of empire.

Huitzilihuitl had two sons by the daughter of Tezozómoc: Motecuhzoma Ilhuicamina ("Angry Lord Shoots Arrows at the Sky") and Chimalpopoca ("Smoking Mirror"). It was Nahua custom that power and responsibility within families passed from brother to brother rather than from father to son. When Huitzilihuitl died, it would have been normal for his capable brother Itzcóatl to assume leadership of the Eagle lineage and therefore the state. However, it was known that Chimalpopoca had become Tezozómoc's favorite grandson. Although only ten years of age, he was elected revered speaker by an Eagle-dominated council obviously playing judicious politics.

The dynastic-minded old Tezozómoc was pleased. Both Mexica cities were now governed by his seed and had his favor. But the Azcapotzalca aristocracy was not pleased. More and more the great men of the Tepaneca saw the Mexica as rivals, and their governors as men who might even come to rule over Azcapotzalco.

About 1427 Chimalpopoca got permission to bring water from the springs at Chapultepec to Tenochtitlan by aqueduct, for the once-clear lake had become polluted from the dense population growing up around it. The Tepanec nobility were furious and Tezozómoc's own officers plotted to use this special favor as an excuse to assassinate Chimalpopoca and reduce the upstart Mexica to their former station. Tepaneca popular opinion was behind them.

And now old Tezozómoc, who to keep his arthritic bones from pain had had to be wrapped in quilted cotton blankets and laid between two charcoal braziers, died peacefully in bed. He had caused much grief and bloodshed in his 106 years; now, his dying was to create more.

The old tyrant had designated his eldest son his heir. But a younger son, Maxtla ("Loincloth") who had been put off with the governorship of a minor city, Coyoacán, was too much his father's son in ambition and cruelty. Maxtla rebelled, induced the lawful heir to exchange places, then murdered him.

During this deadly game of state, young Chimalpopoca of the Mexica made two mistakes. He first sided with the murdered brother; then, he hesitated in sending demanded tribute. Maxtla, very aware that his kinsmen in Tlatelolco and Tenochtitlan had a blood-claim to the throne of Azcapotzalco, had assassins strangle Chimalpopoca and drown the lord of Tlatelolco, Tlacateotl ("Godly Chief") in the lake.

The murders, however, set off a wave of fury in the cities. An angry Eagle aristocracy designated Itzcóatl ("Obsidian Snake"), the son of Acamapichtli and the slave girl, as ruler. It was a shrewd choice, for Itzcóatl was a powerful warrior, hard-minded, but also open to the advice of the cleverest of all the kinsmen, Tlacaélel. Tlacaélel ("Liverish Chief") counseled that a united Mexica should be called to arms and that help should be sought among all the surrounding cities that feared and hated the power of Azcapotzalco.

The war drums boomed, and the Tenochca rose en masse, while in Tlatelolco the new chief Cuauhlatoa ("Talking Eagle") roused the people with flaming speeches. Itzcóatl sent runners east, over the great volcanoes guarding Anáhuac, to the still independent realm of Huexotzingo, where they cried of murder and tyranny in the Valley, begging for aid.

Nezahualcóyotl of Texcoco, now twenty-one years old, was then in exile at Huexotzingo as a respected guest. He persuaded the Huexotzinga to send an army. The neighboring Nahua republic of Tlaxcala also sent warriors from its mountain eyrie. The combined forces marched west under command of Tenocelotl ("Jaguar Lip Plug"), a famous Huexotzinga general.

Meanwhile, young Nezahualcóyotl rushed ahead of the army to Texcoco, to a joyful reunion with his father's old and loyal warriors; the Acolhua people rose against Azcapotzalco, and another army marched westward.

Later Mexica chroniclers did their best to obscure the true events of the days that followed, because the true story damaged Mexica pride and conscience. For most of Anáhuac rose against the usurper Maxtla and his haughty Tepaneca. Little Tlacopán, or Tacuba, in the shadow of the overlord, joined Tenochtitlan. Even the crushed Otomí tribesmen of Xaltocán dared to dispatch warriors.

The Mexica were powerful fighters, but without Nezahualcóyotl, the ultramontane contingents, and the general rebellion they must have been overwhelmed by the greater and experienced forces of Azcapotzalco. They gratefully accepted the leadership of the Huexotzinga warlord Tenocelotl, and it was this warrior, not Itzcóatl or Nezahualcóyotl, who commanded the combined armies against the enemy.

After taking Tenayuca, the allies marched against Azcapotzalco.

The Tepaneca tribe now paid the final price of empire. Its men were killed, its capital overrun, and the great parks and pyramids razed and burned. The people were made serfs or slaves. From this time onward, the plaza of Azcapotzalco was known as a slave market. The long career of Tezozómoc ended in blood and smoke, and the destruction of his people.

Maxtla escaped the slaughter, fleeing to Coyoacán. But he died here, or in Taxco.

The Tlaxcalteca mountaineers and the army of Huexotzingo went home with their booty. Their part in the liberation of Tenochtitlan was subsequently minimized, though it could not be denied, by Mexica scribes.

The myriad small city-states around the lake were free, or so it seemed. Prestigious Texcoco might have been expected to assume a general ascendancy, but Nezahualcóyotl was no imperialist. It would have been better for the countryside, probably, had this prince been more ambitious, because he was wise and tempered by adversity, with a clear mind and a great sense of justice. But as so often happened in human history, it was not the cultured Texcoca but the still half-barbarous Mexica, numerous and warlike and now led by a clever aristocracy, who were to prove that in the long run wars of liberation can rarely be distinguished from struggles for preponderance and power.

7

RED TIDE OF EMPIRE

Loved and tender son,
This is the will of the gods.
You are not born in your true house
Because you are a warrior. Your land
Is not here, but in another place.
You are promised to the field of battle.
You are dedicated to war.
You must give the Sun your enemies' blood.
You must feed the earth with corpses.
Your house, your fortune, and your destiny
Is in the House of the Sun.
Serve, and rejoice that you may be worthy
To die the Death of Flowers!

From the prayer of the Mexica midwife.

The two greatest men of fifteenth-century Mexico were a prince of Texcoco and a prime minister of Tenochtitlan. Nezahualcóyotl of Texcoco and Tlacaélel of Tenochtitlan were both highborn; they were both supremely intelligent, and both lived long lives at the core of power. But while Nezahualcóyotl was a cultivated intellectual given to reflections on the fleeting grandeur of the world, Tlacaélel was a brutal-minded patriot, intent above all else with his country's wealth and power.

Mexican historians understandably prefer the image of the former to that of the Mexica *cihuacóatl* ("Snake Woman," the symbolic title of the second officer of Tenochtitlan). But as chief justice and high priest and chief minister of the Mexica, Tlacaélel did most to shape his times. He never held a throne, but he was the power behind thrones he twice refused. He understood the difference between dominant influence in the state and the cares of exercising power and had the wisdom to prefer the first.

He was of royal blood, a nephew of Itzcóatl, and showed early ability in the rebellion against Azcapotzalco. From this time he was always one of the four great councillors of the tribe, one of the four men who, in the name of the twenty clans, administered the state, advised the ruler, and in effect chose every ruler from their own ranks.

Tlacaélel's name remained almost unknown for centuries, but he was the principal architect of the Mexica or Aztec empire. He dreamed vast dreams in the smoke of Azcapotzalco, and while Nezahualcóyotl, the child of fickle fortune, looked upon the work of Tezozómoc and despaired, Tlacaélel was able to transmit his dreams to his warrior uncle and to all his tribe. He could have seen no omens in the faces of the wailing, enslaved Tepanecs, or in the revolt he had helped engineer.

And while Nezahualcóyotl wrote poetry about the vanity of men and the mutability of fortune, Tlacaélel planned a new course of empire.

The rulers of the three victorious cities of Anáhuac—Tenochtitlan-Tlatelolco, Texcoco, and Tlacopán—struck a pragmatic alliance in the ruins of Azcapotzalco, realizing that between them they had enough power to dominate the Valley; the Mexica and the Texcoca were great warriors, while the Tlacopaneca could provide a commissariat of corn. Under the terms of this alliance the lords of Tlacopán and Texcoco became members of the Mexica council—though power remained with the four members from Tenochtitlan.

The alliance easily asserted its power over the Valley. But while the Texcoca merely reestablished their hegemony over the northeast corner of the lake, the Mexica, urged by Tlacaélel, filled the power vacuum on the *ocotl*-covered slopes of the west by annexing not only the lands but the tributary cities of Azcapotzalco. The Mexica were already overcrowded on their muddy isles, but this proved to be an irreversible step toward empire.

Tlacaélel was ruthlessly practical, with only one purpose: to increase the power of Tenochtitlan. His Toltec education gave him knowledge of things that went back to Teotihuacán—but it had not eradicated his true Mexica nature, barbarian, bellicose, parochial, with an island mentality and a thoroughly tribal mind. His genius—and he had genius—lay in his ability to blend his knowledge and his qualities into empirical actions. The precise chronology of his acts is unknown. They began with the destruction of Azcapotzalco about 1431 and continued until his death in 1480, when he had irreversibly fixed the destiny of the Mexica nation.

When the Mexica seized the western shore of Lake Texcoco they were still a homogeneous grouping of fierce warrior-peasant clans who could have more readily harassed and ravaged the Valley than created and maintained an empire. But it was at this time that Tlacaélel, Itzcóatl, and the small group of Culhua-descended *pipiltin* were able to make vast changes in tribal society.

The first step was to create a military aristocracy that would be a true instrument of empire.

Until now tribal territories had always been held by the clans, who assigned fields to families according to ability and need. But Tlacaélel and Itzcóatl refused to permit the newly conquered lands to be added to the communal holdings and disposed of them in different ways.

Much of the new land was designated as *pillali*, or fields of the nobles, assigned to distinguished warriors who were to hold them for life, with the right to command the labor of the conquered population on them. The sons of *tectecuhtzin*, the feudal landholders, had the right of succession to both privileges, though the lands reverted to the hueytlatoani's office if a lineage died out. Itzcóatl also decreed that the military honors and distinctions won in the war were hereditary. Here, at one stroke, the rulers of Tenochtitlan created a powerful military aristocracy and the beginnings of a militaristic caste system.

The conquered people who were forced to work the *pillali* were known as *mayeque* ("handy ones"). As serfs bound to the soil, they were only permitted to keep enough of the fruits of their labor to eat, the bulk of it going to their landlords. There was also a whole class of people less fortunate than the *mayeque*, the slaves. Serfdom and slavery were old in Mexico.

The slaves, however, were not chattels like Negroes in North America. They kept certain rights; they could contract marriage and beget free children; and they could buy back their freedom and even have slaves of their own. The slave class came from prisoners of war, criminals who did not merit death, and certain people who could not repay obligations.

The distinction between slaves and *mayeque* serfs, clear at first, began to blur.

Tlacaélel believed that a powerful, militaristic class, freed from economic production, was necessary for empire. But he also drew on old forms of organization to create and subsidize the burgeoning bureaucracy that any organized, civilized state required—the administrators, judges, scribes, public engineers, teachers, and junior professional military ranks. For this purpose other fields were set aside: the *tlatocatlalli*, or fields reserved for the revered speaker and the upkeep of his office; the *tecpantlalli* ("palace estates") which supported the growing horde of officers of the hueytlatoani, the "state" bureaucracy; and lands designated as Shield or War Fields, which provided provisions for the professional warriors, and for extended campaigns. All these lands were worked by serfs.

In an agricultural society which had no notion of money, this was the only means of creating a state treasury and of rewarding public servants. The actual ownership of all land was still communal, that is, it came from the tribe or state, but now the ruling clique designated its use. Tlacaélel also founded a new class in addition to the skilled groups that the palace subsidized, the *pochteca*, or merchants. The *pochteca* formed a caste or guild; they were not entrepreneurs, but rather agents who carried on a strategic commerce for the palace. In fact, throughout Mexic society everyone except the family head on his communal plot in some way worked for or was dependent on the "state."

These actions obviously drove deep class divisions between the Mexica tribesmen, separating the people into *pilli* or nobility, and ordinary tribesmen, or *macehualtin*, with certain public-supported intermediate skilled ranks.

The Mexica rulers were consciously trying to recreate the previous imperial social orders. Tlacaélel planned to solve problems, not to create them. There could be no gain in wealth or power without social diversification, specialization, and stratification, and since civilization rested on small cornfields, the directors, sustainers, and war-makers had to be freed from primary labor. There could be no palaces and fine parks, no aqueducts and paved roads, and no soaring pyramids without the labor of thousands of people straining at subsistence level. All of the Meso-American cultures built their capital, and their civilization, out of peasant sweat.

Obviously, power and direction passed to the land-and-office-holding aristocrats after 1431. But the life of the *macehual*, the common clansman on whom the real power of the Mexica nation rested, did not really change. The creation of a landed aristocracy and a palace bureaucracy affected the common farmer very little because foreign peoples supported these structures. The *macehual* kept on living in a common house, working common land with his close relatives, and there is no evidence that he disliked or opposed the changes in any way; in fact, he seems to have considered the rising nobility still his kinsmen, and he saw possible opportunity for himself, through war.

At clan level the Mexica were yet a remarkably homogeneous and cohesive folk, while the new aristocrats and sustainers of the state stood outside the clan organization, and so arose a peculiar dualism.

The old tribal cohesiveness provided a hard core around which to form a remarkable military force. Tlacaélel, whose interests had no boundaries, completely remade the army along Toltec lines, again blending the old and new—the war-band clan feeling of the people and military hierarchies developed by the lords of Tula.

The basic fighting unit was a squad of twenty men, led by a minor officer or chief. Twenty such "twenties" formed a squadron or battalion of four hundred men. These squadrons were always drawn from a single clan, and had to be commanded by an officer of that clan. Twenty squadrons comprised an army of about eight thousand. This, with bearers, allies, and auxiliaries, was the basic field unit with which the tribe made war.

The speaker was supreme general, and the field general, who commanded several armies of Mexica and allies, was normally an aristocrat of Eagle blood. Below the *tlacatécatl* ("Chief of Men") and *tlacochcalcatl* ("Chief of the House of Arrows"), the *tecuhtli* who commanded the clan battalions were also of the military elite. The army was hierarchical and completely disciplined.

Outside of the straight military rank structure there also existed a vast proliferation of military honors, elite orders, and hereditary warrior castes. The common warrior, or *yaoquizque*, was awarded special feathers, ornaments, and other distinctions for valiant deeds. The warrior who captured four enemies in battle was honored, with a title and a special chair. The best warriors formed the elite orders of Jaguar, Eagle, and other "knights," which the Mexica adopted from the Toltec culture and which fought as special groups. Virtually all commanders and officers were chosen from these ranks.

Despite this strict hierarchy and the fact that such distinctions were made hereditary, the army was the main road to social mobility. *Macehual yaoquizque* could and did rise through valor and ability; they could become recognized warriors, leaders, and even feudal noblemen. And all judges, palace officers, priests, and bureaucrats were usually appointed from among distinguished fighting men. Such appointments were still more accessible to the sons of aristocrats, the *pipiltin*, but even they had to prove themselves in war.

Officers and elite warriors wore elaborate masks and feather headdresses, and colorful insignia of rank—fantastic trappings from the barbarian Nahua past. A Mexica army was a disciplined mass of men, commanded by proven officers, supported by an organized commissary, and sustained by a special treasury of palace lands when in the field. The warrior did not have to feed himself; bearers and slaves carried along thousands of baskets of tortillas or corn cakes. And yet the army was still made up of savage, barbarically colorful warbands, hordes of clansmen fighting shoulder to shoulder, blood brothers marching against the world.

However, the institution of a militaristic nobility and the organization of a vast tribal army did not automatically bring about an empire. Tezozómoc had conquered Anáhuac with a similiar social and military organization—although it lacked the Mexica tribal core—and had carved out only an ephemeral dynastic state, which fell apart at his death. Tlacaélel's genius was superior. He had a new rationale for empire, a new vision: a people in arms, committed to a divine mission, driven by mysticism toward a vast collective goal. His great success lay in his ability to give the Mexica a usable past, a myth of superiority, and a vision of glory. Tlacaélel understood human nature and the nature of his bellicose, resentful, barbarian kinsmen very well.

The tribe had an inferiority complex arising from its humiliating past. Tlacaélel dictated new histories that overlaid this past with satisfying myths. The *Codex Matritense* sings:

> *They had kept stories of their past,*
> *But in the reign of Itzcóatl these were burned;*
> *The lords of Mexico ordered this;*
> *So the lords of Mexico decreed:*
> *Their people must not know the old pictures*
> *Because all of them were filled with lies.*

So Tlacaélel rewrote history, his scribes turning out new lies. New books depicted the Mexica, or the Culhua-Mexica, as having always been a great people, the equal of every Nahua nation, who had wandered out of a forgotten paradise. They came as the Chosen of Huitzilopochtli, Children of the Eagle and the Sun, blood heirs of the mighty Toltecs, through Culhuacán. It was a irresistible genealogical myth.

This was harmless compared to the new rendering of the cult of Huitzilopochtli, the tribal deity. Now Huitzilopochtli was offered the most extravagant praise. He was shown to be equal and even the superior of Tezcatlipoca, the powerful Toltec god. He had always required human blood—but now Tlacaélel interpreted the will of Huitzilopochtli in a stunning new revelation.

The Sun God was also the God of War, and he had chosen the Mexica for a great mission—to bring together all the nations into the service of the Sun. The Mexica were to subdue the world and offer Huitzilopochtli continual blood, which he required so that he might continue to rise in the east and vanquish the night. Unless Huitzilopochtli were refreshed and strengthened, he could not replenish the earth. He had called the Mexica to this special service so that they might gain great honor and glory. As agents of the god, the tribe would become demigods themselves, rulers in his name of all the earth.

The warriors who fed Huitzilopochtli, either through the hearts of enemies or by their own blood in battle, were assured of eternity in the East Heaven of the Sun, the most exalted of Meso-American paradises.

Here indeed was a divine mission, promising lordship in this life and heaven hereafter. And the Mexica, as a whole people, seized upon it eagerly. The outstanding characteristic of the Mexica people in their great century was the mystical belligerency that some modern Mexican intellectuals deny and most historians find almost incredible.

Tlacaélel did not invent holy war; he only gave the old Meso-American mythology a new and violent thrust. Blood magic was part of the culture, and religious warfare came down from ancient times. More is known about the empire of Tenochtitlan than the great Mexican hegemonies that preceded it, but since it is known that the Mexica were adaptive rather than creative, the Mexica empire perhaps tells a great deal about those earlier realms.

Like a Caesar, Charlemagne, or Hitler, Tlacaélel found the correct combination of forces for his times. He escaped fame as a great conqueror only because he preferred to remain in the Mexic background, behind the throne.

He created a formidable tool of conquest. History has shown that a homogeneous people with an island mentality, if led by capable rulers and fired with ultrarational goals, burst upon the world more ferociously than others, and fight more tenaciously than heterogeneous societies.

Commanding this instrument, directing it toward goals he himself had devised, Tlacaélel of Tenochtitlan now held history in his hand.

Itzcóatl took only those actions, wrote the Spanish historian Durán, *that were advised by Tlacaélel, to gather together all the nations.* Now the Mexica horde pushed south along the lake. Coyoacán fell, then Cuitláhuac, then Xochimilco, another center built like Tenochtitlan out on its island. Chalco, to the southeast, was overrun.

These cities were populated by men like the Mexica, who spoke similar dialects and worshipped the same pantheon of gods. Perhaps the ruling circle of the Mexica was unafraid that a hungry Huitzilopochtli would refuse to replenish the earth and perhaps the nobility and warriors may have only been dreaming of glory, wealth, and power. But it would be a mistake to consider their warfare pragmatic. Behind it all was a haunting dread. The Mexica tribesmen believed in their war god; they believed in the immortality of the soul; and they believed the universe was ruled by their magic. Thousands fell; the sun was fed; many Mexica won their eternal reward. And each year the power and wealth of Tenochtitlan swelled.

The huge snakehide drum *tlalpanhuehuetl*, which was sounded only to signal human sacrifice or herald war, boomed its dismal message out over the lake. Spaniards who heard it wrote that the monstrous drum could be heard two leagues away, and that its sound made hairs stand up on the nape of the neck. The Mexica continuously found pretexts for war: a refusal to pay tribute, an insult to an ambassador—and Mexica envoys cultivated insults—or interference with traveling merchants. The Mexica were always scrupulous about declaring war and sending advance notice.

The armies of Tenochtitlan would then march forth with advance scouts and flankers to prevent ambush. Picked warriors and priests pushed far ahead; long lines of bearers brought up the rear. Mexica and allies often marched separately, because of the logistic problem, and arrived at a designated battlefield several days apart.

Although the Amerindian warfare took ambush and treachery into account, tactical maneuver was unknown. Foes assembled on a chosen field, usually outside a threatened city. After ceremonial demonstrations and war cries, the actual battle began with a shower from each side of stones, darts, arrows that were usually deflected by shields and did little damage.

When the missiles were exhausted, the infantry charged in closepacked ranks. At this moment the generals lost control; the battle was decided by numbers and mass ferocity, as ranks of warriors clashed.

Men struck with the crude but fearsome *maquauhuitl*, a wooden sword with obsidian teeth, which could sever a head with one stroke, clubbed one another, or thrust with lances or spears.

The first prisoners taken in an action had to be dragged to the rear and sacrificed at once, which sometimes delayed the final assault. The battle ended when one side was overwhelmed.

The Mexica, armed by fury and discipline cut their way into countless towns. The last desperate resistance was always in front of the main *teocalli* or temple-pyramid. When the last defenders were hacked to pieces or driven off, the Mexica set the temple afire. The Mexica pictograph for a captured city was the drawing of a ruined temple, sometimes with a spear driven through it.

The fallen center was then drawn into the hegemony of Tenochtitlan. Long lines of bound prisoners were herded back for the altars of Huitzilopochtli. Most of the conquered people were not molested, but for the rest of their lives they would pay tribute, which the Mexica had learned the hard way from Tezozómoc. Now, they were insatiable and cunning in their demands—corn, fowl, metals, jades, paper, slaves—all of which they kept a permanent record.

Itzcóatl, at the head of his armies, conquered almost all the Valley of Mexico in ten years. These bloody raids made further expansion easier, for the fame and terror of the Mexica spread. When Itzcóatl led an expedition beyond the Valley for the first time, into southern Morelos, its people surrendered without a fight. The Mexica always permitted a city to surrender, and if it rendered homage and paid tribute, its people were permitted to retain their property and lives.

Because the Mexica were victorious everywhere, this warfare added yearly to their wealth and power. Nor were their losses in men serious. The Texcoca fought with them, and other subject peoples were sometimes made to join their ranks.

Most of the peoples who submitted or were overrun spoke Nahuatl and had inherited Toltec culture. Even the Tlahuica of Morelos were Nahua. It would have been possible, at this time, for the Mexica to have founded some sort of great society, or to have erected a powerful Nahua confederacy in the highlands—a union that might have been able to stave off invasion in later years. But the Mexica never again followed the precedent they had set with Texcoco and Tlacopán in seeking allies. They either subjected every other people with whom they came in contact, or made them pay tribute, and failing this, made perpetual war. They did not incorporate the fallen centers into their political structure; they made a sullen empire of rulers and ruled.

The Mexica, though not lenient, left subdued cities under their own rulers, especially at this time because they lacked the political sophistication to devise any other method of controlling or collecting tribute. The defeated rulers had to swear allegiance to Itzcóatl, and this made for frequent rebellion.

By 1440 the Mexica were utterly dominant throughout Anáhuac.

In these same years, Nezahualcóyotl of Texcoco symbolized a different facet of the civilization. This prince ruled over warriors who were the equals of the Mexica, but he was not really interested in expansive war. He fought with the Mexica in their wars, but he made quite clear that he had no belief in the cult of Huitzilopochtli. Nezahualcóyotl was intellectual. He admired astronomy, philosophy, engineering, and art, and he gathered a great number of skilled and learned people into his court at Texcoco, acquired the finest library in all Mexico, and had a palace probably unequalled in magnificence. Texcoco in these years was still a more splendid city than Tenochtitlan; in fact, Nezahualcóyotl built causeways and aqueducts to service his allies in Tenochtitlan.

Nezahualcóyotl showed that he sought intellectual rather than magical-militaristic answers to the questions of the universe. He was interested in popularizing a new syncretism, by which all the old gods would be held to be One, a single giver of life. However, this esoteric view never caught on outside his circle of philosophers.

Even so, a sort of humanism was sprouting in Texcoco, which could not possibly arise in Tlacaélel's Tenochtitlan. Tenochtitlan was too overwhelmingly devoted to social purpose, and too constructed like a human anthill, for any true humanism to take hold.

Nezahualcóyotl did live the good life of a Mexic prince. He enjoyed his splendid apartments and great library and the services of a vast harem. He sired over a hundred children by these wives and concubines. He was greatly admired for this by his people, and also for the disciplined manner in which he ruled his household. Nezahualcóyotl's name was a byword for wisdom and justice; his courts were considered the fairest of all in Mexico, because several of his own children were sentenced to death for public sins.

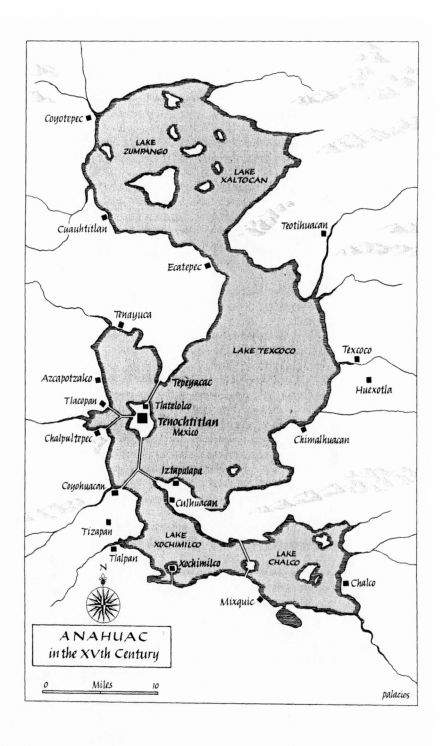

Coyotepec

LAKE
ZUMPANGO

LAKE
XALTOCAN

Cuauhtitlan

Teotihuacan

Ecatepec

Tenayuca

LAKE TEXCOCO

Texcoco

Azcapotzalco

Tepeyacac

Huexotla

Tlacopan

Tlatelolco

Tenochtitlan
Mexico

Chalpultepec

Chimalhuacan

Coyohuacan

Iztapalapa

Culhuacan

Tizapan

Tlalpan

LAKE
XOCHIMILCO

N

Xochimilco

LAKE
CHALCO

Chalco

Mixquic

ANAHUAC
in the XVth Century

0   Miles   10

palacios

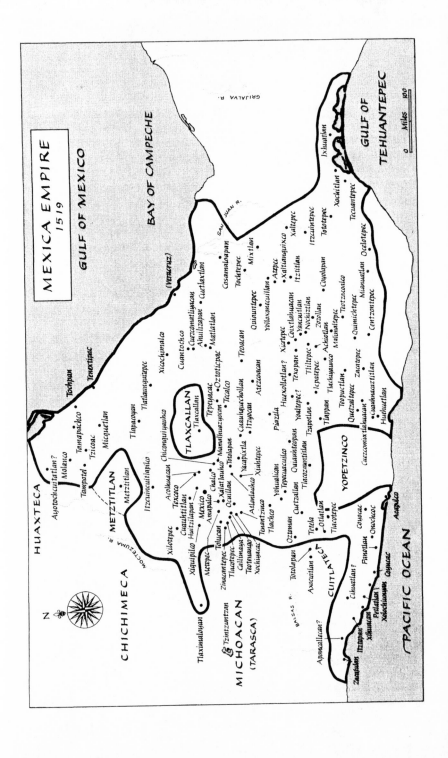

The prince of Texcoco was living evidence that the Amerindian civilization could and did create a high level of intellectual culture. But even Nezahualcóyotl's court was repeating old concepts and forms and breaking no new ground. The art of his engineers never equalled that of the Classic Age; for hundreds of years Amerindian engineers and architects were accustomed to applying old techniques without ever considering the concepts behind the techniques they used.

There was another small island of humanism in these years at Huexotzingo. However, the Mexica of Tenochtitlan were far more representative of the Nahua culture of the age. The vast majority of men were dominated by custom, deference, and devotion to a bloody-minded magic. The Mexica were only more warlike, and better organized and inspired than most.

Itzcóatl the Conqueror died circa 1440. But this marked no watershed in the history of Tenochtitlan, for Tlacaélel had done his work too well. Utterly dominant in its own near-universe, Tenochtitlan had no rational cause to go beyond the volcanoes. But Tlacaélel still lived and gave advice, and ultrarational notions are easier to infuse than eradicate.

The ruling council, including Nezahualcóyotl, offered Tlacaélel the revered speaker's seat, which was by now almost a theocratic throne. When the prime minister refused, the brother of Chimalpopoca, Motecuhzoma Ilhuicamina, was ceremonially installed with rites and nose plug, in the traditional year 1-Dog.

Under Motecuhzoma warfare became the *causa causans* of the Mexica state. The upper echelons of Mexica society had become totally militarist, and the prosperity and employment of the burgeoning aristocracy and bureaucracy depended upon a constant growth of the palace estates. The common man was fired by mystic theology and saw war as his only means of mobility. Such pressures were irresistible. And Motecuhzoma did not try to resist them; he led his armies beyond the mountains into Morelos, and with this act the Mexica empire passed its final point of no return.

Motecuhzoma raped and reduced all Morelos. Then he marched south for the first time, into the series of valleys and broad plateaus that made up the Oaxaca region. Here he encountered the Mixteca (Nahua: "Cloud People") on the snow-capped slopes. The Mexica did not subjugate the Mixtecs, but they soon drove these inheritors of Monte Albán and the builders of Mitla southwest along the same path they themselves had pushed the Zapotecs.

Motecuhzoma lived in the midst of an imperialist furor; he and Tlacaélel, who continued in office, sought new excuses for war. Together they planned new campaigns beyond the mountains.

With the Mixteca country thoroughly ravaged, Motecuhzoma turned to the east. The Mexica twenties marched between Iztaccíhuatl and snow-bound Popocatépetl. They arrived at Huexotzingo and forced that city to become a vassal. They conquered Cholula and exacted tribute. Finally, Motecuhzoma came into the country of Tlaxcala. Here, as at Huexotzingo, the Mexica ignored old debts. The Tlaxcalteca were ordered to submit to Motecuhzoma, and Motecuhzoma attacked them when they did not.

The four great clans of the Republic of Tlaxcala resisted stubbornly. Tlaxcala was ensconced in the cordillera like an eagle's nest. The forces of Huitzilopochtli failed to prevail over Mixcóatl, whom the Tlaxcalteca worshipped as their principal deity. Checked, the angry Motecuhzoma by-passed Tlaxcala and invaded the regions lying along the Gulf coast.

Near the present city of Veracruz the Cempoalteca had created a size-able nation. Motecuhzoma made war against Cempoala. The decisive bat-tle here was a hard-fought, near-run thing, and it was finally won only by the efforts of the Tlatelolca contingent led by the lord of Tlatelolco, Moquihuix the Drunkard. The Tenochcas cousins became very boastful over this success, which angered Motecuhzoma. In the end, the Mexica armies returned to the west, leaving Cempoala looted and subdued, its people seething. This campaign was to bear several kinds of bitter fruit for the Mexica.

Now, Motecuhzoma had conquered a wide crescent of territory that stretched out east and south from the Navel of the Moon. And with these conquests, spearheaded by the warriors of Tenochtitlan, the internal nature of the triple alliance began to change. Motecuhzoma hardly recalled the heady days of the common war against Azcapotzalco. He handled his allies at Tlacopán and Texcoco almost as haughtily as the people of Huexo-tzingo and Tlaxcala. This again was a bad omen for the Mexica future.

During this imperialist expansion there was an even more ominous change in the nature of the Mexica state. About 1450 a series of unprec-edented natural disasters struck Anáhuac. After a serious drought, there were four consecutive years of snows and killing frosts; the normal seasons went awry. The corn supply failed, and the whole civilization was in danger of starvation. Such things had happened regularly in Mexico, but the Mex-ica tribal memory had no record of a disaster of such magnitude.

However, every Meso-American was steeped in the knowledge and fear that his gods, Tezcatlipoca of the Night, Tláloc of the Rain, and Huitzi-lopochtli the Sun, could and would visit communal destruction on the whole race. The common people at Tenochtitlan took these disasters as evidence that the gods were displeased. In the face of mass panic, the rulers of Tenochtitlan themselves panicked, and they undertook enormous efforts to appease the gods.

Despite the institution of human sacrifice which began with the Magi-cians, there is not much evidence that the practice had really gotten out of hand. Symbolic destruction had been kept at symbolic levels; it probably was not much more extensive than comparable practices among the ancient Syrians and Mesopotamians, or the barbaric Germans and Celtic Druids. A few warriors were killed ceremonially to please the Sun, and a few virgins sacrificed to assure the sprouting of corn. But now the Mexica reacted violently according to their culture. The slant and dynamism that Tlacaélel had given the cult of Huitzilopochtli resulted in a vast orgy of destruction.

Motecuhzoma mounted expeditions to the south and east to find thousands of new victims. According to the Mexica's own records, the fury did not cease until ten thousand men were slaughtered at Tenochtitlan.

This sacrificial orgy was unparalleled in all of human history. And it seems to have spread over much of Mexico. There was no essential difference between the Mexica and most of their tributaries and enemies. The Mexica, however, had greater opportunity to seize victims.

The final tragedy was that in Amerindian eyes this magic worked. Following the shower of hot blood the frosts ceased and the sun again warmed the earth. The corn flourished. The lords of Tenochtitlan took credit for averting disaster, and Tlacaélel urged the people to build a newer and more magnificent temple to Huitzilopochtli. And from this time forward mass ceremonial murder was not only institutionalized but uncontrollable. The rulers could not have halted the practice had they wanted to.

This sacrificial ardor had effects beyond the destruction of human life. After 1450 the empirical nature of Mexica imperialism began to change. The ancient Tolteca militarism had been pragmatic in its struggle for predominance and power, but now the Mexica armies tended to see the purpose of warfare more and more as a search for sacrificial victims. The warrior who took four live captives was honored over one who merely killed four enemies in combat.

The perversion produced one unique manifestation. This was the development of the so-called Flower War. The Mexica met both their enemies and their subject cities in prearranged ceremonial battles, whose sole purpose on each side was the seizure of prisoners for sacrifice. The Mexica fought these especially with Tlaxcala, Cholula, and Huexotzinga. A Flower War ended by agreement when one or both sides had taken all the victims it needed or desired. All cities killed their prisoners basically in the same way, for the same reasons.

Being taken in a Flower War and dying on the altar was an honor. The Amerindian culture never escaped its primordial belief that the manner of a man's death was more important in eternity than the manner of his life. The mass orgies of destruction that swept the highlands could not have been carried on so long had there not been passive acceptance even among the victims. Warriors tried to die well.

Besides the cardiectomies, flayings, and burnings before the gods, there

Fire and Blood

was another form of sacrifice called "gladiatorial combat" because it somewhat resembled the bloody customs of the Etruscans and Romans. The
victims were sent unarmed, or otherwise handicapped, against a series of
picked warriors in a narrow court, while spectators watched from the walls.
A prisoner who defeated five warriors could win his life, and the Mexica
had records of such cases. There were also records of prisoners who won
freedom but, in the throes of exaltation, insisted on fighting until they
died.

These perversions of the practical purposes of war fatally flawed the
Amerindian military art and in the next century did much to ensure the
civilization's downfall.

In Motecuhzoma's later years he began to handle friend and foe alike
with contempt—even old Nezahualcóyotl was hard put to avoid trouble
with the Mexica ruler—and his manner pointed up the complete political
failure of the Mexica's drive for empire. They were steadily conquering
their world, but they were failing utterly to create a greater society or a
Mexic universal state. The tribe allowed no other people except the
Texcoca an honorable place in their empire. Thus they turned what might
have been a promising confederacy or a Pax Mexicana into a world of
lords and slaves, a world seething with perennial revolt.

When Motecuhzoma Ilhuicamina died in 1468 this rebellion boiled over.
The Eagle council again offered Tlacaélel the throne; again he refused it.
The choice then fell on Axayácatl, another royal scion.

Axayácatl ("The Scourge") was no Maxtla, presiding over the collapse
of a jerry-built hegemony, because he had a united Mexica behind him.
When long-subdued parts of the Valley revolted, he quickly crushed them.
He marched through all the dominions, again reducing cities and severely
punishing anyone who opposed Mexica rule. He removed some refractory
local rulers, dispersed some tribes, and established permanent garrisons in
others. All these moves emphasized the Mexica inability to create a lasting
political infrastructure; they were experiments in subordination.

The lords of Tenochtitlan now were having serious problems even with
their cousins in Tlatelolco. The sister city was Mexica, but its rulers traced
their lineage from Azcapotzalco rather than Culhuacán and had retained a
separate identity. A terrible jealousy had grown up between the two
branches of the dominant race, as each city considered itself to be the true
seat of empire. Tlatelolco had the finest marketplace in all Mexico, but the
Tenochca were more numerous.

A long-simmering hostility reached flashpoint when the lord of Tlatelolco, Moquihuix the Drunkard, won the important victory at Cempoala.
He was neither temperate nor tactful, and though he had married a sister of
Axayácatl, this relationship now provided the Tenochca with an excuse
for war.

The sister, Jade Doll, probably never adopted her husband's interests; she seems to have served as a spy for Tenochtitlan. Moquihuix sent her back to her brother, along with certain insulting remarks about her supposed lack of feminine charms. Axayácatl used these insults as a pretext to invade the northern island, which was connected with Tenochtitlan by a causeway, in 1473.

The Tlatelolca resisted bitterly; even naked women and children battled the invaders. But the Tenochca were prepared; the Tlatelolca taken by surprise. The head of the war chief of Tlatelolco was mounted on a pole and carried into the city. Moquihuix himself was killed in fighting at the main temple-pyramid, and with his death resistance ceased.

Axayácatl annexed the northern island to Tenochtitlan; he installed a Tenochca governor and ended the existence of Tlatelolco as an independent city. Hostility continued, but soon the two areas rapidly grew together as the lake was filled between them. When the Spanish arrived, Tlatelolco with its still splendid market plaza was merely the northern quarter of Tenochtitlan.

Axayácatl had crushed all opposition in the Valley by 1473. Now he hurled the power and the fury of the Mexica once again beyond Anáhuac, this time to the north and west. They quickly conquered the valley of Toluca and then invaded Michoacán.

But in Michoacán, in the high cool region around Lake Pátzcuaro, the Mexica met their match and received their only serious check from the Tarasca tribe, which had carved out a miniature empire with a capital at Tzintzuntzan ("City of the Hummingbird"). The Tarasca were fierce and innovative warriors; they set imaginative ambushes and fought with copper weapons. They were untrammeled with ritualistic conceptions of warfare, and they cut Axayácatl's first expedition to pieces in their pine forests.

The Mexica mounted another invasion in the 1470s, but once again were defeated and thereafter avoided Michoacán. The Mexica scribes drew accounts that depicted the Tarasca as a brother warrior people, descended from the great peoples of fabled Aztatlán. The slant-eyed Tarasca were dubious relations of the Mexica in any case, but the fiction undoubtedly soothed Mexica pride.

Like Motecuhzoma, Axayácatl also failed to reduce Tlaxcala, although he was able to conquer all the territory that surrounded the mountain enclave. Some historians attribute this failure to deliberate policy: the Mexica preferred to maintain Tlaxcala as strong neighbor to supply them with captives, and on which to hone their arms, but this theory does not fit the Mexica character. Axayácatl would surely have subordinated the Tlaxcalteca could he have done so at supportable cost.

From the 1470s on perpetual warfare ensued between the two peoples. This conflict may have been an exercise for the Mexica, but it was an intolerable burden for the Tlaxcalteca, and it sowed a lasting hatred which has not even disappeared entirely between the two regions in the twentieth century.

Although Nezahualcóyotl died in 1472 and Axayácatl in 1481—the same year in which the Mexica completed the great calendar stone that was to become a national symbol of the Mexican Republic—it proved to be the spirit of Tlacaélel that lived on in Mexica events.

The succession passed to Axayácatl's brother, Tizoc ("Blood-stained Leg"), who appears to have been a great builder. The immense temple-pyramid advised by Tlacáelel was pushed to completion, and all Tenochtitlan now was beautified with palaces and gardens that surpassed those of Texcoco. But the imperial course set by Tizoc's predecessors left him no room for maneuver. Expansion and the search for victims was caked by custom; they had become the entire rationale of the nobility and warrior castes of the Mexica state.

Tizoc either was not a warrior, or was an unsuccessful one. Some accounts claim he took a hundred thousand Huaxteca and Tlappaneca prisoners by war, but these were exaggerations. The aristocracy seems to have grown steadily disenchanted. In 1486 Tizoc died, apparently poisoned in his own palace, perhaps by his own kin of the Eagle dynasty.

Ahuízotl, third son of Motecuhzoma Ilhuicamina, received the nose plug and throne, and he was to be a speaker after the fiercest Mexica hearts. The imperial dynamism that faltered under Tizoc revived; again Mexica armies struck out almost by reflex. They cut through to the Pacific in the vicinity of Acapulco and they reentered Oaxaca to the south. Ahuízotl ravaged a wide territory and then stationed a permanent garrison in Oaxaca, at Cuilapa.

Ahuízotl ("Water Dog") took thousands of Zapotec prisoners, dominated Chiapas, and, according to some accounts, sent an expedition as far as Panama which sent back either tribute or trade goods from South America.

Then, avoiding the stubborn Tarasca and Tlaxcalteca, Ahuízotl went north against the remaining civilized peoples of Amerindian Mexico, ravaging the country of the Huaxteca as far as the River Pánuco, and scouting out the primitive regions beyond the river, including barbarian-inhabited northern Mexico. These poor and arid territories did not interest the Mexica. Ahuízotl halted the path of empire at the Pánuco. Dragging thousands of unfortunate Huaxtecs in his train, he returned to Tenochtitlan.

The great new temple of Huitzilopochtli might now be properly dedicated to the god. Ahuízotl made this event a religious and triumphal ceremony. All the lords of Meso-America, ally, tributary, or foe, were invited to attend, and to see the extent of Mexica power. Indeed, the temple-pyramid and its complex was the largest structure built during the historic period (though in total size the temple of Huitzilopochtli did not approach that of the court-citadel of Teotihuacán). The outer walls enclosed some twenty-five hundred square yards and eighty-odd lesser temples and palaces. The walls embellished with carved serpents copied the older styles, and the courtyards were paved with polished stone. The great pyramid that dominated the court rose three hundred feet above six terraces. Two square squat towers jutted another fifty-six feet from the broad, flat apex of this pyramid. Between the towers stood an enormous idol of Huitzilopochtli. Ceremonial fires burned eternally beside this monstrous image.

The temple complex was erected in a central quarter of the city, almost where the present-day cathedral stands. The palace of Axayácatl bordered the temple on the west, with public armories and granaries on the other sides. This area, with its enormous, paved plaza, was the public and ceremonial heart of Tenochtitlan.

In the dedication ceremony, thousands of Matlazuica, Zapotec, and Huastec captives were herded across the plaza; the column was reputedly three miles long. Besides the principal altar atop the pyramid, there were some six hundred minor altars situated throughout the courts for mass slaughter on important occasions.

The great drum always boomed its dread noise over the city and surrounding lake when a sacrifice began. The hueytlatoani, as supreme commander, supreme judge, and supreme priest, usually performed the first sacrifice assisted by other dignitaries in red robes.

The sullen, but unresisting victims, painted with blue or yellow chalk, sometimes holding small banners, were seized one by one and stretched out on the rough stone altar. According to Diego de Landa—and Mexica pictographs, which are quite vivid—the celebrating priest pressed the point of an obsidian knife just beneath the victim's left nipple, gave the blade a thrust and a powerful, circular twist, and then, he plunged his hand into the gaping wound and jerked out the still-pumping heart in a gout of hot blood. The smoking organ was immediately placed on a platter and rushed before the image of the god; his stone face was smeared with bright arterial blood; sometimes the fresh heart itself was placed between his gaping stone jaws. The symbolism was exact: the god was fed.

Cardiectomy was the favored method of sacrifice in the highlands, although some earth or fertility deities liked their victims stretched out on racks, blood dripping to the ground. Huehueteotl, god of fire, who was the most ancient god of all, was honored by victims who were given a narcotic, thrown into a fire, and then pulled out before they died of burns only to have their hearts extracted. The Mexica also practiced a ritual cannibalism on occasion. Parts of arms and legs were eaten, never for food, but out of the most ancient Amerindian belief that certain properties reside in the flesh and can be passed on by its consumption. Most tribes of the Southwestern United States practiced ritual cannibalism into the nineteenth century.

After the sacrifice, the corpse was usually beheaded and the skull placed on a rack. In 1519 Bernal Díaz, Cortés' soldier, estimated he saw a hundred thousand such skulls around the main plaza of Tlaxcala.

The speaker and high officers began the ceremony, but the labor quickly fell to the horde of lesser priests, who Bernal Díaz described as being hooded, with long, matted hair and uncut fingernails, smelling of sulphur and rotted blood. They abstained from women and led austere lives, much revered by the populace. The priesthood did far more than perform sacrifices and maintain the temple fires. They were keepers of the calendar, teachers, and sustainers of the ancient arts. They also deliberately courted irrationality and hallucinations, by eating certain mushrooms, Jimson weed, or peyote. Divinatory hallucinations were a very old, and very important part of Amerindian religions, particularly throughout southwestern North America. The Chichimeca apparently carried these customs deep into civilized Mexico, and it is likely that the dominant surrealistic vision of the Meso-Americans was connected with such drug-taking.

The Mexica boasted that at least twenty thousand, and perhaps eighty thousand captives were destroyed to celebrate Ahuízotl's triumph. All Tenochtitlan was pervaded by a hideous stench. The already undrinkable waters of the lake were further ruined; there were outbreaks of disease.

Because of the deliberate self-identification of modern Mexican intellectuals with the Mexica nation, the whole question of human sacrifice is now treated with understandable reluctance in Mexico. Ritual cannibalism is emotionally denied, and the currently fashionable view is to ignore or play down the bloodletting, which the nineteenth-century European writers so obviously enjoyed.

The fact of human sacrifice, however, cannot be expunged. The Nahua accounts themselves are too explicit. One problem, historically, is that the Spanish conquerors made judgments and played with numbers inflating the numbers of victims either to prove how religiously barbaric the natives were or perhaps to justify the Spaniards' own crimes. Bernal Díaz recorded—probably with accuracy—that he saw daily sacrifices in some localities. Zumárraga, the first bishop of Mexico, estimated that twenty thousand died by the knife every year before the Conquest. Historian Francisco López de Gómara raised the figure to fifty thousand, while the missionary-author José de Acosta mentioned only five thousand, but admitted that on special occasions, such as the dedication of Huitzilopochtli's temple in Tenochtitlan, as many as twenty thousand might be killed. But other Spanish priests played down the whole business. Bartolomé de las Casas, whose purpose was to protect the Amerindians from his countrymen, swore that only one hundred per year were sacrificed.

The Mexica themselves certainly saw human sacrifice no more as an abomination than the Spanish, in the main, saw their own Inquisition as evil. This magic served a major social purpose. The Amerindians of Mexico were no more, nor less, monsters than other men. If there was a genuine gangrene in their civilization, it came from the vision that made symbolic destruction, and even auto-sacrifice, important and holy. Even so, the immense faith of the Amerindian culture in the immortality of the soul made the culture contemptuous of death itself, especially if it seemed to serve a useful purpose.

Ahuízotl's dedication of the temple marked the flood tide of empire for Tenochtitlan. The central highlands had been subdued. Ahuízotl's power and influence ran beyond his actual writ, in fact, because many independent peoples beyond his conquests wisely sent him symbolic tribute and presents. Since Ahuízotl had found the arid northlands undesirable, he had turned the major thrust of empire toward the south, toward Oaxaca and beyond. There the inhabitants were more civilized than the savages of the north, and there was more desirable loot, like prized feathers and green jade.

As tribute poured in to Tenochtitlan and thousands of slaves sweated to support its projects, scores of lesser pyramids, palaces, and public buildings rose. The array of vast monuments stretching from Tlatelolco to the entrance to the city compared favorably with the vanished splendor of the forum in imperial Rome. And there was no contemporary market, anywhere in the world, to compare with Tlatelolco's great trading square.

When Ahuízotl died in 1502, he had, in enlarging his hegemony, carried on the tradition of his ancestors; his character lives on in the modern Mexican-Spanish word *ahuizote*, which stands for someone violent, vindictive, and fierce.

THE HALLS OF
MOTECUHZOMA

*When we saw so many cities built out on the water, and so many
great towns on dry land, and that straight long causeway that led
toward Tenochtitlan, we were amazed and said that this was like the
enchantments described in the legend of Amadis . . . And then,
when we entered . . . the appearance of the palaces in which we
were lodged! How spacious and well built—of beautiful stonework
and cedar wood, and woods of other sweet-smelling trees—with
great rooms and courts . . . all wonderful to behold.*

*Then we entered the orchard and garden, which was so wonder-
ful to look at and walk in that I never tired of looking at and
smelling the many trees, and the paths covered with roses and other
flowers, and the fruit trees, and the pool of fresh water. Large
canoes could pass into the garden from the lake. And everything
was cemented and splendid, the stones with pictures on them, which
gave us much to think about. Then the birds of many kinds came to
the pool . . . I stood looking at it and thought, never in the world
would there ever again be discovered other such lands as these . . .*

*Of all these wonders that I then beheld, today all is overthrown
and lost; nothing is left standing.*

From the history of Bernal Díaz del Castillo.

Although Motecuhzoma Xocoyotzin (literally, "Sun Burning Through the
Clouds"; symbolic Nahua for "Angry Lord, the Younger") was the son of
Axayácatl the Scourge and a Tolteca princess and of the most exalted

lineage, he had a warrior brother who was considered better fit for the speaker's throne. Therefore, the brother was schooled for rule and war, while young Motecuhzoma was trained to be a high priest. He would surely have been far happier had fate permitted him to live out his life amid the mysteries, ceremonies, and amateur wizardry he adored.

But the warrior brother died in an insignificant skirmish with the Huexotzinga and the ruling Eagle Council designated Motecuhzoma as next in line for power. He strove valiantly to fill the role, marching with the armies toward Tehuantepec, and, in a few years, amply proving his valor and aptitude for command. When Ahuízotl died in 1502, Motecuhzoma II was installed as speaker of the Mexica tribe.

He earned a place as one of the great warrior-imperialists of his line. Motecuhzoma II reduced some forty towns in the Oaxaca area, strengthened, solidified, centralized Ahuízotl's conquests, and pushed the Mexica power steadily to the south, toward the Pacific.

In the early sixteenth century Motecuhzoma ruled over a vast realm that comprised almost half of Middle America. This territory held probably between eleven and twenty million people—an immense population for the time—and there was no one, as Cortés was told in 1519, who was not Motecuhzoma's vassal. The Spaniards saw Mexic political relationships in feudal terms, but in regarding Motecuhzoma as an emperor, they were hardly wrong.

Actually, Amerindian Mexico was a series of swarming human ant hills, with the apex of the whole complex at Tenochtitlan. The empire was not so much ruled by the Mexica race as dominated and administered by the revered speaker through his "palace" aristocracy. And even the ruler's agents, governors, and bureaucrats did not attempt to handle every detail of empire. The allied cities, such as Texcoco, continued their own, even older local hegemonies over the countryside, and most tributary cities continued to collect taxes in the name of the speaker at Tenochtitlan. Most of the ancient centers served as provincial capitals for Motecuhzoma, and this fact, plus the forms of self-government most of these cities retained, led some observers to describe the Mexica political structure as a vast Amerindian confederacy.

This was wrong; Motecuhzoma's realm was no more a genuine confederacy of self-governing tribes and cities than the ancient Greek and Asian cities gathered within the Roman Empire. Both systems left the incorporated cities no real freedom; they were part of a hierarchy of order and control.

In fact, even great Texcoco lost its independence. Nezahualpilli ("Fasting Prince") had succeeded his father, Nezahualcóyotl, in 1472. Nezahualpilli was a true son of his father: he married a daughter of Motecuhzoma I and later ordered her execution; he served as the first elector of the

Eagle Council; he continued the court of Texcoco as a haven for astronomers, wise men, and engineers, and he took an enormous number of young
women as consorts. But when he died in 1516, Motecuhzoma Xocoyotzin
put his own choice of the Acolhua line, Cacama, upon the Texcoca throne.
This arbitrary act was an obvious move to end the independence of
Texcoco as an ally and bring it under the complete sway of Tenochtitlan.
Ixtlilxóchitl, the great-grandson of the first prince of that name, opposed the
selection of his brother Cacama and gathered an important faction of
Texcocan aristocracy around him in rebellion. Within a few years Motecuhzoma was to pay dearly for this interference in the affairs of Texcoco.

A number of the other old cities preserved a sort of shadow freedom.
Cholula and Huexotzingo maintained armies; they regularly met the Mexica in the stylized "flower wars." But these cities were truly subject to the
will of Motecuhzoma; they were tributaries and resented it.

Motecuhzoma's writ ran over about half of modern Mexico; the resources of Tenochtitlan were extended almost to their natural limits. Some
dangerous enemies remained beyond the speaker's power. The Tarasca
were belligerently independent, ruling in Michoacán. Another state, called
Metztitlán, maintained its freedom high in the northeast along the Pánuco. The arid regions between these two nations, which Ahuízotl had
explored and abandoned, were still a fount for savage Chichimecs. But the
desert tribes were no threat as long as the morale and organization of the
Mexica empire remained superior.

The peninsula of Yucatán was known to the Mexica, but it was beyond
their range. The Maya were no danger to Tenochtitlan, because they had
virtually destroyed their civilization through internal wars.

The Oaxaca and Guerrero regions, however, were far from subjugation,
although the main thrust of the empire for two generations had been toward the south. The Mixtecs and Zapotecs were learning to put aside their
ancient enmity toward each other and to combine against Tenochtitlan.
Once Motecuhzoma's befeathered warriors went beyond the volcanoes,
they were actually masters only of the ground on which they stood, and in
fact, one of Motecuhzoma's expeditions was destroyed in the south.

Tlaxcala, guarded by a high wall, clung to its independence in the eastern mountains, despite continual harassment by Mexico. More important,
Tlaxcala was surrounded by a sea of sullen resentment toward the lords of
Tenochtitlan. Chalco, Cholula, Cempoala, and Huexotzingo were civilized
centers before the Mexica came out of the desert and felt no loyalty toward
their rapacious overlords, who collected tribute—food, gems, slaves, and
sacrificial victims—relentlessly.

Actually, when Motecuhzoma came to the throne the hegemony had
reached a highly unstable and very dangerous phase. Motecuhzoma's forebears had forged an empire of the sword maintained by fear. The Mexica

never envisioned any better means of organization or incorporation than to conquer other peoples and force them to pay tribute.

Ironically, the Mexica hegemony was probably better administered than any subsequent regime in Mexico. The Mexica tribe had qualities vital to a ruling race: they learned quickly and adapted or improved all the ancient Mexic techniques of empire. They employed principles of hierarchy and bureaucracy that went back to Teotihuacán, and used military concepts handed down from Toltec Tula. They fused all of these into their own militaristic cult of the Sun. And they were practical: Axayácatl, wearied of rebellions, imposed garrisons and dispersed troublesome tribes. Ahuízotl put his own governors on many local thrones. By Motecuhzoma's reign the system had become regularized. The hegemony was divided into thirty major provinces, each with its administrative capital and governor, answerable only to the speaker.

Tenochca officers were arrogant and hard, but they were efficient and almost incorruptible. Careful records were made of all tribute demanded and paid, and every item inevitably reached Tenochtitlan. The empire was moving steadily toward centralization under autocracy, but without political integration, since all power remained in the hands of the Mexica.

This communication greatly expanded Nahua culture and language. By the sixteenth century Nahuatl had become the dominant language throughout the highlands, and this predominance was to survive the Conquest.

The tribe's ruling classes, who carried the speaker's commands from sea to sea, had also changed greatly over the past century. The Mexica lordlings and bureaucrats had learned all the old skills and traditions. They planned, built, and used splendid houses, temples, causeways, bridges, roads, and dikes. They carried on all the ancient arts and crafts, though without the charm and elegance of the true Classic civilization, or the inventive elán of militaristic Tula.

There is no evidence that Mexic civilization was making any progress, especially when measured against what had preceded it. But the Mexica themselves were caught up in a vast social transition.

The odd dualism between tribal and imperial forms that had begun with the reforms of Tlacaélel continued. At heart, the Mexica were enormously conservative. Toltec ideas and practices were only a sort of aristocratic patina on top of a basic warrior-peasant tribal framework, and did not destroy the tribal social organization. While the speaker gradually ceased to be an elected war chief and became a king, and a growing landed aristocracy and palace bureaucracy came to administer the conquered empire through an increasingly professional military caste, the common tribesman was still organized into communal kinship clans. The old community remained almost intact, though hierarchy and ideology had been imposed.

The majority of Mexica may scarcely have understood that anything had changed. The transition from a warrior-peasant democracy into a warrior-priest theocracy, presided over by an autocrat and articulated by a military aristocracy eternally engaged in war, had occurred so naturally as to seem inevitable. The average Mexica profited greatly, both in material benefits and pride. Vast numbers of the tribe were now wholly supported by tribute. There is no evidence that the horde of commoners resented any of the changes, or cared that elected local clan chiefs no longer exercised any real power in the tribe or state.

Under Motecuhzoma II, however, the speaker's bench had become an almost godlike throne. Motecuhzoma II was not above a certain self-deification; he loved ceremony and subordination. Motecuhzoma's ancestors had been shrewd but crude war chiefs elevated from among a body of theoretical equal lords. But before Motecuhzoma II, all ranks of men in Mexico had begun to act as slaves.

Even high lords were no longer allowed to come into the Speaker's presence wearing fine clothing or adornment. All men approached Motecuhzoma II as beggars.

To come near the throne, the messenger or suppliant first had to reverence it and intone "Lord." Recognized by the ruler, men came forward, again reverenced the sacred throne, and said, "Great Lord." Only people of rank were permitted to look Motecuhzoma in the face.

Throughout the empire, every Tenochca officer was a petty Motecuhzoma, wearing elaborate and costly dress, exacting enormous deference. Cortés' men once observed a Mexica delegation near the Gulf coast. These agents of the throne arrived arrogantly in fantastically-colored costumes, carrying roses which they sniffed diffidently from time to time while demanding men for ritual sacrifice—the odor of the lesser tribes seemed to offend them, or perhaps such business wearied them.

The Mexica had adopted these forms, not invented them. Since the Classic civilization, all Mexico had been a deeply stratified, ceremonial, utterly deferential society. The habit of deference and subordination was engrained in the Mexic soul, and the Conquest hardly affected it.

Four generic orders of nobility had emerged at Tenochtitlan. The highest rank was that of *tlaloque*, an officer who governed a province by royal appointment and was a born aristocrat. The next rank, generally of the same basic social class, provided most of the high military and civil officers; they had been made feudal landholders for life, or were the sons or grandsons of such men, and as such had become almost a caste.

The clan elders or chiefs ranked as nobility, and so did heads of families; however, despite their important military and civic duties, they had no real power over the throne, nor could they influence the direction of the state. They were honored to carry out the orders of the great people.

Yet the Mexica considered themselves all kinsmen and class feelings or tension were absent. The nobility were rich or powerful uncles, the leaders in a vast family enterprise. The bonds of tribal community were powerful; the same sense of community that squelched all individuality also prevented class consciousness. In time, both genuine feudalism, or a form of Caesarism feeding on class conflict might have appeared—but not for generations.

The tribe was not divided merely into nobility and common warriors, however. The empire itself had encouraged a great proliferation of all kinds of intermediate ranks. A civilized state required learned priests, judges, artisans, engineers, teachers, scribes, professional junior military officers, and bureaucrats. The palace created all these ranks, or encouraged and supported them, including the hereditary merchant guild, the *pochteca*. But none of these "middle classes" should be confused with a European bourgeoisie, because they were created or supported by the palace solely to serve the needs of the speaker and the state. Their ethos was entirely different from the Western middle class or bourgeoisie, which more often than not saw the state as their enemy. The skilled classes were neither independent nor self-employed, and therefore they could never become a true middle class in the Western sense. They were a middle rank, rather, fed by the labor of *mayeques* or serfs, invariably employed in the service of the palace on public duties or great public works.

The *pochteca* or so-called merchants were a case in point. Tlacaélel, who foresaw everything, created this guild, whose place in the empire—and the place of commerce itself in Mexico—is often misunderstood. There was nothing resembling European commerce in Mexico.

In every town a brisk barter trade was carried on in floating marketplaces; it had emerged millennia earlier and is carried on today. The market plazas were places of exchange, where peasants and tradesmen met to mutual advantage, exchanging vast quantities of onions and squash, beans and tomatoes, chilies or peppers, pumpkins, squash, cacao, dogs, ducks, metalwork and clothing, slaves and fish. Market days were gala occasions, and when they ended the plazas were deserted; the "tradesmen" disappeared. This commerce was not mercantile, and it did not give rise to either a money economy or a merchant class.

Certain items, mainly cacao beans, copper, precious stones, and quills of gold dust, came to have recognized value, but these were never money in the Hellenic or European sense. Wealth from first to last consisted of land, or land use, of cornfields and men to work them.

The *pochteca* had little to do with the market plazas. They did not deal in bulk goods for the masses but in long-range trade, to secure luxury goods—stones, precious feathers, metals, and artwork—the official classes wanted and were dependent upon the state and aristocracy. They were also frequently mentioned in written accounts as having acted as Mexica spies. This trade was necessitated by the demands of fashion at Tenochtitlan. By the 1480s sumptuous dress and ornamentation had become very fashionable. Great personages sported elaborate headdresses and brilliantly-hued feather capes; they wore ocelot skins and pyrite mirrors, and covered themselves with ornaments of gold, rare stones, and jade. Few of these things were found in Anáhuac; they came from Oaxaca, Guerrero, or points south. The love of colorful feathers was so strong that already certain tropic birds had become extinct.

Above all, the ruling classes valued *chalchihuite* or Mexican jade. Like turquoise, jade was considered much more valuable than gold; from ancient times it had symbolized high rank. Nobles affected ear, lip, and nose plugs as status symbols, and also as actual rank-badges. The lobes of some highborn ears, plugged young, were stretched down to shoulder level by manhood. But sumptuary codes forbade common men to wear, or even possess jade; therefore it could not become a currency.

Meanwhile the common tribesman lived as he always had, in a growing city of magnificent buildings, but in a tight, communal society surrounded by kith and kin. By now he was less a farmer than a semiprofessional soldier of the state. He was hardly opposed to this, because the tribute of the Mexic world supported him at Tenochtitlan, and further, his real hope of social advancement or luxury lay in war. Valiant warriors were socially mobile within the tribe.

But his motivation was not all this modern—every Mexica was caught up in the fear of Huitzilopochtli and devoutly sought to serve his gods.

Both the dualism and the stability of Tenochtitlan was served by a remarkable system of schooling and training. Though every manchild was born a warrior and dedicated to Huitzilopochtli by his midwife at birth, with prayers that he might spill the blood of enemies and eventually feed the gods with his own, his destiny was not left to chance. In the Mexica training primordial instincts were combined with quite sophisticated methodology.

Boy children were soon separated from their sisters and given chores around the house and fields to teach them obedience and discipline. Discipline was a fetish with the tribe. To rebel against a father could bring death. For disobedience or other offenses boys were punished by being cruelly bound and sometimes punctured with cactus spines. For speaking to a male, which was forbidden, a girl might be forced to inhale the searing smoke of burning peppers. The Mexica, like other Amerindians, were rarely wantonly cruel to children; family relationships were warm and close and the young were valued. But children were taught by physical pain to suppress individualism and to obey.

Between the ages of six and nine, all boys of common families were entered in the *telpochcalli*, or communal clan school. Each clan ran one or more *telpochcalli*. The instructors were warrior-priests of proven courage and sense, and were invariably kinsmen of the students.

Here boys entered a closely-knit, rigidly disciplined, strenuous life. They were not allowed to have anything to do with girls. They were forced to learn the religion, history, ceremonies, and customs of their clan and tribe. This indoctrination was ruthlessly carried out.

However, the *telpochcalli* did not teach reading, writing, or any of the higher arts; these were not for *macehualtin*. Nor did the school concern itself with any occupation or craft. Boys were required to learn farming, or a family trade, outside of school. The *telpochcalli's* purpose was to make good warrior-priests for the state.

Above all, the boys were instilled with the rationale and art of war. By their early teens, they were exercised with real weapons, the sword, the macana or club, lances and spears. They learned to use cotton armor and the shield, and they practiced daily with arms, to learn skill and to gain endurance and strength.

At about age fifteen, boys were sent out on field expeditions with the battalions of Tenochtitlan as bearers, laborers, and messengers. They were hardened and got the feeling of real war.

No Mexica youth avoided this training, or failed to take it seriously. Malfeasance of any kind brought severe and painful penalties, and there was actually no place for a youth who failed to become a warrior. He was put to death, or made a slave.

A boy stayed in the clan schools until he had captured an enemy in combat—this brought instant warrior status—or reached maturity, took a wife, and was assigned a communal house and land by the clan. But his training was not over. All males were regularly mustered for exercises by the sound of the great drum, even when there was no war. The Mexica could summon all their twenties within the hour, and most young warriors were eager to seek glory for themselves and gore for their god.

The clan schools served the needs of basic society as the Mexica saw them. But a very different kind of school was organized to prepare the sons of the higher priests, nobility, and bureaucrats—and a few selected young *macehualtin*—to serve the needs of the greater world of Tenochtitlan. This was the *calmécac*, which was the Eton and university of the Mexic society combined. At the end there were six of these preparatory schools in Mexico-Tenochtitlan.

The *calmécac* was a school of, by, and for the aristocracy; the future speaker and all judges were graduates. Here young men were taught all the Mexica had learned of the ancient culture: pictographic writing, astrology and astronomy, theology, mathematics, and metaphysics. The curriculum was particularly strong in discipline and ethics, for these boys were to be the leaders of the tribe and were trained to sustain the civilization.

They were also schooled in warfare, even more strenuously and ferociously than the *macehualtin*. Leaders in a warrior society that fought hand to hand in packed ranks had to have more courage, strength, and ability than the ordinary soldier.

Young aristocrats also learned by rote the songs, rituals, and poetry of flowery, inflected Nahua—which the writing could not convey—studied etiquette and ceremony for their station, and were encouraged to compose their own poems and practice the finer arts. They passed out highly disciplined, tough, and genteel young barbarians—the ideal of the militaristic Toltec mind.

The schools were close bands of kinsmen, taught by blood relatives. By the time any Mexica entered a school he understood that the individual, great or small, stood for nothing against the greater community of the tribe, and as in all communal societies each person lived in a chain of custom and circumstance he could never break. There was no personal rebellion; probably few individuals even grasped the concept. The enormously stabilizing effect of the Mexica school and training system is obvious.

Girls were hardly schooled at all, since females played no civic, military, or political roles in Mexica society. Young girls were required to learn religious duties and domestic arts, and they were taught most of what they were expected to know by their mothers. Women were under strict discipline all their lives. The Mexica were enormously puritanical, as most societies overwhelmingly devoted to social purpose tend to be. Females were normally chaperoned, and they were expected never to interfere in the warriors' business. One Mexica proverb indicated that the men preferred women with both ears plugged and their mouths stopped up.

There was a dualism in this puritanism, just as there was between the old tribal life styles of the masses and the emergence of a Toltec-type aristocracy. The revered speaker and the lords of Mexico were permitted huge harems, but sexual license, and even sexual liberty, did not extend to the common people.

Another conservative influence was the Mexica's remarkable judicial system, a blend of old and new, a primitive yet quite sophisticated system that served its society extremely well. And like the schools, Mexica justice may have had an irrational and primitive basis, but it was wonderfully pragmatic in its execution.

Amerindian Mexico had very few written codes or laws; the speakers had not taken to issuing edicts as emperors. The great basis for law was tribal custom and community discipline. Almost all law-breaking therefore consisted either of a disregard of discipline or customs. The nature of the society made either of these serious crimes against the people, the state, and the gods themselves.

Almost anything that went against good order was a crime, from adultery and cowardice and refusal to obey lawful orders, to bad manners in public.

On the other hand, strictly private crime was rare. There was very little private property, and a society which did not permit private initiative or private enterprise gave little opportunity for a private life, let alone private crime. Even private vengeance was virtually unknown. Offenses were community matters and were handled publicly. And as a rule, public offenses were punished more severely than purely private crimes, such as murder. A man might kill another man and be let off with a fine, provided the offended family agreed. People who defied custom or the conventional wisdom of the tribe were invariably executed or enslaved.

Penalties and punishments were bloody and brutal. Death was meted out by hanging, drowning, stoning, strangling, or even burning alive. Refusal to obey orders was considered treasonous, and called for death and also the enslavement of the traitor's close kin. The Mexica did not keep prisons, but only cages to hold persons awaiting judgment, or prisoners of war. Nor were felons sacrificed to the gods, because this was held to be the most honorable death.

Higher standards were expected of aristocrats, who derived their status from public office or position. Their offenses brought execution that commoners could sometimes avoid. Nezahualpilli put some of his wives and children to death, including the daughter of Motecuhzoma I. This royal consort had taken numerous lovers and had statuettes made of them which she called "her gods." Whether Nezahualpilli condemned her for adultery or impiety is not entirely clear; the highly public nature of her actions brought the retribution.

The actual administration of Mexica justice was superb, and could be copied by many cultures more technically advanced. The judiciary was decentralized, yet state-supported and held under hierarchy and discipline. In every town, there was a judge who had the equivalents of a sheriff, clerk, bailiff, and crier at his call. A higher magistrate sat in each provincial capital city, to handle important cases, or to pass judgment on appeals. At Tenochtitlan a supreme tribunal, on which sat some of the most important officers of the empire, passed judgment both on appeals and on the actions of the lower courts.

The speaker, as supreme judge, supreme priest, and supreme commander of the tribe, could also hear disputes or pass judgment on princes, but even he could not set aside verdicts rendered by the Tenochtitlan high court.

Bad or unwise judges at all levels seem to have been found out and punished or removed. The system, which was admired even by the subject peoples, did not require advocates or torture. The nature of the community made both superfluous. The Mexica believed there was little lying in their courts, and they were probably correct—not because lying was punished painfully if found out, but because false swearing was considered a desecration of the gods.

Repeating offenders almost never survived, for the simple reason that recidivism was felt to be blasphemy, a temptation of fate and gods.

The system's decentralization and public nature made trials and justice swift, and the disciplined hierarchy of magistrates kept them uniform and fair. Above all, the judges enforced the conventional wisdom in each case. The community, the accusers, and the condemned thus easily comprehended each decision; esoteric points of law simply did not exist. The terrible punishments and executions were not imposed by the rulers—they were demanded and approved by the community at large. The rights of individuals might be violated, but they had no rights against the needs and judgments of the tribe.

The weight of the community and the subordination of the people to custom was so pervasive that even felons condemned to a hideous death often did not need to be imprisoned. Men ordered to stay behind a line drawn on the ground usually did so. This pattern of human subordination to authority, like deferential manners, was so deeply ingrained in the Mexican psyche that it still has not been eradicated.

While the Mexica hegemony was held together by armies, disciplined training, and pervasive justice, the whole civilization still rested on the forces that had created it—the ancient religions, which permeated all life styles, custom, and law.

The original religious vision was the *causa causans* of the culture and civilization. It was the awesome force that held communities together, it made men erect temples and pyramids at tremendous social cost, and practice continual symbolic destruction, and it made the universe and life and death bearable, if not understandable. The original beliefs had risen from primordial fears and the Mexic civilization remained pervaded by fear of unexplained disasters, monstrous beings, capricious forces, and vengeful gods eager to punish men. These fears, never rationalized or conquered, impelled the whole race to serve the desires of the gods, at whatever cost.

Therefore, the Mexica and other related peoples never saw their religion as an oppressive force. They had no concept of a separation between "church" and "state," or between the hideous pantheon and the people. The original error—the substitution of mechanistic magic and blood sacrifice for rational observation and intellectual exploration—persisted, and from it emanated the same kind of literature, architecture, and art. This vision, so weird to those unaccustomed to it, permeated everything except a very few areas of life.

Oddly enough, the Amerindians saw medicine as outside religion, and therefore their practice of it was excellent and pragmatic. They based medical care on cleanliness, herbs, and natural healing—that is, on observed results, and ironically, Amerindian medicine was superior to European, which had sacrificed observation and experiment to fear and ideology. Engineering, mathematics, and astronomy were also pragmatic; they had probably emerged before the notion of symbolic destruction took such a fierce turn. But these empirical pursuits remained static during the last millennium of the civilization, probably because of the overwhelming dominance of the surrealistic vision that bloodied altars and kept Mexica armies on the march.

The world view even of the Mexica was pantheistic and tolerant; they accepted all regional gods or forces, until there were more than thirty major deities in their pantheon. The most ancient gods, Fire and Rain, dating back to village life, were still worshipped. The superstitions and magic of the first magicians and farmers mingled with the sophisticated rites and world views of the priest-rulers of Teotihuacán, and upon these essentially peaceful cults stood the savage war gods of the Nahua and Chichimeca invaders. Every people who entered Meso-America carried their own special deity or totem, but no gods were supplanted; more were continually added to the pantheon. Warfare, such as the historic conflicts between the highlands and the Gulf coast, enlarged this pantheon in both directions. Even the Mexica, on their forays through the southwest, discovered new deities and brought these back to Anáhuac. The Maya, in turn, adopted Mexic gods. But throughout the highlands the war gods of the barbarian invasions—Tezcatlipoca of the Tolteca and Huitzilopochtli of the Mexica—had become dominant.

The whole history of Meso-American religion was not the blood orgy it had become in the Mexican empire of Tenochtitlan. The primitive Mexica had ceremonies disgusting to their more civilized Nahua neighbors, but mass destruction seems not to have occurred at Tenochtitlan-Mexico until the terrible years of the 1450s. But from that time onward the cult of Huitzilopochtli lost all rationality; even its instigators found it beyond control.

For all Motecuhzoma's prestige and power, he ruled a theocratic nation whose directions he had no authority to change or control.

Year after year, therefore, long lines of doomed warriors trudged their last mile to the pyramids of Tenochtitlan and countless other centers; they died shrieking while their arterial blood splashed smoking over rough stone altars. Reeking priests held up pulsing organs and danced about in orgiastic frenzies while snakehide drums boomed. The people chanted prayers to the great gods they fed human hearts: to Huitzilopochtli, Bright Hummingbird, Great Face, Lover of Hearts, God of War, Hunting, and the Nobility, Protector of the Eagle, Patron of the Children of the Sun, Slayer of Enemies, Drinker of Blood; to Tezcatlipoca, Shining Disk, Moon of the Night Sky, Lord of the Dark, the Jaguar, Foe of Quetzalcóatl, God of Coyotes, Phantoms, Visions, and Monsters, Beloved of the Priests; to Tonantzin-Cihuacóatl, Snake Mother, Feeder of all Beasts; to Tláloc-Tlamacazqui, Lord of Waters, Maker of Rain, Hurler of Thunder, Dweller on the Mountaintop; to Xipe Toltec, Our Lord the Flayed, Sprouter of Seeds, Honored in Bloody Skins; to Huehueteotl, the Fire, the Most Revered Ancient God, pleased by the screams of burning men.

There were countercurrents; not everyone was dominated by the nightmare visions of hallucinating priests. Throughout Nahua-land were small numbers of *tlamatinimi*, intellectuals or wise men, most of whom gathered in tiny sanctuaries at Huexotzingo and Texcoco. Nezahualcóyotl and his son Fasting Prince were members and patrons of this order, who were mostly astronomers or engineers—men whose trade made them look for observed or intellectual answers rather than magical solutions to existence. The *tlamatinimi* considered the swollen Mexic pantheon of monsters ridiculous.

The *tlamatinimi* believed rather that there was one god, whom they gave different dimensions and names. He was Tloque-Nahuaque, or "Lord of the Near Vicinity," all pervasive over the countryside; or he was Ipalnemohuani, ("the Giver of Life"); or Ometeotl ("God of Duality"). The *tlamatinimi* conceived of monotheism, with a strong feeling toward yin and yang, to explain the workings of their universe.

In later times the speculations of these Mexic intellectuals received probably much more attention than they deserved. They were not important in the civilization. These cold, highly philosophical ideas did not reach, let alone influence, even the aristocracy of Anáhuac. The peasantry were completely ignorant of them. While in time these wise men might have changed the complection of their culture, time was running out for Mexic civilization.

Tenochtitlan was the largest and grandest of all the centers, in kind as well as degree. The built-up mud islands in Lake Texcoco had become one of the great imperial centers of the world. From the colorful, buzzing market plaza of Tlatelolco on the north to the magnificent palaces at the ceremonial center to the causeways that joined at Xóloc, Mexico-Tenochtitlan surpassed in many respects its contemporary imperial sisters, such as Venice or Istanbul. Scores of temples squatted throughout the city; there were eighty-odd lesser temples within the great complex of Huitzilopochtli alone. Public arsenals and storehouses—for this capital was still a great communal enterprise—faced broad paved plazas. All around, thousands of lime-washed stone houses gleamed in the bright sun.

The capital had aviaries, zoos, splendid botanical gardens and flowering parks; the Amerindians loved color in nature as well as dress. And the rulers ceaselessly built palaces, plazas, temples, and other monuments.

The palace of the second Motecuhzoma, like that of his father Axa-yácatl, stood near the immense temple-pyramid complex of Huitzilopochtli (this site was almost precisely where the National Palace of independent Mexico was later built). Spreading out from the revered speaker's house were hundreds of lesser palaces, which housed the nobility, high officers, and bureaucrats, as well as the skilled artisans employed by the imperial state. The Mexica could afford such splendor because they could call on forced labor from half of Mexico.

The majority of buildings were made of *tezontle*, a soft, red lava stone, which was easier to work than marble or granite. But the palaces of the great people contained apartments of porphyry and alabaster, with the interiors finished in rich, rare woods. These rooms had stuccoed walls and polished, level, mortared floors. The most magnificent palace was not in Tenochtitlan, but the residence of the lords of Texcoco; however, the island city had many like it.

Sculpture, following the precedent if not the exquisite styles of Classic Meso-America, was integrated with architecture. Outer walls were covered with carved images and murals, painted in red and black, or in bold blues and greens.

Lime whitewash coated the rough exteriors of gray or reddish stone and gave the city its dazzling, silvery appearance in the high, clear air.

Many buildings had towers and roof crests, resembling fortresses. These towers often intrigued the arriving Spaniards. The roofs of most houses were flat, covering broad chambers. There were center courts, or patios, with trees, orchards, and clear pools containing exotic fishes. From these patios and on the walks between the towers men could observe the night stars and carry out their regular religious and astrological ceremonies; or they could stroll along porticoed walks amid flowering, fragrant loveliness.

Mexic beauty, however, was mainly an exterior, public thing: the interiors of buildings and houses were dark and gloomy. People feared the night, and the monstrous things, human and inhuman, it might harbor. Rooms had either no windows, or else tiny slits set high in the walls, to carry off the acrid smoke from flaring torches. Large houses or palaces usually were built with two exits, one opening on the narrow, corridor-like streets that ran between outer walls, the other providing access to an interior waterway or the lake itself. Tenochtitlan was built on a mud-fill and it was honeycombed with canals and surrounded by open water. In fact, canoes were a favorite means of transportation and communication within the capital.

There were perhaps some sixty thousand buildings in the city, sheltering as many as 250,000 people by the sixteenth century. Common folk lived in houses similiar to those of the poorer classes of Mexican citizens today—built from wattle, with mud floors and thatched roofs. These dwellings were relatively impermanent and ugly; they usually had only one large room occupied by a large assortment of kinspeople of all ages. Here, in the smoky, dark, houses women worked tirelessly, squatting over their mortars and pestles and patting corn cakes.

The whole island, as a center of empire, was a place of restless sound and ceremony. The race liked intimacy, and noise. Regular military drills were held on the great, wide plazas, and around the temple-pyramids, there were always either thrilling, bloody sacrifices or, at night, quiet star-sighting and gentle prayers. Boats and runners sped about. A constant stream of bearers and bureaucrats crossed the three long causeways that linked the city with the mainland on each side.

Human ants patiently carried in the millions of items of tribute which made Tenochtitlan great. Tenochtitlan, and even the market at Tlatelolco, was parasitic. It drew its metals, bright feathers, figbark, vegetables, tobacco, beans, and jade, and even its maize, from the myriad subjected lands around it.

An aqueduct brought clear, fresh spring water down from Chapultepec, enough for all the people, and an efficient gravity sewer system flushed the city's wastes into the darkening, polluted lake. No contemporary city or capital had anything to match the Amerindian engineering in this respect.

The Spaniards lucky enough to see Tenochtitlan in its glory agreed that it was incomparable, and these men included soldiers who had seen Istanbul and Rome. They were awed by the very extent of the city, enormous by their standards, and fascinated by the color, activity, and variety of the bazaars. The Spanish were unimpressed by the enormous pyramids and stone towers; they came from a land of great, grim fortresses and powerful stone walls set high above the arid countryside of Castile. What caught their interest was the sheer luxury of upper-class Amerind life. The splendid gardens and placid pools, exotic with colorful birds and tropic fish, the sweet-smelling shrubs and carefully tended trees—there was nothing like this in medieval Spain or Europe. The climate of the Mexican highlands, under a burning sun but ameliorated by high, cool altitudes, permitted a wonderful blend of tropic and temperate flora and a most un-Castilian mode of living. Remembering the glory of those courts, which they destroyed, at least one austere Spaniard mourned the utter destruction of Tenochtitlan.

It is impossible to assess the civilization of Motecuhzoma II against the entire panoply of human civilizations; civilizations can only be judged by their survival, and finally, what they leave behind. The Meso-American civilization—as opposed to Amerindian cultures—did not survive, and it left behind only artwork and weed-grown walls. It left no lasting legacies like Mesopotamia, Greece, or Rome.

But this culture was unique in a way that the Eurasian civilizations could never be, because it was isolated and apparently totally original. This originality did not mean that it was utterly foreign, but it was alien enough to make it seem simultaneously attractive and repellent.

The tendency of many Mexican intellectuals to identify emotionally with their remote ancestors tends to confuse and distort assessments. On the other hand, the disdain toward indigenous America felt by so many Europeans over the past four hundred years is equally distorting. The civilization *was* abortive, but it deserves a better epitaph than that. The great problem has always been the lack of a real continuity or tie between American civilizations and the others, and of any bridge between the Meso-American and Western, even modern Hispanic Mexican traditions. The parts of Amerindian culture that survived—the *milpa*, certain languages and tribal customs, marketplaces—all preceded Amerindian civilization.

In many respects this civilization reached a very high order. Its calendar was better than the Mohammedan, Roman, or Christian. Its architecture was immature in technical terms but it was magnificent in its scope and execution. The great buildings are all the more impressive when measured against the admitted technical inferiority of the culture, which built without steel or wheels. But always overshadowing these great achievements is the fact that Mexic courses were laid not to serve human beings but to honor supernatural monsters and built by wretched slaves.

The literature of Amerindian Mexico was far more respectable than is generally believed, especially considering the handicaps of pictographic writing under which scribes worked. Only random documents have survived. The vast libraries were burned for the same reasons the library at Alexandria was destroyed. But the existence of this literature is known, as the memory of the culture was preserved, through the efforts and energy of the Spanish ethnologist priests.

Perhaps ironically, the efforts of these sixteenth-century scholars and conservationists were hardly known, and in no way admired, until very recent years. For almost four hundred years, most Europeans were indifferent to the destruction of the civilization of Meso-America.

Motecuhzoma's society was enormously ceremonial, in a way no modern culture is; it needed music and poetry of a high order, and it created them, along with dancing. But the poetry could not be finely written down, and so, even if it had not been burned, only a few colorful fragments could have survived. The poetry of the post-Conquest age, written in Spanish-Nahuatl shows what the original must have been—symbolic, beautiful, filled with color, grace, and fatalism.

The Mexica made music with primitive instruments: flutes, reeds, rasps, rattles, and drums. The tonal scale is and was monotonous to Western ears—but so is almost all Oriental music. And most authorities suspect that this music, like the ceremonial dancing, was not nearly so primitive or barbaric as the few examples the Spanish permitted to survive, or which were bypassed and lived on in remote regions. All Mexic music, dancing, and poetry in some way served the gods, and therefore, in Spanish eyes, the devil.

Because all the higher art forms of the ancient culture vanished or were ruthlessly destroyed, it cannot be correlated or judged by surviving fragments. Modern Amerindian dancing and the pole ceremonies reinvented for tourists are probably as far removed from the ceremonies at Motecuhzoma's court as children's Maypole prancing from dance steps at Versailles. Many lower forms of Amerind culture lived on to be assimilated into later Mexico, but everything that went to make it a distinct, high civilization died.

Only Mexic art and architecture ultimately remained, and these from periods far removed from the era of the Conquest itself. All examination of Meso-American civilization tends to begin and end with these. This has meant, perhaps unfairly, that other cultures have always measured Meso-Americans by their artwork. But then all vanished peoples are remembered mainly through their art, which in all times and in all places tends to reveal the real aspirations of any human heart or mind.

The nature and quality of Meso-American art has been, is, and probably always will be controversial. Its uniqueness denies correlation or comparison. It arose from visions that seem alien. It was surrealistic and nonobjective to the core. It depicted scenes that never were, and things that never walked the earth. The great idols and massive frieze-work of Mexico appear hallucinatory to Western minds. The ancient artists saw their world as a place of magic and mystery, blood and horror, in which men could not defeat fate, and they saw it through a filter of darkest night, or in a violent blast of sun blaze. It is wrong, probably, to see the results as the products of a carefully cultivated taste. The artwork monstrosities of Mexico were honest renditions of what the artists understood.

The artists and artisans of Motecuhzoma II were endlessly repeating old and standard forms, but they saw nothing wrong with these.

Until the twentieth century, Westerners generally considered Mexic art as barbarous, or beneath their notice. In fact, few Westerners could easily conceive of it as art; it was not easy for them to grasp. Frederick Catherwood, a great nineteenth-century English etcher and draftsman, once tried to reproduce on paper some of the lines and proportions of stelae uncovered in the forgotten city of Copán. He worked for hours and yet was defeated.

The problem was not technical but psychological. To Catherwood's European mind everything about Maya art was *wrong*: its proportions violated all his senses of the real world. He could copy it only with tremendous effort; he could not begin to appreciate any of its nightmare qualities.

The monster serpents and beast-mouthed things that walked Mexic walls lack the symbolic, almost serene quality of European or Chinese dragons. The Mexic monsters were misshapen, fang-faced, with mutilated and agonizing proportions. They did not just symbolize power or horror—they shrieked it.

Ironically but logically, Western interest in Mexic art evolved only as the Western world began to doubt and repudiate its own rationalistic visions, and to lose its traditional tastes and culture. Its interest in the nonrational qualities of Mexic surrealism has gone hand in hand with a post-Christian loss of certitude in its own past. Mexic art and sculpture did not depict misshapen monsters because its artists lacked technical skill—the people who built splendid pyramids and laid out perfect sewers could have carved realistically had they chose, just as Picasso might have painted sedate landscapes. The visions of ancient Mexico were human visions, and it is not impossible that men may see them once again.

Mexic pottery and figurines were either primitively sophisticated, or grossly crude, depending on the viewer's taste. The earliest work shared the quality of freshness and spontaneity of other very primitive art and is usually the most prized. All subsequent pre-Columbian art lost originality and gained little or nothing in technical perfection; in fact, a general regression occurred during the civilization's last millennium. Motecuhzoma's artisans could duplicate the massive piles of Classic Mexico, but not their esthetic grace.

The very finest Mexic art ranks alongside that of Egypt, Mesopotamia, and other ancient cultures; almost none of it compares favorably with the Greek. After the first flowering of Classic civilization, all the ebb and flow of ancient Mexico failed to reach its earliest heights. Unquestionably, the series of natural and psychic disasters that overtook the civilization exacted a savage toll. Renascence followed degeneration, but the waves of Nahuas who overran the highlands also took a serious toll. This new blood, and the incessant internecine warfare it engendered, barbarized Mexico.

The great failures of the civilization were psychic and political, and the militarism of Tula and Tenochtitlan, however dynamic, was culturally sterile and artistically uninspiring.

This barbarization showed up in places other than politics and artwork. Although the Nahua peoples seized upon all the old techniques, they

spread war gods like Tezcatlipoca and Huitzilopochtli and warlike aris-
tocracies throughout most of Mexico. They infused dynamism into the
primordial habit of human sacrifice. They loved fantastic headgear, exotic
ornamentation, and practiced physical mutilations. Despite their practice of
cleanliness—it exceeded that of contemporary Europeans—this childlike
love of adornment and ceremony were recognizable barbarous traits.

The Mexica rulers embodied a blend of ancient civilization and recent
barbarism. In them, old arts, ancient erudition, tribal customs, and a savage spirit battled continually. Motecuhzoma was not an ignorant man but
the product of an ancient culture—and, at the same time, as his actions
were to prove, he had the soul of a superstitious savage.

One problem of assessment is that it is unfair to measure the world of
the Motecuhzomas against the Christian calendar. In world terms, Mexico
did not live in the sixteenth century, or even the three thousandth year of
Mediterranean civilization; its universe must be measured on a different
time span. A common comparison has been that the Amerindian civilization was a few hundred years behind the Western technically. This analogy
is invalid. True, the technical explosion that caused Europe to forge ahead
of the ecumene had just begun when the Mexica carved out their empire—
but the Amerindians, as civilized men, were vastly behind all Eurasians in
total human experience.

The great cycles of history tend to show that ultimately very little civilized experience is ever really irrevocably lost. The great societies of Syria
and the Mediterranean rose and fell, came again and were gone, yet a vital
thread of human inheritance continued throughout. A fantastic sum of
present human knowledge, feeling, and attitudes still dates back to Babylon. The successes and failures of Motecuhzoma's world become more
understandable if that world is put in its true historical position against the
world clock of human civilization.

Dating from the vital discovery of agriculture, Mexic civilization was not
a contemporary of Catholic Spain, or even of medieval Europe. It was a
contemporary of ancient Sumer, one of the oldest known civilizations.

This historic, energetic, and brilliantly inventive culture, which arose in
the Middle East about 3500 B.C., eventually failed politically, within and
without, as a result of internecine war and fell about 2300 B.C.

Culturally, psychically, and politically, the Mexic world was closer to
Sumer than it was to its sixteenth-century ecumene. Strikingly similar de-
velopment can be traced between Sumerians and civilized Amerinds. Meso-
American religions, ideals, fears, and social structures were on the level of
Sumer; Cortés invaded a people living on an experience plane equivalent to
the Old World in the third millennium B.C.

The Tarasca, more barbarous than the Mexica, had just started to experiment with copper weapons. The following centuries might have seen

the rise of a greater empire centered on Tzintzuntzan, which again might have failed, as Sumer's empire failed. The Amerindians were a long way yet from creating Babylon. They were living out their version of the story of mankind, nothing more, nothing less. But in world terms, because they invented agriculture very late, they lagged millennia behind.

Thus the world of Motecuhzoma Xocoyotzin was a recognizable Oriental society, linked psychically if not physically with its remote Asian past. It was ceremonial, deferential, given to extravagant symbolism in thought and deed; it was a world of wonderful monuments and striking loveliness, instilled with grace and charm. It was also a bloody and brutal ant hill where all men were subordinated to the whole, and the individual personality was considered worthless. The small, dark, tireless, essentially cheerful peoples of the innumerable valleys had become subjugated not only by ruling castes and dynasties, but by chains of custom and circumstance. They bore life patiently, often callously; like all men they possessed a great spirit and they were capable of collective greatness or collective horror. For the moment they were trapped in an endless cycle, in a self-contained universe that smelled both of flowers and hot blood.

The Mexica really cannot be measured or judged by modern men. They can only be observed as people of their world and times. They struggled upward out of the abyss of history, now hopefully, now valiantly, now fearfully and irrationally, against all the troubles inherent in man and civilization. Even to their direct descendents in the Republic of Mexico, they seem hopelessly remote.

9

STRONG MEN ARMED

*. . . Every kingdom divided against itself is brought to desolation;
and a house divided against a house falleth . . . When a strong man
armed keepeth his palace, his goods are at peace; but when a
stronger than he shall come upon him, and overcome him, he taketh
from him all his armour wherein he trusted, and divideth his spoils.*

From St. Luke xi, 14.

The indigenous accounts of the last days of the Amerindian civilization are
fragmentary, and most of them were written after the Conquest. Naturally,
they contain errors in chronology, because of an imperfect sense of cause
and effect, and of time itself. But they are vivid. If they are less sophisticated and detailed than Bernal Díaz' *Historia* or Cortés' own *cartas de
relación*, they are also less self-serving; and above all, they show the true
nature of Mexic society, of its state of heart and mind as the end approached.

The awesome, bloody Mexica religion had a side effect. The belief that
the sun would not rise, that crops could not grow, and that time itself might
cease unless the gods were continually fed with blood imbued the people
with a pervading fear of total, imminent disaster. Their culture was fatalistic, pessimistic, and anxiety-ridden. Meso-Americans looked back to a
calamity-filled past to discern their future. Priests, magicians, and fortune-
tellers abounded, and even the most intelligent and rational people studied
all natural phenomena for portents or omens. The superstitious emotions
of the masses were easily aroused, and the rulers, though just as superstitious, tended to be fatalistic.

Motecuhzoma II was a mystic. He had been raised a priest, not a warrior; his hobby was wizardry, and he preferred the company of seers and magicians to that of the martial nobility on whose arms his power rested. Motecuhzoma was all-powerful—he could order men, families, or whole tribes put to death at a whim—but perhaps because of this he was wary of destiny and troubled by prophecies and dreams. In ordinary times, Motecuhzoma's mysticism was a relatively harmless exercise—but he would react to crisis with a peculiar mixture of mysticism, treachery, and fatalism which the Western intellect could only partially understand, and which, when confronted by the technical superiority and single-mindedness of purpose of Europeans, almost invariably failed.

The accident that killed his brother and made him ruler of Mexico looms large. Historians cannot help but speculate what might have happened had a bloody but clear-minded barbarian like Itzcóatl held his throne. Motecuhzoma, to the sometime despair of his counsellors and kin, was often blind to the practical problems of his realm. He was not entirely typical of his race.

But he was not unique. Nezahualpilli, lord of Texcoco, also lived under a cloud of irrational doom. He once told Motecuhzoma that Texcoca fortune-tellers had prophesied that Mexico would be ruled by strangers. When Motecuhzoma laughed at this, the argument was put to the acid test, a game of ritual ball, which Nezahualpilli won; later, this result returned to haunt Motecuhzoma's mind.

The Mexic codices and histories, from which this chapter is largely drawn, are understandable only against this frame of mind. Both rulers and ruled watched and worried over any event that seemed unusual, or broke the rhythm of existence. And beginning about the year 1509, the Mexic accounts are filled with a series of strange and ominous events. The exact nature of these phenomena is rather obscure, but the interpretation and reaction of Motecuhzoma and the Mexica is clear enough.

The first terrible omen was the sudden appearance of a great light, "bleeding fire like a wound in the eastern sky," which rose up at midnight, a glowing pyramid-shaped cone above the volcanoes. The populace of Tenochtitlan moaned and wailed through the streets; they beat their palms against their mouths in the Amerindian fashion and feared the end of the world.

The second sign was a mysterious fire that consumed the towers atop the pyramid of Huitzilopochtli. The temple woodwork inexplicably burst into a flame all the bucket brigades of the city could not extinguish until the towers burned down.

Soon after, the temple of the fire god was struck by lightning. The bolt came during a gentle drizzle, when no thunder was heard. It seemed to be a blow from the Sun.

The fourth portent set mobs howling and weeping at midday: it was a bright, three-headed comet searing the sky from west to east and obscuring the sun—a very bad omen.

The fifth wonder was a sudden rising of Lake Texcoco. Water boiled up when there was no wind, collapsing many houses.

The sixth omen was even more spine-chilling. A female voice was heard wailing in the night, crying out: *O my children, you are lost; where shall I hide you?* This *llorona*, out of the dark legends of ancient Mexico, was taken to be the Snake Mother Cihuacóatl, weeping for her human children. The wailing of Cihuacóatl did not just frighten children; when the news was reported to Motecuhzoma, he was shaken.

The seventh wonder was a weird thing taken in a fisherman's net, an ashen-colored bird with a magical mirror on its head. It was taken immediately to Motecuhzoma in the House of Magical Studies, where the ruler spent much of his time. When Motecuhzoma looked into the bird's mirror, he recognized the stars of the constellation Taurus—in Mexic astrology a very potent sign. Looking again, he saw a plain over which a vast host advanced toward Mexico. But when Motecuhzoma called the priests and wizards to confirm and interpret his visions, they confessed they saw nothing.

The eighth omen was the reported arrival in Tenochtitlan of human monsters, men with two heads. But before any of these monsters could be brought before Motecuhzoma they vanished.

The Nahua interpreted these signs and rumors as terrible predictions, perhaps of the end of the world, or the end of the race.

Motecuhzoma reacted characteristically when such ominous portents arose. He commanded his chiefs and lords of towns to send the greatest wizards and magicians to his court. When a great assemblage of seers had knelt before the throne, he demanded: "Have you seen these things? The omens in the sky, and walking the earth? A weeping woman, or strange men? Phantasms and such things?"

But the magicians could not advise Motecuhzoma, and he ordered them all held prisoner, until they should tell him the truth, against their will. Motecuhzoma knew that the magicians were afraid of the custom of ritual murder of any bearer of bad news. He sent the steward to them, to demand the truth: was the coming disaster to be sickness, hunger, insect plagues, drought, or a war? They were not to hide the truth, however terrible. Above all, had they heard the voice of Cihuacóatl, always the first to predict catastrophe?

But the magicians answered the steward's questions: "What can we say? The future is decreed, and obviously, Motecuhzoma will suffer a great mystery. If our lord demands we speak, we can say only that what is decreed must come to pass and he must await it. He will know soon enough."

Motecuhzoma now remembered the predictions of the dead Nezahual-pilli, and remarked with some wonder that the magicians' reply coincided with the fears of that lord. But he would not let the men be; he asked for more details: where, when, and how?

The steward went to question the seers again, but found that they had mysteriously vanished from their prison—probably carrying out a judicious escape. Wailing, the steward prostrated himself before Motecuhzoma, protesting that he had taken every precaution, but obviously the magicians had made themselves invisible and flown away by night, as it was well known they could do.

Motecuhzoma replied: "Let the villains go. But take warriors and go to their towns and villages; kill all their women and children, and destroy the magicians' houses."

The wives of the magicians and wizards were hung up with ropes, and the brains of their infants were dashed out against stone walls. Their houses were torn down, even the foundations removed.

Now, to avert approaching disaster, Motecuhzoma ordered the orthodox solutions. He took comfort in Huitzilopochtli the Sun, who would not turn his face from the chosen people. An immense new sacrificial stone was muscled over the causeway from Coyoacán and drenched with hot blood. The temple of the Sun was plastered with gold and gems until it glistened. To make this possible, armies were dispatched to harry the south; the *pochteca* were commanded to surrender one third of the value of all their goods, and tribute was raised. The subject peoples were now taxed in blood as well as corn and jewels; they must send warriors to be sacrificed at Tenochtitlan.

There were nobles among the Tenochca who warned Motecuhzoma against this course, saying the people of Chalco, Cempoala, and other towns would not tolerate it. But protest ended when Motecuhzoma had his own high treasurer put to death for dissent. Gentle and even kindly in his personal life, the slender Motecuhzoma could be a raging jaguar on the throne, fearful, arbitrary, cruel. He sought divine favor to save his kingdom, and he sought in the only way he knew.

He now also inflicted disastrous wounds on the body of the empire. The subject peoples and the resisting Tlaxcalteca were driven to despair. And Motecuhzoma, for obscure reasons, also destroyed the old alliance with Texcoco. He forbade the electors of Texcoco to choose their new lord when Nezahualpilli died in 1516, arbitrarily placing his nephew Cacama, apparently a flatterer of his powerful uncle with a similar cast of mind, on the throne.

But another son of Nezahualpilli, the second Ixtlilxóchitl, was the choice of the warrior nobility of Texcoco, and he rebelled against Tenochtitlan. Cacama held Texcoco, but beyond the city, half of the Texcocan countryside upheld the rebels. Motecuhzoma sent in an army, which Ixtlilóchitl surrounded and whose leader he had burnt alive.

Then a peasant from Cuetlaxtlan on the Gulf coast, appeared begging audience with Motecuhzoma. This *macehual* had come of his own accord to see the ruler—a fact made much of by the scribes, because such things never happened in Amerindian Mexico. He fell down before Motecuhzoma and said: "Our lord, forgive my boldness. But on the shores of the Great Sea I have seen a small mountain, floating on the water. It moved about, never touching the shore. Our lord, no man has ever seen the like of this."

Motecuhzoma did not punish the man, but thanked him and offered him rest. However, he had the peasant incarcerated, while he sent for a ranking priest and a high officer of his household. He appointed these men his grand emissary and ambassador, and ordered them to proceed at once to the coast.

When the two officers and their retinue arrived at the coast, they conferred with the chiefs of the local tribes. They were informed that "two towers or small mountains" indeed stood out to sea. The Mexica climbed a great tree that looked out over the Gulf and saw two floating towers—a sixteenth-century galleon with castles—and a party of strange human beings who left these towers to fish in a small boat.

The two officials, amazed, hastened back over the mountains to Tenochtitlan. They knelt before the ruler. "Our lord and master, it is true. Strange men have come to the shores of the Great Sea. They were fishing with rods and a net. Then, they returned to their towers out on the sea. We saw fifteen men, some with blue garments and some with red, and others in black and green. Some had very dirty coats, and others had no jackets at all. They wore red bands on their heads, or fine scarlet bonnets, or large round hats, for the sun. All these men have light skin, much lighter than ours, and they all have long beards, and their hair comes only to their shoulders."

Motecuhzoma sat stunned. The isolated, ingrown universe of Meso-America could not account for different breeds of man. Odd happenings were, and had to be, magical. Motecuhzoma's mind could only grasp at ancient legends: Quetzalcóatl, the "white" god, the "bearded one," who had disappeared centuries earlier into the Great Sea, promising to come again one day to reclaim his rightful throne.

At last he said to the messengers: "You are chiefs of my palace and officers of my house; you have never lied to me." But he ordered them to go with his steward and to bring back the original messenger.

The *macehual* could not be found. Greatly afraid, the officers rushed back to Motecuhzoma. The ruler, however, said only: "This is a natural thing, because these days almost all are magicians. But hear now what I tell you, and if you reveal any of it, I shall have you buried beneath my halls; your wives and infants shall be killed, and your property taken, I will root out the foundations even of your houses, down to the water, and have all your blood and seed put to death. Now bring before me in secret the two greatest artists among the silversmiths, and the two finest lapidaries, who can work emeralds."

When the artists came and reverenced Motecuhzoma, he said: "Fathers, come here. I have called you to do certain work. But take care you do not reveal this to anyone, for should you do so, it will mean death for you, and for your kin, and the destruction of your houses. All will die." Then he commanded them to make two objects apiece, working in the palace in secret.

They fashioned chains out of gold, with insets of rich emeralds, and golden bracelets. They created great fans of brilliant feathers, festooned with precious metal, armlets of gold and feathers, and bracelets of gold set with green stones—the regalia of the god, Quetzalcóatl. Further, Motecuhzoma had his steward gather secretly quills of gold dust, precious plumage, and emeralds and chalchihuites of the best quality.

When the work was done, it was the finest ever seen. Motecuhzoma was pleased. He ordered the steward: "Give these our grandfathers rich clothing, and clothing for their wives our grandmothers, and cotton, chiles, corn, seeds, and beans, the same to each."

Then the speaker gathered together the principal officers of his palace, the prime minister, the chief of the house of arrows, and the keeper of the chalk. He informed this council of the arrival of the "white gods." He showed them the artifacts and precious objects he had assembled and told them: "This treasure must be guarded well. If anything at all is lost, your houses will be rooted out; the children in the womb shall die."

Word went out to the chiefs and lords of the towns of the coast to keep constant watch. At Nauhtla, Tuztlan, and Cuetlaxtlan, men were assigned to continual vigil beside the sea.

But the strange apparitions had disappeared. Although artists painted pictures of the weird people, with white-daubed faces, and drew crude sketches of the odd sea-towers on henequen-cloth and sent these to Motecuhzoma, the originals were no longer to be seen. Motecuhzoma, who had drenched the altars throughout his realm with prayerful blood, sighed in relief. His supplications were effective; his magic worked.

But his mind was haunted; this was the year 12-Rabbit. The calendar advanced inexorably, and soon it would again stand at the year *Ce Acatl*—1-Reed. Even the children of the telpochcalli knew what that might portend.

The winged sea-towers the coastal artists drew on henequen were the ships of Juan de Grijalva, would-be conquistador.

A chain of events fatal to the civilizations of the New World lay behind the appearance of these strange craft off Mexico.

While Ahuízotl ruled, the obscure Italian seaman called Cristóbal Colón, or, in the Latin affected by learned men of the day, Christopher Columbus, blazed his sea trail to America and as the motto of his descendents would say, gave a new world to Castilla, or Castile. Columbus, thinking he had reached the fringes of India, named the islands he found *las indias*, or the Indies. His voyage was not the isolated phenomenon it appeared. In the crackup of the old orders and certainties of the European Middle Age in the commercial or capitalist revolution and in the emergence of the kingdoms of the Western rimlands as dynamic, enlarged city-states, all Europe was aswarm with restless, rootless people who still thought in medieval imagery but whose aspirations had found modern form. It was a world in which that peculiarly European concept, *money*, had taken root, destroying social orders and replacing them with social classes; and Europe was a society in which the old, individualistic, piratical ethos of the embattled medieval towns had been transmitted and transmuted into a dynamic commercialism. There were important local differences and variations from Tuscany to the Low Countries and from England to Castile, but by the fifteenth Christian century no European, prince, prelate, or peasant, could hope to live effectively without silver or gold.

This society, in which social mobility had almost become a disease and which strained against a fixed supply of precious metal, was ready to burst out on the greater world. Princes and obscure navigators like Columbus, a weaver's son, dreamed of reaching the fabled riches of the Orient, where houses were supposedly roofed with gold. Cut off from land routes to Asia by the upsurge of the fanatic, warlike Osmanli Turks, the Eurasian rimlands turned outward to the sea. Men had discovered America before, but the great significance of Columbus' voyage was its timing. In the same decade Vasco da Gama also burst into the Indian Ocean around Africa, beginning a vast European explosion of men and energy around the whole world. Europe had governments and individuals ready and eager to exploit the new discoveries. For his second voyage, in 1493, Columbus was besieged with fifteen hundred volunteers.

The dynamism of this peculiar Western society is best seen by a comparison with fifteenth-century China, which was a larger, more populous, and inherently more civilized empire than all of Europe combined. Not long before Columbus sailed, the Chinese empire mounted a great sea expedition to the other regions of the East, reaching the coasts of India. But China, whose people had invented paper and porcelain, printing and gunpowder, was a stable society ruled by a mandarin class which exalted art and service to the state but denigrated commercial, or in fact any personal enterprise. The Chinese government saw no good reason for opening contacts with outer barbarians, and the emperor forbade all future voyages, in the same age when the Court of Portugal was energetically sponsoring navigation and the building of heavy, ocean-going ships. Probably, no European court could have stopped the Western explosion; none wanted to. The European ethos was instead leading all of them toward a great competition for empire. Fernando V of Aragon, the canny and unscrupulous co-monarch of Spain with Isabel of Castile, acted entirely characteristically, by procuring papal title to all non-Christian lands lying in American longitudes, except for the part he adjudicated with the king of Portugal.

But even the consolidated kingdoms of Iberia did not possess vast armies and fleets which they could have spared to explore the outer world. There would have been no European seizure of the American continents without the commercial revolution that had broken the age-old ties of men to their soil and bound them within their social orders. For the exploration and seizure of the Americas, though sponsored by royal governments, was always carried out as individual enterprise. Europeans left their shores to serve their God and their kings and queens, but, as Bernal Díaz the conquistador admitted cheerfully, also to get rich.

Columbus himself was the prototype of all the men who sailed. He was atypical only in his monomania about sailing west. A man of no rank or accomplishment, born in Italy, he arrived at the Court of Spain after repeated failure, burning with bourgeois ambitions and a scientific interest in the real, or physical world, spouting scriptural justifications for all his views, scientific or otherwise. He almost lost his great chance because he refused to sail unless the royal government guaranteed him the hereditary Admiralship of the Ocean Sea, the governance of all lands he discovered, and ten percent of their proceeds. Columbus could only have emerged from the rich, complex society of early modern Europe—and only European monarchs would ever have granted his outrageous requests.

On his voyage into nowhere he asked God to lead him where he might find gold, and when he found strange islands at the far rim of the Ocean Sea, he hardly paused to investigate them but sailed on and on to find one at last that provided gold. It is often overlooked that Cristóbal Colón died a bitter failure in his own, and his sponsors' eyes, precisely because his voyages produced no vast material benefits. He did give Castile, almost by accident, a New World, but Vasco da Gama's maiden voyage to India returned its cost sixty times.

The fifteen hundred volunteers this Italian took to *La Ysla Española* (Hispaniola, or Haiti) were men of his same stripe, though they were Spaniards, inherently rebellious individualists, all of whom were in some

way circumscribed or frustrated at home. There were a few ruined gentlemen who, unable to cope in a society where money had become power,
dreamed of finding storehouses of gold. There were some adventurous,
idealistic priests, most in some sort of trouble either with their calling or
the Church. The majority, however, were very ordinary men: runaway
peasants and boys, whore- and dancing-masters, swineherds and restless
artisans, and a few murderers and thieves. A miasma of social ambitions
wafted out with every Spanish ship that slipped the quays at Sevilla and
Cadíz.

This was not uniquely Spanish; it was European. In this same age Al-
meida and Alburquerque looted the Indian Ocean areas in a welter of
cannon smoke and Asian blood, and in following centuries people with
similar motives and expectations would plunge into North American forests or seek out India's coral strand. Their descendents, understandably,
would find such ambitions worthy.

The Spaniards who poured into Hispaniola were only minimally in the
service of God and king. They were engaged in personal enterprise; in fact,
all *successful* European colonial ventures were some form of private enterprise. But because under Spanish law the Crown held all title to all lands in
the New World, every emigrant was automatically an *adelantado*, or advance agent, of the Hispanic Church-State, and he held rights only through
the sanction of the Crown, which, however, was easily obtained.

While the Portuguese grew rich in the real Indies, the Spanish found
their own *Indias*, which were tropic wildernesses of great beauty, disappoint-
ingly devoid of cities, spices, and gold. The natives of these islands were
naked savages who met the newcomers with hospitality, and even awe.
They lived by gathering and fishing, under a rudimentary village organization with local *caciques*, or chiefs. They did not even understand the concept of trade; they blended into the tropic foliage almost as naturally as the
iguanas and bright-plumaged birds. They had nothing to offer the Spaniards, or the Spaniards them.

The Spanish still thought that these islands, and the vast coastlines of
South America Columbus had scouted, were fringes and barriers to India.
Until Magellan's circumnavigation, the size of the world was greatly under-
estimated. The Spanish poured across the Atlantic in cockleshell ships,
trying to find ways around this barrier. They found Cuba and Jamaica,
explored the lesser Antilles, and reached Darien. In these years, and afterward, they paid a fearful price for admiralty. They were never good sailors
like the Portuguese; Castilians went out by dead reckoning and the grace of
God and met reefs and hurricanes and littered the seabed with their bones.
But thousands of them arrived in the Indies, men and a few women ready
to dare anything and risk everything in pursuit of their personal dreams.

They planted the red and gold banners of the conjoined kingdoms of

Spain on every beach. Notaries read the lofty proclamation of the pope, giving the lands and bodies of the bewildered indigenes to the Crown of Spain. Spaniards would have seized these islands and subdued their Arawak and Carib inhabitants in any case, with or without the sanction of the pope, because human history at root is the relentless diffusion of power from place to place and people to people.

But with this diffusion of European civilization into the New World began an enormous human tragedy whose effect on the Americas will probably never be erased.

The Europeans could never blend into this tropic paradise. Whether runaways, swineherds, or hidalgos, they were all completely economic men, stemming from an Indo-European culture in which forms of hierarchy, serfdom or slavery, and private property had been institutionalized for thousands of years. The Spaniards were neither more nor less ethnocentric than other peoples, but they were powerful, and thus ready to impose their own ways. Two things were inevitable in this contact: that the Europeans would try to incorporate America, and that they would try to recreate their own institutions in the New World.

Some adventurers had brought sugar cane shoots with them in 1493. They carved out plantations, and sugar spread over Haiti and Cuba like a golden plague. If there was very little gold, sugar could still be sold across the ocean at an immense price. The European could neither blend into this world nor leave it alone; he had to bend the world and nature to his will even if both were destroyed in the process.

The actions of the Spaniards toward the Amerindians were cruel but true to the oldest logic. The stronger took advantage of the weaker. The first forays were those of an undisciplined, but powerful and organized horde; the settlers robbed and raped the indigenes and exacted support from them. The Spaniards behaved no better—but no worse—than European armies have in any age of colonization—something often overlooked. The Spaniards' claim by conquest of millions of leagues of virgin lands on the islands enabled any common immigrant who could develop this soil to become a gentleman. There was, in fact, far more land than there were men to seize it.

The economy and society of Castile was diverse and complex, but the economic ideas of the ragtag colonists were very simple in the main. They were to acquire lands and the labor to work them; such landholding in Spain involved immense prestige as well as wealth. Columbus, as governor and admiral, was unable to prevent the virtual enslavement of the gentle Arawaks. Spaniards parceled out vast tracts, rounded up the Amerindians, and forced them to plant and harvest cane, or scour streams for gold. The immigrants were greedy and ruthless—but for these practices which were quickly institutionalized in the *repartimiento* and *encomienda*, the Spanish had ancient religious, political, and legal rationales.

The *repartimiento* grew out of European feudalism as it had been applied to the *reconquista* of Muslim Spain. This was a grant that permitted the grantee to exact unpaid or forced labor from conquered infidels; under it thousands of Moors had erected castles, built roads and bridges, or tilled fields for the warlords of Castile. The *encomienda* was a form of contract or trust: under it the inhabitants of a village or region were "entrusted" to the protection of a lord or landholder, in return for which he might collect taxes or tribute. Both practices were obsolete in Spanish Castile, where serfdom had been finally abolished by Isabel, but in the more backward Aragon serfdom persisted. But *repartimiento* and *encomienda* were recognized and limited under the old codifications of Castilian law, just as chattel slavery, though rare, persisted in Christian Spain.

Historically, neither *repartimiento* nor *encomienda* (which quickly blurred into a common form of serfdom called *encomienda*) were unusually intolerable or onerous; the vast majority of European and Muslim peasants still lived under some such system and bore similar burdens, as had most agriculturists since civilization rose. The conquered Moors had been subjected to this serfdom and survived. The Spanish came to consider the *repartimiento-encomienda* a first step toward the incorporation and assimilation of non-Christian peoples into Spain, and in the sociology and technology of the times, the *encomienda* had merit.

Columbus was reluctant to enslave or enserf the aborigines, but he could not stand against the colonists' angry demands. He accepted a *repartimiento* himself. Besides the greed of the settlers and the obvious political necessity of incorporating the indigenes into European society and economy, the natives had to be Christianized and saved from Hell. Though this mission was far more important to clerics and lawyers than planters contracting a sugar crop in Spain, the indigenes could not be easily converted until they had been gathered together and put to work.

The great horror of the *encomienda* was that the *indios* were not Moors, and they could not work like Moors. They were primitives with no millennia-long history of psychic subordination. They *were* men, of the same species as the Spaniards, as Spanish anthropologists, theologians, and humanists forced Crown and Church to accept—but the Spanish-European world view simply could not penetrate the Amerindian; the European could not comprehend the Indian world view, if he granted there was one at all. The *indios* could be rounded up and parceled out as slaves by Spaniards with superior arms and organization—but they could not be broken to accept fruitful labor in anything like the time frame the greedy and hungry planter-*encomenderos* demanded. The *indios* had trouble grasping the rationale of such work, let alone a brutal, endless labor for the benefit of other men. Old World peasants would have bowed their necks and endured. The *indios* instead rebelled, ran away, or when escape was impossible, sank into a deep apathy from which there was no return. They had no immunity to most Old World diseases; they rapidly died off. Those who lived on in slavery did not propagate.

Only a few of the *encomenderos* were monsters, but as a group they reacted in fury. They hunted down runaways with guns, horses, and hounds; they whipped and massacred rebels; they burned them at the stake as public examples to make the others work. Under the Spanish law, an *encomienda* serf who rebelled could be reduced to a chattel slave without any human rights; many Spaniards abused this by seizing peaceful Amerindians as rebels or "war captives." The colonists, with their primitive economy, faced hunger or failure if they could not secure native labor; hence their cruel reaction. A few slaughtered *indios* callously and carelessly, but there was never a Spanish policy of extermination in the islands. Genocide was alien to the Spanish-Catholic nature, and the Spaniards were not racists in the later, nineteenth-century European sense. They were fanatic religious bigots, but it was understood from the first that the American indigenes were not stubborn infidels like Jews or Moors, but simple, uninstructed pagans. The Spanish did burn a few who returned to paganism after "accepting" Catholicism, but the Church insisted upon the basic humanity of the *indios* and also their right to salvation. The natives were not persecuted nor slaughtered on racial or religious grounds; in fact, the Spanish crown very quickly determined that as subjects of the Catholic kings they had certain inalienable rights—rights the crown, however, from the first was unable to enforce.

The true horror was that the peaceful, very primitive people of the Indies were virtually exterminated in a few years by a tragically mistaken policy. But it was a policy—that of incorporating the indios in *encomienda* —whose obvious failures few Europeans could consciously accept. It was soon clear that if the minds of the indigenes were impenetrable to Spanish logic, their bodies were easily penetrable by European viruses. Their souls were perhaps most vulnerable of all, not just to forced conversion to a faith they could not possibly understand, but to cataclysmic changes in their circumstance that made their lives a horror and cracked their universe. Within a generation, the inhabitants of all the major islands were dead.

When Queen Isabel learned that Columbus had dared to enslave her distant "subjects" she screamed abuse. But hers, and hundreds of other royal and churchly laments were to be, in effect, crocodile tears. Isabel the Catholic, the heroine-queen of Castile, ordered an end to the *encomienda* and the treatment of the indios as serfs or slaves, but as the crown well understood, such orders were never obeyed. The reasons have often been attributed to the pressing need for American revenues; or the impossibility of policing the American frontier, where local governors could always fail to implement unpopular laws; or the fact that the colonists had powerful allies in the royal bureaucracy. The *Casa de Contratación*, a sort of Board of Trade, was set up in 1503 to regulate such matters in the Indies, but its members—from the president, the bishop of Burgos, to the lowest clerks—either held *encomiendas* in the Indies, or received direct emoluments from these.

But what actually paralyzed the Church and crown, and even Spanish lawyers and humanists in this, the one great age of Spanish humanism and law, was something so deeply ingrained in the European ethos that it was ineradicable. The great problem was not that the *indios* had to be gathered for conversion into Catholicism; even Bartolomé de las Casas, the former *encomendero* who took holy orders and then spent his life trying to protect all Amerindians, justified the conquest of America on this ground. It was that Europeans believed the *indios* must be made into productive, economic men. They could not be allowed to live on in their present state of nature; it was intolerable economically, morally, and religiously to the European mind. But they could be made to work only by utmost force, and the necessity for them to work was more powerful than Las Casas' damning arguments or Isabella's tears.

Against this pervasive necessity, Las Casas' *Very Brief Account of the Destruction of the Indies* did far more to blacken the Spanish name than it did to preserve the Indians. Las Casas himself understood the fundamental problem. He saw that the *indios* were a different kind of man, who could not be incorporated into European civilization even as slaves. The *indio* died too easily; he even preferred to die. The Andalusian friar grasped at two possible solutions. One was to solve the labor problem on New World plantations by importing African slaves, which the Portuguese could now supply in quantity. Las Casas saw that the African slave endured where the Amerindian native either provoked massacres or died. Although he did not invent the idea of Negro slavery in America, he did encourage it, to protect the Indians, for whom he had acquired something very like a proprietary interest. His second solution was that the Spanish should leave the indigenes to follow their primitive, communal way of life, contacted only by missionaries, who then could gradually instruct them in European religion and culture.

The first remedy was so hideously successful that the black trickle into America became a torrent, and every European people who came to the Americas copied the Spanish practice. Black slavery took deep root, causing a second destruction of the Indies, infecting the islands and both great continents with an incubus of evil that they may never entirely throw off.

The second remedy, leaving the *indios* in peace, could only have been enforced by a powerful, determined government. It was not to be implemented until later centuries in the Spanish mission system on the mainland. For all the romantic legends the missions spawned, and despite the fact that the concept refused to die in Spanish-Catholic hearts, the system was a dismal social failure. Neither the Spaniards, nor any other European invader, were to discover how to transform the Amerindian into a successful European. The minds of Amerindians and Indo-Europeans would not fuse.

Besides the destruction of the Caribbean tribes and the introduction of black slavery, two other things emerged from the tragic experience of the Indies. One was the definite appearance of a subtle but powerful Spanish racism toward all *indios*, whom the Spanish regarded with exasperation and contempt as undifferentiated, inferior people. The Indians went naked; they were pagan and some of them were sodomites; even when treated kindly they failed to respond to reason. The almost unbelievable horrors perpetrated on the natives, in fact, seem to have been caused largely by this failure of the *indio* to comprehend the white man. If the *indio* serfs had worked like Moors it would have been entirely in the interest of their masters to preserve them.

Out of this growing racial antipathy and view of the Amerindians as *gente sin razón*, that is, people impervious to European reasoning, grew attitudes that became decisive to Spanish policy, despite arguments of theologians and humanists and the passage of countless laws. Neither laws nor arguments can ever change basic attitudes. Spanish-Catholics could not dismiss the *indio* as vermin, as some other white men did; they had to consider his soul. The Church was prepared to love the *indio*, and even save him where it could, but with a patronization almost as deadly as European disease: it began to see the *indio* as a child to be exempted from the Inquisition as incompetent, and to be led like a child toward European rationales. The *encomendero*, meanwhile, understandably came to look on all *indios* as stupid, sullen, intractable savages, who seemed to understand torture better than any other argument. The *indio* might be human, as the priests argued, but he had to be ruled with an iron hand.

These views ran together and often fused. *Encomenderos* sometimes treated their charges like retarded children, and generations of priests came to believe with passionate sincerity that *indios* could only be taught the curse of Eve with the whip.

This concept of the *indio* was to have more effect on the course of the Spanish Empire in America than all the laws, rationales, theories, reports, and arguments with which the Spanish confused posterity.

And when, by 1517, Spanish ships from Cuba began searching other islands for slaves to replace those fast dwindling on the larger islands, the experience of the Antilles rode with them.

The first expedition out of Cuba was piloted by Alaminos, who sailed with Columbus as a boy; it was commanded by Hernández de Córdoba. The winds between the south of Cuba and the peninsula of Yucatán are contrary for sailing ships; and this is why the Spaniards, despite their island sojourn, were unaware of mainland Mexico. Córdoba, however, met a storm and was blown onto the Yucateca coast, which he mistook for an island.

Here, Córdoba found the first signs of civilization in the New World. He saw stone-walled towns, temples set on pyramids, and natives who dressed in cotton cloth. Here, too, the Spanish made first contact with bloody altars and white-robed priests, who let their hair grow and stank of carrion.

Córdoba's expedition also encountered a great mystery. The local tribe, which was Maya, greeted a landing party with shouts of *castellano, castellano!* Lured by smiles and being recognized as Castilians, a hundred Spaniards went with the Maya into their town. Here they were attacked by hordes of cotton- and kapok-armored warriors. They fled under a hail of javelins and arrows, losing half the party. Córdoba himself was severely wounded, and died shortly after his return to Cuba. The Spaniards, who had only met friendship and deference from the coastal tribes before, were greatly amazed.

In Cuba, the governor Diego Velásquez was far more interested in the report of stone houses and towns than in Córdoba's fate. The news created a certain furor; obviously, there was something of value in the west. Velásquez, a scheming pinchpenny who took no risks himself, commissioned Juan de Grijalva to return to Yucatán for exploration.

Grijalva's ships arrived off Yucatán in 1518. He avoided the region where Córdoba had met disaster, landing farther to the north in the present-day state of Tabasco. He found natives willing to communicate. Despite language barriers, the local people made Grijalva understand that this was a very large island indeed, with a great kingdom or empire in its interior. Grijalva then sailed north, finally arriving at the present-day San Juan de Uloa. His orders had been to explore; now, not knowing what to do, he sent one of his officers, Don Pedro de Alvarado, back to Santiago de Cuba for further instructions. He engaged in fishing for some days; then, when his biscuits turned wormy and the coastal mosquitoes became unbearable, he too sailed for home.

Meanwhile, Alvarado's report caused excitement. Velásquez now knew he was on the verge of success; the mainland held thousands, if not millions of potential workers, and, very likely, rich cities. It might even be India, at last. Condemning Grijalva for not exceeding his orders, Velásquez cast about for a leader of more initiative and spirit for the third expedition. He chose his private secretary, a man of education who had lived in the islands as a successful planter for some years. This man, whom Velásquez believed had superior qualities, might also be expected to be loyal to his patron. The governor chose splendidly, and also disastrously for his own fortunes, as it turned out.

Don Hernando, or Hernán, Cortés de Monroy was the son of an obscure squire of Extremadura, the poorest province of Spain. Las Casas wrote of Cortés' family that "it was *said* to be hidalgo," or gentle; apparently Cortés sprang from that large, economically-ruined class which clung stubbornly to pretensions, true or false, of gentility. He had been a sickly child, a dreamer who read law for two years before throwing it up in search of a more glamorous future. He considered taking service with Gonzalo de Córdoba in Italy, but finally sailed at the age of nineteen for the Indies. He arrived with nothing but his Latin and his coat of arms, both of which proved helpful. Although when he was offered an *encomienda* he made his famous statement that he had not dared the Ocean Sea to till the soil like a peasant, but to find gold, he eventually accepted the life of a sugar grower, living by the sweat and destruction of the island *indios*. After a scandalous seduction, which almost resulted in his execution, he married Catalina Xuárez, a girl of poor family.

Now, at the age of thirty-three, Cortés was notorious mainly for his love affairs. However, he had the same openhanded liberality that made him popular with the common sort; he was known as a good fellow and a spender as well as a *burlador*, or deceiver; he had even become an *alcalde* or magistrate. This aging adventurer's consuming passion, however, was neither women nor money, but fame—a raging thirst that ruled his life.

The governor was prepared to commission Cortés only if he put up two-thirds of the cost of the expedition. Cortés accepted these terms, fully aware of Velásquez' nature and the fact that he was being used as cat's-paw. The conquistadorial milieu was one of private enterprise with official sanction; Cortés knew that Velásquez was reaching for the western lands on his own initiative, but if the expedition succeeded he would take the credit and a lion's share of the proceeds, while his patron Fonseca on the Casa de Contratación would back him up. Cortés planned to succeed, then plead his own case with the King.

He began to raise a private army with enthusiasm and no particular respect for the limits of his commission. He recruited a few gentlemen, who could help subsidize the voyage, and a host of restless roughnecks. He seized arms and stores, including some from the governor's storehouse. He took some guns Velásquez had specifically forbidden.

The conquistadorial world was one of constant conspiracy and treachery, as jealous and ambitious men collided beyond the reach of royal law. Cortés had enemies who reported his every indiscretion. Velásquez, sensing that Cortés would not easily be controlled, decided to revoke his commission. But the Extremaduran had his own coterie. He got word of the revocation, and moving swiftly, shipped a vast quantity of supplies and beat out of Santiago harbor with his ships.

From Cortés' legal training, he knew the governor's writ did not run where the governor's warrant could not be served. He sailed off the coasts of Cuba for ninety days, recruiting more men through agents on shore, and even slipping on board additional stores and guns. He suborned the majority of Grijalva's returning sailors and men-at-arms; he had already appointed Alvarado his principal lieutenant.

At last, with some five hundred and fifty fighting men, sixteen horses, ten brass cannon, four falconets, and sixteen arquebuses—all he could find on the island—and eleven tiny ships, he caught the wind for Mexico on February 19, 1519.

He had already demonstrated the salient gifts and characteristics that made his career: ambition, audacity, a legal mind, an awareness of the vital importance of detail, an ability to grasp opportunity, and a refusal to be thwarted by authority, circumstance, or fate. Cortés had an ancient Roman mind—pragmatic on one level, almost inhumanly determined on the next. He was a great captain, a general, and more. He had the personal charm and power of personality to hold and bend an unmanageable band of cutthroats and freebooters to his ends. From this day forward there was to be a continuing unfolding and reaffirmation of these traits.

It is a mistake to pass Cortés off as a pirate. According to his own lights, he was a Christian knight, whom God had generously granted an opportunity to become another Alexander the Great. With a tiny army, Hernán Cortés was prepared to conquer any kingdoms that might be encountered in the west, for glory, God, and gold. Not only was he misunderstood by later men; he was far from typical of his own time and place. He was a considerable cut above all other Spanish conquistadores, especially murderous swineherds like Almagro or Pizarro.

Although ruled by his ambition for personal glory, he was an honest patriot to his country. Determined to conquer a kingdom for himself, he was still entirely loyal to Carlos I, a king he had never seen—more loyal, in fact, than that suspicious Hapsburg ever really understood. He wanted gold, but as a resource, like gunpowder or iron; gold made his world go round. He promised his men gold and women, and his officers titles, each to be a *marqués*, at least. He considered fame and honor of a higher order than mere wealth.

Cortés could be brutal—no gentle soldier in that age could have long survived—yet he instinctively preferred to avoid bloodshed whenever possible. He was crafty and could be murderously cruel—but his cruelty invariably derived from policy. Cortés would employ any amount of force to succeed, but when he was victorious he was genuinely magnanimous to his enemies. He was pragmatic and coolly accepted the world—and yet few men who ever lived have been so stubbornly single-minded in pursuit of a goal. He was also honestly and deeply religious, as religion was commonly understood and practiced in his day.

He needed no special rationale to seek out hidden kingdoms; no Spaniard or European of that time did. It was enough that the world was suddenly open to them. Cortés cannot be weighed against anachronistic values; he can only fairly be measured against his times. His faith must be seen against the fanatic Catholicism of sixteenth-century Spain. His ambition must be put against the bursting vanity of the Renaissance, when fame was everything. His brutality and cruelty must be compared with the treacheries and tortures accepted everywhere in Europe, and his morality balanced against the cesspool of amorality and intrigue that Italianate politics was making from Fernando's Aragon to Tudor England.

If Cortés had been born a prince, he might have been one of the world's remembered kings. As it was, he was born in obscurity and had to win a kingdom on his own. And while he has been condemned for the miseries he brought that kingdom, the aftermath of his conquests was not his fault.

His ships dropped anchor off the shores of Yucatán. Cortés put Pedro de Alvarado, who was considered experienced in these regions, ashore with a landing party. The fair-haired lieutenant, who was as handsome and valiant as he was to prove thoughtless and evil, immediately looted a native village of "gold, clothing, and forty chickens"—the last a form of indigenous fowl. Alvarado also seized three hapless Amerindians and would have tortured them to see if they had gold had not Cortés intervened.

These acts sent Cortés into a fine rage. He now did something no Spanish conqueror in the New World had so far done. He set out to conciliate the *indios*. He freed the captives and restored all the looted property. He tongue-lashed Alvarado, telling him in front of everyone that they had come to conquer a kingdom, not to rob poor Indians, and that if they committed such acts they would turn the whole country against them.

While his rough crew stood by in amazement, and possibly some amusement, the captain-general enticed the frightened *indios* back to their homes. But he struck down all the native idols he could find, and ordered the company to erect a great cross and an icon to the Virgin Mary in the village center. He commanded the chaplain—there were priests, official and otherwise with every Spanish party—to convert the village population and then say Mass. Padre Bartolomé de Olmedo held Mass and also claimed a general conversion. The Maya-speaking tribesmen here may have accepted their "conversion" peacefully, because the cross was known to them as a symbol of Tláloc, and it had other religious significance, also. But Cortés' hardbitten bandits now dared not scoff. He had struck deeply into their own superstitions and beliefs.

This was a bloody age, when God's mercy meant something different to men than it might mean in later times. But it was also a time when all ordinary Spaniards believed in heaven and hell, however they might spurn the former and assure the latter. Europeans might defy their God; none did Him the ultimate mockery of disbelief. They were terrified of the Devil. Religion shaped and colored the world of the Spanish almost as thoroughly as that of the Amerindians in this century, though the Spanish, unlike the Amerindians, could separate the world and spirit if they could not separate Church and state. The Spaniards, particularly, were heirs to eight centuries of intermittent warfare with Arab-Berber invaders, a struggle that always had religious overtones. Their forefathers had conquered and re-Christianized a score of Moorish emirates with the sword from the Pyrenees to the Palisades. This religious conflict with Islam had inevitably infected Spanish Catholicism with a warlike spirit. Spain's patron, St. James the Apostle, or Santiago, whose bones were supposedly discovered in a tomb at Compostela about 850, was one result of such crusades. Santiago did not emerge in the Middle Ages as Christ's gentle fisher of men, but a war-spirit who rode armed and armored high in the heavens above the charging Christian host.

Crosses had been raised everywhere in the islands. But no one, except the Admiral Cristóbal Colón, had ever really worried about incorporating the helpless indigenes into the People of God, although some friars baptized a few *indios* immediately prior to execution for their crimes. Cortés was immensely more enlightened and religious than the normal conquistador. He was honest in his desire to create a new Christian kingdom in the Indies. But what he accomplished—and there is no doubt that he knew this—by his various acts of conversion and piety was not to save the Indians but to enlist the God of the Spaniards in his cause, at least in Spanish minds. His ship banners proclaimed this, and his rankers believed it. Ironically, perhaps, Cortés the conquistador, who slaughtered many Amerindians did more to obviate any future *Spanish* trauma over the Conquest of Mexico than his fellow former *encomendero* Las Casas, who failed to preserve the *indios* but immortalized the Spanish crimes.

In Yucatán, the expedition learned that there were two Spaniards near the coast. And now, an earlier mystery was solved. Some years before, a Spanish ship had foundered off Jamaica; the survivors were blown onto the Yucatán peninsula in a small boat. The Maya seized and sacrificed all but two of these Spaniards to their gods. The two who were spared were Gonzalo Guerrero and a priest, Jerónimo de Aguilar.

Guerrero went native in all things, and it was he who warned the Maya against Spaniards and had instigated the attack on Córdoba's landing party. Aguilar wanted to be rescued—though there is some variation in the old accounts about this—and while Cortés was in Yucatán, made his way to the coast and by the narrowest of margins was sighted and picked up by a Spanish ship.

Gonzalo Guerrero was not heard from again. But Padre Aguilar joined Cortés' expedition. During his stay among the indigenes he had learned the Maya language, and this fact was to prove of incalculable importance to the Conquest of Mexico.

Tiring of the barren limestone plains of Yucatán, Cortés went northward along the coast, to Tabasco. However, the people who had welcomed Grijalva were now hostile. This tribe ambushed the landing parties, who were saved not by firearms, or courage, or cold steel, but by their horses. The Maya of Tabasco believed the invaders to be supernatural creatures— man and horse enjoined. Terrified, the Maya surrendered, teaching Cortés a lesson he never forgot. The sixteen horses, carefully tended and husbanded in the holds, were to be worth more than their weight in gold.

Gathering the awed *indios*, Cortés made a speech to them through Aguilar, informing them of Christianity, and also accepting them as vassals of King Carlos I of Spain. Padre Olmedo celebrated Mass. Then, following their own customs, the new vassals presented Cortés with food-tribute, and twenty nubile girls.

The Spanish accepted both with equal grace, though the girls had to be baptized before they could be used. Cortés forbade his army to sleep with pagans. This was hardly sophistry; Cortés considered himself a Christian knight, and crusaders did not consort with idolators.

Here, again, Cortés seemed almost favored by the Deity, for one of the wenches was a Nahua-speaking captive of the Maya, called Malintzin. Malintzin, or Malinche, was the daughter of a petty Nahua lord; like Aguilar, she had learned the Maya tongue in slavery. Through Aguilar, she could communicate with the Spanish, and also with anyone who spoke the dominant Nahuatl tongue of Mexico. Malintzin was first given to a Spaniard named Puertocarrero. Cortés, when he learned her background and talents, took her for himself. She was baptized Marina, and the Spanish, who were as conscious of birth and rank, though hardly as obedient as Amerindians to it, called her "doña Marina"—the title *doña* being roughly the equivalent of the Nahua suffix *tzin*.

Cortés, still hearing tales of the magnificent kingdom which none of his informants, including Malintzin, had actually ever seen, followed on Grijalva's track, to San Juan de Uloa. Finally, he set foot in Veracruz, on Good Friday, April 21, 1519. Now, at last, two vast kingdoms would meet.

Within hours of Cortés' landing, Motecuhzoma Xocoyotzin was aware of it. Hardy runners sped through the mountains from the coast; the same men sometimes carried fresh sea-fish for the speaker's table. The coast had been watched for two years, as Motecuhzoma had commanded; the year 13-Rabbit had come and almost gone. Mexica scribes recorded the effect of Cortés coming on the ruler of the Mexic world.

"The news of their coming was brought to Motechuzoma . . . it was as if he thought the new arrival was Our Prince Quetzalcóatl. This is what he thought in his heart: He has come! He has returned! He will come here, to Tenochtitlan, to reclaim his canopy and throne, for that is what he promised ere he left us . . .

Then Motecuhzoma Xocoyotzin, moving like a man in a dream, called forth five warriors and superior priests of holy sanctuaries, all Jaguar knights. "Come forward, my Jaguar Knights, come forward. It is said Our Lord Quetzalcóatl has returned to this land. Go to meet Him; go to hear Him. Listen to everything He says—listen and remember!" He had the accumulated treasures brought out. "Here is what you will bring Our Lord. This is the treasure of Quetzalcóatl!"

It was a great treasure: a serpent mask inlaid with turquoise, breast decorations and collars, a shield ornate with gold and mother-of-pearl, all decorated with quetzal feathers. There were mirrors and atlatl encrusted with blue stones, jade bracelets with gold bells. These were the most valued objects Motecuhzoma's realm afforded.

The speaker believed that Quetzalcóatl was returning with a coterie of divinities. In the offering was also included the regalia of Tezcatlipoca of the Night: a helmet set with gold and stars; earrings, mirrors, and bells, and a breastplate of exquisite shellwork. He gave the messengers the traditional regalia of Tláloc: headdresses of green feathers, jade earrings, ornaments of fine gold, a serpent wand, and a cloak. And the finery of the god Quetzalcóatl, taken from the temples: a diadem of jaguar hide and feathers set with a great green stone; jade collars and turquoise earrings, golden bells, and a golden shield.

Besides these, there were other divine ornaments, fit for gods, in the offering. This treasure was packed in wicker baskets and loaded onto bearers' backs. Then Motecuhzoma said: "Go now. Do reverence to Our Lord the God. Tell him: Your deputy, Motecuhzoma, has sent us. Here are the presents with which he welcomes you home to Mexico."

Motecuhzoma's gods were capricious and dangerous; however, it was well known they could be propitiated. If the new arrivals were gods, Motecuhzoma had done the right thing; perhaps they would go away. And if they were not gods—and Motecuhzoma had a grain of doubt—then they could still be destroyed. If they were merely human, he could send all the power of Mexico against them in good time. But first, he had to ascertain whether the strangers were gods, or agents of the gods. Thus, temporizing, Motecuhzoma wrote his own death warrant and his empire's as well.

The five Jaguar Knights hastened to the Gulf, keeping the treasure-laden baskets under close guard. At Xicalanco they embarked in swift canoes and paddled along the coastline until they saw the winged towers rising from the sea. They approached with apprehension, and were hailed in Nahuatl by Malinche, who spoke through Jerónimo de Aguilar to Cortés.

When the messengers said they came from the City of Mexico, the strangers lowered a rope ladder and took them aboard. When the leader, Cortés, was pointed out to them, they reverenced him by touching lips to the deck—the traditional earth-kiss by which men adored the gods. They told him: "We beg the god to hear us. Your deputy, Motecuhzoma, sends us to render homage. He holds Mexico in care for you."

Then, the messengers broke out the treasure and dressed Cortés in godly finery: turquoise mask and decorated vest and sandals on his feet. But when the Captain was adorned with turquoise and jadeite and mother-of-pearl, he did not appear pleased.

He asked, "Is this all? Is this your gift? Is this how you greet people?"

"This is all, our lord," the messengers said.

Then Cortés had the messengers put in irons, and he fired off a cannon as a demonstration of his power. The frightened messengers fainted away. Cortés had them raised up; he released them and gave them food and wine.

Remembering their orders, the messengers were not too frightened to observe everything.

Cortés told them, "I have heard the Mexica are great warriors; their fame has reached even Castile. But I am not convinced. I want to know if the Mexica are truly brave and powerful. I will give you swords and bucklers, and tomorrow we shall fight in pairs, at daybreak. So we shall learn the truth!"

The messengers protested: "Oh, our lord, we were not sent for this! What the lord demands is beyond our authority. If we did this, it will anger Motecuhzoma, who will put us all to death."

But the captain said sternly: "No, this must take place. Therefore, eat early, and good cheer!"

Having played his psychological warfare to the hilt, Cortés then allowed the five knights to leave his ship. Grinning, he watched them leap into their canoes and paddle furiously away—those without paddles pushing the water with their hands. He knew they would hasten back to Motecuhzoma. And the messengers shouted to each other: "Faster, faster! Nothing must happen to us, until we report what we have seen!"

Back on shore, they ran to Xicalanco, and from there to Cuetlaxtlan. They paused only to eat, although the local official begged them to stop and rest. "No, we have seen terrifying things, and we must report them to our lord, Motecuhzoma."

Meanwhile, the lord Motecuhzoma had been comfortless; he could neither eat nor sleep, nor could any mortal speak with him. He was immersed in gloom. Once he said aloud: "What will happen? Will anyone outlive this? Ah, once I was content, but now I feel death in my heart." He revealed the thing that worried him most: "Will they come here?"

He gave orders to the palace guards to wake him, even if sleeping, the instant the messengers returned.

Finally, five exhausted nobles trotted up the causeway to Xoloco in the middle of the night. When the sentries came to Motecuhzoma, they found him wide awake. He said: "Tell the messengers to go to the House of the Serpent; tell them to go there. And have two captives painted with the chalk. . . ."

They assembled in the House of the Snake. The two captives were dragged in and sacrificed; their chests were torn open, and the messengers were sprinkled with the hot and holy blood. Then, after this ritual, the knights knelt to Motecuhzoma and spoke.

They described the cannon, how it roared and deafened and caused warriors to faint; how it shot out sparks and a rain of fire, and gave off an odor like rotting mud—and how its ball could shatter a mountain and splinter a tree.

And they reported: "Their arms and clothing are all made of the white metal, iron; they dress in white metal and wear it on their heads. Their swords are of iron; their bows are of iron, and their shields and spears are of iron. They have deer which carry them wherever they wish to go. Our lord, these deer are as tall as the roof of a house!

"They cover their bodies, except for the face. Their skin is white, like lime. They have yellow hair, though some have black. Their beards are long and yellow, and their mustaches are yellow. Our lord, their hair is curly, with fine strands.

"Their food is like human food, but strange. It is like straw, with the taste of a cornstalk, but tasting also as if of honey . . .

"Their dogs are enormous, with yellow eyes that flash fire. The dogs' bellies are hollow, and they have long and narrow flanks. They are powerful and tireless. They are spotted, like the jaguar, and they leap about, with tongues hanging. . . ."

The Mexica scribes wrote, "When Motecuhzoma heard this report, he was filled with fright. It was as if his heart fainted, as if his heart shriveled. It was as if he were conquered by despair. . . ."

Cortés knew he had found his hidden kingdom. Even the soldiers of his band understood that the gifts represented artwork of a high and delicate order, although they did not contain much gold, and the stones so precious to the Amerindians were worthless baubles to Europeans. Ironically, Cortés himself had brought along the sort of trade goods one presents to naked savages, toys, trinkets, glass beads, and some cloth.

The Spaniards now speculated about this revealed kingdom. It was certainly one of the realms described by Marco Polo or Sir John Mandeville. Cortés, holding that it was the Golden Chersonesus, where King Solomon acquired his gold, began to lay plans, his mind afire.

Having discovered a kingdom to conquer, Cortés' first problem was not the conquest, but to make certain he did not conquer it for the benefit of Diego de Velásquez, under whose commission he sailed. Cortés' facile legal mind was still working. He convinced his army that they should now found a Spanish town here in the sand dunes, and constitute themselves as its citizens. This was not the mere exercise of a Mediterranean urban reflex, as some historians thought. Under Spanish law, the citizens of a town gained certain privileges, one of which was to be governed directly by the crown. At one stroke, then Cortés might obviate the whole problem of the governor of Cuba.

Thus Cortés founded the city of Veracruz, and dispatched a ship directly to Spain to inform the king. The army—which had no love for Velásquez, who sent others to do his work—voted Cortés their captain-general, and also voted him a fifth share of all booty, in addition to the fifth that would go to the crown.

As for conquest itself, Cortés knew exactly what he intended to do, but he would make plans only as he gathered sufficient intelligence. The more he could learn about Mexico and its people, the better.

And meanwhile, Motecuhzoma began that peculiar series of embassies and contacts that led inevitably to his country's doom. Like Cortés, he was wary of acting until he knew more. Unlike Cortés, he had no firm resolve; haunted by magic and prophecies, he wished only for the strangers to go away. Here began a process of contact and conquest that was to be repeated in various forms again and again during the next centuries, between Europeans and other peoples of the world. Cortés was the technically superior, self-assured, morally confident, energetic, single-minded aggressor, able to play upon his opponents' weaknesses and fears; Motecuhzoma was the highly civilized but superstitious potentate, swamped in fatalism, reared in a static universe unable to cope with blinding change. The very appearance of outsiders began to shatter his world. He began the game with the power to destroy these strangers on his shores; he could not find the will to use it.

This was the beginning of a Western dominance of the entire world.

Motecuhzoma still retained the initiative. Now, he sent a deputation of wise men to study and spy upon the strangers, and if possible, to wreak mischief upon them. Characteristically, he chose wizards and magicians for this task; his faith in wizardry was unshakeable.

The seers brought food and gifts to Cortés, and at Motecuhzoma's orders, they sacrificed some captives before the Spaniards, to honor and feed them. The Mexica account of this ceremony is striking:

". . . But when the white gods saw this done, it was as if they were filled with loathing and disgust. They spat upon the ground; they closed their eyes and shook their heads from side to side; they wiped away tears. When food sprinkled with hot blood was offered them, they struck it away, as if it sickened them, as if the blood were rotted . . .

The magicians were badly shaken by this reaction; doubtless they recalled that the god Quetzalcóatl had abhorred human sacrifice and had futilely tried to abolish it. The magicians called upon Huitzilopochtli, through rites and incantations, to direct a wind against the strangers, or to cause them to grow sores, or to die or vanish. The charms did not work. The strangers ate the fruit and corn cakes they were offered, without blood, and prospered. Discouraged, the wizards hastened back to Motecuhzoma and assured him the strangers were invincible to Mexic magic.

"O our lord, we are no match against them; against them, we are as nothing."

And Motecuhzoma was even more frightened; surely these were the agents of gods, if his wizards could do nothing against them.

Now, another stroke of luck favored Cortés. Several Totonac-speaking people from the subjugated state of Cempoala wandered into camp. When Cortés explained to them he was the agent and vassal of a great king across the sea, they asked bitterly how anyone could not be subject to Motecuhzoma. For the first time, Cortés began to understand that the kingdom of Motecuhzoma was comprised of many different peoples, and that all was not well with it. Smelling opportunity, Cortés set out for the city of Cempoala, leaving strict orders that his men must avoid trouble in his absence.

His party struggled through dense bamboo stands and forests to a town built around a great square, which shone whitely in the tropic sun from its lime-wash. The Cempoalteca greeted the strangers with fruit and rose garlands. The lord of Cempoala quickly enlightened Cortés as to the true nature of Motecuhzoma's empire; he was a fat chief who made clear his hatred of the Mexica and their continual demands for tribute in kind and blood. While Cortés considered this, he had another stroke of luck. Five tax collectors arrived from Tenochtitlan. These richly-robed men, carrying crooked staffs and roses, arrogantly demanded twenty Totonacs for Mexico's altars.

The lord of Cempoala would have obliged, but Cortés stopped him, seized the Mexica envoys and imprisoned them. The Cempoalteca were startled by such boldness, then badly frightened; Motecuhzoma's wrath would surely fall upon them.

Then, secretly, Cortés released the angry tax-gatherers, and through Malinche asked them to report back to Motecuhzoma that he was the speaker's friend, who had aided his people against rebellious Totonacs.

Cortés, steeped in Roman history and law, understood the principle *divisa et impera*. He had forced the Cempoalteca into an alliance before their chiefs quite realized what had happened.

For all their hatred of the Mexica, the Totonac Cempoalteca followed identical practices: every day they sacrificed three or four captives. Cortés would not put up with this. He ordered fifty soldiers to climb the main pyramid and tear down the idols. The priests shrieked protests and the warriors of Cempoala notched arrows to their bows, but Cortés held the lord of the town, and all the priests, under his sword, and through these hostages, he made the people acquiesce, and also learned something about Mexic subservience.

The temples were cleansed of blood; a Christian altar was installed, and Padre Olmedo said Mass. Four priests were bathed, given haircuts, and placed in charge of the new shrine. Then, Cortés returned to the beach, taking along six Totonac girls—the gift of the lord of Cempoala.

He found many of his private army disgusted by now with the whole enterprise. Mosquitoes drove the idle Spaniards mad, and thirty men had already been killed by tropic fevers. Cortés was urged to sail back to Cuba—but he had other plans.

Before his force quite knew what was happening, he set fire to his fleet. Now, there was nothing for the army to do but strike inland. On August 19, 1519, with forty Cempoalteca warriors, two hundred native bearers, and about four hundred Spaniards, Cortés left the beach. In the whole history of mankind, probably, no more audacious march has ever been made.

In his palace Motecuhzoma heard this disturbing news. He knew Cortés was asking questions about his vigor, and appearance, and he understood that the strangers intended to come to Tenochtitlan. Motecuhzoma was terrified that eventually he must confront these strangers, that Cortés would demand his throne, and that he would not be able to decide what to do.

His fears communicated themselves to the populace. Pessimism and terror was expressed everywhere; it was recorded that many Mexica greeted each other with tears.

"The children were caressed and comforted; they were comforted by their fathers and mothers," the Mexica accounts sing. But there was no one who could comfort Motecuhzoma Xocoyotzin.

10

MARCHES
AND MASSACRES

*. . . They have sold themselves in their terror. See the scum of
Tlaxcala, the great cowards of Tlaxcala, the guilty ones of Tlaxcala!
They were beaten by the Mexicans, and now they bring strangers to
defend them . . . O you frightened beggars, you have surrendered
the immortal glory won by your heroes, who were of the pure blood
of the ancient Teochichimeca. What will become of you, you traitors?*

From the *Historia de Tlaxcala*, Diego Muñóz Camargo.

Don Hernando Cortés, captain-general by the authority of the Villa Rica de
la Veracruz, that Spanish colony marked out, proclaimed, and notarized,
but so far unbuilt on the coast of Mexico, did not intend to strike directly
for Motecuhzoma's capital. The Cempoalteca advised him of the Tlaxcalan
confederation, the Amerindian republic that still held out against the power
of Mexico. After leaving a small garrison at Veracruz under Gonzalo de
Sandoval, Cortés commanded only some four hundred troops. Under his
divide-and-conquer strategy, Cortés wanted some warrior allies.

The army sweated up out of the mosquito-infested lowlands, the *tierra
caliente*, into the eastern cordillera. It passed under mighty Orizaba, the
highest snow-capped peak in the country, and climbed into a mountain
pass ten thousand feet above the sea. Cortés now crossed the most spectacular scenery in Middle America, and some of the most unusual in the
world, as he marched up out of the fetid tropics into the highlands, through
forests and deserts and into endless mountain valleys, green with corn and

maguey plants. At the van of this army marched the warlord of Cempoala, who guided Cortés on his way. And so the invaders came to the high wall of Tlaxcala—a stone barrier about nine feet high that stretched across the mountains for mile after mile.

All the events that now occurred have never been entirely clear. The Amerindians left colorful accounts, some of which fit into the *cartas de relación* Cortés sent his king and the *True History* that Bernal Díaz, a petty officer in the ranks, wrote years afterward; other indigenous tales have no such corroboration. The Mexica and Tlaxcalteca with their imperfect sense of chronology, undoubtedly mixed times and places, but their statements ring of truth.

The Cempoalteca had sent messengers ahead, and the Tlaxcalteca already knew about the coming of the white men. They also knew about the continual embassies between Motecuhzoma and Cortés; they did not know whether the strangers were friends or foes. The chiefs of Tlaxcala—whom the Spanish called *caciques*, like all native lords, after a word from the islands—had been besieged for generations. They suffered from a powerful fortress-psychology. They feared letting strangers, even possible allies, enter their lands; at the same time, they did not want to offend these people, if they should prove useful. They hit upon a truly characteristic Amerindian subterfuge.

They allowed the invaders to cross the wall and arrive at a village inhabited by a tribe of Otomí, subject to Tlaxcala. Here, the hordes of Tlaxcala suddenly converged upon the Spanish van. If the foreigners were driven away, well and good; they were no use as friends. But if they triumphed, then the attack could always be blamed on the lowly Otomí.

Here accounts differ. The Amerindian records say that the strangers utterly destroyed the Otomí; they divided their ranks, fired cannon through the open spaces, shot them with iron arbalest bolts, then charged with sword and buckler—tactics the Spaniards had already made famous in Italy. The natives perished.

But the Spanish wrote that they survived a series of combats only with the greatest difficulty, and that if the Tlaxcalteca had not been so imbued with the corrupting influence of "flower wars"—trying to take sacrificial victims—they might have been hurled back. Cortés' rank and file began to complain bitterly. How could they hope to continue to Tenochtitlan and defeat the admittedly mightier Mexicanos if they could not cut their way across Tlaxcala?

The lords of Tlaxcala met again in council and decided to greet the Spanish as allies, lest Tlaxcala be destroyed. "Therefore, the lords of Tlaxcala went out to them, bringing many good things to eat; fowl and eggs and the finest corn cakes. They reverenced the strangers, saying, Our lords, you are weary; rest!"

The Spanish were understandably wary. "Who are you, where do you live?" Malintzim asked.

"We are from Tlaxcala; you have come upon our land; we are from the City of the Eagle."

And the Spaniards were guided into the city, with its great idols and racks of human skulls; they were paid honor, fed, and given the daughters of Tlaxcala. The Spanish officers were acquiring an entourage of local concubines; they were living like Amerindian lords.

From the Tlaxcalteca, Cortés learned much about Tenochtitlan, especially that it was only three days' march beyond the mountains, and that the Mexica were indeed ferocious warriors who had conquered most of Mexico.

Here, in the midst of numerous and very powerful allies, Cortés changed his policy of Christian conversion. He was affronted by the captives held in cages pending sacrifice, and insisted these be released; but the better part of valor induced him to forbear smashing the idols. Nor did he have opposition from Bartolomé de Olmedo. Olmedo, an honest priest, had become cynical of overnight mass conversions by people who could not even speak a Christian tongue. A compromise was accepted: the God of the Europeans and Mixcóatl and the pantheon of Tlaxcala were to be considered equals, for the present.

During these events, Motecuhzoma stirred himself from his apathy only to keep sending envoys and embassies. He used poor tactics. One embassy would beg that Motecuhzoma was too poor to offer the strangers suitable hospitality, so they should not come to Tenochtitlan. The next would offer to pay tribute if the strangers stayed away, and tried to feel out how much would be required. Finally, with the white men in Tlaxcala, Motecuhzoma resolved to try a different, desperate gambit. He accepted Cortés' demand to visit Tenochtitlan—but insisted he come by way of Cholula.

In Cholula, Motecuhzoma planned an ambush. He sent officers to Cholula, ordering that city to receive the strangers and to provide them with a large escort for the final leg to Tenochtitlan. On the march, this escort, joined by secretly armed bearers, was to fall upon the strangers and kill them all.

Motecuhzoma's fortune-tellers said an oracle foretold that Cholula would be the strangers' grave. And the ruler felt safe in attempting this treachery, for who could connect him with it? Motecuhzoma believed that these strangers were the agents of gods, but he had no concept of an omniscient deity. And he would find out if these were only men, who could be killed.

Two things went wrong with this plan.

The first was that the Tlaxcalteca and the Cholulteca were historic and virulent enemies; they considered each other sodomites and women, and worse. The Tlaxcalan allies warned Cortés against Cholula. There is one indigenous account, which may have been invented by Tlaxcala, that the Tlaxcalteca sent a respected ambassador to Cholula, advising that city to join with Cortés. But in contravention of all normal practice and decency, the Cholulteca skinned the ambassador's face and his arms up to his elbows, they cut his wrist tendons, and sent him back with insults. And for this, Cortés promised his new allies revenge. When the Spaniards set out for Cholula, the Tlaxcalteca sent along an army of six thousand men, led by the greatest warlords of the confederation.

The second thing that went wrong was Malintzin. Although the Mexica knew there was a Nahua-speaking woman from Teticpac with Cortés, Motecuhzoma paid no attention to this; females did not figure in warriors' business. At Cholula, while the Spaniards were hung with garlands and regaled with music and dancing, Malintzin became friendly with a certain woman of the town and smelled out Motecuhzoma's plot.

The Spanish and allies had been quartered in the enclosure of the great temple-pyramid, but they knew that runners were coming and going across the city, and that the lords of Cholula—the co-rulers *tlaquiach* and *tlalchiac*, lord of what is above and what is below—were in continual council with their chiefs. Alerted by the Tlaxcalteca and warned by Malintzin, Cortés determined to strike first, and to make a signal example of Cholula.

If there is one villainess in Mexican history, she is Malintzin. She was to become the ethnic traitress supreme. The modern Mexican view, however, is totally emotional rather than accurate. Malintzin was not a symbolic traitress, but an unfortunate and intelligent Amerindian girl, who made the best of the situations life handed her. She was made a slave by her own race and presented to the Spaniards as a concubine, and as Doña Marina, Cortés' mistress, she enjoyed more prestige and consideration than almost any woman of Mexico had ever had. She remained with Cortés voluntarily. She was not Mexica; there was no reason at all why she should have felt loyalty to the overlords at Tenochtitlan. Nor could she have understood the total ramifications of the Conquest when she served Cortés. When she revealed the plot at Cholula, Malintzin would have been bewildered by a charge that she betrayed the Amerindian race—a concept she would not have understood.

Cortés called the lords and nobility of Cholula, most of the priests, and his proposed escort into the temple compound where he camped. Most came unarmed, not suspecting counter-treachery. When they were assembled, Cortés had the enclosure sealed off. Then, he set his soldiers upon them, with pike, sword, horse, and gun. The result was a massacre—and one in which the Tlaxcalteca gleefully engaged.

The hapless Cholulteca were literally cut to pieces; hundreds of priests were driven up the pyramid and pushed off to their deaths. Probably, the vast majority of these victims never knew why they died. Then, the Tlaxcalteca stormed through the city, killing all they could find.

The slaughter at Cholula has been put down to thoughtless brutality or Spanish bloodlust, but while the Spanish army had plenty of both, this was hardly consistent with Cortés' style. Cortés felt he was punishing treachery, and he did it thoroughly, as a symbol—Cortés' brutalities always served some purpose. He was a leader from the age of Machiavelli. The Mexica and Cholulteca ascribed the attack to the success of the Tlaxcalteca in poisoning the Spanish minds; ironically but understandably, they were most affronted, not by the bloodshed, but by the fact that Cortés violated all the ceremonial precepts of Mexic war. He should have given a ritual warning, and taunted his victims, first.

The Spanish toppled the idols and set fire to the temples of Cholula, thus razing the principal shrine of Quetzalcóatl and doing symbolic damage to a very ancient religion. The temples were looted, and a great cross was erected on the main pyramid that had survived from Preclassic times. This had an enormous effect on the Tlaxcalteca, who saw at firsthand the efficacy of the strangers' God. From this day forward, the warriors of Tlaxcala adopted the Spanish war cry, *Santiago!* and they made St. James —the Spanish Iago the Iberians had invented as an invocation to counter the Muslim y'*allah*—their especial patron.

Cortés, however, stopped the utter destruction of Cholula, and the slaughter by his allies. He explained that the conquered people were now subjects of the Christian king, and as such, they had the protection of the Spanish crown. He immediately went about bringing the shattered people into his greater alliance, along with Cempoala and Tlaxcala.

Shortly afterward, the Spanish and Amerindian host took the road west to Tenochtitlan. Bernardino de Sahagún, years afterward, recorded the indigenous descriptions of this army:

"They came on in battle array, the conquerors, with dust rising in whirlpools from their feet. Their iron spears shone in the sun; their pennons fluttered in the wind like bats. Their armor and swords clashed and clanged as they marched; they came on with a loud clamor, and some of them were dressed entirely in iron . . .

"Their great hounds came with them, running with them; they raised their massive muzzles into the wind. The dogs raced onward, before the column; they dripped saliva from their jaws."

When Motecuhzoma heard the story of Cholula, he was horrified; these creatures *must* be gods, or sent by the gods. Surely, the magic of Huitzilopochtli, or propitiation, could save him. He prepared new embassies to meet the Spaniards in the mountains east of Tenochtitlan, this time sending on substantial presents of gold, and ordered the way cleared for Cortés.

These presents, delivered by a high envoy, came to the column when it was in the Pass of the Eagle, high in the mountains between Popocatépetl and Iztactépetl. For the Amerindians, the effect of the yellow gold on the Spaniards was extraordinary:

"They burst into smiles; their eyes gleamed; they were delighted by these gifts. They picked up the gold; they picked it up like monkeys; they were in ecstasy; their hearts were made full.

"The truth is, they longed and lusted for gold. Their bodies swelled with their greed, and they were hungry; they were hungry like pigs for that gold."

Many of Cortés' men were growing tired and worried as they moved deeper and deeper into Mexico; nothing could have rejuvenated their courage like Motecuhzoma's offerings.

The envoy, perhaps on Motecuhzoma's orders, tried to pass himself off as Motecuhzoma himself. But the confederates from Cempoala and Tlaxcala, the "shrewd and treacherous" allies, knew better.

"He is not Motecuhzoma, our lords," they said. "It is only the envoy, Tzihuacpopocatzin!"

The envoy persisted, but they yelled at him: "You cannot fool us, you cannot blind our eyes, nor can Motecuhzoma hide from us!"

Having thrown oil on the fire, the envoy hastened back to Tenochtitlan.

Once more Motecuhzoma fell back on wizards. He ordered a party to intercept the strangers before they entered Anáhuac, and to work some mischief on them—anything to turn them back.

The wizards went out reluctantly. Before they met the Spaniards, they encountered a man blundering down the road. He was dressed like a Chalca; he made the gestures of a man of Chalco. And he was drunk.

The drunk shouted at the wizards: "Why do you come here? Why? What do you want? What is Motecuhzoma doing? Has he still lost his wits? Does he still tremble and beg? Motecuhzoma has committed a multitude of errors; he has already destroyed many people. . . ."

This may have been a classic case of *in vino veritas* exhibited by some unknown citizen of Mexico. But the wizards thought it must be divine intoxication, with the man speaking in oracles, or else the Chalca was a god disguised as a man. Quickly, they built an altar and a bench of grasses for him. However, he refused to be worshipped, and kept shouting: "Why have you come? This is useless. Mexico will be destroyed. Go back, go back!"

And the wizards were struck by a common vision—they believed they saw all Tenochtitlan in flames; temples burned, and schools, and palaces, all in flames.

They told each other, "We should not have seen this thing, for it was meant for Motecuhzoma's eyes alone. This is no man. It is the god, Tezcatlipoca!" When they finished debating, they realized the man had vanished. They forgot their mission and rushed back to Motecuhzoma's house.

"Our lord, we are completely helpless; we cannot blind the eyes of the strangers, nor overcome them in any way."

They described the happenings on the road, and their awful vision.

Motecuhzoma hung his head, and for many moments he was unable to speak. At last he said, "What help is there for us, friends? Can we climb a mountain? Can we run away? No, this would disgrace the Mexica race. We can only wait. Ah, pity the old men, and the old women, and the small innocents. We can do nothing. We can do nothing. We shall be judged and punished. It will be as it will be."

Motecuhzoma wanted to run away, but he could not. His counsellors advised him either to seek the Place of the Dead, or hide, but he could do neither. In the end he mastered his terror, but only through fatalism. He withdrew into himself and prepared to meet his fate.

Now, the vanguard of the Spanish-Tlaxcalan army came in sight of the vale of Anáhuac. They saw vast pine forests and shining lakes, a green expanse in which countless towns glittered like silver in the sun. They marveled over tall white towers rising out on the still waters, and the leagues of growing corn. They could see for miles in this high, clear air. They told each other that this must be an enchantment, as in the story books. A few of the more timid suggested it might be time to turn back, and to find more Indian allies. But Cortés smiled at that, and the army began to move down the mountains. It camped partway down the volcanic range.

The next events are not corroborated in Cortés or Díaz' writings; they are described only in fragmentary indigenous accounts. But again, whatever their chronology, they have a ring of truth. While most histories relate that the Spanish continued on to Ixtapalapa, where they could see the towers of the capital five miles away out on the lake, some Nahuatl accounts indicate they went first to Texcoco.

According to these, Prince Ixtlilxóchitl and some of his brothers met the invading army in the mountains; this area was within the hegemony of Texcoco. Cacama, lord of Texcoco, was in Tenochtitlan with his uncle, and the rebel forces were in control of the country. Ixtlilxóchitl came and made obeisance to Cortés, and Cortés replied with a bow. Both were wary of the other at first—but both needed allies. The prince marveled at the light skin of the Spaniards; meanwhile, the Europeans were impressed by these Texcoca aristocrats. One of the brothers was lighter-skinned than most Extremadurans; he could have passed for a *gallego*.

Cortés was invited into Texcoco. The people welcomed Ixtlilxóchitl and his new friends with ceremony, and it was said that Nezahualpilli's prophecy had come true.

According to these legends, Ixtlilxóchitl was instructed in the Christian faith by Cortés, and asked to be baptized. This was done, and the prince was christened Hernando, after his sponsor. Once the prince had become a Christian, twenty thousand more Texcoca wanted to be baptized, but they could not all be accommodated.

The queen mother Yacotzin, however, refused to attend this ceremony. She told Ixtlilxóchitl he had lost his wits, to be cozened so easily by a band of barbarians. The new don Hernando replied that if she were not his lady mother, he would have her beheaded for such talk. He gave her an ultimatum to be Christianized, and the same account tells that in the end Yacotzin submitted. She was renamed doña María, which Cortes felt was symbolic, since Yacotzin was the first woman in Anáhuac to be baptized.

Meanwhile, Motecuhzoma was aware of these events, and realized the strangers were coming on to Tenochtitlan. He called a final council, this time not of wizards, but of the secular lords. Motecuhzoma asked how the strangers should be welcomed.

Cuitláhuac, his brother and a true son of Axayácatl the Scourge, answered boldly that the enemies should not be welcomed at all.

Cacama disagreed, saying that the strangers were at the gates, and it showed a lack of courage not to let them in. Cacama said that these people were obviously the envoys of a great lord, and it was unseemly to turn them away. He added that if they proved insolent, warriors could then be called.

No one else had a chance to speak. Motecuhzoma ended the council by saying briefly that he agreed with Cacama.

Cuitláhuac rose and said: "I pray to our gods you will not do this thing. They will cast you out of your own house and overthrow your throne, and you will not recover either!"

All the lords of the council silently indicated that they agreed, but dared not speak. And so Motecuhzoma ordered Cacama to guide the strangers into Tenochtitlan, and instructed his brother Cuitláhuac to welcome them in the palace of Ixtapalapa where they would spend the night.

At dawn, November 8, 1519, Hernando Cortés led four hundred armed Spaniards, pikes, crossbowmen, arquebuses, artillery, and horse, down the causeway toward Tenochtitlan. Motecuhzoma himself, accompanied by a great entourage of officers and nobles, met him at Xoloco, where the causeway joined that from Coyoacán. The revered speaker was carried through an honor guard of knights on his litter. Behind him at the ceremony, in file, stood Cacama, the lord of Texcoco, and the lords of Tlatelolco, Tlacopán, and a high officer of Tenochtitlan, representing ritually the four corners of the world. Masses of people thronged the causeways, and the lake was dotted with canoes.

The Spaniards were drenched with brilliant, aromatic blossoms. Motecuhzoma hung golden necklaces upon the Spanish officers, prostrated himself, and licked the earth. Cortés dismounted from his horse and would have embraced Motecuhzoma, but the speaker's noble companions prevented this—the gesture was not understood. So the captain-general hung a string of cheap glass beads around Motecuhzoma's neck.

Then Motecuhzoma made a short speech of welcome. "Our lord, you are tired from your journeys, but now you are here. You have arrived at your city, Mexico. You have come to sit upon your throne; you have come to sit beneath the canopy.

"The lords who have gone before, they were your representatives who guarded and preserved it for your coming again. The Speakers Itzcóatl, Motecuhzoma the Elder, Axayácatl, Tizoc, and Ahuízotl ruled for you in Mexico. They protected the people by their swords and shields . . .

"Do these rulers know the destiny of those they left behind? Are they watching now? If only they might see what I now see!

"This is not a dream. I do not walk in my sleep . . . I have seen you at last; I have met you face to face. I was in agony for many days, with my eyes fixed on the region of Mystery. But now you have come to sit on your throne.

"This was foretold by the rulers who governed your city, and now it has come to pass. You have come back. Rest now, and take possession of your royal house . . ."

When he had finished, Malintzin began to translate. How much of this speech Cortés received or fully understood is problematical. He said only: "Tell Motecuhzoma we are his friends. There is nothing to fear . . . tell him we love him well and that our hearts are contented. We have come to his house as friends. There is nothing to fear."

Thus two civilizations met face to face, but there were planes on which they could never meet.

The Spanish and a great many Tlaxcalteca allies were housed in the palace of Axayácatl, west of the great temple. Slaves brought food for the guests, and when they had eaten, Motecuhzoma brought more presents— sufficient cotton robes for every man. At this time he said he would accept Cortés' lord as his own, and do all the captain asked. But he also said he was not nearly so powerful or wealthy as was supposed.

The Spanish had already realized this; they had noticed the streets of the capital were not paved with gold. In fact, they examined everything, and were disappointed that very little precious metal was to be seen.

Cortés then positioned his artillery to command the plaza, posted sentries, and the army bedded down. How many Spaniards slept through the first night in the city of Huitzilopochtli can only be speculated upon.

The conquistador ostensibly had already conquered Mexico. But he had problems. He did not and could not trust Motecuhzoma; at any moment this dark-skinned, peculiar emperor, surrounded by a hundred thousand pagan warriors might lose his apathy and superstitious fears. This was one problem, and a fearful one. Another was his own men. This was not a disciplined army; it was greedy, fearful, rebellious, and the rank and file were superstitious and suffering from culture shock. The squat temples and demon idols, the incense and perpetual fires and sullen drums unsettled them. Sooner or later, Cortés knew, some incident would provoke war. He decided to seize Motecuhzoma and hold him hostage.

Within a few days, he picked a small bodyguard and went to Motecuhzoma's palace. The ruler greeted the Spaniards courteously and offered Cortés one of his daughters, but Cortés dismissed the offer and stated coldly that he had learned of a clash back at Veracruz, on the coast, in which Spaniards had been killed by Mexica. This was true, but Cortés had had the news for many days—now it served him as a convenient pretext. He said that Motecuhzoma was responsible for this treachery, and because of it he was to be imprisoned in the palace of Axayácatl. If he resisted, he would die here and now.

Motecuhzoma wept but did not resist. He was carried on his litter in a circle of armed Spaniards to the palace of Axayácatl. The officers of his palace did nothing; some Mexica accounts relate scornfully that the high officials ran away.

The populace, however, filled the streets, allowing the Spaniards and their hostage to pass through only at Motecuhzoma's behest. A great mob gathered in the plaza before Axayácatl's palace. Cortés fired off a cannon, and the detonation sent the mob fleeing in all directions, "as if they had eaten the mushroom that distorts the mind, or had seen a dreadful vision." The people and the nobility of the capital remained restless, troubled, and confused.

Here began a weird episode that was to last six months. Through Motecuhzoma, Cortés ruled the empire. Motecuhzoma did everything Cortés asked, with one exception—he refused to give up Huitzilopochtli or his native gods. There is no insight into the speaker's mind during these months. The Amerindians no longer had close contact with him; the Spaniards, who professed a certain affection for him, did not care so long as he obeyed their orders.

Cortés promised Motecuhzoma that he would continue to hold the throne, and that he would also rule additional kingdoms that Cortés would conquer for him, though in the name, of course, of Carlos I. But Cortés' soldiers thought only of gold, and he had no choice but to provide for their satisfaction and pay. Motecuhzoma was pressured to reveal his wealth.

He led them to the public treasure house, the *teucalco*. This was filled with arms, artifacts, and ornaments which contained gold and precious stones. The Spanish went wild, rushing about, grabbing everything of value, quarreling among themselves. They destroyed countless art objects, tearing out the gems, melting down the goldwork. They selected only the clearest emeralds and jade; the Tlaxcalteca allies, however, were delighted with their leavings.

When this house was looted, Motecuhzoma revealed his personal storehouse, which was in the *totocalco*, or zoological gardens. The Spaniards took him with them to this place, under close guard, and what happened here was reported and carefully handed down to Bernardino de Sahagún:

> "The Spaniards grinned like little beasts and pounded on each other with delight. When they entered that hall of treasures, it was as if they had arrived in Paradise. They searched everywhere and coveted everything. They were slaves to their greed. All that belonged to Motecuhzoma was brought out: the fine bracelets, the necklaces with large stones, the ankle rings with golden bells, the diadems and all the royal costumes—the things that belonged to the ruler and were his alone. But they seized these treasures as if they were their own, and as if this plunder had come to them by good luck. They took it all and heaped it up in the middle of a patio.

After this exercise, the girl Malintzin—who was becoming perhaps drunk with power—climbed up onto the roof and shouted to the nobles and palace officials who stood watching outside. "Mexica, come forward! The Spaniards are tired and hungry—bring them food and clear water!"

The command was obeyed. This society, so organic that every person had his function and place, had one terrible weakness. All individual initiative had been destroyed. If Motecuhzoma had given the order, tens of thousands of armed warriors would have fallen on the invaders; but without such orders, not even the highest officials dared act. Some of the nobles, including Cuitláhuac, did express hostility, however, and Cortés took these potential rebels as hostages.

At Cortés' orders, Motecuhzoma summoned all his lords and, with tears streaming down his face, commanded them to accept the Spanish dominion. They were to help the Spaniards collect gold from all parts of the empire, because the king of the Spaniards needed gold. And so a large treasure was assembled, and continually divided: a fifth for the king, a fifth for the captain-general, the rest distributed among the rank and file.

Cortés also halted human sacrifices on the pyramid; he even toppled the great idols of Huitzilopochtli he found there. He held Catholic services on this pyramid, and drove the Mexica priests close to rebellion. The situation was unstable. Although Motecuhzoma, apparently hoping that when the Spanish had enough gold they would depart, remained meek and courteous, this state of affairs could not have gone on long. Cortés was astride the tiger. But when the break came, it was caused by events outside Mexico.

The governor of Cuba, who had support in the homeland, was furious at Cortés' defiance. After Cortés' departure, Velásquez assembled the largest force ever put together in the Indies, fifteen sail, eighty guns, and some nine hundred soldiers. He sent this force under Pánfilo de Narváez to Mexico to seize Cortés and to return him to Cuba in irons.

Narváez landed near Veracruz and marched to Cempoala, broadcasting that Cortés was a traitor to the Spanish king, who would shortly be hanged. However, he failed to capture Sandoval and the small garrison at Veracruz. Sandoval instead captured two of Narváez' army and sent them, bound and trussed up in hammocks, to Cortés in Tenochtitlan.

Cortés reacted vigorously and characteristically. He released the two frightened Spaniards, charmed them and showed them the wonders of the city, and he gave them a quantity of gold. He promised more gold and all the native women a man could want, if Narváez' troops would join him. Then he sent the two back to Cempoala, to subvert his pursuers.

He followed them closely, with two hundred men, about half his total force. Cortés knew he had to do something about this threat in his rear, before Narváez could bring all his efforts to ruin. He placed Pedro de Alvarado in command at Tenochtitlan.

Cortés was brilliantly successful on the coast. Under the cover of a tropical downpour, he infiltrated Narváez' camp and seized Narváez himself before resistance could be organized. With a sword at his throat, Pánfilo de Narváez immediately capitulated. Cortés then embraced Narváez' bewildered officers, welcoming them as old friends, and described his successes at Tenochtitlan. Before morning, the whole army had voted to desert Velásquez and join him. Cortés then prudently destroyed Narváez' ships, put Narváez in irons at Veracruz, and led more than a thousand men back into the interior.

Long before he arrived, Tlaxcalteca messengers brought him news of total disaster back in Tenochtitlan.

The great feast of Huitzilopochtli, which was celebrated once a year, had come round. The Tenochca prepared an elaborate statue and brought it into the temple enclosure next to where Pedro de Alvarado and the Spaniards were housed. Motecuhzoma granted permission for the ceremony to be held; hundreds of picked warriors were prepared to dance in the temple courtyard. All the Nahuatl accounts agree that the Mexica planned no violence, but were eager to impress the strangers with their dancing and magic. Alvarado, whom the Mexica called *Toniatuh* (the Sun) because of his golden hair, had been told, and he had agreed that the dance could be held.

But the *Toniatuh* was in a very unstable frame of mind. Cortés had left him with two hundred men in a delicate political situation; further, he was worried sick about what might be happening on the coast. He was a brutal fighting man, a good lieutenant, but totally unfit for this kind of command. When the Dance of the Serpent reached its climax, with howling, frenzied warriors leaping about, some urinating as they danced, Alvarado apparently was driven mad by the screeching, just when, as the indigenous accounts said, "the dancing was most beautiful, and song was linked to song." The Spaniards convinced themselves that the natives were working themselves up for an attack, and that they would all be sacrificed on the altars of the Sun God. Then, Alvarado remembered how his captain had handled the treachery at Cholula.

He blocked the exits of the temple enclosure with armed men, and the Spaniards, armed and armored, suddenly attacked the dancers, without warning and without mercy.

> *They attacked the man who was drumming and struck off his arms. They cut off his head, rolling it across the floor. They attacked all the celebrants with swords and spears. They struck some from behind, and these fell with their entrails dragging. They beheaded some, or split their heads to pieces . . . arms were torn from bodies. Some tried to run away, but their intestines dragged the ground. There was no escape . . . The blood of warriors flowed like water and gathered into pools . . . and the stink of blood and entrails filled the air.*

Mad with blood lust, the Spaniards pursued Mexica who crawled over the walls into nearby communal houses. They slaughtered anyone they found.

A shock wave spread over Tenochtitlan as the word was passed. *The strangers have murdered the young warriors!* A great roar of grief and rage rose up everywhere. People beat their palms against their mouths, ululating their laments. But there were also sharp war cries among the despairing shrieks. Officers called their twenties up out of the clans.

A horde of armed men poured toward the bloody courtyard. Brought to his senses by a hail of missiles, Alvarado barely got his murderous crew back into Axayácatl's palace. *A cloud of spears and arrows covered the strangers like a yellow cloak.* Inside, however, gunfire and a volley of iron crossbow quarrels dispersed the attack.

Several thousand Mexica had died in the massacre. Lamenting kinfolk gathered up the torn bodies; they were taken to clan houses first, then all the victims were brought together and cremated. A sullen silence settled over the city.

Alvarado, in a panic, had Motecuhzoma chained like a wild beast.

The silence still held when Cortés brought his troop through the capital. Cortés was dangerously angry; he told Alvarado that he had behaved like a madman. He might have hung the lieutenant on the spot—but he was forced to work through such imperfect instruments. It was this kind of conquistador—uncontrollable but also irreplaceable—that made the advance of Spanish power such a ghastly affair.

The fortress palace was surrounded by a sullen, hostile mob. Cortés ordered Motecuhzoma to salvage the affair. Protesting he only wished to die, Motecuhzoma and the governor of Tlatelolco were taken to the roof of the palace. The lord of Tlatelolco tried to issue a royal proclamation: "Mexica, lay down your arms. You are not strong enough to fight the Spaniards. See, they have bound Motecuhzoma in chains—his feet are bound in chains. He commands his people to go to their homes."

A terrible tumult arose; men shouted back they were no longer Motecuhzoma's slaves. Missiles showered the roof; Motecuhzoma was struck in the head. The Spanish quickly sprang forward to shield him, and the cannon dispersed the mob.

The Mexica had been totally outraged by the sacrilegious nature of the attack in the courtyard. War they understood, but an attack without a declaration of war—after which ambush was of course acceptable—and the murder of worshippers violated their strongest religious beliefs.

The Tenochca put the palace under total siege. Some people, loyal to Motecuhzoma, tried to enter; they were put to death. Motecuhzoma's palace stewards and servants—who could be identified by their glass lip plugs—were hunted down and slain, because of a suspicion they might bring food to Motecuhzoma. The purge got out of hand—even innocent bearers, bringing tribute or provisions into Tenochtitlan, who had no knowledge of events, were halted, questioned, and cut down as traitors, and many others were executed for "imaginary crimes."

Fighting continued for several days. The Spanish wreaked great execution on the Mexica with their bolts and guns, but the crowded city, with its twisted canals and streets and houses set wall to wall, prevented them from clearing and holding space outside the palace. Cortés' food was running out. He sent one of the noble hostages outside with orders to reopen the markets and bring in food. He made a bad choice: the valiant Cuitláhuac.

Cuitláhuac, the brother of Motecuhzoma, assembled the phratries and took direction of the war. The causeways were breached, to bar a Spanish escape. But after a week of violent clashes with Spanish firepower and hard steel the Mexica abandoned direct assaults.

Cortés realized he had to leave.

He had a portable wooden bridge constructed to span the breached causeways and demolished bridges during the retreat. All the booty the Spaniards had accumulated, except for the fifths belonging to Cortés and the king, which was loaded on horses, was piled in a heap for the common soldiers. Significantly, Cortés' veterans took very little, while Narváez' former soldiers loaded themselves heavily.

At night, under the cover of a gentle rain, the army came out. The Spaniards led, with the Tlaxcalteca allies pressing close behind. They actually reached the first causeway before a woman saw them and began to scream.

The priests of Huitzilopochtli beat the alarm drum from the top of the great pyramid. Thousands of warriors poured into plazas with shield and spear. Many leaped into canoes and raced through canals to cut the invaders off. Pursued by the sound of the drum and thousands of screeching men, Cortés' troops jammed the portable bridge at the first demolished bridge. They were trapped, up against the dark waters of Lake Texcoco, at the second break, over the Canal of the Toltecs. The *noche triste*—the unhappy night—of the conquerors had begun.

Canoes converged on the causeway. Bowmen loosed a hail of wooden shafts into the packed ranks. Other Mexica swam to the causeway and dragged Spaniards into the water. The Spanish answered with gunfire and crossbows.

The column piled up at the Canal of the Toltecs, but the closepressed Tlaxcalteca rearguard, which suffered worst this night, pushed it on. Screaming men, concubines, and horses fell over the lip of the breach. Hundreds, weighted down with loot or armor, drowned. But the men behind them piled on, until the survivors crossed over a bridge of corpses.

The same horror was repeated at the next break, and the next.

All the guns were lost. The treasure vanished somewhere in the night. The camp-followers died—only Malintzin, with Cortés' protection, and two others survived. Only twenty horses were saved. When the first survivors reached the mainland, at Popotla near Tlacopán, the retreat had become an utter rout.

Cortés himself stayed on the causeway all night, trying to salvage as much of his army as he could. At dawn, he sat exhausted under a large cypress tree, with tears running down his face. His army was huddled along the shore; less than half his original force had reached the mainland. The greatest casualties, aside from the allies, were suffered by Narváez' poorly disciplined new arrivals.

Cortés gathered the survivors and pushed them on. But as he entered Popotla, the dawn was split by new war shrieks, and a horde of warriors attacked. The entire dispirited Spanish force could have been destroyed, but the Mexica failed to press the attack home—the only thing their leaders wanted were Tlaxcalteca captives for sacrifice. The allies suffered grievously, while the Spanish vanguard was harried into Tlacopán.

When the victors had taken all the prisoners they wanted, they were content to let the survivors go.

No one knows for certain how Motecuhzoma Xocoyotzin died. Before the Spanish left Tenochtitlan, they rolled his corpse, and that of the lord of Tlatelolco, down to the water. The Spanish insisted he was killed by his own people. More likely, however, the Spaniards murdered all their hostages before the retreat. A number of Motecuhzoma's children and kinfolk, whom he had commended to Cortés' care, also died. The casualties among the warrior nobility were very great. However, Cuitláhuac lived, and the high council elected him speaker in Motecuhzoma's place.

Cortés' real test as a great captain came in the next few days. He had seized an empire by treachery and intrigue, and lost it, with more than half his men. He was surrounded by leagues of hostile country, and harried by an enemy no longer paralyzed by superstitious fears. On the western shores of Lake Texcoco only a great spirit could have saved the Spanish force from total destruction. Somehow, Cortés rebuilt his own morale and that of his army. He marched north, to skirt the lake and return to Tlaxcala—which, with this turn of fortune, might prove a very doubtful refuge.

His luck held. The Tepaneca people remembered the destruction of their own greatness by the Mexica and were friendly. A Tepanec prince guided Cortés part of the way, only to be killed in a skirmish with the Mexica. Village chiefs gave the Spaniards food. Except for this, they had only wild cherries and ears of corn to eat. Cortés was finding Mexico filled with ethnic traitors: the Mexica had made them everywhere their twenties marched.

The bedraggled, exhausted army reached the northern tip of the lake and struck directly east for Tlaxcala. Now, they passed the grass-covered ruins of Teotihuacán, and here, in the valley of Otumba, Cortés faced his greatest crisis: a Mexica host was drawn up to stop the Spanish. And here was fought the decisive battle of the Conquest, oddly overlooked by historians.

Cortés had no possibility of maneuver or retreat; he had to fight his way through or die.

The Spaniards had lost all their firearms. They were low on missile ammunition. Much of their armor had been discarded in the retreat. They had only their swords, pikes, and shields, and between twenty and forty horses; the accounts vary on this. At the sight of the Amerindian host, the

Spanish wept, but Cortés called forth their courage with all the considerable power at his command.

Cortés, like most conquistadores, had never had any military training or experience in Europe, but he now employed tactics of Alexander the Great. Cortés formed his four hundred foot soldiers into a front broad enough to meet the attack of an enemy battalion and used cavalry to sweep his flanks. The Spanish formation, part square, part phalanx, had a flexibility which the Amerindians, in their stylized warfare, lacked.

Thousands upon thousands of feathered warriors filled the valley of Otumba. They were mainly allies and tributaries of the Mexica Cuitláhuac had called to arms. The warlord or general was carried on his litter, Mexic fashion, close behind the van, from where he could direct the action by various signals and drum beats. As the Mexic host advanced, war cries, drumming, and raucous horn calls beat against the Spanish ranks, who stood silently behind their spears.

Javelins, stones, and arrows whistled through the air. The Spaniards turned most of these upon their shields or armor. When missile ammunition was exhausted, the front battalion of the Amerindians charged home with obsidian swords, spears, and shields.

The Mexica fought in close-packed columns, expecting the day to be carried by the press of men upon men. Their battalions exerted mass and concentration, but despite their huge number, these tactics permitted them to confront the Spanish with only some four hundred men at any time. The Spaniards formed a line of steel, and one by one, the Mexica battalions crashed into it and were shattered. The sheer press of numbers would have pushed Mexica warriors around the Spanish flanks, but the Spanish horsemen prevented this with their lances and with sudden charges up the attackers' flanks.

For the Spanish, it was fight or die a terrible death on stone altars. But there was nothing really remarkable in the fact that they withstood the enemy for hours. The tribesmen were splendidly valiant, excellent fighting men, frightening in quantity, but an aimless mass without maneuver, in which only a small vanguard could actually fight. Any sixteenth-century European infantry would have defeated them. Cortés' ragged band held them at bay, charge after charge.

Sheer numbers might have worn the Spanish down, had not Cortés identified the enemy commander close behind the fighting ranks. This officer had no notion of the shock power of the European horse. Cortés led a charge toward the general and with his own hand cut the startled Mexica officer down. The Amerindian army, valiant to the death while under authoritarian leadership, then lost its heart and became a thousand fleeing knots of panicked men.

The battered Spanish force rested and moved on. But from this day forward, all the Spanish were totally confident that they could cut through any Mexic host.

The Tlaxcalteca met them at the edge of their country with sympathy and tears. Although the Tlaxcalans had suffered hideous casualties from this alliance, and although Cuitláhuac sent embassies, begging for a great indigenous alliance against the invaders, Tlaxcala had suffered too much from Tenochtitlan, and they knew that once the strangers were destroyed, Tlaxcala would be punished in turn. They raised new armies to aid the Spaniards.

And this was as far as the greatest of the Spanish conquistadores was going to retreat. He began planning his triumphant return to Tenochtitlan.

11

BROKEN SPEARS

Broken spears lie in the roads . . .
The houses are roofless;
The walls are red with blood.
Our city, our inheritance
Is lost and dead;
The shields of our warriors
Could not save it.

Our wails rise keening,
Our tears fall down like rain;
Tlatelolco is lost,
Tlatelolco is lost!
Weep, weep, our people,
For we have lost Mexico.

Taken from Nahuatl codices, composed circa 1523–1528.

After the *noche triste* and the retreat of the Spaniards to Tlaxcala, the Amerindians tried to carry on the ceremonial cycle of their lives, while Cortés stubbornly resumed his efforts to conquer his kingdom. His single-mindedness and constancy, undaunted by signs, omens, fears, setbacks, circumstance, or even conscience, was a peculiarly European trait, as was a total belief in cause and effect. He did not *want* to cause the deaths of thousands of people, even *indios*, nor did he desire to raze splendid cities. But if Mexico could be reduced in no other way, so be it. It was this characteristic, along with his enormous personal ability that differentiated Cortés from other men, and gave the Spanish a thrust into Mexico the indigenes could not withstand.

The Mexica believed the strangers had been defeated on June 30, 1520, on the bloody causeway leading to Tlacopán and they did not expect to see white men again. After the battle, people scoured the roadway for abandoned arms, armor, and loot. Some was found in the lake by divers. The battleground was also littered with the corpses of Spaniards, Tlaxcalteca, women, and horses. The Mexica dragged the white bodies, and the remains of the horses, into Tenochtitlan as curiosities and threw the indigenous corpses into the rushes along the lakeshore. Although bits and pieces of the treasure were taken by individual searchers, much of it was never recovered from the lake.

The Mexica rebuilt and redecorated the temple of Huitzilopochtli, which the strangers had defiled, and resumed their festivals. But it was not easy to restore the old tenor of life. Motecuhzoma, Itzcuauhtzin, Cacama, and many of Motecuhzoma's household were dead. The priests, certain military officers, and the clan chiefs continued to root out all who had submitted to the hated invaders. The surviving great lords were outraged by this popular purge, and stopped it. Although Cuitláhuac had assumed the throne, a thread of dissension and uncertainty ran through Tenochtitlan.

Cuitláhuac did try to destroy the Spanish finally by turning the eastern tribes against them, but the Tlaxcalteca and others were still more afraid of the Mexica than of Cortés. Then, any possible warlike operations out of Tenochtitlan were halted by a new disaster.

One of Cortés' men had apparently brought smallpox into the capital in June. This disease, painful, disfiguring, and dangerous for Europeans, was lethal for Amerindians, who lacked the hereditary immunities acquired by Europeans over centuries. Some warrior touched an infected corpse, and by September, 1520, an epidemic swept Anáhuac as far as Chalco.

Most of Tenochtitlan was infected. Pustulant sores erupted on faces, stomachs, and breasts; the victims became too sick to move about. Thousands of people lay helplessly screaming in pain. The worst cases died quickly, but many more thousands, with milder cases, died of hunger or neglect. Even the survivors were pockmarked, and a few were blinded. The death toll was very high; neither age, sex, nor rank were spared. The revered speaker, Cuitláhuac, died.

After some seventy days, the plague receded. The capital was left weakened both in numbers and effective leadership, and the lords passed the throne to Cuauhtémoc ("Falling Eagle"), a nephew of Cuitláhuac. Cuauhtémoc was a youth of high courage and spirit, but he was not experienced at war, and he lacked the brutal intelligence that so many of his ancestors had displayed.

Meanwhile, Hernando Cortés was still the child of fortune. He had retreated to Tlaxcala empty-handed with barely four hundred men. But new

Spanish expeditions were arriving now off the coast of Mexico; somehow, the word of its treasures was out. Caravels came in from Jamaica and Hispaniola; even the inept Velásquez, still trying to control the situation from Cuba, sent more ships. Cortés managed to charm, recruit, or suborn all these crews, and their vital equipment. Within a few months he had assembled nine hundred Spaniards, with a hundred horses and many guns. The appalling casualties he had suffered in the interior did not dim the newcomers' lust for women and gold.

Cortés realized the key to the conquest of Mexico lay in the subordination of Tenochtitlan. Alvarado's stupidity had destroyed all hopes of a bloodless conquest; the Spanish were no longer regarded as gods. But Cortés could still rely on political skill and judicious force.

With a combined force of Spaniards and Tlaxcalans, Cortés took the entire region betwen Anáhuac and the coast. He employed the rationale that Motecuhzoma had surrendered his realm to the Spanish king, and that any resistance now constituted treason. Cortés systematically had any Amerindian who killed a Spaniard burned alive. Cities which held out were destroyed, and the eager Tlaxcalteca were permitted to slaughter their inhabitants. But in every case Cortés tried to avoid bloodshed and to make new allies. Huexotzinga and many other historic enemies of the Mexica joined him, and Cortés made sincere efforts to protect such allies, both from the Mexica retaliation and his own men.

His greatest problems came from his own unruly troops, who looted everything and complained continually they were being cheated because the comeliest women were reserved for the officers.

While forging a great Amerindian confederation against the Mexica, Cortés made plans for Tenochtitlan. Remembering the deadly shower of missiles upon his retreating army from canoes, Cortés knew the city could not be stormed from the narrow causeways that led in from Tlacopán, Coyoacán, and Tepeyacac. He set a skilled Spanish shipwright to work with Tlaxcalteca carpenters building ships. Sails, rigging, and essential ironwork were brought in from Spanish ships stripped at the coast. Cortés wanted a Spanish squadron on Lake Texcoco when the crucial campaign began.

By December 1520, although these ships were far from built, Cortés led his army to Texcoco, where the prince, don Hernando Ixtlilxóchitl, provisioned it. From this base Cortés now planned to isolate the capital.

He marched around the entire lake, and reduced the country as far south as the modern Cuernavaca. Many cities, like Chalco, went over to his side. There was a battle at Xochimilco before it fell, and Ixtapalapa resisted so strongly it was sacked and burned. By April, Cortés controlled all of the Valley except the island capital.

This second conquest gained its energy not only from Spanish fury and the obstinate determination of one man, but also from the willing support of countless thousands of Amerindian allies, who fed, supported, and fought beside the Spanish force. The history of the Mexica nation created the great, hostile Amerindian confederation that now surrounded and isolated Tenochtitlan, but it was Cortés who forged it and held it together. The alliance made the Conquest easier, and in the end allowed the Spanish to take over the country with far less bloodshed than if they had had to battle every city and tribe, because a European conquest of Mexico was inevitable. Whoever arrived there first—Dutch, Portuguese, French, or English—would have dominated. And as all later American history has shown, Amerindian culture was destroyed in every case.

The effort by some modern Mexicans to depict Hernando Cortés as a twisted syphilitic cripple, the epitome of depraved rapacity and cunning, stems more from the emotional rejection of the Conquest, and its aftermath, by those with Amerindian blood than from objective evidence. Cortés probably did suffer from syphilis, and his energy was affected in later years. But a despicable image contrived for Cortés does more to demean the Amerindian race he conquered than it demeans him. Cortés employed torture less frequently, and shed relatively less native blood, than any other conquistador.

His politics were so successful that in 1521 only one indigenous people, the Tarasca of Michoacán, considered sending aid to Tenochtitlan. And here again ancient enmities prevented action.

The Spanish-Tlaxcalteca-Texcoca assault upon Tenochtitlan began in May 1521. The island fortress was defended by a still numerous, still warlike and valiant race. It was also one of the greatest and most beautiful cities in the entire world, and Cortés had hoped to capture it intact, to serve as the capital for his new kingdom. He wept genuine tears when he could not—but he was not stayed. No conquest would ever be secure so long as the Children of the Sun held out.

Cortés divided his forces. Pedro de Alvarado was given responsibility for the sector that included the causeway leading out from Tlacopán; Gonzalo de Sandoval held the causeway terminal at Tepeyacac; and Cristóbal de Olid, another lieutenant, under Cortés himself prepared to attack outward from the mainland at Coyoacán. Holding all the entrances to the city, Cortés now tightened the siege; nothing could come in or out on foot.

Alvarado's men pressed down their causeway and fought their way into the quarter of Tlatelolco before being quickly forced back; his second assault was repulsed, almost without loss by the Mexica, by a storm of arrows from converging canoes. Sandoval accomplished nothing out of Tepeyacac. The swarm of Mexica canoes also frustrated the siege in another way: it was impossible to prevent the besieged from slipping onto shore by night and bringing back supplies and food.

From Coyoacán, however, Cortés had a limited success. He led his men-at-arms into Acachinanco, a place just outside the edge of Tenochtitlan, and set up his personal headquarters. None of a series of violent Mexica attacks could dislodge his toehold.

After some ten days of such indecisive combat, Cortés' long-awaited ships appeared, carried down in sections on the backs of thousands of Tlaxcalteca warriors to the lake front at Texcoco. Thirteen brigantines, shallow draft vessels carrying oars and sail, and constructed with forward castles to mount guns, were quickly reassembled. The masts were raised and set, the cannon emplaced, and then, manned by Spanish sailors, gunners, and crossbowmen, with a horde of eager indigenous rowers at the oars, the squadron set sail under Cortés' command.

Cortés now had complete command of the lake. He trained cannon on the walls and houses of Tenochtitlan and began a naval assault against the northwest portion of the city, supported by forces from Tlaxcala and Huexotzingo. Cortés' ship, flying a great linen standard sewn with his arms, led the squadron into shore. The Spanish beat drums and sounded trumpets from the ships, raising a loud, martial din. They were met by a horde of Tlatelolca in canoes, and they found little maneuvering room. Cortés shifted the point of attack southward, against Tenochtitlan, near the Xoloco, and created panic in the population, and a sort of paralysis among the Mexica commanders.

A great exodus began from the houses and tiny farms at the edge of the city. Men, women, and children leaped into canoes and fled. The Spanish and allies came ashore and plundered all the abandoned houses.

Canoes packed with warriors converged on the Spanish flotilla from the Tlatelolco quarter but could not prevent the Spanish from landing and looting. A party of Spaniards fought their way into Xoloco, demolishing with cannon shots a high wall the Tenochca had erected across the roadway.

The outer fringes of Tenochtitlan-Tlatelolco comprised a jumble of houses cut through by narrow canals and wandering streets. The inner waterways were too narrow for the brigantines, so the attack was channeled along the causeways, which the Mexica breached at canal crossings. The Mexica also blocked the roadways with high walls. Although the Spanish fire and steel could push the Mexica before them, this was almost impossible military terrain.

Meanwhile, Cortés dispatched part of his squadron to destroy the flotilla of canoes. The Amerindians, ignorant of the power of cannon, approached with their craft tightly packed, the paddlers protected by upraised shields. Spanish gunners fired into the thick of the harassing canoes, smashing many of them; crossbowmen mounted in forecastles shot swarms of iron quarrels, which snapped through the flimsy shields, ripped flesh, and sank boats. Dozens of the Tlatelolca garrison were killed; others, too badly hurt to swim, drowned in the scummy lake. The frothed waters reddened with spreading streams of blood. The remaining canoes scattered. The Spanish pursued them, sounding trumpets and guns.

Now a sort of panic must have swept through Tenochtitlan. At Xoloco some Tenochca warriors turned on their own officers, murdered them, abandoned Xoloco, and retreated into Huitzillán, where they hid behind another great wall that had been prepared.

The brigantines, after pursuing the remaining canoes, trained their cannon on the blocking wall and blew it to dust, scattering the cowering warriors.

Men debarked from the ships and quickly filled in a prepared breach in the main causeway with rubble. When this break was bridged, the cavalry, heavily armed and armored, galloped into Tenochtitlan. They struck up against a mass of warriors in front of Motecuhzoma's palace, and a bloody engagement began.

Spanish foot soldiers followed the horsemen to the Eagle Gate, from which rows of magnificent stone columns led directly to the central temple square. Large numbers of Mexica lurked behind these columns, and more waited on rooftops and behind walls. Warriors had already learned to take shelter from arbalest and arquebus fire, which caused frightful casualties in their usually close-packed ranks.

The Spaniards dragged up a heavy gun and smashed the Eagle Gate, and the pillars behind it. When the black smoke had cleared, they advanced with swords to the courtyard of the temple of Huitzilopochtli. Frenzied priests were on the pyramid, beating on the great snakehide drum, until Spanish soldiers ran up the steps and cut them down. The large cannon was wheeled into the courtyard and mounted on a great sacrificial altar stone.

But now resistance was stiffening, as warriors poured into the area from all parts of Tenochtitlan. Several important war chiefs who had been fighting in the canoes returned and rallied the clans. The Spaniards were quickly surrounded by a screaming horde. The air was noisy with arrows; the ground shook with the pounding of advancing feet.

The Spanish retreated, to avoid entrapment. They were forced to abandon their cannon, which the Mexica managed to push into a deep canal.

The Spanish pulled back all the way to the base at Acachinanco, while the Mexica reoccupied the Xoloco. Both sides, exhausted, rested as night fell.

Two days of fighting at the southern tip of the city set a pattern that was to be repeated for many weeks. The heavily armed Spanish, with cannon, arquebuses, and cavalry, could battle their way into Tenochtitlan, but they could only clear or control small sections of the city. With darkness, they were forced to withdraw. And with night, the defenders returned, and again breached new holes in roads and causeways and repaired broken walls.

As long as the Mexica fought on, the only one way to reduce the capital was to blow it apart, piece by piece, and to kill its defenders, man by man.

The first Spanish foray into the center of the city sent the citizens streaming into the northern quarter of Tlatelolco weeping, and carrying possessions and small children. Priests carried the wooden image of Huitzilopochtli to safety in Tlatelolco. The Tlatelolca—who, despite their incorporation into the larger city had not lost their identity and strong sense of clan pride—seem, for some reason, to have borne the great burden of the fighting from this day on. Cuauhtémoc, who had not been conspicuous in the resistance, also retreated into Tlatelolco. The clan leaders of the Tlatelolca did not share the Tenochca panic. They rallied their people, shouting: "We can save our city. We are Mexica! We are Tlatelolca!"

Alvarado, once again trying to advance along the causeway into Tlatelolco from Tlacopán, was routed.

The next day, however, when the Spanish brought up ships and landed a powerful force in Nonohualco, they were able to march at will through Tenochtitlan. The entire city was eerily silent and deserted. But when they and an army of Tlaxcalteca tried to move into the northern quarter, they were defeated in a heavy combat, with considerable loss on both sides.

Tlatelolco could not be reduced like a European city, by breaching its walls and sending in troops. When the Spanish and their allies had taken a house, or cleared a plaza, they were still masters only of the ground where they stood. Beyond were other plazas, thousands more houses, defended by a stubborn clan in arms. Even women took up weapons and fought.

However much irresolution and panic the Amerindian nobility had shown at the appearance of white men, no defense of a country in world history transcends in courage and tenacity the struggle of the Mexica *macehualtin*. Vast numbers were killed; yet day after day their courage held.

Cortés tried to induce the Tlatelolca to desert the people of Tenochtitlan. An officer, Castañeda, made an embassy to the defenders, and brought a party of Tlatelolca warriors into Nonohualco, where Cortés had set up field headquarters in a great house. The warriors met with Cortés, Malintzin, Alvarado, and Sandoval, along with the chiefs of most of the indigenous allies.

"Come forward," Malintzin said imperiously to these envoys. "The captain wants to know what the chief men of Tenochtitlan can be thinking about, to have no mercy on the women and children of the city. Must even the old men die? Is Cuauhtémoc a stupid, willful boy? *Hai*, see the lords of Tlaxcala, of Huexotzingo and Cholula, of Chalco, Acolhuacán and

Cuauhnahuac [Cuernavaca]; here are the lords of Xochimilco, Mizquic, Cuitláhuac and Culhuacán; all are with us!"

One of these allies told the Tlatelolca they should abandon the Tenochca and avert senseless self-destruction.

But the Tlatelolca refused to give up the fight.

Cortés, unable to take the city by storm, began to starve the defenders and destroy their houses. His ships, prevented canoes from bringing in supplies. The aqueduct that carried fresh water down from Chapultepec was broken. This was a serious blow, for the waters of Lake Texcoco were unpotable. He made continual forays into the city, and the cannon and falconets of his flotilla ceaselessly pounded at its walls. When gunpowder ran short, a brave Spaniard went down on a rope into the smoking crater of Popocatépetl for sulfur to make more. Rocks were loaded into the guns in place of roundshot. The siege—always the most horrible form of human warfare—continued. By the end of the month, half of Mexico-Tenochtitlan was a smoldering ruin, and the island smelled of carrion.

But the Mexica won small victories. They quickly learned that the terrible guns were deadly only in a direct line of fire; when cannon were trained on them, they broke to the side, or lay down on the ground. They cut innumerable small holes in the walls, so that they could pass through and escape from pursuing cavalry. They dropped stones from rooftops, and they sank arrows in any attacker who unwarily exposed himself. And twice they routed and seized captives from parties of over-confident Spaniards.

Fifteen Europeans were snatched out of a group that had landed from the fleet, stripped, and sacrificed while those who had escaped back to the brigantines were forced to watch.

At the end of June 1521 a contingent made up of Spaniards and many allies from Tlaxcala, Chalco, and Xochimilco advanced with flute and drum on the great market square of Tlatelolco and were suddenly set upon from all sides by Mexica under the great war-captain, Hecatzin. The Spanish, instead of retreating in good order, "blundered like drunkards" through the streets to the lakeshore, where they were bogged down in the mud. The Mexica now reaped a great harvest of Spaniards and Amerindian allies, who, along with four horses, were sacrificed on the pyramid at Yacacolco. The Spaniards, fifty-three in all, were decked with feathers and made to dance, while many of the Spanish army watched the scene from out on the causeways. After the last screaming victim had died, the fifty-three human and four horse heads were set on spears, facing the sun. The Mexica did not bother displaying the allies' heads.

This setback almost destroyed Cortés' alliance. It was a bad omen, and thousands of the local confederates slipped away. To rebuild morale, Cortés suspended all action for some three weeks.

But by now there was terrible suffering in Tlatelolco-Tenochtitlan. The starving people ate lizards and birds; they pulled up saline grass and water lilies from the stagnant lake. They chewed on old corncobs and deerhides, and in their agony, many stuffed their stomachs with dirt. The weak began to die.

The polluted water, meanwhile, gave many a crippling dysentery.

Then, in August, Cortés began the assault again. The sick, starving Mexica were pushed back from wall to wall. The stone slabs were hideous with dried blood; the adobe walls, no longer whitewashed, stank in the hot sun. The lakeshore was awash with decomposing corpses. The wailing children died from lack of water and food. But still the courage of young Cuauhtémoc and his war chiefs held. They fought on.

Finally, the Spanish forced their way into the great marketplace. Horsemen galloped across it, butchering anyone in their path, but then withdrew. Others set the principal temple of Tlatelolco afire, and as the flames and smoke rose high over the city, the population wailed in horror. A canopy was erected for Cortés in the market plaza, when finally it had been cleared, and a catapult, under the direction of Castañeda, was set up atop the main pyramid, to hurl stones randomly against the surrounding quarters.

Cuauhtémoc tried magic as well as courage. In the hope of terrifying the enemy and winning favor from the gods, a selected warrior was dressed in the regalia of his great father, Ahuízotl. The power of Huitzilopochtli was believed to reside in this costume, with its brilliant quetzal feathers and golden ornaments. The Spanish were startled by the sudden appearance of this apparition on a rooftop, but it had no other effect. Cuauhtémoc also ordered that any captives be brought directly to him, and once he personally sacrificed three.

The area under his control rapidly diminished as the defenders were driven back into the northwestern corner of the island. Cortés again tried to persuade him to surrender through the agency of a captive ranking priest who was sent to Cuauhtémoc with a message.

Before receiving him, Cuauhtémoc assembled his surviving lords and asked their advice. All were eager to hear the message, and an officer was dispatched to hear it from the priest and relay it back to the war council.

This officer reported: "The 'god' and Malintzin send word to Cuauhtémoc and the other lords that there is no hope for them. It is all over. Have they no pity for the old men, old women, and little children? You are to deliver up women with light skins, and other tribute. You will have no other chance. You must choose whether to surrender or be destroyed."

Some wanted to surrender, others held out. Cuauhtémoc himself was stubborn. He asked the fortune-tellers: "What do you see in this?"

A priest answered him: "Our prince, hear the truth we say. In four more days, eighty days will have passed since the siege began. It may be the will of Huitzilopochtli that we shall be saved. Let us wait four days." The nobles and Cuauhtémoc discussed how much tribute they might have to pay. Cuauhtémoc appears to have been more sanguine than the others. But they did nothing, and the Spaniards renewed the carnage.

A few nights later, in a soft rain, noncombatants and even many warriors began to stream out of the city on the causeways. At first there were many killings, because some of the warriors still carried clubs and shields. But as the stream grew into a torrent, and the Spanish realized what was happening, they merely searched the refugees and let them go. Those Mexica who had boats or canoes or rafts paddled away in the night. Others struck out into the lake, trying to reach the mainland. Many drowned.

Yet resistance continued. August 12, 1521 was a day of heavy fighting, but also of slaughter and rapine, as the Spanish, aided by thousands of eager allies who had returned to the war, began to sack Mexico-Tenochtitlan. The sack was as horrible as the end of any historic siege. Alva Ixtlilxóchitl, a descendent of the prince of Texcoco who led his warriors into the Mexica capital that day, claimed that the Texcoca pitied their former allies, and protected many women and children against the hideous deeds of the Spanish, the Tlaxcalteca, and the other Amerindians, who now revenged themselves for generations of wrongs and humiliations. The Mexica accounts make no such distinction.

At nightfall the sack halted. Cortés, Ixtlilxóchitl, and the other leaders agreed to finish the job the next day, which was the Feast of San Ippolito the Martyr.

Along the causeways the Spanish and allied soldiers dealt brutally with the refugees throughout the night. Many of the Mexica women had dressed themselves in dirty rags and covered their faces with mud—but the Spanish stripped and searched them all, for some did have golden objects hidden beneath their skirts.

A few of the obviously young and strong men, were put under guard and a "G" for *Guerra* ("war") branded on their cheek or lips, to denote that they were slaves taken in war.

Those lucky enough to pass through the Spanish-Tlaxcalteca-Texcoca cordon with nothing more than humiliations scattered along the shoreline, crawling naked into nearby villages, huddling in the drizzling rain under trees, or up against walls. Not all who fled were *macehualtin*—some of the greatest lords and their families escaped naked from Tenochtitlan.

The refugees were abused, reviled, or killed by the inhabitants of the mainland villages into which they fled.

At daybreak on August 13, Cortés marched through the last quarter of Tlatelolco-Tenochtitlan. The Spanish had to tie kerchiefs around their noses because of the stench. Out on the lake, the brigantines maneuvered against the last stream of refugees.

There was no more resistance. Mexica men and women who remained in the city crawled out on roofs to watch the Spanish pass; the women and old men wept. The city was a bloody, smoldering ruin; the surviving warriors were dazed and starving.

Some of the nobles escorted Cuauhtémoc to a waiting canoe. There are two versions about what happened next. Either Cuauhtémoc was paddled to the Spanish to surrender, while the watching Mexica moaned and wept or he tried to escape with a large escort of Tlatelolca nobles in canoes, but was overtaken by a brigantine commanded by García de Olguín. Recognized by some of the native allies, with Olguín's crossbowmen towering over him, he threw down his sword and shield.

Either way, Cuauhtémoc and several captured nobles were dragged by their cloaks to stand before Cortés.

Cuauhtémoc put his hand on Cortés' belted dagger and said bitterly: "I beg the lord to kill me. It would be fitting to end the lordship of Mexico, for you have already destroyed my city and killed my people."

But Cortés had no intention of destroying Cuauhtémoc at this time. He patted him on the head, and ordered a chair brought for him. He asked the captured prince to tell his people to lay down their arms, and Cuauhtémoc climbed a tower and did so in a loud voice. With this, the some thirty thousand Mexica still alive in Tlatelolco-Tenochtitlan finally dropped their clubs and shields. A few nobles came forward to comfort Cuauhtémoc.

Ixtlilxóchitl of Texcoco, according to his historian descendent's *relación*, arrived in a Spanish brigantine carrying other captured nobles, including a son of Motecuhzoma II and the widow of Cuitláhuac. The Texcoca prince grasped Cuauhtémoc's hand; there is no record of Cuauhtémoc's response.

Out on the lake, Spanish gunners fired off their cannon in celebration. Then, a great, morbid silence descended over Tenochtitlan. There were no more shots or screams, only the buzzing of myriad flies. So ended the day 1-Snake of the year 3-House, the day the Mexic calendar ended, and Mexic civilization died.

Alva Ixtlilxóchitl summarized the final destruction of the great capital as well as any:

> The siege of Tenochtitlan, according to the histories, paintings, and accounts, lasted exactly eighty days. Thirty thousand men from the kingdom of Texcoco were killed, out of the more than 200,000 warriors who fought on the Spanish side. Of the Mexicans, more than 240,000 were slain. Virtually all the nobility perished; there remained alive only a few lords and knights and the little children.

12

THE CONQUERED

Nothing remains
But flowers and sad songs,
In Tlatelolco and Mexico,
Where once there were
Warriors and wise men.
   From the *Cantares Mexicanos*, Nahua poems written circa 1523.

The Mexica, or Mexicanos as the Spaniards called them, had paid the final price of military empire: hundreds of thousands of their warriors had been killed, their lands overrun, their cities destroyed, their women raped, their possessions taken. The fall of Mexico-Tenochtitlan represented the destruction not only of an empire but of a whole people. And while the Mexica had suffered hideously in the war, this was as nothing compared to the trauma they suffered in defeat.

Cortés ordered the survivors of the siege to evacuate the city, now a bloody, stinking shambles. He had the scattered corpses buried or thrown into the lake; then, Tenochtitlan was set afire and its standing walls razed to the ground. The remains of the great temples, and the palaces of Axayácatl and Motecuhzoma, and the artifacts of the tribe, were lost in the rubble.

The evacuated Mexica joined those who had already fled to the fields and villages along the lakeshore. All were ragged and hungry. The Tlaxcalteca and Texcoca warriors had stripped the Mexica of their feathers and jade; the finery went to allied nobles, while common warriors divided up the humbler ornaments and cloaks. The villagers scorned, harassed, and sometimes killed the refugees.

The surviving clan chiefs of Tlatelolco gathered in the town of Cuauh-titlan. They were overcome by grief, but they had no time to mourn. Their kinsmen were desperate, and all desired to return to their houses and tiny farms out on the lake.

The chiefs agreed the only course was to beg mercy from Cortés. They understood only too well the Spanish greed for gold. Therefore, the leaders ordered all the Tlatelolca to deliver up any golden objects they might have brought away and also had the people searched. Several baskets of golden ornaments were thus found and carried by several trusted leaders to Cortés at his Coyoacán headquarters. The chiefs addressed Cortés through Agui-lar and Malintzin.

"Your servants, the chiefs of Tlatelolco, beg you to have mercy. Your servants are being molested by the people of the villages; they scorn us and even kill us by treachery. We beg you to hear us, and we have brought you these baskets of gold."

Cortés and his lieutenants frowned at the small accumulation of precious metal. Malintzin said venomously, "Is this how you have wasted your time? For this little bit of gold? Why have you not brought the treasure that fell into the Canal of the Tolteca? Where is that? We must have it!"

"Cuauhtémoc gave it to the *cihuacóatl* and another lord," the Tlatelolca replied. "Ask Cuauhtémoc and the lords of Tenochtitlan; they know where it is."

In the degradation of defeat, old wounds had reopened between Tla-telolco and Tenochtitlan. Each quarter of the city had begun to blame the other for the disaster; the Tlatelolca ballads and accounts were particularly derogatory. Very little of the large treasure accumulated while Cortés held Motecuhzoma hostage had been recovered; most of the gold bars cast by the Spaniards had probably sunk forever into the mud of the lake. The Tlatelolca knew this, but strove to put the blame on their kinsmen in Tenochtitlan.

Cortés put the envoys in irons, but later he had Malintzin tell them: "The captain says you may go back to your people. He is grateful to you for what you have done. It may be true that the Tlatelolca are being mistreated. Tell your people they may return to their houses in Tlatelolco —the captain desires that they come back. But no one is to go into Tenochtitlan; that is now the property of the gods."

Cortés understood the strategic and symbolic importance of the Navel of the Moon to central Mexico; he recalled the former beauty of the island and wanted to restore it, and found a Spanish city there.

The clan leaders returned to the refugees, and gradually, they picked their way back across the breached and bloody causeways. The Tlatelolca survivors were no longer molested by the Spanish, and they were allowed to reoccupy their communal houses in peace. Some of the chiefs, either out of bitterness or fear, remained away, and several died in exile.

As Cortés' actions with the Tlatelolca showed, he was not obsessed with the vision of golden treasures. In the calm of total victory, he dreamed of new cities and a great Christianized Amerindian realm under the king of Spain. As he promised Charles I in one of his five letters of explanation, he intended to make the capital of Mexico greater and grander than it had been before. Now that the natives were his subjects he seems to have sincerely wanted to protect them and make them useful subjects of the crown. He was intensely loyal to king and country, and to the mystique of Christian Spain, but he had not conquered the empire as an agent of the crown. He led a private, unofficial army, held together only by his personality and constant promises of reward. The vast majority of this army was mercenary, loyal only to personal greed. Men had deserted Velásquez, Narváez, and other captains under the spell of Cortés' charm and the expectation of enormous booty at Tenochtitlan. This army was not interested in the glory of Spain or future kingdoms; it had dared much and suffered much, and now the rank and file expected to be paid.

The loot was inconsequential; all the personal ornaments and lip plugs, divided among nearly a thousand soldiers, amounted only to a few ducats for each man.

The treasure lost on the *noche triste* had represented most of the gold mined in Middle America over many centuries. The treasure had never been as extensive as the Spanish had hoped, and now even that was lost. But the army would not accept this fact. The soldiery was of two opinions: either Cortés had cached all the gold for himself or the natives had it. The army quickly turned rebellious; the ambitious officers looked at the captain-general calculatingly.

Cortés had already faced and surmounted one rebellion, before the siege. He had hanged the ringleader, but he had had no choice but to pardon all the common soldiers who had entered into the plot. The army, only nominally under control once the fighting ended, was dangerous to Cortés himself; and what happened now can only be understood in this light. The great tragedy of the Spanish Conquest lay not in the war that humbled the Mexica, but in the terrible aftermath in which the unpaid conquistadores had to be appeased.

While Cortés was supervising the razing and burning, he had Cuauhtémoc, the cihuacóatl, Tlacotzin, the lord of Azcapotzalco, called Oquiztzin, the lord of Ecatépec, and a royal steward brought before him. They had been able to commandeer a few Spanish bars of gold recovered from the lake, along with several helmets, disks, and personal ornaments. The Spanish lieutenants snatched their offering up, while Cortés demanded through

Malintzin: "This is all? Where is the gold you are hiding? Bring all of it!"

Tlacotzin answered boldly: "All the gold we had was in our palaces, and we gave it to the lords in Motecuhzoma's time. Did not our lords take it with them when they left Tenochtitlan?"

Malintzin answered, "Yes, this is so. The gold was taken then and stamped with our seal. But it was lost in the Canal of the Tolteca in the night, when your warriors took us by surprise. Now you must give it back."

Tlacotzin said, "That battle was fought by the Tlatelolca, not the warriors from Tenochtitlan. We do not fight from canoes, as they do. It is possible the Tlatelolca took the gold."

Cuauhtémoc added: "Yes, this may be so. Our lords have seized the wrong people—everything indicates that the Tlatelolca took the gold. We have brought all the Tenochca had."

"This little bit?" Malintzin asked.

"Perhaps it was stolen," Tlacotzin suggested. "Why do not the lords search for it? Why not look for it, and bring it to light?"

But Cortés demanded that Tlacotzin find him two hundred bars of gold; he had Malintzin indicate the size of the wanted bars with her hands. The Mexica chief argued, perhaps derisively: "Mayhap some woman has hidden it under her skirts. Why do you not search there for it?"

One of the other Mexica officers explained what Cortés, however reluctantly, must have known: that all the available gold in Motecuhzoma's realm had been brought to Tenochtitlan and given to the Spanish by Motecuhzoma's command; there was no more.

Cortés ordered that the five chiefs be placed in irons and taken to Coyoacán. The next morning he acquiesced to his followers' demands and allowed all of them to be put to the torture, to make them confess where the gold was stored. Like all pirates, Cortés' army had enormous faith in the powers of torture, a faith equivalent to their belief that their victims had always hidden gold. Cuauhtémoc's feet were thrust over a brazier of red-hot coals. Although Cortés tried to temper this torment by having the captives' feet rubbed with oil to prevent permanent injury, the torturers pursued the question with such angry stubborness that the Mexica's feet were charred and destroyed. All of the men suffered terribly.

Cuauhtémoc bore up stoically; when one of the other tortured princes screamed to him, he is reputed to have said bitingly, "Am I myself in a pleasant bath?" None of the Mexica confessed, and Cortés halted the proceedings before any died.

Meanwhile, the army, out of hand, was conducting less official treasure hunts. The chief priest of Huitzilopochtli died under similar torture because he would not deliver the god's finery. All surviving Mexic priests were handled ferociously. The Spanish considered them servants of the devil, who deserved the fire in any case. When the treasure of Huitzilopochtli was at last ferreted out in Xaltocán, where two chiefs had taken it for safekeeping, the Spaniards left their corpses dangling on the road to Mazatlán.

Some gold was found in the palace of a minor lord in one of the nearby towns. The son of a royal steward, who had been entrusted with eight bars of the stamped gold, fled before he could be questioned, and only four bars of this store were recovered. The army went on a rampage. It hanged Macuilxóchitl, the lord of Huitzilopocho, and the lord of Culhuacán, who had fought on the Spanish side at Tenochtitlan. The indigenous accounts recorded these atrocities to the highborn. The torture of ordinary Amerinds was so commonplace it escaped recorded notice.

The soldiers had discovered that their great hounds terrified the natives. They delighted in setting these vicious beasts on helpless men, either to make them reveal hidden treasure, or simply for sport. Ranking priests were fed to the dogs; the slavering hounds and the blood of the victims were depicted with striking clarity in several Mexica books of pictographs. According to one codex, three unarmed wise men, journeying from Texcoco with their books, probably to pay homage to Cortés, were set upon and slain by the Spanish hounds.

The Meso-Americans, especially those who had been the longest civilized, were terribly vulnerable to the conquerors. The indigenes' utter lack of individual initiative permitted a few hundred armed men to tyrannize and destroy them. The Mexica, and other tribes, continued to look to their hereditary leadership until the last of the aristocracy was destroyed and there was nothing to replace it. The civilization fell with the tiny minority which had always sustained it; only the sullen, ineffective hatred of the Amerindian mass remained, showing its resistance more through apathy than open revolt.

The Nahuatl accounts of Chimalpain Cuauhtlehuanitzin shed some light on Cortés' first dreams for the reorganization of Anáhuac. According to this source, Cortés had the five lords he had put to the torture brought before him again and Malintzin asked them certain questions concerning the political status of the Chalca, Xochimilca, Acolhua, and Tepanec peoples.

Again it was the last *cihuacóatl* of the Mexica, rather than the youth Cuauhtémoc who answered him honestly: "The Mexica had no lands when we first came here; the Tepaneca, the Acolhua, the Chalca, and the Xochimilca, all had lands. We made ourselves their lords with arrows and shields. We took their lands. But what we did was no different from what you have done, our lord, for you came with arrows and shields to take our lands and cities from us."

Cortés turned to the others and said firmly: "You hear this. The Mexica came here with arrows and shields to seize your lands. They made you their slaves. But I have come to set you free. You are no longer slaves of the Mexicans. Your lands belong to you again!"

Tragically, Cortés would not and could not keep his promise. Mexico had been freed from one subordination of the mind and heart only to fall under another, perhaps even more terrible, of the body and soul.

In the end neither those at Tenochtitlan who stood with Cortés or against him were spared. The fall of Tenochtitlan was more than the fall of a great capital and empire; it signaled the rapid destruction of an entire way of life.

Of all the sufferings borne by the Amerindians in the Conquest, demoralization was perhaps the worst, and the one thing Amerindian hardihood and courage could not fight. Their universe was upended and their values utterly destroyed. Demoralization, perhaps, killed as many Amerindians in the long run as Spanish swords or Eurasian disease, for men whose deepest beliefs are shattered seldom have the will to live. The superficial patina of Christianity and European culture did not really replace the old culture for generations. Trauma and neuroses linger still, and may never be entirely overcome. For the Spaniards, in Mexico, did not commit genocide; they committed culturicide.

The civilization itself did not reach deeply into the mass of men—it could not have, or else it could never have been so easily forgotten and destroyed. In the final, impartially cruel analysis, its loss had little effect on the world. Scientists and sentimentalists may mourn needless destruction; blood descendents of the Amerindians may feel an ancestral outrage. But the Amerindian civilization had nothing that the Old World had not discovered, and discarded for the most part, millennia before. The things that America had to offer the world—lands, mineral wealth, and above all, native foods—were all preserved and disseminated.

The great contributions of America were the native plants—the tobacco, chocolate, potatoes, and other immensely valuable crops which in some way changed human life across the world.

When the sun broils down on the wasteland that now surrounds the Pyramids of the Sun and Moon at Teotihuacán, and the moon shines across the tree-tumbled ruins of Palenque or Copán, as priests and warriors and slaves parade on endless friezework, and as beast-fanged stone monsters mouth their eternal, silent screams, even the untrained observer senses that these are surviving relics of something terribly old. The mistake is to think of them going back only five hundred, or a thousand years. Even to the descendents of the people who built these things, they are incredibly strange, belonging to another world.

Yet when the moonlight falls in certain patterns on the sacred squares, and animals scream in the inky jungle blackness beyond the ancient walls, the hairs on the nape of a modern man might also rise in fear or wonder, just as Bernal Díaz' hair quivered to the boom of Huitzilopochtli's drum. For these ruins are part of mankind, and they both record and foretell man's fate.

PART TWO

The Tyranny of Conquest: The Spaniards

13

THE SPANIARDS

Undoubtedly the greatest single fact in the history of Spain was the long Roman occupation, lasting more than six centuries. All that Spain is or has done in the world can be traced in greatest measure to the Latin civilization which the organizing genius of Rome was able to graft upon her.

Charles E. Chapman, *A History of Spain.*

The sixteenth-century Spaniards who poured through the Indies and landed armed and armored on the shores of Mexico were a people peculiarly fitted for empire.

The very qualities some other Europeans considered Spanish weaknesses or aberrations were in effect enormous imperial strengths. The Castilian captains were warlike and ruthless highlanders. The Spanish race was proud, intolerant of infidels, and determined to destroy false gods. The Spanish were neither maritime nor mercantile; they were like the Romans who crossed water but who remained economically naive. They were a people who developed an immense sense of lordship. In fact, they very much resembled the conquering Mexica of Middle America in many ways. The Spaniards conquered millions almost by sheer will.

Like all truly imperial peoples, the Spanish did not bargain with alien civilizations and cultures they found; they struck them down. They were not sailors, merchants, colonizers, nor refugees; they were conquistadores.

Everywhere the Spanish went, they carried their civilization and implanted it with immense success.

Conversely, the other Atlantic-European peoples were not truly imperial. The Portuguese, Dutch, English, and French went out for trade, or to found colonies. They sent out successful traders, and they planted some successful colonies, usually in relatively wild and uninhabited regions. They also forged hegemonies over alien cultures from Suez to the Celebes, following certain patterns: they established trading posts and fortified them; they were drawn into local politics and wars; through superior technology and organization they gradually created local hegemonies. Great trading companies exercised a sort of rule, collecting taxes or tribute from native populations and eventually recruiting native soldieries from them. But all this thrust was economic; the Dutch and British and Portuguese never perceived an imperial purpose nor undertook a "civilizing" mission until the twilight of their hegemonies, when it was too late. Their "empires" proved ephemeral, though some of their spun-off colonies endured and grew.

The Spanish alone made a true empire in the Roman fashion, something not always seen. They did this because the Spanish alone of all Europeans possessed an imperial consciousness and past when the great navigators opened up the world.

The sixteenth-century Spaniards were a mixed, dark, tough, combative breed which had not essentially changed for two thousand years. They were still the same lithe, olive-skinned, longheaded people the Phoenicians had found in the peninsula they called the "remote country" or *Span* in the eleventh century B.C. The ancestors of this race, a dark Caucasian folk, probably migrated across North Africa out of the Middle East in very ancient times. Over the centuries this people, whom the Greeks named Iberians after the River Iberus or Ebro, mixed with fairer, distinctly Indo-European Celts who passed through the Pyrenees and settled in the high northwest; with Greeks and Phoenician-Carthaginian merchants and their Numidian-Berber mercenaries in the south and east; with Sephardic Jews and Germanic overlords who arrived from different directions in the Roman Empire's evening. Then came new waves of Eastern peoples: the related Berbers, with a sprinkling of Arabs, Syrians, and Slavs at the high tide of Islam.

All the conquerors who entered Spain came in small numbers. They were armies of conquerors, not migrations, who established military hegemonies over the existing tribes. The physically-similar Punic peoples and their Berber allies sank their seed into Spain without trace. The Romans ruled from colony-cities and military camps; they did not destroy the people on the land. The Visigoths, a tiny minority, merely introduced a warlike aristocracy, and the Muslims did the same. The Goths were assimilated; while the Muslims recruited the vast majority of their subjects from turncoat Christians. Throughout every change the old Spanish blood survived, Indo-European in the north above the Ebro, predominantly Asian in the mixed race of the east and south.

The primordial characteristics of the Iberians survived, traits bred into the people by their land. Behind the green and deceiving Mediterranean coasts and fertile southern plain, which always nurtured a softer, sprightly race, the interior of Iberia was and is a high, harsh, largely arid series of mountain ranges and vast tablelands. The heart of the land, rising between the Gaudalquivir and Ebro, is a great, impoverished mesa, historically more damaged than improved by man.

In ancient times the Spaniards, herdsmen with an instinctual Mediterranean dislike for trees, began to demolish the irreplaceable Pleistocene forests of the highlands, cutting swathes of destruction—to this day— across the land with the over-graze of sheep. And for millennia Spanish tribesmen lived on these high, barren plateaus, chilled by winter frosts, burned by summer suns, pounded by infrequent torrential rains. Here vultures have soared on mountain updrafts since the present world began. The land's harsh mesas and deep gorges are cut apart, isolating each region and valley. This country shaped a certain kind of man: violent, valiant, contemptuous of both comfort and pain, clannish and austere, and conservative to the bone. The serrating mountains drove a deep separatism into the Spanish soul.

This separatism, sometimes miscalled individualism, made the race intolerant of discipline and neighbors. The Spanish people have oscillated between violent social anarchy and imposed despotism throughout their history—the latter almost inevitable if there were to be an Hispanic social order at all. The Iberians would cooperate only when ruled by force—or rarely, when caught up in some overriding drive toward ultrarational goals.

The supreme event in the history of this people was its conquest and incorporation into the Roman Empire. The six centuries of Roman presence were decisive. They destroyed all the older languages, cults, and even consciousness. The organizing genius of Rome replaced the ancient Indo-European Iron Age culture of the Iberians with a Latin civilization. In the first century B.C. Hispania comprised Rome's fairest western provinces; the southern plain was dotted with her colonies and became the home of Seneca and Trajan, Hadrian and Martial, an integral part of the Roman world at the floodtide of Imperial art.

The Romans transmitted a vast reservoir of culture and civilizing influences with their language, literature, and law. But they also transmitted all that the Greco-Roman civilization had altered or debased: hieratic monarchy articulated by a crushing bureaucracy; a rigid social order now devoid of original Indo-European aristocracy; a distaste for commerce or industry among educated men; a rhetorical cast to education and thought, with argument supplanting fact and evidence; a late-Roman passion for juridicalism and regulation; and an agricultural system in which huge landed estates became a way of life. Above all else, Rome at last planted in Spain the religion which the Roman mind had inevitably made into a vast legal system, with a God like a judge-emperor, and in which canons and dogma and form extinguished the vital early Christian ethic.

All this was a Latinity that took permanent root in Iberian soil. Its tap roots could not be eradicated; they would grow back again and again in the face of adversity.

The invading Visigoths, Vandals, and other Germans ended the Roman Imperium, but the Gothic kings, who ruled a turbulent Spanish state from Toledo, abandoned their native language and cult for late-Latin and orthodox Catholicism. In the same period thousands of the Sephardim (Hebrew: *Spaniards*) or Jews who had settled in Spain after the Diaspora also adopted the Latin language and life style, although they held on to their tribal faith. The Germans at first tolerated the Jews, but when the Visigoths turned Catholic, the Sephardim were persecuted.

The Muslim wave that broke over Iberia in the eighth century submerged a decadent but still Latin Spain. The Arab-Berber horsemen carved out rural estates and established a new military aristocracy. The Muslims left most of the towns to the Christians, many of whom became Muslim converts in time. The conquerors also made practical working arrangements with the formerly persecuted Jews, for in this age no hatred existed between Jewry and Islam. The Sephardim administered Muslim estates and were tax gatherers and ministers. Together, the Muslims and Spanish Jews, drawing mainly on the knowledge of the Byzantines, created a splendid but ephemeral civilization in southern Spain. In the tenth century the caliphate of Córdoba was the richest and most powerful state in Western Europe.

Almost accidentally, some pockets of Latin Christians survived in the misty Atlantic northwest; they barely held their own for two hundred years. In the eleventh century the Cordovan caliphate collapsed, split into warring emirates, and the Christian Asturians were able to debouch back onto the great central plateau. Like all Spaniards, the northern Christians tended to splinter into several minor kingdoms.

But the Christian pig-farmers of Asturia and Galicia joined with their half-Frankish Catalan brothers in the high northeast to battle the Muslim overlords. Poor, tough, primitive and hardbitten, these semibarbarians, petty warlord and vassal alike, began a pressure on Muslim Spain that was never to cease. The two cultures met in the eleventh century along a long, fluid frontier that split the peninsular highlands from Saragossa to Guadalajara, and from Talavera to Toledo. As this frontier shifted slowly south and east, fortresses arose, giving it a new name: *Castilla*, the land of castles, or old Castile.

As the clash went on, power inevitably flowed to the more virile warders of the frontier. Castilla grew from a war march to a petty kingdom, and subsequently into Spain's most unified and powerful state. Castilla grew from conquests, and as she grew, her warfare with the Muslims, blazing now and again from brutal power struggle to jihad and crusade, forged the mind and soul and shape of early-modern Spain.

New hordes of fanatic Berber horsemen continued to pour into Spain. Constant war required powerful, able Castilian kings who were able to control the innately turbulent *condes* or counts. Meanwhile, their magistrates ran the kings' writ in the reviving Spanish towns, and their ever-present officers destroyed the bases for republican self-government.

By the thirteenth century, Castile had overrun all of Muslim Andalusia except the enclave of Granada, and Alfonso X, the Learned, could assert the tradition that all the legislative, military, judicial, and monetary powers of the Castilian state were inalienable prerogatives of the crown. He codified such traditions into law. His successors, despite constant rebellions by the nobility, increased the actual and theoretical powers of the throne. What these rulers achieved was much more than a personal despotism. It was nothing less than the gathering of *all* governmental legitimacy under the unshakeable symbol of the crown. The Castilian king *was* the state. This concept of legitimacy sank deeply into the Spanish consciousness; it could not be shaken by prolonged bouts of anarchy or even weak kings; it was to bring about the Spanish Empire as well as immense problems for the whole Hispanic world.

The slowly but entirely successful wars of the Reconquest shaped Spanish society in other ways, making all Spaniards identify themselves first and last as Catholic Christians—their religion was the basis of their nationhood.

As the frontier advanced behind successful campaigns and crusades, successful warlords and the fighting religious orders that sprang up everywhere in Spain were granted huge rewards by the crown. The kings entrusted great nobles and orders with vast territories and the conquered populations upon them. *"Se os encomiendan"*—"to you is given in trust" —the feudal charters read, and these territories became known as *encomiendas*, regions from which the trustee might command tribute. By the *repartimiento*, the *encomendero* could also command the labor of the population, especially for public works. First held in feudal trust, the *encomiendas* were gradually turned into personalty and protected by primogeniture under a reviving Roman law; the agrarian workers became serfs. Broad fields and towns thus became the property of important lords, and the basis of the *latifundios* that settled as a permanent social and economic incubus over much of southern Spain.

More important, probably, was the immense psychic result of this *Reconquista* of rich lands, and hordes of servile Muslims and Jews. The effective classes, the warlords and their retainers, the counts and knights saw the true function of the Christian as the exercise of arms, and *señoría,* the exercise of lordship or rule. These ideas affected in some degree the entire Christian mass. The knights and peasant-spearmen from a high, harsh, barren, economically primitive land became the lords of millions of vastly more civilized and economically sophisticated Muslims and Jews. The nobility could easily adjust and tolerantly despise the peculiar talents of the Muslim merchants and artisans and Jewish bankers as the traits of inferior races and religions. But in the midst of huge, differentiated populations which they despised but with whom they were soon forced to compete, the poorer classes, muleteers and gentlemen, could find no such tolerance. As Christians and victors, they held to the outlooks and biases of their lords, and the great majority inevitably made everything the Jews or Muslims excelled at ethnically and religiously suspect. Thus the Spaniards came to despise Jews and Moors and what was seen as the Jewish-Moorish way of life.

The Western urge to entrepreneurism and stewardship were fatally damaged in Christian Spain.

The Spaniard, whether noble, a knight, a landowner, or a serf was motivated by forces beyond his conscious control to assume symbolic pretensions of nobility. The true nobility, secure in their estates, could afford it; the common men who had to earn their bread by the sweat of their brows or their brains, could not.

The aftermath of the Reconquest made fusion of the value systems of the Castilians and the Muslims and Jews impossible. The Spaniard whose blood was pure (meaning he stemmed from three generations of unblemished Christian ancestry) whether starveling or vagabond or thief, felt compelled to put on the *señor*. Here rose the exaggerated, ridiculous pride of the Spaniard, gentleman and commoners alike, too poor to live according to their lights, too proud to engage in the work of Moors or Jews. This insidious form of racism was to have disastrous effects on Hispanic civilization.

But if this subtle racism barred the Spaniard from careers in commerce or industry, there was still a splendid substitute for *señoría*—office. The second sons, the secondary, serving nobility, and most of the small class of bourgeoisie ached to find a post in the service of the Church, the orders, or the king. Office was not only respectable; it was almost the only avenue of social advancement. In the Spanish system it inevitably became a means of rewarding service rather than of service to the state. The medieval Castilian looked on the crown's grant of a post, almost always secured through favoritism or as a reward, as a sort of fief, almost like the award of an *encomienda* or an estate. And he used it more as a personal fief than a public trust, enjoying its privileges and emoluments exactly as true *señores* enjoyed their estates. This attitude toward office, deeply implanted in the middle ages, would be sown from Manila to Mexico.

The Reconquest was not just a social disaster; it created an imperial spirit and an imperial past, and in some aspects was an immense ethnic and religious success. As the Christian kingdoms of the north seized Muslim emirates, they absorbed large heterogeneous populations of subjugated Old Christians, *renegados* or Muslim converts, Muslims, and Jews. The Spanish kingdoms were able to incorporate and assimilate these peoples. The territories were joined organically under the Spanish crown, and three major states emerged: Castilla and León, Aragon, and Portugal. The two larger Spanish kingdoms were hardly homogeneous even in themselves. They were a series of lands and older kingdoms and counties incorporated under a single crown; the incorporation usually left older political and legal boundaries and even older regional consciousnesses intact. Laws, rights, customs, and languages varied from place to place. Aragon, in the east was more heterogeneous than Castile, though Castilla had her *gallegos, asturianos,* and Andalusians. Through the seizure of the most of the rich southern plain, Castile became the richest and most powerful Iberian state, and through her size and vigor began to exert a certain cultural dominance.

Though not a true national coalescence, it laid, in the middle ages, the foundations for Spanish world power, and the practice of conjoining separate kingdoms through conquest or royal marriages set the precedents for the formation of the Spanish Empire. Where other European peoples had to wrestle with the constitutional problems of the status and governing of overseas or alien territories, the Spanish had already learned to incorporate them.

The Reconquest was completely decisive: it not only broke Muslim power forever, it wiped out the Muslim-Jewish cultural presence. The great mass of Spanish *moros,* themselves of Spanish descent, turned renegade again; they were absorbed as New Christians. Many of them had always remained more Spanish than Moorish, except in faith. When Granada fell in 1492, its several millions spoke the Andalusian-Castilian dialect and they were hardly distinguishable physically from Spaniards. Arabic and Berber had fallen out of use, though Arabic persisted in the Islamic courts. Galician was actually the patois of the Granadine palace because of the preference of the rulers for blonde concubines. Rebellions and resistance of the Granadine Muslims, who were conquered late, continued into the seventeenth century; but on the whole the Andalusians passed into the Christian masses peacefully.

The Sephardim were very much an elite, but their entire world view was anathema in Christian Spain. For a true assimilation, the Spanish Jew not only had to surrender his religion but his whole way of life—the Castilians despised and detested bankers as much as infidels, since they consciously linked the two. Thousands of Sephardim did convert, but this very conversion lay at the bottom of the peculiarly Castilian institution, the Holy Inquisition. In 1492, perhaps twenty thousand Spanish Jews were killed in the tumults of the expulsion, and approximately one hundred and sixty-five thousand left Spain. A full quarter of the Jews chose to convert, and many of the exiles eventually returned. These people, together with the converted Muslims, left a residue of perhaps thirty percent of the Spanish population at the close of the middle ages who were either religiously or culturally suspect. The Inquisition's huge popularity was due to it rooting out not only infidels but non-Castilian attitudes and life styles as well.

The former Jew who used his peculiarly "Jewish" talents or skills to prosper or rise in the social scale—as thousands did—was virulently hated by the impoverished caballeros or hidalgos, men who were nobles under the laws of Castile but whose function and prospects had vanished with the war frontier.

Of the values of the Sephardim, nothing remained at all. The New Christian had to be more Castilian than the Castilians to survive; thousands did not; and it was no accident that so many of the most active Inquisitors and soldiers of early-modern Spain had Jewish blood.

Columbus sailed the same year that Granada fell and Fernando and Isabel expelled the Jews. Inevitably, the Castilian mind saw the lands opening up beyond the Ocean Sea as new extensions of an old frontier.

A people who could not tolerate religious or ethnic differences at home and who had been assimilating alien populations forcefully for five hundred years, whose wealth and raison d'être came from conquest, would logically expend prodigious efforts to incorporate new servile populations and to Christianize such peoples as a matter of course.

The marriage of Fernando II of Aragon (usually called Fernando V, in deference to the line of León and Castile) and Isabel of Castilla allowed the final fulfillment of the Castilian Dream: the last holy crusade against the Moors on Spanish soil; the destruction or expulsion of all infidels; the enactment of the vision of a people gathered under a single Church and crown. The Spaniards did not yet perceive a nation, and the marriage bed of Fernando and Isabel did not forge a nation-state. Castilians had put their faith in the faith and in the house of León and Castile. Now, these two things alone united them. Castilla and Aragon were to continue as separate legal entities for at least two hundred years.

Still, the union of the crowns opened enormous opportunities for a still-divided Spain, allowing for a common policy abroad, if not always at home. Against the structure of an emerging, not-yet-modern Europe, this union gave the conjoined crowns great power. And Spain *was* powerful, in her energetic and intelligent rulers, in the élan of a crusading faith, in the warrior ethos, and in the endurance of the Castilian race. But the two kingdoms remained poor, arid, comparatively backward countries. The dominant ethic of Castile was far more attuned to the age that was going out than the capitalist-commercial era that was arriving.

Out of a history of a centuries-long Reconquest and an amalgamation of kingdoms and peoples interspersed with bouts of anarchy—the last of which almost kept Isabel from her throne—a separatist, heterogeneous grouping of peoples, dialects, and hostile classes somehow emerged into the modern world caught up in a vast spiritual fusion. The fusion gave her monarchs the freedom to act. It infused thousands of Spaniards with a will to act. Other than this, Spain had only a numerous, warlike, essentially frustrated chivalric class, a source of captains, and a poor, tough, peasant people, yearning for symbolic nobility—a source of stubborn infantry. It was enough to set the world on fire.

Out of the peninsular experience and history had come the concept of the *español*, or patriotic Spaniard. The concept was not national in the modern sense, or even territorial. The true *español* was a person, *catalán, asturiano,* or *aragonés,* who whatever his station or his sins, was above all else loyal to the Holy Catholic Church and the Most Catholic Kings. As an idea, this linking of cross and crown was powerful and pervasive, the first great European national ideal. It allowed all Spaniards to submerge their suspicions and hatreds of each other in a common hatred of the enemies of the Church and crown and a common fury against all subversive elements within and without the state.

The concept led inevitably to the Inquisition and totalitarian persecutions. It led to forced expulsions of Muslims and Jews, because the Spaniard who was out of order in faith could not be *español*. Finally, under the direction of the Catholic kings, it led to the erection of a vast church-state.

The crown was the dominant element in this fusion of Church and state. The crown, while supporting a fanatic Catholic faith, was able to make the Spanish Church an arm of state. The Inquisition was far more a Castilian than a Catholic institution, reporting to the king rather than the pope. Fernando and Isabel were able to wrest control of the Spanish Church almost completely from Rome. Isabel defeated the religious orders which opposed her claim to the throne and dominated them; Fernando acquired the *patronato real,* the right to select prelates for Granada and the Americas from the Holy See. Patronage and patriotism as Spaniards knew it, kept Spanish clergy loyal to the crown.

In this new church-state prelates often held high public office and staffed royal councils. Laymen held some important offices within the Church. There was no clear distinction between Church and state.

The newer, almost mystic loyalty to the church-state provided the Catholic kings with great opportunities to destroy much of the middle ages in Spain. They brought the anarchic, rebellious military aristocracy of Andalusia and Galicia to heel. They destroyed all usurpations of the royal prerogative and revenues by the nobility, and abolished serfdom in Castile—a great blow to feudal power. They replaced the counts and great magnates who traditionally dominated royal councils with new men, the *letrados*, commoners lettered in the Roman law. The kings ran the state through a new bureaucracy, loyal only to themselves.

Far more than the feudal powers of the aristocracy was destroyed. The once-vigorous Castilian *cortes* or parliament, in which the towns and middle classes had a voice, was packed with the kings' creatures; equally fatally, it was allowed to die of neglect through disuse. The privileges and liberties of the Castilian towns were reduced, as the monarchs came to appoint all local councilmen and magistrates. Isabel strove to reform the still-medieval structure of the Church. Prelates and wealthy orders and slack convents were severely disciplined. Some clerics quit Spain in disgust, but the regular clergy was largely brought under strict form and discipline. And while Isabel was unsuccessful in purifying the secular clergy—priests continued to keep concubines and cardinals bought offices for their children as before—she at least controlled it.

The reduction of the whole apparatus of government to the royal wills allowed the Crown to increase taxation, create a new monetary system that would one day serve half the world, and to raise an almost-modern army. Regiments of guns, pikes, and horse were now recruited by conscription on the villages and paid professionally, both improving Spanish arms and further destroying the function of the old aristocracy. Fernando gave the new army good captains and prestige and sent it to serve his interests in Italian wars.

While Isabel revived the Inquisition to purify the faith, Fernando quickly understood its use as a terrorist tool. In Spain heresy was treason and lèse-majesté heresy, and the Holy Office investigated opponents of the king. The Inquisition crushed all opposition to royal policy. Accused Catholics more often than not escaped the fire, but Fernando and his principal inquisitors regularly divided up large estates, for few men accused in Spain emerged from prison with their wealth. This single instrument, in a fanatic age, gave the crown fantastic power over the higher reaches of society, and all intellectual life.

The first effects, however, were energizing. The monarchs were active and intelligent, destroying outmoded things, and the spirit of fusion and action, the currents of the Renaissance wafting out of Italy, and a sudden Spanish élan under strong leadership made the one great age of Spanish humanism and science. The first Castilian grammar was printed in 1492, an event in its way as important as Columbus' voyage, the fall of Granada, and the expulsion of the Jews from Spain. A vigorous Castilian literature evolved; other regional languages were driven out. Castilian became the court and literary tongue. Spaniards excelled in certain earth sciences, in history and in law, and a Spanish jurist envisioned the first concept of an international law.

All this was modern. Even the despotism of the crown and the totalitarian terrorism of the Church were more modern than medieval in ethos and form. But on the other hand, it has been said that all that emerged in Spain was only a new leaf on an old Castilian root. Behind all the bright modernity, Fernando and Isabel continued and strengthened things that were very old.

The royal treatment of the military aristocracy was an unhappy compromise. The great landholdings of the Reconquest, which already paralyzed the economy and social life of southern Spain remained; the revived Roman law and a new primogeniture maintained them. While the kings removed the aristocracy from effective participation in affairs of state they scrupulously preserved all the old concepts of hierarchy by confirming the nobility's privileges at law. Isabel gathered the magnates around the court as a glittering if sterile elite, bribing them with titles and hats, making them dukes and grandees. Thus was confirmed in Spain an hereditary hierarchy of great wealth and social prestige which was devoid of genuine aristocracy. The worst aspects of feudalism, which was once a rational contract, were frozen into the worst of social and economic worlds.

And if the structure of the church-state was new, its spirit was that of the bygone crusades. The Spanish religious vision emerged from medieval Christendom in the very age when that world view was cracking beyond repair. The new-model army in Italy made the western Mediterranean into an Aragonese lake, but it also destroyed the Renaissance and the modern Italianate world in those regions. The papacy, under Spanish pressure, was dragooned back into accord with the ideals of Castilian Catholicism, and thus a certain medievalism was restamped into Italy and Rome that would endure another four hundred years. The Spanish, whose armies dominated Rome, fell into the common but tragic trap of believing that one people's truths were or could be universal.

Ironically, the Spain of 1492 was in many ways the most modern and effective state in the West, but the very forces that impelled her to greatness promised to destroy her.

Yet, as the sixteenth century dawned, the Castilian dream seemed destined to culminate not only in a great society in Spain but in Spanish world power. The great age of Spanish arms and politics in Europe had begun. Fernando was mastering Italy, spinning dynastic webs to confound France and make Spain predominant. Isabel dreamed of loosing her fleets and soldiers against Muslim Africa, even freeing the Holy Land. In the New World, the Spanish were carving out a fantastic empire without competition. The improverished gentility who had once won their honors against the Moors were caught up in these plans and wars, and the ragged Spanish masses in mass enthusiasm. All Spaniards believed that *voluntad*—will— could achieve any dream. After eight centuries of adversity, the Spaniards had retaken their homeland in a bitter but brilliant imperial exercise; they were active and enthused, poised to burst out on the world.

This remains the era in which Spain made her greatest contributions and had her greatest effect, and in which her efforts, for better or for worse, from Italy to America were far from failures. It was an age shot through with contradictions. The exploration of the New World and the glory of Spanish arms in the Old were stained by rape, murder, plunder, and de- struction. The splendor of the emerging Castilian art and literature would never drown out the frightful screams from Castilian inquisitions, or cover the stench of burning flesh at festive mass executions. The great faith of men who believed they had discovered Truth was marred by breaking of faith with countless, hapless Muslim peasants of Granada, and essentially loyal Hispanic Jews. And the great spirit of Spain itself was inseparable from a totalitarian tyranny over the Spanish mind and soul. Spanish will left no room for opposition and Spanish truth left no place in Spanish hearts to comprehend Spanish tragedy. The fusion of spirit that gave Spain such élan and power was ephemeral. The great church-state was a human institution erected over an imperfect human landscape, filled with hidden chasms.

The Spaniard, like his isolated barbarian ancestors, was still hostile to any discipline. He still tended to personalize everything with which he came in contact. If this trait kept Spaniards from dehumanization, it also isolated them from one another. They oscillated wildly, in their souls and politics, from sheer rebellion to insistence upon orthodoxy and dictator- ship. Their separatist natures ran to jealousy and uncooperativeness. Few Spaniards trusted another; no ruler trusted the ruled, especially the Span- ish kings who had learned their subjects' fractiousness from long experi- ence. The crown demanded total loyalty but permitted vast malfeasance; the Church required scrupulous outward observance but put few, if any, inner demands upon the faithful. The profuse and constant expressions of loyalty that marked all Spanish life obscured a deep urge to anarchy and rebellion.

The Spaniard could not easily merge his personality with any social role; he was thus almost the social opposite of the civilized Amerindians, who oriented themselves completely to their society. The Spaniard was always at odds with circumstance, too much aware of his symbolic pride and dignity. He instinctively identified things with himself, never himself with institutions or things. Thus he was more inclined to try to adjust the world to his desires, by will, than to adjust himself to the real or physical world by observation and experience. His willingness to drink wine when there was wine, water when there was not, was not stoic adaptation, it was a refusal to accept those things which were necessary to assure the flow of wine. He would always founder angrily in vast, impersonal forms of human organization, becoming impatient with any process unresponsive to his personal will, whether in science or politics.

Among such people, style was immensely important, and rebellion was always mixed with heroism. Spanish history was filled with the *bandido en heroe*: the bandit who became a hero, and the hero who became a rebel bandit. It was a spirit that made life and politics chaotic unless tyrannized. The Castilian codes of honor were essentially the old señorial codes of conduct. The ideal aristocrat, therefore the ideal Spaniard, admitted neither error nor shame; he turned wrongness into virtue and triumphed over adversity by sheer will or force of personality. He scorned any form of productive labor, and the fact that he needed money was an affront to his sensibility. He also scorned ambition, itself a pejorative word, except toward lordship. Arrogance was the mark of a real man. Candor, meanwhile, was ill-bred and showed a man up as a fool. To be responsible meant to be too tightly wound or bound, while compromise implied a sell-out, both of manhood and the soul.

None of these were exclusively Hispanic traits; they were aristocratic values once shared by all the warrior castes of Christendom. But in Spain the medieval war-march lasted longer, and its ethos was vastly more refined and suffused through a whole population. This was the true heritage of Reconquistadorial Spain.

The effective, or would-be effective Spaniard was a man who came to see most forms of labor as servile, or a curse. He looked on financial or commercial talents and even stewardship as suspect, the peculiar properties of despised races. God provided, or should provide, for Christian gentlemen.

This heritage gave him a powerful racist pride. He saw the end of ambition as the holding—not necessarily any fruitful use of—vast landed estates. Office was almost the only respectable avenue to position or wealth. Here was an ethic that was never the true ethic of the ordered world of medieval Christendom, and was the reverse of the ethic that won out north of the Pyrenees. The dominant Western ethic, whatever it was called, was one in which productive work came to be seen as a virtue, wealth as a reasonable basis for status, and prodigality verged on sin.

The Spanish ethic, so aristocratic, persisted after the true concepts of aristocracy—the rule by effective persons—were erased. From the sixteenth century the Spaniard confused racism and hierarchy with aristocracy. The aristocratic social orders collapsed as effective orders in the modern church-state, but society remained rigidly, sterilely hierarchical. Effects were profound and often cumulatively paralyzing: Spanish silversmiths would not draw water; pages would not groom horses; knights would not clean armor; lawyers would never dirty their hands. Each rank had an enormous sense of what was right and dignified for it and would do nothing else. It was no accident that just as the Spanish put together the first European bureaucracy since the Roman Empire the powerful Spanish kings discovered they had to operate through and within a vast series of petty hierarchies. They could order and order, and were obeyed and obeyed, while very little ever got done. In truly aristocratic or oligarchical societies, men tend to follow leaders; in a hierarchical society the great emphasis has always been to *be*, not to *do*.

The Spanish never quite passed through the true European feudal experience, and what they forged out of the Reconquest was neither tribal nor contractual government, but a hieratic despotism. The Church never quite became an independent social order; it became a tool of state. The town bourgeoisie never quite established an independent existence or ethos; they succeeded only as agents of the crown. Thus the Spanish middle classes were bureaucratized in spirit as few middle classes have ever been.

Spain emerged neither as a feudal holdover, as she has been described, nor as a Western nation in the pattern of England or France. Modern Spain came into the world more as a reemergence of an ancient, late-Roman, Mediterranean civilization, with a Roman Church much as its function had been envisioned by Constantine; monarchy as Diocletian had understood it, and a society—hierarchical, ostentatious, corporate, and bureaucratized—like that which Theodosius had ruled.

There were economically wasteful but socially powerful *latifundia*, held by an elite which no longer played an effective role in either culture or government. There was a horde of imperial agents, with an ineradicable taste for petty regulation. There was a Roman economic naivete, confusing unproductive lands and metallic resources with true wealth.

Finally, there was a dying Rome's greatest contribution to her successor states: a religion that had become almost a legal system, a Church that was at the same time a stimulus to higher civilization and an institutional incubus.

Throughout history, men have created mainly out of their own ideals, experience, and consciousness, and all that was Spain came with Cortés to Mexico.

14

THE CONQUISTADORES

They do nothing but command. They are the drones who suck the honey which is made by the poor bees, the Indians. . . . They come out very poor from Spain, carrying only a sword. But in a year they have gotten together more goods than a drove of animals can carry, and they must have the houses of gentlemen.

From the Spanish of Fray Toribio de Benavente (Motolinía).

A handful of Spanish adventurers had displaced or destroyed the former lords of Mexico in the summer of 1521. The shock waves of the destruction of Tenochtitlan spread far beyond Anáhuac. Almost all of Motecuhzoma's empire became subject to Cortés through the subjugation of the Mexica; the tributary tribes were awed by Spanish power. And in the immediately following months, Cortés' captains were able to conquer adjoining lands and peoples that Motecuhzoma had not cowed. A single campaign by Alvarado incorporated the Mixteca and Zapoteca of Oaxaca; the Tarasca of Michoacán submitted without a fight. By 1522 most of central Mexico acknowledged the Spanish king.

The pattern of these later conquests was the passage of a few Spaniards, accompanied by hordes of native allies, through the mountains and valleys. The passage was often brutal. Cortés had deliberately burned alive some Mexica officers who had reputedly killed Spaniards, and Alvarado and others followed such precedents. The effect of seeing their lords and priests burned at the stake for rebellion or recalcitrance usually left the Amerindian commoners thoroughly cowed. The soldiers also widely used the fire, water, and rope tortures (as they faithfully recorded in their reports) to force the natives to deliver up tribute of food or gold.

The Spanish passage, however, was hardly more cruel or destructive than the progress of sixteenth-century armies in Europe in this age. Until the eighteenth century all armies, poorly paid and more poorly disciplined, regularly ravaged occupied country, almost destroying European civilization where they camped. The Spanish treated the Amerindians hardly worse than they treated Italians, Flemings, or French.

The aura of rape that hangs over the conquest, however, ironically stems more from European attitudes in modern Mexican minds than from trauma visited on the Indians. The sedentary peoples lacked such European sensibilities. The Spanish normally were offered a surfeit of nubile maidens wherever they went without demanding; from Cortés' first contact with friendly natives the Spanish march was a long debauch.

The millions of villagers scattered throughout the civilized highlands acquiesced to Spanish rule, in what proved to be one of the most decisive conquests recorded. There was not to be a single serious rebellion against the Spanish within the old Mexica empire for three centuries. There were a few pitiful uprisings, like that of the Tlaxcalteca in the seventeenth century, when this once-proud people realized that the Conquest had destroyed them as much as the Mexica, but these were quickly crushed.

Cortés' grandeur as a conqueror was assured by this utter decisiveness, but his greatness, however, lies not in his cruelties but in the fact that he caused permanent change. He never intended to loot and leave Mexico, as he explained from the first in his *cartas de relación* to his king. He was conquering a kingdom to add to the Spanish empire. He planned no genocide. He did plan culturicide, however, and this is probably why the modern age, with its enormous biases toward self-determination, cannot forgive him.

All the major diffusions of civilization over the globe, and the Spanish Conquest was exactly that, have been in some sense crimes against humanity. In the broadest perspective, it is impossible to apply criminality or morality across ethnic lines. This is part of the human tragedy, and the Spanish Conquest of Mexico was a vast human tragedy. And Cortés himself must in some sense rank beside Alexander, Caesar, or William the Conqueror.

Cortés intended to remake Mexico into an Hispanic kingdom. He operated out of his own instincts and historic background. He planned nothing more and nothing less than what the Romans had done to his own race, and the Spaniards to the Moors and Jews. Some of his concepts were brilliant; some were totally impractical.

He had decided out of the precedents of warfare and Hispanic law that the lands and bodies of the Mexica, as "rebels," were forfeit. There was some expediency in this: he had an army to reward. Many Mexica survivors were branded as slaves taken in war and all the public lands and their serfs seized.

Cortés intended to divide these fields as land grants to veterans according to rank. However, Cortés recognized the clan leaders and intended to permit them certain lands. And he did intend, as he stated, to return the lands of the Mexica-dominated peoples such as the Chalca and the Xochimilca to those tribes.

These tribes, most of which had assisted materially in the destruction of the Mexica overlords, were to be free vassals of the Spanish crown. They were to pay taxes or tribute, but to be ruled by their own chiefs or *caciques*, as the Spanish called them, from a Caribbean term the conquistadores carried into Mexico. The Tlaxcalteca, without whose help the Spanish would have been destroyed, were to be excused from all tribute. In these circumstances, most of the Amerindian population would be better off than the majority of European peasants, and most of the inhabitants of Castile.

Cortés expected to settle his soldiers and future emigrants upon farms and to build towns and forts across the land. He would import Catholic missionaries from the disciplined orders, such as Franciscans and Augustinians. He had noticed, like Bernal Díaz, that the pagan priesthood were devoted, austere men who abstained from wealth and women and were revered by the people. Like many Spaniards, Cortés easily made a clear distinction between his faith and the peculiarly corrupt, prideful, and womanizing secular clergy of Spain; he wanted to loose nothing like those priests on Mexico.

The settled veterans, the rising towns, and the teaching brothers would soon seed a flourishing Hispanic civilization throughout Mexico. The *indios* would be instructed and lured into that civilization. This Roman concept could have worked—except for the fact that sixteenth-century Spaniards for all their Roman heritage were not Romans, and Cortés' followers were early-modern Spaniards, not Roman-peasant legionaries. Spain had only hordes of hungry adventurers, looking for rewards. Cortés should have seen this, because he himself epitomized the true conquistador.

And there was another problem confronting this dream of Hispanicizing Mexico. Spaniard and Nahua lived in separate universes of the spirit and mind, far more unfusable than the worlds of Castilian Christians and Sephardic Jews. The *indios* might be Hispanicized, but they would never become true Spaniards.

Whatever the possibilities, the manner in which the Spanish came into the New World was to prove disastrous for European-Amerindian fusion. Mexico had in fact been discovered by a slave-hunting expedition out of Cuba that lost its way, and the old hands in the Cortesian army carried fatal precedents and attitudes from the Indies. Alvarado had started treating continental, town-living *indios* exactly like the slavefodder of the Indies. A permanent vision of the *indios* as labor to spare all noble Spaniards from such indignity was engrained in Spanish minds. In the absence of gold, *indios* were wealth.

Cortés himself had fueled these visions of reward at the expense of the indigenes. He recruited his army, suborned men from Velásquez and Narváez, and kept them on their feet through disasters and countless sleepless nights with promises of El Dorado. His facile tongue had fired vast dreams; he vowed that common soldiers would ride saddles of gold and that brave captains would become *marqueses* at least. He had motivated incredible heroics by playing on the fact that every Spaniard had come out to the Indies determined to be *señor* where he stood.

In the shock of finding no treasure in Tenochtitlan, Cortés could put off his captains with more promises and visions; he believed these himself. Like Alvarado they rode off to find more kingdoms beyond Anáhuac, or like Montejo, to conquer the vast peninsula of Yucatán that had been left behind. Actually, gold or slaves seems to have motivated most Castilian captains as little as they did Cortés. They dreamed of conquests and power. Old Pedrarias, now past eighty, still schemed at Darien. Pizarro, ex-swineherd, was already rich with plantations in Panama before he sought out Peru. De Soto found his fortune, threw it away, then died in the swamps of Mississippi pursuing new dreams. Whatever drove them, these captains from Castile could rarely retire or settle down. They won a world —but most of them died by fever and arrow, by assassination, in duels, or by execution or in prison and disgrace.

The rank and file of Cortés' army, however, was not put off with more promises. They had no more dared this mysterious empire to plow the soil like peasants than had Cortés himself. The bulk of them were Andalusians, volatile, irreverent, mutinous, and swaggering, with a southern style of speech and an ethos and affected gallantry that, unlike Castilian gravity, were to become the Spanish norms in the New World. Frustrated in Tenochtitlan, they were ready cheerfully to cut their leader's throat. They vociferously backed the royal treasurer Alderete when he demanded the torture of Cuauhtémoc. When Cortés offered them estates, they demanded lordships—*encomiendas* far more magnificent than any in the islands, encompassing villages and towns.

Only a very few of these conquistadores were noblemen. Many of the officers were impecunious hidalgos, with a tenuous claim to gentility like Cortés. The ranks were neither gentle nor bourgeoisie. The small Spanish middle class had no interest in the New World then or later; their ambitions lay in acquiring letters and gaining offices in the bureaucracy. Some of the army were not Spanish but Greeks, Venetians, or Portuguese. Some were criminals. They all had the great Spanish cultural disease: they were not interested in finding farms, trading with the natives, or setting up various businesses. They had sailed to become *señores*. Their genuine valor and enormous endurance and energy was expended to this end and set certain patterns of race relations in conquered Mexico.

All of Cortés' actions after the Conquest must now be seen in the light of his desperation to remain the ruler of his conquered kingdom. He could only hold power by catering to his armed men. The qualities of a Christian knight and the qualities of an early-modern prince were two entirely incompatible things, and now Hernán Cortés began to stain his reputation. He allowed the crippling of Cuauhtémoc by torture when he knew there was no gold in Tenochtitlan. He knew in his heart that he should protect and conciliate the *indios* of Mexico; he had expressed this many times. But he conciliated his army instead. He began to award *repartimiento-encomiendas* which soon went far beyond the Mexica fields and, made his Spaniards lords over the Chalca, Xochimilca, Texcoca, and a dozen other tribes.

He needed the loyalty of his men to survive the power struggles that caught up all conquistadorial politics. He was still involved in a great game with Velásquez. Early on, he had sent two gentlemen, Quiñones and Ávila, with letters of explanation and presents to the king. These couriers characteristically disobeyed orders, stopped in the islands, and thus alerted the furious governor of Cuba. Quiñones got himself killed in a tavern brawl; Ávila at last reached Spain. Cortés dispatched Puertocarrero and another officer with more treasure and further letters to argue his case at court after he took Tenochtitlan.

A violent controversy swirled about the court at Valladolid. Juan Rodríguez de Fonseca, bishop of Burgos and president of the Casa de Contratación, the regulating body for the Indies, and Pánfilo de Narváez, who had lost an eye fighting Cortés in America, represented the claims of Velásquez. They demanded Cortés' recall and arrest. Cortés, however, had secured his own support in the Duque de Béxar, the Conde de Aguilar and other notables who had been fascinated by his deeds, and who protested his unwavering loyalty to the king despite a pinchpenny and backbiting Cuban governor.

Charles of Ghent, Carlos I of Spain (usually known as Charles V, his German Imperial title, outside of Spain) was the Hapsburg grandson of the Catholic kings, barely secure on the Castilian throne. He had forced an unlawful coronation, since his demented mother Juana still lived. Carlos had demanded to be king rather than regent, had arrogantly assumed the unwonted title of Majesty, and increased taxation, while irritating all Castile with his imperial ambitions and his Flemish favorites. A *junta* of Castilian towns revolted and was quelled only when certain democratic tendencies of the rebels alienated the bulk of the upper classes. While Cortés was conquering Mexico, Carlos I was executing hundreds of rebels and extirpating the last liberties of the Castilian towns. Plagued with this revolt and already enmeshed in European schemes, Carlos seems to have consciously waited for the dust to settle in the Indies before he took a hand in the distant quarrel.

Cortés held his own, beating off an attempt by Garay to seize the Pánuco region from Jamaica, and forcing an official sent out by Fonseca, one Tapia, to retire from Coyoacán, despite his possession of legal orders to supercede the conquistador. By 1522 it was obvious that Cortés was in control in Mexico, and the king refused the complaints of the Fonseca-Velásquez faction, confirming all Cortés' actions.

Cortés was appointed governor, captain-general, and chief justice of New Spain—the name he had given Mexico—and empowered to appoint subordinate officers and exile his enemies. But Carlos also dispatched four officers, ostensibly to oversee the treasury, with private instructions to spy on Cortés.

The king often is represented as ungrateful to a man who had presented him with a domain holding more people than all of Spain. But Cortés was a new, nameless adventurer, a proven rebel, with qualities of leadership that any Renaissance prince must have viewed suspiciously. Cortés was perhaps the most completely loyal Spaniard in the Indies, but the king could not know this. The great thrust of the Spanish monarchy was toward total consolidation and centralization of power in the crown, and Spanish kings trusted no one completely. And the drive of the crown was incompatible with Cortés' dream of ruling in New Spain as a loyal but virtually independent prince. Carlos I treated Cortés with consideration now and later, but the king and the men around him had no intention of permitting any Spaniard to gain genuine power in America.

The king understood the chaotic condition of the governance of America. He revived an old plan of Fernando, creating a new *Consejo real de las Indias*, or Council of the Indies, which was actually a considerable bureaucracy. This superceded the Casa de Contratación, which remained a board of trade, in the regulation of the overseas empire.

Carlos also issued an order forbidding the inhabitants of New Spain to be granted in *encomienda*. The *indios* were to be considered free vassals of the crown. The king had two apparent motives. Loaisa, the president of the Council of the Indies, who was a member of Las Casas' Dominican Order, and a number of other influential persons at court had developed powerful reservations concerning the enserfment of the native Americans. They had Las Casas' evidence it was not working economically and was actually destroying the Indians. Furthermore, the crown did not care to establish a new, powerful aristocracy overseas. Mexico seemed to be a populous, potentially powerful country, and a class of *encomenderos* might become, like the now-cowed nobility of Castile, a threat to the throne.

Cortés received this order in 1523 and coolly refused to obey it. His courage was probably based on the fact that his new *encomenderos* were more dangerous to him at the moment than the king. He wrote to the king that the *encomienda* was essential if a handful of Spaniards was to hold New Spain. The country could not be Christianized and without the labor of the natives the conquerors would not be able to maintain themselves. He further recommended that grants be made perpetual or hereditary, because if granted for the usual single lifetime there was a temptation for the beneficiary to work his commended *indios* to death.

Cortés was correct in one thing: without some form of *encomienda* his freebooters would leave. The army would starve unless it lived off local labor. The policy of the crown was to invest nothing in the exploration and conquest of the New World, though the crown claimed a fifth of all profits and proceeds. The crown had no ships and no army prepared to take over an occupation of Mexico; even in Europe Spanish armies lived more from looting than from regular pay. All the arguments against the *encomienda* and the exploitation of the *indios* broke against this fact. The crown was still not prepared to make an investment in America, but the Spanish were even less prepared to relinquish Mexico. Cortés' defiance angered Carlos, but the king really had no choice except to let Cortés' arrangements stand.

Cortés continued to award Amerindians to his followers lavishly, and he took for himself large tracts of land and peoples north of Tenochtitlan, in Cuernavaca, and in the Zapoteca area of Oaxaca. Some historians estimated these territories included as many as two-hundred-and-fifty thousand natives. If so, this made Cortés a vastly greater territorial lord than even the dukes of Castile.

Cortés also granted *encomiendas* under the Spanish system to many native lords. The two surviving daughters of Motecuhzoma, for instance, received large awards of their own people. This secured them a place in Spanish society and made them quite attractive to some members of the conquering race. Both married Spanish noblemen.

Actually, as it was defined by Spanish law the *encomienda* was not a bad system. It was legally hedged with duties and responsibilities for *encomenderos* by regulations lovingly drawn up by jurists and clerics at Sevilla. The masters were to furnish their charges with clothing, housing, and other necessities and instruct them in religion in return for labor or tribute. The commended were not allowed to move away from their land, but all their other basic rights were to be respected as free men. The Spanish law went to great lengths to indicate that this form of serfdom was not slavery in any sense. As written, *encomienda* regulations were actually superior to many feudal contracts still in force in Europe.

Spanish theory was superb, Spanish laws were enlightened, but both theory and laws were virtually unenforceable. They totally failed to take the reality of conditions in America into account. To have expected the Spanish conquistadores to behave much differently than they did was incredibly naive, but it was a naivete continually written into Spanish law. Because the Spanish councils insisted upon legislating morality which could not be enforced there was always a terrible gap between Spanish ideals and Spanish reality.

Queen Isabel's rages had not saved the *indios* of the islands, nor the passionate arguments of Las Casas with which almost all educated Spaniards agreed. The edicts continually issued through Sevilla were mere discharges of conscience.

Cortés was typical in his violent tensions between his ideals as a Christian knight and his actions as a sixteenth-century destroyer. His whole people was torn between contradictions of the flesh and spirit, instinct and intellect, love and the law, the fear of God and the temptations of the Devil. It was instinctive for Cortés and his army to conquer Mexico and set themselves up as lords—but they had to assuage their Christian consciences with interminable rationales to permit or disguise what came naturally. The Spanish spirit insisted on making codes the Spanish flesh could not keep, so they evaded those laws by tortured legalisms. They arrived preaching the love of God for all *indios* but destroyed Indians for Christ's sake; they admitted the humanity of all men while they deliberately dehumanized those different from themselves; they professed peace while they instinctively made war. The Spanish did one thing and said another, but in this they were anything but unique.

This fact has confused Hispanic-American history. There were to be many threads to the Spanish presence in Mexico—social, economic, political, religious. But beginning with Cortés' conquest, there was to be only a single theme: the subordination of one people by another. The Spaniards came to become lords in Mexico, and they would stubbornly maintain themselves as lords, against even law and morality and humanity, until the end. Given this fact, all that the Spaniards did and were to do in Mexico makes it own sense.

Cortés and the king understood this, and if it grieved either of them, it never stayed them.

The few turbulent years that followed the Conquest were crucial. Cortés ruled for three years, and if he could not carry out a true Roman colonization of Mexico, he did enforce a decisive subordination. From Pánuco through the isthmus of Tehuantepec most of the sedentary Amerindians were brought under Spanish rule. Enduring patterns were laid. The *encomienda* system was fastened on central, civilized Mexico. This was not a terrible time for the native peoples; the *encomienda* was the substitution of one form of lordship for another. And Cortés also enforced some regulation of the *encomienda*. He required *encomenderos* to be married, to raise horses and keep arms for the defense of the realm, and he prevented wholesale despoliations. His regulations did have a serious flaw—he failed to set strict limits on what might be required of the Indians. But in Mexico, unlike the islands, a shortage of *indios* seemed inconceivable.

Cortés was keenly aware of the beauty of the site of Tenochtitlan, and also of its strategic and symbolic location. Cortés now dragooned thousands of Mexica into clearing the fallen walls and rotting bones. After a cleansing by fire, the remaining palaces and *teocallis* on the southern isle were torn down. Their stones went to form the foundation for the new city. Sunk into the spongy mud, thousands of these stones and abandoned artifacts were again uncovered in the 1960s when the underground transportation system was built.

The new, Very Noble, Notable, and Most Loyal City of México was laid out in rectangular Spanish fashion. Cortés boasted it would soon rise, more splendid than before. Under the surviving clan leaders, who were indispensable to the conquerors, thousands of native workers were brought in from the surrounding area. They came across the causeways for work each day, bringing corn cakes and beans. Far more men were put to this labor than were needed, but this had been a Mexic tradition in their ancient building projects. The conquered Mexica saw nothing strange in this communal labor, carried on mostly without tools, although their own role was reversed, and they bore it stoically. Some men died in the careless construction, but the Amerindians were used to this, also.

The former ceremonial center at the south end of Tenochtitlan was made the heart of the new Spanish town. The plaza was set out where the great temple complex and the palaces of the speakers had stood. Cortés designed this plaza with a municipal hall and shops, with a church to be erected on the site of the destroyed temple pyramid. This area is now the modern Zócalo of México, and the church, many times rebuilt, is the present cathedral. The present National Palace occupies the site of the vanished palace of Motecuhzoma II. Cortés did not build these structures, but he laid out the locations.

Broad avenues went out from the great plaza in all directions to the lake. The houses of the conquistadores were planned along these streets. Laborers sweated blocks of soft gray lava stone, and the red tezontle the Spaniards especially preferred into position for these great houses, and they brought down thousands of cedar and cypress logs from the mountains for beams. Within a few months the outline of Cortés' capital was taking shape. Dull red palaces and bright, whitewashed walls again threw their reflections into the still lake. The massive houses of the conquerors were erected around open patios, but within they were still dark and dank, because the Europeans feared the night air as much as Amerindians.

While the building was in progress Cortés organized a civic government at Coyoacán. He appointed aldermen to represent the crown; these councilmen then elected their mayor, and the municipality then began to regulate through the proclamations dear to the Hispanic heart, setting the price controls, sanitation standards, regulations and curfews that the Spanish believed they could not live without.

An ordinance assigned the natives to Tlatelolco; they were forbidden to live in México. This was not, of course, enforceable. The indigenes were building México, and besides every conquistador had his retinue of native servants and girls. The rising houses were filled with *indios* and *indias*, house servants, and a swelling band of half-breed children. The great mass of *indios*, however, remained outside this transplanted Hispanic civilization, within their own clans.

This first city of Nueva España set a style for all future Hispanic cities across the country. All slavishly followed Spanish forms, in design, architecture, and government. Within a few years they would rise up in the mountain valleys, from a distance almost indistinguishable from towns in Old Spain. All would be erected by forced native labor, though for centuries no native was to have a real place inside them. With their urban instincts and traditions most of the Spanish in New Spain sought to dwell in cities, which were the Spanish governmental and social units, exercising jurisdiction over the surrounding countryside. All offices in the towns were held by Spaniards, who eagerly competed for such posts. Most *encomenderos*, whose lands and commended Indians might lie far distant in the hinterlands, kept a town house.

Cortés requested all the things from Old Spain needed to make this country into a truly Hispanic kingdom: mules, cattle, horses, sheep, and swine, chickens, rice, sugar cane shoots, fruits, and vines. Above all, the Spanish were impatient for wheat seed and mill machinery to grind flour for bread. The conquistadores were sick to death of living on beans and tortillas, the cakes made from maize. The conquerors, in fact, never were to acquire much taste for indigenous foods or products beyond tobacco. They introduced wines and beef and wheaten bread into New Spain, traditions that would remain in the central highlands among the Europeanized class.

The natives continued to tend their ancient *milpas*, but Cortés with the introduction of work animals and the wooden plow, revolutionized agriculture. Oxen and donkeys soon became indispensable to the *indios*. They would always prefer their native corn; however, those caught up in the *encomienda* had no choice but to cater to their masters' tastes and needs.

They worked wheat fields and watched over herds of Spanish cattle and sheep. Spanish goats and Spanish chickens also entered their lives.

With new Spanish towns and European agriculture, the highlands soon began to take on an Old World look they would never entirely lose.

There were also less fruitful imports into New Spain. The news of the Conquest sent a newer horde of rootless Spaniards pouring into America. Hundreds landed at San Juan de Ulua, usually with only a rusty sword, their pride, and the clothes upon their backs. Cortés' kingdom needed Europeans, because there was now and always would be a great lack of Western skills and knowledge in Mexico. Unfortunately, most of the immigrants were the wrong kind to build the kingdom Cortés visualized. They were the same kind who had gone out before.

The authorities did try to limit emigration to married men with families, people with useful trades or skills, and those who could prove they were free of taint of Jew or Moor. In practice, these regulations were as unworkable as other codes. Only a few Spaniards were free by birth or circumstance to leave Spain and these were adventurers in the main. They had no concept of a New Jerusalem, but they did have a strong urge to find El Dorado. Many who were married conveniently left their wives behind and never sent for them. Craftsmen who were desperately needed in New Spain sailed to put all that behind them. Even purity of blood was no problem; certificates could be bought from an obliging officialdom. The bureaucratic maze that entangled the Casa de Contratación did not so much regulate emigration as tend to slow and restrict it, so that the trickle never averaged more than about one thousand Spaniards per year. This was more than sufficient, since they came not to work but to live off the Amerindians.

The constant arrival of new Spaniards caused problems for the governance of New Spain. Cortés siphoned off many for his explorations, but they could not be prevented from harassing the *indios*, and many gathered, turbulent and volatile, in the capital, jealous of all authority and full of complaints and accusations.

Cortés was also disappointed in the first missionaries sent out from Spain, who were Flemish Franciscans and who were headed by a bastard of the king. The Spanish disliked such Nordics almost as much as Moors or Jews, but it would have been impolitic for Cortés to reject them, so he shunted them off to Texcoco.

He was much pleased by the second contingent, which arrived in 1524 and which was made up of true Spaniards, Martín de Valencia and eleven Franciscan friars, probably some of the most dedicated members of their order. They were to prove the best and most vigorous representatives of European culture in the New World.

Cortés made a great show of the coming of the friars. He met them, trudging barefoot in the apostolic fashion over the mountains from Veracruz, with his court and a great assemblage of Indians. He knelt at Valencia's feet and kissed the coarse hem of the priest's habit. This may have astounded the gentle Franciscans; the effect on the native notables was even more profound.

The fathers, who knew nothing of the country, its people, or languages, immediately began building convents at México and Huexotzingo.

These years were the summit of Cortés' career.

For now the stresses of holding power were changing him. Weariness, insecurity, and perhaps disease had begun to warp his judgment and cause acts that tarnished his brilliance. All that really damaged Cortés' image came after the Conquest and stemmed from his stubborn determination to hold on to power. He was continually fearful that other conquistador captains would encroach on his domain, and because of the conquistadorial nature and the undefined boundaries of the fiefdoms in the New World, his fears were not unfounded. But after having coolly held off Garay of Jamaica with arms, bluff, and diplomacy, Cortés finally proceeded in 1524 to throw everything away.

The wily Pedrarias was expanding his conquests northward from Panama. Cortés held that all Middle America was his territory, and to thwart Pedrarias, he sent Pedro de Alvarado down the Pacific coast into Guatemala, and Cristóbal de Olid by sea to seize the country of Las Hibueras, now Honduras.

The unimaginative but brutally efficient Alvarado faithfully annexed the Guatemalan highlands to New Spain. Olid, however, fell prey to fatal conquistadorial disease: in the Honduran forests he decided to erect his own kingdom. The news threw Cortés into a rage. Uncharacteristically, the leader who had survived countless crises with an icy temper now gathered a force of Spaniards and Indians and rushed off to the south, through country no European had explored.

Had Cortés stopped to think, he would have left the disciplining of Olid to his lieutenants, or at least have gone by sea. And in leaving he made only makeshift provisions for government in his absence, by appointing a committee of three men. Of course, Cortés had no idea of the horrendous terrain that lay between Honduras and Anáhuac, the mountains, jungles, rain forests, and vast swamps, nor any notion of the months it would take to cross the barriers. He expected to be absent briefly, but he took along Malintzin, and also Cuauhtémoc and the former lord of Tlacopán, because he feared to leave such potentially dangerous native leaders behind in Mexico.

He was soon lost in the swamps and forests south of Tehuantepec, country where even his native guides had never trod. Men sickened and horses starved. Cortés himself grew ill, and he was never again to regain his former energy. And here he committed the act for which modern Mexicans will not forgive him.

Under attack by hostile savages. Cortés was informed by one of the Mexica who attended Cuauhtémoc that the captive lordlings had hatched a plot against his life. Cuauhtémoc and his kinsmen of Tlacopán were to attack the Spaniards, kill them, and then lead the local Indians back for a liberation of Mexico. Fanciful as this undoubtedly was, a feverish Cortés immediately seized Cuauhtémoc and the other lord, and though the last speaker protested his innocence calmly, had them hanged from a ceiba tree. The Falling Eagle behaved with courage and dignity to the last.

Cuauhtémoc was killed from expediency; he was a dangerous captive for Cortés in his present perilous circumstance. But this political murder was carried out hastily under conditions that made even the brutal Spanish men-at-arms mutter, and Bernal Díaz was to write uneasily years later that Cortés had erred.

The two princes were buried in the rain forest. Cuauhtémoc was to become a symbolic hero to most Mexicans, the embodiment both of Indian virtues and the Indian tragedy, and above all, a symbol of the oppression of the native race. Modern claims of the discovery of his bones sparked much political and ideological—but little scientific—controversy among twentieth-century Mexicans, proving primarily that Cuauhtémoc had become a martyr, and the man who killed him an ogre, in the modern Mexican mind.

The conquistador arrived in Honduras only to find that Olid's revolt had been put down by loyal officers and Olid himself beheaded. The weary and wasted Cortés party now took eighteen months to march back to Aná-huac.

This journey accomplished nothing for Spanish arms or exploration. Cortés only accomplished one thing: he disposed of Malintzin. Passing through Malintzin's native country, he endowed her with a large estate and married her off to Juan Xaramillo, a Spaniard perhaps attracted by the splendid dowry. Like Cuauhtémoc, Malintzin had served her usefulness; her fate was presumably happier.

A great crowd assembled to welcome Cortés' miraculous return; he had been believed dead. But now he learned of new disasters in his absence.

The deputies he had left in charge had immobilized each other, while carrying a virtual civil war with the *encomenderos*. New Spain devolved into anarchy, while the *indios*, without protection, had been exploited mercilessly. Cortés' legion of enemies had sprung up, firing off accusations and complaints about him to the council and crown. Cortés was charged, in his absence, with eight crimes ranging from robbing the king's treasury to the murder of his wife.

The charges were probably totally specious. Las Casas, no friend of

Cortés, refused to credit any of them. Cortés was scrupulous in his accounts, and, while his wife Catalina Xuárez died suspiciously soon after arriving unbidden from Cuba, the rumor that he strangled her arose only after he left the city.

Cortés was guilty of poor judgment, and this gave the king an excuse to remove him; he dispatched Don Luis Ponce de León, a young courtier, to strip Cortés of his governorship while he investigated the charges against the conquistador.

Cortés was not, however, in any sense disgraced. He was allowed to retain the captaincy-general of the military in New Spain. The king sent him a letter in the royal hand assuring Cortés of his regard pending his justification.

Cortés retired to his palatial residence surrounded by a bitter crowd of old comrades-in-arms and friends. In 1526, Ponce de León died before he could accomplish anything, and a successor also followed him quickly to the grave. The third special commissioner selected by the council to govern New Spain was himself part of the original problem; Estrada, the royal treasurer was one of the officers Cortés had left in command at México. Estrada immediately proved himself so incompetent and so biased against Cortés that he was removed. In 1527, the Council of the Indies, with the king's approval, appointed an *Audiencia Real* or special royal commission to rule. This body consisted of a *presidente* and two judge-commissioners or *oidores*, who collectively exercised full executive and judicial powers.

Cortés himself was now commanded to appear at royal court. This was not to try him, since his future trial was to be in the New World before the *audiencia*, but a judicious move to get him out of New Spain. He sailed in 1528, taking along an entourage of old captains like Tapia and Sandoval, many *indios*, and much treasure. His arrival in Spain and his passage to the court at Toledo was a triumph. Mobs cheered him, crowding the roads to see the strange *indios*, and great noblemen feted him along the route.

Carlos received Cortés with exquisite courtesy. He believed none of the charges, and he created Cortés Marqués del Valle de Oaxaca. A marquisate was still a great title in the early sixteenth century, and this was to be the only ennoblement of a conquistador, and the only granting of a patent in New Spain for almost a century. Cortés' land grant was also confirmed, binding forever his score of Indian towns and thousands of native servants. The king further approved Cortés' marriage to Doña Juana Zúñiga, a great lady related to the houses of Béxar and Aguilar. There were other honors —but Carlos would not grant Cortés the one thing the great conqueror really wanted, a second chance to govern Mexico. The Crown was wary of charismatic captains.

Meanwhile, the first *audiencia* continued the existing chaos in New Spain. The appointments of bureaucrats and clerics on the council of the

Indies had been naive. The man made president of the *audiencia* was Nuño Beltrán de Guzmán, former governor of Pánuco. Nuño had quickly made a reputation foul even among the worst conquistadores, by selling thousands of Huasteca tribesmen as slaves to Caribbean planters. He was a man without a single redeeming virtue, but his career tells something about the Spanish ethos on the raw American frontier. Nuño de Guzmán was energetic and powerful, with the peculiar morality of a leader who even in outlawry kept scrupulous accounts with the crown, sending the royal treasury a peso for each slave sold—and his sword did extend the Spanish jurisdiction in Mexico. Nuño had supreme contempt for most men, *indios* and Spanish alike, hanging both for specious crimes; he once had a man nailed by the tongue to a post, for insolence. His two *oidores*, Delgadillo and Matienzo, lacked Nuño's bestiality but shared his greed.

For two years these three milked New Spain. Nuño sold *encomiendas* to his cronies of the worst sort and allowed them to ravage the enserfed *indios* unmercifully. Natives were declared in rebellion so that they could be made chattel slaves; it was the frightful experience of the islands repeated in Mexico. Nuño also persecuted any real or suspected friends of Cortés. He recalled Alvarado from Guatemala and threw him into prison.

Only one Spaniard in New Spain dared cross the powerful president. Juan de Zumárraga, a Franciscan friar who was now the first bishop of the Diocese of México, was a stubborn Basque, intransigent in his religion but also fearless in his protection of his Amerindian charges. He denounced the *audiencia* from the episcopal pulpit and wrote letters to Spain. Nuño de Guzmán's spies intercepted most of these letters, while his bullies very nearly assassinated Zumárraga on one occasion. Finally, a smuggled letter did reach the council, which could not doubt the bishop's honesty. The first *audiencia* was recalled in 1530.

The council and the crown were now disenchanted with setting up one conquistador to rule the others. The council recommended to the king that a viceroy be appointed over New Spain. The great problem was authority and legitimacy, and the finding of a governor who would be responsive to the government in Spain. The *letrados* believed that a *virrey*, a viceroy, would embody some of the mystique that surrounded the Spanish crown and bring order to New Spain, which was too far away to be governed directly by the royal bureaucracy. The new viceroy should be a grand señor, a nobleman who stood so far above the assorted riffraff in the Indies that he could never be enmeshed in their endless quarrels. The king agreed.

But Carlos was off to Flanders, caught up in his own endless European wars. He left the selection of the right man to the queen-empress and the council. Few noblemen wanted any part of the dangerous American shore;

finally, a royal chamberlain, Don Antonio de Mendoza, Conde de Tendilla, accepted but needed time to settle his affairs.

Mendoza was an excellent choice. He was descended from perhaps the most illustrious ducal house of Castile, an aristocrat but a thorough and trusted royalist. While he made ready to go, the council appointed a second *audiencia* to rule New Spain.

The new *audiencia* was selected with great care. The president was Don Sebastián Ramírez de Fuenleal, bishop of Santo Domingo in the Indies; the *oidores* were the *licenciados* or licensed lawyers Vasco de Quiroga, Alonso Maldonado, Francisco Cainos, and Juan de Salmerón, known to be competent and humane.

When they arrived at México with the authority to depose and arrest Nuño de Guzmán, the former president gathered an army of partners in crime and *indios* and fled into Michoacán, claiming his mission was to pacify the northwest country for the church and crown. The Tarasca had paid homage to the Spanish king and made no warlike moves against Nuño de Guzmán. He rewarded them by seizing and ravaging Tzintzuntzan and torturing the lord of the Tarasca to make him reveal his treasures. The tribute arrived too slowly, and the lord was burned alive. Nuño ravaged the whole region, killing native chieftains indiscriminately. When the Tarasca fled to the mountains, he moved on, into what is now Jalisco and Sinaloa, raiding into Nayarit. He was able to carry on for six years before he was finally caught up with on the east coast and brought to justice. He was disgraced, but his services were considered too important to the crown for him to be punished severely. He did draw the Spanish upward into the west, which was called New Galicia, and his one lasting act was to found a settlement called Guadalajara, which was some years later moved to the site of the present city.

Ramírez de Fuenleal and his lawyers made great efforts to repair the damage. The *audiencia* revoked the *encomiendas* granted by Nuño de Guzmán, and it also outlawed the branding and enslavement of natives supposedly taken in war. This ended the taking of Mexicans as slaves for the most part throughout central New Spain. Enslavement of Africans, however, was still legal and even encouraged by the Church, and some blacks were now arriving in Mexico.

The *audiencia* also organized the government of the millions of *indios* who were still outside private *encomiendas*. These were considered free vassals of the crown; they were to continue owning their communal fields and their villages were to be ruled by the *caciques*, most of whom were now officially designated *regidores*. The Spanish, however, failed to see the elective nature of much of this leadership, and they made the office of *regidor* hereditary, as in Spain. They appointed salaried Spanish officers, who reported to the *audiencia*, to supervise the village *regidores*. This system was called the *corregimiento*; the duties of the salaried officer or corregidor were to collect the assigned tithes and taxes, keep order with constables or *alguaciles*, dispense justice, and assist in the conversion of the Indians.

The *corregimiento* was in reality nothing but a royal *encomienda*, operated by crown officers rather than private *encomenderos*. The concept stemmed from the same blend of despotism and feudalism and paternalism that characterized all Spanish institutions. The *audiencia* believed the *corregimiento* would prove far superior to the *encomienda* because it was thought that crown officers would afford better justice and fairer regulation than proprietors who profited from native labor. The system, obviously, fell back on the hope and trust in competent and incorruptible officials at all levels of the hierarchy, an optimistic notion.

But under the second *audiencia*, all systems seemed to work reasonably well. There was peace. Towns rose, at Puebla and other places. Friar-missionaries began to arrive in effective force. The conquistadorial era had ended in the heavily-populated, long-settled fertile regions of central Mexico, though it would continue for many years on both the northern and southern frontiers.

Hernán Cortés did not fit into the new scheme. He returned to New Spain in 1530 with his mother and his new bride. The charges against him were neither dropped nor brought to trial, probably judicious royal policy on both accounts. At Cuernavaca Cortés erected a great house with walls and battlements. He lived here in princely splendor, captain-general and first gentleman of the country, although he had no role in government. He quarreled continually with the *audiencia*, whose members were suspicious of his ambitions; Cortés, never content with his sugar mills and score of Mexican towns, still dreamed of great projects in the west.

Cortés organized expeditions to explore the Pacific coast at his private expense. Much of this activity proved of lasting value. He built shipyards at and founded the ports of Zacatula and Acapulco, and sailors in his service mapped the coast between the Isthmus of Tehuantepec and the sea which still bears his name. Cortés became fascinated with California, the bleak, beautiful peninsula named from a chivalric romance, but his effort to plant a colony in Lower California failed. Cortés was an incurable romantic; he still dreamed of finding fresh kingdoms. The dreams were no more grandiose than before, but now there were no more kingdoms within his reach.

After ten years, refused the command of an expedition that fell to Coronado, Cortés returned to Spain. Here he offered various services to the king, fighting Moors in Africa, always hoping to rewin the governorship of Mexico. He died in 1547 in Spain. His bones were carried back to Mexico at his request and buried very near the spot where he and Motecuhzoma first met.

A son by Juana Zúñiga de Cortés succeeded to his titles and estates. The line died out in the fourth generation. Some of the income from the vast Oaxacan properties went to endow a hospital founded by Cortés at México; the rest passed by inheritance to the Italian house of Monteleone, which held and enjoyed this in absentia until the Mexican Revolution.

No public statues have been raised to Cortés in Mexico. Probably, none ever will be. Modern Mexicans side emotionally with the Amerindians in the Conquest; the Republic has made a symbolic hero out of the hapless Cuauhtémoc. Modern biases, however, cannot set aside historic fact. Cortés conquered Mexico and left it forever changed; he was a founding father. Even the Spanish-speaking, blended race that now professes to despise him is unthinkable without Cortés.

15

NEW SPAIN

In the midst of all the fiery and unregulated spirit of a colony like Mexico, he sustained the dignity of his office unimpaired . . . he was successful upon all occasions except in the enforcement of the complete emancipation of the Indians. . . . History must at least do him the justice to record the fact that his administration was tempered with mercy.

Brantz Mayer, on the Viceroy de Mendoza, 1850.

Don Antonio de Mendoza, Conde de Tendilla, first viceroy of New Spain, debarked at San Juan de Ulua in 1535, the year the Spanish empire in Mexico properly begins. The broad patterns of society and subordination had already been set in the *encomienda* and the *corregimiento*, which now applied to all the sedentary Amerindians of the old Mexica empire. The Spanish domain was not yet made; exploration and warfare continued in the north and in Yucatán. But the great fertile regions of Mexico had been taken. What remained was to bring together the chaotic satrapies of the conquistadores under the Spanish crown.

The viceregal system was designed to keep order in the Mexican wilderness by protecting the native mice and also belling the Spanish cats, but above all it was designed to hold an empire for Spain.

Mendoza came as Viceroy, and the personal representative of the Crown, as president of the *audiencia*, which was expanded and retained to serve as a viceregal council and highest court, and as head of government and chief justice of the realm. As captain-general, he exercised all military powers. As vice-patron of the Church, he controlled religious patronage, with the power to appoint and discipline the clergy. As superintendent of the treasury, he held full power of the purse. He had power in every field; even his moral influence in these circumstances was apt to be profound.

The viceroy was not, however, sovereign in any sense. He could not make law—there was no legislative power in the Indies—and his proclamations always reflected decisions made in Spain. While the viceroy's office was to be supreme, or nearly supreme in the New World, it was to be kept totally subservient to the crown of Spain.

The viceroy, appointed at the king's pleasure, could be removed at any time; later, his term was limited to a very short period. His *audiencia* which took over on his removal or death, was appointed independently out of Spain, and it could go to the crown over the viceroy's head. The viceroy was subject to the laws and orders of the Council of the Indies, of which the king was actually president. Finally, he was subject to two potentially humiliating devices: the *visita* and the *residencia*. *Visitadores* or special inspectors armed with warrants could be sent out by the king; they could supercede the viceroy while he could not interfere with them. The *residencia* was a full scale investigation of the acts, finances, and failures of a viceregal administration.

The system was hastened by the demonstrated failure of the conquistadores to regulate themselves; however, it derived directly from the centralizing despotic tendency of the Hispanic world. The Spanish no longer had any genuine form of local government; if city councils were permitted to elect mayors, the individual councilmen were all appointed by the crown. The Spanish instinct was more for regulation than law; therefore their government had emerged almost entirely as a government of men instead of laws. Its pervasive and persistent rationale was that of benevolent despotism and enlightened directives articulated through a hierarchy. If the despotism were not benevolent, however, there was no remedy short of violent resistance or revolution.

In the creation of the viceregal office New Spain was not treated more cavalierly than Castile. In fact, in Mendoza's day the Holy Inquisition did not cross the Atlantic, and neither colonials nor *indios* were forced to pay anything like the crushing burdens already fastened on the merchants and peasants of Spain. There were certain privileges in the older kingdoms granted by former kings. The crown had no intention of granting any new ones in the New World; however, certain rights that applied to privileged corporations, the clergy, the military, the engineers, entered with the professions themselves. The Spanish society was almost paralyzed in time by the exemptions and privileges of privileged corporations—but the total power of the crown made such institutions necessary: some filter, something, had to stand between individuals and the arbitrary power of government. Without privileged corporations, a theoretically all-powerful monarchy might have been able to tear up Spanish society from the roots.

The creation of viceregal government in Spanish territories made differences between Spanish and British America that went beyond even the marked differences between the two peoples. Spain stopped all colonial experimentation in government. The English, who had great difficulties developing any sort of genuine imperialism, and whose monarchy was beset with peculiar problems in the seventeenth century, allowed their settlers in North America great latitude in the first century of colonization. These colonists actually developed something new in self-government, though it sprang from English county traditions. Whether Spanish America could have created something new is moot; it had no opportunity.

Consolidation of the Spanish empire came at a crucial period, when the Spanish kingdoms were the greatest power in Europe. Spain had superb confidence and also a necessary sense of self-righteousness. She threw up highminded, confident men. The inherent racism and intolerances had not yet festered, under pressures, into gangrene. Cruel as it was, the Spanish Inquisition was still a creative tool; the inquisitors were not consciously destroying so much as remaking.

The Virrey de Mendoza began his triumphal march to the highland capital from the pestilential through-port of Veracruz. The Spanish were as thoroughly ceremonial as the Amerindians, and the month-long progress of the viceroy was magnificent. At Segura de la Frontera, the outpost founded by Cortés, Mendoza was honored with pennants and drums. At Puebla de los Angeles, a new town, the *regidores* vied with each other in lavish courtesies. The viceroy was announced with fiestas or public celebrations, bells, and guns.

The old nobility of Cholula and Huexotzingo reverenced Mendoza as they had once bowed to Motecuhzoma. These ancient cities were not much changed, because in these years the conquistadores had not yet impinged heavily upon them, though the Franciscans were in them building churches.

Outside the towns the countryside was changing rapidly. Wheat and orchards sprang up beside the ubiquitous Indian corn, and there were native herdsmen guarding flocks of sheep.

At the causeways that still led out to the Very Noble, Notable, and Most Loyal City of México, the viceroy was welcomed in a blaze of red and purple cloaks and polished armor, as the *audiencia* surrendered its powers and all the rich and important personages of the Diocese and *ayuntamiento* bowed to the Viceregal baton. There were banners and trumpets and the bright feathers and green jades of assembled Mexic lords. Notaries read the king's proclamation, and Don Antonio de Mendoza entered into his kingdom.

This was the beginning of the greatest and probably the happiest era in the life of Spanish Mexico.

Mendoza was excellently equipped to be a viceroy. He was a Renaissance humanist and statesman and by the standards of his times remarkably humane. He was deeply interested in the rudimentary sciences, the arts, and education; he brought a printing press to Mexico. Beyond that, he was a rarity among Spanish noblemen: cool rather than passionate, hardworking but not driven, cautious but firm when he had made up his mind. He did not come as an aristocrat, but as the best of bureaucrats.

These qualities, and his circumstances, paved the way for a splendid reign. His instructions from the king were liberal. He was to protect his Amerindian subjects, see to the state of public worship, discipline the clergy where required. He was authorized to establish a mint to advance the prosperity of the realm. He was to be generous with grants and concessions, both to natives and conquistadores.

In the 1530s Spanish attitudes toward America were more generous than they were to remain. The crown still lived handsomely off its Flemish and Castilian revenues; Castile was prosperous and the disastrous revolt of the Netherlands lay in the future. Europe was bearing the burden of Carlos' ambitions and wars. America had not proved to be a treasure-house, and Spanish authorities looked on the New World more as a region to be developed than to be looted, whatever the dreams of the conquistadores. The crown got its revenues from *encomienda* taxes and *corregimiento* tribute. Neither taxes nor tribute were excessive by any standard.

In this decade both institutions seemed to be working well. There were two reasons for the apparent, and probably very real success. The first was that even with the exorbitant demands of some *encomenderos* and the massive building programs in the new Spanish towns, the very numbers of the conquered peoples made the burdens of supporting a few thousand Europeans negligible. The ratio of Spaniards to Amerindians could not have been more than one to five thousand in New Spain; the houses of the conquistadores, Cortés' fortress-palace at Cuernavaca, and the great church-convents going up put no strain on the indigenous economy. The demands of the Mexica, probably, had been more onerous, certainly in waste and blood. Previously, at least a third of the daily hours of the common people had been devoted to various religious ceremonies, and Meso-American agriculture, without plows or draft animals, was minimally productive. The Spanish introduction of the steel axe alone worked a technological revolution; in 1535 Amerindian Mexico was probably more productive than it had ever been. If masses of Indians were being dragooned for Spanish projects, these were no more expensive in terms of time and labor than the former pyramids.

The second reason the system was working was that the second *audiencia* followed the rationale that the native population was to be assisted toward full citizenship. The casual torture, killing, and enslavement of sedentary Amerindians was halted. The missionary program was in full swing, but the paternalism of the Franciscan padres was not yet deadly, for these priests saw themselves in a truly parental role, and one that had a finite goal. There is considerable evidence that the conquered population worked cheerfully in the 1530s. Mendoza himself was always ready to hear complaints of the indigenes; he corrected abuses, and he had a great reputation for fairness with the native population.

The viceroy also was extremely successful in handling the previously turbulent Spanish settlers. The viceregal throne had its desired effect by awing the conquistadores, and also, these men appeared pleased and flattered even at the condescension of a Mendoza. And there was as yet no sense of separation between Spaniards and colonials; all adult Spaniards in the New World were still *peninsulares*, that is, they had all been born in Spain.

And in this period the Spanish conquerors were free to indulge themselves in almost any vice or pleasure so long as they did not infringe upon the prerogatives of the crown. Mendoza was not only good-humored toward colonial extravagances; he catered to them. The viceregal court was surrounded by pomp and ceremony; the viceroy sponsored fetes and balls and supped in many of the rude palaces of the ruder conquistadores.

The lives of the small Spanish master class quickly devolved into a round of hunts, feasts, bullfights, and in this century, the immensely popular tournaments or jousts. These were then the sports of the high European aristocracy and kings. The creation of this quite wealthy leisure class in New Spain soon threw a patina of cultivation over colonial society. The transplanted Spaniards in the city of México were not ungenteel, and in outward appearances México soon compared favorably with almost any capital in the world. But this was, and would remain, a colonial society; it was an appendage that drew its sap and sustenance from Old Spain.

Mexican-Spanish society was different in several vital ways from that of Spain or Europe generally. Besides obvious marked ethnic differences between the ruling Spaniards and the indigenous Amerindians, there was no infrastructure between the small class of Spaniards and the Indians. Above all, New Spain lacked two groups that formed the backbone of European society: the gentry, and an independent bourgeoisie, whose professionals, artists, and merchants created most of the forms and ethos of Western civilization.

The conquistadores, for all their aristocratic pleasures and airs, vast landholdings, exacted tribute and forced service, did not rule. The *encomendero* class had no role in the governing of New Spain, and thus could not emerge as an aristocracy. The civic posts they held were prestigious and even held out opportunities for graft, but they were not policy-making. The *encomenderos* therefore could not emerge as a leadership class like the landed squires, merchants, and lawyers of early British America because they held no magistracies and there were no local legislatures. The class, in fact, had no real public role at all. Their theoretical functions were to provide military service by holding down the *indios* and to impart Hispanic culture to the native population; in effect, they immediately left such functions to the viceroy and the friars. Thus they formed merely a privileged social elite, but without even the traditions of the European aristocracy. They and their descendents gave the capital of New Spain polish and social glitter, and little else.

There seemed to be immediate, enormous progress toward civilization in the Spanish New World primarily because of the creation of this tiny, immensely wealthy leisure class. Mexico soon had universities, palaces, printing presses, and fancy dress balls. All this was enormously more impressive than the appearance of the rude, turbulent, and inherently equalitarian North American frontier with its endless lands and shortages of labor. The glittering Spanish capitals of Lima and México, however, were very exotic growths. They were mere reflections of Europe cast over the New World. Uncreative, they produced nothing new; like the great houses of the *encomenderos*, which except in size and massiveness never approached the grandeur and refinement of the great houses and palaces of Europe, then or later, the reflection of glory was rather pale compared to the source. The imported Hispanic civilization in the Spanish provincial capitals failed to take native root. Its members would still be looking back to the Old World for their sap and sustenance after four hundred years.

This does not mean, however, that there was no seeding of a vital *Hispanidad*; it simply was not the work of the conquistadores. The work of the sword was followed immediately by the labors of the friars, in a direct continuation of the dreams of Cortés. The missionary effort in Spanish America was the one thing that kept the lordship of Spain from becoming just another ephemeral imperial venture. Spain's free hand in the New World gave governors, bishops, and missionaries a chance to change America forever. This era coincided with the greatest flowering of Hispanic civilization, the time of Spanish hope and power and glory from the reigns of the Catholic kings to the abdication of Charles of Ghent.

The priests and teaching brothers planted two roots of culture, language and religion, imperishably in the native populations. Thus they changed the very environment forever in the New World. The efforts of the mission system *were* a failure and must be described as a failure—but *only* in the sense of the system's self-imposed goals of making fully Europeanized, fully equal subjects of the Amerindians. This did not happen for a host of reasons, some historic and some human, but the work of the missionaries was to prove more effective in the long run than the work of soldiers, merchants, or conquistadores.

The utter collapse of the Amerindian civilizations of America in the face of Spanish challenge increasingly fascinates modern historians, because it was a phenomenon experienced nowhere else during the four-hundred-year European mastery of the outer world.

The single greatest reason was probably the stagnation (though a few scholars deny that Mexic culture was static when Cortés arrived) and the inherent brittleness of the indigenous civilizations. To destroy nations, the Spanish conquistadores had only to destroy tiny lordly-priestly elites.

In Mexico, not only the Mexica but the lords and priests of all the civilized communities were immediately paralyzed by European technology and power. The paralysis was followed by deep demoralization. When the Spanish came, the sun continued to rise in the east and the corn grew without the services of the priests and without the replenishment of human blood; the white men, mocking all idols and ceremonies, carried everything before their shields, guns, and spears. Killing alone would not have destroyed the Mexic priesthood; Mexicans had been killing themselves for thousands of years. The Europeans cracked their whole universe, and unable to cope with Spanish material power, the native ruling classes never began to cope with Spanish ideas.

The priests were the carriers and preservers of all Amerindian knowledge, and this died with them among the demolished temples and toppled idols. Amerindian *civilization*, with its rituals, techniques, traditions, writings, and world views, vanished utterly. But very large elements of Amerindian *precivilized culture* survived. The communal village societies, primitive agriculture, and indigenous customs and foods all survived vestigially in remote areas and even within the shadow of the Very Noble City of México. These were things that had remained outside of or untouched by the rise of indigenous civilization, and much of this primitive culture remained beyond the reach of Hispanicization. The Amerindian tribal village was already an anachronism in Motecuhzoma's empire; only the fascination of so many anthropologists and the emotionalism of modern Mexicans toward their past has obscured the fact that most precivilized indigenous survivals have actually handicapped the advance of civilization in modern Mexico. They have had no other effect, in any case.

If Amerindian blood and some vestiges of Amerindian cultures were to reassert themselves, Amerindian civilization was dead a generation after the Franciscans came. If Mexico remained an Amerindian nation, as so many modern observers have claimed, it is necessary to define what is meant, and to recall that blood has never been a determinant of human civilization. Benito Juárez was not in any real sense an Indian, except as Indians came to be defined in the Mexican caste systems and in the Mexican mind.

The swords of the conquistadores and the intolerances of their chaplains created a spiritual vacuum in Mexico, filled quickly, it seems, by arriving missionary friars who took the former ruling elite's places. The *encomenderos*—who preferred to live in Spanish towns—were merely a brutal set of warlords becoming enervated by ease and wealth. Catholic priests, instead, in a real sense came to rule and direct the lives of the Amerindians, because the *encomenderos* gladly left both the conversion and the Hispanicization of the natives to the friars.

From the rise of the first Magicians, Meso-American society had prepared its peoples for the friars' role. The failure of the ancient magic made a race as inherently religious as the Amerindians desperately hungry for replacements. The Meso-Americans had never developed a rational world view that could give meaning to their lives without religion and ritual. More than a hundred centuries had conditioned the sedentary Amerindians to accept the domination of a priestly elite. Therefore, a few score missionaries, usually operating alone amidst millions of Indians, were able to remake the cultural map of Mexico.

Their accomplishments may be questioned on many grounds; that they made Amerindian Mexico more "Catholic" than even Old Spain cannot be. Surely, idols remained behind some Roman altars, but such superstitions survived the higher religions everywhere, even in Europe itself. Roman Catholic Christianity, with its spectacular rituals and sacrificial theology fitted splendidly into the native traditions. The satisfyingly bloody and agonizing sacrifice of one Man, strongly emphasized in Spanish consciousness, was immediately recognizable and esthetically appealing to peoples accustomed to an endless procession of mangled bodies and racks of drying skulls in the appeasement of god-forces. The natives could appreciate the Mass and the symbolism of Christian sacrifice, which was as much based on the shedding of blood as their old religion. They probably could not grasp the concept of a triune God or fully comprehend the Judaeo-Christian ethic, but the conquerors hardly understood the finer points of these themselves. Spanish Catholicism, like the native religions, placed its great emphasis upon ceremony and observance, not internal intellectuality. And if the God in Three was not quite comprehensible, the ancient Mediterranean religion had thrown up a full assortment of lesser deities in its saints to replace all the minor, local gods of the Mexic pantheon.

Indigenous needs and the qualities of Hispanic Catholicism do not quite explain the fantastic progress of the new faith in Mexico. A great deal was due to the quality of the missionaries. The Spanish clerical orders had been recently disciplined and purified by Queen Isabel and were at the height of their organization and élan. The friars of the regular orders, Franciscans, Augustinians, and Dominicans, were anything but refugees from the world —they were active, intelligent, dedicated men who expected to perform active roles in the world. Friars became bishops in these days, like Zumárraga; like Loaisa they served as presidents of royal councils. They went barefoot among the people; they taught at the greatest universities. The orders perhaps represented the finest products of the Church in this century. The priests and brothers who volunteered to take the dangerous passage to the New World in the service of their God were neither a cloistered band nor the still-ignorant, medieval-minded parish clergy of hinterland Spain. The friars of the century included men who had been soldiers, lawyers, farmers, and bureaucrats. The orders were meritocracies in which noblemen, the middle classes, and peasants' sons all found excellent careers. They were bound to discipline and austerity but at the same time forced out into the world and into vast affairs. In a society and an era suffused with great faith, they were the best among the best. Their coarse robes and simple habits, their keen knowledge of the true world, their erudition, and above all, their demonstrated humanity and burning convictions could not help but make immense impressions upon the Amerindian mind. The friars themselves, in their humaneness and humanism must have made a more profound impression than their theological arguments.

The orders in this age accepted and believed in the theory that the *indios* were being prepared for citizenship. The native disciples believed this, too; otherwise, so many Amerindians would hardly have repudiated their heritage. Few indigenes seem to have clung stubbornly to familiar ideas and old institutions; the ancient conservatism of the Amerindian world cracked completely. The friars had not come to destroy but to build, with tools and techniques and education as well as sermons; they directed the erection of hospitals and schools and laid out model farms along with church and convent walls. And if they were intransigent against the old religions, they immediately defended the natives from abuses by their fellow Spaniards. Some, like Las Casas, were old hands at this internal warfare from the Indies. All of them were soon involved in it.

The missionaries approached the natives with an immense charity. They seem to have been free of real racism in these decades. They did abominate the native cults and saw little or nothing to admire in the indigenous civilization, which may reveal as much about it as about Renaissance Catholicism, because the Spanish friars never considered any course but eradication. The efforts of the friars went to save souls and bodies, not native arts and manuscripts.

Most of the destruction of the indigenous art and artifacts was carried out by native converts. In countless cases, zealots closed their minds to their former lives and showed their new faith by energetically destroying temples and altars. The destruction of the Amerindian religion and civilization was directed by the Spanish but carried out by willing native hands, which made the destruction singularly effective.

The missionaries were particularly charitable toward the *indios* because they were seen as uninstructed children, but not toward *indios* who were exposed to truth, professed it, and then in some way recanted. The first bishop of México burned a lord of Texcoco for secretly fostering the old worship. Invincible ignorance was tolerable—free choice, despite Catholic rationales and teachings, was not.

Significantly, the friars went among the *indios* and tried, as one friar wrote, to overcome the Devil by studying the ways of his deceived disciples. Most learned Nahuatl and other local dialects and also taught Spanish. Many priests tried to wrap up Christianity in native symbolism. The indigenes were devoted to the dance, and most friars soon decided that a ceremony once done in honor of Tláloc did not dishonor the Christian God. They also taught bibilical stories by means of plays put on in the native fashion, in which the native actors freely substituted their own life styles for Hebraic practices. Honorifics that were once for Quetzalcóatl were applied to Christ and quite a few *indios* probably confused the two.

These practices, combined with the life styles and humble attitudes of the friars, did vastly more to convert the *indios* than the tactics taken by certain too-intellectual priests, who tried unsuccessfully to prevail with scholastic debates and arguments over even a demoralized native priesthood and aristocracy. Some of the first missionaries held meetings and preached sermons, but significantly, Peter of Ghent squatted in the dirt with common *macehuales* and *indio* children, playing games with them until he learned the Nahuatl dialects. He then opened his school in Texcoco, teaching crafts, the use of metal tools, and the catechism. He quickly drew the sons of the native nobility, accustomed to elite schooling. The Spanish developed ideas and procedures from this missionary system that influenced all subsequent European efforts.

Late in the year 1531 the missionaries were provided with an enormous breakthrough to Amerindian hearts. According to the story, a poor *indio* who had been baptized as Juan Diego had a dazzling vision of the Virgin Mary at the northern terminal of the causeway from México at Tepeyac. The Lady spoke to Diego in his native tongue:

"Beloved son, go you to the bishop and tell him to build a church to me on this spot, so that from it I may give help and protection to the Mexican people in their sorrows and calamities."

Juan Diego rushed to the bishop, Juan de Zumárraga, but was turned away. Again the Virgin appeared to him, instructing him to climb the hill of Tepeyac, a blasted spot covered with snakes and cactus, but where he now found a profusion of Castilian roses. He gathered them in his native cape, and at last was ushered in to see the bishop. As he spread the roses, it was seen that the cape had become imprinted with the image of a radiant, dark-featured Amerindian maiden.

Zumárraga has been accused of inventing this useful miracle. The story, however, has the aura of Amerindian visions. In any case, the vision, which became accepted by the Church as the miracle of the Virgin of Guadalupe, had an explosive effect in Mexico. The Spanish Church admitted that the Mother of God could appear to a poor *indio*, speak to him in Nahuatl, and if she chose, show herself as a dark-faced Amerindian. The cult of the Virgin of Guadalupe was peculiarly appealing to all with native blood. From that time forward the Lady of Guadalupe was the patron of Mexico, venerated under many names: Our Mother, La Morenita (Sp: "the little dark one"), Our Lady of Sorrows; to this day *indios* approach the altar of her shrine on the hill of Tepeyac on their knees.

In the next fifteen years, nine million Amerindians were baptized.

This work was carried out by a mere handful of men. In 1524, only fifteen Franciscans were in New Spain, including both Peter of Ghent's and Valencia's bands. Dominicans, who were already in the islands, arrived in 1526, but the Augustinians did not come till 1533. The friars suffered casualties; there were not more than two hundred Franciscans in Mexico after twenty-five years.

In these days, there was little of the infighting and backbiting that was to envelope the Spanish Church. The three major orders divided the country into missionary zones. All were represented in the capital; the Franciscans continued with the Tlaxcala-Cholula-Huexotzingo region and also received Michoacán. The Dominicans took the south, Oaxaca through Chiapas. The Augustinians had to settle for the more barbaric north-northwest.

The friars, operating in ones and twos at first, laid out enormous church-convent complexes in or near major indigenous communities. Some of these, like Puebla de los Angeles, were to become Spanish cities, though normally, by deliberate choice, the native and the Spanish communities were removed from each other.

The style of these new compounds was European but with a touch of Mexic exoticism, which gave Mexican church structures an almost oriental look. The first churches rose in the massive, late-Gothic pattern then still dominant in Spain, with great, vaulted ceilings and buttressed walls. The overall effect of these complexes was one of somber grandeur set in native stone, resembling the austerity of the great medieval monasteries of Spain. But the decorations of the churches and chapels were given over to native artists, who painted frescoes and carved sculptures in Meso-American styles, portraying centaurs sporting quetzal-feather plumes.

For generations these great structures rose to dominate the landscape of central Mexico, but natural disasters and time destroyed many of them. The churches were rebuilt, centuries afterward, in newer styles.

Outside the church-cloister compounds the friars laid out shop buildings, schools, and gardens. The surrounding *indios* were catechized, baptized, and strictly disciplined. The friars had a great problem with native sexuality, especially the custom of Mexic chiefs to take multiple concubines and wives. The *indios* were accustomed to religious ceremony and holidays, and they made Catholic holy days into colorful fiestas and market days. New instruments and new tonal scales taught the natives by the friars livened religious ceremonies, plays, and fiestas with cheerful music that would ever afterward be a feature of Mexican public life.

The missionaries considered a full education of the indigenes to be a vital part of their effort; they taught writing, craftsmanship, and art along with religion and morality. The Texcoco school became a genuine aristocratic academy, a replacement of the former *calmécac*. The friars consciously attempted to train a leadership class of converted, Spanish-speaking Amerindians.

In 1536, with both Zumárraga's and Mendoza's approval, the Franciscans started the College of Santa Cruz in the native quarter of Tlatelolco. This institution was designed to educate the sons of the old nobility, considered by the friars to be a natural leading class, in Latin, theology, and philosophy. The Franciscans wanted to prepare natives for holy orders in this college, and other universities.

Many of the attitudes and practices of the friars were remarkably enlightened, but Spanish policy did not remain enlightened long, and the Spanish orders themselves decayed terribly in the later demoralization of the Hispanic world. The racial and religious bigotry that came later blighted the work and even the memory of the early friars, but the chronology of Spanish humanism is as important as the chronology of Imperial Rome. The memory of Roman grandeur survived the hideous decay of the twilight of empire; the glory that was early sixteenth-century Spain has not.

For a generation, however, the Catholic prelates, all chosen from among the friars, were actually dominant in New Spain. With Mendoza's blessing they built and ruled while the conquistadores either wore themselves out searching for new El Dorados or sank into luxurious apathy. Zumárraga, who had demonstrated that *indios* had equal access in the eyes of the Church to the Catholic Mother of God, was a powerful administrator and educator. He risked his life against Nuño de Guzmán in protecting Indians, sponsored schools, built hospitals, and supervised the printing of the first books in America. He enlisted the pope in the cause of founding a university, which began life as the Royal and Pontifical University of México soon after his death. Angered by the stubborn insistence of some conquistadores that the *indios* were really animals or submen, Julián de Garcés, first bishop of Puebla, got the pope to issue a bull stating that the Indians were true men, who must be converted to Christ by the word of

God and by the example of good and holy lives. Since the Spanish settlers were hardly given to "good and holy living," Garcés tried to keep the races apart, unsuccessfully.

Vasco de Quiroga, *oidor* and now bishop of Michoacán, erased the trauma that Nuño de Guzmán's passage had left among the Tarasca people. He protected the tribe ferociously, brought in Spanish cattle, chickens, new crops, and artifacts, and founded a university. Tata (Tarasca: "grandfather") Vasco was a benevolent despot who tried to organize Tarasca society along the lines of Sir Thomas More's *Utopia*, of which the learned lawyer was very fond. He created a community too good to be true, even with the Amerindians' communal traditions, and it could not last—but Tata Vasco left a living legend of kindness and benevolence throughout Michoacán.

In Chiapas, Bishop Bartolomé de Las Casas battled vigorously for native rights. He was hated by the conquistadores, because he was not only energetic and articulate, but had the ear of important personages up to and including the king.

Most of these men were genuine humanists, and genuinely kind. But they also were leaders in a Spanish society that had a total faith in its own truth. Their curiosity and genuine love of learning clashed with their mission among the Indians. Diego de Landa, bishop of Yucatán, burned or buried every Maya stela or pictograph he found, but he also studied them assiduously and from them and observation wrote an anthropological description of the Maya culture that alone preserved this knowledge.

The Zumárragas and Landas were once admired for their protection of the Amerindians; but as their motives and rationales have become incomprehensible to later ages they are mostly remembered for their destruction of the books and artifacts of the indigenous civilization, and their determined persecution of heresy. Zumárraga burned both the lord of Texcoco and his priceless library for being in the service of the Devil. Ironically, however, other priests, like Landa, preserved much of the native heritage —in fact, almost all of it that has survived. Bernardino de Sahagún Latinized Nahuatl and encouraged his converts to write down in both languages all the traditions of their past they could recall. The mission schools produced some amazing and beautiful pictographs with Spanish and Hispanicized Nahuatl captions. Some found their way to European archives and thus survived, important records of indigenous life styles and thought processes, and also contemporary natural history. Sahagún's history is brilliant by any standard, and Benavente, who lived among the natives as Motolinía (Nahua: "Poor Man") wrote a manuscript second only to it. Against the valid charge of vandalism is an equally valid record of deliberate preservation, which was usually carried out as a labor of love. Many of these friars were Renaissance men, not seventeenth-century Catholic bigots.

The charge of paternalism must also cling. The whole Spanish society from the crown down was organized on essentially despotic paternal lines. However, the tyranny was hedged by customs and habits and tempered by love. Spanish priests could behave no other way, and their paternalism, like that of the whole society, only became deadly to the Amerindians when development reached a dead end. The Quirogas were consciously training their children to be free. Later Spanish friars, consciously or unconsciously, were only playing eternal father roles, with the logical effect on their stunted "children."

Interested in people, uninterested in slaves or gold, friars penetrated remote, barren areas. Later anthropologists have been startled by Amerindian tribes in remote places, who showed no trace of European blood or obvious contact with Spanish culture but who spoke a pure Castilian as their *native* tongue.

In the sixteenth century Spain became the greatest civilizing power since Rome. It was no accident that the first Catholic bishops of Mexico have remained the greatest, and that the first viceroy's memory was always venerated by the sons of the conquistadores as the greatest in his long line. These men, for all their efforts, could not make Mexico a paradise, or even prevent the inexorable tragedies that were to come. But they did, more than is now recognized, make Mexico into a genuine New Spain.

16

THREE DISASTERS

The liberty of the Indians is of more importance than all the mines in the world, and the revenues they yield to the Spanish Crown is not of such importance that all divine and human laws should be sacrificed in order to obtain them.

From the Spanish of Don Luis de Velasco, II. Viceroy of New Spain.

While the friars and bishops labored to make central Mexico a New Spain, there was still death and destruction on the outer fringes of the march of European civilization. The conquest of Motecuhzoma's empire came in a brilliant, whirlwind campaign. But beyond the edges of the Meso-American civilization, the Spanish began to encounter more primitive lands and tribes. Most of these regions were inherently unattractive to them, because the Spanish form of colonization, both secular and religious, required settled indigenes to support it. The mission system did not work among very primitive and essentially warlike savages who could not even be successfully congregated. This did not prevent the Spanish from stubbornly pursuing it for two hundred years, from disaster to disaster on the far northern frontier.

During the sixteenth century the conquistadores and friars gradually seized all of the *meseta*, or central highlands, founding important towns as far north as Guadalajara in the west, and in the east, Monterrey. This settlement followed the cordilleras and the sedentary *indios*. Beyond this, the *tierra despoblada* or deserted regions began: Sonora, Chihuahua, Coahuila, Nuevo León, Tamaulipas, inhabited by wild Indians, to be penetrated successfully only by soldiers or armed settlers; even the peaceful friars had to dwell in forts. The Spanish were pulled into the great, forbidding central bowl between the northern cordilleras for reasons other than Indians, and here they began to fight the first interminable Spanish-Indian wars. These were guerrilla campaigns that lasted many years, and they invariably ended in the death and destruction of the Indians, by guns, swords, disease, and drink.

Climate, soil, and the existence of exploitable labor, both for friars and *encomenderos*, confined the heaviest Spanish settlement in New Spain to the general extent of the old Mexica empire, particularly in the great volcanic bowl of Anáhuac. Secondary areas of settlement were in Oaxaca, Chiapas and Tabasco, Michoacán, and the beautiful, watered country of Nueva Galicia or Jalisco. There were forts or ports in other regions, handfuls of adventurous or law-fleeing Spaniards everywhere, but in the north the Europeans were repelled by the vast deserts and wild Indians, and on the coasts by the heat and deadly fevers. The Gulf coastal regions, like the whole Circum-Caribbean area, were made almost uninhabitable by the importation of malaria and yellow fever, introduced with other diseases by African slaves.

The flat, arid, limestone plains of Yucatán were a special case.

Cortés had entrusted the conquest of this bypassed region to his captain, Francisco de Montejo. Montejo and his son tried to carry out the usual brief conquistadorial campaign against the Maya tribes, who were sedentary but the heirs of a long, internal degeneration. This very degeneration thwarted the Montejos. The Maya were less civilized now than the peoples of the central plateau, but they were also much more warlike. The Spanish could not be thrown out of the country, but they could not pacify it or break the Maya to be their slaves. Here began a bitter, bloody, cruel struggle that was to continue for twenty years.

The Montejos were in effect allowed a free hand by the *audiencias* and the viceroy; Yucatán, separated by mountains and jungles from central Mexico, was too remote to be controlled in any case. The Spanish were continually replenished with arriving conquistadores, they had superior arms and organization, and they could exert endless pressure as long as the Montejo family had the will. Repulsed, the elder Montejo passed the job on to his son.

In this struggle the Spanish finally learned the intricacies of the centuries-long Maya civil wars, which had never ended. The tribes were still bitterly, almost insanely split between the old factions in the fallen cities, the dynasties of Xiu and Cocom-Itzá. Montejo used the Cortesian example of *divisa et impera* by joining the Xiu. Now Maya destroyed Maya in the Spanish service until the remnants of the Itzá retreated into the fastnesses of Guatemala, where they were not finally reduced until late in the next century.

When the warfare petered out, the Spanish controlled the peninsula.

Though a few Jaguar priests escaped Landa and held out secretly for more than a hundred years, most Maya tribesmen forgot their writings, their history, and even their ancient cities, now hidden under trees and shrubs. But the Maya were one of the few Amerindian peoples who preserved their language, their sense of identity, and their basic, if primitive way of life. They kept their old agricultural methods. The Spanish conquered them, and exacted tribute from generations of Maya serfs, but their resistance tended to keep the Spanish settlers absentee landlords bottled up in the coastal towns of Mérida and Campeche, which grew exotic colonial societies more on the order of the Indies than of New Spain. The Spaniards were planters whose orientation was more to the Indies and the outside world than it was to mainland America; like the Maya they became separated from the rest of Mexico. Thus the racial, cultural, and social patterns of Yucatán, both Spanish and Amerindian, diverged from New Spain. Yucatán remained one of the most primitive and backward regions in what was to become the Republic of Mexico.

The Yucateca war did not siphon off all the restless souls in Spanish Mexico. The example of Cortés still haunted a rootless generation of voyagers who put out from Spain. It was now known that the Americas were two vast continents which still might hold more kingdoms ready to topple with the wave of Toledo steel. Such dreams were fired by the swineherd Pizarro's looting of Peru between 1531 and 1535. Pizarro for the first time found storerooms of gold. Pánfilo de Narváez, Cortés' old enemy, scouted Florida. His expedition was wrecked by a storm on the Texas coast, and a few survivors dragged themselves up on the sands.

One of these men, Álvar Nuñez (who preferred his mother's name of Cabeza de Vaca because she came of higher family than his father) made his way through the southwestern part of North America and arrived after eight years on the Pacific shores of Mexico. Cabeza de Vaca spun a fantastic tale of the Seven Cities of Cíbola, in a kingdom called Quivira, which was supposed to be far richer than fallen Tenochtitlan but which he had not seen. He had learned of it from friendly Indians.

Viceroy de Mendoza dispatched a Franciscan, Fray Marcos de Niza, and a Moorish slave, Estéban, to investigate. They walked through deserts and mountains, reaching present-day New Mexico, where the friar thought he saw a great city gleaming in the sun. He planted a cross, claimed all the country in the name of God and the king, and walked back to the City of México.

Mendoza had never been one to believe much in El Dorado, but now his imagination was fired. He organized a large expedition, financed it himself —giving the equivalent of several millions of dollars—and he chose Don Francisco Vásquez de Coronado to head it. Coronado was thirty, energetic, the governor of Nueva Galicia, and also rich; he was able to advance fifty thousand escudos for horses and arms.

In 1540 Coronado headed north with some three hundred armored Spaniards and a larger train of *indios*. Few Spanish expeditions were greater or more bitter failures, though few spawned more romantic legends. Still, this *entrada*, together with Hernando de Soto's thrust inward from the Gulf, was to have an important effect on Spanish policy in New Spain.

Coronado came to Cíbola, which proved to be a wretched *pueblo* or cliff village of Zuñi Indians on the upper Rio Grande. Cursing Fray Marcos, who was with them, the frustrated conquistadores annexed the country, pacified the region by burning a number of Zuñi elders at the stake, to teach the tribes, as Coronado wrote, to obey the will of God and the king, and rode out in various exploring expeditions.

A Coronado lieutenant actually rode to the Grand Canyon, which chasm he seems to have viewed with less wonder than disgust, because it halted his advance. Coronado himself marched through the high plains of Texas, and perhaps as far as Kansas. After much hardship, he returned to the Rio Grande pueblos, whose inhabitants had sensibly run away, taking their food with them.

At last, after nearly starving, the dispirited army trudged back to New Spain. Coronado had expended prodigious efforts, as he assured His Majesty and the viceroy, but he was disgraced. Fray Marcos himself was struck down by a seizure on his return, which the army called God's justice to liars.

Coronado's and de Soto's experiences—Hernando de Soto had died in Mississippi—chilled Spanish enthusiasm for the apparent wastelands of the northern continent. While parts of the land were rich, and there were millions of bison, which the Spanish sarcastically named *cíbolas*, neither these plains, forests, nor animals had much appeal. The Spanish had already explored more territory, an area forty times the size of Spain, than they could absorb or settle. Fifty years later an expedition was mounted to settle the pueblo area; but no real effort was made to go back into what is now Texas for a hundred and fifty years.

Meanwhile, a serious *indio* war had broken out in the large, amorphous region in the west, Nueva Galicia. This uprising was directly attributable to Nuño de Guzmán; he and his men had raped the country without really trying to settle or pacify it. The Amerindian rebellion—as the Spanish, of course, considered it such—was the beginning of several hundred years of continual racial conflict on the northern frontier. Here the scattered Spaniards, a few thousands among millions of Indians, were seized and killed; some were burned alive. The rebellion, instigated by the Amerindian priests, caused a wave of fear in the capital. The Tarasca and the Tlaxcalteca seemed also on the verge of revolt. Mendoza sent Pedro de Alvarado, the most experienced Indian fighter in New Spain, to Guadalajara and tried to repair old alliances with the pacified tribes.

Alvarado was defeated and mortally injured in a fall while trying to stem a Spanish rout. Guadalajara was besieged. Inside, Alvarado died at the age of fifty-six, replying to a question whether he was in pain that he "hurt only in his soul."

The viceroy himself took the field, with an army of three hundred Spanish horse and one-hundred-and-fifty Spanish foot—all the Europeans who could be raised. Mendoza, like Cortés, was brilliantly successful in raising Amerindian against Amerindian. The Tlaxcalteca, the Cholulteca, the Huexotzinga, the Texcoca, and even the Tarasca provided perhaps fifty thousand warriors for the viceregal host. Mendoza gave the native chiefs Spanish horses and arms.

Again, the indigenes destroyed each other for Spanish benefit. The tribes of Neuva Galicia were destroyed defending their mountain fortresses. Mendoza did ameliorate the conflict by halting the practice of taking and branding natives captured in war as slaves. He also extended a general amnesty to all *indios* who stopped fighting. His arms crushed the indigenes and destroyed their war chiefs and priests, but his humaneness sealed the peace. This outbreak, called the Mixtón War, was the only serious Amerindian uprising against the Spanish throughout the entire *meseta*. There would be Indian wars in Mexico through the nineteenth century in the north, but these were merely the savage struggles of various Chichimeca against advancing civilization.

Some of the Tlaxcalteca and Texcoca allies, themselves former enemies, settled in the Jalisco region. They provided a buffer for Guadalajara, which was to become the most important Spanish town in New Spain, outside of México City.

The Mixtón War, Coronado's quest, and the pacification of Yucatán all belonged to the conquistadorial era. By the 1540s, central New Spain had enjoyed a prolonged era of peace and stability. The indigenous peoples were accepting Christianity; they were losing their old culture. Mendoza's benevolent despotism was firmly in control. The Cortesian vision of a New Spain was coming true: sixteenth-century Spain, it seemed, would recreate a flourishing civilization in America, a civilization that would draw on the finest currents of the European Renaissance, and one in which millions of Amerindians would peacefully and happily enter into Western culture.

The millions of Amerindian villagers and peasants would not have entered into the millennium, however, because European civilization itself was no paradise for the millions across the sea, and Spain was implanting her own sins and errors with her governors and priests, but even this partial paradise was not to be.

In the 1540s three major disasters began to reshape the entire society of Mexico. The seeds of these disasters lay in the nature of the conquerors, the conquered, and the Conquest itself.

Twenty years after the Conquest, the permanent relationship between the conquerors and the conquered peoples had still not been decided, in theory and rationale. The crown and Church both operated, if imperfectly, on the principle that the theoretically-free Amerindian vassals were to take their place as full Spanish subjects once they were Hispanicized and Christianized. The *encomienda* serfdom had been grudgingly accepted, and the mission system had been enthusiastically pushed on the assumption that the *indios* required a certain period of tutelage before they could be expected to live as a free Spanish peasantry. The Church was already educating a native elite and was considering conferring holy orders on the best of the indigenes. Such moves could not help but raise and institutionalize the status of the native Mexicans to that of Spaniards.

Meanwhile, Spanish jurists, humanists, and clerics continued to protest the enserfment of the *indios*. Many influential Spaniards never accepted the Cortesian compromise. Their opinion was hardened by the bloody horrors of Pizarro's conquest of Peru, which profoundly shocked the homeland, and by the Mixtón War, which the king believed was a direct result of conquistadorial oppressions. The crown convened a special council to recommend solutions to the *encomienda* question.

This council was composed of eminent jurists and theologians, whose conclusions were eminently sensible and humane: the granting of *encomiendas* should be stopped, the existing ones should be abolished at the death of the present incumbent grantees, and all *indios* should be guaranteed the rights of free vassals of the crown. Carlos I incorporated these recommendations into royal commands, the so-called New Laws of 1542, and dispatched *visitadores* or special inspector-generals to proclaim and enforce them in the Indies.

The New Laws failed to take into account political and financial power and basic human nature. The New Laws would have totally, if healthily, torn up the Spanish society of New Spain, and that society was bound to resist them.

In the 1540s there were 1,385 Spanish heads of families in New Spain by Mendoza's count. Of these, 577 held *encomiendas*. These families formed a wealthy and influential elite, the real Spanish society of New Spain. The other Europeans were mainly officials or immigrants without a permanent stake in the country. The *encomendero* class had become corrupt, unproductive, and inherently parasitical. It was ferociously jealous of its privileges; its survival depended on them.

Few *encomenderos* wanted the *indios* to be freed and they argued that without the *encomienda* the *indios* could not be Catholicized and Europeanized. This argument was not really valid by the 1540s, after almost a generation of Spanish rule.

Although the *encomenderos* were a theoretical military feudality, they did not provide any real armed force for the viceregal government. The sedentary Amerindians were totally pacified; the Spaniards who were still fighting on the various frontiers were primarily adventurers and freebooters. A small royal army, maintained in New Spain and buttressed with Amerindian allies, could easily have replaced this supposed function. The *corregimiento* was governing the vassals without military force, and the friars already had most of the *indios* in a far firmer and more lasting grip than any occupying armed force could have maintained. Six hundred-odd tribute-collecting *encomenderos* in no way stood between the *indios* and rebellion; in fact, they were more apt to incite rebellion with their demands, which the viceroyalty constantly had to regulate and ameliorate. The *encomenderos* had left the conversion of the natives, even within their grants, to the friars.

The *encomenderos* no longer had any real military, governmental, or religious function, even had they wanted one, but as a class, they were prepared to defend themselves.

When the Visitador Francisco Tello de Sandoval arrived at Veracruz and began his month-long passage to the capital in 1544, he was surrounded by agitation. Every *encomendero* delayed Sandoval and argued with him; wives and daughters begged him with tears not to destroy a genteel Spanish society. Grave, hospitable *regidores* warned him he was destroying the prosperity of loyal families who had bravely served the crown; all Spaniards in Mexico prophesied revolution, destruction, and ruin if they were beggared and driven out. Lawyers, who were already numerous in New Spain, insisted for their clients that the New Laws were an unwonted and unconscionable innovation upon the customs and established laws of the realm.

Shaken but not daunted—his orders from the king were clear—Sandoval reached México. Mendoza affirmed his loyalty to the king, and supported the visitador. The New Laws were officially proclaimed; Sandoval began to remove *oidores* and *encomenderos* who appeared to him particularly corrupt or detestable, including those most strenuous in their arguments.

The *encomenderos* reacted with threats of violence. Sandoval and Mendoza became cautious, and Mendoza became convinced that the New Laws, in whose spirit he believed, simply could not be enforced, at least by a visitador without an army at his back. Mendoza tactfully interceded with Sandoval and worked out a compromise. A delegation was to be sent to

Spain to plead the case of the *encomenderos*. This would include two official envoys, the provincials of the monastic orders, and several persons of wealth and eminence among the society of New Spain. No Indians were included.

The passion, rhetoric, and judicial and theological arguments obscured the real question, which was whether or not the Spanish were to be maintained in Mexico permanently as *señores*. Bribery by *encomenderos* certainly changed some Spanish officials' minds. The king was not corruptible in this way, however, and the New Laws would have stood except for the fact that finally almost irresistible pressures were brought against the crown. Mendoza advised the king to relent, and at last, so did Sandoval. The real defection came from the Church itself. The Franciscan, Dominican, and Augustinian provincials of New Spain, representing the orders which had most vigorously fought for Amerindian rights and damned the abuses of the conquistadores, counseled the crown that the New Laws were ill-advised and that there should be no change.

The clergy feared violence and disorder among the Spanish in Mexico. They also realized their progress was still superficial. There was already a growing understanding among the friars that the great mass of *indios* were many years away from becoming genuine Europeans, or even genuine Christians, despite their adoration of ikons of the Virgin, the crucifixes among their earth gods, and their songs bewailing the death of Jesus and the contrariness of Eve. Above all, the friars were disturbed about anything which might interfere with their work. They had devoted their lives to the Indians, though many almost came at times to hate their charges for their baffling behavior and closed-mindedness. The orders sincerely wanted to preserve the Indians, but almost unconsciously they wanted to continue them in their preserves. Many friars believed the *indios* would be better Christians if they avoided Europeans altogether. The friars did not really want slavery—but they felt the Indians required more tutelage.

The great, pervasive, carrying argument, which all Spaniards came to believe, was that the *indio* was different and therefore inherently inferior. The *indio* did not understand European concepts of work, and money; therefore, he was not ready for civilized society. For very different reasons then, the Church and the conquistadores entered into an alliance lethal to the Amerindian.

Carlos I, reasonably sincere and genuinely liberal toward all Indians, could not withstand the alliance. He would not erase the New Laws; the crown's prestige was behind them. But Spanish lawyers quickly devised compromises through "exceptions." The sons of the conquistadores were granted exceptions for one or more lifetimes, some to the sixth generation, but all to expire with the extinction of a lineage. Money wages were decreed for *repartimiento* laborers, at a fair and decent rate, along with other supposedly strict regulations.

The real theory behind the *encomienda* was not changed or even attacked. What in effect was now institutionalized was a *permanent* "tutelage" of the *indios*, though what had really been decided may not have been obvious at the time. It is a fact that, sincerely or cynically, Spanish churchmen and officers were still predicting a quick conclusion to this tutelage in the eighteenth century, long after the last sixteenth-century *encomienda* had lapsed or been returned to the crown, and the guidance of the Amerindian had been continued in various other, ingenious ways.

Meanwhile, the Amerindians had begun to disappear. Smallpox had become endemic once it had been brought in by Cortés' men; it recurred about every seven years. New Spain was never again free of it, and as late as 1779 a smallpox epidemic killed twenty percent of the people living in the City of México. Measles was almost as fatal for Amerindians.

African plagues like malaria and yellow fever made the coasts and low regions almost uninhabitable. The most lethal epidemics, however, came from a virus or infection described in contemporary medical records as either a form of typhus or a peculiarly virulent influenza. This disease, which seemed to strike only at elevations above three thousand feet, above which height the majority of the Indian population lived, ravaged the central highlands.

Spanish records are either nonexistent or extremely inexact. But in the year 1545 at least eight hundred thousand Amerindians died. In 1576 a recurrence of this epidemic took two million lives. Wildfire epidemics were aided by the crowded, communal living habits of the natives.

Disease heightened famine, and whole communities died of starvation after an epidemic. In 1784, three hundred thousand Amerindians died of respiratory infection accompanying a famine. This was not the first time; it was simply the first time the Spanish recorded such an event. Except for when epidemics raged totally out of control, very little official attention was paid to the destruction of the indigenes by disease, but it was a slow, steady process that soon cast a terrible pall of suffering and death over all central Mexico. Death, and the constant consciousness of death, were imbedded indelibly in the native mind. No family was unaffected; the scourge lasted for generations, and the awareness of living eternally in the presence of death strongly shaped the Mexican world view. For one thing, death certainly aided the grasp of the Catholic Church upon society. Disaster heightened religious fears and feelings at the same time it completed the demoralization of the old culture.

This bloodless destruction of the indigenes was anything but deliberate. The Spanish were as appalled by it—though more conditioned to it in those times when most men at forty already carried their seeds of death—

as they would have been had all their livestock died. The whole economy of New Spain rested on the backs of Amerindians. Spaniards were not immune from epidemics or disease, though none suffered from a lack of care or starvation. Syphilis, which may or may not have been Motecuhzoma's revenge—authorities are still divided as to whether this infection was indigenous or imported from Asia—ravaged the European community.

There were probably at least eleven million Amerindians in the conquered regions in the 1520s. Apparently, no more than six-and-one-half million survived into the 1550s. After the terrible fevers of the 1570s, there were no more than some two million by 1607. By 1650 only about one million Amerindians remained, those with some immunity to European disease. After 1650, the indigenous population began slowly to grow.

The economy of New Spain was based on *indio* labor, and as the *indios* vanished, fields lay idle and towns began to stagnate. Heavier and heavier burdens were thrown on the *indio* survivors to support the Spanish lordship. When five thousand *indios* were available to support one Spaniard, tribute levels had been light. By 1550, however, one-third as many males were rendering the same amount of taxes or tribute. The situation worsened tragically for the Amerindians as the ratio of indigenes to conquerors continued to fall. It was approximately 65 to 1 by the 1570s; 20 to 1 in 1600; no more than 10 to 1 at best by 1650, as the European population continued to grow slowly while the *indios* vanished. While the viceroyalty did set aside tribute payments in particularly disastrous years, it did not and really could not make any basic change in a society where officials, ecclesiastics, landowners, and mine operators all insisted upon immunity from manual labor. The demands of the *encomenderos* fell heavily on the survivors; despite strenuous exploitation many *encomendero* families sank into a bitter, genteel poverty as their *indios* died off.

The greatest exploitation and destruction, however, fell on the indigenes who remained outside private *encomiendas*. As the numbers of *indios* decreased, the *corregidores* destroyed the old village and clan structures they had originally permitted to exist; more *indios* were congregated and brought directly under the supervision of the crown; the native towns and centers were no longer allowed to rule themselves and cultivate their own, communally-held fields. Corrupt officials supplied the supposedly free crown vassals to town councils and to private landowners for unpaid labor. Constables forced the "free" natives to work in wheat fields so that Europeans might have bread, and they in effect sold their services to private contractors. These encroachments on the lives of the Amerindians continued in direct proportion to depopulation, until few villages in central Mexico were unaffected. Thus the economy of central New Spain turned rapidly from a situation in which a small master class drew tribute and labor from a basically undisturbed mass of civilized Amerindians into an economy in which the conquerors began to parcel out bonded labor to their landed estates and mines. Most of what was done was illegal under the law; corrupt *corregidores*, however, operated in close alliance with town councils and with landowners and Spanish contractors. They supplied forced labor beyond the limits permitted by law, and they cheated these *indios* of the wages due them under the law. The *corregimiento* emerged exactly the opposite of what it had been envisioned by the humane officials of the second *audiencia*: worse than the *encomienda*. Hereditary *encomenderos* had a stake in preserving *indios*. Brief-tenured, usually poor and ambitious Spanish officers set over the Indians had only a stake in exploiting them. Despite continual complaints, the situation was not corrected—it could not be, so long as the Spanish population in Mexico was determined to live as *señores*.

The *indio* way of life was quickly corrupted and destroyed, as all natives one way or another were parceled out to the dominant race. For a brief few years, the ordinary Amerindian had in some sense been liberated by the Conquest; now he began to be destroyed by it.

This destruction was exacerbated by a third great disaster, which most Spaniards saw as a tremendous blessing. In 1546, Juan de Tolosa found a fantastic mountain of silver—La Bufa—at Zacatecas in the Chichimec region, the forbidding, arid central bowl several hundred miles northwest of the capital. The discovery of silver changed the whole economy and outlook of Spanish Mexico. Armed men poured into the rugged mountains that fringed the settled regions and rapidly discovered huge deposits of silver ores. Eventually, silver was discovered in eleven of the modern Mexican states, ranging from Guerrero into Sonora; the richest strikes, however, were in the north, beyond the fringes of civilization.

Mexico was the richest silver-bearing country on earth. Once a method of separating silver from its ores was perfected in 1557, a treasure-hunt mentality and a mining camp psychology arose that was never to disappear. Five thousand Spanish mines soon produced an incredible flow of silver ingots and rough-struck pesos, creating an enduring image of Mexico as a great storehouse of mineral wealth, where fortunes might be made overnight. This was true, and remained true for centuries, but these sudden riches had a terrible effect on the long-term growth of New Spain.

There was some good, of course: silver sucked Spanish exploration into the grim central bowl. The Bajío region was developed as a way station and support area for the mines in the lunar landscape to the north. Silver stimulated local economies in these mountains, and mining camps like Guanajuato grew into important cities. Former Spanish muleteers could become millionaires overnight and endow magnificent churches. The splendid, ornate churches that rose in many remote places were paid for by pious miners who had struck it rich.

The main effects, however, were wholly bad.

The Spanish mentality confused precious metals with real wealth. The discovery that Mexico was a great mountain of silver ores—which also contained gold as a by-product—blinded the crown and viceregal government to everything else. The viceroyalty, after the middle of the sixteenth century, began to shape the entire public economy to support the flow of silver out of the country and back to Spain. Soldiers and forts were placed in the north to guard the silver packtrains; the communications network was directed to and from the wastelands. Even communications with Spain were dominated by bullion flow. Sailing schedules were set to coincide with treasure shipments, which had to be convoyed across the ocean. Meanwhile, normal commerce stagnated and goods piled up and rotted.

The hunger of the Spanish for ready money while understandable, was fatal. The viceroyalty, under increasing pressure to supply money to the crown, lost interest in agrarian development. No roads were constructed into the rich farming areas, and so hundreds of thousands of Amerindians starved in epidemic years, while the corn to feed them often went to waste only a hundred miles away. The government was hardly bothered. The bullionist psychology of the Spanish, which was general to all Europeans in this age, was so deep-seated that it was never overcome. The agrarian economy, already hard hit by the loss of Amerindians, worsened. The government even ignored or discouraged the development of mining for anything but silver or gold.

The stimulation of the economy was mainly around the mining camps. Many Spaniards in Mexico did acquire vast wealth from silver mines, but there was nothing to do with this money except to sink it into huge, vaguely-defined *latifundia* throughout the central plateau. With a shrinking work force, the landowners turned more and more to stock raising, an enterprise that was not very profitable but required few Indians.

In Spain the large share that went into the royal coffers caused running, disastrous inflation which destroyed the rudimentary economy. An apparent endless stream of bullion encouraged the crown to spend recklessly and to involve Spain in grandiose wars. Oddly, Spain was the envy of all Europe because of her American mines; few contemporaries understood the real reasons why the crown was eternally bankrupt and thousands of Spaniards were in rags.

All mineral deposits, under Spanish law, were the property of the crown. The discoverer, however, was normally granted a concession to exploit a *single* mine. Spanish mining enterprise was therefore carried out by a horde of relatively small contractors or concessionaires. Mine operators paid a fifth, the *quinto real*, of their proceeds to the crown; this was reduced to a tenth after mercury, essential to the Mexican mining process, was made a crown monopoly and sold out of Spain to Mexican miners at exorbitant prices. Other taxes, fees, and duties for refining, assaying, and blasting powder, a crown monopoly, added at least an additional twenty percent to mining costs. Precious metals by law had to be stamped by royal officials to indicate that all duties were paid; cheating was a capital crime. But there is no doubt that it was widespread. Soon, the crown required bullion to be crudely coined at the Casa de Moneda, or mint, at México, both for convenience and to curtail smuggling.

A horde of Spanish mine-seekers poured into the arid mountains of the northern frontier. At Guanajuato and beyond, they erected litttle towers that were forts in every sense above their claims. Hundreds of these long-abandoned structures still stand starkly on the blasted slopes of the mountains of Zacatecas and Guanajuato.

Mexican silver ores were mostly very low grade, plentiful but assaying no more than fifteen ounces to the ton. This fact, and the enormous profits demanded by the crown through its fees and monopolies, meant that Mexican mines needed vast amounts of labor, and cheap labor, besides. It was inevitable that the Spanish immediately began to dragoon the nearest available Amerindians into working their mines. The mine concessionaires looked to the *corregimiento* system to provide forced labor under the *repartimiento*. This could be justified, although the mine operators were private businessmen, because the mines were legally crown property, and therefore mining was a "public" enterprise. Whatever the law, the labor was at hand and would have been provided in any case; but here the forced labor of the *indios* was particularly cruel.

The mines were hundred of miles beyond the homes of the nearest pacified Indians, which were the Tarasca of Michoacán. Zacatecas lay four hundred miles from Anáhuac, across arid stretches inhabited by savage tribes of Chichimecs. But the *indios* were rounded up and forced to walk to the mining camps; they were expected to provide their own food on the road. The distances made an extreme demand for workers. To keep ten men working continually in one mine, for example, at least thirty had to be away from their homes and fields: on a journey that took weeks, ten had to be going out and ten coming back from their forced labor period at any given time. Spanish accounts tell that the vulture-picked bones of countless hapless *indios* soon marred these trails, as *repartimiento* Indians became victims of thirst or savage Chichimecs.

The Spanish used the *de rato*, or shortest route, method of mining; they followed ore veins by tunneling. The English corrupted this name to "rat-hole," and the mines were indeed ratholes—narrow, twisting, precariously timbered, connected from level to level by rickety ladders—some going down fifteen hundred feet. In these torchlit breathless tunnels, the *indios* hacked out ore which had to be carried to the surface in leather buckets. Workers carried two hundred pounds of ore on each trip, up ladders and through narrow passages on their knees, and they worked twelve hours a day. No few Indians died in these foul holes.

Under these conditions, the *corregidores* who supplied *indios* for a price to the operators soon had to use slave labor methods to ensure the supply. Men were rounded up by the *alguaciles*; they were kept chained or locked in pens. Both *corregidores* and the mine operators began to use the whip—although the law required fair wages for this forced work, few *indios* ever saw a piece of the silver their sweat brought forth, and they could be inspired to the tremendous efforts demanded of them only by brutal punishments. The concessionaires naturally made the most of them while they could. Tortured, chained, starved, these *repartimiento* miners were slaves in everything but name.

These evils were recognized by authority. The clergy protested. But potential profit, historically, has always been an enormous spur to slavery; energetic men and governments will acquire necessary labor one way or another. The *audiencia* really dared not interfere with a flow of silver back to Spain. The hard fact was that the distant mines could not be exploited without forced Amerindian labor. If any officer had halted the *repartimiento*, his motives might have been applauded, but he would have been removed. For more than fifty years, abuses were ignored, or hidden under elaborate rationales.

The institution of permanent serfdom, disease and depopulation, and silver and slavery corrupted the promise of the Cortesian kingdom, and they stained the civilizing efforts of the friars and first two viceroys. By the 1540s there was no longer any hope—if actually there ever had been—of a Hispanicization of Mexico that would follow the course of the Romanization of Gaul and Spain.

The once colorful and busy human beehive of Amerindian Mexico was becoming a great, grim, barren silver mountain, surrounded by stunted, almost empty fields; two different kinds of men, Spaniards and Amerindians, conquerors and conquered, were sinking into permanent patterns of tyranny.

17

CASTES AND COLONIALS

Colonial Mexico made men into hypocrites.
Octavio Paz, twentieth-century Mexican Poet.

In 1550 Don Antonio de Mendoza was requested to take the newly-created viceregal throne of Peru. The Crown would not let him retire; it needed his presence in the turbulent Inca territory. Mendoza conferred with his successor at Cholula before he sailed in 1551.

Don Luis de Velasco, the second viceroy of New Spain, was an aristocrat like Mendoza. He continued the policies of Mendoza—which were those of the king—almost unchanged. He probably had secret orders to oppose the *encomienda-repartimiento.* Velasco shared the distaste of most Spanish aristocrats and jurisconsults for Indian slavery, and tried to regulate the *encomenderos* and the *corregidores* rigidly. There were continual protests against his severity, but he was able to maintain full authority and control. Velasco could not, however, change the system; this had proved even beyond the crown's control.

Velasco continued support to the new Royal and Pontifical University of México, which now acquired the same rights and privileges as Salamanca. He also continued Mendoza's work of shipbuilding and sea exploration of the Pacific, which earlier had been carried on privately by Cortés. The coasts had been scouted and charted from South America up into Oregon; there were regular sailings from Acapulco to Panama. Now, the thrust was across the Pacific, toward the Philippines. Velasco was organizing a Spanish-Mexican expedition to conquer these islands when he died in 1564, and the work was carried on by Juan de Legazpi, who founded Manila on Luzon. Soon, Spanish galleons were plying the vast distances between Manila and Acapulco, and the Orient began to play a significant role in the life of Spanish Mexico.

Velasco was unsuccessful in an effort to seize Florida by sea, but he directed explorations in the north of New Spain. Don Francisco Ybarra found more veins of precious metal beyond Zacatecas, and founded a new mining boom town, Durango, in the north.

Silver mining had created a military and logistics problem in the Chichimec country. The Chichimeca were adept at guerrilla campaigns, though they were not very numerous. These tribes put up no organized resistance to Spanish encroachments, but they raided Spanish settlements and mines, killed *repartimiento indios*, and robbed the silver pack trains of their mules. Velasco posted garrisons made up of a few Spanish soldiers and allied Indians between México and Zacatecas and Guanajuato. Some of these posts or forts grew into important towns: Querétaro, San Felipe Yztlahuaca, San Miguel el Grande, later San Miguel de Allende. This was the beginning of Spanish settlement in the so-called Bajío—the "low country" that was actually a temperate, fertile highlands beyond the high volcanic bowl. This settlement of new country was to have profound effects on the development of New Spain. Here, the Spanish and Amerindians laid the groundwork for a newer society—but this was to be centuries in developing.

The so-called Chichimec War began between these settlers and garrisons and the savage tribes and lasted fifty years. Finally, toward the end of the century, the wild tribes gave up, congregated around the Spanish settlements and missions, and quickly became extinct through demoralization and disease.

For the colonials, Velasco's era was still an age of splendor. He ruled over them with paternal sternness, but also with tolerant good humor. While he tried to enforce the laws protecting the Indians, he permitted colonial luxury and eccentricity. There was no Inquisition in New Spain, nor much royal taxation.

There are several views of this colonial society, and all are valid. On one plane, New Spain was flowering and undergoing rapid improvement. The capital and the other towns such as Puebla and Guadalajara were growing into large, well-kept, beautiful cities. Already, many of the older, hastily-erected Mexican-Gothic monstrosities were being replaced with more graceful buildings. Some of the older palaces, like Cortés' in México, which now housed the royal mint, were used for public buildings, while newer, splendid municipal halls, hospitals, schools, convents, and private mansions rose. The capital did not begin to approach the former size of Tenochtitlan, but it was well-ordered, remarkably clean, and broad-avenued. The Spanish colonials invested much of their wealth in architecture, public and private. The first Spanish church on the Zócalo was soon to be removed; in the 1570s it was replaced with the great cathedral which still stands.

México, Puebla, Valladolid, and Guadalajara were Spanish. The indigenes lived in them only as servants; though masses of *indios* huddled on their fringes, as in Tlatelolco. The cities as yet contained no slums; they were the territory of a master class. Despite their soaring churches and flowering parks, they were rather sterile. There were exotic marketplaces and thriving shops, great town halls where grave *regidores* met and courts where lawyers matched rhetoric, but there was little of the raucous bustle and raw excitement that pervaded great, heterogeneous capitals like London or Paris. Even in this age of building there was already a little ennui and somnolence.

The *encomendero* class tended to be eccentric in some respects, fully understandable in a class that had nothing to do, ferocious in the defense of its racial privileges, and determined not to be provincial. Along with fine palaces it built large libraries, importing classics from Europe wholesale; it studied Latin and philosophy at the university; it supported printing presses and local theaters lavishly. Some families began to build luxurious country houses on their estates. Many of these fine seats, and scores of neat shooting boxes on private game preserves, ringed the capital and major provincial towns. Cortés had commanded his *encomenderos* to raise horses for military purposes; blooded horses became an especial love of the wealthy class.

The members of this class left many records that show them to have been reasonably educated, genteel, and thoroughly satisfied. They had hunts in the country and elaborate, extravagant masquerades and balls at which the viceroy might appear. They loved fiestas. They were gregarious and well-mannered, more so than Spaniards in the old country. They lived with more thought of the day than of the morrow; after all, they were people striving for nothing and going nowhere. Prodigality was admirable in the Hispanic ethos; otherwise, one might appear too much a Flemish banker or a Jew. Rich men at México broached casks of imported European wines—a tremendous luxury—in the streets on fiesta days; such acts were much admired and usually duly recorded. Of course, by living for the day, many colonial families were soon sunk in deep, if arrogant, poverty.

This society, and the country generally, usually impressed visitors and newcomers most favorably. While some Spaniards tended to mock colonial eccentricities, most arriving bishops, *oidores*, and viceroys were entranced with the luxury and apparent vitality of New Spain. The vast mountains, volcanoes, green valleys, huge vistas, and mild climate had no more impressed the hardbitten conquistadores, on the whole, than the jungles, swamps, hurricanes, and Amerindian arrows. But the scholarly friars and the men who were emerging from the Royal and Pontifical University in the 1550s were fascinated with the things of the country and the elegance of Mexican life.

This culture had the rapid polish and gentility so often acquired by slave-holding societies. The Spanish invented no new forms—they drew on Western Europe. Their colorful social life, even their vices, were in sincere flattery of the lives and vices of the European aristocracy. Their literary efforts—however remarkable for a transplanted society—were generally mediocre. The important works, from Sahagún to Balbuena, came from men born in Spain. The colonial writings have survived primarily as curiosities rather than literature.

The arbitrary differentiation of society along racial lines left no real middle class. Arriving European shopkeepers and artisans, even workmen of mediocre quality, were relieved of manual labor, and neither they nor the many petty officials formed a true bourgeoisie. This robbed society of creativity and vitality. The elite was emasculated at birth, because it did not exercise and grow as an aristocracy. The Spanish bureaucracy—which unfortunately is often confused with a true middle class—regulated and directed both colonials and Indians.

Meanwhile, under the facade of viceregal benevolence and colonial luxury serious social antagonisms were brewing, between American and peninsular-born Spaniards. Separated by the Atlantic, with imperfect communications, the two countries gradually grew apart in some respects. The generations that began to emerge in America now contrasted sharply with the young men who still came out from Spain.

The colonials, who came to be called *criollos* or Creoles (which in Spanish territory always signified American-born individuals of supposedly pure European blood) actually did not change as much as the people in Spain. Their speech, mentality, and styles were less adulterated than the constantly affected styles in European Spain; the Andalusian-accented Castilian of New Spain remained a purer language than the metropolitan tongue. Colonial attitudes and eccentricities represented the swashbuckling styles of the Renaissance—but by the 1550s, Spanish officialdom already reflected the newer, more somber age of Felipe II.

The austerity of these grim clerics and *letrados* clashed with the gay, egoistical irresponsibility of the sons of the conquistadores. Metropolitan society was now beginning its long, painful regression from the great hopes and brilliant humanism of the Carlist era into the gloomy, arrogant intransigence and obscurantism of Philippian times. Eternal war against most of Europe, in which the homeland Spanish confused Hapsburg dynasticism with the defense of Catholic Christianity not only drained the royal treasury; it warped and desiccated the Spanish mind. The full force of the Protestant Reformation polarized and paralyzed Spanish thought. It was impossible for the Spanish to turn Protestant; however, the cracked cosmos of Christendom gradually turned the Spanish to a fortress mentality. The Inquisition, which had once, with good intentions, ferreted out infidels became a frightened exercise in bigotry and cruelty. It began to hunt down *erasmistas*, the liberal Catholic humanists who offered an enlightened alternative to the grim Spanish Counter-Reformation. In the second half of the sixteenth century the surviving Franciscan friars who had tried to humanize Mexico were to feel the Holy Office's deadly grip. The humorless, suspicious Felipe II both instigated and applauded such destruction.

There was at first no rigid policy that all high offices in the New World must be held by native Spaniards. But the crown's suspicions, intensified under a distrustful Felipe II, custom, and the fact that *peninsulares* fought as jealously for privileges as Creoles fought for their status vis-á-vis the Amerindians, solicited this practice. Almost all the policies and practices that were to characterize Iberian government in New Spain were hardened in this reign. Power was consciously reserved to the *gachupines* (a term of uncertain origin, which perhaps meant "spurred ones") who from this time forward formed a dominant faction in the government and affairs of New Spain. The *gachupines* or *peninsulares* arrived feeling themselves different from and uncomfortable among the colonials, whom they called *indianos*—inhabitants of an Indian country.

What rapidly grew up was not a divergent nationalism but a sort of patriotism of faction. The *criollos* were loyal to the crown and Church; even tenth-generation Creoles still thought of Spain as "home." But in New Spain factionalism between peninsular Spaniards and *criollos* was already widespread. There was enormous resentment among the Mexican-born that every official of rank and power invariably was appointed out of Spain.

A conspiracy against Iberian officialdom began to take form in the last years of Velasco's regime. The exact nature of this conspiracy is unknown; the record shows mainly spectacular but unproven charges brought by the Spanish government. Apparently a group of idle, frustrated young members of the elite, barred from prestigious offices and mightily affronted by the real or implied insults of the royal officers in power, began to meet secretly, and probably, to discuss full-scale armed revolt.

Alonso de Avila Alvarado and his brother Gil, rich young roisterers about México, emerged in the forefront of this "revolution." When Don Martín Cortés, Marqués del Valle, the eldest legitimate son of the conquistador, returned to New Spain in 1563, the Avilas tried to engage him as their leader. Martín Cortés was an arrogant, pampered young coxcomb, apparently given to braggadocio. Whether he actually joined the Avilas is not known, but he associated with them constantly.

The Viceroy Velasco, fully aware of this tavern talk, seems to have understood that the bulk of the *criollos* were not prepared to separate from

Spain, and he did not fear men like the Avilas, Cortés, and their spoiled entourages. But then, in 1564, Velasco died while organizing an expedition to the Orient, and playing at revolution suddenly became very dangerous. The *audiencia*, composed of the *oidores* Orozco, Villalobos, and Zeinos, took over the government of Mexico; they were given neither to aristocratic assurance nor humorous tolerance of young men.

The only overt act of the conspirators was the symbolic crowning of young Cortés, dressed like a conquistador, by Alonso de Avila, got up as Motecuhzoma. The notion of a new *criollo* kingdom titillated them. They may have tentatively planned an uprising. But the Avilas were fatuous young fops and the second Marqués of the Valley was a coward. The *audiencia*, informed by spies, arrested the Avilas and most of their companions. Martín Cortés, his brother Don Luis, and his half-brother Martín, Malintzin's son, were all jailed in México. Although a full investigation of the Avilas turned up no real evidence, the brothers were convicted of treason. Almost all the important Creoles of New Spain tried to save the Avilas, but they were immediately beheaded, as became their noble rank, and their skulls exhibited on lances from the roof of the Casa de Cabildo.

The marqués was saved, though not exonerated, by the arrival of Don Gastón de Peralta, Marqués de Falces, the new viceroy. Peralto was a humane aristocrat; concluding that the *audiencia* had been overzealous, he stopped the proceedings and released the prisoners.

The *oidores'* reports alarmed the always-suspicious king. Peralta was accused of joining the conspiracy and of raising an army of thirty thousand men. These were totally unfounded, ridiculous charges, but they reflected upon the character of the age. Felipe II really could not accept the charges made against Peralta and Martín Cortés, who had been raised at his court —but he could not quite dismiss them, either. When he failed to hear from Peralta, whose reports were intercepted by his own disloyal *oidores*, Felipe sent out the *licenciados* Muñoz, Jaraba, and Carillo as investigating judges, with full powers to supercede Peralta and return him to Spain.

The lawyer Muñoz, as president of these *jueces pesquisidores*, deposed the viceroy and assumed the government. Peralta retired to the fortress at San Juan de Uloa to await a ship. He had already released Martín Cortés, who immediately left for Spain, where he was not exonerated until 1574. His estates were confiscated during this time. The estates were allowed to pass to his heirs, but the Marqués himself was barred from New Spain for life.

At México, Muñoz and Carillo began a reign of terror. They arrested hundreds of *criollos*. Any resistance was considered treason. Muñoz entered into a round of seizures, tortures, and executions. The Martín Cortés who was Malintzin's son was put to torture in the hope that he might confess some crime. But this Cortés, the only descendent of the conquistadorial captains who played the man during this episode, defended his half-brothers to the end.

How were these judges, backed only by a few constables, able to tyrannize a whole society? A handful of colonials in arms could have stopped Muñoz and the persecutions, which everyone knew were unjust. But the *criollo* elite had pride without a concept of responsibility or leadership, and all Spaniards were rendered helpless by the fact that Muñoz exercised the authority of the crown. Since Muñoz held letters from the king, he was above all law except a revocation of his patent by the king. The final irony of the reign of terror was that it was ended, not by colonials, but by the very *oidores* who had instigated Muñoz' appointment. For the lawyer overstepped himself, treating even Spanish officials with such contempt that they began to fear for their lives. The former *oidores* sent the king overwhelming evidence of Muñoz' errors and crimes, causing Felipe II to send out a new *audiencia*.

In Spain the Marqués de Falces was exonerated. Muñoz had to be confronted in a monastery, where he had sought refuge, with the king's order. But he meekly complied, returned in disgrace, was abruptly silenced by the king, and died immediately—whether by royal command is not known.

In these two years the right of *peninsulares* to rule had been harshly established, and the *criollo* population was thoroughly cowed. Succeeding generations of colonials hardly dared criticize the government, even in satire.

The line between *criollos* and Spaniards also was now rigidly drawn. The determination of a suspicious monarchy to rule, and of Spanish councils to maintain a complete monopoly of all offices in their hands is completely understandable; these were totally human manifestations, and Hispanic politics allowed no remedy for them. But, again humanly, rationales began to grow up around these drives. The peninsular colonies within New Spain gravely asserted that there was something debilitatiing in the Mexican climate or air—Europeans deteriorated in the tropics—which meant that *criollos* or *indianos* had become inherently inferior. Colonials were irresolute and irresponsible and pleasure-seeking, also lazy, they could not be entrusted with important affairs. Some theorists went much further: they stated that there was something in the New World that prevented all native living things, human, animal, or vegetable, from reaching a full maturity. The indigenes therefore remained children, the *criollos* adolescents.

Less subtle, but immensely more crushing, was another source of imputed *criollo* inferiority. This was the notion that all *indianos* possessed at least some Amerindian blood. There was a great deal of truth in this. Most conquistadores had wed native women. Few Spanish women survived the passage to the Indies. In 1646, a century after the Conquest, there were still nine males to every European female in New Spain, and the native *criollos* were at a serious disadvantage in competing against the *peninsulares* even for these. The "old" families almost always had an Amerindian ancestress of whom they were usually proud, especially those who could trace their lineage back to Motecuhzoma. But for the general run of *criollos*, this *indio* blood became suspect. Arriving *peninsulares* never forgot it, or allowed the colonials to forget it. The snide reference, *se dicen español*, was applied to the "so-called Spaniards" in the same way that Spaniards put down "so-called hidalgos," those colonials who put *don* before their names and mysteriously acquired a coat of arms. The Mexican elite writhed under these sneers. The children of the conquistadores retaliated with jokes and doggerel about starveling Spaniards who came out to the Indies with their gloomy faces and went home counts—but the *gachupines* sat in the seats of power, and formed the brilliant court around the viceroy. What they thought and said had far more weight in society than the opinions of the *criollos*.

Creole maidens jumped at the chance to marry even impoverished *peninsulares* of good family—and they sometimes were sent "home" by their husbands when they were with child, so that the infant might avoid the stigma of being born in the New World. Members of the *audiencia* in time were forbidden to marry in New Spain in order to prevent them from making attachments and alliances with the colonials.

The full-blown racisms that now grew up throughout New Spain and Spanish America affected the mentality of Spanish America and strongly colored the emergence of its society. The attitudes should never be seen as quintessentially Spanish, or even European. Spanish society was inherently racist in its attitudes toward Jews and Moors. However, the racism of the Indies grew directly out of the colonial situation and society. Some such system or systems were inevitable because of the determination of the Spanish to rule over the Indians, and of the peninsular Spaniards to dominate the colonies.

Cortés himself and most of the conquistadores had been quite free from any prejudice based on skin color or appearances. The Spanish were not "white" in the sense the northern Europeans were; skin pigmentation never figured strongly in the Iberian consciousness. Spanish racism was based on ancestry rather than physical appearances. The Amerindians were never physically repugnant to the Spanish, and the conquistadores, at least, never doubted their humanity. The Spanish put far less emphasis on color than on religion, social rank, and ancestry; and there was a definite chronology to the growth of racist tendencies, just as there was a definite chronology in the growth and regression of Spanish humanism.

Cortés insisted that his *encomenderos* marry, and this meant that almost all of them had to marry native women. The priests concurred; they were appalled at the sexual license of a country where nubile females were constantly made available. The two races blended well, often producing strikingly lovely children. No stigma attached either to these marriages or their offspring, who were accepted as Spanish. Motecuhzoma's daughters wed Spanish noblemen and produced a race of Spanish *grandes*, who were proud to assume the name Montezuma. Cortés and Malintzin's son became a knight, and Bernal Díaz' half-Amerindian son a *regidor*. This whole generation passed easily into *criollo* society.

But it became harder and harder for Spaniards to respect native aristocrats when the whole body of *indios* had been effectively enserfed. Soldiers and adventurers without women had few prejudices, but wives were arbiters of society, and when a few Spanish women arrived and as a distinctly Spanish society grew, race lines hardened. By the last half of the sixteenth century, interracial marriages were officially discouraged, though never illegal, and they virtually ceased.

Racial prejudices, caste lines, and racial rationales had to follow, once the incorporation of the *indios* had ceased. The Spanish colonials resisted incorporation of the natives for social and economic reasons, but these had to be, and were, buttressed with rationales, the most pervasive and enduring of which was that all *indios* were *gente sin razón*. The whole edifice of the *criollos*, had to depend on an assumed inferiority, incapacity, and inability of the Amerindians.

It made no difference that, compared to the island natives, the "childlike, incapable" Mexicans had developed a high civilization, if it was technically and rationally inferior to the European. They had an elaborate hierarchical social structure not much different from the Spanish, and their engineers erected cities greater than any in Spain. The friars who were closest to the Amerindians came to admire them and never doubted they could eventually be recivilized as Europeans. The Franciscans deliberately, with Zumárraga's and Mendoza's support, had begun developing an Hispanicized native elite.

From all accounts, Pedro de Gante's academy, and the colleges at Tlatelolco and Michoacán were great successes. They were in fact too successful, both for the *encomendero* class and Spanish officialdom. Officers whose instincts were to maintain their domination were frightened to see native aristocrats seizing European philosophies and techniques, and, as one wrote the king, reciting the language of Tullius with more skill than the heirs of Rome. An educated native aristocracy, which the friars were doing their best to create, would almost certainly assume an equal footing with the conquerors, and the leadership of the Mexican people.

Hierarchy among the *indios* was dangerous to the developing *criollo* society. King Felipe's decision to deny the entry of *indios* into holy orders was a fatal blow to Mexican education. When all social advance was to be denied the race for an indefinite period of "tutelage" there was no reason for offering it higher education. The college at Tlatelolco, where students had orated in Latin and drawn up excellent Nahuatl and Spanish books and manuscripts, degenerated into a sort of elementary school, and soon disappeared.

Discouragement went beyond denying higher education. Spanish guilds, Spanish doctors, artisans, shopkeepers, and smiths, now establishing themselves in New Spain, were successful in barring *indios* from all professions and skilled trades. Guilds and professions were exclusionist in Spain and throughout all Europe, but in America the exclusion took on a definite racial connotation.

By the last half of the century, the Spanish recognized only one form of hierarchy among Amerindians. They permitted selected *caciques* to act as local village headmen, whose purpose was to transmit Spanish orders. Such men, inevitably, became toadies and tyrants. Meanwhile, the indigenous nobility, many of whom had loyally served the Spanish, denied both the old education and the new, could not maintain itself and sank into the oppressed mass of *indios*. By 1600 it had disappeared.

The Spanish official rationale was always one of protecting the *indio*. He was made a ward of the state, and suffered the fate of all such wards. Powerless, he became a stranger in his own country. The laws required *indios* to live separately from the Spanish; forbade them to acquire any debt greater than forty reales or five pesos, and denied them European dress, horses, and firearms. All these laws were "protective" in theory— they were to keep the *indio* from being corrupted. In effect, they kept him in slavery, with no chance to better himself.

The law did make it difficult for an Amerindian to be executed for anything except a return to heathenism, and *indios* were not normally subject to investigation by the Inquisition. However, the laws allowed *indios* to be whipped for an enormous assortment of crimes and misdemeanors, and many *encomenderos* and *corregidores* had Indians beaten to death. Thus the laws of New Spain destroyed and justified the destruction, by making the *indio* into exactly what he was claimed to be: an incapable, childlike, irresponsible, uncooperative human being, a *cerrado* who failed to grasp European reasoning.

The Amerindian spirit was strong, but it broke. The hardworking masses who once cheerfully supported a vast, surrealistic but impressive civilization and who had eagerly cooperated with the early friars changed drastically over the years. All early Spanish accounts described the *indio* as curious, energetic, good-humored, and cooperative. Now, Spanish writings showed them as withdrawn, sullen, and sometimes vicious, with a deep hatred veiled by a pose of apathy and stupidity. The *indio* increasingly showed an inability to understand commands and to carry them out intelligently, exasperating the masters and driving them to more restrictive codes.

According to all indigenous records, the excessive use of alcohol was unknown, or forbidden, in the old culture. In his unhappy new world, the Mexican *indio* retreated into drug use. He began to stupify himself with pulque, an unsanitary fermentation of the juice of the maguey plant. Normally sad and passive, the drunken *indio* often exploded into violence and murder. Alcohol abuse became endemic among many Amerindians and completed their destruction. The Spanish came to believe that *indios* could not handle alcohol, and modern studies, showing certain physiological differences between Europeans and Amerindians, have confirmed a physical basis for this belief.

The conquered *indio* had been carefully, if not entirely consciously, made into what he was. The Spanish rebuked and penalized the *indio* for not being a European while at the same time making it impossible for him to become a true European. Nothing in this was unusual in master-slave relationships between two races; it had happened before in many parts of the world.

The hardening of racial lines made the status and situation of a growing population of mixed bloods increasingly anomalous. The first generation of the blended race entered freely into *criollo* society, even though they might bear a slight stigma in peninsular eyes. But as the whole Amerindian mass degenerated and legal marriage between Spanish and *indios* grew unthinkable, the mixed bloods who had not been adopted as legal Spaniards found their position even more uneasy than that of the Amerindians. From the first gift of girls to Cortés' soldiers in Tabasco Spaniards had been making babies indiscriminately in Mexico; the children of casual unions far outnumbered those legitimized. As in all such situations, the miserable offspring were caught in tensions between two races and cultures; they were accepted neither by Europeans nor Amerindians. And while it is true that thousands of native women in New Spain deliberately sought to bear Spanish children—in the hope that such children would be relieved of slavery or serfdom—an aura of rape hung over all such liaisons. The mothers had no power to protect themselves or their mixed-blood children, and the Spanish fathers often abandoned them.

The end of legal intermarriage did not stop the production of mixed bloods. If he could not fill his house with nubile *india* servants, the Spaniards came to maintain a *casita*, or little house, where he maintained an illegitimate family. The position of such families was anomalous. The bastard children not only had the stain of illegitimacy before the society and Church, but they carried a supposed blood taint, which they believed themselves. However, the bastardized population grew rapidly proportionally to the surviving Amerindians, because its members inherited greater immunity to European diseases. By 1650, there were at least one-hundred-and-sixty thousand mixed bloods in New Spain.

In a society where the races had become sharply delineated, mixed bloods had to be officially recognized. Therefore, a person with mixed parentage could not be regarded as wholly European or *indio*, and systems had to be devised to classify him. These systems, which the Spanish pioneered in the New World, had many shadings. The Spanish did not create a single, brutal racial bar, but rather a system that had many hurdles and doors. They believed in the theory of "dominant blood." The Spanish broke people of mixed blood down into many different categories and gave them a certain hierarchy of status according to predominant white, Amerindian, and African genes. This led some observers to believe that the Spanish had no acute sensibilities to racial matters in America— a notion refuted by the enormous attention they gave to the system of classification.

Spanish bureaucracy and training in Roman law, which tended toward exact definitions, created a socio-racial structure of marvelous complexity in the New World. All mixed bloods were called *castas*, or breeds. There were *castas*, or castes, of the European or white, the Amerindian, and the Negro races:

Castes of the White Race (Criollo or Peninsular)

European father and Negra mother	=	Mulatto
European father and India mother	=	Mestizo
European father and Mulatta mother	=	Cuarterón
European father and Mestiza mother	=	Criollo
European father and China mother	=	Chino blanco
European father and Cuarterona mother	=	Quintero
European father and Quinterona mother	=	Blanco (white)

Castes of the Indian Races (All):

Indio father and Negra mother	=	Chino
Indio father and Mulatta mother	=	Chino oscuro
Indio father and Mestiza mother	=	Mestizo claro
Indio father and China mother	=	Chino cholo
Indio father and Zamba mother	=	Zambo claro
Indio father and China chola mother	=	Indio
Indio father and Quintera or Cuarterona mother	=	Mestizo pardo

Castes of the Negro Race:

Negro father and Mulatta mother	=	Zambo
Negro father and Mestiza mother	=	Oscuro
Negro father and China mother	=	Zambo
Negro father and Zamba mother	=	Negro
Negro father and Cuarterona or Quintera mother	=	Mulatto oscuro

"Corruptions"

Mulatto father and Zamba mother	=	Zambo miserable
Mulatto father and Mestizo mother	=	Chino claro
Mulatto father and China mother	=	Chino oscuro

The tables, which in some respect influenced all European racial attitudes in the New World, show the enormous Spanish interest in ancestry. The definitions actually were hardly scientific but arbitrary and inexact. They varied in different times and places, and more than anything else, the classifications were descriptive. Some castes were considered highly attractive (especially where the bloodlines bred beautiful women) while others were regarded so pejoratively that in time the very names became deadly insults. The dark-skinned Spanish, many of whom possessed some Asian blood, paid little attention to skin color in determining castes. Race was determined officially, in case of question or doubt concerning parentage, by examinations of hair shades and structures. Short, woolly hair marked the African; straight, coarse locks or an inability to grow body hair the Amerindian.

The caste system did allow *castas* to breed themselves back into the white race—the children of whites and *quinteronas* were white—but it did not allow for castes springing from European mothers and non-white males. Apparently this was unthinkable. The authorities also gave up any attempt to classify castes of the bewildering mix of East Indians, Malays, Chinese, Japanese, and Filipinos which entered through Acapulco after 1600. All Asians were lumped together as *chinos*, or Chinese.

All non-white *castas* were more or less equally excluded under the law; however, castes of the white race had legal status that distinguished them from African or Indian castes. Castes of the white race enjoyed a limited citizenship. They were subject to taxes, fines, prison, and the death penalty, and fair game for the Inquisition. They could be conscripted, and therefore they had none of the special "privileges" of *indios*. On the other hand, they could not legally enter the professions or hold office, carry lances or knives, or live in certain European neighborhoods. In many ways the *mestizos* and such white *castas* were worse off than *indios*. They were subject to all Spanish punitive laws and burdens, but without any of the theoretical protections of the Amerindians. The great majority were out-castes, accepted and tolerated by neither society. Thousands of them were vagabonds, slum dwellers on the fringes of the towns. Many were a sort of street people, without homes or steady occupations.

These street people, who huddled, starved, and begged on every corner of the towns of New Spain, were known as *léperos*. Social lepers, they begged, did odd jobs, and robbed. By the seventeenth century, mobs of *léperos* thronged the capital and constituted a growing threat to public order. They could be wantonly destructive, even murderous, when sparked by some incident. Out in the countryside, *léperos* formed a bandit class. They were the first Mexican bandits, and by 1700 mixed-breed brigands infested the road between Veracruz and the City of México.

According to Spanish records, almost all the violent crime in New Spain came from *castas* or *léperos*. *Indios* never seemed to have engaged in banditry, though they sometimes murdered when drunk or enraged. The *lépero* was forced to survive by his wits in a society that gave him no place. Cold, hungry, miserable, and worst of all, despised, the *lépero* lived as he could. Descriptions show the *léperos*, men, women, and children, as ragged and diseased, existing day to day, obsequious, whining, ready to cut either a throat or purse, begging for food or work, screaming under the whips of the town authorities who frequently ordered them chastised.

The *léperos* appalled the *criollo* upper class, which believed that the half-breeds inherited no virtues but magnified the vices of both races. To the dominant society, the *léperos* were sly, lazy, untrustworthy, lacking the manly courage of the Spaniards and the stoicism and patience of the Amerindian. The leaders of the bandit gangs were almost always *criollos*, and this fact reinforced the racial myths of the dominant classes.

Yet, thousands of *léperos* survived; they formed families; they made their devotions and dropped their *óbolos* in the offering boxes. Ironically, the *léperos* were to survive, grow, and finally, inherit modern Mexico. They proved, not the degeneracy of man, but mankind's tenacity in the face of hideous adversity. Meanwhile, they suffered hideous damage as a people, which would take centuries to undo.

History has shown that the relationships of conquering and conquered peoples have always devolved either into a form of slavery or serfdom, a caste system, or miscegenation, the last necessary to reform into a reasonably homogeneous people. The Spanish empire in America invented nothing new and solved no unsolvable problems. Uniquely, the Spanish employed all three methods—serfdom, castes, and interbreeding—in the building of the emerging Mexican society.

Felipe II decided that New Spain was ready for both the alcabala, the peculiarly regressive Castilian sales tax, and the Inquisition. Before, Spanish taxes and the Holy Office had not been applied to Mexico; the *encomenderos* paid a light tribute and the Bishop of Mexico acted as chief inquisitor, and attention had been paid only to heathenism among the Indians. Now, some sixty special taxes and assessments, collected through the Church and the viceregal government, were fastened on New Spain. And in 1570, a branch of the Holy Office was assigned to Mexico to ferret out possibly dangerous aberrations and eccentricities among the *criollos* and *castas*.

The entry of the Holy Inquisition was enormously unpopular in New Spain, where a sizeable number of the population had actually fled Spain to escape it. But no serious voices protested the digging of a prison and the start of special investigations at the capital. The inquisitors began to assemble files on suspected *conversos* or converts from Judaism or Islam, and also on suspected Protestants, sorcerers, witches, warlocks, blasphemers, and a few flagrant eccentrics. The holy office decided that Bernardino de Sahagún's superb history of the Amerindians should not be published, though fortunately the book was not lost to posterity. It destroyed the indigenous efforts to preserve written Nahuatl, either in the original or in its Latinized alphabet. Sahagún himself came close to treason as it was then defined. Although the inquisitors actually investigated or seized only a few people out of the whole population, no Spaniard could write, speak, or probably even dare to think without taking into consideration the public humiliations, fines, torture racks, and fires of the holy office. The crown never interfered with its operations, even when the Inquisition arrested people close to the king.

The most celebrated victims of the Mexican office was the family of the Carvajales, who were of Portuguese-Jewish origin. The Carvajales were prominent in New Spain; one became governor of the province of Nuevo León. Don Luis Rodríguez de Carvajal, nephew of the governor, was a secret Judaizer, who could not refrain from proselytizing. He, his mother and his sisters, after repeated investigations and hideous tortures, were finally burned in 1596 in the plaza of San Ipolito, before a brilliant gathering of all the notables of the Most Loyal City of México. Each was strangled at the stake before burning, however, because of last minute recantations.

Very few persons were actually burned in New Spain, but lesser punishments were very common; even if eventually exonerated, few suspected persons escaped with their reputations and fortunes.

No law was ever enacted that distinguished between colonists and native-born Spaniards. But the suspicions of the crown, and the natural interests of the *peninsulares* insured that born-Spaniards would always be favored with all the important posts and offices in New Spain. The few exceptions, ironically, as with two viceroys, were the sons of men who had the misfortune to be born in the Indies while their peninsular fathers governed. In effect, the *criollo* civic councils had no jurisdiction over a true Spaniard, who could appeal to his compatriots on the *audiencia*. The Creole *regidores* ruled only over the miserable *léperos*, since they did not even rule themselves. One viceroy summed up the real situation truthfully if tactlessly by saying that so long as a single mule remained in La Mancha (a backward province of Spain) that animal possessed the right to govern everything in the Indies.

The *criollos* were confirmed in their landholdings, and for all their irritations and resentments, this held them to the crown and scheme of things. However, native Spanish secured almost all the various economic favors and privileges the government could impart. All profitable monopolies and franchises went to them; *peninsulares* made up the small merchant classes and professional bodies of New Spain.

When the flood of American silver and gold began to destroy homeland industries by pricing them out of European markets through inflation, the merchants and guilds of Sevilla seized upon the Indies as a privileged marketplace. Royal ukases forbade the colonials to trade through any port except Sevilla, and at the same time, Spanish firms were granted monopolies to trade in the Americas. Far worse than this, restrictions were placed on the kinds of goods New Spain might produce, so that there could be no local competition with the homeland. New Spain thus became a dumping ground for shoddy Spanish merchandise, sold at exorbitant prices, while native industries and enterprises were destroyed. One such victim was a burgeoning silk industry, which had been built up by the Dominicans for the Indians, with worms and mulberry trees brought out from Spain.

Paper, chocolate, and alcoholic beverages, all of which were easily produced in Mexico, had to be imported through Seville. Chocolate, once drunk freely by the poorest Amerindians, became an enormous luxury, available only to the richest landowners, officials, and churchmen. Other ordinances stopped the manufacture of finished textiles in Mexico. The *indios* were restricted to making the roughest cotton cloth, soap, and a crude pottery, thus destroying a once flourishing indigenous craftsmanship. The natives lost all such skills and the *criollos* were not allowed to replace them. Economic barbarism was imposed on Mexico, hardly more than a generation after the friars had begun to find such promise among the indigenes.

By the close of the century, proud, haughty, dark-cloaked Castilians passed in and out of the Indies, dominating the halls of power, gathering the riches of the country. The crown now deliberately made their tenures short, so that they might acquire no interest in the Americas; this also made them more rapacious, since they had only a brief time in which to get rich. The impression created in all Mexican minds by this horde of mostly middle-class *letrados* and bureaucrats was that a natural perquisite of officialdom was to make money from office on the side. This was in fact, the only social mobility Hispanic society allowed.

The supposedly sallow and enervated *criollos*, with their silver-mounted saddles, flashy clothing, *india* concubines and a bitter though not quite resolute pride, lived in their town houses, or rode out to their country places surrounded by servile entourages. They were masters only in their own houses. They swallowed their resentment, or expressed it in sly verses or jokes. Their manhood began more and more to express itself in sexuality, a natural manifestation for men who are otherwise restricted, humiliated, or deprived. No *criollo* could engage in public affairs, go to war, or stand up against the government. They developed a peculiar cult of "machismo" that centered primarily on male domination of the female sex. The status and education of *criollo* women was even more stultified, and very similar to that of Mexica ladies. They were confined to the home and restricted to affairs of religion and the heart. They were passive, but terribly important, sex objects in the *criollo* culture.

Criollo life at best was splendidly luxurious, at worst comfortable. It was isolated from work or care. Every *criollo* was consciously a member of an elite, respected even if he had wasted his patrimony, spared the hard knocks of the European upper classes, which suffered constant wars. But disquiet and discontent lay over the Mexican elite and deeply shadowed its collective mind. Despite the piety of its women and the reckless, feckless ardor of its gallants, the class had no destiny, and seemed to know it.

Another form of destruction was working within the missionary church in Mexico. The Inquisition, symbol of the polarizing minds in Europe, paralyzed all the promising Catholic humanism. The friars, whose numbers increased as the *indios* declined, lost most of their former optimism and moral righteousness and certainty. In old age Sahagún believed his life had been devoted to cosmic tragedy—it would have been better to have left the *indios* alone. The contact of European civilization had killed them. However, the mission system, sliding into apathy and failure, was institutionalized. The convents were fastened on the land, and the orders were now quarreling among themselves over the dwindling carcass of Amerindian Mexico, trying to exclude the newer Jesuits, defending their privileges against the encroachments of the viceroys or the crown.

The *criollos*, churchmen, and even the *peninsulares* lived increasingly purposeless lives, while the *indios* and *léperos*, intent on survival, endured. So the century closed.

Far away, in the magnificent Escurial erected by American revenues among a starving but impressed peasantry on the high, cold plains of Castile, Felipe II lay dying. The greatest monarch in all Christendom, owning half the world, the king was bankrupt. He had mortgaged the silver of the Americas, *esos reinos* as his councillors called them, those kingdoms beyond the sea. He had done great damage to Castile and Aragon.

Worse, he had mortgaged the future of New Spain.

18

SPAIN, THE WORLD, AND MEXICO

Then every thing includes itself in power,
Power into will, will into appetite;
And appetite, an universal wolf,
So doubly seconded with will and power,
Must make perforce an universal prey,
And last eat up himself.

Shakespeare: *Troilus and Cressida* I, III.

The history of every nation is bounded, and the power and glory of Spain was ephemeral.

The power system that carried Spain to greatness also carried the seeds of its own destruction. The mystique of monarchy that allowed Fernando and Isabel to rule effectively and reform the Church and state permitted their grandson Carlos I to extirpate the last liberties of the Castilian towns, and their great-grandson Felipe II to reign as a complete despot. The same modern bureaucracy that the Catholic kings erected to articulate their government burgeoned, until at last, directed by inbred, inept monarchs more concerned with pleasure than a sense of purpose, it regulated the nation into bankrupt stagnation.

The confusion of Spanish nationalism with ideological fervor for the medieval Church involved the country in endless, futile wars; the Spanish mistook the interests of the house of Hapsburg for the interests of their faith. The drive that freed Spain from Islam turned her on terrible, useless, impossible crusades against distant Protestants.

That same faith and drive made Spaniards destroy two valuable minorities, the Moriscos who worked the southern fields and the Sephardim who had administered the kingdom. The forces that raised great cathedrals also dug dank torture pits. The long struggle to preserve the Castilian vision of truth, that gave the conquistadores such utter confidence, almost destroyed the Spanish soul in a changing world. In the end, the defense of Castilian Catholicism paralyzed Spanish liberalism, humanism, and independent thought.

The Spanish tragedy was that for a century Spain did not lose her dynastic-ideological wars of the Hapsburgs but destroyed herself trying to win them. Victory was always just beyond reach. And the ideological nature of the struggle and the dead grip of the Inquisition did not allow Spaniards to admit tragedy. The holy office had reduced Spaniards intellectually to the point where they could not decide, Hamlet-like, to be or not to be—they could no longer pose the question.

The self-destruction was far gone long before the Armada sailed, and complete before the *tercios'* myth of invincibility was finally shattered at Rocroi in 1643.

The Spanish economy, always primitive at best, fell apart under the strains of unprecedented royal expenditures and the great inflationary stream of bullion from America. By the 1550s Mexican silver had fueled a serious inflation in Castile, pricing Spanish products out of European markets. Meanwhile, money flowed out of Spain to support the foreign wars. The towns decayed and the roads filled with ragged vagabonds in the same era that King Felipe enjoyed the greatest revenues of any European prince.

The bureaucracy countered by debasing the coinage and forbidding the export of specie. It could not attack the root problem. Carlos I, for the maintenance of the court alone, spent ten times the sums expended annually by the Catholic kings. His successors were even more extravagant. By the reign of Felipe III the nation was bankrupt.

The promise of the silver fleets from Mexico permitted Felipe II unlimited credit. He borrowed wildly against American revenues. His military and political expenses caused a royal bankruptcy and default in the 1590s, the decade in which New World shipments of specie reached their highest total. None of this wealth was spent on the Spanish state or people. All of if flowed through to foreign bankers; little of it reached the army, which lived by begging door to door at home, and by looting abroad.

When, after 1600, the supply of bullion from America fell radically, dropping to approximately what it had been before the great silver strikes of the 1540s, the crown found it impossible to admit error or readjust. In the same century that the Spanish-American silver peso or piece-of-eight reales became the trading currency of half the world, the Spanish government was forced to replace good money at home with the copper maravedí. This base coin, part cause, part symptom, created more inflation and misery. The Spaniards, according to a contemporary joke, had become the northern bankers' Indians.

The crown used desperate means to raise revenue. It sold offices, titles, and privileges. For a price one could now ennoble a dead grandfather. It taxed every use and function, controlled most prices through monopolies, and sold religious bulls or privileges. The crown put any title from a dukedom to the privilege of putting "don" before one's name up for sale, along with certificates of *limpieza de sangre*, or "clean blood." While constantly increasing taxes stifled the economy, the constant additions to the "nobility" dried up the tax rolls, because nobles were exempt from taxes. In Spain the *hidalguía* or gentry were classified as noble, and the passion for titles proliferated its numbers beyond those of any Western nation. The clergy was also excused from taxation. In 1541, there were one hundred thousand nobles against only eight hundred thousand tax-paying free subjects in Castile. In the next century, one Spaniard in seven was officially noble. In all, a full quarter of the male population had the privileges of the nobility, the clergy, the military, or office by the eighteenth century; thus one-fourth the population was removed from taxation and productive labor.

In the Hispanic world, all forms of enterprise were penalized, and it was no accident that sensible persons got out of enterprise as quickly as they could. Merchants bought land, which they did not work, and entailed it; they sent their sons into the bureaucracy or Church. By the 1600s, except for a few large, royally-favored monopolies, most Spanish business was in foreign hands. Foreigners dominated the commerce of Seville.

The image, and the reality, of Spain as an economically backward, socially stagnant, and over-bureaucratized country was made while the Spanish Hapsburgs remained Western Europe's major military power.

Unlike the English and French, the Spaniard emerging from the Middle Ages was unable to bring forth a new world view. The French were beginning to create their modern mind in the concept of the *honnête homme*, the person honest with himself and the external world, socially virtuous, his intellect in control. The French ruled passion with reason. The English were formulating the Elizabethan world view: that loosely-ordered realm in which common sense ruled both passion *and* intellect. The English were making a cool assessment of the real world, allowing neither passion nor intellect to dominate, and thus attempting to dominate that world.

The Spaniard showed no ability to compromise or change. He remained the *hombre de honor*, the man of honor, and honor as he held it brooked no accommodation with the external world. The Spaniard could not study or adjust. He had found truth; he was right; if the world differed, then the world was wrong. Here the Hispanic culture began to separate emotionally and intellectually from the dominant forces in modern Europe.

In the early sixteenth century, the man of honor was Hernán Cortés, daring Motecuhzoma's hordes, translating attitudes into action. The friars were also *hombres de honor*, changing an entire civilization by acts of faith and will. But when the Invincible Armada's battered survivors returned to Spain, and the *tercios* in the Netherlands were held off by Maurice of Orange's new tactics with firearms, action was becoming impossible. By the time French regiments destroyed the Spanish armies at Rocroi, the Spaniard had become utterly disillusioned with the world. It no longer responded to his acts and will.

The terrible tension between faith and reality produced a brilliant art in Spain. The age of Spanish self-destruction was Spain's cultural golden century, the *siglo de oro*, the age of Cervantes and Lope de Vega, Alarcón and Calderón and Quevedo, El Greco and Velásquez.

The great thrust of Spanish art and literature was a reaffirmation against fears and doubts. Lope de Vega's *comedias*, which were part of a genuine national theater, extolled the qualities of faith, fealty, love, and honor, embodied in changeless characters dominated by will. While Lope held forth against the night, doubts produced another kind of art from the pens of Cervantes and the Mexican-born humpback, Alarcón.

Cervantes wrote one of the world's great novels, a tale of delusions and dreams and tilting at windmills by men mired in brutal reality, and subtly posed the question whether dreamers or the world was mad. Cervantes' genius was not blunted by the Inquisition's thought-police, which now had gone beyond ferreting out heretics and infidels to exercising thought control, but like Alarcón, he had to write carefully.

Alarcón, perhaps because of his American birth, had a clear vision of the whole Spanish concept of the century as a lie, a monstrous illusion fostered by society and state. Ingeniously, when the characters in his *comedias* are known to be telling lies, they assume the forms and cadences of Lope's verse.

These artists wrote when there was still hope and made Hispanic literature predominant in their age. But as the nation proceeded to final disaster in the Thirty Years War, art increasingly showed the Spanish exhaustion and disillusionment. The age became *barroco*, or baroque, not only in the embellished styles of Churriguera, but in its life styles and the shadows on its mind. It was an age of people too aware of death and destruction, unable to find alternatives, and no longer assured of their souls or their souls' salvation. The fear of death grew, with the knowledge that for all a society's collective will and glory, every man dies alone. Such fears and doubts could not be voiced in Inquisition-ridden Spain, but heros on the Spanish stage and in the Flemish trenches joked about death—not because they were fearless, but because they were desperately tired.

Faith was becoming more and more an external thing, and so was sin. Both sin and the regular *autos-da-fé* performed for cheering audiences had become meaningless acts. God was real—but he had deserted Spaniards. The world still had form, but it had lost all meaning.

Now, on the stage, in life, in war, at court or church, form and style was all there was. *No hay realidades, solo hay palabras* wrote Quevedo: there is no reality, only words. Still holding fanatically to all her forms, Spain sank into a morass without true moral codes or meaning, disillusioned, but still hungering for a worm-eaten glory.

The authorities debated endlessly what was wrong. Some blamed the times, some foreign influences. As Spain turned from aggressor to the besieged, she succumbed to a siege mentality. Foreign knowledge was banned; students forbidden to study abroad. The great universities of Salamanca and Alcalá, once brilliant in law, medicine, and botany, became backwaters where pedants squabbled over form. The damage was profound.

In the last stages of decay between 1580 and 1680, Spanish life began to have an unreal quality, reflected in the arts. The world was now seen as an *engaño*, a snare and delusion. *La vida es sueño, y los sueños suenos son* Calderón wrote: life is a dream, and the dreams themselves dreams. His sophisticated audiences of *desenganados*, cultivated men and women undeceived with the world, appreciated the futility of action, and rejected the notion that man, half brute, half angel, might raise himself by his own bootstraps. This was the final failure of will, verging on anarchy of the soul.

Fatalism grew. In this new world where everything he believed in went wrong, the Spaniard degenerated intellectually. The *cultos*, the educated, followed sterile styles colored with cynicism; the *vulgos* or ignorant retreated into gross superstitions.

The first hero of the century had been the Cid, the man of action, loyalty, and honor, changing the world with his sword. The final hero was the *burlador*, the joker, the deceiver of women. Tirso de Molina's Don Juan was a rebel, desperate for something real to rebel against. He could only assert his manhood by deceiving as many women as possible, and by defying the laws of man and God. His anarchy of soul was followed, inevitably in Spain, by an anarchy of politics and culture. Everything collapsed in stupor, ending the Spain that Fernando and Isabel had wrought.

At the end of the seventeenth century, Spain existed in stasis, the final loss of will to act. Carlos II, *el hechizado* or the bewitched, was human and king but not a man, taking decades to die. Meanwhile his country had become the sick man of Europe, a pawn among the other powers. The English eyed the empire greedily; the French desired the Spanish throne; the Austrians waited to seize Spanish provinces in the Netherlands and Italy. By being, as they thought, true to themselves, the Spaniards had turned power into dust, and glory into despair. At the last, Spain herself was like Don Quijote on his deathbed—sane, but drained and devoid of dreams.

Most of the destruction visited upon seventeenth-century Spain did not occur in Mexico. After the Muñoz visitation an almost idyllic peace held throughout the civilized parts of New Spain. Mexico was undisturbed by the great designs of Felipe II and the baroque madness of the Thirty Years War. The natives of the fruitful regions had been conquered and pacified and the rebellious spirit of the *criollos* broken.

The Wars of Religion affected Spanish America only in the occasional thunderclap of English, Dutch, or French raids along the coasts. However, the Spanish had imbedded themselves in the American highlands and built cities instead of trading posts; unlike the Portuguese, their empire could not really be threatened by the maritime powers. The nature of the Spanish did not let them use Mexico's strategic position between Europe and the Orient to make the colony a great *entrepot*; the Spaniards were not oriented to the sea. But their land empire was almost invulnerable. Sea-raiders could seize ships and towns; they could not displace the Spanish.

The enemies of Spain harassed commerce and forced the treasure ships to sail in convoy; they sacked some coastal cities such as Veracruz, Acapulco, and Panama. They could not halt the flow of specie, hold outposts on the mainland, or threaten Spanish rule of the continents.

The conflicts in Europe probably made the raids, which the Spanish considered piracy, inevitable, but Spanish policy in the New World also brought a certain retribution. The Spanish claimed the entire Western Hemisphere, except for Brazil: Spanish law proclaimed the death penalty for trespassers. Also, most would-be trespassers were northern heretics, to be burned, hanged, or, mercifully, sent to the galleys. Both policies made peripheral warfare endemic in America, between the Spanish authorities and sometimes entirely peaceful foreign traders or would-be colonists. The Spanish in the sixteenth century hanged a colony of French Huguenots in Florida "not as Frenchmen but as heretics"; revenge was taken by other Frenchmen "not against Spaniards, but against murderers." Various forms of Spanish treachery or mistreatment, entirely justifiable within the Spanish world view, created hordes of vengeful buccaneers. There is considerable evidence that the Dutch and English, particularly, would have preferred to trade than raid or fight, and that "piracy" was often caused by Spain's intransigent insistence upon a closed-door policy.

It was almost impossible to observe morality, laws, or niceties between heretics and papists. In 1568, John Hawkins arrived off Veracruz with five ships and a cargo of African slaves, contraband, but for which there was a ready market in New Spain. The new viceroy, Almanza, arrived with a fleet immediately afterward. A storm brewed, and Almanza, eager to reach port, made a truce with the English slave traders. But, with the advantage and after weighing his fealty to Church and king against a "promise made to a pirate," Almanza had his ships attack the unsuspecting English. Only two English ships escaped, one Hawkins', the other captained by a young sailor, Francis Drake, who swore bitterly to make the Spanish pay for their treachery.

Hawkins left a hundred English sailors ashore who were marched to the capital by Don Luis de Carvajal, a hero before his Judaizing relatives brought him into disgrace and prison. They were imprisoned and "severely examin'd" by the Inquisition. The survivors were paraded as heretics in the great square. Three were burnt, sixty were whipped and sentenced to the galleys, others were made slaves.

Hawkins had his revenge when his new ships and long-range culverins battered the Spanish Armada in 1588. Sir Francis Drake kept his promise in fire and blood from the Pacific to Cádiz. His name enraged the king and frightened viceroys, and *El Draque*, the bogeyman, for centuries frightened the children of New Spain.

The coasts and commerce were never entirely safe. The Dutch landed and looted Acapulco in 1624; Piet Hein captured the plate fleet, the great treasure convoy from New Spain off Florida in 1628. Later, the English sacked Veracruz, collecting vast sums in loot and ransoms. But terrible as the appearance of pirates was to the coastal towns, these raids hardly disturbed the tenor of life inside Mexico.

The older English historians seem to have wilfully misrepresented the quality of life in New Spain because of their insurmountable biases against Spain. It was true that the viceregal government was despotic, the Amerindians were oppressed, the Inquisition practiced terrorism, and society grew corrupt. But all this has to be weighed against conditions and events in the outside world, at a time when Europe was both making enormous cultural advances and trying to destroy itself. The Spanish empire was spared many of Europe's horrors. Ten times as many persons were burned for heresy in sixteenth-century England than during three hundred years of Inquisitorial history in America; some petty western German principalities destroyed more people for witchcraft than were brought before the holy office for any reason in all New Spain.

The Inquisition was despised by most of the Spanish population and the clergy of Mexico, and it seems to have lost much of its Iberian virulence in the new climate. The whippings and burnings in the Alameda park at

Mexico, viewed by the viceroy and the *audiencia*, were never quite the semi-hysterical fêtes they became in Spain. The fact was that the people were loyal to the Church. The state of religion, then and later, was much stronger and healthier in New Spain than in the old, where religious faith and practice was almost a matter of form, though powerfully institutionalized. The Cortesian decision to entrust the conversion of Mexico to the orders rather than the secular clergy had lasting effects, even after the Mexican Church was secularized in the seventeenth century. The friars provided a powerful element of humanism and social protest, which though often submerged ran through a portion of the Spanish clergy.

There was, of course, immense superstition in New Spain. The Amerindians were illiterate and half-heathen, the *léperos* grossly ignorant, and the *criollos* intellectually lazy. Also, Mexico continued to suffer from the same kind of natural disasters that aroused religious fears and feelings among its earliest peoples. Thousands of men, women, and small children took the fever and died within days; smallpox regularly broke out in the Spanish towns. Earthquakes and volcanic eruptions shook central Mexico, toppling buildings and aweing millions. In one year, both a violent earthquake and a snowstorm were recorded in the Valley of Mexico. In the face of such seemingly random, irrational acts of Nature, in a society of declining population where death was constantly forced on the survivors' consciousnesses, intense religious feeling combined with the grossest superstitions.

Mexico was honestly loyal to the concepts of Hispanic Catholicism, and a series of tolerant and quite capable viceroys kept the whole population loyal to the crown. The viceregal term of office was reduced to three-to-five years, though it was often extended at the pleasure of the Council of the Indies. This, and the enormous salary viceroys were paid—an annual sum equivalent to more than a million dollars in modern purchasing power —were expected to keep the viceroys free of American interests and personal corruption. The policy was reasonably successful. It is evident that if the viceroys did little to improve New Spain—changing the social system was beyond their powers, just as it was beyond the powers of the friars— they did nothing to damage the country, either. Some of the viceroys were genuine statesmen, and their job was easier because of the immense distance that separated them from the cesspool of jealousy, vice, and intrigue that swirled through seventeenth-century Madrid.

Don Luis de Velasco, Conde de Santiago, later Marqués de Salinas, son of the second viceroy, and eighth viceroy of New Spain, was welcomed with great ceremony and rejoicing in 1590. He had grown up in Mexico, and held various posts before his accession, and was considered a native by the *criollos*. Velasco wanted to develop the country and to halt the continuing abuses of the Indians. In 1601 and again in 1609 laws were passed that restricted the use of the *repartimiento*, especially in the mines of the grim northern frontier. The new codes forbade the requirement of long travel, and required the mining contractors to pay portal to portal time, furnish meals, and to pay cash wages at a fair rate. Corporal punishment such as the use of whips and stocks was banned. Like most Spanish laws, these were easily evadable, but a combination of depopulation and a radical decline in the skills of the native masses made slave labor in the mines, and in the towns where venal *corregidores* provided labor for private contractors, councils, and wheat farmers, unprofitable. The mine operators and most towns had to institute a system of paid, free labor to attract sufficient workers. By the middle of the century, mining was still a dirty and dangerous occupation, but now, trained, skilled, and willing *indios* went into the dark holes for a reasonable wage.

The City of México, situated on a lake that had been gradually drying for a thousand years, had begun to experience serious flooding as early as the administration of the first Velasco. The problem was that the Spanish had deforested the ocote and cypress-covered slopes of the three central lakes, Xaltocán, Texcoco, and Zumpango; now water cascaded off the mountains and soil erosion began to silt up the lakes. The lakes in Anáhuac had never drained to any sea; and during seasons of unusually heavy rains the water level lapping against the capital rose dangerously. After an inundation in the 1550s, the viceroy had rebuilt the old Mexica dikes; by 1604 no dams or levees could hold off the rising water. The second Velasco set the engineer Enrico Martínez to solving the problem.

Martínez dug a tunnel four miles through the encircling mountains to drain off the excess water. Many thousands of local *indios* were dragooned into this task and driven harshly to complete the job within a year. The task was done in eleven months, at an enormous cost in Amerindian hardship and lives. Unfortunately, while the idea was sound, the construction was shaky. The tunnel tended to cave in, and it was not large enough to handle a serious flood. For some twenty years, huge numbers of *indios* were kept laboring to clear the tunnel and shore it up; then, in 1629, a simultaneous rise in all the lakes choked the tunnel. The destruction was enormous, and some parts of the city remained flooded for four years.

The engineer Martínez was again called upon. Now, he converted his disastrous tunnel into an open ditch about thirteen miles long and about two hundred feet deep. This ditch, called the Tajo de Nochistongo, required ten years to put in operation, and work continued on it for more than a century. The draining of the Valley occupied a whole series of viceroys, used up most of their revenues, and laid terrible burdens on the surviving Anáhuac Indians. Nor was the drainage problem really solved, though the Capital was kept out of the mire. Drainage, and the subsequent sinking and shifting of the porous lake-bottom soil is still a monstrous engineering, architectural, and financial problem for México.

The abolishment of the *repartimiento* was accompanied by a phase-out of the *encomienda*. The *encomienda* was not officially ended until 1720, but by the seventeenth century, it was dying out. As grantees died without legal heirs or went bankrupt and disappeared, their villages and territories escheated back to the crown. Such events made little or no real change in the Mexican social and economic system; a basic reality simply changed its legal forms. There were no longer enough Indians to support Spanish overlords under the old system, but the new one was still based entirely on the enduring concept of the inability and incapacity of the Amerindian— which by this time Spanish policies had made true.

A new system of landholding and social organization made rapid advances. This was the *hacienda* (Sp: "estate or wealth," derived from "enterprise"), which in Mexico came to mean a very large, landed property. As the villages shrank or disappeared, much of the land in central New Spain became vacant, both within the *encomiendas* and the crown-supervised *corregimiento*. These lands began to be granted or sold to a newer class of landholders, the *hacendados*. The hacienda, or *latifundio*, could not have grown so rapidly without a radical depopulation. Although some tribal titles to land continued to be disputed into the eighteenth century, private landowners began to snap up large tracts, to surround whole Amerindian villages, and to encroach steadily on the smaller, European wheat fields and orchards. Depression and depopulation aided the growth of huge estates; also, successful *criollo* mine operators had large fortunes to invest in land. Haciendas expanded rapidly when the indigenous population dropped to about one million. Large acreages of former *encomienda* territories were converted into hacienda holdings, and private estates absorbed much of the communally-worked crown lands, which had belonged to the supposedly free-vassal Indians. The crown sold much vacant land; also, corruption was rife in the bribery of Spanish officials entrusted with the welfare of the Amerindians. Fields were declared vacant and sold, with money changing hands throughout the whole hierarchy in a process that never really ended under one form or another until the Mexican Revolution.

Contemporary studies had already shown that the natives fared better, usually, under the private *encomienda* than the theoretically superior *corregimiento*. Private holders tended to protect their *indios* from the roads, tunnels, and mines, and found it profitable to assure each man or family a plot of land; while the *corregidores*, officials who came and went, found it profitable to make their fortunes out of the *indios'* labor. They "sold" slave labor freely and also, with a short time to make their office, which they usually purchased, pay, they mulcted the Indians in every possible way. At best, they left the indigenes neglected wards of the state, to be tyrannized by petty *caciques* and *regidores*.

The hacienda should have provided a great advance over the *encomienda*; its purpose was not to extract tribute or services but to provide products for sale or export. The workers were now free men under the law, due money wages. The hacienda was basically plantation agriculture, and historically, whatever its social effects, plantation agriculture usually marked an economic advance because it produced, or should have produced, surpluses. But in Hispanic society, land ownership gave immense prestige, but neither the social system nor system of taxation provided any spur to its efficient use, or even use at all. It rarely occurred to a *hacendado* to try to increase his profits through development and experimentation. Mismanagement of all enterprise was inherent in the Hispanic world view. The hacienda system developed in a country where landholder and worker were separated by enormous racial, social, and rational gulfs. In a very real sense, the hacienda was less designed to improve agriculture than to continue the subordination of the Amerindian.

The peculiarly Mexican institution of debt peonage also began in the sixteenth century. The law required that free men be paid adequate wages. The Spanish invented minimum wage codes in the modern world. But the law, also, ostensibly to protect the *indio* from acquiring large debts, did not allow him to borrow more than forty reales or five pesos, and further, despite much protest from the clergy and Indians, prevented any employee from leaving his master while in debt to him. Debts were made hereditary. These rules assured the complete immobility of the *indio*. The codes that protected him from large debts prevented him from ever acquiring capital or buying land, and small debts which he could never pay off chained him to the soil. The peon, or farm worker, became a debt slave. Landholders easily kept ignorant workers eternally in debt by small advances of wages.

The institution of peonage or debt slavery cannot be understood without understanding the continuing determination of the European society to remain masters of the land and people. The effect was that the *indio* did not live from wages, but rather from small wage advances, which kept him effectively enslaved. The practice became so engrained that even in the twentieth century many Mexican laborers still expected to receive wage advances and considered being in debt to employers a natural condition, habits baffling to foreigners.

The hacienda, efficiently run, might have made New Spain into an important exporter of agricultural products, as the North American British colonies became. Actually, the system deepened economic stagnation and social degradation. The rapid growth of vast estates meant that the land was soon closely held; a few families owned almost all crop land in every region. Since the laws barred the Amerindians from almost all occupations except primitive labor, the *indios* remained tied to the soil. In one sense, the hacienda continued the old indigenous custom of land assignment, with one great change: the Indians no longer had any collective or communal rights to the soil; they were not at the mercy of the tribe but of the *hacendado*. The *hacendado* assigned fields to work, rather than managing the whole estate with hired labor or tenants. Each family of peons scrabbled on its own plot, continuing a million inefficient little operations as before, with any surplus going to the landowner. The *indio* remained completely at the *hacendado's* mercy; the greatest of all punishments was to be evicted from the land, because in this economy the Amerindian had nowhere to go. Conditions varied; many *hacendados* were decent men and took a paternal interest in their *indios*; others regarded them as animals; worst of all, some absentee *hacendados* hardly realized the *indio* peons existed. But everywhere the system was inherently degrading. The *hacendado* was the master, now relieved of even governmental watching and regulation of the *indio*; the peon, supposedly free, was always a humble supplicant, hat in hand, suffering any indignity to obtain his miserable security from the *patrón*.

The hacienda was not really an economic enterprise; it was a self-enclosed, self-sufficient, very limited socio-economic system. Most great haciendas, which contained their own churches, primitive factories, and "company" stores, were more a way of life than a business, and it was a way of life that peculiarly stifled economic gain or social change. The viceregal government apparently did not approve the transformation of the *encomienda* into the hacienda, because it had less control over landlords who held *latifundia* in fee simple and entail. However, in its preoccupation with extracting mineral wealth and getting silver to Spain, the government did nothing to aid or improve either society or agriculture.

The haciendas spread over most of the older, long-settled regions of central New Spain; they tended to grow as small landholdings were bought up and more Amerindian community lands were alienated and enclosed. The *hacendado* became the most important man in his area; although, like the *encomendero*, he had no real role in politics or government, on his estate he was a petty king ruling over hundreds or even thousands of people. The old outlooks and ethos of the *encomendero* class were continued almost unchanged. All the *hacendado* had accomplished, by securing free title to his lands, was to rid himself of certain annoying hindrances of the crown. He could sell, mortgage, or entail his hacienda, and although his workers were now paid hands, he actually had more power over them than before.

Some *hacendados* erected great, fortress-like mansions and commuted to the capital. Others hardly ever visited their estates, and some families even lived in Europe for generations, leaving operations to *mayordomos*, or managers. The *mayordomo* usually operated in an atmosphere of owner disinterest or disdain, and this gave him tremendous opportunity for various grafts and cruelties. Although no *hacendado* had the right of justice, the whipping post became a feature of many haciendas.

In the absence of governmental or owner concern, agriculture was not particularly profitable. Crops were produced either for markets in New Spain, such as the mines and towns, or for export. Sugar cane was important; like wheat, it always had a European market. Corn, the major crop, was unpalatable to Europeans. In the seventeenth century millions of acres of cornfields went out of production, and much of this land was replanted in maguey plants, which required less labor and produced the profitable if socially damaging intoxicant, pulque. Through this kind of mismanagement, New Spain frequently failed to raise sufficient food, and in the absence of a communications system, thousands of *indios* died in local famines. Bureaucratic regulation destroyed or prevented the production of many potentially profitable crops. The cotton cloth industry, like the making of silk, was ruined; vanilla, chocolate, and tobacco were crown monopolies. Many products easily raised in Mexico had to be imported at great cost. Still, New Spain produced some fifty million pesos in crop value, which vastly exceeded that of all the silver mines and which easily could have been doubled, had anyone cared.

All exported produce had to pass through the Spanish *entrepot*, and all sailings were bound to the convoying of the plate fleet. Ships sailed sometimes only every four years. Goods rotted in the meantime. New Spain did develop a thriving commerce with the Orient, through Acapulco and Manila—but this trade was in Spanish hands, and it was largely an exchange of Mexican silver for various Asian finished goods. In both directions New Spain suffered from heavy imbalances in trade. There was at best a 3 to 2 import-export ratio, which drained the country of its specie as fast as it was produced.

Stock raising quickly became important, since cattle and sheep suited to a depopulated countryside. Many haciendas had thousands upon thousands of the tough, longhorned, African-breed cattle. But here again bureaucracy and stupid legislation destroyed a possible meat industry. Butchering was strictly regulated and was a monopoly in every town, and meat was actually scarce and of poor quality in a country overrun with livestock. Meanwhile, the law provided one hundred lashes for any *indio* caught killing a cow—which despite the law forbidding execution of Indians was a death penalty, depending on how the whip was applied.

Millions of cattle were raised and killed for their hides and tallow in the absence of a meat market, and this was a pattern that was to be lasting in Mexico.

The religious orders soon entered into the hacienda system. The Jesuits, who arrived late in Mexico, bought lands and seem to have been especially efficient in management; however, the older orders, with their original mission largely completed, became sterile. The orders and the secular church, which entered Mexico in the seventeenth century, collecting the *indio* tithes, rapidly became wealthy.

In a pious, death-conscious, superstitious Mexico, all branches of the Church were deluged with gifts and bequests. This was an old evil in the Mediterranean Church; now in Mexico, the immortal institution's wealth could not be alienated or taxed, and soon it became the largest land-owner and landlord in New Spain. This was extremely unhealthy for both the economy and the Church itself. Church property was not well-managed on the whole, and clerics, presiding over ever-growing wealth, became tinged with avarice. The Church, which itself had done so much to destroy the banking ethos in Spain, now lent plentiful money at extremely low rates and required principal to be repaid only at the debtor's death. In the profligate *criollo* society, this policy produced more wealth for the Church.

By the 1630s, as Thomas Gage saw and recorded, the missionary orders had largely turned from serving and protecting the *indios* to living extrava-gantly off them. The Franciscans, Dominicans, Augustinians, Carmelites, and Jesuits had erected four hundred convents by 1600. These no longer served any real social or economic purpose, but they had to be supported by native sweat. Many of the friars had become pervasively lazy and corrupt. They spent nights drinking and gambling with cards and dice, finding various legalistic pretexts to evade their vows.

Felipe IV in effect secularized the Mexican Church by turning over the collection of *indio* tithes—every subject paid ten percent of his income into the Church; if the *indios* had no money, they paid with portions of their crops, or goats or chickens—to the secular clergy. The established orders, however, remained ensconced in Mexico, very jealous of each other and of their privileges. Despite the fact that the Church as a body was rich and that it collected tithes and retained eight-ninths of these, one-ninth going to the crown, in Mexico high fees were demanded for every service. The clergy refused to perform marriages, baptisms, or burials except at exorbitant cost.

By 1616 one of nineteen Europeans in New Spain was a cleric. The very thing Cortés had feared occurred: the secular clergy poured in from its impoverished benefices in Spain, bringing along its arrogance, ignorance, and sexual laxity. With the secularization of the Church in the 1620s, the higher prelates no longer came exclusively from the more disciplined orders. The whole outlook of the hierarchy changed. Where once the bishops had battled for native *indios* to be admitted to holy orders, now the prelates petitioned the crown to prevent even Spaniards born in the New World from entering the Church, on the argument that the Church would soon be dominated by an American clergy of doubtful loyalty. And while one Indian, exceptionally, became a bishop in the seventeenth century, and Creoles were ordained, it became almost impossible for *indios* to take orders or for *criollos* to advance in the hierarchy. Throughout the colonial era, seven of eight bishops, all canons, and the vast majority of *curas* or pastors were *peninsulares*.

Despite popular misconceptions and the deep religious feelings in Mexico, there was no little controversy within and toward this Spanish Church. In 1644 the *ayuntamiento* of México protested against the erection of more monasteries, of which there were already twelve in the capital, and petitioned the king to prevent the Church from acquiring more real estate. These protests continued, but nothing was done despite the fact that the Church came to own at least one-third of all the buildings at México.

The Mexican Church was an integral and useful arm of government, just as in Spain. It supplied the crown with large revenues (these were not taxes on the Church; they were collected from the people through the Church in the form of *bulas*—certificates of dispensation—and tithes). The archbishop of Mexico regularly collaborated with the viceroy on all affairs of state; the relationship was so close that the archbishop was frequently appointed an interim viceroy; ten such prelates assumed the viceregal throne. The viceroy, as vice-patron, had the power of approval of all appointments, though as a matter of policy the viceroys usually approved candidates for bishop, canon, and curate in the order in which they were submitted; his power was the negative one of veto, like the pope's. With offices, power, and money involved, there could not help but occur constant quarrels between the "gospel and the sword," as they were termed. These were terribly bitter, but for all the anathemas hurled and the priests expelled, they were family fights that never disturbed the system.

The Church was an enormously stabilizing influence on society and state. Its effect on the Amerindians was profound, for it replaced the destroyed indigenous priesthood in dominating and regulating most aspects of native life. It had almost an equal effect on the European society, because the Church taught that disloyalty to the crown was heresy. The Church was integral and augmentative to a system that came to be seen as evil and oppressive. But the great marvel is not that the Catholic Church in Mexico grew corrupt and arrogant and shot through with avarice and superstition, since priests and bishops sprang from a common society with *hacendados*, *corregidores*, and bureaucrats and shared a common ethos, but that the Church retained any social consciousness at all. Lay society did nothing either to preserve the Amerindian heritage or the Indians, but a long line of clerics, whether enlightened humanists or narrow-minded but humane missionaries, did. The Church, in Mexico, threw up some of the worst men who ever disgraced the Catholic calling, and some of the best. If arrogant, aristocratic prelates and lazy friars ground down the poor *indios* with threats of hellfire and sipped costly chocolate while they added up their revenues, the Kinos and Junipero Serras devoted their lives to a burning faith, and the Torquemadas and Clavijeros continued the work of Sahagún and Benavente in preserving the memory of ancient Mexico. The Mexican Church was never a monolithic organization. Part of the Church was reactionary and oppressive; the other, usually, but not always, at the level of the lower clergy, held the love and loyalty of the people and remained a potential source of change and glory.

The sourness with which the Church is now regarded, both abroad and in Mexico, probably stems primarily from its enormous success as part of the system. It successfully taught that obedience to Church and crown were supreme virtues, and that rebellion and free thinking were the worst of vices. Clergy in other countries tried similar inculcations, but with far less historic effect.

Spanish data is either suspect or nonexistent; the Spanish kept poor records and even many of these were destroyed; and the historian finds few reliable statistics. But Mexican society by 1650 had taken on the patterns it would hold for centuries.

About one hundred and twenty-five thousand Europeans lived in New Spain by 1646. Most were native-born, and half of them lived in or near the capital. The City of México, because of its population, its position as the capital, and its role as the center of Hispanic culture, always dominated. Beyond México, the European population was very largely confined to the Spanish-built towns that sprang up throughout the *meseta* during the sixteenth century. Puebla and Guadalajara were important centers, and there were smaller regional capitals from Valladolid to Monterrey. These towns had private palaces, great churches, convents, and municipal buildings and seem to have been unusually clean; they did not yet have ancient litter and raucous slums. These municipalities reigned over a somnolent but quite impressive countryside.

Thomas Gage, who traveled mostly in the regions south of México was impressed mainly by the immense variety of the land and its peoples. He was impressed by the docility of the *indios*, the richness of the churches, the color and courtesy of the *criollos*, and the excellence of their horses—things that have struck almost all Mexican travelers since his time. Compared to the Europe of the Thirty Years War, Gage found Mexico a rare and beautiful place.

To his eyes, whatever tyranny there was rested lightly on all races. Gage reported no discontent, and as an Englishman who eventually disavowed his Catholicism and rejoined his anti-Roman people, he had no reason to be favorable to the dominions of the king of Spain. His accounts of real conditions show clearly, when compared to existing Spanish rules and regulations, that the colonials were blithely oblivious of them in many respects. Few if any Europeans of the seventeenth century, the era of violent intolerances and particularly cruel wars, would have seen anything reprehensible in the orderly beauty of colonial Mexico. In fact, at this time almost all Europeans envied the Spanish in their possession of America. The English would have changed places gladly and traded their icy forests and gloomy woodlands on the northern Atlantic slope for the dominion of Mexico—where, as Marlowe wrote, "Indian Moors do obey their Spanish lords," and silver poured out of the mountains.

The rich society of the Creoles was becoming more complex. Spaniards, although they still arrived seeking fortune through office and their competition with the *criollos* for white women, posts, and privileges was a constant irritant, could no longer expect to arrive in America as *señores*. A few tradesmen, merchants, professionals, and artisans had begun to arrive. As *peninsulares*, they had advantages over the colonials and also filled a void. The early Spanish masters, *encomenderos* and friars, had been able to erect a whole civilization out of redirected Amerindian efforts. *Indio* engineers and architects and carpenters built the ships and dikes and palaces and cathedrals of the sixteenth century. When the indigenous skilled classes had been wiped out by policy and neglect, someone had to replace them. This void was filled by immigrant Spaniards of the lower class, from carpenters to grocers.

The *criollos* universally regarded these peaceful fortune seekers as gloomy misers. They did what the *criollo* ethos and outlook did not permit: they worked hard and tried to take advantage of the opportunities inherent in a new country. They opened shops, peddled wares, served as *mayordomos*, and kept the accounts for haciendas. They tended to be austere, clannish among themselves, and arrived with set prejudices against *criollos*, half-breeds, and *indios*. But they created an essential social infrastructure. They got ahead in the world, and many a poor Spanish ragpicker made money, married a local heiress, and bought a patent of nobility. Ex-peddlers and muleteers became counts, which exasperated the indolent *criollos* who forgot their own ancestry, who cordially detested the newcomers, and who looked on their industry with jealousy and fear. These poor Spaniards left a homeland that had no opportunity, and with their petit-bourgeois mentality, they in some ways became as much the Spanish fathers of Mexico as the earlier conquistadores.

Creole society still continued to be wealthy and elegant, but nothing in the arts or creativity compared with contemporary activity and advances in Europe, even in Spain.

Alarcón, significantly, though educated at the Royal and Pontifical University of México sought a career in the peninsula. He was a practical artist who wrote only to support himself while waiting appointment to a sinecure.

Sor Juana Inéz de la Cruz and Carlos de Sigüenza were prodigies alienated from their times and backgrounds. Sor Juana's beautiful lyric poetry survived, but her keen mind made the *criolla* beauty an anomaly in Mexico. She retreated to a Carmelite nunnery and died in an epidemic at thirty-four. Sigüenza y Góngora, a polymath trained at a Jesuit college, the only rational academies in New Spain, might well have ranked with Leibniz or Newton if he had been born in another place. He was competent in poetry, astronomy, cosmography, and history—the first of a new generation of Jesuit-trained men regaining an interest in pre-Columbian Mexico. Most of Sigüenza's work was never published and was lost.

Behind these two prodigies there was unfortunately little intellectual infrastructure. Two *mestizos* descended from the indigenous nobility, Alvarado Tezozómoc and Fernando de Alva Ixtlilxóchitl, wrote histories of the Conquest from the viewpoint of the century—when the day Tenochtitlan fell was celebrated as a great national and religious holiday—and from the viewpoint of the Amerindian allies. Mendieta, Juan de Torquemada, and the Jesuit priest José de Acosta wrote Mexican histories which, though primarily concerned the history of Catholicism in the country, revealed a deep interest in native things.

This culture was of a tiny, largely clerical elite. The life styles of the *criollo* leisure class were the antithesis of intellectuality. Wealthy *criollos* cut fine figures in dress and manners; they were devoted to old friendships and family, but they were also colonials, terribly caught up in an emotional pride and insecurity. *Hacendados* insisted upon assuming the noble honorific "don," to which few of them had any social right. The famous story of the two Mexican gentlemen whose coaches met in a narrow alley, and who sat unbudging for days before a Solomon-like viceroy had them both back away at equal speed, reveals more about *criollo* society than studies in depth.

Men spent their days on horseback, and their nights at fêtes and in the conquest of women. Ladies spoke in vapid pieties and dreamed sexual fantasies. The rich, like all classes, knelt in the dusty streets when the Host passed; they lived extravagantly and endowed churches and convents on their deathbeds.

This whole society, *gachupines, criollos,* and clerics alike, rested on a much diminished understructure of Amerindians. The *indio* population seems to have bottomed out at about one million around 1650. Most now labored on haciendas or were clustered, like the few thousand remnants of the Tlatelolca and the Tenochca, near the towns. They were now largely Hispanicized in religion and language. Only a few friars among the Spanish ever bothered to learn Amerindian tongues. The conquered had to learn the master's speech, and meanwhile, their own dialects lost their means of expressing higher concepts through a lack of education.

Some Indians, certainly, in the high sierras or in remote valleys rarely if ever saw a European other than a priest. These were tribes who had remained outside the Mexic civilization, and they would remain outside the Spanish, only to be slowly destroyed in the twentieth century by culture in other forms. The *indio* had no future. If he did not actually die in the shadow of the white man, his culture withered.

In a society where European males still outnumbered white females ten to one, legal and illegitimate miscegenation went on. By 1650, New Spain already had some one-hundred-and-sixty thousand half-castes or *mestizos*; they outnumbered the Spaniards. The *castas* bred faster than Europeans and survived better than *indios*. Their population curve was rising sharply against those of the other races. Slowly, painfully, and almost unnoticed, the *castas* were growing, and while most of them remained little better off than the Indians and lived in insecurity and misery, many were filtering into bottom layers of Hispanic society. *Castas* could not hold office or enter professions, but they could be watchmen, semiskilled workmen, day laborers, jailors and the like in the Spanish towns. They filled a great infrastructure of undesirable occupations just above the *indios*. In time, the differences between Hispanicized Indians and the half-castes or *mestizos* would blur, leaving only a sharp distinction between the propertied and professional white classes and the great mass of dispossessed.

This heterogeneous country was remarkably tranquil throughout this century, and the next. Although the Hapsburgs kept no army in New Spain, there were no wars, rebellions, or conspiracies. The internecine quarrels between *gachupines* and *criollos*, and between the Church and state, and between secular clergy and orders drew more fulminations than blood. There was no such tranquillity in Europe, where every nation fought internal wars, usually based on religion, as well as international conflicts, and in Spain Cataluña rebelled. The crown left the defense of America to the viceroys but failed to provide them with military forces beyond whatever local levies they might raise. The Indian warfare on the northern frontier, campaigns in Guatemala, and similar excursions were entrusted to private commissions, much as they had always been.

Centuries of subordination to their native lords and priests, the swords of the conquistadores, and the magic of the friars, together with the death and destruction caused by Old World pestilence left the natives thoroughly broken. The *indios* submitted meekly to Spanish whips. Indian rage and rebellion was usually self-directed; *indios* murdered each other in fits of drunken rage. The enslaved could not even unite in opposition to the masters, because they were separated into 150 different and even hostile tribes. In Oaxaca, Zapotecs and Mixtecs could not forget old hatreds.

The Spaniards throughout the century were much more concerned with possible rebellions of the small body of African slaves, who showed more spirit than *indios*. Some slaves rebelled, but the Spanish handled slave protests cruelly. The authorities sometimes hanged Negro men and women and left corpses rotting on the gallows, merely to allay public fears and assuage public opinion. The black, however, was a disappearing problem. Most slaves were imported in the sixteenth century, and their descendents were gradually absorbed into the general *indio* and *casta* population.

The one flaw—and a dangerous, if unseen portent—in the peace were occasional riots of the *léperos*. In times of recurrent famine, which never affected the Europeans and during which the *indios* stoically starved and died, the miserable mixed-blood proletariat sometimes rose in rage.

A great riot took place in 1624. Don Diego Carillo Mendoza y Pimentel, Conde de Priego and Marqués de Gelbes, one of the few totally unscrupulous viceroys, through a Mexican agent, Mexía, used his powers to engross the maize crop. Mexía went through New Spain, buying up the entire production at dictated low prices, which the law provided in case of famine so that the poor might be relieved. *Hacendados* and grain merchants sold, believing famine existed in some other region. With the whole crop in his warehouses, the viceroy then declared no famine existed, since the crop had been good. He and his agents stood to make enormous profits out of public misery.

Alonso de la Serna, the archbishop of Mexico, condemned the viceroy, and after much dispute, excommunicated him and Mexía. Gelbes' officers seized the archbishop and hustled him onto a ship at Veracruz. This act aroused rage and consternation among the *criollos*, though no pious colonial raised a hand for him.

Certain *criollos*, however, played on the misery of the half-caste masses, inciting the poor people of the city. A huge mob gathered in front of the viceregal palace shouting "*¡Viva el Rey! Muera el mal gobierno! Muera el Luterano!*" The divine right of kings made it impossible to threaten the crown and risk hellfire, but the Hispanic world, like the English, made a separation between the crown and its administration. The cry, "*Death to the bad government!*" was often raised in Spain. The viceroy was branded as a Lutheran, or Protestant—rather than *comulgado* (Sp: "excommunicant")—because this was the vilest epithet known to New Spain.

Gelbes had loyal officers, but no army. The police conveniently vanished. The mob surged forward and sacked and burned the palace. The viceroy fled to a Franciscan monastery.

But the leaderless *léperos* became frightened as their rage abated. They scattered with their loot, and the constables reappeared to track them down. The *criollos* laughed up their sleeves. The riot caused the king to relieve Gelbes and send a visitador. The *audiencia* hanged those rioters who could be found.

There were other disturbances. In an exceptionally wet year, the waters rose and grain mildewed and famine again struck the poor. In 1692 a great mob again descended on the palace of the viceroy. The Conde de Galve, then viceroy, who had done all he could to alleviate the suffering, barely escaped with his life while the palace burned. The Casa de Cabildo also went up in flames; it contained the archives of New Spain. Sigüenza himself rescued a few precious documents.

The capital mob of 1692 contained many *indios* and a few propertyless *criollos*, and it appeared briefly that a general massacre of Spaniards and the rich might ensue. But again irresolution and fears prevailed; as the Casa de Cabildo collapsed, the mob dribbled back into its alleyways.

Eight people were executed and many more whipped publicly, as it was almost legally impossible to execute an Indian. The Conde de Galve tried to disperse the hordes of wretched slum dwellers and homeless persons and he tried to control the sale of pulque to the poor. But the society of New Spain had been gradually built by inexorable events, and only other inexorable events could undo it.

Such thunderclaps could not bring change to the social and governmental system of Mexico. Riots, but not consuming revolutions, could be made by the dregs of society, whose valid protests turned into futile criminality. Nor was there any hope that tumults in the cities would spread to the masses of subordinated Indians, or that *criollos* would join *mestizos* in a common hatred of the *gachupines*.

A small army of *criollos* could have driven out every peninsular, and by the 1640s, it is extremely doubtful if the Spanish crown could have reconquered Mexico. Portugal had successfully rebelled; and the Dutch controlled the seas. But whether because of their Catholicism, a sense of loyalty to the remote king, a sense of Hispanic nationality, or the fear that *criollo* society could not stand by itself against the Indians, there was no desire. And if there was a lurking thought for independence, it was carefully hidden, because the flashy Creoles themselves had become irresolute in the face of haughty Castilians.

Spanish government of the Indies had grown much more lax after the death of Felipe II. Viceroys and *audiencias* made less effort to enforce the myriad ukases and taxes as the century progressed. The dynasty radically decayed in Spain. The kings were weak or imbecilic; the ruling favorites, like the infamous Conde-Duque de Olivares-Sanlúcar, had little interest in America beyond the arrival of quadrennial plate fleets. No bureaucracy could be effective without discipline and a sense of national or some higher purpose. The whole Spanish nation had lost its sense of purpose, if not its pride, and the corruption of the bureaucracy destroyed effective despotism. Less and less was now collected out of America, and less and less of that reached the coffers of the crown.

Corruption of Spanish officialdom was widespread, beginning at the top.

The Marqués de Gelbes, who cornered corn, never suffered for it. He was eventually vindicated and honored by Felipe IV, while Archbishop de la Serna was banished to an obscure see. Gelbes' successor, Pacheco Osorio, Marqués de Cerralvo, made a fortune by monopolizing salt while viceroy. The Duque de Escalona, Grandee of the First Degree, sold concessions and grafted grandly. He made his Spanish stableman commissioner of pulque sales and collected fifty thousand pesos in kickbacks. By the 1640s most offices were being sold, both in old and New Spain. The post of *alguacil* to the *audiencia*, or high sheriff, went for one-hundred-and-twenty thousand pesos. Men would invest such enormous sums, not for the honor, but because they could expect to retire rich from any high office in a few years. Justice was venal. Judges purchased their robes and split imposed fines with accusers. The Holy Inquisition burned few persons, about fifty (forty-one evaded arrest and ninety-nine were burned in effigy because they had sensibly removed themselves from Mexico) but in a single *auto-da-fé*, in 1649, the crown and inquisitors divided some three million pesos in fines and penalties. Money could abrogate almost any law.

Corruption in the highest places inevitably spread down to the lowest clerk and constable. The time came when no legitimate business could be done, no permit secured, no certificate honored, without a payoff. Corruption made the system work. Without bribes, the jails would have been overflowing and administration halted, because no society could operate under the fantastic burden of regulation the well-intentioned *letrados* ground out. The seventeenth-century Spanish politicized *everything* with their totalitarianism and tried to regulate every aspect of existence in order to protect or improve it, and corruption allowed the individual his only escape. What was wrought in this century in Hispanic Mexico would not soon disappear.

The burden of corrupt government fell mainly on the poor, who could neither bribe nor evade taxation. The *hacendados* and Spanish merchants could usually avoid full payment of taxes or duties by paying officials *mordidas* (Spanish: "bites") or bribes, except in the carefully controlled mining industry. Much troublesome regulation could also be obviated by judicious pay-offs. The greatest irritation of the *criollos*, except their exclusion from office, was the restrictions placed on Mexican commerce by the peninsular regime, which resulted in drastically inflated prices for imported goods. Nonetheless, New Spain carried on a thriving illicit trade, smuggling silver to the English and Dutch and Chinese in exchange for contraband. The smugglers and corrupt officials allowed the rich Creoles to live well, though the growth of healthy, homegrown industry or commerce was blighted. The poor stayed poor and enjoyed few comforts. Mexican historians enraged by the treatment of colonial Mexico, however, have not always understood that the same burdens of extortion and taxation fell even more heavily on the middle classes and free peasantry of Castile.

The inefficiency of Spanish administration allowed men to survive. *Indios* gave up their corn and ducks and goats and eggs in taxes, but the imposts were levied inefficiently by the *corregidores* and monasteries. The taxes in kind also rarely went beyond the collector, almost never into the coffers of the government. Few Mexicans of any rank were driven into the vagabondage or outlawry that was common in Spain, and few rich *criollos* ever faced extortion by the Inquisition as in Spain—where a failure to grant the government a loan might bring on an investigation. In Mexico, crown officers never had much success collecting the wonderful "king's alms," donations taken by priests going door to door for the support of the monarch's palaces and mistresses. While *criollos* screamed to high heaven about taxes and duties, the evidence is clear that the colonial society was not really bled dry. If the poor stayed poor, the rich remained rich.

The great damage done was more institutional and moral than economic. In this age official corruption became a way of life. As long as the law was one thing, enforcement another, conditions were actually quite bearable. Throughout the last half of the seventeenth century Mexico was the superior of Spain in peace, piety, and prosperity. For all its flaws, the society in America appears more appealing in these years than the degraded, disillusioned Spanish nation.

But Mexico was inextricably part of a greater Hispanic world, and as the core decayed so all the branches were affected. The Spanish vigor that made an empire sank into stasis, and the stasis seeped into the New World. The *peninsulares* were utter arbiters of New Spain; year after year they brought out their styles, notions, and aura of decay. While *criollos* cursed grasping officials and laughed at comic-opera vanities of *letrados* raised to high office, they were also absorbing Hispanic corruption, obscurantism, and ennui. What happened in Spain eventually crossed the ocean sea to Mexico.

The Mexican Church fell into obscurantism and ignorance and mindless intransigence, for seven of eight American bishops were always Spaniards. The once-promising colleges decayed, with one exception, the Jesuit institutions. The Spanish hierarchy, invariably more Catholic than the pope, blighted education. The Royal and Pontifical University sank into pedantry and sterile rehashings of Thomist philosophy and finally, into obscurity. Education consisted of literacy and the catechism for the laity, and the wealthier laity at that. There were no free schools, and no education was provided for the *castas* and *indios*.

The late-Spanish philosophy of the masses—the emotional but sterile assertion of manhood in terms of sexual pleasure, and the defiant refusal to face consequences or a tomorrow that might never come—invaded and further enervated the upper classes of Mexico. *Criollos* stood on their honor while they exhausted their patrimonial estates. Like the Spaniard, the *criollo* tended to become world-weary, past-oriented, and indifferent to the future. The *criollos* were not oblivious to their decadence, and the knowledge of it sometimes even made them vicious. While the more powerful nations were humiliating Spain, all Hispanic Americans were trapped in a hierarchy of inferiority: the *criollos* bowed to *peninsulares,* the *castas* begged from *criollos,* and the *indios* knelt before everyone. The constant reminders of this inferiority ground a deep sense of collective humiliation in the whole population, high to low. It was not to be easily erased.

The splendid qualities of Hispanic life, the guarding of home and family, the warmth of blood relationships, the benevolence of old friendships, the respect for artistic ability, the personal piety of so many, remained more and more behind the walls of Mexican houses. They could not be carried out into daily society. The Hispanic person was thus often two men in one: one face to the world, another among people he knew and loved. It would be utterly wrong to say that the people of New Spain were corrupt, for there was warmth and love and morality behind countless private walls.

The public stasis was the final self-inflicted wound. What happened to the Hispanic world was less a "decline" than a failure to keep pace with a world and civilization it had briefly led. The Hispanic world had failed to face or accept the trends and dislocations upon which France, England, and the Netherlands were making newer societies. Unfortunately for the entire Hispanic world, the power of faith and the sword, the arbiters of the medieval cosmos, had given way to the power of fact and reason and economics and industry. To see the "decline" in true perspective, it should be remembered that in 1500 all Castile had not produced so much woven cloth as one Flemish town, Bruges. The Spanish never bothered to learn to make good gunpowder. As time passed, the disparity grew and grew. Like China, Spain became disillusioned and stood still, trapped in ideals and forms she could not break—and she held Spanish America fast with her.

New Spain, as the many travelers wrote, was a colorful, peaceful, almost-brilliant society in the seventeenth century. Its social injustices were unremarkable in that age, for all Europe was filled with horrors as well as splendors. But fateful patterns had immutably began to form. New Spain would fail to keep pace in a restless, constantly changing ecumene. Mexico was falling behind, as she had once fallen millennia behind in the era of the Amerindians.

Ironically, Spain had destroyed the stasis of the Amerindian civilization of Mexico only to impose a newer stagnation.

19

LA RAZA

The virtues of the Mexican people are to be found in the mixed race.

José Luis Mora, nineteenth-century Mexican intellectual.

The complex and rigid class-caste system had become clearly delineated by the beginning of the eighteenth century in New Spain.

The Hispanic superstructure consisted of a small, directing elite of landowners and clergy in the countryside, and a Spanish culture centered in a number of cities and towns. Spanish civilization, except for a patina of language and religion, had not penetrated much beyond the walls of the towns. The capital, Guadalajara, Puebla, Valladolid, and other cities were predominantly Spanish in population throughout the entire colonial era; the European population lived in the cities and made them deliberately exclusive. The *indios* and mixed-bloods who lived in Spanish cities comprised only the necessary supporting classes, and the considerable Hispanicization of Amerindian servants and laborers within the towns was more accidental than planned.

For the whole Spanish civilization in Mexico had become deliberately exclusive, in an almost complete reversal of Cortés' intentions and the visions of the early friars. To assure the *peninsulares* superiority over the *criollos*, and the *criollos* mastery over the *castas* and *indios*, the rulers prevented the ruled from sharing in the imported civilization in any meaningful way. Most striking was the change toward the Indians. The optimistic effort to reeducate and assimilate the *indio* population as citizens had been abandoned, and the whole *indio* mass had been cemented into a bottom caste.

In an age when there was no secular education, *indios* were effectively if not completely legally, barred from holy orders, and the Church discriminated sharply against *criollos*. There were no free schools in eighteenth-century Mexico, therefore education was rationed to the rich, and for *criollos* it largely consisted of literacy. Education for *indios* was limited to the catechism.

Because the cities of New Spain, however, were centers of culture and civilization set and supported amid a very primitive agrarian countryside, the rather splendid aspect of these towns contrasted sharply with the continuing barbarity of the Amerindian countryside. A peculiar and permanent dichotomy had begun in Mexico, between urban areas that were genuinely part of European civilization and surrounding plantations and valleys teeming with Amerindians barely removed from tribal barbarism.

Even without the racial and cultural bars that separated civilized, urban Mexico from its hinterlands, the economic system buttressed the trends of society. The ownership of large landed estates was the pinnacle of prestige in the Spanish world. Every successful person tried to acquire land, and because land could be entailed and was taxed lightly according to use instead of value, the growth of haciendas continued inevitably. The severe depopulation hastened the trend, and deliberate marriage alliances put together larger and larger estates. By the eighteenth century most of the land that had not fallen to Church ownership was very closely held. In every region there were a few great landowning families. Haciendas engulfed wheat farms and small private plots and drove them out. The constant urge of successful mine operators or men who made fortunes from office to buy land put steady pressure on the remaining small farms and the *ejidos*, or remaining *indio* communal tracts.

The growth of haciendas would not have been so pernicious had landowners developed or used their holdings. The haciendas could have produced great surpluses, creating great wealth. A great landowner, however, was perforce a gentleman, and Hispanic gentlemen did not concern themselves with agricultural profits or markets. *Latifundia* represented the social ideals of the most effective men in society and therefore were irresistible—but the Spanish concept of landownership did not extend to its fruitful or profitable use. The tax system reflected the dominant attitude toward enterprise, for land taxes were assessed against use, never inherent value.

The hacienda system was self-sustaining. Merchants, miners, and successful bureaucrats left enterprise as quickly as they could, becoming idle landholders. Hacienda workers lived at a bare subsistence level, and they produced little for export, but the size of the average hacienda was so immense that its owner lived in considerable luxury.

The growth of haciendas paralyzed the economy of the countryside.

There was nothing to draw the European population beyond the towns. The Spanish were aware of certain successes of the English and French in settling large numbers of European farmers in America, and the government, particularly under the Bourbons, wanted to emulate this. Two things, however, made this impossible. The first was that Spain herself had a dwindling population throughout the seventeenth century, and French farm workers were imported to harvest the crops of Aragon. Few peasants could be spared for the New World. The second factor was the Spanish ethos and social system, which killed any pioneering spirit. Those Spaniards who were settled in America at crown expense in the eighteenth century refused to till the soil. A lack of people, and this attitude, made a successful Spanish colonization of North America impossible. The Spaniard in the New World invariably prefered to continue in poverty, or seek office, or to go into the professions or small trading ventures in cities or towns—never to face the wilderness axe in hand. The friars braved the backwoods in search of souls, but they themselves could not found a continuing Spanish society. Thus three hundred thousand Spaniards who emigrated to New Spain over three hundred years congregated in the old cities and left the countryside to priests and a handful of great *hacendados*.

Spanish intellectuals understood most of the disadvantages of *latifundios*, but the ethos of society made *latifundios* inevitable.

In the absence of immigrants willing to work small freeholds, and in the face of the persistent belief that the *indio* was incapable and must be kept in permanent tutelage, there could be no change. The crown did defend the remaining Amerindian tribal communities against further encroachment by the *hacendado* class until the close of the colonial era. Amerindian communities could and did win suits at law in protection of their rights throughout the eighteenth century—but this again represented a freezing of the social and economic system.

One possible alternative, the establishment of the native race as a viable peasantry or yeomanry with the help of the crown, was destroyed by a total, fanatic resistance by all *criollos* and Spanish officials in Mexico. It is also relevant that although this was proposed by Spanish theorists, there was no such class in Spain, and the concept of private freeholds was foreign to the Mexic Indians. Arguments in favor of a return to the old Amerindian communal land system, also made, broke against the Roman law and the urge of great men to hold land. In fact, the hacienda continued most of the features of Indian village life, except that the landlord, not the tribe, owned the land the villagers worked, and therefore dictated the life of the tribe.

The large landowners, high Spanish officials, and the prelates formed the social and economic elite of colonial Mexico. Officials and bishops were overwhelmingly peninsular, while *hacendados* quickly became *criollo*, but together they formed a tiny upper class. The landowners did not have a public role, and the bishops played too much of one, laying a basis for enormous problems if the ruling officialdom were ever removed. However divided in some ways, this elite was united in one thing: defense of the status quo.

The Mexican cities and towns were dominated by the officeholders and professional men who formed the bureaucracy, a peculiarly Hispanic middle rank. Lawyers, jurists, minor officers, and petty magistrates enjoyed more power and prestige in a highly regulated society than they would have in either an egalitarian milieu like British America or an aristocratic society like England. Such professionals did not legislate, but they regulated and directed ferociously. The first-generation Spanish immigrants held the offices or acted as tradesmen; as they married and their children became *criollos*, new Spaniards took their places.

The great majority of the *criollo* population were professional men or property holders. While a great many sank, almost unnoticed, into genteel poverty through improvidence, the class-caste system permitted all *criollos* to maintain themselves as a distinct, privileged group vis-à-vis castes and Indians. Because of the dominant ethos, there was no entrepreneurism among such townspeople. Those who could afford education preferred to seek a minor office or a place in the Church, or to become a lawyer or other professional man. There were a few great merchant enterprises in New Spain, but these were anything but entrepreneurial—they were monopolies granted to favored houses by the crown. Such businesses were managed themselves like bureaucracies, and they were closer in spirit and practice to tax-farming than to private business. The majority of genuine businessmen in Mexico probably were engaged with English or other smugglers and thus outside the law.

Caste laws, delineating status, and permissible occupations, trapped the mixed-bloods and *indios* into social immobility. Economics forced those *indios* outside the *ejidos* or communes into the peonage of the haciendas, while the law froze the *ejido* Indian in place. In rural areas, *castas* tended to become peons exactly like *indios*. On the haciendas, it was difficult to tell a pure *indio* from a quarter-breed, and in fact, under the class system of the hacienda a *indio* or *mestizo* peon was treated the same and had the same prospects.

However, for generations the law and social prejudices—of *indios* as well as whites—kept most *castas* in the towns, where most of them lived as *léperos*, confined to lowly occupations. The caste system was well defined, but even without it, the society and economy of the country provided little opportunity in cities like Valladolid or México for a *casta* to improve himself or gain a better life. There was no free education, no free lands, no free enterprise—no private sector in the cities through which a capable *casta* might rise. Barred from official posts and favor by his supposed blood taint, the *casta* still faced a class situation not always recognized. He was a member of a proletariat completely constricted by a lack of class opportunities. And historically, the Hispanic class system was to prove far more troublesome to the *casta* and the *indio* than the peculiarly colonial restrictions placed on them because of ancestry.

The gulfs between the silver-buttoned *hacendado* on his blooded horse, the lace-collared lawyer in the towns, and the humble, horny-handed peon in straw hat and cotton pants or the cringing *casta*, were too great to be overcome by any simple evolution. And there was no evolution, since the system had solidified and was self-perpetuating. Nor could it be changed by law, even if such laws could have been imposed. There had to be some new ingredient, for without it the society of New Spain was freezing as solidly as Han China or ancient Egypt.

Fortunately for the evolution of Mexico, it had a frontier.

The full meaning of the Mexican frontier was long overlooked; it was not brought home even to Mexicans until the twentieth century. New Spain was no more impressed with the raw lands to the north of the City of México than old Spain was with her American possessions, except as a source of wealth. The great mass of the population, and the center of gravity of New Spain always remained within the old Cortesian kingdom. Most Mexicans were always to be oblivious of the northern frontier—a remote region, which did not seem important to their lives. Yet here in a very real sense the later Mexican nation was to be made.

Although New Spain extended from southern Guatemala through Yucatan into North America with no defined limits short of the Arctic Circle, to the Spanish New Spain meant the Mexica empire, with scattered additions along the cordilleras from Guadalajara to Monterrey. For the *criollos*, nothing much existed beyond the town walls or their estate boundaries. The tribal *indios* for centuries rarely thought beyond their valleys. Despite this, New Spain developed a frontier that was to play at least as great a role in Mexican history as the western frontier of the United States.

The Spanish treasure seekers found the country extending beyond Michoacán and the present state of Hidalgo for a thousand leagues into Texas, Arizona, and Colorado to be mostly desert, inhabited by scattered, nomadic, mostly savage Amerindian tribes. They termed this country *tierra despoblada*, or unpopulated lands, and considered most of it worthless. The memory of the pueblo-dwellers Coronado discovered along the upper Rio Grande, however, led them to colonize the province of New Mexico in 1598.

In the same decade that saw Monterrey established in the eastern cordillera, the governor and Captain-General Don Juan de Oñate led a large party of priests and settler-soldiers through El Paso del Norte and upward along the Rio Grande (which the Spanish in Mexico came to call the Rio Bravo). He reduced the sedentary Zuñi and other Amerindians of the Puebloan culture and soon subordinated them to Spanish landowners and mission priests, but the Puebloans resisted the loss of their old religion and sacred rites more than many Indians. The Spanish were unable to provide the reduced *indios* full protection from ancient enemies like the fierce Apaches. The Puebloans revolted in 1680, driving all the Europeans south after a general massacre.

The Spanish returned ten years afterward, suppressing resistance in fire and blood, powerfully aided by the smallpox. However, the missionaries now pragmatically permitted the northern *indios* to keep many of their ancient practices alongside the Mass. The result was that these indigenes, who had felt only pale emanations of the Meso-American culture, were never fully Christianized or Hispanicized.

The New Mexican outpost failed to grow. It had a thin, isolated population scattered along the river. When Anglo-Saxon explorers and traders found it early in the nineteenth century, New Mexico was still living in the seventeenth century, following life styles as primitive as the lances and shields still carried by its horsemen. On the other hand, this colony inadvertently had a decisive effect on the Spanish North American frontier, by dispersing horses among the Amerindians. Oñate had brought thousands of cattle, sheep, and horses north. The tough Spanish mustang came into the hands of Apaches and the even deadlier Comanches, who exploded the horse culture on the North American Plains, changing the Indians' whole way of life and enormously increasing their war-making power. The fierce Comanches, who never numbered more than a few thousands, were now to be instrumental in halting the final Spanish advance along the Rio Bravo.

But New Mexico, and other scattered settlements from Texas to California that developed in the eighteenth century, were never—as the Marqués de Rubí reported to Carlos III—the true frontier of New Spain. Set down imposingly on maps, they delineated a mythical frontier that gave Spain a claim to the country that was more apparent than real. The real Mexican frontier was much farther south: it began, in the sixteenth century, a few miles north of the Valley of Mexico.

This semiarid expanse, inhabited by barbarous cousins of the settled Nahua tribes, had no more appeal to the conquistadores than the empty leagues of Texas or the wonders of the Grand Canyon. They might have left it alone for centuries but for the silver deposits there. Silver was the major basis of all the currencies of the world until the nineteenth century, and it pulled the Spaniards north. Raw, roaring mining camps coalesced into important towns at Potosí and Guanajuato; Querétaro and San Miguel grew up as way stations between the capital and the mines. The hundreds of miners and thousands of *repartimiento* Indians who went up into the arid, inhospitable central bowl between the sierras, did not so much carry the culture of New Spain with them as create a newer one.

The socio-economic effects were immediate. Settlement was sucked into the Bajío. There were large stretches of fertile lands around Guanajuato, and the broad valley surrounding Querétaro was suitable for grazing stock. Farms and cattle ranches sprouted to support the distant mining camps, which were hundreds of miles from the old sources of supply. In time, the Guanajuato region was to become the richest and most fruitful agricultural district in Mexico, and the plains around Querétaro gave birth to the remarkable cattle culture that would one day reach as far as Canada.

Here, New Spain found her frontier, with all that a true frontier implies. The most adventurous, energetic, and least tractable Spanish and *criollos*, were drawn to the new, available lands. Here there were no *indios* who could be reduced to slaves. This required new patterns, new arrangements. One was the birth of the *rancho*, which in Mexico, unlike its North American derivative, always meant a small ranch or farm, worked by its owner with no more than a few hired hands. The ranchos provided meat and vegetables and pulque, leather goods, burros, and horse gear to the mining camps and new mining towns. They had markets; they were economic enterprises rather than exercises in social prestige and *señoría*.

Here there was action and interaction, beginning in the sixteenth century and carrying on for two hundred years. The subordinated society of the south was caught up in custom and bound by rigid laws and traditions. Spaniards were Spaniards, hoarding the best offices, monopolies and shops; *criollos* were *criollos*, propertied people sharply distinguished from *castas* and *indios* by class and blood. *Mestizos* were mostly *léperos*, unable to find dignity or a decent life. The *indio* remained an *indio*, even when he spoke Spanish, went to Mass, and donned a straw hat and cotton pantaloons. The *casta* could not enter business; the *indio* could not own land, ride a horse, or carry arms.

But in the Bajío country, as on any frontier, where conditions are hard and men are scarce, men had to be accepted and valued for what they could do more than for what society said they were. While the *gachupines* and *criollos* were dominant, the Bajío country became the *mestizo's* land of opportunity. Here, it was possible for a miserable *lépero*, if he had the will and energy, to become a *ranchero*—lord of his own acres, a cattleman on his fine horse, with his broad sombrero and braided jacket, his silver buttons, and spurs. The almost-white *mestizo* was accepted as a man in ranching or business, and soon, he became accepted as a *criollo*.

Most *mestizos*, of course, did not become rancheros, those proud, independent souls of northern Mexico. The less able or less fortunate, however, could find steady work as *vaqueros*, or cowmen, wage earners separated from their employers more by class than caste. *Vaqueros* were poor, but equally proud, because it took a good, valiant man to ride the dangerous stretches of Chichimeca country, warding off skulking Indians and chousing the near-wild longhorned cattle. They became fine horsemen on great wooden Mexican saddles, in deerhide jackets and rough work trousers and goatskin chaps, quick and skilled with rope and knife. These men developed a new society, the camaraderie of the cow camp. Some of them were bandits in the rough country, but most acquired a new loyalty, to their patron, their rancho, and its symbol, or brand.

There was enormous opportunity for the *indio* who could enter this frontier country, too. Here, where other *indios* were naked savages, speaking unintelligible dialects, and where they considered a Spanish-speaking Mexica or Tlaxcalteca a "Spaniard," to be robbed, tortured and killed like a white man, the *indio* could not quite stay an Indian. His lot was cast with the *criollos* and *mestizos*. Nor could an Indian herdsman be bound up in all the restrictive laws of New Spain when he began to work in the region around Querétaro. He had to ride a horse to herd wild range cattle; he had to go armed with lance and knife; he had to ride independently and use his own native intelligence on lonely patrols. The laws were waived or ignored. The Hispanicized *indio*, like the *casta* or *mestizo*, became a splendid horseman, skilled with lance and rope. Like the *mestizo*, he could find a man's pride in his work, something forever denied him in the hacienda or *corregimiento* of New Spain.

Quickly, little distinguished the Spanish-speaking *indio* from the *mestizo* in this country, except perhaps a darker skin. Wearing "European" clothing and following the same life styles, these *indios* tended to merge into the caste population; they were considered *mestizos*. The Bajío had become a genuine melting pot, where *indios* merged into *mestizos* and *mestizos* tended to be accepted slowly into the "white" race. Class, as on almost all human frontiers, was more important than ancestry, and men became "white," "mixed," or "Indian" more according to their social rank than their actual race. This was important, because in the Bajío society was vastly more flexible along class lines than farther south.

While the south remained overwhelming *indio* in racial complexion, dominated by a tiny, distinct white elite or master class, the whole north country, reaching out from Querétaro to Sonora, through Chihuahua to the Rio Bravo was becoming neither distinctly Spanish nor Indian. History proceeded differently in the north of Mexico.

The native populations of the south-central regions won their long struggle against extinction by 1650. The fate of the *indios* of northern Mexico was different. The original Chichimeca close to the Valley of Mexico quit fighting at the turn of the sixteenth century, but when they were congregated beside missions and towns they were almost completely exterminated by demoralization and disease. The same pattern was to continue as the Mexicans slowly pushed north. The very warlike, nomadic tribes that held much of these regions could not be reduced by the mission system, although the Franciscans stubbornly erected missions until almost the close of the eighteenth century. The frontiersmen of New Spain warred continually with these savage peoples, while the fort and mission system that was carried north virtually exterminated the more peaceful tribes, from the miserable Coahuiltecans to the Caddoans of East Texas. The missions were a failure in the north. They destroyed far more Indians than they reduced. The Church never accepted this failure, however, and left behind its contemporary arguments against the military policy as an enduring Spanish-Catholic myth.

A few tribes, very tough or ensconced in inaccessible country, such as the Yaquis—who were uncivilized cousins of the Nahuas—and the *indios* of Nayarit, survived all efforts to destroy or displace them into present times. Most northern Amerindians, however, suffered the fate of the once-numerous and powerful Tarahumares of Chihuahua and Sinaloa. Following the silver, the Spanish pushed into Tarahumare country with forts and missions in the early seventeenth century. But soon, either the intolerant discipline of the friars or the arrogant abuses of the Spanish officers alienated the tribe; both Spanish missionaries and soldiers in the north never learned that they were not dealing with the cowed, obedient, and long-subordinated peoples of south-central Mexico. This led to frightful *indio* uprisings, both in the Tarahumare country and in New Mexico. In 1649, the Tarahumares rose in fury, burning Spanish barracks and churches and missions, and the padres in them.

The governor of Nueva Viscaya, as the Spanish called this region, did his best to quell the revolt from Parral. But the Indians held the sierra passes and maintained their freedom for twenty years. The Tarahumare war was finally ended in 1670 by betrayal and massacre, when an *india* girl led a viceregal army into the mountain valley where most of the Tarahumare warriors were encamped. After this, the Tarahumares sank gradually into the present degenerate skulkers in the remotest canyons of Chihuahua—a once-proud barbaric people reduced to miserable savagery, facing mortal enmity from the Mexicans and no future except eventual extinction.

In the north, few Indians were conquered or Hispanicized; the empty spaces were filled with *mestizos*.

The Amerindians who seized horses, the predatory Apaches of Arizona, New Mexico, and Sonora, and the terrible, hard-riding Comanches of the Texas plains, presented the northern frontier with a problem the Spanish never solved. By the eighteenth century, New Spain and these tribes were locked in a savage struggle that was really a war of extermination on each side. Thousands of Mexican frontier settlers and soldiers were killed in raids, while official and unofficial campaigns of extermination were waged in retaliation. Spanish cavalry made punitive raids, bounties were paid for *indio* heads and hair; massacres and mass poisonings were tried. The eighteenth-century viceregal government erected a vast, expensive chain of forts across the northern deserts from Sonora to San Antonio; it maintained more soldiers on this frontier than Cortés had used to conquer Motecuhzoma's Mexico. But the horse Indians were neither conquered nor pacified. They defeated Spanish arms severely in Texas in the 1750s; they destroyed Spanish settlements everywhere on the frontier. They did worse: Comanches and Apaches raided hundreds of leagues beyond their territory into New Spain. The terror continued until the second half of the nineteenth century, when at last civilization, in the form of cooperating military campaigns between Mexico and the United States, destroyed the wild Amerindians.

There were three basic reasons why the Spanish Empire could not advance against these few, scattered, but highly warlike Amerindians, a fact that severely bounded its territory and history. In the arid regions and vast distances involved, Spanish-Mexican soldiery simply could not mount successful campaigns against mobile enemies who were expert at guerrilla warfare. It was estimated that at least five thousand troops were needed for the Texas frontier alone, and the crown would never support such efforts, although it jealously wanted to retain its North American territories. There was also a paralyzing jurisdictional struggle between the secular military authorities and the missionary Church over how the problem should be handled: the Church wanted generations to try to reduce and pacify the Indians, while the military was determined to exterminate them. Considering the nature of the enemy, and the Spanish means, both concepts were futile. Finally, and most decisive, the Spanish Empire put no real population pressure against these hostile Indians. Spain, unlike Great Britain, did not hurl streams of colonists against her North American frontier, men and women who could destroy the Amerindians by destroying their native wilderness. New Spain, like old Spain, threw out too few pioneers.

The Bajío region developed the only true pioneering people in New Spain. In the eighteenth century, thousands of settlers, taking their livestock with them, marched north into the present Coahuila, Tamaulipas, and Nuevo León. Significantly, these pioneers marshalled at Querétaro for the Rio Bravo. They were *criollo* and *mestizo*—again significantly, the viceroyalty began to issue land grants to *castas* who were willing to go to the far frontier as early as 1690. Such families were considered Spanish officially, and *mestizo* families received thousands of crown grants that reached beyond the Bajío into the present United States. Just as the

Hispanicized *indio* blurred with the predominantly Indian-blooded *castas* in the north, the white and almost-white rancheros merged.

But the thinly populated old frontier north of Mexico had exhausted its energies and its human resources by the time, in the 1750s, it had pushed permanent settlement up along the Rio Grande. The Bajío pushed out a hardy, stubborn culture which clung along the Bravo but could go no farther. Here, a few thousand *indios* on horseback halted the course of empire.

The great struggle, and in effect, the destiny of Mexico, was left primarily to ambitious people who wanted new lands, new freedoms, and whose social position in the civilized regions was at best suspect. Few of these pioneers found their dreams; even in the new country only a handful of rancheros rose above their station and class. But the struggle had enduring effects on the whole emerging population.

The *norteños* or northerners grew into a much more active, independent, and self-reliant people, vastly more belligerent than the cowed masses of subordinated southern Indians and enervated *criollos*. Indian wars made Chihuahua a breeding ground for Mexican soldiers. The northerners were bred in New Spain, and not quite Spanish however the whitest of them might assert their Hispanidad—but the enormous differences between them and the Yaqui, Apache, and other savage tribes, the cruelties exchanged and the smoldering hatreds and blood feuds between these *indios* and the Mexicans, kept the mixed race of the north, whatever its ultimate ancestry, from ever considering itself "Indian." By the 1700s, the people north of the city of México were a population beginning to search unconsciously for a nationality.

The empty, arid spaces and savage horsemen did not stop the advance of culture. Moving into the ecology of the Sonoran Plain that reached across much of northern Mexico up into south-central Texas, the Spanish-Mexicans developed new economies, new outlooks, and new life styles. This country was splendidly suited to the grazing of the tough African-blooded cattle and horses. Thousands of animals were turned loose to graze; loosely herded and supervised, they grew into millions. The men who eked a poor, but exhilarating existence from horses, hides, and tallow, in a country where men were valued for their hardihood and bravery and not their hair and skins, infused new attitudes into New Spain. This was an outlook and a value system that came to be called *charro*. The *charro* was more than a horseman or a cowboy; he represented an evolving, if limited, culture.

The *vaquero* on the frontier was soon subtly different from the humble hoeman and the whining, servile *lépero*. Most *vaqueros* were socially and even legally peons, for class systems and debt slavery went everywhere—but they worked on horseback; they were elevated over other men. They fought Nature and wild Indians; they ranged independently over wide *estancias de ganado* and ranchos or haciendas where the lean, longhorned cattle ran free. The country, the cattle, the dangers, the horses, and the evolving ranch economy built new traditions and myths. The qualities of the good *vaquero* or *charro*—the ability to ride any horse that lived, to face wild men and wild beasts, to be brave and skilled with knife, lance, and rope—were social and economic necessities that quickly solidified into genuine folk-culture. The *charro* was valiant and loyal, as in any frontier society, to his patron and his peers. He was both a bullfighter and a lover, since he was an extension of the culture of Spain. He had the mystic camaraderie of the lonely camp, and an aristocratic disdain for any work that could not be performed on horseback. The *vaquero* became a hero.

The values, styles, and even the clothing of this horse and cow culture had become standardized before the eighteenth century, though their great impact would come much later. The wide sombreros with pointed tops, the broad leather belts with silver buckles, the buckskin jackets and tough, canvaslike horsemen's pants, the half-boots and goatskin *chaparreras*, and the casual sarape thrown over the shoulder marked the emergence of a native costume. This was working dress, not the effete, stylized, black *charro* costume later worn by fat street musicians who never mounted a horse. It was a mixture of native and Spanish styles, just as the *charro* was a mixture of Hispanic and native blood, and his food was a mixture, too: chiles and beans, tortillas and beef, *chorizo* or sausage and the roasted suckling kid, or *cabrito*. The language was Spanish, but with a developing working jargon—*corral, bronco, loco, arroyo, lazo, la reata, rodear, adobe, pinto, mesteño, caballado, rancho*—that would one day, either in pure or adulterated form, be recognized around half the world. Deep in the Bajío, the cattle culture and what North Americans would some day call the Old West, began. Both would be carried to the Rio Bravo and beyond, following the trails from Texas to Calgary.

This was a stultified society and culture for all its wild freedom and exhilaration, lacking art and intellectuality. It was shot through with deep class cleavages between owners and ranchhands; it was poor, barely existing from rangy cattle in an arid land. But here men had found a certain valor, and they looked forward—the people who went north forgot "Aztec" glories and their Spanish grandfathers, two things the south could never put behind.

They were forming "la raza," a new bronze race, and becoming Mexicans.

20

THE INDIAN SUMMER OF NEW SPAIN

The population of New Spain is composed of three classes of men: to wit, whites or Spaniards; Indians, and castes. . . . All property and wealth is in Spanish hands. The Indians and the castes till the soil; they serve the upper class, and live only by the labor of their arms. This puts, between Spanish and Indians, contrary interests and mutual hate, which easily arises between those who have everything and those who have nothing—between masters and slaves.

From a letter to His Majesty, King Carlos IV, from the bishop of Valladolid, third richest man in Mexico.

The transfer of the Spanish crown from the extinct Hapsburg line to the Bourbons created the War of the Spanish Succession in Europe and cost Spain the last of her European empire. Spain had become a prize to be fought over rather than a prime mover among the European powers. When the French dynasty was confirmed on the Spanish throne and began, as the other nations had feared, to act in conjunction with France, this did not create a new Bourbon ascendancy in Europe. Spain did not possess such power; by 1700, the empire was sunk into apathy and backwardness.

The Bourbons did bring new vigor to government, and after 1760, Carlos III instituted a great reform of Spanish administration. But the Bourbons could not reinvigorate the nation. Their changes were more changes of style, and no reform of government could cure the sicknesses of Spanish society, for they were malaises of the soul. The Bourbon dynasty merely papered over the deep chasms of Hispanic society for a century; its progress and power were far more apparent than real.

The turmoil of the succession in Europe caused hardly a ripple in New Spain. The empire accepted the dynasty unquestioningly. In 1700 Mexico was neither politically alive nor much aware of the outside world. But Spain no longer had any sort of monopoly in the New World. The French were in Louisiana, defying the Spanish crown's ukase against all "foreigners" in the Gulf of Mexico; the British were expanding in North America and their sail outnumbered the Spanish six to one in the Caribbean; the Russians were exploring the north Pacific coast. The great age of competition for empire had begun, and New Spain became caught up in it.

The first Bourbon, Felipe V, was a weak ruler, dominated by his Italian wife. However, the new dynasty at Madrid effected a slow but pervasive change. Although Felipe V made no incisive reforms, the Bourbons had a knack for selecting good officials, level-headed and honest men who reflected much of the consciousness of the eighteenth-century Enlightenment, and who were a new breed of European aristocrat, forming a social class rather than a feudal order. They were devoted not only to class privileges but to the state. And the Bourbons saw themselves as first gentlemen of the realm rather than suspicious liege lords ruling over a rebellious hodgepodge of kingdoms. What slowly came about was a sort of aristocratic revolution that ended the crown's old alliance with middle-class bureaucrats and provided that phenomenon of the times, enlightened despotism.

The Bourbons, their ministers, and high officers were secure men who understood each other and operated free of the mystical aura that had formerly surrounded the Spanish crown. The Bourbons did not create a new liberty in the Hispanic world, but they let in a little French clarity.

The new viceroys who arrived in Mexico reflected these changes. Their stately portraits set one by one in the viceregal palace were those of eighteenth-century men of the world rather than somber Castilian grandees. They brought color and a certain gaiety to the capital, and a newer attitude toward religion: they were decidedly, though secretly, anti-clerical. The Bourbons brought the Masonic order to Spain and thus to the American empire. Freemasonry was then in Latin countries an aristocratic club. The king and his officers could not abolish the Holy Inquisition, for not even theoretically absolute monarchs could break up the bureaucratic and institutional mazes of the *Ancien Regime*, but they could and did denigrate the holy office and make it less terrible. The new viceroys no longer trembled at the anathemas of the Spanish Church.

The Marqués de Casa Fuerte, whom Felipe V kept in New Spain for many years, revitalized the government with his energy and personality. Wholesale corruption and Spanish bureaucratic laxity were assaulted by

Gallic notions of uniformity, rationality, and centralization. Government became more effective. However, this vigor and enlightenment was strictly at the top and had great difficulty seeping down. Most of the patterns and attitudes frozen in the Hispanic world did not change, and in fact, they were hardly to change through the twentieth century. The Bourbons made a slow administrative revolution, but whatever spiritual revolution they fostered was confined to a few.

Felipe V (1700–1746) and Fernando VI (1746–1759) presided over very little pervasive change in New Spain. The only real vigor was shown on the northern frontier. Back in the 1680s the concern of the viceregal government had been drawn north by activities of the French in Louisiana and Texas. First, this led to the founding of Monclova in Coahuila, as the viceroys tried to extend the frontier. In the early 1700s, as the French tightened their grip on the Louisiana coast and furnished firearms to the Texas Amerindians, the Spanish began to extend their forts and missions into Texas, which, as later officers pointed out, lay far beyond the true frontier of New Spain. Generally, all the efforts beyond the Rio Grande were failures, but the reigns of Felipe V and Fernando VI did accomplish an extension of the real frontier several hundred miles across northern Mexico, from Sonora to the Gulf. These efforts rounded out the lands that came to comprise modern Mexico.

The royal agent, Colonel Don José de Escandón, brought hundreds of *criollo-mestizo* families out of the Querétaro area and settled them in new towns, ranches, and haciendas south of the Rio Grande from Nuevo León to the Gulf of Mexico. Escandón seeded Mexican-Spanish civilization permanently, because he brought colonizing families to this high frontier. The settlement stopped along the great river, for two reasons, the hostility of warlike Amerindians in Texas and the lack of sufficient Hispanic pioneers. There was no lack of royal will to push the Spanish settlement of Texas, for the crown spent millions maintaining forts and futile missions in the northern deserts. Flags and forts with cannon, however, could not substitute for thousands of Spanish-speaking people on the land.

If the crown had been able to settle a sizeable Hispanic population into Texas, Arizona, California, and the Louisiana and Florida territories it claimed, the entire course of Hispanic culture in North America would have been unalterably changed. But the Spanish empire in North America, despite the efforts and expenses of the government, remained a mythical empire, imposing on maps, underneath a hollow shell.

The Spanish misunderstood this historic reality, for after they acquired the Louisiana territory from France in 1762 they relaxed the efforts to colonize Texas. That Spanish cannon controlled the Mississippi seemed sufficient. Russian penetrations drew the Spanish into California, in the service of both majesties, God and king, as the missionary Junípero Serra and the Visitador José de Gálvez agreed. San Diego was founded in 1769, San Francisco a decade later. But lacking pioneers, the northern empire had to depend on scattered forts and the frail hope that the thinly-scattered North American aborigines could be Hispanicized. The fortress-mission system from San Antonio, Texas to San Diego, California, was more the result of imperial policy than a religious exercise. But suitable *indios* did not exist to be reduced, as in the Cortésian kingdom, and these missions failed utterly on the far frontier. The Spanish penetrations left a patina of place-names, but few people.

The two dominant concerns of the Bourbon dynasty in America were the military defense of the empire against other European powers, and the increase of American revenues through better administration.

To accomplish the first, the crown tended to make military men viceroys; they devoted their attention to the northern frontier and to strengthening the defenses of the Mexican coasts. They paid less attention to civil administration, from which they were gradually relieved. The soldier-viceroys—who in retrospect are among the greatest who ever came out from Spain—built new forts in the north, supported the missions reluctantly, and mounted cannon from Mérida to the Mississippi. The final effort, which most historians have agreed was self-defeating for the crown, and disastrous for Mexico, was the raising and training of a colonial army in New Spain.

This defense effort was logical in its time and place. It should not be denigrated, for all its lack of success against either Anglo-Saxons or wild *indios* on the northern frontier, because it may very well have preserved the integrity of the southern continent and Middle America. In the expanded, worldwide struggles that became a feature of the eighteenth century, the confident British took hard knocks from Cartagena to Buenos Aires. While sweeping the French from India and seizing colonies from the Dutch, British naval power failed to seize a foothold in Spanish America. In fact, the British were driven from the Gulf and Florida in the 1770s. In the era of the viceregal lieutenant-generals, the empire reached its greatest extent. The Lions and Castles flew over San Francisco and Spanish guns guarded St. Louis in the Missouri territory. In this brief age, Spain again was taken seriously, and the final failure of the empire was beyond the powers of the eighteenth-century Bourbons.

The second major concern of the Bourbons, making the empire pay, was carried out by reforms in administration. New World revenues had fallen to almost nothing in the seventeenth century. Incisive changes came only with Carlos III (1759–1788), the greatest of the Spanish Bourbons. He was eccentric but effective, and he surrounded himself and filled his offices with similar men. The high officials of his reign stand out in Spanish history.

The Bourbons were active despots who ruled the colonies less as distant "kingdoms" than as dependent provinces. The screws that Felipe II had forged, and which had been allowed to rust under his successors of the Hapsburg line, were oiled and turned. The new pressure was rational, for the eighteenth-century state was neither paranoid nor fanatic as a century earlier. But it came as a great shock to the *criollos* in the New World. During a century of decadent government, the Europeans in America had almost forgotten that they were ruled from Spain. The new men who arrived as royal agents not only reminded them of their status, but made them feel even more like provincials. *Criollos* whose great resentment had been exclusion from power and office, now found that old laws were being enforced, taxes were collected, and smuggling was becoming more difficult, under officers who brooked no argument.

The greatest change in administration under Carlos III was the restructuring of the colonial government on the model of contemporary France. The Visitador José de Gálvez, whose family produced two viceroys, made a thorough study while serving as secretary of state for the Indies. He cut through the complex maze of *audiencias, corregidores,* governors, and *alcaldes mayores,* feudal trappings which splintered government, and revamped administration under twelve new regional intendancies.

The intendancies were provincial governments, whose borders generally followed the lines of the major modern Mexican states. The intendants, who under Carlos III were career soldier-statesmen, were directly responsible and responsive to the viceregal chair. They assumed almost all of the civil and financial administration. Again, because of social pressure and the office mania of the society, few of the older posts were abolished; they remained as useless ceremonial offices. Power, however, flowed around them. In one thing there was no change: the intendants were always *peninsulares.* This further angered the *criollos* who had been allowed to buy offices as *alcaldes* and *corregidores,* for the titles they came to hold were meaningless in terms of power.

The new administrators, while cutting through bureaucratic mess and corruption, did not improve the economy or the lot of the *indios,* though this was claimed. The society was too rigid to be reformed by better administration. The intendants did uphold the rights of the tribal *indios* against *criollo* claims, and they scandalized the great landowners because they could not be bribed easily and collected due taxes. But this infuriated the rich without really changing the condition of the poor, who in the end bore all taxes. No change could have been made in their condition without a radical change in land tenure or an industrialization, as the bishop of Valladolid, Abad y Queipo, informed Carlos IV. The defense of the *ejidos* and the enforcement of laws protecting the *indios* merely continued their alienation and subordination.

Bishop Abad y Queipo was one of numerous Spaniards who argued for an agrarian law to redistribute millions of *varas* of idle hacienda lands among the poor. With land reform, he believed that the *castas* and *indios* would be able to acquire property and become true citizens. He argued the abolition of the humiliating tributes and head taxes every *indio* was required to pay, and he also wanted the crown to permit the establishment of cotton and woolen industries. These ideas were logical, but psychologically and politically impossible. The *criollos* would not hear of any kind of land reform; the textile industries of Spain had become utterly dependent on their monopolies of the captive American market.

The undisputed result of Bourbon reform was that the intendants extracted six times as much money in taxes as the Hapsburgs. By European standards of the time, this taxation was not devastating—but all of it was money that left New Spain; it was a drain. The Bourbons spent much on local defense, but the vast majority of the monies they extracted went to support Spaniards and Spanish administration. Nothing was used for capital investment in Mexico. Therefore, increased revenues hurt rather than helped the economy and the poorer classes, while the *criollo* establishment, accustomed to a century of successful tax avoidance, was outraged.

The cost of administration rose steadily to meet increased revenues. In the second half of the century a succession of viceroys began many public works and projects, which were more for ostentation or sanitation than genuine capital improvements. Some of these projects were deliberate make-work by government, designed to relieve the misery of the poor by providing employment. Bernardo de Gálvez laid out gardens in the capital and added new towers to the still-unfinished cathedral. Since the cutting of the Nochistongo, the sediment-filled lakes around the city had dried; the water was retreating south, where eventually the only remnant of the great lakes of Anáhuac would be the muddy canals of Xochimilco. Gálvez put thousands of workers to clearing and filling the slime and refuse-choked canals in the city. His monument, however, was the fortress-palace of Chapultepec.

This lovely, larch-covered hill just beyond the capital had become a viceregal retreat. At a cost of more than a hundred thousand pesos Gálvez erected a splendid seat. He justified the expense, immense in an era when one peso purchased one hundred pounds of corn or two hundred of beans, as a project to create work for the poor.

Other projects made work for the *léperos* and also modernized the cities. Viceroy Revillagigedo (1789–1794) cleaned and widened the streets of the capital and installed turpentine-burning lamps. He created the first botanical gardens since Motecuhzoma, built new public buildings and aqueducts in several towns. A few roads were laid out—the first in two hundred years. Revillagigedo and similar-minded viceroys also patronized the Mexican arts in the Academy of San Carlos with the active encouragement of Carlos III.

In this era most of the surviving architecture of colonial Mexico was built. Exquisite churches, palaces, and public halls threw a patina of magnificence over New Spain. The Alameda, no longer used for burnings, became a splendid promenade, where Spanish and *criollo* notables displayed fine horses and coaches on the Paseo before retiring to their gaming tables, mistresses, or private balls. The changing face of Mexico represented progress, but it was superficial progress. The new public magnificence was paid for by mining fortunes or revenues and such expenditures were not investments that improved the stunted economy. The Spanish loved monuments and ornamentation at the expense of utilitarianism—the Hispanic mind, educated or ignorant, had a fine contempt for utility.

The viceroys did improve sanitation and import German hydraulic and metallurgical engineers for the new School of Mines, but much of the new European knowledge and techniques could not be applied to the primitive Mexican economy and society. Although the Condes de Gálvez and de Revillagigedo were fine examples of the Enlightenment, a handful of aristocrats at the top could not drag all Mexico into the eighteenth century. The viceroys Lieutenant-General Don Antonio María de Bucareli and Teodoro de Croix, and officers like Hugo Oconor and De Anza and Ugalde, who commanded on the northern frontier, were hard-minded pragmatists who understood basic problems. They recognized the failures of the mission system in the north, where raiding Indians were devastating Sonora, Chihuahua, Texas, and Nuevo León. De Croix finally won reluctant approval from the ecclesiastics for a war of extermination against the Apaches, although the requisite troops were never found. The rulers of New Spain were men of greater vision, ability, and even good humor than has usually been recognized. Although most of them were soldiers, most had wide interests: Bucareli founded the Monte de Piedad or national pawnshop which still operates beside the National Palace; Revillagigedo poked into everything, inspecting his realm like a British naval captain ruling his warship. With the full power of the Bourbon kings behind them, the viceroys had immense authority—in fact, greater power than Carlos III in Spain, where the royal prerogative was opposed by a maze of ancient local charters, privileges, and rights. The king's officers were a terror to the lax bureaucracy. But they neither deeply reformed the government, nor changed the country and society.

The viceroys and their intendants threw a finish of efficient regulation and enlightenment and good intentions over a sterile social situation. The Bourbon officers only papered over the yawning chasms left by previous centuries; the pastel colors of their despotically-enforced Enlightenment hid the dark barbarism of rural Mexico but did not dispel it. Neither Spain

nor Mexico really entered the world of Galileo and Descartes, or understood the findings of Locke or Newton. The Bourbons and their officers
ruled over an empire that appeared again to be a great world power, whose
cannon controlled vast coastlines and whose flag waved over whole continents. But this was an empire in which the dry rot of the past still spread
under a modernistic veneer of fashion.

The population was still mired in superstition and the cultivated people
caught up in barren *conceptismo*, confusing thought and style with action.
Spanish society was still organized as if there had never been a commercial
revolution. Spanish thought, which never quite fully emerged from the
Middle Ages, ossified. The Royal and Pontifical University of México was
as stagnant as Salamanca—both took scholasticism seriously.

The Church had lost all sense of mission. Its dominant mood was
blackness, portrayed over every altar by stark images of bleeding Christs
and tortured saints. Its ambience was mind-numbing ritual: bells, processions, robes, and candles. Thousands upon thousands of hooded penitents
marched through the streets of Mexico on holy days. Flagellants beat
themselves until the blood ran. The missions had failed, but idle friars
walked the plazas with their whores and seduced virgins through the confessional. Spanish Catholicism had lost all ethic, retreated into ritual and
mysticism. Whores wore crucifixes and murderous bandits carried images
of the Virgin around their necks. Nothing was demanded of the Christian
except observance, but that ferociously; nothing was unpardonable but
free thought or heresy.

Just as Spanish architecture in Mexico remained baroque far into the
century, the whole culture, under a veneer of fashion, lagged at least a
century behind developments in Western nations. Technology and organization and design were out of date.

The common people of the empire, and the Church as an institution,
never accepted the modernizations of the Bourbons, and a cultural gulf
yawned between the Church and people, and the rational, directing aristocrats. It is obvious that the eighteenth-century Spanish elite that Carlos III
brought to power despaired of both Church and people, their customs and
superstitions. There was no high bourgeoisie in the Hispanic world to seize
on the Rights of Man—ironically, the Spanish Enlightenment, so far as it
went, was an enlightenment forced by aristocratic despots. There was in
fact an intense aristocratic reaction among Bourbon officialdom, sick to
death of obfuscating churchmen who were institutionally part of government, and a population of all degrees they considered mired in ignorance.
The Bourbons' men were authoritarian to the bone; Teodoro de Croix
said: "The folk of New Spain are born to be silent and obey and not
meddle in affairs."

Ironically, this remark was occasioned by public protests in Michoacán over Carlos III's suppression of the Jesuits and their schools—and on this occasion the people were right and the crown wrong. The expulsion of the Jesuits from Mexico in 1767 destroyed the only element in the Mexican Church that was free of medievalism. The Bourbon officials meant to erase a competing institution, but the true effect was the destruction of all educational standards in New Spain.

In any event, the Bourbon reforms came too late. They did not begin to bite incisively until the administration of the second Conde Revillagigedo, when the capable Carlos III was already dead. For all the fact that every reform was designed to benefit Spain and the crown, not Mexico, they laid a basis for profound change. The Viceroy Flores (1787–1789) created a new colonial army with three regiments of native militia: the *Puebla, México*, and *Nueva España*. The commands went to prominent *criollos*; the officers were native whites, and the ranks were largely *mestizo*. Theoretically, this force was to fight the northern *indios*, but Creole militia was useless on the frontier. Revillagigedo put eight companies at San Antonio without solving the Indian problem, and after 1790 the frontier situation deteriorated even more. The colonial army was not intended to forge colonial pride and self-reliance but to reduce the crown's expense of keeping regulars—just as the reduction in the controlled price of mercury for the mines, and the Royal fifth to a tenth was intended to increase revenues. But colonials organized into armed regiments created a new kind of Mexican.

In the same way, the new laws that made *indios* citizens and opened the ports of Spanish America to the world at last opened immense opportunities. The commerce of New Spain quadrupled in a few years, though citizenship of *indios* meant less since the debt peonage laws were retained. The reforms were unsettling for two reasons. They raised expectations, as reforms always do, and they also reminded the *criollos* and *mestizos* of the inequities that remained. And, enacted arbitrarily and in an authoritarian manner, they made the colonials acutely aware of the fact of Spanish tyranny over their lives.

Carlos III certainly intended to go farther. Before his death he approved a grand design for an Hispanic Commonwealth, in which the viceroyalties would be ruled as virtually independent countries. This could only have been implemented over violent protests by various interests in Spain, and the idea died with the ablest of the Bourbons.

New Spain, however, had been managed as a bankrupt's estate for too long. What centuries had made could not be undone by a few royal *cédulas* and good intentions out of Madrid. The fresh air of the reforms, entering a fossilized structure, tended to weaken it without really changing it. As history was to prove, what had been wrought in Mexico could not be quickly or painlessly changed even by the Mexicans themselves.

Yet this age was still a sort of Indian summer of the Spanish Empire, and of New Spain. It was the best of times since the sixteenth century; conditions were improving, although irritations were soaring.

Mexico was not turbulent. The *indios* were passive, except in Yucatán. Here, in 1761, the Maya rebelled against excessive tributes to absentee landlords and the bloody floggings which had become a grim feature on the haciendas. The Maya rejected use of Spanish, and all of the tribes had not been completely subjected until the eighteenth century. The rebellion was crushed; eight leaders were disemboweled as examples. While there were troubles with miners at Tepic and some *indios* at Tehuantepec, there was nothing that could be called an Indian revolt. The hacienda and *ejido* workers were silent throughout the century.

Life was neither better nor worse for the *indios*, whose numbers were now increasing. The Bourbons protected the rights of each *indio* village to its square league of land, and in some cases forced *hacendados* to disgorge lands they had sequestered illegally. However, the survival and growth of the *ejidos* was no longer a triumph of justice—it marked a failure to Europeanize the Indians.

The *indio* villages were trapped on marginal lands, continuing a primitive agriculture and social structure. They were partially Hispanicized in religion and language. If their Catholicism was half-pagan, the Amerindians still often showed more genuine faith than white men, and the one Hispanic institution they were loyal to was the Church, which had consistently cared for them. While some *indios* remained totally outside the Church, in Chiapas, Nayarit, Tehuantepec, and of course the wild tribes of the north, most looked to the priests for help and leadership. In some places they got it; in others the Church merely lived off them.

The reemerging mass of villagers had become an insoluble element in the midst of a supposedly-Spanish Mexico. There were 2.5 million Amerindians in late eighteenth-century New Spain, comprising some forty percent of the total population. They were, through no fault of their own, a laggard mass within a stagnating civilization.

The direct burdens placed on the Amerindians were no longer disastrous. The crown taxed them lightly, and all tributes had been commuted to cash payments. However, the head tax was an instituted humiliation, and the *indio* was still restricted as a member of a conquered race. *Criollos* did not pay tributes or head taxes, and the taxes they paid were not collected like the Indian duties—tribute rendered to the *corregidores* by humble Amerindians.

The growing numbers of *ejido* Amerindians comprised sixty percent of the indigenous population, but forty percent were employed on haciendas. Here, these peons were merging with the *castas*, who by now were more and more simply classified as *mestizos*, or mixed-bloods without further subclassification. There were at least two million *mestizos* by 1800, far outnumbering the Europeans, and now rapidly overtaking the *indios*. *Castas* and *mestizos* also had begun to take the *indio's* place as laborers; the vast majority were either hacienda peons or *braceros*, manual laborers in or around the cities. Although the caste distinctions continued, the *casta* and the Indian in Mexico were becoming indistinguishable, especially in the north. Once an *indio* had learned Spanish and put on European-style dress, he became "*mestizo.*" The process was easy, but slow, because the Amerindians showed a reluctance to be deracinated and detribalized.

Almost all true *mestizos* were propertyless. They were barred from professions still and rarely could achieve an education, except for a handful who were able to enter holy orders. They were entirely a supporting class and caste, much closer to the *indios* than to the Spanish-*criollo* upper class. Further, since they were by nature deracinated, their whole condition was insecurity. Unlike *indios*, whose humble place was secure, *mestizos* inhabited ghettos and roamed aimlessly from place to place seeking employment. There were at least thirty thousand indigent *léperos* in the capital alone. They provoked official distaste and distrust. Otherwise rational officials like the Marqués de Croix believed that floggings had a salutary effect on this human flotsam, and above all, kept it in its place.

In rural areas, the *lépero* bandits who had come to infest the country sometimes became heroes to the Indians. Under the prevailing social system, the bandit could often appear a Robin Hood, and banditry had become a serious problem. A special police force, the *acordada*, was set loose on brigands and road agents, empowered with the right of summary executions. This was a harsh age for criminals everywhere, but the *acordada* behaved in ways that revealed the deep class and racial hatreds beneath the surface in Mexico and gave a hint of future horrors. This constabulary took to crucifying captured thieves and robbers in prominent places along the roads. The executed took days to die in public agony, and their tarred corpses, held to the crosses by nails, warned passersby for months.

Significantly, the *mestizos*, even in banditry, were beginning to show certain traits, especially more individualism, energy, and rebellion than the *indio*. Against almost impossible odds, the *mestizo* had to make his own new world. Scarred with illegitimacy, naturally emotionally unstable, given to great mercies and greater cruelties but increasingly resourceful, the *mestizo* was proving the enormous powers of endurance of men under frightful conditions. Universally disdained or abhorred, the swarthy *mestizo* was slowly but inevitably inheriting Mexico biologically—a fact few *criollos* noticed, even while they added to the *mestizo* population.

Despite a multiplicity of caste and racial bars, which tended to grow stronger—before the eighteenth century, the term "white" was seldom used to distinguish Europeans, but now the *criollos* were increasingly conscious of a role as "white men"—thousands of *mestizos* were also passing into Creole ranks. The caste system always allowed this, through the principle of dominant blood. The process was easiest on the northern frontier beginning at the Bajío. The census taken by Revillagigedo in 1793, the first and last under the crown, certified more than one million Europeans, about twenty percent of the population. This percentage was patently impossible, because *criollos* had not increased so fast, and there were only seventy thousand Spanish-born. By 1770 *mestizos* were beginning to pass for Europeans in growing numbers. The contemporary authorities revealed this in their writings, by indicating that of the "Europeans," no more than eight to ten percent were pure-blood *criollos*.

In this era, the *criollos* resented furiously any implication they had Indian blood, since no one had any pride in it. The law certified many families—whiteness could be bought, like offices and titles—but there were also many cases of acute embarrassment, when marriage alliances produced suspiciously dark or hairless children, and many *criollo* families had relatives with whom they preferred not to associate.

What was created was a small but very important infrastructure of *mestizos* who, as certified *criollos*, were becoming a sort of middle rank. Because they could go nowhere as *mestizos*, the ablest *mestizos* got themselves classified as white; this trend was obvious on the northern frontier. These near-Spaniards of course identified with *criollos*, and now began appearing as priests, lawyers, rancheros, merchants, and minor bureaucrats. But though they were part of an elite, it was not a rich or highly privileged elite. Such men rarely acquired substantial property or social position. They were working *criollos*, far beneath the mine operators and magnates. They appeared an upper class simply because the chasm between them and the supporting classes was so wide and difficult to cross.

The "new" *criollos*, by the nature of their emergence and existence, had to be among the shrewdest and most ambitious people in New Spain. Their attitudes resembled those of the poor Spanish still arriving in Mexico to be bookkeepers, managers, and traders, but they lacked the born-Spaniards' assurance and arrogance. The new *criollo's* position in society was anomalous and he knew it. He was made to feel insecure with subtle slurs against his ancestry. The combination of ability, ambition, and handicaps they could not overcome made "certified" *criollos* angry, irresolute, and often vicious in their attitudes. They were volatile, corrosive souls, at the same time socially promising and socially dangerous.

Bandits and rebels of all kinds were more apt to rise from these "so-called Spaniards" than from the propertied eight percent of the upper class. The rich *criollos* hated the arrogant *gachupines*, but they were completely locked into a defense of the whole social system. The crown sent officers to rule them and taxed them, but the crown also secured their property and status and ease. Thus the *hacendado* class, like the *indios* but for different reasons, formed a great obstacle to any pervasive social or political change in Mexico. The wealthy could buy minor offices and impressive titles under the Bourbons; the viceroys apparently deliberately created scores of ceremonial offices for this purpose. *Criollos* became colonels, *alcaldes*, and *corregidores*, though the centralization of administration under the intendants took the last shreds of power from such offices. The rich found their exclusion an irritant, but not nearly so great an irritant as was put on. The *hacendado* class did not want the burden of real power, because it had no sense of responsibility. This had been destroyed by centuries of Spanish despotism.

It was that part of the elite who had neither silver mines nor *sitios* and whose minds were insecure who found the inequities of the colonial system intolerable. The twelve or so percent of *criollos* who still had fortunes to make were infuriated by the snubs and the advantages of *peninsulares*; the new *criollos* found it almost unbearable when at last they achieved privileges and offices, only to find these devoid of power. As a class, the new *criollos* were growing richer, but at the same time acutely more aware of the injustices and stupidities of the colonial system. To understand the mind of this class, it must be understood that life under the Bourbons for the *criollos* was not onerous, but it was flagrantly inequitable. Doors opened for the meanest clerk out of Sevilla that remained closed to families that had been two hundred years in Mexico.

The Spanish taxes did not hurt the elite; *criollos* paid about 18 pesos per capita annually under the alcabala, which actually was levied less heavily than in Spain. The transactions tax really damaged the poor, by adding to the price of goods. The Spanish monopolies, however, were flagrantly inequitable. All license and commercial contracts were given to born-Spaniards. Mexico was a dumping ground for cheap Spanish wines and shoddy manufactures, which were sold at exorbitant prices. The manufacturing picture in Mexico was dismal. The few textile mills were primitive sweat shops operated by debt slaves. Local industries tooled leather and turned out crude pottery for a local market; beyond this, there was nothing. Even food was imported from Spain or from the Orient. Chinese silks and porcelains arrived in quantity, but through monopolies in the hands of a few favored Spaniards or the government.

The government controlled mercury, chocolate, alcoholic beverages, and tobacco through royal monopolies—virtually all the extremely profitable commodities. After the Bourbons tightened administration, the crown drew huge revenues from these sales. For example, the revenues from the sale of pulque, the universal drink of the working classes, amounted to four million pesos in 1746 from a population of three million. In 1800 they came to twenty million pesos, out of a population that had merely doubled. The tobacco monopoly produced four-and-one-half million pesos, which exceeded the royal revenues from the mining industry. However, even Bourbon efficiency was efficient only on a Spanish scale: administrative costs were ridiculously high in every government enterprise due to the bureaucratic proliferation of offices and processes. The tobacco monopoly spent more money, for example, on administration than it did for both labor and raw materials.

The Spanish monopolies and colonial restrictions on trade were seriously aggravated by an almost incredibly inefficient shipping system. The Spanish merchant marine was not sufficient to supply the empire to begin with, and continual wars made Spanish shipping vulnerable to English sea power. Only one vessel sailed annually from Manila to Acapulco, and while only one of these was lost to the English, the restriction of trade to a singly yearly galleon kept prices exorbitant. And trade restrictions, the monopolies, and the shipping system paralyzed trade, making smuggling a profitable business. When Revillagigedo opened Mexican ports to world shipping in 1789, the legal trade increased fourfold—but whether this marked a real increase in true volume is hard to tell. The reform came too late in any case, because the Spanish Empire was soon caught up in the wars of the French Revolution and the Napoleonic era.

The Spanish colonial mercantile system had destroyed Mexican economic development even more thoroughly than the land tenure system or the social system. Throughout the century the production of silver and gold rose. The mining income was no longer crucial to the government— but New Spain could never shake its addiction to a mining-camp psychology, and mining did provide most of the spendable wealth and what stimulation of the economy there was in Mexico.

Mexican silver, which was coined into milled pillar dollars after Felipe V installed mint machinery in 1732 at México flooded the world. The Mexican dollar circulated in Europe, was the basis of currency throughout most of the other European colonial empires, and was to become the unit of account of much of the British Commonwealth—because most of this silver ended up in British hands. The English had now established a maritime and commercial ascendancy, and while Mexico poured out millions of dollars every year, most Mexicans remained outside a money economy, and the currency of Spain herself was still the miserable copper maravedí. In the late eighteenth century, there were more silver dollars in the British-American colonies than in Spain.

In 1790, fifty-five percent of all Spanish colonial revenues came out of Mexico, and New Spain paid far more taxes into the royal treasury than the kingdoms of old Spain. This inequity, piled upon all the other inequities and stupidities of an archaic colonial economic system, created a smoldering discontent among all educated *criollos*. The knowledge that the Spaniards, both the crown and the *gachupines* in New Spain, were milking Mexico fomented anger among the poorer *criollos* more than any intellectual notions. In any case, ideas like the Rights of Man, ascendant in France and colonial North America provided no rationales for the continued superiority of the white elites over the mixed-bloods and the Indians. Between 1775 and 1794, therefore, neither the American nor French Revolutions stirred any real emotion in *criollo* minds or breasts.

Carlos III clearly saw that the successful revolt of the British American colonies posed two dangers to the empire: one, from the example, and second, from a vigorous, independent, Anglo-Saxon state on the northern frontier. He chose to side with the American colonies only because England was considered the greater danger, and this decision apparently allowed Spain to strengthen her position in America vis-à-vis the British, as the traditional enemy was swept from Florida and the Gulf. Most Creoles in New Spain rejoiced in the English humiliations between 1775 and 1783; over centuries they had become conditioned to think of England as both the national and ideological foe.

Through the close of the century, despite enormous underlying grievances and irritations, there is no evidence of revolutionary sentiment in New Spain—nothing like that which already was fermenting further south. Protests were limited to radical chit-chat in drawing rooms. The huge reservoir of *indio* and *casta* discontent—of which the *criollos* themselves were not really aware—was growing, but invisibly.

Most of what is known about New Spain in this era comes from the Prussian traveler and geographer, Alexander von Humboldt. Apparently, he loved Mexico, but he tried to record everything about the country with fine impartiality. He painted no paradise; however, he found conditions better in Mexico than in many other countries. He saw the absurdities of the colonial system as no worse than the absurdities prevalent in Europe under the *Ancien Regime*, and his careful analysis indicates that after 1789 conditions had improved rapidly.

However, Humboldt's comparisons were drawn against the Eastern Europe with which he was most familiar, and where most of the people still lived in serfdom. White serfs beyond the Elbe were probably no better off than Mexican peons. Prussian peasants lived under a rigid class system, paying forty percent of their incomes to landlords and government. New Spain was hardly unusual in the worldwide societies of the Old Regime, where small, sometimes brilliant elites, culturally and often ethnically separated from the masses, showed cultural vigor amid social and economic stasis. México was a greater capital than Berlin, and the Mexican upper class on the surface no more lazy or corrupt than the upper classes of the Austrian or Russian empires. *Castas* were as well treated as Christian peasants in the Balkans under Turkish rule. Humboldt saw the miserable *léperos* of the urban ghettos but considered these no more unsanitary nor murderous than the Paris or London mobs.

He could not judge Mexico, because the Prussian baron lacked insight into dominant world trends, into the vital role of a bourgeoisie in the Western world, and into the differences that the democratic revolutions would make in the Prussian and Hispanic milieus. Prussia had a disciplined population and an energetic, patriotic, and authoritarian upper class, devoted both to its own interests and the state. Together, these elements could build armies and bureaucracies in the nineteenth century that would bring Prussia perilously close to world domination.

Humboldt's lack of understanding of the differences between New Spain and his own part of the world was to be reflected often in the nineteenth-century Hispanic world, where men greatly admired the Prussian experience and wondered why they could not emulate it. But the Hispanic elites were very different, and were to lead the Hispanic nations to a different kind of destruction.

Humboldt, and most *criollos*, felt that if the more ridiculous restrictions of the Spaniards were removed, and the Spanish stopped from their eternal milking of Mexico, the country had enormous promise—but this view failed to take into account the true nature of the *criollos*, their lack of aristocracy, and their centuries of psychic subordination and sense of ingrained humiliation.

The Indian summer of Spanish-American society was an age of certain splendor in the visual arts, but the sterility of thought and education stifled intellectual creation. If Mexicans had an active life of the mind, they left little evidence. The country produced tinkerers and journalists, and writers who rehashed worn-out styles, no Sigüenzas or Sor Juanas, but minor figures impressed with personal conceits.

The Enlightenment did have one strong effect, however, in creating a growing interest in things native to Mexico. Carlos III, through his viceroys, encouraged the sciences and practical arts. By the 1770s several men were carrying on studies of Mexican antiquities and minerology, geology, and geography. The expulsion of the Jesuits hampered these, but had another unexpected effect. Some of the Jesuit exiles were *criollos* who in Italy found themselves longing for, and finding a new identity with the country of their birth.

The new perspectives of these men made them aware that they were not really Spaniards. Out of nostalgia for his homeland Padre Francisco Javier Clavijero wrote the *Ancient History of Mexico*, drawing upon Sigüenza and new codex sources he found at Rome. Clavijero, whose researches revealed to him the extent of the Amerindian civilization, strongly rejected the notion that the ancient *indios* could have been *gente sin razón*.

Other priests made earth studies, showing an expanding consciousness of identification with Mexican soil. Significantly, these men, all *criollos*, began to identify with Mexico, and therefore, in some manner with the Indians. They found inspiration in the forgotten ruins of Amerindian greatness.

The brilliance of a people who were generally unintellectual and who had been forbidden free inquiry, however, had to lie in the visual arts. These were channeled into religious themes, because all expression was still dominated by the Church. It should be seen that the exquisite religious art and architecture of colonial Mexico did not always represent feverish faith—there simply was no other outlet for artistic expression. The Church destroyed the possibility of individual responsibility or independence among the people, but it continually patronized native arts that were devoted to the glorification of religion, and the skills that died out in the sixteenth century were in fact revived in the eighteenth by religious patronage, both among *indios* and Spaniards.

Sigüenza had indicated that thousands of paintings were produced in the seventeenth century, but little of this baroque art was valuable, or survived. Miguel Cabrera, the greatest of Mexican colonial painters, appeared in the next century. He was a Zapotec Indian but his inspiration was entirely Hispanic. He decorated dozens of churches with canvases and painted portraits of viceroys and other famous men. Some of these show a crude, New World vitality, somewhat similar to North American primitives, but they show nothing of the indigenous, or the Amerindian.

The eighteenth century was the great age of church building. Stately edifices rose everywhere in south-central Mexico and especially in the Bajío. The early churches, even the great cathedrals, had a certain air of grossness and medievalism, still seen in the cathedral at México and certain enormous shrines and convents. The artwork on the old buildings was a weird blend, Judaeo-Christian themes carried out by Nahua minds. On the newer buildings, which soon had a universal form—two imposing towers fronting a great dome—an art style evolved that in some ways was a fusion of Western Christianity and indigenous, oriental exuberance. It was basically baroque. The form was Hispanic; the intricacy of the ornamentation went back to Palenque and Teotihuacán. The splendor and detail of this ornamentation, the carved facades and burnished woodwork, the baroque mass of delicate curvatures, are indescribable. They created joy for the anonymous builders and carvers, and wonder for all succeeding generations. Next to ancient Amerindian monuments, these eighteenth-century churches are the most important architectural attractions in Mexico.

Like the ancient Amerindian cities and temples and pyramids, this burst of creativity must be seen as much a spontaneous manifestation of native energy and art as the Gothic period in Europe. It produced magnificent and hardly less spectacular monuments.

This outburst, however, ended before the close of the century. Nativism, the blending of Spanish baroque and indigenous imagination, withered before the French importations of Manuel Tolsá. Tolsá was a Spain-born classicist who logically found favor with the viceroys. Tolsá's palaces, public buildings, churches, and equestrian statues reflected the neoclassicism of Europe that began with Versailles and seeped with the Bourbons into Spain.

New Spain also produced some excellent medallists in this century, who struck or cast thousands of portraits, mostly in praise of, or on the proclamations of the Bourbon kings.

These monuments of eighteenth-century New Spain reveal clearly the distortions and terrible inequities of society. Silver mine operators who made millions of pesos overnight, and an enormously wealthy Church, expressed their thanks to God by endowing altars covered with silver and gold, at which a ragged population prayed and received the Host.

José de la Borda paid for the exquisite church in remote Taxco, where he became a millionaire. "God gave to Borda, and Borda returned to God," as he said. There was a new-rich ostentation behind most of the Bajío churches. Antonio Obregón erected a marvelous church on a steep mountainside overlooking Guanajuato, known popularly as *La Valenciana* —from the name of his glory hole. Some of these men were muleteers, like the Conde de Regla before he struck it rich, and most of them, like Regla, purchased titles with their silver.

Men who grew rich from lucky strikes or oppressed labor built monuments to themselves and God in remote places, adding architectural glory to Mexico.

The Church in these years, now without a mission and with more revenues that it could use, lavished huge sums on similar projects. The notion of spending for social benefit was foreign to clerics as well as the whole society; the Church raised its own monuments. By 1790, it held one-third of all the houses in the capital along with many haciendas everywhere in Mexico. The rents from this property were unnecessary to religious operations, for the Church was amply supported by enforced tithes and taxes, and on top of this, priests charged high fees for every service, every dedicated Mass, marriage, christening, or funeral. The clergy also charged handsomely for the meager learning it imparted through convent schools. The money created surpluses, which went into architecture and high salaries for the ruling hierarchy.

A measure of the wealth of the eight Mexican dioceses is shown by the annual incomes allotted to the bishops. The archbishop at the capital drew

130,000 pesos, twice the salary of the viceroy. This provided a purchasing power of at least two million modern dollars in terms of services and labor. The bishop at Puebla was paid 110,000 pesos, of Valladolid 100,000 pesos, and of Guadalajara, 90,000 pesos. And these emoluments must be measured against relative pay scales in an economy where a skilled workman might earn three pesos per week and hacienda peons rarely saw any money. It must stand to the eternal credit of some of these prelates, who like the bishop of Valladolid, Abad Y Queipo, that they could protest to the king the continuing misery of the poor and demand reform. But the majority, sipping expensive chocolate in their splendid refectories and receiving reports of mounting revenues, were completely trammeled up in managing a business. Even Abad could not quite bring himself to propose giving Church property back to the people—the thought was sacrilege, because the Hispanic Church had long confused giving to the Church with giving to God.

Tithes, bulls, fees, and bequests from the faithful covered altars and railings with gold and choked chapter houses with bags of pesos. All of this wealth was withdrawn from circulation. Finally, it was distributed very unevenly within the Church. A few miles from the episcopal palace, a dedicated parish priest might be allowed to retain only one hundred pesos annually in support, less than earned by a common soldier. The parish clergy among the poor was itself very poor.

This property ruined the Church more insidiously than its position as an arm of government. A great bishop was now a great builder, administrator, or patron, rarely a great theologian or pastoral leader. Property drained the hierarchy of spirituality. It remained only on those levels where vows of poverty were enforced by miserable salaries, and only on those levels did the clergy retain influence among the people. The Spaniards in purple knew this, but the bishops were more inclined to obstruct efforts of the priests among the people than the supposedly anticlerical government.

The Church had not wasted all its power and influence. The question was how that wealth and power would be used, if it were used at all.

The Mexican landscape, except in the harsh deserts of the north, was complex and colorful and peaceful as the century ended.

The things unbearable to Western minds about colonial Mexico—the arbitrariness and corruption of government, the economic stagnation and naivete, the rigid class and caste systems—did not weigh all that heavily on the Mexican consciousness. Hispanic society, and Hispanic colonial society, were never utilitarian in concept like the English or the Dutch. Life was not ceaseless action; its goals were being and feeling as much as doing. If on the practical plane Mexico had become stagnant and inefficient—if nothing got done on time, or never got done at all—the Mexican spirit soared and excelled in other things. Every house however poor had flowers; the streets and even the fields were filled with music. Almost everyone could play some instrument and sing and even compose songs. Everyone took sheer delight in color, from the hues of the dashing costumes of the caballeros to paint smeared on village walls. Mexico was a dazzling mélange of whites and reds and greens under a brilliant sun, and if life were directionless, there was always time to feel, to absorb, and enjoy. If government and society were bad, family life was close and warm. The *indios, criollos,* and *mestizos* had great, extended families that were a bulwark against the world.

Latin temperaments and Amerindian consciousnesses had combined to reinforce a different sense of reality. Finery, manners, rhetoric, generosity were admired immensely more than capabilities. Sheer courage counted for more than demonstrated results. To fail gracefully was as important to the Hispanic mind of the post-sixteenth-century world as to win. Men were prepared to accept all consequences with a calm and melancholy dignity. The Hispanic-Mexican consciousness, in fact, had somehow taken the Castilian and Amerindian vices and cloaked them with charm and dignity and grace. It found solace in a sense of destiny, and a philosophy that respected death as much as life. Such concepts, feelings, and qualities, of course, made and reinforced a world that was intolerable in many ways— but the same qualities helped Mexicans endure it. Hispanic Mexico was more like the Orient than England, or even Spain, and to live gracefully the Mexican had to find an almost oriental sense of time, matter, and the mind. The Hispanic world lived badly, but it knew how to live. Alexander von Humboldt never forgot the wonderful spectacle of white-capped mountains rising up over green tropical foliage on the road to México City, and a blond *criolla*, a belle who was "the most beautiful woman he had ever seen." New Spain was a land of contrasts, an ancient country and an aging colony in a New World, with enlightened despots reordering everything and changing nothing, a gay, high society living as though tomorrow would never come, a growing mass of outcasts beginning to search for tomorrow, at least in their secret hearts, a Church trammeled up in the things of this world in the midst of death and living faith, millions of primitive Amerindians determined to endure whatever tomorrow might bring. It was a country of rare natural beauty and marvelous monuments, of sunny splendor and lavish hospitality and deep antagonisms, hauteur, and cruelty, where men piously rendered up their *óboles* to their God and just as piously applied the whip and nails to their fellow men.

There was beauty as well as misery to this age, and it left its glories behind in vast structures and ornamented walls. But the spirit that had created this Mexico was almost dead, and New Spain was an empire held together only by a small, imperious band of enlightened aristocrats holding wearily against the coming night.

PART THREE

The Tyranny of the Past:
The Mexicans

21

THE CONSPIRATORS

Those who liked to use the language of Rousseau talked of interpreting the sovereign will of Mexican people. What they really desired was the rule of a native white minority released from the trammels of Spanish legalists and bureaucrats.

If the Creoles had been more resolute and better organized, this is what they might easily have achieved. But the men of birth and property who formed the most powerful element among them were too hesitant to move quickly or decisively.

From *Mexico: A Short History*, Sir Nicholas Cheetham.

At the beginning of the nineteenth century, Spain collapsed as a world power and the Hispanic empire dissolved.

The failure of the Spanish Empire was far more than an inevitable evolution of the American dominions into independent states. For example, the British colonies in North America south of Canada separated from the mother country and re-formed into a new, vigorous nation without doing any essential damage either to the homeland or themselves. The new United States soon restored old commercial ties with England, under more favorable terms, and in the long run the English-speaking world was immensely strengthened. The disintegration of the Spanish-American empire, however, was profoundly different. The successor states in America emerged primarily because of a general disintegration of the cement of Hispanic civilization, at the beginning of an era in which neither the old country nor the emerging independent states could maintain any stable internal order. The British colonies characteristically united; the Spanish dominions dissolved, not only into almost a score of nations, but into societies within nations that were fundamentally divided.

The Hispanic world was one which simply could not cope successfully with either the democratic or the industrial revolution, the two major sources of power in the modern world.

Under the impact of Anglo-Saxon and French ideas, ideals, and demonstrated success, the old forms of the Hispanic world became intolerable to large numbers of its people. Hispanic society, everywhere, tended to become deeply divided between *continuistas* who believed in building a better society upon existing roots through adopting Western techniques and those who were *reformistas*, who believed society was already made and merely needed to be changed by radical social reforms. The terms conservative and liberal, which were and are conventionally used, do not fit exactly. In Mexico, for example, in the nineteenth century the greatest and most influential "conservatives" desired radical changes in industrial and economic techniques but without an abrupt change in the civilization or social order—in other words, a modernization on the order successfully carried out by the Germans and Japanese. The "liberals," more ideological, fought to reform society, but were intensely hostile to technological and other progress. Both mainstreams were pulled and torn by true reactionaries on one side—people who resisted all change—and by pure radicals on the other—men who wanted to destroy everything. Both liberals and conservatives, in the Hispanic world, remained a small elite, because the vast majority of the population was still outside a true money economy or modern politics.

In the broadest perspective, with all the shadings of ideology and the tumults of personalities and prejudices laid aside, the great argument was whether to seize the utilitarian concepts and techniques of the Western world without first creating a Western society—in other words, whether to put into operation Western social and governmental forms while utterly ignoring the social basis from which those forms evolved.

If the Bourbon dynasty had remained vigorous, such a revolution might possibly have been imposed gradually from the top. Carlos III had done much to modernize Spain. But his successors were totally unfit. They could neither lead nor surrender their prerogatives, and the same was generally true of the upper classes in almost every Hispanic country.

When the traditional leadership patently could not cope with new ideas and techniques—as, for example, the Spanish monarchy and nation could not cope with the French Revolution and Napoleon—great cracks and hideous struggles had to appear. The Hispanic anarchy of soul that existed from the seventeenth century was at last translated into an anarchy of society and government.

Compared to the contemporary democratic and industrial revolutions, the Hispanic revolution was abortive. There was too much struggle against problems of the mind and spirit as well as physical realities, as ideals and aspirations, now noble, now naive, ran far ahead of possibilities. And Hispanic revolutionaries, whether conservative or liberal, took too much of their aspiration and inspiration from outside Hispanic culture; xenophobic and desperately desirous of dignity on one plane, they were abject on another. They tended to reject an essential nativism when they should have been creating a newer culture out of their own historic depths.

The conservatives refused to face the fact that after the twin Western demons were released on the world, the old Hispanic order was intolerable to too many people who were prepared to die rather than accept a gradual transition. The reformers, however, invariably ignored the equally salient fact that the human and social material to make a democratic revolution on the French or North American order simply did not exist in the Hispanic world. The democratic revolution was a revolt not of the masses but of the independent, propertied, Western bourgeoisie. No such middle class had ever evolved in the Hispanic nations—probably, none would ever evolve, because the value system that created such people in other parts of Europe never existed in Spain.

The Hispanic culture could not create either a modern democracy or a modern industrial-commercial economy without first totally changing the very roots from which all Hispanic conservatives and reformers sprang. The French and English could reorder their societies relatively quickly to meet democratic and industrial trends without changing the essential nature of the state, or of the inherent value systems. When Hispanic civilization destroyed the crown and Church, legitimacy and religion, it had nothing to replace them. French and Anglo-Saxon ideas of society, technology, and government were exotic transplants, that either were rejected, became encysted, or grew noxious, sickly weeds in Hispanic social soil.

But the struggle was inevitable, and its very nature had to produce civil, social, and psychic horror. Once truth was repudiated and legitimacy fled in the general collapse at the beginning of the nineteenth century, no Hispanic culture was to find more than a generation of internal peace and order. Violent revolutionary periods were followed by disillusioned post-revolutionary eras, and in turn by new disintegrations. This trend was universal throughout the Spanish-speaking world. The cycles of anarchy, civil war, pretorianism, liberalism, *caudillaje*, rampant reform and crushing reaction were similar everywhere from Argentina to Mexico to Spain with only local variations, but they did not occur at the same time. Mexico's dominant political problems were very little different from those in Spain, because they grew from the same ethos. From decade to decade each country found different solutions. Events were unsynchronized; the pattern was much the same.

Mexico was and is uniquely part of a greater culture and civilization. All Mexican intellectuals have recognized and admitted the enormous problem

of Mexican "identity" for almost two hundred years, without recognizing
or admitting the root of the problem itself. The Spanish Empire grafted its
civilization onto many quite different human stocks from Patagonia to the
Rio Bravo, and onto many variant basic human societies. The graft was
dominant *everywhere* in the things that compose civilization: language,
law, religion, organization, ethic. Far too much attention has been paid
intellectually to the Amerindian trunk of Hispanic America, which has
sometimes actually prevented Hispanic-American intellectuals from seeing
their problems for what they are: Hispanic problems. Strangely enough, in
the present century, a tightly integrated intellectual Hispanic world con-
tinues to exist, from Madrid to Lima to Mexico, however its members
deny its survival in political terms.

In the early nineteenth century, Hispanic civilization seemed determined
to destroy itself, and in a real sense, the battle became one between civilization, however imperfect, and barbarism. The degradation and destruction in Santa Anna's Mexico was matched in Rosas' Argentina, in Spain,
Bolivia, and Peru. Territorial integrity of the successor states of the old
empire was preserved mainly because the British, and later the North
Americans, guaranteed this, keeping Spanish America as their particular
preserve, for economic if not imperial penetration. The Hispanic world
lost only a few fringe territories, mostly those North American regions it
had never successfully populated.

The currently dominant, liberal Mexican view of national history, which
forms the conventional wisdom and is taught in schools, tends to be
anachronistic—that is, it begins with the present century and looks back.
Mexicans have tried to take the twentieth-century social revolution as a
culmination, and therefore they have consciously shaped their past to point
toward 1910 and 1917. This does provide the theme, intellectual order,
and form so important to some intellectuals; it connects the anarchic
events of the Hispanic revolution with a thread of purpose. Above all, such
a view creates the myths and heroes new nations need.

In the dominant Mexican view, all who worked for racial or social
equality and for economic reforms, whether failures, great men, or bandits,
have become national heros. Those who stood for tradition, even if patriots and nation-builders, are tarred with villainy. A few such villains, like
Lucas Alamán and Lorenzo de Zavala, are grudgingly respected, because they dealt with facts. Against this dominant view there has been a
minority report, the themes of traditionalist, rightist, writers, who easily
point out the failures of the reformers—but finding little to be proud of,
often indulge in national self-degradation.

Neither viewpoint deals with the fact that Mexican history forms part of
a worldwide Hispanic time of troubles, or admits that the Porfiriato was as
essential to the emergence of a modern Mexico as Hidalgo's insurgency.

And as Madariaga wrote, men can only be judged against the forces, necessities, and possibilities of their times, not by later standards. Ideological viewpoints make for intellectual order, but human history by nature is random and disorderly, like any organic growth. Its grandeur is made by its essential tragedy.

The history of Mexico is not a story of heros and villains, martyrs and oppressors, good against evil, or different rationales and interests pitted against each other, so much as the story of a struggle by very human men and women to make a livable present and future out of an intolerable past.

Carlos III of Spain died in December, 1788. His death marked the collapse of a culture and empire, and his ministers had waged a valiant, personal, and eccentric war against the fall of night; briefly they had made Spain and her empire a great power again. But they only delayed history.

The great Viceroy Revillagigedo was actually an afterglow of this reign. He was appointed after the king died, but while his ministers still had control of the government. The reforms of the early 1790s—the opening of Hispanic ports, the curtailment of Spanish monopolies, the stimulation of arts and sciences, and others—were thus doubly doomed. They not only came too late, but they were quickly obviated, reversed, or rescinded by the newer breed of men who came to power in Spain.

Carlos IV was a handsome, amiable, near-imbecile, and a cuckold whose queen's lover ruled the kingdom. He soon replaced the capable ministers with Spaniards who wiped out a century of rational reform.

In 1792 a soldier of the royal guard, the pretty adventurer Manuel Godoy who was the queen's lover, was elevated to chief minister of state. Godoy, who was made Duque de Alcudia and afterward a prince under various names, was twenty-five years old. Godoy had talent as well as ambition. He did work at the job, but he was not capable of managing an empire, and the very nature of his preferment, the pervasive moral corruption of his coterie, and the inherent weakness of Spain doomed his ministry. Now, only the most capable, farsighted, and powerful of men could have coped with the dangers ignited by the French Revolution and the Napoleonic era in Europe. Godoy's fate was first to disgrace the crown, then virtually destroy it through his actions.

Carlos III's ministers had instinctively opposed the revolution that convulsed France in 1789. Godoy, however, honestly thought that Spain should continue the French alliance between the two major branches of Bourbons. As France became in turn a constitutional monarchy, a republic, and finally, a dangerous imperial power running amok in Europe with revolutionary élan, Godoy's policies turned a weaker Spain into a French pawn, directed by changing regimes in Paris. Thus Godoy went into a disastrous war with England, out of which Spain could have gained nothing and in which the Spanish fleet was destroyed; he allowed Napoleon's armies into Spain to operate against Portugal, a British ally, which led to Napoleon's occupation of the peninsula and the dispossession of the Bourbon dynasty. This event, by its very nature, destroyed the Spanish Empire.

In the meantime, Godoy's administration created havoc across the Atlantic in New Spain. Revillagigedo was summarily dismissed in 1794. His replacement, the Marqués de Branciforte, a relation of Godoy, was uncaring, incompetent, and utterly corrupt.

Branciforte began his regime by smuggling a large quantity of personal goods through Mexican customs, making a huge profit from their sale. He was so openly corrupt he held office only a year, which was enough, since he departed with some five million pesos and the "curses of the entire populace." His successors were hardly better. They were a series of the worst viceroys who disgraced the baton; they broke their own laws and regulations for profit, and tacitly permitted their appointees and officers to do the same.

The abrupt change from men like Bucareli and Revillagigedo to officials of this stripe, and the abrupt change of direction of *gachupín* government from enlightened despotism to naked avarice shook Mexican sensibilities and eroded unquestioned loyalties. Injury was added to insult as Godoy became involved in unfortunate continental wars, since the crown increased American taxes to pay for these. The Church was pressured for money, which caused it to call some of its dormant mortgages. A capital levy was extracted from the endowed religious charities in Mexico. The poor bore most of these taxes, as always, but they aroused a deep sense of outrage and malaise among all colonials.

The *criollos* of New Spain were in some important ways different from the Creoles of the other American viceroyalties. New Spain had always been more "Spanish" and under tighter control; both its European and Amerindian populations had been more tamed than on the southern continent. Mexican *criollos* had not engaged in *comunero* movements or tried to depose viceroys. As one Spanish official said bitingly early in the nineteenth century, all that was needed was to show the *criollos* of New Spain an official seal for them to kiss the hand or fall on their knees. And the half million or so of the pure-European propertied class were almost impervious up to now to the ideals and concepts of the American and French revolutions. The pamphlets issued from these upheavals circulated quite freely, despite the opposition of the Church; the North American Declaration of Independence and the United States Constitution were on the Inquisition's index of forbidden tracts, along with the writings of the French philosophers, but most educated people had seen them.

The notions of independence for the Americas, expulsion of the bloodsucking *gachupines*, abolition of the Inquisition, and secular control of education had occurred to the *criollo* class without the revelation of French *philosophes*. The concurrent ideas of the Jacobins—free republics, racial and social equality, land reform—however totally destroyed the appeal of revolutions for the true *criollos*. A rich *hacendado*, queued up to kiss the viceroy's hand, flushing under Castilian arrogance, was still locked by interest to the crown and empire. Above all, the Creoles possessed a tremendous identity problem. They were European and glad of it in a heavily Amerindian country, even if the *gachupines* would not let them be truly Spanish. They had very little sense of "American" nationality, though one genuine oddity was the tendency of some pure-blood descendents of the conquistadores to try to identify with the ancient Mexica rulers of Mexico. Such men studied pre-Columbian artifacts, and liked to think of themselves as heirs of the "Aztecs." The contemporary *indios*, meanwhile, had completely forgotten their mighty ancestors.

In South America, *criollo* elites had already become small oligarchies which could produce leaders like Bolívar and San Martín. The Mexican Creoles were much more emasculated by history, with profound effects for their country.

In New Spain the negative aspects of the democratic revolutions—that is, the things and institutions liberalism attacked, such as despotism and inequality—struck responsive chords mainly in a *criollo* minority at the bottom: the half-million *criollos*, lawyers, doctors, and petty officials who had some education but no mines or estates. They struck home even more deeply in the few of the two million *mestizos* who could read and write, mainly men who had gotten a clerical education. The Creole lower half, and the upper ranks of the *mestizos*, were privileged compared to *léperos* and *indios*, but they easily saw the contradictions and inequities of the empire. Many of these men were ripe for radicalization. The *léperos* and *indios* did not count, or seem to count. They were apart from "society," and far too poor and apathetic to engage in political activity. They were good only for a riot now and then.

The *criollo-mestizo* lawyers and rancheros had allies in an unsuspected place: the Church. The poorer parish clergy contained many *mestizos*, because the Church had always provided a means of social mobility—if not too far. Parish curates and assistants resented their poverty in a rich institution, and also the *óbolos* ground out of their hungry flocks. They were men of some learning, who could understand that arbitrary and actually ridiculous inequity was not ordained by God.

The lower *criollos* and *mestizos* (who often could not really be distinguished from each other, as many *mestizos* were certified *criollo*) may have appeared to form an elite vis-à-vis the bottom castes, but they were both insecure, and ambitious. There were hundreds of able priests who knew they would never be made canon, and hundreds of lawyers who knew they would never be favored with the kind of position they craved, simply because of their birth or circumstance. This class did not hate the rich *hacendados*, because its real enemies were the *gachupines*, who hoarded the civic and clerical posts it desired. Hidden underneath ambition, also, was the smoldering dissatisfaction of almost all men who had indigenous blood—whether they admitted it or not—against a system that made them anomalies, citizens but still slightly less than human.

This radicable class was not then, or a century later, a true middle class as the Western world defined a middle class, which never existed in the Hispanic world. This apparent middle rank in Mexico (and other Hispanic areas) had dreams and ambitions that began and ended with securing some form of public employment—an office that was the only road they knew to *señoria* and true dignity.

This class of petty bureaucrats, priests, apothecaries, teachers, and lawyers, and the ranchero stock from which much of it came, could, however, play the role of revolutionaries, and this class became the primary revolutionary force in the Hispanic world. But while the North American revolution was waged *against* government, the Mexican revolutionaries always wanted to seize their government to exploit it. A successful revolution thus was a completed coup d'etat. An unsuccessful revolution, begun over a subterranean volcano of misery and humiliation, was likely to devolve into the horrors of class struggle and civil war.

The class open to radicalization unfortunately could find little in its past to support revolutionary change. There was no concept of rule of law, sovereignty of the people, or local government or freedom of choice in the Hispanic heritage. The revolutionaries were hybrids who did not know who they were, or even what they wanted to be. Hated institutions like the crown and Inquisition could be erased, but the consciousness of the Spanish mind made such things as a "free citizenry," a "republic" or "free choice" as meaningless as the idea of a "free market," which had never existed, and in which no Hispanic mentality could quite believe.

A tragedy of the so-called liberalism in New Spain was that its leadership, for all the splendid, idealistic, and honest men, never had a single creative genius. Therefore, all Hispanic revolutionaries were driven to borrow foreign concepts and ideologies—tragic, because French and North American or English liberalism was alien to the Hispanic ethos. The concept of popular sovereignty proved fascinating to all Mexican revolutionaries, who invariably identified "the people" with themselves. In New Spain, however, there were no "people." There were only separate and unequal classes and castes arranged in rigid hierarchies. A still-powerful religion denied the concept of the sovereignty of the people as heresy. Under the Church and crown, Spaniards, *criollos*, *léperos*, and *indios* lived in separate countries—there was no such thing as a Mexican, in the way that Frenchmen were already French.

A certain Mexican consciousness had emerged out of the native studies encouraged by Carlos III. The thrust was scientific, but an emotional feeling for native soil proceeded from this in men like the mineralogist, Manuel Mier y Terán. The academies, especially the Jesuit schools, helped forge this Mexican consciousness among certain intellectuals. These men could not be active politically under the existing church-state, nor put any of their ideas into political form. But the very creation of a new Mexican consciousness could not help but have political implications.

Men like Carlos María de Bustamante, who edited the periodical *El Diario de Méjico*, and Fernández de Lizardi, the so-called "Mexican Observer" who wrote perhaps the greatest Mexican novel, worked to create an indigenous literary medium early in the nineteenth century. Their language was Spanish, but their focus was on the things of Mexico. Significantly, these men secretly favored independence long before the notion could be broached, and they had come to think of the Spanish Conquest as an usurpation of their native country—although they were Spanish by ancestry. The concept was more emotional than practical, because there were no longer any "Aztecs" waiting to be liberated—but it was also to become the source of marvelous intellectual confusion in Mexico.

The Mexican problem was political—the arbitrary, tyrannical rule of one Hispanic country by another. The Amerindian past was buried forever. But the search for identity, terribly important to insecure *criollo* intellectuals, led them to try to resurrect it. The identity crisis and search were more European than Amerindian, for the surviving *indios* knew all too well who and what they were. Here, in the first years of the nineteenth century, began the interminable Mexican argument over whether Mexico was an "Indian" or a "Spanish" country. One of the ironies was that those people most intent on establishing the Indianess of Mexico were elitists far removed from the contemporary *indios*.

While Godoy's henchmen looted New Spain, there were minor, but increasing signs of disaffection. French Jacobins—about half of all foreigners in Spanish America were French—circulated propaganda and sometimes nailed provocative placards on México City walls. The only overt rebellions were comic opera: in 1798 some barbers, wigmakers, and petty functionaries plotted a coup; other conspirators planned to arm the *lépero* mobs with machetes in 1799. Other dissidents met to discuss blowing up Chapultepec Palace, and once the viceroy had been miraculously disposed of, the equally miraculous erection of a new Mexica empire. All these plots were abortive. The *audiencia* knew of them and made some arrests, but wisely refrained from making martyrs. The government understood that those Mexicans who talked of restoring the old Amerindian throne faced an insurmountable problem—the only survivors of Motecuh-zoma's line had become dukes and *grandes* of Spain.

The idea of American liberty, engraved on the medals that were sur-reptitiously passed about, was only an idea, until Napoleon undercut the whole order of things in the Spanish empire.

Napoleon, emperor of France, had troops in Spain in 1808 ostensibly to fight the British ally, Portugal. Godoy trusted Napoleon, although he had already betrayed the Spanish trust by selling the Louisiana territory to the United States, after these possessions had been returned to France by Carlos IV on the promise they would never be alienated. Napoleon planned to seize control of the peninsula. Godoy seems to have realized the emperor's duplicity too late, and in any case, both the minister and his royal fool were helpless because they had both lost the confidence of the entire Spanish population.

The hopes of Spaniards had fastened on the Infante Fernando, who although *macho* and a firm believer in the divine right of kings, was idle and faithless. When Napoleon put his armies in Spain, the Infante Fer-nando organized an opposition to Godoy and French influence, and finally forced his father Carlos IV to abdicate. He took the throne as Fernando VII.

Napoleon refused to recognize the accession. His marshals had control of the peninsula, apparently, because French battalions were everywhere. At Napoleon's orders, the entire royal family was hustled off to Bayonne. Here, in a disgraceful episode marked by both filial and paternal treachery and total cowardice before the French ruler, all the Bourbons surrendered their rights to the Spanish throne in favor of Napoleon—who then granted it to his brother, Joseph Bonaparte.

These events aroused popular fury throughout Spain. In May 1808, there was a genuine spontaneous uprising against the French in Madrid. The French army easily crushed the Madrid mob and cowed the Spanish forces, but the Spaniards countered with that most characteristic of all Hispanic actions, the guerrilla war. The French, superior in arms, training, and discipline, quickly overran the peninsula, but they were masters only of the actual spots on which they stood. Local leaders arose among the middle ranks and the peasantry to fight the invaders, and juntas sprang up at Oviedo and Seville proclaiming themselves governments and trustees for Fernando VII, now in French captivity. These juntas were dominated by Spanish liberals, and they were intensely jealous of each other. Again characteristically, every junta claimed supremacy; none could organize the country. What now happened was that Spain sank into a decentralized and quite horrible guerrilla warfare, in which hideous atrocities were com-mitted on all sides.

The French held but could not pacify the country; until they gained the aid of Wellington's British forces, the Spanish could not eject them from the fortresses and towns.

These events crashed against the American empire like shock waves. The Americas universally rejected the Bonapartist claim to the throne; both the viceregal administrations and the *criollos* declared for Fernando VII. But these events damaged the mystique of an already tarnished crown, and the prestige of the dominant Spaniards themselves. Besides this, the captivity of the recognized king left Spain without a truly legitimate government, causing utter confusion in the viceregal administrations.

In South America, *criollo* juntas quickly sprang up as spontaneously as those in Spain and claimed the government in the name of the king. With this began a war with Spanish officialdom for jurisdiction. Armies of the juntas and the viceroys clashed in vast, decisive campaigns. In the end the Spanish party was defeated, and the successful juntas broke up into a series of national states, despite the desires of Simón Bolívar and other Creole aristocrats to hold the regions together in one great Hispanic federation modeled on the pattern of the United States.

In New Spain, the most influential *criollos* were strongly anti-French and far more conservative than their southern cousins—so much so that they were hostile to the peninsular juntas, considering them illegitimate, too liberal, and also tools of the English heretics. But while the *criollos* of the southern continent took advantage of events to throw off peninsular rule and soon proclaimed for independence, the Mexican upper class remained entirely too irresolute to do anything decisive.

Many prominent *criollos* did agree that New Spain should ignore the authority of the peninsular juntas and elect its own junta to rule until the king was restored. This would mean the displacement of the *gachupín* governmental hierarchy, which the Mexicans desired as much as the South Americans. The *peninsulares*, meanwhile, found themselves in the uncomfortable position of having to uphold dubious Spanish liberal juntas which they secretly despised, in order to legitimize their continuing authority.

Don José de Iturrigaray, the viceroy, was caught in the middle. He was a Godoy appointee, distinguished mainly for his grafting, and he knew that if the juntas were able to extend their jurisdiction to New Spain, his career was finished. Therefore in his own interest, he tried to curry favor with the most prominent Mexican Creoles. In this age in which obscure adventurers and soldiers were becoming ministers and kings in Europe, it occurred to him that he might even become the first monarch of an independent Mexico. In August, 1808, he convened both the *audiencia* and the *ayuntamiento* of the capital, but the two bodies disagreed on everything. The *audiencia*, made up of Spanish jurists and clergy, denounced the mere notion of an elected Mexican congress or junta as heresy. The *criollo*-dominated council of the capital insisted upon an American junta.

Iturrigaray was able to use the presence of competing delegates from both Oviedo and Sevilla, each claiming jurisdiction, to delay all action until September. The viceroy and his major *criollo* allies, however, were incompetent, irresolute, and more given to talk than action. At this time, the *criollo* leadership in Mexico could easily have seized the government, and against a million native Europeans the eighty thousand *gachupines* could have done nothing. Any strong Creole leader might have aroused the whole country against the Spaniards and ejected them. But the emasculated rich men of the capital hesitated, beseeching the viceroy to assent to the election of a congress, which at last he did.

The smartest of the *peninsulares* knew that they stood to lose everything if a *criollo* congress assumed power. A few of them resolved to strike first. Yermo, a Spanish sugar planter of Cuernavaca, organized and paid several hundred "volunteers for Fernando VII"; he bribed the viceregal guard; and at midnight, September 15, 1808, these men invaded the palace and arrested the viceroy. Yermo confiscated Iturrigaray's personal fortune and hustled him onto a ship at Veracruz. Seven of the most active *criollo* leaders were also arrested, two of whom, the lawyer Verdad and the friar Talamantes, were to die in prison.

Then, as part of a general Spanish conspiracy, the *audiencia* met and appointed an elderly soldier, Don Pedro de Garibay, as viceroy. Garibay was only an interim choice. Yermo eventually pensioned him off, and he was replaced with the Archbishop Lizana, a stern defender of *gachupín* rights.

This 16th September was a fateful day in Mexican history. Two things had happened: the Spaniards had staged an illegal coup d'etat, badly damaging the prestige of the viceregal throne while creating a purely cynical *gachupín* tyranny over Mexico; and the native leadership permitted it. In the face of outrages that would have sent Virginia planters and Boston merchants and the whole population of Buenos Aires to arms, the *criollos* of México did nothing. The richest, most ancient, and prestigious families rushed to kiss the new viceregal hand. There were a few scurrilous *corridos*, the street ballads composed to satirize current events, and a few unhappy meetings of parlor secret societies. The 16th September made it plain there were no Washingtons, Jeffersons, or Bolívars among the great families of New Spain.

There was, however, a bit more outrage in the provinces, especially in the Bajío, now a rich area of great haciendas and numerous jewel-like Spanish towns, graced with elegant baroque churches and filled with colonial treasures. It was also a region where the new, Mexican, *mestizo* race began and where many small farmers still struggled against the encroaching *latifundios*, and where the mining camps still had something of their old, unruly character. The rich towns had attracted many *gachupines*, who were universally hated, but they also held thriving societies of *criollos* and almost *criollos* who were becoming politically aware. The great estates and mines were worked by Hispanicized *indios* and *castas*, people who were too low for politics or public affairs, but who formed a vast reservoir of human frustration and misery, unseen and unfelt by all except themselves and their parish priests.

Nursing their resentments against the *gachupines*, the *criollos* of the Bajío began a conspiracy. It proceeded cautiously, since an open protest at Valladolid in 1809 was quickly suppressed with Spanish troops. At least a score of secret societies met and railed against the tyranny and cynicism of the newly-illegitimate *gachupín* regime by 1809; the most important nucleus formed at the crossroads city of Querétaro, disguised as a literary group.

These men did read French and North American tracts, and they were impressed by the notions of liberty, fraternity, and equality, which they translated mainly as liberty and equality for themselves. They did discuss representative government and racial equality but rarely thought them through. The Querétaro conspirators were neither republicans nor anticlericals; they were royalist and Catholic, and what they really wanted was to get rid of the Spaniards who dominated them on Mexican ground, and to take their places and jobs. These men were true cousins of the South American liberators. As events proved again, they were far less vigorous, courageous, and decisive.

The organizer and original dominant personality of the Querétaro "literary society" was Capitán Don Ignacio Allende, a *criollo* landowner of the nearby town of San Miguel. Allende, like many of the elite, had secured a commission in the Bourbon-organized native army. Aside from parading in his handsome, yellow-tailed dragoon uniform, his major interest had been bullfights—until his fitness, and the fitness of any Creole to be a captain had been sneeringly questioned by a Spanish superior at the capital. Don Ignacio was a gentleman, and his pride smarted under the implied inferiority of his race. He was one of the first Mexicans to show what the *criollo* militia of Buenos Aires had already proved—that the organization of an American army, the greatest of Bourbon successes in the defense of the empire, was also the Bourbon dynasty's greatest mistake.

Allende's friends included many officers of this army, such as Juan de Aldama, and officials like Miguel Domínguez, the *criollo* corregidor of Querétaro. He found they shared his frustrations; he recruited them. Allende saw that the *gachupín* regime was loved by no one and supported by only a handful of Spanish-born troops; he knew that any determined uprising by a Mexican leadership could unseat it. Allende did not ignore the *mestizos* and *indios*; he assumed that they would obey the orders of the native elite and march behind *criollo* generals. His great hope lay with the *criollo*-officered standing army. He thought these officers must support his concept of a rearrangement of the empire, still under Fernando VII and the Church, but in which New Spain achieved full equality as a kingdom with the old. Like Allende, most junior officers hated their Spanish commanders. He saw himself as the general who would lead his country and his class to dignity, equality, and glory, in a bloodless coup.

While his major plan was to subvert the officers of the army, he recruited *criollos* of all kinds. One man he found was the parish priest in the dusty little town of Dolores, a few miles from San Miguel. This was the curate, Miguel Hidalgo y Costilla.

Miguel Hidalgo was a tall, gaunt man in his late fifties, whose family was second-generation "*criollo*." He was impressive in appearance, with a fringe of white hair and expressive green eyes in a dark face, and he had a dominant personality. Hidalgo had been trained at the Jesuit college at Valladolid, and had later instructed seminarians. He was widely read, in religion, Spanish, and foreign literature—in fact, he had a great fondness for French writings and ideas. This affection, and his lifelong sympathy for the downtrodden *indios* and *castas* had kept him in bad odor with the Inquisition and the hierarchy; despite his brilliance, he had been shunted off to the insignificant parish of Dolores, where his pay barely supported his sisters and his cousins who were dependent upon him. In a more rational system where merit or humanitarianism were recognized, Hidalgo might have been a great bishop. In New Spain, his birth and feelings condemned him either to be a rebel, or to obscurity.

At Dolores, his impetuosity continued to get him in trouble with the authorities. Appalled at the poverty and squalor of the poor *indios* and ranchero farmers in this arid district, Hidalgo tried to teach them to grow olives, vines, and mulberries for silkworms. This violated the law, and Hidalgo had to stand by in bitter frustration while constables came and chopped down his poor parishioners' trees and rooted out their vines. Hidalgo was a man of culture, imprisoned by irrationality, and a man of action, bound up in tyranny. He joined Allende willingly—but he did not quite share all the young gentleman's notions. Hidalgo believed, and said, that the revolution would have to depend on the people rather than the army.

By the middle of 1810, some three thousand persons throughout the Bajío were included in the conspiracy, and now Allende decided to stage his coup in December, at the great fair of San Juan de los Lagos. It would begin with a proclamation of Mexican independence under the crown of Fernando VII, which he felt would bring the whole country to his cause.

So widespread a conspiracy, and the fact that Allende tried so vigorously to convert the army, made total secrecy impossible. Several *criollo* officers who were approached, including Agustín de Iturbide at Valladolid and Joaquín Arias at Querétaro, reported everything to the government at México. At least one Spanish priest also revealed secrets entrusted to him in the confessional. The *audiencia* had a justified contempt for *criollo* conspiracies, but the government was getting on firmer ground. The juntas at Oviedo and Sevilla, incapacitated by the French army, had been replaced by a board of regents operating from the Spanish island of León and acting for Fernando VII, who was in exile in France. This regency sent a new viceroy, Don Francisco Xavier Venegas, to New Spain, who was accepted by the *gachupines* and installed in office on September 14, 1810. Meanwhile, the *audiencia* had already issued orders to arrest Allende, Hidalgo, and other leaders, and to seize an arms cache they were known to have at Querétaro.

The government did not know that the corregidor Domínguez was in on the plot. This fact would have meant very little—for Domínguez was seized by total irresolution in the crisis of receiving orders to arrest his friends and fellow conspirators. He locked his wife, Josefa Ortiz de Domínguez, in her room while he temporized, because she was a flaming liberal in her own right, and he was afraid she would do something "stupid." Josefa, a remarkable woman, now became a heroine. She got word to Allende and Aldama, who were at San Miguel on the night of September 15, 1810. Panic-stricken, the officers rode to Dolores to alert Hidalgo.

What happened from this moment forward is not only history, but the stuff of Mexican legend. There has always been a tendency either to admire the ideals of the Mexican Insurgency and ignore its horrendous calamities and failures, or else to denigrate the persons and ideas of the insurgents in a brutal bath of cold reality. Neither view is entirely instructive. Mexican historians have always tried to judge their people less against what they actually accomplished than what they set out to do. Mexican history has made Mexicans love martyrs, and Hispanic culture has always had its love affairs with hopeless rebels, and these attitudes are rightly questioned by utilitarian societies. But the Mexican viewpoint that has made Hidalgo a national hero and the father of his country in the twentieth century is far from wrong. Hidalgo, instinctively or intellectually, had a deep historical sense: he knew the colonial system *was* intolerable, if a Mexican people ever were to emerge into a modern world. Sooner or later, it would have to be torn down. Hidalgo's great tragedy was that he was far ahead of his times; his ideals were impossible because of the very nature of the three hundred years of history he wanted to obviate. The blame, as he himself came to see, did not fall entirely on Spaniards or reactionaries, but on a whole population struggling against circumstance.

When Allende and Aldama pounded on Hidalgo's door at two o'clock on the morning of 16 September, they and their class were surrendering the initial thrust of the Mexican revolution. Allende wanted to go into hiding.

Hidalgo, putting on his boots, said that the only remedy was to go "hunting *gachupines*." He put a pistol in his belt and sent for relatives and trusted companions. When a few armed men assembled, he seized all Spaniards in Dolores and lodged them in the local jail, whose inmates he released. Hidalgo quite calmly relinquished Allende's dream for a bloodless coup presided over by the elite and prepared to implement his own dream: the declaration of a popular revolt and the arming of the people.

Hidalgo, and men like him, were coming into the leadership of the Mexican nation by default.

And with daylight Sunday morning, the 16th of September, 1810, he ordered the church bells rung, to summon the people from the countryside.

22

THE CRY OF HIDALGO

A great expense of powder and shot was saved by the cutting of the throats of prisoners . . .
Don Félix María Calleja, Lieutenant General and later Viceroy of New Spain.

The nature of Miguel Hidalgo y Costilla, who is now enshrined in the pantheon of Mexican national heros, is as difficult to assess as the nature of any true revolutionary. Like his country itself, Hidalgo was a mass of contradictions.

He was steeped both in rational French Enlightenment and the older Hispanic tradition. He was both a nineteenth-century liberal and a Spanish Catholic zealot. He was a kindly man whose fanaticism forced him to be impersonally cruel. He had a great vision of a Mexico whose social inequities were removed, and against this vision the ends outweighed the horrors of the means.

Hidalgo was a priest with a pistol in his cassock, nothing unusual in the Hispanic world. He was part of that continuing paradox of the Spanish Church in Mexico, which put up the best and worst of priests, whose grossness contrasted with austerity, and whose humanism battled crushing authority. He was a man in the tradition of Las Casas and Zumárraga, forever on the side of the underdog, and of Fray Servando Teresa de Mier, who was exiled from New Spain for ridiculing the miraculous origin of the icon of the Virgin of Guadalupe. He was a rational enemy of tyranny and superstition—but just as passionate, obstinate, and in his way, as arrogant as his foes. There was always a deep thread of austerity and anger running through the Spanish Church, which cracked the seeming monolith from time to time. And Hidalgo was a born rebel who also chafed against various disciplines of the Church, including chastity, though he had a genuine reverence for its ancient core of belief. He was a peculiarly Hispanic rebel, passionate, anarchic, and emotional despite his intellectual capacity. He was far from unique, as Morelos, Matamoros, and a hundred other parish priests in Mexico proved.

He no more caused the Mexican War for Independence than Luther caused the Reformation. What was peculiarly significant in Mexico, however, was that the European upper class consistently refused to lead in a power struggle that had to come, and when action, and leadership, fell to men like Hidalgo and Morelos the *criollo* caste-class showed clearly that it could not control Mexican destiny. The Mexican struggle for independence immediately became a social revolution.

What Hidalgo actually said to his massed parishioners from his church steps is not known; no definitive record was made. Almost all historians agree however, that he spoke apocalyptically, surrounded himself with almost apostolic sanctity, and told a Big Lie, whose very simplicity and whose source made it believable to the ignorant.

Hidalgo did not mention "independence," "commonwealth," or any of the concepts at the core of the Querétaro conspiracy. He knew such ideas would be meaningless to his *mestizo* campesinos and Indians, who lacked even the concept of a nation. But Hidalgo knew what these people had suffered and what was in their souls; he knew what they loved and hated and what they would risk their lives for. He spoke to the ragged assembly at Dolores of the rich land of Mexico, of which they had been dispossessed by foreigners—*gachupines*. Then, with the crowd drinking deep of hatred and frustrations, he accused the arrogant Spaniards of the worst of treasons. He shouted that the *gachupines* were plotting to recognize José Bonaparte as the king, and deliver the Church into the hands of French unbelievers. He called upon all loyal Mexicans and Catholics to rally behind Fernando VII and to expel the traitors from America. "*¡Viva el rey! ¡Viva América! ¡Muera el mal gobierno!*"

Whether the parish believed all of this, or even understood it, did not matter. Hidalgo had touched their deepest feelings, and above all the hatred of slaves for their masters, and given this hatred sudden respectability. The crowd screamed back: "*¡Mueran los gachupines!*" ("*Death to the Spaniards!*") If Hidalgo had ignited a revolution in the name of a reactionary king and an inquisitorial Church, he fed it from the only possible source— hatred of the oppressors. And if he flinched from the long, ferocious howl of hatred that went up—the *grito de Dolores*—he gave no sign. Hidalgo had a revolutionary's stomach, like Lenin: he did not back away from violence or flinch from terror in the making of his vision.

This spontaneous uprising suddenly exploded the passions, hatreds, and humiliations of three hundred years; it can be explained in no other way. As word flashed through the surrounding *jacales* and huts there on the arid fringes of the rich Guanajuato hacienda-lands, men and women streamed toward Dolores. The backbone of this assembling mob was the tough, bitter, *mestizo* ranchero class, the people who clung stubbornly to their small plots of ground, their few goats and maguey plants, who all their lives and their fathers' fathers' lives had been lorded over by arrogant silver-spurred men on horseback and who had been squeezed dry by grasping Spanish tax collectors and merchants. But these same frustrations were shared by all *castas,* Indians and mulattos, whether they were campesinos or peasants, or held by peonage on the estates or in the towns.

Hatred, and history, put an army in Hidalgo's hand in hours.

Hidalgo knew that this cause had to move, or die. The insurgents, as they came to call themselves, swarmed together, *castas* and *indios,* and, led by Hidalgo, Allende, and Aldama, overran haciendas, smashed property, and looted cattle and corn. Recruits joined everywhere; the insurgents marched.

This was not what Don Ignacio Allende, late captain of the Queen's Dragoons, had had in mind at all. Allende had seen himself as a Bolívar or San Martín, a *criollo* aristocrat leading a proper army in white and blue, a gallant general riding into the capital amid the cheers of his class, while gentlemen applauded and the lovely women threw roses and waved flags. His dream had never been impossible—it had simply proved impossible for his kind to carry it out. Now, Allende and his Creole friends were carried along, half-frightened, half-appalled, in a revolution they hardly understood and almost immediately disliked.

At Atotonilco, a roadside shrine holy to the *indios* of the Bajío, Hidalgo seized the icon of the Virgin of Guadalupe that hung there, and affixed the picture to a staff while all around him the insurgents fell sobbing to their knees. Now, the image of La Morenita, the most holy of all symbols to those who had native blood, went to the van of the army like a banner.

There can be little doubt that the thousands who soon marched beneath the mystic and peculiarly Mexican banner of the Virgin of Guadalupe had little interest in the original concepts of the plotters of Querétaro. They were aflame with joy and fury and the sheer exaltation of such mass movements. Men, women, and children, wild with courage and hot with tears, marched to right old wrongs. Inevitably, some joined them with nothing but opportunity and loot in mind.

The insurgent host poured into San Miguel, Allende's birthplace. Here, Allende was able to subvert a battalion of his old regiment, but here, also, as Spaniards and officials were put under arrest, the insurgency took an inevitable turn. Hidalgo's army began to sack the shops of Spanish merchants; then, as the town *léperos*, loiterers, and proletariat joined the revolution, there was wild rioting in the streets. The rebels broke down doors and looted private homes, terrifying the wealthy families of San Miguel. In this riot, the insurgents hardly cared whether their victims were *gachupines* or *criollos*, for from their viewpoint there was no real difference between a Spaniard and a native-born Creole.

Allende, however, was outraged as shops were robbed and finery dragged into the streets. He flew at the mob with his sword, scattering the looters. In San Miguel, Allende lost a great deal of faith in the insurgency, and a little love between him and Hidalgo was also lost.

The priest remonstrated with the angry young *criollo*, arguing that some excesses had to be tolerated. After three centuries of humiliation and subordination, the lower classes could not absorb freedom calmly. Men who had gone hungry most of their lives must be expected to take things from the rich; after all, the upper classes had never taught them responsibility. Hidalgo stressed he did not condone robbery, but also that this was the only army the patriots possessed. The *léperos* and poor *indios* must be catered to, to hold the army together to free Mexico from the Spaniards. This clash between Hidalgo and Allende—which was never quite reconciled—showed that there were going to be far greater problems in forging a Mexican nation out of a rich *criollo* elite and a mass of ragged Indians and *mestizos* than either Allende and his conspirators or the priest dreamed of, or bargained for.

The insurgent mob, now strengthened to four thousand by workers from the town sweatshops, servants, and tough-muscled miners with their picks and hammers, rushed toward Celaya, another small Bajío town. Here it sacked more town houses and palaces of their treasures and art, dragging along terrified Spanish hostages in its wake. Laughing peasants tossed handfuls of silver pesos in the air; others carried chests filled with gold, rich silks and plate. And after this triumph—everywhere officials and Spaniards fled—Hidalgo's forces swelled to at least twelve thousand. Now, the priest pointed his column of human ants toward Guanajuato, which, with its silver mines, was the jewel of the Bajío.

Hidalgo was no soldier or organizer; he was merely leading a raucous mob. But he refused to let Allende exercise any sort of military command, whether from pride or distrust is not clear. Hidalgo named himself "Captain-General of America"; he already had visions of this revolt spreading beyond the borders of New Spain.

At Guanajuato Intendante José Antonio Riaño had little warning. Riaño was a capable officer, but he had only a few soldiers in the provincial capital. He rightly feared that the miners and town proletariat would join the revolution; therefore there was no chance at all that he could defend the whole city. He ordered the local Spaniards to withdraw, with what treasure they could collect, into a huge stone building in the city called the Alhóndiga de Granaditas, or government granary. Some measure of the wealth of the Spaniards in Guanajuato was revealed by the fact that some three million pesos in coin and bullion was stored in the Alhóndiga within a "few minutes' time."

Riaño set cannon in the walls of the granary, and his troops dug trenches outside. As the insurgent thousands streamed into the town, on September 28, 1810, Riaño refused Hidalgo's demand for surrender.

Hidalgo attacked the stone warehouse with at least 12,000 men; some of the local miners immediately joined him, but most of them gathered on the hillsides above the city to watch. Their feelings were clearly shown by the prints of the Virgin of Guadalupe which most of them waved from poles. These workers knew very little about Frenchmen and kings—but they understood the differences between white men and dark, and poor people and millionaires.

For the first time, the insurgents met fierce resistance. Riaño's cannon and muskets mowed down charge after charge of rebels armed only with knives, picks, and slings. The outcome was uncertain until one of Allende's troopers shot Riaño in the head as he was directing the defense.

While various officers quarreled over who should command, the soldiers withdrew into the granary. Again, massed gunfire from windows and roof-top slaughtered Hidalgo's men. But a young miner called El Pípila grabbed up a huge flagstone with his mine-hardened arms and used it as a shield as he put a torch to the granary's wooden doors. The woodwork caught fire, and when the door crumbled, the howling mob of insurgents pressed against it. The defenders stopped shooting and first tried to divert the mob by tossing out golden *onzas* from the roof and then by running up a white flag—too late. The *gachupines* were butchered, their blood spilling over their hoarded silver. None survived.

The granary was swept by five o'clock in the afternoon, but the insurgent horde ran wild far into the night, gutting the shops and houses of Guanajuato, burning down taverns, and, misunderstanding the nature of the new freedom, smashing the machinery of the mines. Massacre and pillage went on by torchlight, despite the efforts of insurgent leaders to stop it. Hidalgo was now as horrified as Allende. But the rebel host had been bloodied; they had met no opposition before, but after Riaño's men had piled rebel corpses up in front of the *alhóndiga*, blood called for blood.

One young *criollo* of Guanajuato, Lucas Alamán, never forgot this horror as he hid with his family behind locked doors listening to the blood-roar of the mob and the cries of the victims. Alamán, who was to grow up to become the greatest conservative spokesman of independent Mexico, never again believed in any concept of the "Mexican people"; the rape of Guanajuato haunted him all his life.

Here, Hidalgo won a great battle, but he lost his war. His shining vision of a free and just Mexican society was not emerging; it was crumbling before the imperatives of the past. Appalled by the massacre, the surviving *criollos* of Guanajuato refused to have anything to do with the government Hidalgo now tried to erect within the smoldering city, although the priest offered important posts to persons of distinguished family. Most Creole families were for freedom from the *gachupines*, but they were horrified at anything that smacked of social revolution.

Hidalgo forced some men to serve, and filled other posts with people from the poorer classes. He marched then toward Valladolid in Michoacán with fifty thousand uncontrollable barefoot followers in ragged cotton pants. Now, he could only hope that his revolt would succeed quickly, to stop the bloodshed, and he still believed that the ends justified the means. Allende and the *criollo* rebels had no choice but to go along, although Allende warned that Indian armies would never conquer all New Spain.

At Valladolid, another splendid, ancient provincial capital, where Hidalgo himself had studied and taught, Bishop Manuel Abad y Queipo placed the priest of Dolores under anathema and the ban of excommunication. Abad y Queipo had been Hidalgo's friend as a young man, and had often remonstrated earnestly to the authorities against the slavery of the poor, but the bishop was a Spaniard, a *gachupín*. What Hidalgo was doing was heresy in his eyes. He ordered his cathedral bell melted down for cannon. But there were only a company or two of soldiers in the city, and these men went over to the insurgents, perhaps to save their lives. The bishop's canons discreetly tore down his edict of excommunication and ordered a Te Deum celebrated when Hidalgo entered Valladolid. Abad y Queipo fled.

The abject surrender, however, saved the city from the horrors of Guanajuato. There was no massacre or rape at Valladolid; the insurgents took the capital of Michoacán peacefully.

New Spain was in many parts abruptly descending into anarchy, a phenomenon that was to be again and again peculiar to the Hispanic revolution. The ossified society had not withstood the defeat and occupation of Spain and the humiliation of the Spanish crown. The Hispanic empire had been held together almost solely by traditional loyalties. Godoy and Napoleon destroyed almost all royal mystique, and now, in the New World, the governing *peninsulares* were left to defend themselves. Their own morale and mystique had vanished, and Spanish rule was crumbling everywhere. This same year the *criollos* of South America began the military campaigns that eventually drove the last Spaniards from their shores.

In New Spain, the northern, predominantly *mestizo* regions were ripest for the form of revolt that suddenly erupted with the *grito* of Dolores. This region, stretching from the Bajío through the wastelands of distant Texas, had a greater, if almost unconscious, sense of nativism and of being Mexican, rather than *criollo* or Amerindian. In the north, without Hidalgo—though influenced by what he had begun in the Bajío—there was an almost completely spontaneous uprising against the *gachupines*.

After Guanajuato, the mining town of Zacatecas declared for the insurgency. In Jalisco an illiterate campesino called Torres seized the great city of Guadalajara in the name of the revolution and the Spanish fled. This sudden, spontaneous rise of an indigenous leadership was historically Hispanic. Such phenomena almost never occurred in the more disciplined, if more flexible societies; their constant recurrence in the Hispanic world was not a sudden freeing of social chains, but more a measure of anarchy caused by the bankruptcy of the upper class.

Herrera, a friar who had marched briefly with Hidalgo in the Bajío, rode to San Luis Potosí, which surrendered without a fight. Unfortunately, a local bandit, Iriarte, almost immediately looted the defenseless city. Some aspects of the Hispanic revolution could not be separated from sheer banditry; some outlaws became genuine heros in a patriotic revolution, but hundreds reversed the pattern. As authority collapsed, mounted raiders rode through the northern sierras, robbing pack trains of goods and silver; mobs sacked haciendas. Anything was justified if the victims were Spanish, or suspected of the wrong politics.

A mine foreman, Jiménez, a lieutenant of Allende, seized Saltillo, and after this, the provincial governments of Nuevo León and Texas proclaimed for the insurgents. Aside from harassment of *gachupines*, there was less social turmoil in the north, which had neither the completely stratified society of the south, nor its rigid racial distinctions.

This northern uprising was proclaimed everywhere in the name of King Fernando VII. Men had to have some rationale. But a growing sense of nativism and a deepening determination to break the patterns of the past was emerging in the mixed society of the north. The reaction of the northern frontier, which, did not affect the millions in the south and central intendancies, was extremely significant only for the future, because it showed the birth struggle of a Mexican nation.

At Valladolid in October, Hidalgo held the rich Bajío and Michoacán; the north was liquidating Spanish rule, and his agents were penetrating as far south as Acapulco. Eighty thousand rancheros, *braceros*, peons, and *indios* had joined him in Michoacán, along with a nucleus of leaders, such as the *mestizo* curate José María Morelos, and Ignacio López Rayón.

Hidalgo had an excellent chance of carrying everything before him with numbers and sheer momentum. The capital lay only a few leagues over the mountains, and if his ragged masses seized México, the power of the viceroyalty would be fatally damaged; the *gachupines* must be driven out.

The new viceroy, Venegas, was weak, and slow in responding to Hidalgo. Venegas had less than thirty thousand troops of all kinds. It was a colonial army, despite its *gachupín* generals. The rank and file were almost all *mestizos* or Indians (though they were considered "Spanish"). The officers were mostly *criollos*, but the bulk and above all the most active were either propertyless adventurers or even, like the Teniente Agustín de Iturbide of Valladolid, *mestizos* who passed as Creoles. The ranks were trained to blind obedience to their officers, and the officers were generally loyal to their Spanish generals, despite their Mexican birth. Stemming from two warlike peoples, the Mexicans made superb soldiers, provided they were well led. The rot, however, in this colonial army lay in its officer corps, which was corrupt even by eighteenth-century standards.

The era of Godoy had ruined the generals. Most were much more concerned with privileges and graft than with war. They owed their posts either to purchase or favoritism, and they expected their commissions to pay. The malaise at the top filtered down, though there were many excellent professional mercenary officers in the junior ranks. Napoleon's battalions had brushed aside the Spanish army in the peninsula like dust, and with one exception, the Spanish generals were no better in New Spain.

The Bourbon colonial army in Mexico was in no sense an elite force, except in the privileges of the *fuero militar*. The military, though having authority over civilians, did not come under the civil law and could be controlled only by a powerful central authority in the crown.

Venegas in October, 1810, compounded his precarious situation at México by sending the larger part of his army north to San Luis Potosí under Félix María Calleja, his one capable Spanish commander. This act left only seven thousand troops, under the general Trujillo, to defend the capital.

Hidalgo, meanwhile, for all his success, faced enormous problems at Valladolid. His greatest problem—and greatest failure—was to bring some order to his revolution. Hidalgo was no soldier, and he was a better orator than administrator, and for all the fire of his personality he had no staff to back him up. Allende, Aldama, and other *criollo* officers sulked in their tents both over his abrupt seizure of the leadership and the direction of his revolt, which they still wanted to turn into a purely military coup by subverting the viceregal forces. Hidalgo, conversely did not trust the military, because he did not really believe the *criollo* officers would support a genuine social revolution. Actually, the army *was* subvertible, but not for Hidalgo's social goals; furthermore, no numbers of *indios* would, in the long run, be able to defeat disciplined regiments. Hidalgo wanted the support of both the Creoles and the castes and Indians. It was unattainable.

At Valladolid he did try to win support among the Mexican-born upper classes, by proclaiming the real object of his insurgency was to establish an elected Mexican congress which would govern in the name of Fernando VII, and also by offering various influential *criollos* generalcies and high civil posts in his "government." But at the same time he insisted upon catering to the *indios*. His "government" abolished all tributes and returned various hacienda-possessed *ejidos* back to Amerindian villages. The fact that Hidalgo continued to arm *indios* and to rely on the poor masses to fill his army, in the aftermath of the sack of Guanajuato, was too much for the privileged *criollos*. Hidalgo won favor for his Indian policy only among *mestizos* and a certain number of young intellectuals, such as the law clerk, Andrés Quintana Roo. Almost all property owners and professional men, and the Church hierarchy, believed he was fomenting a murderous revolt of the poor people that would end in the massacre of all the upper classes. Racial fears as well as property interests dominated the European mind. It was only a few years since the blacks of Haiti, enflamed by the opportunities of the French Revolution, had slaughtered their white masters, sending shock waves throughout all colonial America.

The Spanish-dominated Church also now formally excommunicated Hidalgo, and this undoubtedly had a profound influence on the *criollos*.

Instead of coming over to his cause, the upper class now began to support the viceroy. Creoles raised money for the government to arm and pay troops, and many *hacendados* ordered their workers into the viceregal army. By the end of October 1810, Hidalgo's insurgency was no longer a revolution waged against *gachupines*. It had become a full-scale civil war.

At the end of October, Hidalgo finally moved on the capital. The dry season had begun, suitable for large-scale military operations. The insurgents climbed over the high, forested mountains between Valladolid and Toluca, eighty thousand men and women, some carrying babies, hauling carts with food and driving small herds of sheep and cattle. Most of this horde was only primitively armed, and Hidalgo had been able to form it into only the sketchiest of organization.

Trujillo, with his seven thousand soldiers and a few guns, chose to defend the Valley of Mexico at a pass called Monte de las Cruces. Allende sought to take command of the insurgents, by leading the former government soldiers in the attack, while he ordered the mass of poorly armed *indios* to the rear. The army would not obey him and swarmed forward, into the face of Trujillo's guns. Some Amerindians who did still not understand the nature of cannon tried to stop their discharge with straw sombreros.

Trujillo held the pass for some hours. At last the insurgents surrounded the viceregal army and Trujillo retreated.

Trujillo had been driven from the final line of defense. Although he claimed he had won a victory, the viceroy knew better, and so did the residents of the city. They panicked. Venegas led a procession to the cathedral and invoked the Virgin of Remedios in the European cause by laying his baton at the feet of her image. Remedios, unlike Guadalupe, was carved with blue eyes and a white face, and Venegas, more for the crowd than out of his own belief, proclaimed her captain-general of the viceregal army in an effort to reinvoke Cortés' war against the Amerindians.

The miracle happened. With nothing between the capital and his eighty thousand, Hidalgo for some still unfathomable reason paused. The fanatic priest may not have been able to face the moral responsibility for the rape of México. There was also the worry over Calleja, who was known to be hastening back from Potosí; Hidalgo had some fear that the capital could prove a trap, that his *indios* would be taken in the rear and massacred while they indulged in a sack of the city. Further, the insurgent force was disorganized, tired, and almost out of ammunition. Insurgent councils were divided. Allende pleaded to go forward, but Hidalgo hesitated.

To have brought the insurgent host even this far was a great feat, but now Hidalgo waited for three days—and when he finally decided to move back toward Toluca in early November, half his followers had already melted away, cold, hungry, and disenchanted.

Hidalgo's plan was now to move into Querétaro, avoiding Calleja on his march south, and to make it his base while Allende, Aldama, and the few soldiers among the insurgents transformed the army into viable regiments. But Calleja, with good intelligence and moving swiftly, crashed into the strung-out insurgent host at Aculco, a place not far from Toluca. Calleja, a cruel but excellent officer, threw his battalions forward with the bayonet, against which no untrained, undisciplined troops could hope to stand. The whole rebel army fled, losing its baggage, loot, arms, and even its Spanish prisoners.

Allende was wild with fury over what he felt was an unnecessary disaster. He gathered his Creole followers and deserted Hidalgo, fleeing toward Guanajuato. Meanwhile, left with only two faithful friends, Hidalgo rode for Valladolid. To his own surprise, he was welcomed in Michoacán, and soon had seven thousand more recruits. But he now believed the only chance was to retreat to Guadalajara, where El Amo Torres still held that city in his name. Before he rode northwest, he replied to his condemnation as a heretic. "I am a true Catholic," he stated. "Our enemies are Catholics only out of politics—their God is money."

Hidalgo and his seven thousand followers were welcomed coolly but obsequiously at Guadalajara. Hidalgo now tried to formalize his revolution by organizing a rebel government and proclaming its full ideals and goals. He ruled Guadalajara, a strong Creole city, as generalissimo, and the clergy did not dare oppose him. He sat through a Te Deum offered in his honor, under a canopy usually reserved for visits of the viceroy. Meanwhile, he issued propaganda with a captured newspaper and edicts to be enforced until an elected congress could be assembled. Hidalgo abolished slavery and crown monopolies, intending to make better use of the resources the "Sovereign Author of Nature bestowed upon this vast continent." He appointed a minister of justice, and secretary of state.

It was all too late. Hidalgo's movement, among virtually all propertied and educated men in New Spain, stood more for anarchy and bloody revolution than liberalism or liberty as they understood those things. Thousands of liberals in the north who had proclaimed for the rebellion were trying make amends with the viceroy. And Guadalajara, despite being in the north, was a disastrous base for Hidalgo; it was heavily *criollo* and conservative at heart.

Guadalajara was not loyal to Hidalgo, and before long his dark-skinned followers had worn out their welcome in the provincial capital. With peculiar *criollo* quiescence, the influential people failed to oppose Hidalgo. They did offer some support to the Spaniards. Hidalgo, outraged, demanded in a broadside: "Americans, is it possible that you take arms against your brothers? This war could be won in a day if you would not help the Europeans in their battle!"

So it would—but Hidalgo's revolution had polarized light and dark skins, elite and disadvantaged, rich and poor. After three centuries, there was desperately little brotherhood in New Spain, and none at all based on a common Mexican birth.

The revolution was also sinking into a bloody mess of reprisals and counter-reprisals.

The nature of Hidalgo's insurgency inevitably aroused fright and viciousness among the upper classes. After the desperate battle for the capital, the viceroy ordered that every rebel "taken in arms" should be summarily executed. Such orders and actions were perfectly legal, but the mercilessness and even relish with which General Calleja began to shoot prisoners showed that the government had decided upon a campaign of counter-terror. And murder inevitably begat murder.

After Hidalgo abandoned Guanajuato, the leaderless proletarian rebels there massacred the remaining Spanish hostages in the Alhóndiga. When Calleja recaptured the city, he took vengeance upon the whole Indian and half-caste population by ordering a decimation, a procedure long established under Spanish military law. He erected gallows in the plaza, and after the soldiers had rounded up all the *indios* and *mestizos* that could be found, one man in every ten, chosen by lot, was hanged. The innocent died with the guilty; guilt or innocence, in this kind of conflict, was beginning to be determined on either side less by deeds than by skin shade and social position.

After this, Hidalgo's army at Guadalajara carried out its own decimations of Spaniards in that city. Scores were marched outside the town, garroted, and their bodies hurled into the *barrancas*. The crime of these men was that they were *gachupines*.

Colonial Mexico had always had a horrendous mortality from famines and epidemics; the natural death rate was higher than anywhere in the world outside the Orient. All Mexicans grew up with fatalistic attitudes toward suffering and death, as only one of every two children survived. Now, once the bloodshed started, casual executions and sadistic reprisals became a fact of the insurgency. The leaders of both sides indulged in dehumanizing barbarities, sowing a savagery that would not end with the war.

Esquivel invented the practice of burying enemies alive in quicklime. Regules cut off men's ears; Bustamante shot all prisoners as a policy; Moctezuma enjoyed torturing women. Vicente Gómez, after earning fame as a castrator of Spaniards, joined the royalists as a captain and gelded his old comrades. The final horror of all this cruelty was that there was nothing truly ideological behind it; it seemed to well up from some dark cavern of human despair. It stained the country, and the war. Rosains, who was welcomed by Hidalgo, tortured liberals and conservatives with equal savagery depending on his current loyalty; a perfect monster, he ended up a senator of the Republic in 1824. Calleja put out in writing that he had the throats of bound and helpless captives cut in order to save powder and ball. Whatever the true reasons, they went deeper than problems with logistics.

After decimating the *castas* and *indios* of Guanajuato, Calleja marched toward Guadalajara with some six thousand picked troops. Though Hidalgo had lost the upper classes and the Church, his volunteer forces numbered again at least eighty thousand. Allende, realizing that the rebels must stay together or die separately, joined Hidalgo with a small force. He urged Hidalgo not to risk a battle with Calleja, despite his overwhelming numerical superiority. Allende, who had been a soldier, had no faith in numbers of *indios* in the face of disciplined firepower. But again he was overruled; Hidalgo was determined to fight.

The insurgent host defended at the bridge of Calderón on the Rio Lerma outside Guadalajara in January, 1811. Calleja attacked, although he was outnumbered more than ten to one. The insurgent army fought extremely well, repelling the attack hour after hour; it might even have prevailed, except for the fact that untrained, uncoordinated, and undisciplined fighters were always vulnerable to any sudden change of fortune or startling event. Calleja's guns set an ammunition wagon ablaze in the insurgent rear; this exploded and started a roaring grass fire. In the smoke and confusion, while the insurgents wavered, Calleja ordered a violent advance. The now panic-stricken insurgents were cut to pieces.

Everything was lost: army, baggage, even the guns that Allende had placed to command the river. Hidalgo, Allende, and the group of *criollo* officers from the original conspiracy—who all now held the rank of general in the insurgent army—barely escaped with their lives, fleeing toward Zacatecas. These surviving generals now demanded that Hidalgo give up the leadership and put Allende in charge. Hidalgo had no choice, for he was now their prisoner.

Allende, desperate, decided to join his lieutenant Jiménez at Saltillo, but his real hope was to secure assistance in the United States. The Anglo-Saxon frontiersmen throughout the Mississippi Valley hated Spanish tyranny and also hungered for Spanish lands above the Bravo. Allende hoped that thousands of armed North Americans could be recruited for the insurgent cause, especially if the lure of Texas were dangled before them. Gutiérrez de Lara went ahead to Kentucky, and eventually did succeed in raising a North American filibuster against Texas. But Allende, Hidalgo, and the other failed insurgents never reached the Bravo.

At Saltillo, with Calleja in rapid pursuit, the remaining revolutionaries, now almost all *criollos*, decided to leave López Rayón in command while the leadership went north to the United States. The party set out with fourteen coaches and a large amount of money looted from various Spanish and royal treasuries, guarded by about one thousand men. This money was to buy arms in Washington.

Now the betrayals began. The provincial capitals of San Antonio, Texas, and Monclova, in Coahuila, had again changed sides. The insurgent commander in Coahuila, Elizondo, a *criollo* captain, had been insulted by Allende's refusal to appoint him a lieutenant-general. Elizondo saw a new way of achieving his generalcy, and turned his coat once more, back to the viceregal side.

At the wells of Baján, Elizondo ambushed Allende's straggling detachments one by one as they approached the wells around a curve in the road through the hills. Allende was seized in his coach, after an exchange of gunfire that killed his young son. Hidalgo was taken and disarmed in the saddle.

The four principal leaders, Hidalgo, Allende, Aldama, and José Mariano Jiménez, were taken to Monclova and put in irons, then sent to Chihuahua, a month's journey across the desert, for trial. The junior officers captured at the Wells of Baján were shot out of hand by firing squad. The common soldiers were condemned to hard labor and parceled out as slaves to local haciendas.

At the remote town of Chihuahua, Hidalgo's revolution ended in whimpers and volleys. Allende asked for mercy, while Aldama tried to shift the blame from himself. They and Jiménez, were soon condemned by a military court and shot.

Hidalgo, because of the privilege of the clergy, had to be handled differently. The priest had to endure three month's imprisonment while ecclesiastical authorities entered his examination, because no priest could be judged in a civil or military court. Hidalgo was jailed in a dark hole, but otherwise well treated, even by his *gachupín* warden. Hidalgo neither asked for pardon—"Pardon is for criminals, not for defenders of the country"—nor tried to put the responsibility for what he had done on anyone but himself. He did suffer deep remorse for the futile suffering he had caused. He also wrote a retraction of his revolution, which some Mexican historians claim was written under pressure or else was forged. But Hidalgo surrendered none of his ideals; he had only come to understand from terrible experience that they could not be realized in the Mexico in which he lived.

The one thing that hurt Hidalgo terribly was not remorse, or his condemnation to death. He was haunted by his degradation by the Catholic Church. Hidalgo had believed in the charity of the Church and God toward the humble and oppressed. But he was convicted of heresy and shorn of his vestments, and the power of consecration was symbolically stripped from his fingers as he was turned over to the royal authority by his religious superiors for execution.

He was shot by firing squad at first light July 30, 1811. An *indio* was paid twenty pieces of silver to strike off his head. It was taken, with the skulls of Allende, Aldama, and Jiménez, to be hung in an iron cage outside the Alhóndiga de Granaditas at Guanajuato.

23

MORELOS

Lord, if I have labored well, Thou knowest it, and if badly, I take refuge in Thy mercy.
From the last prayer of José María Morelos, December 22, 1815.

The priest of Dolores had loosed something that would not die. The continuing tragedy of Mexico was that while Hidalgo's demands for a just society could not be achieved, the determination to break the chains of the past could not be totally destroyed by muskets and bayonets.

Hidalgo had failed for two main reasons: no successful revolution could possibly be forged by the impoverished, illiterate lowest classes in New Spain, even had Hidalgo's *indios* brushed aside the army, and the very nature of the insurgency alienated the great majority of the upper and middle ranks of society; and the priest had never been able to give his revolution organization. The *grito de Dolores* merely caused an explosion whose effects were quickly dissipated; the viceregal general, Calleja, re-established Spanish authority in the north as rapidly as Hidalgo's agents had destroyed it.

The Insurgency never overcame its two principal faults. Its anarchical nature could not appeal to the stable classes that had to form the nucleus of any civilized society, and it never gained a centralized leadership. Every upsurge of the Hispanic revolution tended to sink into a struggle between an outmoded society and barbarism.

The Hispanic revolution gave most intelligent, civilized men who were not overcome with grievances, emotionalism, or ambition merely a choice between two destructive tigers.

After the heads of Hidalgo and his fellow conspirators were rotting in a cage at Guanajuato, and Calleja was stamping out insurgency in the north, Ignacio López Rayón tried to give the revolution order and form. In some ways López possessed more generalship than Hidalgo. He recognized that the regulars could not be overwhelmed with masses of poorly armed Indians, and that towns and cities could not be held by rabble. He avoided battle with Calleja and retreated south with the remnants of the insurgent army, from Saltillo in Coahuila to Zacatecas, and from there into Michoacán. This retreat required considerable strength and skill, because López Rayón commanded a ragged, heterogeneous, and usually mutinous force, and he was now operating in hostile country. The viceregal army had reoccupied Potosí, Guanajuato, Valladolid, and all the major centers.

López Rayón ensconced himself and his followers at Zitácuaro in Michoacán, which lay in a remote, almost inaccessible valley guarded by dense forests and towering mountains. He fortified the valley around Zitácuaro and tried to legitimize the insurgency by causing the local people to elect a junta and form a provisional government in the name of Fernando VII. López Rayón still held to the original aims of the rebellion: to drive out the peninsulars, but to remain loyal to Church and crown in a Spanish commonwealth. He established secret communications with dissident intellectual groups in the capital, and he acquired and operated an insurgent printing press. He carried out some of these classic guerrilla operations by instinct, some by plan.

Whatever the peasantry of Zitácuaro thought of becoming the Supreme Junta of Mexico, López Rayón exerted great appeal for many intellectuals in México City, who had organized themselves into clandestine groups, like the so-called Guadalupes. The Guadalupes were composed primarily of young *criollos* and *mestizos* of professional or semiprofessional rank, such as the doctor Cós and the law clerk and poet Andrés Quintana Roo, both of whom slipped away to join him in the mountains. Romantic revolutionaries, like Quintana's bride-to-be, the lovely heiress Leona Vicario, smuggled letters and pistols to the insurgents, and Leona herself, discovered, was smuggled out of the capital by the Guadalupes. These revolutionaries carried on a propaganda war against the regime, often in opposition to their own parents, who were more conservative, and some of whom actively supported the viceroy.

López Rayón had to hold a privileged sanctuary in the mountains, from which he could direct and coordinate the revolution. His great weakness was that he could not control or direct the men who were now actually carrying on the resistance in the south.

After the *grito de Dolores*, anarchy swept into the south-central intendancies just as it had the north, but here it took different form. The cities were Spanish and Creole, and much more resistant to the rebellion than places like Zacatecas and Saltillo on the frontier. The insurgency coalesced in the high sierras and remote valleys, under scores of local chieftains, who sprang from the mixed race—though a few were pure Indian—and from the lower classes. They were tough countrymen who went heavily armed and rode hard, with a few disciplined followers. Except for an almost universal anarchic tendency and mutual jealousy, these local chieftains followed no pattern. Some were patriots with some notion of a large view; the majority were rebels whose main thrust was sheer banditry. These *heroes en bandidos* made no effort to lead the *indios* to freedom, nor did they worry overmuch about constitutions. They believed in independence, mainly for themselves, and in killing and robbing *gachupines* and Creoles. As Albino García, the petty guerrillero chieftain of Michoacán, told López Rayón, he recognized no "highness" but the hills, and no "junta" except the coming together of the rivers.

These local rebel chiefs made a shambles of the southern provinces in 1811. They and their followers were hardy horsemen, skilled with the machete, rope, and musket. García himself could whip regular officers from the saddle with his lariat, with which he was deadlier than any pistol. The guerrilleros raided haciendas and towns; they robbed pack trains and killed and burned. Osorno dominated the mountains overlooking Puebla; Fernández, a former law student from Durango, plundered the road leading up from Veracruz; a Huastec who called himself Emperor Julián I threatened to exterminate all Europeans around Tampico. There were in all more than a score of such leaders and bands ranging from Zacatecas to the Gulf and to the Pacific above the port of Acapulco. They lived in the mountains, frequently fighting among themselves over who controlled which territory while they murdered Europeans. This form of insurgency, unlike Hidalgo's and López Rayón's, was almost impossible for the regular army to fix, fight, and destroy. If a regiment were sent against them, they faded into the vast, tumbled countryside, or hid their weapons and pretended to be peaceful agrarians—only to reassemble and ride again when danger passed. These were the men who carried on the revolution.

They also destroyed it. Their activities alienated virtually every civilized Mexican who may have wanted independence, but who also longed for law and order.

López Rayón and the majority of the true liberals who desired a constitutional independence hated and feared these petty warlords as much as they did the *gachupines*. López Rayón, significantly, had shot the bandit Iriarte at Saltillo—although Hidalgo had welcomed him to the revolution— partly because Iriarte's loyalty was suspect, and partly because he was a bandit.

The Viceroy Venegas, more concerned with López than with bandits, ordered General Calleja to march to Michoacán. The general was prideful, cruel, and was feared by his own officers—but he was also coolly and thoroughly efficient. Calleja's reputation was so fearsome that López Rayón's forces did not even try to defend their fortified valley at Zitácuaro when the Spanish general attacked it in January 1812. All the insurgent artillery, which had been assembled with great effort, was abandoned. Although López Rayón escaped into the mountains while the unfortunate Tarasca village was burned, his own reputation was destroyed. Leadership in the kind of war that now emerged fell to Morelos, the greatest of all the insurgents.

José Mariá Morelos was a *casta* of mixed Spanish, Amerindian, and Negro origin. Born in obscurity in Michoacán, he had worked as a laborer and muleteer until he was twenty-five, then, starving himself to gain an education, he had entered holy orders through the College of San Nicolás, where he had studied under Hidalgo. This struggle foretold something of Morelos' quality, but in colonial Mexico he was only allowed to become the curate of Carácuaro, a Tarasca hamlet. When Hidalgo's revolution engulfed Michoacán, Morelos joined the insurgency, as did so many poor, *mestizo*, parish priests. He was a short, squat, dark man, taciturn and humble, barely five feet tall and ravaged by malaria and constant headaches, against which he wore a tight bandanna over his bald head. He was also a genius, by any standard.

Hidalgo grandly commissioned him to raise the south in 1810, sending him out with twenty-five men and no weapons. The way Morelos went about this immediately revealed his genius. Back at his parish, he took only a few, tough horsemen who could live on dried jerky and plunged into the horrendous, wild country of the Pacific sierra south of Michoacán, the region that is now the state of Guerrero. He found entire villages and towns where the *indios* would have followed him en masse, but, unlike Hidalgo, Morelos would accept no volunteers for whom he lacked weapons. As he captured muskets, swords, and lances from the Spanish, he enlisted and trained a tight, disciplined little army.

Morelos also had what Hidalgo lacked: the ability to judge and command all sorts of men. He was able to secure excellent officers: *mestizos* like the blue-eyed ranchero Hermenegildo Galeana and the priest Mariano Matamoros, his "good right arm," and the part-African campesino, Vicente Guerrero, whose father was a loyalist; and Don Leonardo Bravo and his brother, *criollo hacendados* of Chilpanzingo who were driven into insurgency by Spanish officials who would not respect their desire to remain neutral in this tragedy.

By the end of 1811, Morelos commanded nine thousand well-armed, reasonably trained fighters, under competent lieutenants, and his authority extended over a vast region reaching from Acapulco—still held by Spanish forts and guns—almost to Anáhuac. He was moving to support López

Rayón in Michoacán when Calleja took and burned Zitácuaro. His horsemen were raiding into the outskirts of the capital.

When Calleja marched south against Morelos in February 1812, Morelos prepared to give battle at Cuautla, on the open plain below the volcanic strike. From here Morelos had been exacting tribute from the sugar haciendas as far as Cuernavaca, while Leonardo Bravo, assisted by the poor, placed guns and fortified the thick stone buildings of the town.

Calleja's force included heavy artillery and two regiments newly arrived from Spain. However, Morelos believed he could hold Cuautla against assault, and that with the rainy season, the climate of the hot plain below the mountains would immobilize the Spanish guns and weaken Calleja's troops with sickness. Unlike the natives, Spaniards and *criollos* from the highlands found the tropics below the volcanic regions unhealthy and intolerable.

Calleja tried to seize Cuautla by direct assault and was repulsed. Calleja still was not overly concerned. He thought that no guerrilla force could long withstand a siege and bombardment.

Morelos' troops and the townspeople withstood siege and shelling for seventy-two days; they ate bark, lizards, and soap. In this defense many heroic legends were born, soldier and civilian. But the spring rains that were to immobilize and sicken Calleja's army failed to come. By May 1st, Morelos was desperate, although he refused offers of a pardon with surrender.

Two hours past midnight on May 2nd, Morelos led his forces in a breakout. The townspeople, knowing Calleja would show them no mercy, went with his column. The insurgents easily broke through the Spanish pickets, and most of the fighting men escaped into the open country by night. The women and children of the town, however, were caught and massacred by Calleja's troops, and Don Leonardo Bravo was captured. Calleja took over a ruined and deserted Cuautla.

Calleja was worn down by the siege and had to move back to Anáhuac. He claimed a victory, but his reputation had been damaged. Cuautla was a great moral victory for Morelos.

Morelos' army reassembled, and operating out of the rugged country that took its modern name from his lieutenant, Guerrero, was now invincible. Within a few weeks Morelos reoccupied Cuautla and then marched into the eastern cordillera. He made a base at Tehuacán, from which he could command communications between México City and the Gulf and threaten the capital itself. His raiders seized the rich tobacco region up from Veracruz and burnt the government stores—a serious blow to the viceroy, who depended upon the tobacco monopoly to pay his troops. Morelos captured enough firearms to equip an army of ten thousand by fall.

It was becoming extremely difficult even for strong loyalist parties and convoys to move throughout Morelos' zone of operations. Nicolás Bravo, the son of the captured Leonardo, snapped up two hundred regular soldiers in one ambush. Morelos offered to return these men for the life of the captured father; the viceroy, however, insisted upon having the elder Bravo strangled publicly in the capital. Morelos ordered his prisoners murdered in reprisal. Nicolás Bravo refused to shoot these helpless men and set them free. This was so unusual that it was recorded and remarked by everyone in Mexico. Morelos failed to appreciate the act, and it did not happen again.

With fall, the insurgent army seized Oaxaca. Afterward, Morelos took his army into the steaming hills above the green lagoon of Acapulco. Although he had not been able to bring siege guns over the mountains and could not blockade the port, it surrendered in August 1813. Now, Morelos controlled, or at least deprived the government of all of south-central New Spain from north of Veracruz on the Gulf to Acapulco, save only the major cities of Veracruz, Puebla, and México, strongly defended by government troops.

He had not only paralyzed the government and the economy, he was now beginning to bring his own kind of order. He collected taxes, appointed local governing bodies and officials, and tried to enforce an insurgent law, which, although he did order looting insurgents shot, was not entirely successful. The priest of Carácuaro was the virtual dictator of this vast region; however, he remained taciturn and humble, refusing any title except that of "servant of the people."

It was easier to drive Spaniards out of his territories than to create the new order. By August 1813, Morelos had determined to formalize the revolution and define its goals beyond what Hidalgo and López Rayón had done. As he told López, it was "time to strip the mask from independence"; there should be no more talk of kings but the formation of a republic. López Rayón disagreed, but Morelos now had all the power and the prestige. The priest summoned a congress of eight delegates, one from each major region under his control, to a meeting at Chilpancingo.

In this small, mountain town in the sierra up from Acapulco, Morelos instructed this congress, which called itself the Congress of Anáhuac, in his basic ideas. Morelos believed that sovereignty should be established in the people, that government should be exercised by separate branches, and that government should moderate the extremes of privilege and wealth. His reforms envisioned official racial equality, universal suffrage, the opening of office to every rank and caste, and the abolition of compulsory tithes and the privileges of the clergy and the military. He further believed that a free society could not come about without the confiscation of the *latifun-*

dios, especially idle lands, including Church property. Half of such confiscations should go to support the government, half to the landless poor.

These ideas were wildly popular with the congressional delegates, who were predominantly *criollo* liberals, priests and lawyers. Morelos set them to drafting a new Mexican constitution to implement these ideals.

Morelos' concept of a congress and constitution was excellent, and his notions for society and government, however radical they appeared against Spanish tradition, were sound. But Morelos, who never wanted personal power, also surrendered too much authority, to the "congress," letting these men partake in government. This was to be an enormous mistake, given the Hispanic nature and the fact that the war was far from won. Most of the individual delegates were able men, but collectively they were only another jealous, quarreling junta. In retrospect, also, Morelos' definition of the liberal plans for Mexico was an error at this time. The destruction of the Church and military privileges and the land tenure and social system and the crown, all in one swoop, was far too radical to be accomplished without absolute power. No new converts were won; a million Creoles were alienated to the point of siding against the revolution.

Many thousands of *criollos* who really longed for Mexican independence became active royalists. Morelos was too radical for them. Also, the insurgent style of warfare was destroying the economy. Mines were closed, the roads blocked, the ports isolated, the cities cut off from the countryside, and the fields untilled. This was beginning to hurt everyone except those guerrilleros who were willing to live in the mountains, and even the most patriotic guerrilleros were plunderers. The war was becoming intolerable to the Creoles; their interests were threatened and they were exhausted by disorder. The native-born elite swung solidly behind the viceroy in an intense reaction.

Calleja, who succeeded Venegas as viceroy early in 1813, extracted vast loans to pay troops and he made every European-blooded householder liable for military service. This arming of all *criollos* was a dangerous experiment, as Calleja remarked himself, but he felt the insurgency had to be destroyed before it destroyed New Spain.

With a greatly expanded royalist army—from 1813 forward it is proper to call the government forces royalist and the insurgents liberals—Calleja took the offensive. The north, rebellious again, was thoroughly crushed while Morelos completed his hold on the south. The vital silver towns of Zacatecas and Potosí were occupied, and local insurgent chiefs were killed. General Arredondo, whose army included a young subaltern named Santa Anna who was learning the art of Mexican warfare, pacified Texas by shooting hundreds of captured North American filibusters and cutting the throats of native liberals. By the fall of 1813, Calleja could regroup his various armies and begin to deal with Morelos.

Morelos left the congress of Chilpancingo to its debates and marched north to seize Michoacán. He planned to capture Valladolid and make it the insurgent capital. Valladolid—which the Republic renamed Morelia eventually in Morelos' memory—was invested. Calleja sent a force under the Spanish general Llave to relieve it.

With Llave was young Agustín de Iturbide, the auburn-haired *mestizo* who had proven himself to be an exceptionally capable officer. Iturbide, now a colonel, learned that Morelos had ordered his insurgents to blacken their faces so that they could recognize each other in close combat. Against orders, Iturbide had a troop of his cavalry darken their own faces, and then, after dark on Christmas Eve 1813, he led a reckless mounted charge into the very heart of Morelos' camp. Morelos had set his headquarters atop a steep hill, and because of the time and the terrain, security was lax.

When Iturbide burst in upon the surprised insurgents there was total confusion. Morelos' regiments fired on each other; they were not trained for rapid fire and maneuver in the dark. Men who would have fought bravely under different conditions ran, screaming they were betrayed. The insurgent army dissolved in the face of inferior royalist forces.

Iturbide followed up his advantage with energy. Mariano Matamoros gathered some of the insurgents and made a desperate stand at Puruarán but was decisively defeated. Matamoros himself, the best of Morelos' lieutenants, was taken and shot. After a series of disasters, Morelos' whole force dissolved, and the insurgent chief barely escaped with an escort of one hundred men.

Calleja pounced swiftly, ordering his forces to strike everywhere. A royalist army retook Oaxaca, while another force seized Cuernavaca, Cuautla, Taxco, and finally, Chilpancingo, setting the congress on the run for their lives. Hermenegildo Galeana, Morelos' remaining "good arm," was captured and beheaded. The royalists walked into Acapulco.

Morelos' peasant army melted back into the mountains and valleys from which it had come. Within a few weeks Calleja destroyed everything Morelos had accomplished in two years.

The fact that Morelos had accepted his authority from the congress now proved disastrous for the insurgents. The humble *mestizo* priest was the only man of genius on the liberal side, but the congress threw all the blame for the various disasters on his head and ordered him to surrender his command. Morelos obeyed, saying he was willing to serve the cause as a private soldier. Thus the leadership passed out of the hands of the single man with high ideals, military, and political ability among the liberals and fell to a divided, jealous, quarreling group of petty local chieftains and juntas, none of whom could raise an army from the people, or command one against the royalist professionals. The congress and López Rayón knew only how to criticize and issue propaganda; local monsters like Rosains and Félix Fernández knew only how to raid and kill.

In October 1814 the congress of the Republic of Anáhuac finally put out its new constitution, in Apatzingán in Michoacán. This charter drew heavily on Anglo-Saxon ideas, such as providing universal suffrage and indirect elections, but also retained Hispanic traditions, by creating an executive which was a junta of three persons, appointed by the congress, and a court of *residencia*, and while the constitution was never to be implemented, it was to remain as an ideal for all future reformers.

The royalists were now destroying insurgency. Even many of the country people were now aiding officers like Iturbide, who caught and executed nineteen guerrilla leaders and nine hundred of their followers in Michoacán within two months. As the rebellion was stamped out in this area, the congress tried to reach the dubious safety of Tehuacán, which was still held by an officer who was perhaps the most idealistic and splendid of all the liberal commanders, the *criollo* mineralogist, Manuel Mier y Terán. To make this journey the congress, swallowing its pride, called on Morelos to be its escort and guide.

Morelos and Nicolás Bravo rode with the congressmen. Despite every ruse the old guerrillero could employ, two bands of royalists caught up with them at Texmalaca. Morelos ordered Bravo to escape with the congress, while he and a few devoted followers led pursuit astray with a diversion.

After a futile delaying action, Morelos' party tried to save itself by scattering into surrounding cliffsides. A royalist officer—significantly, one of Morelos' old lieutenants who had changed sides—caught the priest as he tried to remove his spurs in flight and asked him what he would do if the situation were reversed. The priest answered bluntly that he would confess the officer and shoot him. Morelos was taken under heavy guard to México.

Here, lodged in the dungeon of the Inquisition, Morelos was examined for forty-six days, accused of treason, heresy, and lesser crimes. Like most of the rebel priests, Morelos had never believed in clerical chastity and openly acknowledged he had children. He was convicted of treason, branded as a Protestant, unfrocked, and turned over to the secular arm for execution. He was the last victim of the Inquisition in Mexico. He was shot to death three days before Christmas 1815.

He was the one man who had a chance of making a constructive revolution. He joined a growing pantheon of Mexican martyrs. His death was the most tragic of all for Mexico, because his ideals were buried with his bones.

24

TREASONS

Mexico's independence, then, was the achievement of two op-
posed sectors, each working toward a different immediate objective.
One side wanted to separate from a liberal Spain and continue the
system without the motherland. The other side wanted separation
from Spain too, but it wanted to wipe out the colony and establish a
new order—especially a new political order.

Victor Alba, *The Mexicans.*

In 1816 Viceroy Calleja restored his authority everywhere. With Morelos
dead, there was no leader and no cause to hold together the horde of
dissident intellectuals in hiding, the juntas without legitimacy or armies,
and the guerrilla chieftains who were more and more sheer bandits.

The deputies for whom Morelos had sacrificed his life quarreled at
Tehuacán until the highminded Mier y Terán threw them out of town.
Félix Fernández and the evil Rosains, the two principal guerrilleros of the
Veracruz region, fought to control the insurgents operating there. Mier y
Terán arrested Rosains, who escaped and turned coat, as an officer in the
viceregal army. Failure, futility, and despair descended over the revolu-
tionaries, and decent men began to desert the insurgency in disgust.

Once Calleja had full military control, he was recalled and replaced by
Don Juan de Apodaca. The time for ruthlessness was over. Apodaca now
worked against the remaining insurgency more effectively than Calleja
could have done, by offering amnesty to rebels who surrendered, and by
spectacularly rewarding men who changed sides. Insurgent officers, however tenuous their commissions, were offered commissions in the regular,
royal army with only minor demotions and awarded the privilege of put-

ting *don* before their names. No discrimination was made because of former class, caste, or creed. Thus people like Rosains and Vicente Gómez, the gelder of Spaniards, who had robbed, murdered, and tortured countless soldiers and civilians were given the king's commission. Most of the insurgent officers turned traitor with them.

Osorno surrendered near Puebla; Mier y Terán's officers forced him to give up Tehuacán, though the young idealist simply took the amnesty and returned to private life. Guerrilleros now operated only in parts of Guanajuato and Michoacán. Montes de Oca and Pedro Ascencio, holding out in the south, were clearly local brigands.

Thus when Xavier Mina, the Spanish liberal and revolutionary who conspired with Servando Teresa de Mier to separate King Fernando from his Mexican silver, landed in April 1817 it was a futile effort. Mina arrived on the Tamaulipas coast with three hundred North American adventurers and marched inland to Guanajuato. He recruited some rebels, but most Mexican liberals were prejudiced against him because he was Spanish and refused to shoot prisoners indiscriminately; his protests that some Spaniards loved liberty, also, were fruitless. Government forces hunted Mina down in October and executed him. In death, he was accepted by Mexicans, and afterward buried with the other insurgent heros under the Column of Independence at the capital.

In the same months, the last guerrilla chief in Michoacán was murdered by his followers. Then, in December, 1817, Nicolás Bravo and Ignacio López Rayón accepted amnesty. The insurgency had ended.

Two insurgents did not surrender, however. One was Morelos' lieutenant Vicente Guerrero, who held out in the remote sierra north of Acapulco. Guerrero was a simple peasant of white-*indio*-Negro descent, who had worshipped Morelos. Although the viceroy sent his own father, a royalist, to offer Guerrero the usual king's commission and rewards for apostasy, he refused to give up. Guerrero was innately a kind and gentle man, a true hero, and ironically, his greatest misfortune was to be that he was not martyred like his idol, but lived to become president of Mexico.

The other holdout was Félix Fernández, deserted by his men and hiding alone in the cordillera up from Veracruz. He went half-naked in the forests and mountains, fed now and then by friendly *indios*. Driven by a stubborn, quixotic vision, Fernández called himself *Guadalupe Victoria*, symbolizing eventual Mexican victory.

Neither rebel posed any threat to the government of Apodaca, who in 1819 reported to Madrid that he had no more need for Spanish troops. The irony of the insurgency was that all the bloodshed totally failed to achieve Mexican independence—in fact, the civil war actually delayed it. Hidalgo and Morelos were to be honored in modern Mexico for their social ideals, not for what they accomplished. The War for Independence, as the insurgency came to be called, produced few heros, but ample martyrs.

While Mexico was wracked by rebellions, the Spanish peninsula had its own troubles: the great patriotic war against the French occupation turned into a full-scale popular revolt. The leadership of the guerrilla campaigns against the French was predominantly liberal, that is, men deeply unhappy both with the traditional society and their own place in it. These liberals came from that middle rank, not quite a true middle class, of easily radicalized reformers. They were anticlerical and antiroyalist, but as modern studies have shown, they were not quite democrats. Their aim was to seize power. They took and propagated democratic French and Anglo-Saxon rationales because they found nothing in their own heritage to justify the rule of people such as themselves, and in the long run this was to prove their downfall, and the real reason for the failure of liberalism throughout the Hispanic world.

The Spanish liberal juntas that fought Napoleon in the name of Fernando VII were themselves confused in their basic attitudes toward the Spanish empire. As liberals they were forced intellectually to accede that the colonials possessed political rights. As Spaniards, and men who in many cases derived their livelihood from the offices, privileges, and monopolies made possible by the empire, they had no wish to see colonial dominion destroyed. Whether the king of Spain ruled by the grace of God or through powers granted by a constitution, there was no changing the fact that the inefficient industries of Barcelona and Bilbao, the wine growers of Andalusia, and the merchants of Sevilla depended primarily upon the captive markets across the Ocean Sea.

This confusion colored the policy toward New Spain in these critical years. In 1812 the Spanish junta wrote a new Spanish constitution which called for elective city and provincial governments, the abolition of the Inquisition and the privileges of the military and the clergy, and for freedom of the press. The American dominions were to be represented in the new national *cortes*, or parliament, on the same basis as the peninsular cities and provinces, by freely elected deputies. New Spain was allotted seven such representatives. Since in 1812 the Spanish junta controlled only the fringes of Spain, the new charter could not be implemented at home. Venegas, however, was ordered to implement it in Mexico.

These instructions arrived at the time Morelos was at the height of his power in the south and the viceroyalty was surviving mainly because a conservative reaction to the threatened social revolution had begun. They weakened the Spanish grip, but Venegas saw no choice but to obey. He promulgated the new constitution in September 1812.

It was received enthusiastically by the *criollos*, because it met many of their demands. The insurgency, despite its failures, had created a climate for self-government among almost all native-born Mexicans, including the clergy, army, landowners, lawyers, and functionaries. It must be understood that while the upper class fought stubbornly on the side of the viceroy against social revolution, it had become suffused with dreams for a de facto independence from Spain. The Mexican elites possessed a great stake in independence, with an end to tribute and forced loans, monopolies and Spanish arrogance, and the opening of profitable offices to colonials. The *hacendados* had already sensed a great opportunity that the liberal lawyers had not quite grasped: the abolition of crown regulation would give the countryside over to the control and aggrandizement of the landowning class. *Criollo* officers, now holding most of the ranks up to colonel, hoped to remove the disliked peninsular generals. This, of course, was exactly the revolution that Allende had intended—and ironically, if there had been no *grito de Dolores*, it might have come about peacefully in 1812.

When the constitution went into effect, *criollo* Mexico celebrated with bells and bonfires. The city council at the capital changed the name of the Plaza Real to the Plaza of the Constitution. A mob of citizens tore down the royal scaffolds.

Newly elected officials, all *criollos*, replaced the old, appointed, hereditary *regidores*. The new men believed in self-rule. Masses of thanksgiving were dedicated in all the principal churches. The new law permitting press freedom gave birth to a horde of local periodicals, whose editorials attacked Spaniards and their role in Mexico.

Francisco Venegas himself was liberal, appointed by a liberal junta, but he understood that liberalism was leading toward a separation of Mexico from Spain, which his own superiors failed to see. Therefore, in the midst of disorder and rejoicing, he arbitrarily suspended the constitution, using Morelos' insurgency as the excuse. He did not quite dare replace the public gibbets (garroting of the condemned was now carried out in secret) but he threatened to penalize the unauthorized pealing of church bells with ten years' hard labor. Over vehement protests of the newly elected *criollo* officials, the authoritarianism of the ruling clique of Spaniards was completely restored by edict. The Spanish parliament, apprised of the true situation, approved.

This confused giving and taking away of self-government angered almost everyone except the insurgents; Morelos was delighted, because to him it revealed the duplicity of all *gachupines*. The Mexican liberals—only a few of whom actually had joined the insurgency—were dissatisfied with the terms of the constitution, since it still required Mexico to be a Spanish dominion despite the granting of minority representation in the Spanish parliament, and they were dismayed by its sudden revocation. The Mexican conservatives—as this amorphous faction could now be called—meanwhile had been horrified by the constitution's liberal provisions, though they concealed their deep misgivings in the general public rejoicing. The idea of free elections and the abolition of privileges did not appeal to army officers and the higher clergy.

The threat of Morelos' social revolution forced both the liberals and conservatives, however, to swallow the reimposition of viceregal rule.

During the same years that the insurgency was crushed, combined British and Spanish forces drove the French out of Spain. In 1814 Napoleon was overthrown in France, and the royal prisoner Fernando VII was released. He had hardly recrossed the Pyrenees when, driven by the coterie of nobles and ecclesiastics that surrounded him and by his own Bourbon inclinations, he abolished the constitution promulgated in his absence. This began five years of intense reaction in Spain. Fernando, who came back to a smouldering, ruined homeland, the recent scene of massacres, battles, and hideous sieges, found it easy to destroy the incipient Spanish liberalism in the general weariness and the general rejoicing over his return. The Inquisition again became active—one of its victims was the bishop of Valladolid, Abad y Queipo, who was recalled from Mexico on the strength of his letters of protest to the former king written years before—and the liberal leaders of the juntas were soon in jail. Their protégé Viceroy Venegas was recalled and the king replaced him with Calleja, a man much more to the Bourbon liking. Calleja pronounced the Constitution of 1812 dead in August 1815. But Mexico was as ruined and war-weary as Spain, as for the moment as little inclined to serious revolt.

However, during this triumph of reaction in old and New Spain, the southern continent waged its decisive battles for independence. There royalist and nativist *criollos* fought for control, and the patriots won. San Martín and Bolívar led armies from one triumph into other viceroyalties, liberating region after region from Spain; this whetted the Mexican appetite for independence. Finally, the efforts Fernando VII forced on his exhausted country to support the royalist cause in America caused a new revolution in Spain. Spanish peasants and townsmen were being conscripted to die in the mountains and jungles of the Americas, and the concept of Spanish grandeur and material interest did not offset the repugnance to a vastly unpopular colonial war.

In 1820 conscripted troops bound for the Americas revolted, and a new revolution swept Spain. The liberal juntas reappeared. Fernando VII saved his throne only by an apparent, abject surrender, swearing to reinstitute and uphold the Constitution of 1812. Fernando, however, was entirely treacherous. When the equally reactionary Bourbon regime in France, supported by the Holy Alliance, intervened with military force in Spain, the king recanted and began a reign of terror against the liberals. He won out again. Meanwhile, the shock of the latest convolution in the peninsula produced decisive effects in Mexico.

Apodaca, under orders of the ephemerally ascendent liberal parliament, had restored the Constitution of 1812. Once again a horde of separatist-minded *criollos* were elected to local councils, and an anti-Spanish press appeared. But now, the insurgency was finished militarily, and the Mexican conservatives were no longer bound to the viceregal regime by a threat of social revolution. Fernando VII himself, in the confusions of the hour, encouraged the notion of Mexican independence, because the king briefly despaired of Spain and thought that Mexico might provide the Bourbons with a firmer seat.

The total political confusion created a Byzantine political mess in Mexico. The Spanish, engaged in civil war at home, had little attention for America. The peninsular troubles were destroying the last vestiges of Spanish power and prestige in the colonies, and also, the apparent victory of liberalism in Spain in 1820 at last made the Spanish Church in Mexico think seriously of the advantages of independence. The hierarchy was bitterly hostile to the liberal reforms twice promulgated out of the old country, and now began to think that only Mexican independence might preserve the traditional religion and society.

The reforms, such as abolition of the Inquisition and clerical privileges, closure of convents, and confiscation of Church property, were totally unacceptable to the prelates. The Church had played a very great role throughout the entire insurgency. While people's priests like Hidalgo and Morelos had provided the brains behind the revolt, the bishops and canons had provided even more effective financing and rationales to the conservatives. The troubles had brought the Mexican hierarchy and the *criollo* elite into a genuine alliance against a revolution that promised to destroy them both. In the interest of continuing this alliance, the prelates were willing to desert the *gachupín* ascendancy, provided that the *criollos* who came to power entered into a similar governing relationship with the Church. This would be a continuation of the royalist coalition that had defeated insurgency, but with the *peninsulares* no longer in control.

This new twist was neither so treasonous or cynical as it has sometimes been described. It should be remembered that the loyalty of Hispanic traditionalists had never been to a Spanish "nation" but to a Spanish Church and crown. There was more than property and privileges at stake, for the whole direction of foreign-inspired liberalism frightened all traditionalists to their roots. There were emotional reactions that went far beyond a defense of property and privilege; many poor traditionalists had an almost mystic belief in the rightness of the old orderings of Hispanic society.

If nothing but privilege and property had stood in the way of reform, liberalism must have triumphed quickly throughout the Hispanic world. Effective reform, however, required a remaking not only of society but of all the traditions, beliefs, and ethics that lay behind it.

The Mexican Church in 1820, with the rebellious priests dead and the reactionaries fully in control, was undecided only as to whether it should support immediate independence, or await the expected arrival of Fernando VII on a separate Mexican throne. The Spanish prelates saw no treason—to them, the Spanish nation, by turning liberal, had committed treason against the Church and crown. The clerics saw themselves as loyalists in the larger sense. Their view of a continuing Hispanic nation in Mexico was very different from that of the *criollo* liberals, but in these confused times all the forces could coalesce behind a single goal, independence, without a clear definition of the sort of nation independence would bring about.

Therefore, in the spring of 1820 the royalists in Mexico who had fought one form of treason for ten years, began to plot a newer form of treason against the mother country, Spain.

There is still no agreement among historians as to who used whom in this Byzantine embroglio of confused loyalties and politics. The Church, that *bête noire* of the liberals, was active, but not necessarily dominant. What was happening was that in a social milieu in which order had fled and everything seemed to be falling to pieces, those men who best understood how to use the people and forces around them were coming to the fore. These new leaders were a common enough phenomenon in failing or transitional societies. They were usually military men, the *caudillos* or leaders on horseback, because in transitional societies once legitimacy had been destroyed, power could only emerge from the mouth of a gun.

Agustín de Iturbide, the wealthy, ambitious "certified" *criollo* from Valladolid, who had risen from lieutenant to general in the bloody years, was typical of a whole group of officers created by the insurgency and the royalist reaction. Venegas and Calleja had never trusted such Mexican officers, but had needed them. Iturbide, capable and courageous on the battlefield, distinguished himself at Monte de las Cruces and by defeating Morelos in Michoacán. He was in his early thirties when made general. In 1815 he was entrusted with the delivery of the vital mercury to the northern mines, and the guarding of silver bullion in transit to the capital. Iturbide had grown rich through graft in this position, taking a fat percentage for his protection. This was hardly unusual; every royalist commander followed such practices, just as every insurgent leader indulged in robbery. But Iturbide went too far, and was dismissed from service in 1816.

General Iturbide combined ruthlessness and immorality with a superstitious nature and a craving for sanctity, not unusual in men of his type and times. Disgraced, he entered a lay retreat in the convent of La Profesa at the capital, in ostentatious penance for his sins. Here he met with important and disgruntled clerics, and during Lent, he could converse with judges, noblemen, generals, and wealthy miners who came to La Profesa in these days. Gradually, a junta began to meet at the convent, composed of dismissed or disaffected men, plotting to save society as they knew it. The liberal revolution of 1820 in Spain frightened all the traditional forces; Iturbide became the leader of a group that planned a coup d'etat against the viceregal regime.

Iturbide must first somehow subvert the viceregal army. This proved almost ridiculously easy. Apodaca was planning a final campaign against Vicente Guerrero, no danger but a nuisance in the southern sierra. The Spanish clerics who surrounded the viceroy insisted that Iturbide be given command of the southern army. Apodaca agreed, and in December 1820 Iturbide took control of the best regiments in New Spain.

The general outline of the conspiracy called for the young general to win fame by destroying Guerrero, then, returning with his victorious army to the capital, to seize the viceroy's baton and chair with the professed rationale of making Mexico secure for Fernando VII. But Iturbide had his own ideas. This was still the age of Napoleon, and he was dreaming vaster schemes.

He failed to demolish Guerrero, who was unassailable in his wild mountains. Defeated by a small force of guerrilleros, Iturbide, who felt he had no time to waste, opened negotiations with the insurgents. He also seized a pack train carrying five-hundred thousand silver pesos to Acapulco for shipment to the Orient for his own use.

Guerrero did not trust Iturbide, but the general had charm and persuasiveness, and also an almost irresistible bait: a plan for the independence of Mexico, which he circulated early in 1821. Among its twenty provisions were three major guarantees: 1) independence under King Fernando or a suitable Bourbon prince; 2) continuation of Roman Catholicism as the state religion; 3) citizenship and racial equality for all Mexicans. The ideas were not new, but the plan was brilliantly drawn, with something for everyone, and without the usual ideological arguments and complexities of revolutionary documents. Iturbide offered the *criollos* independence, a king, and a continuation of property rights; the Church its privileged status; the masses citizenship and equality before the law. Far better-educated men than the guerrillero chieftain Guerrero did not see that the first two guarantees rendered the third meaningless for the mass of Mexicans. The plan had nothing of Hidalgo's social revolution and embodied none of Morelos' ideals. It continued Mexican society with one change, freedom from peninsular rule.

The plan has always been viewed with distaste by Mexican liberal historians because it failed to revolutionize colonial Mexico, and the dominant later view was that independence achieved this way was a great betrayal. But Iturbide's plan was the only possible one on which the effective men and institutions in Mexico could agree. Hidalgo's and Morelos' ideals had been proven premature; Iturbide's plan succeeded because it fit the realities of time and place.

The simplicity of the plan appealed to Guerrero, who must have believed, with many of the Mexican liberals, that independence and legal racial equality was a great first step toward the nation Morelos had wanted. Iturbide admitted candidly his plan did not solve everything; much would have to be worked out later. He told Guerrero that first the viceregal government must be overthrown, then elections could be held to form the inevitable junta that would decide the country's destiny. Guerrero was swayed. He met Iturbide at Acatempán, where the two leaders embraced before their cheering armies.

With this *abrazo*, and the signatures upon Iturbide's plan, issued at the small town of Iguala between Taxco and Chilpancingo February 24th, 1821, the course of independent Mexico was set.

The Trigarantine army, as the newly combined force was called, raised a new flag: a tricolor representing the three guaranties, white for religion, green for independence, red for the union of Europeans and Amerindians. The irreverent have held that the selection of colors came while Iturbide and Guerrero split a watermelon on a rough table at Iguala.

The viceroy was enraged, but helpless, for in all Mexico only the Masonic order supported him, with a handful of peninsular soldiers. Virtually all the Mexicans hailed the Iguala plan.

The key was the royal army. Iturbide had some trouble in swaying all his soldiers, but he subverted the officer corps with promises of rapid promotion. Apodaca, hoping to heal wounds, had rewarded hundreds of Mexicans who had changed sides, and now he was rewarded in turn by wholesale military treason throughout the royal ranks. Every former liberal or insurgent officer deserted to Iturbide along with the conservatives. Nicolás Bravo and the rest raised the tricolor; Fernández, or Guadalupe Victoria, came out of hiding to praise the plan. The decisive blow, however, was the complete desertion of the army to Iturbide.

Thousands of officers betrayed their oaths to the government, rationalizing the act much like the clerics who deserted Spain. But the army was not all that ideological or traditional; a more profound reason for the reversal was that such things as soldiers' trust and honor had virtually vanished during the age of Godoy. Iturbide made lavish promises: a captain could become a general with a timely declaration. At Orizaba, Captain Antonio López de Santa Anna, son of a penniless Spanish immigrant and *criolla* mother, showed he understood this game superbly. By seeming to hold fast, he secured a lieutenant-colonelcy from the government; promising to switch, he was offered a colonelcy. He emerged on Iturbide's side as a brigadier. After years of dangerous campaigning, men like Santa Anna made their fortunes in a day's intrigues in politics.

The Trigarante movement was assured success when the *criollo* general Anastasio Bustamante, the tigerish commander who shot all insurgents and suspected liberals who fell into his hands, went over to Iturbide with six thousand troops at Guanajuato. Bustamante then had the skulls of Hidalgo and his fellow rebels taken down from the iron cage and buried with military honors.

Guadalajara declared for the tricolor. Iturbide occupied Valladolid. By July 1821, the entire north had swung, and in August he rode into the conservative city of Puebla side by side with Guadalupe Victoria and Nicolás Bravo. Distant Yucatán, never involved in the insurgency, declared for independence. Only the capital, the ports of Veracruz and Acapulco, and the fortress of Perote still flew the red and gold banners of León and Castile.

A new viceroy, Juan O'Donojú, had arrived to replace Apodaca. He was trapped, however, in pestilential Veracruz, where his party and even his family took sick and died of the black vomit. Desperate to escape the fever coast, O'Donojú met Iturbide and agreed to abide by the Iguala plan. Hoping to salvage a treaty of friendship and commercial ties, O'Donojú also signed a pact that recognized Mexico as an independent empire and with a provision that if no Spanish infante took the throne, the choice of ruler would be left to a Mexican congress. O'Donojú was then permitted to go on to México, from where he ordered the last Spanish regiments to proceed for embarkation at Veracruz.

Iturbide chose his thirty-eighth birthday, September 27th, to lead the Trigarantine Army into the City of México. He came on his great black horse, ruddy and handsome in a plumed hat, surrounded by generals in gold braid, followed by sixteen thousand soldiers. The marchers included smart battalions of bluecoated regulars and companies of dark, ragged guerrilleros. The fine ladies on the balconies of the route of march sported green, white, and red ribbons in their hair. The street mobs screamed *vivas* until their voices failed against the crash of field music and the roar of the drums.

Iturbide's army came from Tacuba into the Alameda, then he led it on a wide circle to Plateros, so the whole march might be seen by the reigning belle of México. At the convent of San Francisco the city council presented him with a gold key to the capital. The Virrey O'Donojú received him at the palace—which was now the National Palace, and from which he reviewed his parade. Iturbide then entered the cathedral and sat in the viceroy's chair while the archbishop celebrated a Te Deum in honor of the day.

Three centuries, one month, and two weeks of Spanish domination of Mexico officially ended. This was not a day that would be remembered or honored by Mexicans. The reasons, perhaps, were revealed even on that day by General Iturbide when he issued the inevitable Hispanic proclamation, which read:

"Mexicans, now you have liberty and independence. It is for you to find happiness."

25

THE PRETORIANS

There is a constant clash between the doctrines professed, and the institution adopted, the principles established and the abuses already sanctified, the customs that prevail, and the semifeudal rights that are respected; between national sovereignty, equality, freedom of the press, popular government and the intervention of armed forces, privileged status, religious intolerance, and the owners of immense territories.

Lorenzo de Zavala, Mexican historian.

In 1821 there was no experience in the world or Mexico to show that the building of a new nation out of a long and profound colonial experience would be far more difficult than winning independence. The North American example was a false beacon. The British American colonies had enjoyed local self-rule for generations; they had firm, working laws and institutions; they had remarkable leaders from a class developed on the continent. The North Americans had evolved a flexible, frontier society out of open lands and free institutions, and unlike almost every other country in the world, their land was underpopulated and institutionalized poverty simply did not exist; at its very beginning, the society of the United States was perhaps more splendid in some ways than it would ever be again. The new nation was also remarkably homogeneous, despite the apparent differences from Georgia to Massachusetts. All North Americans had been English-speaking for at least a generation; there were no more than thirty thousand non-Protestants out of some three million; and the population was overwhelmingly white—eighty percent were free citizens. The Anglo-Saxon Americans had established their identity long before independence, and with all these things in their favor they were able to cement a new nation rapidly.

Independent Mexico was almost the reverse in every respect. For three centuries Mexicans had been defined only in relation to the colonial power and never in the country's own right. This was the core of the Mexican problem. If New Spain were now Mexico, and Mexicans no longer Spaniards with the misfortune to be born abroad or pseudo-Spaniards of mixed blood or the remnants of an indigenous race subordinated by conquest, what were they?

There were possible tools to solve institutional problems, but no tools to attack ethnic and psychological troubles.

The *criollos* who gained Mexican independence in 1821 had already divided into two great camps. The *continuistas*, usually but not always social conservatives, saw obvious advantages in continuing the existing colonial patterns, at least until some satisfactory new forms were discovered. They were xenophobic toward foreign ideas, though not toward foreigners themselves. They longed to reestablish a crown and reinvest it with the old mystique. These traditionalists, perhaps incongruously, also saw salvation in industrialism; they wanted to follow the British lead in business and finance. Taken all together, the *continuistas* formed an alliance of nostalgic reactionaries, vested interests, and newer, practical positivists. As a group, they were landed, wealthy, and had tremendous spiritual influence through the Church. But as a group, they were people born of ruined houses and overcome with ennui. They were a would-be aristocracy, emasculated by history before birth.

An exception was Lucas Alamán, the first great spokesman for an Hispanic Mexico. He was undone by the company he had to keep. Alamán's concepts were coldly realistic, but his vision of a rational conservatism mixed with material progress was blasted at the outset by three stubborn facts: the problems of Mexican society were too explosive for positive gradualism; the past was too unbearable to too many; and there was no expertise, energy, or leadership in Alamán's own class. Alamán found himself in strange alliance with superstition, cynical corruption, and dictatorship throughout his life.

Against the *continuistas* ran the argument begun by Carlos Mariá de Bustamante. "Who are we, if in freedom we merely follow in the footsteps of the raper, the usurper, the tyrant, Spain?" Bustamante's form of freedom demanded that Mexicans forget the former master, and find a collective identity in the things of Mexico. His cry found a deep response in the literate *criollo* class. Incongruously, a large part of this elite, which was predominantly liberal, felt a desperate need to find a usable Mexican past. They had to go back three centuries, and to a long-dead civilization, to unearth it. Bustamante represented that obsessive self-searching that Mexicans often have believed was peculiarly theirs, but actually has been experienced by the literate members of every emerging ex-colonial society. As much as Alamán and his conservatives, these men sought legitimacy; they simply could not conceive of the new legitimacy returning in Spanish dress under an Hispanic crown. The Bustamantes were drawn to construct a splendid mythical history and native grandeur to which the moderns were all heirs but which had been destroyed by the conqueror's villainy.

Alamán's self-image accepted the scabrous state of the past and bore its scars; Bustamante's rejected them, and by a great leap of faith identified with the Amerindians. Mexicans must enshrine the national hero, Cuauhté-moc, and avenge the slaughter at Otompán. Above all, Mexicans must destroy the pervasive image of themselves created by the Spaniards: ignorant, blood-spattered Indians, fleeing from horses and guns, kissing the whips of the conquistadores; somber, petty, argumentative, whining colonials, inept beyond rational belief, childish, blood-tainted offspring unable to handle their own affairs. Against this image of a vicious race must be planted shining, noble heros, excellent martyrs, in whose blood and heritage all Mexicans could find pride. This was, of course, wonderful psychotherapy, which the most rational of the traditionalists could never provide.

The Mexican historians, such as Alamán, Zavala, and Bulnes, who whatever their politics tried to show facts as facts no matter how much this destroyed the Mexican self-image, were hated by many liberals precisely for this reason.

The tragedy of the Mexican intellectuals then and afterward was that polemic myth and counter-myth hurled against each other in no way got on with the business of building the nation.

The best of the Mexican conservatives were progressives who wanted to preserve and build; many of the best of the liberals were regressives, searching for a proud past and insisting the nation could be made by pen stroke. Both faced the terrible problem of having no kind of usable past on which to build. The *criollos* who admired the Mexica past could not understand it, and created their own concept of it. Their interest in the Amerindian never extended to concern with the realities of the current Indians. The *continuistas*, who went too far in the other direction praising Spaniards and despising indigenes, meanwhile found themselves crippled by Hispanic holdovers. The Church and army were two problems; the Hispanic value system was a greater one, and much harder to change in the long run.

For a century, the tyranny of the past defeated both the liberals and conservatives, because the Mexicans, high and low, had been too thoroughly shaped by their colonial experience to behave collectively in any other way but as colonial stereotypes: vain, childish, exhuberant or in despair, irresponsible, one minute tearing down what they most hated, the next trying to emulate what they professed to hate most.

Mexico was thus a truer beacon to the world than the United States of North America, showing that there were no shortcuts on mankind's interminable road to happiness.

In the glittering air of its eternal spring, the capital was brave in its bunting and grand expectations through all the fall of 1821. The bishops and those Mexicans who loved a *gran señor* hourly expected the arrival of a king; the liberals had their quiet confidence that kings might come but a republic must evolve. The three guarantees satisfied no one completely, yet everyone to some extent. Even the down-to-earth Vicente Guerrero professed hope. The one thing all Mexicans agreed on was that Mexico, free at last, would immediately take a rightful place among the great nations of the world. The capital was still the metropolis of the Americas, and it was destined in their eyes to become the seat of a great New World empire.

This empire already reached from the mountains of Guatemala, through the Great Plains and high sierras of the northern continent; its flag flew from the Sabine to San Francisco.

The old imperialism was not quite dead. Almost all commerce was still in the hands of thousands of *gachupines*. The ousted Spanish army still clung to the fortress of San Juan de Ulua, commanding the vital port of Veracruz and collecting its customs revenues. Spanish prelates utterly dominated the national Church. Spanish officials and jurists, like Spanish merchants, carried on most public affairs. All this could be uprooted—but no one was sure how to begin.

In the magnificent National Palace the new management, the now Generalissimo and High Admiral Agustín de Iturbide, drawing a salary of one-hundred-and-twenty thousand pesos, appointed a Supreme Junta of thirty-eight and a Regency Council of five to rule the kingdom. There were conspicuously no old insurgents among these men. Iturbide was the darling of the bishops and the turncoat royalist generals, who saw him as their tool, and he turned to where his support lay. He was also, not incongruously, the hero of the capital mob, because with his fine horse, plumed hat, handsome face, and charismatic tongue, he cut a fine appearance before the *léperos*. The mob that tried to burn Cortés' bones cheered the generalissimo.

But the lower half of the *criollos* did not trust Iturbide, and the great men did not love him. He was an upstart, a dictator come from nowhere, and his very power provoked enormous jealousy.

As president of the Council of Regents, Iturbide presided over a euphoric but ruined country. Half the mines were flooded, their machinery wrecked; half the haciendas were idle, their tools and livestock looted. The national treasury was empty, and the government had no apparatus to collect new revenues. The national army, eighty thousand strong—half of them officers, commissioned and noncommissioned—fired off salutes and waited to be paid. Meanwhile, fully half the *criollo* population—according to one contemporary—had made application for public employment. *Empleomanía*, the madness for offices, reigned.

Iturbide's wits now deserted him. A wiser man would have remained with the army, letting others wrestle with the mounting problems, letting someone else absorb the discredit and disillusionment that was bound to come. But Iturbide saw himself as a new Napoleon, not recognizing that independent Mexico was not postrevolutionary France.

The junta supervised elections that produced a Mexican congress in February 1822. The elections were rigged. No Mexican had any experience with the electoral process, and almost none really believed in it; elections were an alien concept but too fashionable to be ignored. Their purpose was invariably assumed to be a ratification of the regime in power. The Anglo-Saxon process, by which men surrendered power and allowed principle to be turned around by a small, fickle plurality remained incomprehensible to the Hispanic mind. An overwhelmingly rich, conservative, royalist congress, sprinkled with a few intellectual gadflies like Carlos María de Bustamante was elected. The Congress arrived believing its purpose was to ratify the coming of a Bourbon king. However, Iturbide already had other plans.

Fernando VII was once again secure on the Spanish throne, supported by the so-called Holy Alliance. He had no intention of moving to Mexico, which he now claimed was still entirely subject to him, and his parliament forbade any Spanish prince to accept an American crown. The Mexican *borbonistas*, in some confusion, began to debate the advantages of a centralist, aristocratic republic. The congress meanwhile neglected the duties of providing a viable constitution and assuring revenues.

There was neither governmental experience, or in fact, any useful public expertise among any of these men—or anywhere in Creole Mexico. Instead of attacking the pressing problems, the congress began to attack the generalissimo. Months now went by in futile deadlock and argument.

In April Iturbide charged eleven members with treasonous actions. The congress retaliated by removing three of his cronies from office. Bustamante added erratic rhetoric to every session, comparing the deputies to Roman senators and Iturbide to Caesar at the Rubicon. While nothing got done, the Trigarantine Army was eating the capital bare.

Iturbide, who shunned the old insurgents and new liberals, rapidly lost all their support. Nicolás Bravo and Guadalupe Victoria entered into a conspiracy and were briefly jailed. Afterward, Victoria returned to his old mountain hideouts.

In May the congress finally proposed to reduce the army to sixty thousand officers and men and to prevent any member of the Regency Council from holding a military command.

On May 18, 1822, there was a sergeants' revolt in barracks. The shout was raised: "¡Viva Agustín Primero!"

The regiments stationed in the capital and the volatile street mobs immediately took up the cry. Great throngs of soldiers and *léperos* massed in front of Iturbide's mansion, demanding that he take the throne of Mexico. Iturbide, who certainly planned and staged this coup, feigned reluctance to become emperor—a title his agents suggested—until the congress ratified the people's wish.

The congress was chivvied into session. The deputies, who in this emergency possessed no traditional legitimacy and therefore no powers of any kind, were intimidated by the roaring mobs that filled their halls, and the massed regiments that impatiently awaited their verdict. They were not so much craven as divided, confused, and helpless. The deputies quickly bowed to the pressures of the hour, declaring Mexico an empire and Iturbide its emperor. Fifteen representatives, however, refused to acquiesce in this hysterical decision.

Agustín I was a prototype of a kind that would continue to plague the Hispanic world: leaders made by military success in a revolutionary milieu. Their success was as dazzling and pernicious as it was usually ephemeral. Men of this kind invariably had talent to plan and improvise and usually possessed great personal charm, but lacked entirely the qualities their societies most needed—and in fact, most despised: patience, firmness, discipline, moderation, a taste for hard work and self-sacrifice. Iturbide and his successors, risen from nothing to the heights, perhaps from an inherent inferiority complex had an uncontrollable appetite for pageantry and personal adulation; they loved appearances; they were frivolous, pretentious, dishonest, and surprisingly, even ignorant of the world. Iturbide and his more famous disciple, Santa Anna, were paragons of all the vices of political figures in postcolonial societies.

Emperor Iturbide spent days designing chivalric orders and inventing titles for his court and planning his coronation, which was to be exactly like Napoleon's. He made princes of his family, and his clients ladies and gentlemen of the bedchamber. After the coronation, in which he appeared covered with borrowed decorations, he instituted the Order of Guadalupe, dispensing many grand crosses. Meanwhile, the imperial treasury was bare and the country still lacked a constitution. Expenses were met by confiscations from rich *gachupines*, who had no protection of laws.

All this apparently delighted the mob and imperial favorites, but it soon soured with the still-sitting congress. Iturbide knew how to organize coups, but he did not understand any true political process.

The Spanish, who intransigently refused to leave the fortress isle of San Juan de Ulua, artfully returned an old exile to Mexico. Fray Servando Teresa de Mier, the iconoclast and razor-tongued liberal who had roamed the world for thirty years, had been elected to the congress in absentia, and from this platform the old man who had ridiculed superstition and ignorance and tyranny in his youth began to slash through all Iturbide's ridiculous pomps and vanities. He had an immediate coterie—the fifteen men who had voted against the Mexican empire.

By August Fray Servando drew such blood that the emperor had him and fourteen deputies arrested. The remaining members, many of whom hated Mier but who asserted congressional immunity, caused so much trouble that Iturbide, emulating Cromwell, forcibly dissolved the body with troops. He replaced it with forty-five new men, actually a hand-picked junta. But the congress-junta refused to draft the kind of constitution Iturbide demanded, or even to legislate taxes. Upon this, the emperor declared a complete dictatorship and stated he would make his own laws. He still had the army.

But he did not have the army, because the generals were not getting paid. The army drank up all the enormous early coinage Iturbide had issued stamped with his image and the crowned "Aztec" eagle of the Mexican empire; running out of bullion, the emperor printed paper money —the first in Mexican history—and made this worthless currency legal tender. Since generals and officials were paid in paper, their indignation was as great as that of the general population.

In his high palace, bemused with his own grandeur, Agustín I no longer smelled the wind. Young Antonio López de Santa Anna did; he was a junior Iturbide with an uncanny nose and sense of timing. Promised lavish promotions by Iturbide in 1821, Santa Anna had fallen out of favor and had been banished to an obscure command at Veracruz to watch the Spaniards. After he had engaged in several schemes, including a defeat for which his superior took the blame, Iturbide ordered him back to Mexico, ostensibly for promotion. Santa Anna knew better, and he also knew that the emperor's credit had run out.

Santa Anna now issued a proclamation calling for a republic—the meaning of which word, he admitted candidly, he did not understand. Guadalupe Victoria immediately came out of the hills and joined him. The two led a small force toward the capital as a liberating army. Checked by a superior imperial army, Santa Anna panicked; he was always a man of moods. He prepared to flee to the United States, but Victoria drily informed him things were not lost until the enemy sent him Victoria's own head.

The army failed to fight for Iturbide. Guerrero and Bravo, moving to their old retreats to the south, were caught—and released—by an Iturbidist general. Then, General Eachávarri at Veracruz, with the main army, published his Plan de Casa Mata. Under this plan, the Mexican congress was to be allowed to meet freely, without interference from the emperor. Most of the generals subscribed to it, and Iturbide's own imperial guards acclaimed Casa Mata with marches and band music.

Overwhelmed by this national ingratitude, the Liberator of Mexico convened the old congress, but was only able to stammer a few suggestions to it. In March 1823, the stalemate ended, when the emperor sent a petulant message of abdication, saying he had been forced to accept the crown, and that furthermore, the nation was in arrears to him by one-hundred-and-fifty thousand pesos. Nicolás Bravo, the old guerrillero, made sure he embarked on a British ship, after congress accepted his resignation and sentenced him to perpetual exile.

Iturbide tried again, in the spring of 1824. He arrived in Tamaulipas with a packet of paper money and printed proclamations, unaware that the congress had voted a bill of attainder if he ever set foot again on Mexican soil. Petty local authorities seized him and shot him immediately. It was a sorry ending for the leader who after all, did at last achieve Mexican independence from Spain.

The years that followed Iturbide's fall, in fact the whole first century of nationhood, were a series of vicious cycles of repeated follies and crushing reactions, of national failure and blasted dreams. Mexico fell even farther behind the advanced world, until the name itself became a byword for instability, revolution, backwardness, and barbarism.

The *criollo* elite who inherited independent Mexico could not define the Mexican nation. They either clung mindlessly to the past, or else tried to impose alien dream structures. It made no real difference whether Mexico was called a monarchy or a republic. Four-fifth of the population was still submerged in the old colonial patterns, *indios* and *peones* and *braceros,* people who still, despite new laws, were considered tainted, and were illiterate, moneyless, and ineffective. As the careers of Hidalgo and Morelos showed; the vast underclass contained explosive grievances.

The Europeanized elite had clearly divided by 1824 into two great camps. This was a division that was to remain, although names, programs, techniques, rationales, and even alliances within the camps continually changed. It is too simple to call the camps *continuistas* and *reformistas*, as they are usually called, because the *continuistas* or traditionalists were constantly forced to try reforms in order to make a nation, while the most radical of the reformers frequently behaved in highly traditional, authoritarian ways.

Each camp was culturally, socially, and racially heterogeneous; each had factions. The *continuistas* over the years came to be known as royalists, centralists, clericals, conservatives, imperialists, *escoseses* (from the Scottish Rite to which many belonged), and positivists. The *reformistas* were called insurgents, liberals, federalists, *yorkinos* (after the competing York Rite), etc. Both camps were vast, shifting, and peculiarly ineffective alliances.

The *continuistas* were based solidly on the *hacendados*, in alliance with the Catholic hierarchy and the army. Yet they did not stand entirely for property and privilege, because many *continuistas* hungered for national greatness which could come only from development. If many traditionalist intellectuals were royalist romantics, there were others who insisted that Mexico adopt English techniques in industrialism and finance. Their outlook was strongly Western; they denigrated the Amerindian nature of Mexico. Many still saw themselves as Europeans who must direct Mexico out of a continuing Indian barbarism toward a full inclusion in the Atlantic culture. In this sense, they were a continuation of colonialism, men who thought of themselves as custodians with a mission to command and civilize.

Their power base was obvious: in the control of the landowners over the dark and ignorant workers on the estates; through the enormous wealth and influence of religion; and in the army, which now gained the right to conscript *indios* and use them as the generals directed.

But they had terrible weaknesses. The alliances were incongruous, bishops and brutal generals, *caudillos* and progressive businessmen, religious fanatics and trained engineers. The realities of this alliance made the excellent basic concepts of the *continuistas* impossible to implement. The nation would never be civilized or modernized until the masses were educated and uplifted, but the landowners and the prelates were adamantly opposed to any such action by government. A modern economy could not be built upon semifeudal *latifundios*, debt-slavery, religious education, and class privilege. Therefore, the *continuistas* had to ignore the misery of the masses and the ambitions of the *mestizos* and were to become entirely dependent upon foreigners to bring capital and technical progress to Mexico.

The *reformistas* tended to be drawn from the middle or lower professional ranks of the *criollos*, with a very important sprinkling of educated *mestizos*. This was a distinct elite of professional men and bureaucrats, but rather than an alliance of property and privilege, the Spanish-hating *reformistas* were groupings of men with social and political ambitions who found their rationales for power in intellectual doctrines that called for extensive reform. The reformers were divided sharply into *puros* and *moderados*—purists and moderates.

They were "liberal" only in the nineteenth-century definition of liberalism, for they were as elitist and undemocratic as the conservatives. They simply stood for different things: they hated monarchy, clericalism, and all the worm-eaten structures of the past; their ideal was equality of opportunity (which meant a chance for office) within a French-style republic.

Their strengths were many. They could draw on the misery of the poor (though the *reformista* leadership was very remote from the poor) and above all, on the frustration of the *mestizos*, who were emerging as the most energetic caste. The nativism of the *reformistas*, however confused, had innate appeal for the majority with indigenous blood. But *reformista* political alliances were also awkward: primitive *indios* on *ejidos* led by intellectuals who thought in French; idealists uncomfortably associated with local *mestizo* guerrilleros and rapacious office-seekers. They were terribly dependent on foreign ideas because nothing in the Hispanic heritage served their ends. The reformers lived in as unreal a world as the Mexican traditionalists. They hoped to remake society by the stroke of a pen, and create a liberal republic without citizens. Their greatest weakness was the fact that Mexican society had few private institutions that could advance society, and the reformers had to institute all liberal changes by decree.

This notion that a few intellectuals in office might somehow forge a citizenry out of peons by enacting liberal laws was as ridiculous as the *continuistas*' insistence upon evolution without reform.

Both camps shared common, basically Hispanic traits. They had a tendency toward intense personal jealousies, for they personalized everything, including politics. Both had the irresistible Hispanic passion to regulate, making governments of men even as they declared governments of laws. The moderates were ineffective, the effective men immoderate. Both leaderships lacked austerity and self-discipline, without which no revolution could succeed. Both were economically naive. Centuries of conditioning made both confuse rhetoric with reality.

A handful of intellectuals played a peculiarly prominent role in each camp, writing contemporary histories and delineating the great arguments, and also playing central roles in government. Unfortunately, these intellectuals spoke mostly to each other and to the outside world. They fulminated brilliantly, and strove earnestly against circumstance, but all were helpless against the reality of the interests, hatreds, ignorances, and idiocies of their countrymen.

Because they wrote and argued well, too much attention is paid to these intellectuals by historians. In the history of any Hispanic nation, attention must be paid less to what men argued, or wrote, and more to events. What actually took place, not what certain men wanted to achieve, was the true reality of the times.

Iturbide's antics had completely disarrayed the monarchists; all the Mexican elite at least professed republican sentiments by 1823. The *continuistas*, disillusioned with kings, now hoped for a centralized regime, a *República de México* organized along the lines of the old viceroyalty; centralism was traditional and lent itself to the control of the whole country by the powerful interests at the capital. However, the liberals or federalists, in the conservative disarray, organized the republic and wrote the Constitution of 1824. The *federalistas* were dominated at this time by the moderate wing, who were lukewarm toward incisive social reform. Therefore, the constitution attacked problems indirectly. It closely followed the North American pattern, providing a national congress and a presidency with "extraordinary powers," but also creating a labyrinth of new state governments, with power divided between the regions and the federal capital. The federalists wanted to dilute the power of the great landowners and prelates of south-central Mexico by making a host of local governments, and more important, expand their own opportunities for office in local statehouses and assemblies. They created nineteen Mexican states and four territories, following the general outlines of the old intendancies though many of the new states received new, independence-related names. Ramós Arizpe, the *mestizo* priest who wrote this constitution, tailored it to his own northern viewpoints. The thinly populated north and other outlying regions were strongly federalist in sentiment. The constitution did make for a broader Mexico than the centralists' designs, which considered nothing important beyond the Spanish cities, the great estates, and the dioceses of the Cortésian conquests.

The constitution lacked two democratic safeguards: it made Roman Catholicism the only tolerated religion, continuing tithes and privileges; and it had no provision for trial by jury. It did, however, create universal suffrage and allowed lay education. It ignored the purists' demands for secularization and redistribution of property. While purists like Valentín Gómez Farías, José Luis Mora, and Lorenzo de Zavala pointed out the obvious discrepancies between a democratic constitution and a society that remained organized on feudal and authoritarian lines, the moderates won, electing Guadalupe Victoria and Nicolás Bravo president and vice-president.

Victoria immediately proved that having become a symbol of rebellion hardly prepared a man for government. The ex-law clerk and popular hero was ignorant and irresolute, incorruptible but also ineffective. He disliked both his predominantly purist intellectual advisers and the arrogant *criollo* gentry of the capital, who dominated society. He did very little to lead, beside putting down able men who tried to rise in his administration and taking the Condesa de Regla as his mistress.

Nicolás Bravo, who was a revolutionary more by inheritance than conviction, also had great prestige but offered little leadership.

The problem, however, was not just the executives but the whole *criollo-moderado* leadership that had organized the government. Their rhetorical educations had not equipped them to deal with problems the country faced. They believed they dared not alienate the army, the *hacendados*, the mine operators, or the Church. They dared not create new taxes, after a generation of agitation over Spanish bloodsucking, and as independent citizens, they were constrained to abolish Indian tributes and humiliating head taxes, and the heavy taxes on precious minerals. But this only erased revenues. And it left the government with customs, excises, and monopolies as its sole source of income.

The Republic soon increased customs duties and the alcabala or transactions tax to approximately three times the levels they had held under Revillagigedo. These were not only regressive but destructive, and they did not even have the rationale of the protection of native industries, because the Mexican economy was in ruins. The new men running Mexico had absolutely no grasp of that elusive European concept, money. In the long run, economic naiveté was to do more damage to the republican Mexico than the landowners, Church, or army. The financial problems exacerbated all the others and caused the government to be organized as a permanent revolution.

By the 1820s, the primitive economy had been sucked dry by eleven years of insurgency and war. Mortgages had fallen due and more productive land passed into the Church's mortmain; the mines were closed or barely operating; the Spaniards who had run the mercantile establishment were put out of business or driven from Mexico. A Spanish merchant or engineer could only remain with a permit, obtainable only through influence or corruption. Great families with enormous capital and thousands of men with needed skills left the country. Meanwhile, the independent government recklessly increased public expenditures. Iturbide's expenses had been enormous, but under the Republic they increased sharply.

Everything that befell, or the government caused, was logical in its way. The pressures to expel *gachupines* were enormous, and it was a fate the Spanish brought on themselves. The pressures to expand the Mexican government were also irresistible, not just because the elite had no financial discipline, but because the army and the bureaucracy were the only means of social mobility and reward in this still utterly static society. Apodaca had begun the process of buying off rebellion with commissions, titles, and jobs. He had made a monster the republicans, liberal or conservative, were never able to exorcise.

This might still have been supportable if the Mexican elite had been able to institute programs to exploit the material and human resources of Mexico. But they did not have such programs on the drawing boards, let alone implement them. The purists' programs—destruction of Church property and privileges and land reform—even if carried out could not have solved the economic problem. The demands for social mobility and jobs coming from the office-oriented educated class kept the government under impossible pressures. The government had to try to meet all demands for employment, which was impossible fiscally. The Republic began with an impossible debt, seventy-six million pesos which it assumed honestly if unrealistically. Early budgets made things worse, because they vastly exceeded revenues.

The army was a major villain. There was an excuse for a large armed force, because Spain refused to recognize independence, still held San Juan de Ulua through 1825, and in 1829 landed troops on the Gulf coast. But army budgets exceeded anything required by the external situation. In 1823 the military budget of over nine million pesos was approximately twice *all* government revenues. In 1825 this was doubled, and although revenues rose, the military expenses were still approximately double all government income. These were not emergency budgets, for the ratios became permanent, peace or war. During sixteen of the first twenty-three years of independence, military appropriations exceeded total revenues. The eighteen commandant-generals, with their insatiable demands, were the root cause of the financial destruction of every administration that took power.

There was no remedy for military activism when legitimacy of government was destroyed and citizenless republics were made. Generals and a few armed men were the only organized, disciplined force in every Hispanic nation by 1830, from Spain to Mexico.

In Mexico the insurgency, the royalist reaction, and Iturbide's coup and Santa Anna's counter-coup subtly but totally ruined the military at the top. Loyalty and honor were destroyed; the men who now became high commanders were the very men who proved faithless and broke their oaths. *Every* general of the line of the Republican army had a background of advancement through treason. The officer corps had become political, and the governments of independent Mexico, liberal or conservative, only made it more so by passing out commissions wholesale to their friends.

The army had been brutalized by the eleven years of civil war. Commanders had grown accustomed to riding roughshod over civilians, looting towns and shooting prisoners out of hand. Many of the general officers of the Republic had carried out such practices on both sides. A soldier could only be tried in a military court. The colonels and generals were increasingly dangerous and troublesome people to have around, but no intellectual in the capital knew how to get rid of them. In fact, they were proliferating. Fully half the entire army consisted of officers; by 1838, there were one hundred and sixty generals of the line for some thirty thousand troops.

The vast appropriations largely went to bribe this officer corps. The line of the army deteriorated rapidly with independence. The ranks were now mostly filled with conscripted *indios*, some of whom had been inducted by press gangs. Neither the officers nor the ranks had any appetite for genuine war. In any sustained action, there was a tendency for officers to change sides, and for the privates to desert. Mexicans, *mestizos*, or *indios*, made excellent soldiers when properly led and trained, but now the only efficient body in the Mexican army was a small group of mercenary junior officers, many of whom were foreigners.

The army still might have provided no problem other than a constant financial drain, with very little to show for the money, if the government had been efficient enough to make certain it got paid. The army as such did not take over with Iturbide, the first Mexican pretorian; after Santa Anna helped declare a republic in 1823 it again stood aside. The basic problem was that the politicians petted and promoted it, then continually failed to find money to pay it. Bulnes arrived at the conclusion, demonstrated by fact, that the army usually began a *cuartelazo* or barracks revolt, deposing a government, only when the fiscal deficit reached twenty-five percent—which of course it did continually.

Guadalupe Victoria's administration compounded its financial ineptitude by borrowing abroad. The British had long dominated Spanish America's external trade, and with independence the English merchants understandably saw Mexican markets—if not the country itself—as theirs. Victoria was able to float more than thirty million pesos' worth of loans on the English financial market, though subject to severe interest rates and discounts. Typically, very little of this money reached the Mexican treasury. Much of it was spent on British arms—relics of the Napoleonic wars—and no real accounting was ever made. It added to an impossible burden, but this was one that had to be paid. As Mexicans were to learn, foreign debtors could not be put off so easily as domestic citizens, because they were backed by foreign governments with warships.

Meanwhile, British private capital began to flow into the country. The British especially invested in mines, and they put many of the richest back into production. Fortunes were made, but many were also lost, without dimming the luster of the eternal foreign concept of Mexico as El Dorado. London capital poured in heavily, along with French and German money, until this capital had largely replaced the former *gachupín* economic hegemony. Many Mexicans, as well as foreigners, believe the great foreign economic penetration of Mexico began with Porfirio Díaz. It was heaviest in the earlier years of the Republic; here began that fateful and fatal train of seeking loans and foreign capital that did Mexico no permanent good, taxed her people, poisoned her international relations, and eventually made the Mexicans xenophobes. Victoria, not Diáz, was the first Mexican ruler to become dependent on foreign capitalism, and he did it not to develop the nation but to pay his bureaucrats and army.

Mexico did have several quite superb, if uncharacteristic, men in this era who could see disasters looming on all fronts. They had that peculiar Hispanic-Mexican quality of being trained and good at cross disciplines; they were many-dimensional men in every respect. One such was the economist José Luis Mora, a *criollo* with an orderly, analytical mind. Mora became the theoretician for the purists. He was allied with Valentín Gómez Farías, a Creole doctor from provincial Zacatecas who combined medicine with liberal politics. Gómez Farías was a person of admirable but cold and theoretical integrity, a brilliant spokesman but a man who placed too much confidence in human nature. With these two was joined a third *puro* theoretician, the Mérida-born *mestizo* Lorenzo de Zavala, now governor of the central state of México, who was a Jacobin but a man with excellent vision who could see exactly the faults and fallacies of the *moderados*, if not his own. Characteristically, Zavala had more common sense and political ability but a little less integrity than the other two. These three, with great force among the literate community, pressed for serious reforms of the society and state.

What they achieved, however, was less a response from the more torpid moderates who held the seats and perquisites of power than a reaction from the briefly submerged conservatives. The conservative alliance had its own theoretician, the engineer-businessman-classic historian Lucas Alamán, a man who combined gentle manners, deep culture, and an unimpressive appearance with a romantic traditionalism and rigid authoritarianism. Alamán was a curious blend of a mind that held romantically to faded royalism and the moth-eaten glories of the Spanish Empire while expounding a sincere conviction in efficiency and imposed progress. If he had been born a great lord, he might have been another Metternich. As it was, he became the backroom intellectual who tried to use reactionary forces and cynical leaders to bring about his own vision of Hispanic civilization.

Collectively, the Moras, Zavalas, and Alamáns were beginning to polarize the *criollo* elite along newer, more rigid ideological lines. In this polarization there had to be some side-switching of the moderates. Nicolás Bravo was the first. In 1827, the vice-president staged an abortive coup in the name of conservatism, which was at once suppressed by the old warrior, now General Vicente Guerrero. Like Iturbide, Bravo was expelled, but unlike Iturbide, he had begun something that would not die.

In 1828 Victoria's term of office expired, and that plain, common-looking citizen who had somehow reached the presidency retired distinguished only by two accomplishments: he was one of few chief executives to serve out his term, and perhaps the only president who left office as poor as he entered it. A power struggle now developed between the *puros* and the *moderados* who were still the dominant faction. The *puros* put up Vicente Guerrero for president, while the moderates—now backed by the conservatives with whom they were merging, nominated an orator and scholar named Gómez Pedraza, former secretary of war in Victoria's cabinet.

Guerrero was *mestizo* and a popular hero; however, Gómez Pedraza controlled the army and through the generals he exerted severe pressure on the state legislatures which were instrumental in choosing the president. He was elected, with General Anastasio Bustamante, an unreconstructed royalist, as vice-president.

The Victoria administration had been elected by the congress, much like Washington in the United States' first presidential election. But subsequent national elections showed that the electoral process was unworkable in Mexico. Mexicans did not understand parliamentary systems, and to the Mexican mind election could not confer legitimacy. The parliamentary-elective political system that the intellectuals had foisted on Mexico was not quite the putting of a loaded pistol in the hands of children, as one historian called it, and it was not the cause of all the troubles, for Mexico could not have solved its problems with any politics. But it immediately became apparent that the electoral process only confirmed or ratified whichever faction already held or manipulated the government; it never revealed the wishes of a nonexistent citizenry. The elections were not honest, because almost no one believed in honest elections, whether liberal or conservative.

One man who sensed this political reality was General Santa Anna, who despite his enormous shortcomings seemed to have an instinctual grasp of the evil of his times and knew how to exploit them. Santa Anna was restive because he felt the *moderados* had not rewarded his services in deposing Iturbide. He understood that the election of Gómez Pedraza was unpopular, and out of the Iturbide episode he had a liberal reputation. In September 1828, Santa Anna dipped into the Pandora's box that Iturbide had revealed to the Mexican pretorians. He said the Republic was being converted into an Inquisition, and issued a pronunciamento in favor of Vicente Guerrero.

Guerrero and the purists, however, had decided reluctantly to accept the electoral verdict. And troops loyal to the government chased Santa Anna into refuge in an Oaxacan monastery. But then Gómez, not yet president but in control of the army, began to arrest leading *puros*, and his soldiers drove Lorenzo de Zavala, the legal governor of a state, from his office. Violence and rebellion quickly flared among the ardent liberals.

In December, Zavala suborned the garrison troops in the capital to his side. There were four days of bloody fighting in the city, during which the *léperos* ran wild and looted two million pesos' worth of goods from foreign merchants and businessmen. Although most of the provincial generals backed him, Gómez Pedraza suddenly fled the country. In steps of a process that were soon to become as ritualized as those of the bullring, Zavala and his friends marched through deserted and rubble-strewn streets to the presidential palace, where Victoria, legally still chief executive, sat alone, abandoned even by his servants. Congress now declared Guerrero the true president, and within a month the provinces acquiesced.

Meanwhile, Fernando VII of Spain, thinking the Mexican Republic was nearing its end, sent over a small invasion force in the summer of 1829. The king thought Mexicans would welcome the Spanish flag. The demonstration combined those elements of comic opera and tragic bloodiness that had become a feature of Hispanic politics. The Spanish military and naval commanders were personal enemies, and the Spanish flotilla put the army ashore at Tampico—a fever-ridden hole with no strategic value— and then abandoned it. His troops dying of the yellow fever, the Spanish commander at Tampico surrendered to Santa Anna, who had rushed to take command of this front by his own authorization. This "victory," assiduously promoted as a great national triumph, made a national military hero of Santa Anna.

Meanwhile, back at the capital, the Mexican leadership marched relentlessly onward toward disaster. The old guerrilla fighter Guerrero, invincible in his mountains, could not cope with the capital. He was ignorant of national and international affairs, and like Victoria, he hated the intellectuals upon whom he had to depend. He also hated the wealthy *criollos* and the bishops, who intimidated him. He vacillated, accepting incumbency in place of action. This presidency of a *mestizo* who could not speak good Spanish offended all the higher *criollos,* and as months passed and Guerrero was not able to give all the *criollo* purists the offices and salaries they thought they deserved, everyone turned against him. Zavala quit the cabinet in disgust. Then, in 1830, Vice-President Bustamante (who had been left in office as a sop to the powerful conservatives) organized and led a military coup.

The regular army seized the capital. Guerrero escaped back to his familiar haunts in the mountain range above Acapulco. Here, with an old follower, Juan Álvarez, he organized guerrillas. His enemies, however, had learned that treachery was the best means of disposing of guerrilleros. The ex-president was lured aboard a foreign ship at Acapulco, whose captain arrested him and turned him over to the Bustamante regime for fifty thousand pesos. After some argument in conservative circles—if his election was declared illegal, it also destroyed the legality of Bustamante's succession—he was declared mentally incompetent and afterward, quietly taken out and shot. Only after the memory of his presidency faded was Guerrero to be enshrined among the thirteen heros of Mexican independence.

The government was now an openly reactionary military dictatorship, whose backroom genius was Lucas Alamán. Alamán stiffened Bustamante into behaving like a Spanish king. Sessions of the congress were held with its hall surrounded by bayonets. Eleven of the state governors and their legislatures, all liberals, were deposed by the army. Alamán saw to it liberal newspapers were suppressed, and purist leaders driven into exile.

This pseudo-monarchy—the best Alamán could achieve—was coldly efficient. The banditry and wholesale evasion of customs that had grown up was checked. The treasury actually began to show a surplus. Alamán provided an orderly, efficient government, but his rationales and authoritarianism could not be stomached by many, above all in the outlying states, which were mostly dominated by liberal *mestizo* politicos. The strength of the government, and conservatism generally, lay in the capital. The so-called liberalism or federalism had its stronghold in the outer districts: Zacatecas, Durango, San Luis Potosí, and the sierras of Oaxaca and Guerrero. These provinces held fewer Creoles and vastly more *mestizo* rancheros and *licenciados*, and also less submissive *indios*—the last important, because they could fill the ranks of liberal armies.

Quite beyond the capital's control, the provinces were developing a local leadership. These leaders, who took the name *cacique*—chief—were exactly that—local political chieftains. They were almost all *mestizo*, like the ranchero Juan Álvarez, a true disciple of Morelos who from his small farm was actually the master of the great sprawling territory of Guerrero. These chiefs, some honest, some corrupt, were not democrats, and they usually rose without legal or constitutional sanction. But they rose from the emerging Mexican people, and it is not too much to state that most of them embodied the will and aspirations of that people. Their chieftainship was personal and autocratic—but it did embody what national consensus existed among the masses.

Like its leaders, this caciquism blended Spanish and native Amerindian outlooks and forms. From this time forward, various *caciques* remained in control of the rural areas, sometimes fighting the national government, sometimes at armed truce with it. The provincial leadership, though wise in the ways of rural, *mestizo-indio* Mexico, was ignorant in the ways of the greater world. Caciquism balanced the rule of the capital; it could not replace it.

Though Alamán gave the Bustamante regime efficiency, it was as corrupt generally as the old viceregal administrations that were its mentors.

Alamán balanced the budget through loans from *agiotistas*, wealthy persons who advanced short-term, high-interest money in return for the guaranties of government monopolies or customs, and who soon realized that they profited more from disorder than order. Their best friends were greedy generals. Thus generals and native capitalists, by milking the government, supported conservative regimes but destroyed them at the same time.

By 1832, General Santa Anna, now ensconced at Veracruz, pronounced against the corruption of government and seized the customs duties at the port. Santa Anna was now becoming a power in his own name and right. He was a good-looking, charismatic man, with no philosophy beyond a thirst for power, who was summed up by a brilliant contemporary as one of the worst men in the world, ambitious, greedy, and unprincipled, already grown rich in the "service" of his country, ever ready for greater adventures. He had enormous appeal. He knew how to stand for what seemed to be the dominant feeling of the times.

The officers Bustamante sent to extirpate Santa Anna at Veracruz, as usual in this age, had no taste for a real contest at arms; the various forces negotiated and skirmished. The highland troops began to die of fever in the lowland tropics, which Santa Anna had skillfully avoided by recruiting local, Afro-Amerindian-blooded soldiers. While this charade was carried out between the pretorians, the northern states, as usual, rose against the central government. By the end of 1832 Bustamante was disgusted, and he passed into exile. The conservatives faded. A jubilant liberal coalition brought Gómez Pedraza back to the palace—his "legal" term still had six months to run—but kept the *moderado* isolated while they sponsored new elections.

In the elections of 1832 Santa Anna, not surprisingly, was made president, and the purist spokesman Gómez Farías his vice-president, and old *puros* like Zavala were returned to office. In January 1833, Santa Anna confused everyone by an uncharacteristic act. He refused inauguration and turned the presidency over to Gómez Farías. This made him an overwhelmingly sympathetic hero with almost everyone, and it was noticeable that foreign observers and newspapers began to praise him as the one honest politician and general in Mexico. The real reason undoubtedly was neither lack of ambition nor modesty, but the fact that Santa Anna was not sure of the true strength of liberalism. He had the discipline and forbearance to hold his power and position while someone else tested the wind and water of the confused Mexican maelstrom.

Santa Anna's political instincts were excellent. Gómez Farías, the epitome of *puro* virtue, cold, honest, intellectual, with no grasp of practical politics or the true motivations of most Mexicans, immediately began to ram a radical purist program through congress. The new congress, rigged and cowed as all Mexican congresses were coming to be, enacted every law proposed. The reforms were especially directed at the Church, which the Hispanic liberals had seized on as their enduring enemy. The Church *was* the foe of all Hispanic liberalism, and reform was in order if modern processes were ever to succeed in Mexico. But the Gómez Farías type of reformer tended to be punitive and radical, intent upon destroying religion as well as the powers of the Church. In this society, where superstition and faith still had a greater hold on the people than in Europe, Gómez went too far, too soon.

He abolished compulsory tithes, the obsolete missions, and established secular public education, all needed reforms. But Gómez also forced through laws that permitted nuns and monks to renounce their vows, that suppressed the clerical University of Mexico, and that required all ecclesiastical appointments to be made by the state. Gómez wanted more than mere reform; he was determined to control or destroy the Church.

At the same time, he pushed through edicts that abolished the military privileges and reduced the size of the army. This was also needed—but both programs were assaults on two of the great power bases of the country.

The religious and military communities, and almost the entire upper class, were antagonized, along with a vast number of pious, nonpolitical people. Unfortunately for the liberals, cholera broke out while these laws were being enacted. The epidemic decimated the capital, while the priests kept churches open around the clock, praying for the frightened, soothing the bereaved, and pointing out the wrath of God had been drawn by an impious government on Mexico. Army officers found a new slogan, *religión y fueros*. Mutterings turned into meetings between clerics and generals.

Santa Anna, while not repudiating his protégé, the acting president, surprised and gratified the bishops by listening courteously to their grievances, and seeming to express sympathy.

Then, in April 1834, Santa Anna decided the time had come to save Mexico. He marched into the capital—he was still legal president—and removed Gómez Farías from office, proclaiming a "holy revolution." He assumed those "extraordinary powers" which even liberals had kept in the constitution. He abolished congress, ostentatiously locked the doors of the Hall of Sessions, and declared all the anticlerical legislation repealed by fiat. He was saluted by the army, with guns and marching bands, and bishops sang tearful Te Deums in his honor throughout the land.

However, the unruly northern frontier town of Zacatecas rebelled. Santa Anna, still with his cold sense of timing, rushed north with an army and crushed the revolt mercilessly, killing thousands. Gómez Farías, Mora, and Zavala fled the country. Zavala went to Texas and cast his lot with the Anglo-Saxon immigrants, seeing in them the only hope of establishing true republicanism in Mexico. He had despaired of his own people, and would not be forgiven by their future historians.

In one swoop, the liberals were destroyed as a national force for a generation, whether by Santa Anna's treachery or Gómez Farías' politics.

Santa Anna was a typical *caudillo* of his times, come too far, too fast. He now lost all sense of discipline and proportion, like Iturbide. Again, that vanity stimulated by a clinging, colonial sense of inferiority knew no bounds. Santa Anna as president began to design incredible uniforms for himself; he rode in gaudy coaches; he demanded near-regal honors and displayed complete irresponsibility. His private life became vulgar and corrupt. He had once been a good soldier, and could still conduct an energetic campaign. But with his fantastic uniforms, callous cruelty, crates of fighting cocks and hordes of passing whores, and his incredible blindness to anything but the superficial, he was a disastrous ruler.

He stood for nothing; he was traitorous to everything; his "holy revolution" may have saved the Church, but pampered two of the worst forces in the land, the army and the *agiotistas*. He issued twelve thousand new commissions, and he gave the treasury over to the *agiotistas* at an interest rate of four percent per month.

Although he shot any enemy who opposed him, he remained a popular hero for decades, surmounting failures that must have destroyed a leader in a more stable society. And in the course of this fantastic career, he almost destroyed his native land.

26

THE END OF EMPIRE

Whatever constitution governs Mexicans is the constitution the colonists of Texas must obey, and it makes no difference whatever what kind of principles form this constitution.
From a proclamation of General Martín Perfecto de Cós, Military Commandant of Coahuila-Texas, 1835.

Independent Mexico did not have time to determine esoteric questions of identity in the nineteenth century, because destiny was already being forced upon the nation, from the north. While the *criollo* consciousness looked backward to Spain and France for cultural inspiration or tried to create a mythology of Amerindian grandeur, the transcendental fact of Mexican national life was the nation's location upon the North American continent and its proximity to the United States. Unlike the Anglo-Saxon republic to the north, the *criollo* leadership did not perceive a purely American destiny until too late.

In 1821 the two independent nations, both infants but already territorial giants, met along the Sabine River between Louisiana and Texas. The differences between these countries and their societies, despite propinquity and a common colonial background, was as great as could exist within the framework of European civilization. Mexican society was backward technically and organizationally, racially differentiated and hybrid, and rigidly stratified. It had been static for centuries, although it was tearing itself to pieces at the top. The Mexican elite produced many brilliant men, but it was so divided, confused, and psychically sick that it could offer little national leadership. Because of insolvable problems, the whole society was sliding into decline.

The United States presented an enormous contrast. It was sprawling but at this time relatively homogeneous, egalitarian, and inherently dynamic. Its population was exploding while Mexico's remained stable. Its leadership tended to be unintellectual but keenly intelligent and pragmatic, possessed of superb strategic vision. The land hunger of its people and the vision of the leaders drew the nation westward across a rich continent then populated only by savage or barbaric Amerindian tribes; North Americans had already conceived of a magnificent *American* destiny, creating a powerful, secure new nation upon this continent.

The march west to the Pacific was a splendid cycle of cause and effect. The North Americans began to spill over the Appalachians, twenty thousand per year, while the British colonies were still struggling to gain independence. The colonists were people with a limited cultural tradition but with an overwhelming utilitarian ethic and instinct. The Mississippi became the western boundary of the United States in 1783 because thousands of hardy, armed, Anglo-Saxon frontiersmen were already in Kentucky and Tennessee. Because they were there, the North American leadership recognized that the United States eventually must control the mouth of the Mississippi. This was accomplished through Jefferson's vision and Napoleon's treachery to Spain. But again, once the United States had acquired the sprawling Louisiana Territory, it was clear that the republic would not be strategically secure upon its continent until it had expanded its boundaries to the Pacific and the deserts of northern Mexico. In the ensuing explosion westward, which went forward at an incredible pace—European and even American observers thought it would take the United States a thousand years to settle up to the Mississippi in 1783—the land hunger and pioneering spirit of generations of frontiersmen was part tool, part imperative.

If the westerners were going forward come what may, the record shows far more scrupulousness on the part of the North American governments toward seizing empire than was displayed by contemporary European nations. Considering the actual weakness of the Spanish Empire above the Rio Bravo, and by Jefferson's time North American explorations had revealed the Latin holdings from Santa Fé to San Antonio were a hollow shell, the United States accorded vast respect to the Spanish and succeeding Mexican flag. The United States was always prepared to purchase the western territories, from Florida to Texas to California. The fact that the purchases, where consummated, were always made with an expanding population already spilling into the desired lands, with the threat of their alienation in any case, caused vast resentment on the Hispanic mind, and profoundly affected Hispanic pride. Pride refused to alienate more territory, and fear also entered in, for between 1783 and 1820 the United States more than doubled its territory, all at the expense of lands the

Spanish Empire claimed. But Hispanic weakness made further severances inevitable.

The North Americans never quite understood this bitter Hispanic pride in appearances, or why Mexico, the inheritor of the Spanish North-American empire, refused to dispose of provinces it could not develop and apparently could never use.

The United States and Mexico in 1821 were natural rivals and inherent enemies both from culture and geography. The two nations were heirs of rival, deeply inimical Anglo-Saxon and Hispanic empires and value systems, and as impinging successor states they had to establish some hierarchy of power between themselves. The view that the United States abused a weaker Mexico ignores the fact that in the nature of things there could not be *two* dominant powers upon the continent. The resolving of the question need not have been more painful or dishonorable for Mexico than for the Canadians. British governments, themselves hostile to North American growth and power, acceded to reality. But the Mexican leadership could not accept reality, and in continuous failure heaped lasting humiliation upon all Mexican heads, for it could not make adjustments gracefully or peacefully.

The still-dominant Mexican view is of the United States as a scheming despoiler, first conniving to get Texas, then fighting a cynical war with a weaker power to seize all the lands between the Rio Grande and the Pacific. It is true that the United States always wanted these territories, but in the broadest sense there was never any plot against Mexico. Mexicans, like many others, were rarely able to distinguish between the often uncoordinated actions and statements of North American citizens and United States governments. The Mexican nation was forced by circumstance to engage in a competition for empire with the North Americans. That half of purported Mexico that lay above the Bravo may have flown the new tricolor, but it was a vacuum which the dominant people and power would eventually fill.

Once the United States stood secure upon the continent, reaching from ocean to ocean and ending any chance of foreign-power footholds, all North American fear and rivalry with Mexicans disappeared. North Americans carried few hatreds over; in fact, they had never hated the Mexicans, for it was hard to hate people they neither admired nor feared. Understandably, the losers in the contest did not so easily forget or forgive, not merely the physical injury of the separation of primitive territories beyond the real borders of historic Mexico, but the psychic damage all Mexicans suffered in the process.

Relations between the two powers were at first uneasy but correct. The Mexican leadership, liberal or conservative, had inherited an historic hatred of Anglo-Saxon marauders that went back to Drake, and the fact that the United States between 1800 and 1820 had doubled its national territory, all at the expense of the purported Hispanic world, disturbed the Mexican mind. The Mexican leadership, while either unable or unwilling to plunge into a genuine development of the northern territories—none of them were sufficiently populated or organized to be states—developed a fixation about the surrender or sale of any more "national territory." The feeling was perfectly patriotic and natural, and was based on very real fears. If the Anglo-Saxons acquired Texas, what was to stop them from peeling off Coahuila, and finally dismembering all Mexico?

The Mexican governments had legality completely on their side, because Washington had recognized Spanish sovereignty over Texas in the 1819 treaty fixing boundaries at the Sabine. Independent Mexico inherited this sovereignty, which the United States did not dispute. It was the Mexicans' option to sell or not to sell, to alienate or not to alienate. But the Mexican governments set too much store in the permanence of this treaty, not recognizing that in the ebb and flow of events in the real world, treaties are continually renegotiated according to changes in conditions, needs, and power.

Just before independence, the Spanish government had granted rights for North American colonists to enter Texas. This was not a new thing: Spain had allowed many immigrants from the United States to settle across the Mississippi in Spanish territory in Missouri in the last century. While the law demanded that these immigrants accept the only tolerated religion, Roman Catholicism, anticlerical Spanish officers winked at this, and one Spanish governor of Louisiana actually deported an inquisitor who tried to make trouble among the heterogeneous population of New Orleans. The Anglo-Saxons had made good citizens. They had played no part in the transfer of Louisiana to Napoleon, and his subsequent treachery in breaking his oath and selling it to the United States. Feeling secure in the 1819 treaty, and desperate to populate the wild, Indian-infested wastes, Spain was willing to experiment; there was hope that assimilated colonists would provide a buffer against their countrymen. This was an enlightened policy, and it might very well have worked—after all, the United States was to populate its own empty spaces with the help of millions of European immigrants.

The local military authorities in the north, most concerned with the eternal Indian problem, pressured the councils and civil authorities of New Spain into permitting North American immigration into Texas. Moses Austin, a former Spanish subject in the Missouri territory before its transfer to the United States, was granted a commission to settle Anglo-Saxon immigrants in east Texas. After his death, the concession was passed on to his son, Stephen F. Austin, who, however, had to lobby energetically at

México during the confusions of the rapidly changing governments between 1821–1824. The Austin grant was at last confirmed in 1824 by the new republican regime, and the way opened for similar grants to other North American concessionaires, or *empresarios*.

Rich lands in Texas were offered to colonists virtually free, since the nominal charge of a *medio real* (about six cents) per acre was usually waived by Austin. Every family head who proposed to raise livestock was allowed a square league, or 4,428 acres. At this time, the public lands of the United States were sold at $1.25 per acre. Men who brought in capital in the form of machinery or slaves were granted extra leagues, or *sitios*; some received more than 40,000 acres. All colonists were to be exempted from customs duties for seven years, and for ten years from all taxation. Under these circumstances, Austin immediately settled three hundred families, and thousands more North Americans soon poured in.

Several facts destroyed the hope of the original plan's success. One was that successive Mexican regimes, busy with coup and counter-coup, paid no attention to Texas. It might have been possible to assimilate Anglo-Saxon North American immigrants had they come into a truly Mexican country, but there were only three thousand Spanish-speaking inhabitants of Texas, almost all settled southwest of the Colorado and not even in contact with the immigrants. Therefore, the North Americans colonized. There were no Mexican schools and no Catholic churches to serve the North American enclaves, and no pressure whatever on the colonists to learn Mexican ways or the Spanish language. While every colonist swore to become Roman Catholic upon entry, it was pragmatically understood by Mexican officials who were Freemasons that this law would be ignored. The Mexican Church, denied the right to collect tithes from the immigrants, refused to send them priests—trammeled up in protecting property and privilege, the hierarchy had no interest in distant heretics.

The immigrants, while they became Mexican citizens under the Constitution of 1824, remained culturally and politically alien. Equally important, a thousand miles of wasteland separated Texas and the real Mexico, and trade and cultural ties remained strong with the nearby United States.

Within ten years the North American colonists outnumbered the old Mexican settlers ten to one. More important, they had felled more trees, cleared more farms, and built more houses and settlements than the Spanish had in Texas over three centuries. The more dynamic culture was overwhelming the static.

Stephen Austin, leader of the North American colonists, was a man of conscience, who understood the Mexican mind, and while he was not over-admiring of Mexicans he was loyal to the Republic. Most of the colonists were satisfied in a country that gave each family head four thousand acres

virtually free and collected no taxes. There were only two major irritations. Mexico had no trial by jury, which offended the colonists' sense of
justice, and justice and government were administered out of Coahuila, to
which the province was attached. Austin worked to overcome these irri-
tants with some success, and he and most settlers sincerely believed that
Texas was heading toward self-government as a Mexican state under the
1824 Constitution. While the colonists were not assimilating, they were
causing no trouble.

What made the Texas colony into a Trojan horse was a succession of
events and fears in Mexico. During the 1820s the Mexican governments
gradually became almost psychotically fearful of the intentions of the
United States government, poisoning relations with Austin's people.

Bermúdez Zozaya wrote from Washington that he was appalled at the
"haughtiness of these Republicans who see us not as equals but inferiors,
and who think that Washington will become the capital of all the Americas," and he predicted, "*They will be our enemies.*" Joel Poinsett, the
South Carolinian who was the first North American envoy to Mexico, was
sympathetic to the country, but saw it and his own as natural rivals. In
these ostensibly friendly relations there was contempt on each side. The
Hispanic contempt was rooted in cultural outlooks that went back to
Rome, and which saw the Northerners as cold, rude, insensible barbarians.
The contempt, however, was tinged with fear and rage at the barbarian
efficiency and material power. The Mexican attitude toward the United
States, therefore, was a dangerous combination of arrogance and fear.
The North Americans were appalled by the inexplicable inability of the
Latins to achieve self-discipline and viable democratic government, and
they were exasperated at the continuing difficulty of doing business with
them. Their attitude stemmed from exasperation but was suffused with
confidence—also for Mexicans a dangerous combination.

Unlike Austin, who knew that the Hispanic mind would accept many
defeats and compromises but only if appearances were observed, Poinsett
broached the possible purchase of Texas in 1825 in a well-meaning public
speech to the Mexican Congress. He was expressing only the honest desire
of his government to buy Texas, but the Byzantine minds at the capital,
trained on plots and counterplots, were thunderstruck. No Mexican government could publicly undertake the alienation of territory, and many
prominent Mexicans concluded that Poinsett was either trying to unseat
the government, or revealing the commencement of an aggressive policy.

Poinsett found himself antipathetic to the conservatives, then in power,
who were both culturally more hostile to the northerners than liberals, and
more intransigent toward selling national territory. Poinsett therefore cultivated the liberals, introducing the York Rite into the country to give the

liberals a Masonic club to offset the highly popular Scottish Rite lodges, which had become conservative strongholds. But he could not really cross the cultural gulf between his rough, pragmatic culture and the liberal gentlemen who proudly wore French ideas and clothes, and who, if they had to deal with barbarians, preferred the suaver English. Furthermore, the British minister, Ward, was quite effective in poisoning official Mexico toward Poinsett and the United States. The English at this period resented any possible North American expansion of influence, hoping to keep the Caribbean and Mexico as their own economic preserve. To Poinsett's disappointment, the liberals he befriended proved as emotionally intransigent as the conservatives on the question of selling Texas. Finally, Poinsett became persona non grata and went home, to be remembered mainly by the *flor de nochebuena* which he took back and renamed the poinsettia.

Influenced by Ward's subtle hints, most leading Mexicans now began to see the North American colony in Texas as a potential Trojan horse in the service of the United States. Ward privately informed his government that the Mexicans spent far too much time worrying about plots in Washington and far too little actually governing Texas, and that when they finally got around to regulating the province, they would find these frontiersmen hard to handle—His Majesty's Government had had some experience with that.

Sparked by fears at the capital and Ward's suggestions, in 1828 the government sent General Manuel Mier y Terán, the old insurgent idealist and possibly the most honest man in Mexico, to inspect Texas. What Mier y Terán saw frightened and discouraged him. The North Americans were taking over the province with their energy and industry, and the contrast between them and the native Mexicans was appalling. The colonists were even organizing their own schools. Mier recommended that the colonization be halted at once. His alternatives, however, were exotic schemes involving the settlement of convicts and the importation of European Catholics. Mexican citizens in fact were offered colonization opportunities on better terms than the North Americans, but the elite was not interested in the hinterlands, and the poor could not move because of circumstance. The government had no money to subsidize except with grants of raw land, which required energy, expertise, and some capital to develop. Austin's colonists were not illiterate backwoodsmen; only three of his first three hundred settlers lacked education. Many of them arrived with tools, machinery, and Negro slaves. Rough and ready as these people appeared, there was no equivalent class in Mexico.

In 1829 the Guerrero government tried to discourage the colony in a roundabout way, by abolishing slavery in Mexican territory. Since chattel slavery (peonage was not affected) existed only in Texas, this was obviously aimed against the North American colonists. But, like so many other decrees from the capital, this one could not be enforced on the frontier.

Then, in early 1830, Alamán, who had come to power as foreign minister under Bustamante, pushed through much more sweeping laws. Alamán was deeply patriotic and hoped for a restoration of the old Hispanic empire; to him the colonists were a present danger even without the machinations of the United States, because they were all heretics and natural federalists.

The decrees of 1830 halted further colonization, reimposed customs duties, and provided General Mier y Terán with soldiers to enforce complete compliance with the new authoritarian regime.

The effect on Texas was predictable. The colony did not and could not trade with distant Mexico, and it was now effectively cut off from New Orleans by high tariffs. The laws were evaded by smuggling both goods and new immigrants. The army which was sent to enforce the laws was a disaster of another kind. Here, the first real, inevitable culture clash began. The Mexican garrisons, fortified by the military privilege and accustomed to dominating civilians, treated the Texan colonists like the people of Mexican military districts. Army officers arrested civilians without warrants and held them in prison without charges or bail, and grafted on the side. The colonists, who believed they had left none of their inalienable rights behind when they crossed the Sabine to become citizens of Mexico, were soon ready to rebel. A revolt broke out in 1832, which might have led to the Texans being crushed by the army that was sent against them, but Austin adroitly convinced Mexican authorities that this uprising was a demonstration for Santa Anna—who just now was proclaiming liberalism in Mexico. A Mexican general inspected Texas, found the people everywhere cheering for Santa Anna (believing he stood for the overthrow of Bustamante and his laws) and withdrew the soldiers stationed there to join the current *cuartelazo* at home.

During the convulsions that wracked Mexico over the next two years, Texas lived in a political vacuum, in which disrespect for Mexican government grew swiftly. The older colonists were still loyal; they had profited before 1830. The newer arrivals were unsatisfied, and more and more were imbued with the idea of joining Texas to the United States. Some of these men, like Sam Houston of Tennessee, were probably unofficial agents of President Jackson, whose vision saw an American nation reaching the Pacific. If they were part of a plot, the Mexican regimes that now came and went made things vastly easier for them.

Believing that the liberal provisions of the Mexican Constitution of 1824, assuring statehood to deserving territories, were to be enforced, the North Americans began something no Mexican official, liberal or conservative, could understand or accept: they took the political initiative. They peacefully organized a political convention, passed resolutions, and sent

Stephen F. Austin to Mexico with petitions for statehood, and for repeal of the discriminatory decrees of 1830.

Austin, who had moved easily in capital society ten years earlier, found things incomprehensibly changed in 1834. All Mexicans, except for a few radicals like Zavala, had become hostile to the *norteamericanos*; the liberals, who ruled by decree the same as conservatives, though they did enact different decrees, were as suspicious of political initiatives as royalists. The North American resolutions and petitions looked exactly like pronunciamentos and plans, and the next step, obviously, was a colonist rebellion. Mexicans who knew better were not able to overcome their natural antipathies and their fear of United States aggrandizement. President Gómez received Austin so coldly that he was thrown into despair, and when the president intercepted a letter from Austin urging the Texans to proceed with the establishment of a state legislature without the sanction of the central government—the way it was done in the territories of the United States in those years—he was thrown into the prison of the Inquisition. He was held here without formal charges, without bail, and without trial, for eighteen months. Then, unexpectedly, he was released along with a horde of various felons in a general amnesty declared when Santa Anna assumed dictatorial powers; since Hidalgo, a feature of every Mexican revolution was to clear the jails. Austin returned to Texas, his health ruined and his loyalties as a Mexican citizen irreparably damaged. He found the Texans ready to fight.

Mexican liberals and conservatives, together, had raised exactly the kind of monster both feared.

Santa Anna, who moved energetically to destroy liberalism everywhere in Mexico, sent his brother-in-law General Cós to Texas with an army. Cós, with perfect logic as he saw it, told the colonists that no matter what kind of constitution Mexico had, they were bound as Mexican citizens to live by it. Santa Anna was repressing revolt at Zacatecas with great brutality. In 1835 the lives of dissidents of any kind were forfeit. Lorenzo de Zavala and the other *puros* had to flee to escape the firing squad. Zavala, believing that the Texans held the last hope for the liberties the dictator was extinguishing, rode to Texas and encouraged resistance to the central government. He joined the *norteamericano* rebels, who began their revolt with the rationale of reestablishing the Constitution of 1824, helped the colonists form an independent government, but died in despair soon after becoming the Republic of Texas' first vice-president.

In this terrible time of dissolution and despair among liberals the actions of Mier y Terán, the last idealist, were less traitorous in Mexican eyes but equally significant. Unable to stomach either the North Americans or Santa Anna, he killed himself.

The campaigns which followed were to become part of North American legend. But what was North American glory as the Texans defended their rights as free men, as they saw it, began a bitter trauma of national humiliation for all Mexicans. Cós was driven out of San Antonio in December 1835 by a horde of armed farmers. Santa Anna, finished with Zacatecas, rushed north across the Coahuilan deserts, killing men and horses and leaving his heavy artillery behind. Arriving in Texas in early 1836, he took the rebels by surprise.

Most of the militia had returned home, believing the war over.

One of Santa Anna's columns, under General Urrea surrounded some adventurers bound on an ill-considered raid of Matamoros, a Tamaulipas border town. These poorly-led men, all volunteers newly arrived from the United States, were no match for Mexican lancers on the open savannahs near Goliad. They surrendered. They were then massacred on Palm Sunday by Santa Anna's express order.

This was legal murder: the prisoners were not members of the armed forces of any nation; they were in fact armed pirates on Mexican soil, and they had surrendered "at discretion"—not, however, believing they would be shot. Urrea and his officers were appalled at the president-dictator's orders, and some of them, along with several Mexican women at Goliad, rescued a few of the captives at the risk of their own lives. Opponents taken in arms had been stood against walls in Mexico since the Insurgency in which Santa Anna was trained, but the slaughter of some four hundred North American adventurers at Goliad destroyed Santa Anna's international reputation as no execution of Mexicans could have done.

Meanwhile, Santa Anna and his main force invested San Antonio, in February 1836. With a force of several brigades but armed only with light field guns, Santa Anna wasted thirteen days reducing an old mission complex, now known as the Alamo, defended by less than two hundred North Americans. The fortress had to be taken by storm, because the defenders chose to die to the last man. Santa Anna again declared no quarter, but in dying the men in the Alamo inflicted ruinous casualties on the dictator's army.

Santa Anna was waging a war of terror; his campaign was planned to extirpate the North American presence in Texas. Years afterward, however, he was still trying to explain his acts, because he failed disastrously.

His terror campaign sent the North American population fleeing toward the Sabine, while the colonist government which declared independence on March 2, 1836, took refuge on an island. But then Santa Anna, contemptuous of his foes, moved recklessly into east Texas with divided columns. Here Sam Houston, a canny natural general, allowed the small Texan army to be "trapped" between Buffalo Bayou and the San Jacinto. Overconfident and lethargic, Santa Anna was sleeping when his column was attacked and overrun by Houston's forces on April 21. Within twenty minutes, the Texan army, composed mostly of colonists defending their homes, bloodily avenged the slaughters at Goliad and the Alamo. Santa Anna, who tried to escape dressed as a common soldier, was taken prisoner.

The dictator had covered Mexican arms with no glory in Texas; now, he added disgrace, by placing his own safety before the honor of his country. He bargained with Houston, ordering the other Mexican columns to retire below the Rio Bravo, and signing a convention by which he agreed to commit the Supreme Government to recognize Texan independence.

The victory at the San Jacinto was peculiarly decisive, because the other generals lacked initiative, and also, the whole Mexican army, confronted with a burnt-out country, was in logistical difficulty. Santa Anna had not prepared for an extended campaign. Some parts of his army had started to retreat even before Santa Anna's defeat; all of it arrived ragged and hungry south of the Rio Bravo.

Once he had squeezed all the advantage he could from Santa Anna, Houston sent him home by way of Washington. Disgraced, he retired to his hacienda at Jalapa. His agreements with Houston meant nothing, because the conservative congress at the capital immediately repudiated them, asserting continued Mexican sovereignty over Texas. However, the ruling conservatives were too fragmented and too involved in local power struggles to reassert Mexican sovereignty in the only practical way, by dispatching new armies. Houston's army of a thousand men melted away as the colonist militia returned to their farms, but the victory at the San Jacinto was allowed to stand.

Congress instead devoted itself to extirpating liberalism, by issuing a new centralist constitution taking away the powers and liberties of the states and requiring property qualifications for voting. The true state of the nation is revealed by the fact that no one, not even an ambitious general, wanted to take the presidency or march against the Texans. Finally, the congress called Anastasio Bustamante, the old royalist, back from exile to take the office.

In these crucial months the United States government had held itself aloof from the Texas revolution. President Jackson wanted Texas, but considerations at home and abroad kept him from annexing it despite offers from the newly-independent republic. Jackson had to respect the United States-Mexican treaty, and Texas had become an issue in the North-South slavery controversy that was starting to tear the United States apart. Most Texans expected annexation, but the new nation was forced to go it alone. If there was a North American plot to seize Texas in 1836, there was little evidence. Thousands of United States citizens supported the

Texan rebellion and most rejoiced in its success, but these were private acts.

The Republic of Texas lasted for ten years. It was hardly a viable nation, despite the fact that it claimed huge territories; it remained a small North American enclave on the upper Gulf coast, underpopulated, bankrupt, and disorganized. Yet, the colonists began at once to create an effective government, and Sam Houston, the president, worked tirelessly to bring about annexation by the United States, although his successor, Mirabeau Bonaparte Lamar, dreamed of making Texas an empire and kept the republic in continual conflict with Mexico.

Texas remained independent, not because the United States protected it for ten years, but because Mexicans of this era did not truly believe in an imperial destiny above the Rio Bravo and had no effective leadership. A struggling little enclave of thirty thousand immigrants separated Texas from Mexico because Mexico was still a sprawling territory that contained seven million inhabitants without any developed sense of nationhood. A united nation under a powerful leadership could have avenged San Jacinto within months.

Here, every Mexican patriot began to eat the bitter bread of national doubt and humiliation, and the urge to find excuses in North American plots and the myth of overwhelming Nordic numbers was irresistible. Mexico had failed as an empire, and the first failure prevented Mexico from effectively challenging the United States' role upon the continent. Although Mexico was still building toward nationhood, the failure was damaging to Hispanic pride and created a national trauma that would not die.

27

THE DEATH OF HONOR

*Mexicans! We have brought this tragic misfortune on ourselves
by our endless disputes.*

From a proclamation of General Santa Anna.

After 1836 the *criollo* elite that ruled Mexico had grown older but scarcely
wiser. General Bustamante was honest enough, and his intentions were
good, but as before, and like so many of the military heros who became
presidents of Mexico, he was led and directed by subtler and stronger
persons who did not themselves want responsibility. The centralist republic
worked no better than the former federalist one. The problem was not the
constitution but the people involved. The *criollos*, as a class, were still
overcome with indolence and ennui; nothing could spark them into sustained activity. They put off everything until tomorrow, and flights of fancy
convinced them that tomorrow could be put off forever. They grew increasingly more past-oriented. Nostalgically, many *criollos* now regretted
the separation from the crown.

And since independence, Mexico seemingly had gone backward. Since
1810 no churches or palaces had been built, and the arts and sciences
stimulated by the Bourbons had fallen into decay. The intellectual elites
were too much absorbed in futile politics, which destroyed them. By 1840
Mexico was a less civilized country than it had been. For a generation,
Mexico had fed off material and intellectual capital stored up under the
crown, without replenishing either.

Many of the better men, vitally needed in a postcolonial society whatever their politics, emigrated or were exiled after independence. Thousands
of skilled Spaniards who were never involved in any controversy were

driven out by a xenophobia that was particularly powerful among *mestizo* liberals. So many wealthy families left the country after 1821 that they took about two-thirds of Mexico's liquid capital. Other families retired to Europe but held onto their estates. This added more evil to an already wasteful tenure system, as revenues went abroad and haciendas were mismanaged by corrupt agents.

The emotional determination of *mestizos* and *criollos* to be masters in their own house was completely understandable, but economically and technically, this was not yet possible. Mexico lacked a native scientific and mercantile class of any significance. The departing Spaniards were not replaced by Mexicans, but by other foreigners. English and German engineers, hired by British companies, bought up, pumped out, and extracted the profits of the silver mines. After independence, silver flowed out of the country exactly as before. Trade went into the hands of foreigners by default. This kind of development need not have been fatal had Mexico provided a stable society and government which could have integrated modern business and industrial systems as in Germany. But Mexico, in the first generation of independence was passing from one kind of colonialism into another.

A process was starting that was to sour Mexico's foreign relations and poison the minds of Mexicans against foreigners for a century. Governments were dependent on outside expertise and capital and were forced to open the country to foreign investment. Meanwhile, disorder and revolutions, for which Mexico was now a byword, destroyed foreign-owned property. As claims were uncollectable in Mexican courts, the foreign investors increasingly looked for help from their own governments. Mexicans were beginning to learn that a nation that could not keep internal order faced threats against its sovereignty.

In 1838 a French fleet appeared off Veracruz to collect some six hundred thousand pesos in damages claimed by French citizens from the riots in the capital in 1828. One of the claims was filed by a pastrycook whose place of business had been wrecked by drunken army officers. This claim, like many others, was exaggerated, and Mexicans sarcastically dubbed the ensuing episode the Pastry War. The French demands for reparation were arrogant—but on the other hand, Mexican governments never attempted to satisfy even the legitimate claims of foreigners unless pressure was brought. All such episodes added to the national feeling of humiliation, because the nation could not prevent the disorder and damages, and while it tried to stand on its sovereignty, Mexico was too weak to prevent forcible collections.

The French warships shelled the fortress island of San Juan de Ulua, whose pirate-proof walls now failed to withstand nineteenth-century gunnery. The French seized San Juan and blockaded the crucial port of Veracruz. Mexico declared war. However, the only action stemming from the declaration was a capital riot against foreigners, in which the *lépero* mobs shouted the curious slogans: "*¡Mueran los judíos! ¡Mueran los sajones!*"— ("Death to the Anglo-Saxons and Jews!")

The crisis again brought the retired Santa Anna into prominence. Leaving his estate and acting with that utter independence and insouciance which in fact most Mexicans admired, he took command of the Mexican forces at Veracruz and led them, without authority, against French raiding parties. He gained nothing and lost a leg to a French cannon ball. However, he wrote florid dispatches claiming victory, calling attention to his wound, and adding that he would die happy, having sacrificed his blood for his country. Overnight, he again became a national hero to a people easily swayed by splendid rhetoric—while Bustamante, in charge and in despair, was forced to buy off the invaders by a guarantee of six hundred thousand pesos from the customs.

This piled Pelion upon the Ossa of the already unmanageable deficit.

The chronic fiscal problem, which caused countless *cuartelazos*, or barracks revolts, among unpaid soldiers, was now beginning to threaten the territorial integrity of the Republic. The theoretically highly centralized conservative regime was unpopular in the outlying states and territories, and it lacked the money to enforce its authority on them. There was never an effective government or military force despite immense appropriations. Mexico began to face a threat of dismemberment.

The vision of the Creole elite rarely extended beyond the capital and the caste-ridden central states, the great Spanish-*criollo* cities of Puebla, Guadalajara, and Morelia-Valladolid, and the fingers of civilization that ran up the eastern cordillera into Tamaulipas and Nuevo León. This Mexico, with its stratified society, baroque churches, vast haciendas, and European elites ruling a mass of *indios* was the conservatives' country. The outer, rough and ready, *mestizo*-dominated frontier regions were seen as barbaric places ruled by upstarts. The capital elite despised the type of lawyer, bureaucrat, and ranchero that assumed leadership in the outer states, a feeling that was reciprocated. The capital could not provide national leadership to the outer states. The quarrel took liberal-conservative, centralist-federalist ideological trappings, but fundamentally it revolved around what kind of Mexican nation, *criollo-indio* or *mestizo*, was to emerge. In the meantime, it prevented any sort of nation from emerging.

After the secession of Texas the prestige of the nation was so low that France and England recognized the Lone Star Republic, and large parts of the north seemed ready to break away, also. In effect, the Pacific areas from Nayarit to upper California were already independent and only remained in Mexico because there was nothing to pull them away. The southern state of Guerrero was ruled by a guerrillero *cacique*. Communications were tenuous with Nuevo México, and existed only because of the trade route that ran from St. Louis to Chihuahua through Santa Fé. The true situation in the northern tier of states in the late 1830s was that the local leadership, whether elected governors or military chiefs, was emotionally separating from the capital. And Yucatán in the far south seceded, its federalist state government allying itself with the rebels in Texas. By 1839, a small Texas navy operated against Mexican shipping out of Yucatán.

Observers believed the Republic of Mexico was disintegrating, and it was widely thought by Europeans that most of the north would eventually be absorbed into the United States. While their various Excellencies at the capital still spoke proudly of Mexican grandeur and beheld the immense Mexican map with satisfaction, most of the Mexican intelligentsia were beginning to despair of national survival.

The mood of despair and national ineffectiveness brought on a new cycle of pretorianism, as the soldiers, sometimes cynically but often idealistically, tried to save the nation. In 1840 General Urrea joined Gómez Farías, returning from exile at New Orleans, in a federalist pronunciamento. The rebels seized Bustamante in his bed and fortified the presidential palace. The government garrison, however, retired to the Ciudadela, the military headquarters in a capital suburb; Bustamante escaped and took command of these forces. Eleven days of cannon and propaganda bombardments ensued between the rebels and presidential troops.

The generals in the nearby states wanted nothing to do with Gómez Farías, but they did not move to support the president. The stalemate was broken by Santa Anna, who rushed in from Veracruz offering to mediate. This news unnerved Gómez Farías and Urrea. Bustamante, in a ritual that was now becoming as established as the pronunciamento and *cuartelazo*, offered the rebels safe-conduct out of the country. The failed revolutionaries chose exile, from which they, in a pattern also becoming customary, kept in close touch with supporters in Mexico. In the fighting few soldiers had been killed, but a great many hapless civilians had been mowed down in the cross fire.

The generals now decided that although Bustamante was one of them, he was ineffective, especially in meeting military pay demands. Most of these generals were men without military honor in the fundamental sense —although they would have had any civilian shot who made the accusation. All of them had reached their posts by the politics of betrayal; their oaths to any regime were worthless; they were loyal only to whatever leader fortune seemed to favor. As fortune seemed to desert Bustamante, his alcoholic but trusted chief of staff, Gabriel Valencia—who had declared Bustamante's rout of the rebels comparable to God's six-day creation of the world—conspired with General Paredes at Guadalajara and

Santa Anna against him. General Valencia, backed by these two, issued a pronunciamento against the government at the capital, and turned the guns of the Ciudadela against the presidential palace.

But now there was bloody fighting, since many of the junior officers observed their oaths and stood by the president. Two rival military factions battled along a line that almost evenly bisected the capital. The artillery exchanges destroyed palaces and houses and killed hundreds of civilians.

This divided army, however, was not prepared to destroy itself in fraternal warfare. The two forces faced each other in what was to become famous as a "Mexican stand-off," threatening and parleying, until Santa Anna and Paredes arrived with many conscripted *indio* soldiers to reinforce Valencia. The trio now issued the Plan of Tacubaya which called for Santa Anna to assume power. When it became obvious that Santa Anna had the superior forces, the pretorians defending the president agreed to a capitulation with "honors" on all sides.

Bustamante himself finally emerged without honor, because he tried the ultimate treason in an effort to remain president, by declaring himself a liberal and promising to restore the Constitution of 1824. The liberals did not rise to the bait, and Bustamante, by agreement, departed again in exile.

Santa Anna rode into the capital behind four white horses, intoxicated with triumph. But he had learned some finesse. When new elections returned a predominantly moderate congress, he turned to Nicolás Bravo, who like so many of the old insurgents was now a complete reactionary. Bravo turned out the congress and supervised the redrawing of the constitution by a junta in 1843. The new document gave the president supreme powers, and Santa Anna then graciously accepted the office.

Believing himself secure, Santa Anna was even more reckless and prodigal in his second dictatorship. Styling himself the "Napoleon of the West," he erected a heroic statue of himself, with its arm pointing north to Texas, in the great plaza. He dedicated a theater to his personal glory. He had his amputated leg removed from its burial place on his hacienda and reinterred it in the cathedral with full military honors. He mourned the death of his wife with a procession of twenty thousand marchers led by the archbishop. He affected the simple clothing and melancholy manner of Napoleon, and to intensify the effect, made his generals wear brilliant, scarlet uniforms in his presence. At formal occasions six full colonels attended his chair.

He made thousands of new officers without giving them duties, and he made military contractors rich. He spent huge sums on parades, fiestas, and cannonades to cheer the populace. He paid for all this extravagance by extracting loans from his friends, raising customs duties to nearly sixty percent, levying taxes on windows, and selling more mining concessions to the British. He thus doubled revenues.

He also doubled expenses, while the revenue measures were ephemeral and self-defeating. Mexicans boarded up their windows and took to smuggling as the supply of saleable concessions ran out. With that irrepressible, cynical sarcasm that so often is the sole refuge of an oppressed people, Mexicans began to refer to the dictator as "His Immortal Three Quarters," to suggest that Santa Anna's statue really pointed to the mint, not Texas, and to deride his new marriage to a fifteen-year-old girl obscenely. When one of the parade of whores who passed through his chambers stole his decorations, society roared.

By 1844 even Santa Anna's genius could find no more money. While the civil bureaucracy was paid in worthless warrants, the generals again were not so simply put off. General Mariano Paredes pronounced against the man he had helped make president. As a soldier Paredes was a drunken incompetent, but the capital mobs now turned against Santa Anna. Gómez Pedraza and the moderates who had been turned out of government seized the palace and proclaimed General José Joaquín de Herrera, an honest but ingenuous officer, president. The fickle *léperos* who had cheered Santa Anna's triumphal entry toppled his images and took his leg from its marble tomb and threw it into the open sewers. Santa Anna fled to Havana, enjoined from returning for ten years.

Herrera faced all the old problems, and a new one that was becoming acute: Texas and the United States. The "war" with Texas had dragged on ten years. A grandiose but harebrained scheme of the Texas President Lamar to seize Santa Fé ended in the surrender of the North Americans in New Mexico without a fight. The prisoners were marched deep into Mexico, treated brutally, and finally released through efforts of the United States minister. Another Texan column invaded northern Mexico, but also was captured; Santa Anna had ordered this band decimated—one in ten chosen by drawing black or white beans from a jar, and shot. This was a traditional Hispanic-Latin method of punishment, and under Mexican law the raiders were pirates, but the act aroused indignation both in Texas and the United States.

The Mexican army made two incursions into Texas in 1842, twice capturing San Antonio. These raids and counter-raids made a settlement of the Texas question difficult.

Herrera was a sensible man. He knew Texas was lost, but hoped to prevent its annexation by the United States, fearing that this would be a first step toward the loss of all the northern provinces. The United States government had delayed annexation because of protest from the northern states against the addition of new slaveholding territories to the Union. Herrera wanted to keep an independent Texas as a buffer, but he was too fearful of appearances to recognize Texan independence. Most literate Mexicans considered the loss of Texas a blot on the national honor and had an almost irrational bloc against admitting the fact. They forced Herrera to move slowly, while time ran out.

James K. Polk, from Tennessee, sought the presidency with only one goal: to gain Texas, and if possible, California. He was an intentional one-term president who was quite willing to fight a war of policy if North American strategic interests could be served no other way. Polk, and an increasing number of his countrymen had become concerned with the British, who were working actively to make an arrangement with Texas to bar the United States from the Pacific, establishing a British center of influence in the west. Sam Houston, once again president of Texas and still an ardent believer in annexation, played skillfully on these fears in Washington, just as the Mexican ambassador, Almonte, tried to stir up animosity in New England against the entry of a new slave state. Early in 1845, after Polk's election, the congress' strategic vision overcame domestic quarrels, and a bill of annexation passed, angering the British government and horrifying the Mexicans.

Herrera's offer to recognize Texan independence, provided there was no annexation, came too late. He was now in a trap of Mexicans' own making. Every regime since 1836 had stated that North American annexation of Texas meant war between Mexico and the United States. Almonte asked for his credentials without waiting for instructions from his government. Mexican newspapers and politicians of all political coloration denounced the act in flaming rhetoric, warning that the United States would be severely punished. Most Mexican officials knew otherwise, but they still hoped for massive malfeasance on the part of New England if there were a war, and also for help from Great Britain. Herrera, fearful that war might destroy his country, was bound by Mexican emotion, which insisted that Mexican honor be vindicated.

He was, however, prepared to accept the inevitable annexation, provided national pride could be salved. The final loss of Texas must be made not to appear a Mexican defeat. To hold power, and to save Mexico, as he saw things, he desperately needed to preserve appearances.

Polk, a backwoods lawyer, was blunt, strong-willed, and unimaginative. He understood no other culture but his own, and he could not comprehend the enormous Hispanic regard for appearances that had kept men sitting facing each other in coaches for days in a Mexican alley until a formula could be found for each to withdraw with honor, and he would have been contemptuous of such things had he understood them. But he did believe in equity; he intended to offer Mexico the best deal it could expect under the circumstances.

Mexico owed the United States a large debt, ratified by international arbitration, but in default. There was also a serious question as to the boundary between Mexico and Texas, which now meant between Mexico and the United States. Texas extravagantly claimed the Rio Grande (as North Americans called the Rio Bravo) as the frontier; however, the Nueces, about 125 miles to the north, had been the accepted Spanish boundary between Texas and Tamaulipas. The Nueces, a short, winding, tenuous stream, made for a poor international line, while the Rio Grande was a clearer delineator, reaching from the Gulf to El Paso del Norte in the west. As the boundary, it would give the United States more, though unpopulated, territory. Polk was prepared to buy this extra territory through assuming the Mexican debt, a fair price at the time. He also wanted to negotiate the purchase of California, which the Mexican government did not fully control, but for which he was ready to pay a high price. It probably did not occur to Polk or his Democrats that the very offer would be taken as an insult by many Mexicans.

Their reaction was that of a new nation, unsure of itself in an unsatisfactory world, whose people were torn between arrogance and fear. A Stephen Austin, Spanish-speaking and fully aware of all the nuances in the Mexican capital, might have brought this off, getting the territory but also allowing Herrera to seem to be the victor. Polk's people wanted to be fair, but were impatient with pampering Mexican sensibilities.

Despite enormous domestic criticism, Herrera informed Polk that he would accept a commissioner to discuss the problems. This was a concession, since diplomatic relations had been broken over the annexation act. Herrera intended to carry on communications outside of formal channels. Polk saw this as nonsense. He sent a minister, John Slidell, who was instructed to regard the annexation as past history and to get on with the important matters, such as the boundary and California.

Slidell, also oblivious to Mexican sensibilities, arrived to do business, not indulge in face-saving games, and when President Herrera almost tearfully begged him not to present his credentials, he persisted in demanding full diplomatic recognition. This doomed the Herrera government.

The conservatives behind Lucas Alamán had grown more and more monarchist during the pretorian anarchy, now believing that only a European prince on a Mexican throne could restore legitimacy to government and restore Mexico's respect among the other nations. They wanted to destroy Herrera's moderate liberal regime. The conservatives therefore led an attack on Herrera, accusing him of selling out the national soil and honor, arousing vast hostility against him among almost all *criollos*. General Mariano Paredes was persuaded to pronounce against the government, and he was supplied with one million pesos in coin by the clergy. Herrera, vilified by everyone, fled the capital in early 1846.

Slidell then tried to present his credentials to Paredes, who contemptuously returned his passports. Furious, Slidell rode to Veracruz and fired off a letter to Washington, saying "Nothing is to be done with these people

until they have been chastised." Just as the mention of past-due debt:
infuriated Mexicans, the refusal to talk business coldly angered the North
American president. He resolved to provoke war to achieve his goals.

The presidency did not yet possess the powers to engage the United
States in a major conflict by executive action; however, Polk skillfully
arranged a confrontation. He sent Zachary Taylor, a superannuated, dila
tory, but rough and courageous Indian-fighter from the Nueces to the
mouth of the Rio Grande. Here Taylor landed a small army and built a for
on the Rio Grande across from Matamoros. His soldiers daily raised the
Stars and Stripes with fife and drum in full view of the Mexican land
owners who held title to the north bank. Mexican cavalry under Genera
Mariano Arista and U.S. dragoons were now patrolling the same disputed
territory, and inevitably, they clashed, in April 1846.

When the news reached Washington, Polk told congress that "American
blood had been shed on American soil." He had his war.

A sour memory still surrounds what North Americans called the Mexi
can War and the Mexicans the North American Intervention. The war
strained the morality of the North Americans by easily extracting half the
purported territory of Mexico, and in retrospect it seemed the deliberate
bullying and robbery of a smaller power by a stronger one. However, a
the time the immense furor that was set off, mostly in the northeastern
United States, was largely political and subsided quickly in the face o
North American success. The opposition Whig Party and antislaver
forces, while immediately denouncing the conflict, never proposed that the
huge Southwestern empire taken from Mexico be returned.

The Mexicans, while maintaining the notion that the whole North
American advance westward was part of a nefarious plot to destroy Mex
ico, were terribly humiliated by their inability to offer any effective de
fense. If the United States surrendered a certain kind of idealism and
honor in this conflict, the Mexicans, considering themselves the injured
party, still could take no sense of pride or honor from the war's events
The loss of Texas could be blamed on Santa Anna—but the whole nation
out of its treasons and ineptitudes, lost the greater war, and consciousnes
of that humiliation affected their attitudes and actions for a hundred years

The northern and eastern states did not rally behind Polk, but this lacl
was more than made up by enthusiasm in the Mississippi basin. Here th
people, descended from pioneers who crossed the Appalachians, believed i
American empire—"Manifest Destiny." Thousands of young men wer
eager to march through Mexico. Their feelings were part patriotic, par
adventurous, part piratical. These volunteers, supported and sustained b
a tiny regular army and navy, were to wage one of the most effective an
decisive campaigns since Cortés entered Mexico.

The North American strategy was simple: to seize the *despoblada* from

Texas to California, which was defenseless, and meanwhile to invade the "real" Mexico, defeat its armies, and force the government to accede to the loss of the northern territories. Despite enormous distances, the first goal was easily accomplished. Small United States forces took Santa Fé, and a naval expedition, aided by North Americans already settled in California, seized that province. The defeat of Mexico below the Rio Grande, however, was a much more difficult problem.

Despite a disparity in power between the United States and Mexico, the North American forces employed in this war rarely exceeded ten thousand men. They were almost always opposed by much larger Mexican armies, fighting on their own soil. The United States military establishment had never fought a war, though generals like Taylor had campaigned against warlike Indians. The U.S. army was no scientific instrument; its generalship was aged and less than brilliant.

The great difference between the two national forces lay in spirit and technique. Despite the much larger Mexican military budgets of the past years, the Mexican army was execrably equipped by corrupt contractors. North American artillery and engineers were infinitely superior to their Mexican counterparts. As all historians have written, the original Mexican ranks were filled with illiterate conscript *indios*, quite different from North American volunteers. The Mexican soldiers made excellent troops when disciplined and trained, and in fact they performed prodigies of dogged valor in these campaigns. The rot was in the pretorianism of the Mexican military class, which loved uniforms, pay, and power, but had no taste for sustained combat.

The greatest problems the North Americans faced were not Mexican commanders, but the horrendous distances, the terrain, and the climate. As always, the Mexican lowlands were deadly for European stock; bugs and bad water killed more invaders than Mexican copper balls. The second greatest problem for the North Americans, after logistics, was the ineptitude of their own generals.

Taylor was a poor tactician and a worse logistician and strategist. He defeated Arista in two sharp battles along the Rio Grande in May 1846 mainly through the quality of his troops. He crossed the river and took Matamoros. But here he hesitated for two months, while thousands of his young soldiers died of disease. Finally, always cautious and lethargic, he marched south into the healthier highlands of Nuevo León. Again, the superior qualities of his infantry smashed the gaudy but antiquated cuirassiers of Ampudia at Monterrey.

The invaders stormed the old city, then marched west and seized Saltillo in Coahuila.

But here Taylor dawdled and did nothing, despite the fact that the United States government had an express strategic plan that required him to move southward into the vitals of Mexico.

These early, less than decisive defeats, however, toppled Paredes at the capital. Paredes and his backers were unable to organize anything effectively. As the president sank into a frustrated alcoholic stupor, the *caciques* in the provinces began an effective insurgency, not against the invaders but against the government. The Yucatecas, who had a liberal-federalist regime, declared neutrality in the war. They were too removed to be affected directly anyway, but the local government now raised a local army of Maya Amerindians—an almost fatal error. In Guerrero, the old Morelos guerrillero, Juan Álvarez, was already independent of the capital As confusion and rebellion grew, the *puros* under Gómez Farías staged a coup and seized the presidency.

Gómez immediately reinstated the Constitution of 1824, which legiti-mized the de facto separatist local state regimes, but did nothing to remove the foreign invaders at Saltillo. Gómez Farías was convinced by the gen-erals that Santa Anna was the only man who could conduct the war Always overly optimistic about all men, Gómez entered into negotiations with the exiled dictator in Havana, offering him both command of the Mexican forces and the presidency if he would return. He preferred Santa Anna to the threat of an imported European prince, posed by the mon-archists.

Santa Anna was most eager to save his country once again. First, how ever, he had to pass through the North American naval blockade. He coolly opened communications with Polk, revealing Gómez' offers, bu promising Washington that once he was in power in Mexico he would after a decent interval to serve appearances, make peace on favorable terms. Polk issued Santa Anna a safe-conduct.

Just whom Santa Anna fooled or sold out is still a matter of some argument. The man had the quality of being able to convince Mexican again and again of his genius and to make them weep at his pronounce ments, while at the same time he could convince foreigners of his honesty in betraying his country.

As acting-president, Santa Anna assembled a large army at San Luis Potosí. Gómez Farías continued to manage the government, as vice-presi dent, on the same arrangement as a decade earlier. This gave Santa Anna the opportunity for glory but left Gómez to raise money and direct an unmanageable population. By January 1847, Santa Anna had equipped between eighteen and twenty-five thousand troops at Potosí, paying for this army partly out of his own pocket, partly from wholesale confiscation of property in the name of the war.

The problems that Gómez' *puro* government encountered illustrated the basic tragedy: no single faction, party, or ideology could unite Mexico Bombarded by Santa Anna's demands for silver, Gómez' congress author ized the seizure and sale of several millions in Church properties. The clergy, despite the national danger, refused to loan or give his government anything. About 1.5 million pesos were raised this way, at the expense of further alienation of the clergy and the majority of the Creole society. At the capital, the *criollo* militia regiments wore religious medals ostentatiously to show their beliefs. Some of the higher clergy said openly that Gómez Farías was a greater danger to the country than the Anglo-Saxons, because it was known that even those heretics did not confiscate Church property in the United States.

Meanwhile, Polk in Washington had become exasperated with Taylor's dawdling in Coahuila. Polk and the war-makers were Democrats, while by an odd circumstance all the senior commanders of the army happened to be opposition Whigs. There is no evidence that this Whiggery turned the generals against the war or added a deliberate malfeasance to their incompetences, but incompetence and politics created two problems for Polk. The first might lose the war; the second made him reluctant to see Whigs win in the field and thus gain all the glory. Polk now tried to solve both problems by ordering an invasion of Mexico through Veracruz. The new invasion force was to siphon off half Taylor's troops, as it was to be the decisive maneuver to seize the capital. Its commander, Winfield Scott, was also a Whig, but Polk hoped to divide the potential credit between the two generals.

Taylor was ordered to surrender half his army and to retire from his exposed position at Saltillo. He reluctantly obeyed the first order, but refused the second. He remained deep in Mexico with less than ten thousand men. His position was precarious, and in fact, he seems almost to have gone out of his way to let the Mexicans destroy him. The North American forces stayed in winter camp at Saltillo, without even an effective intelligence.

Santa Anna saw this opportunity clearly. In January 1847, he marched north from Potosí with forces that outnumbered Taylor by about three to one. He caught Taylor by surprise. Taylor was forced to burn his stores, quickly retreat a few miles north, and fortify a defensive position at a pass through the mountains at an hacienda called Buena Vista. He left a vital stretch of ground undefended on one flank.

The somewhat rough and ready but quite dangerous invading army watched the Mexicans prepare for battle with dread fascination: the brilliant uniforms, drums, bugles, and pennants, the solemn, traditional Mass before the killing. Then, Santa Anna hurled his legions forward. His tactics were flawless—he quickly flanked Taylor on one side—and his conscript soldiers advanced with splendid discipline and determination.

The superior firepower of the North Americans, however, inflicted enormous casualties on the larger Mexican host as it drove through two North American defensive trenches, capturing two colors, and bending Taylor's forces back on their final line. At nightfall, February 23, the North American army hung by a thread, but apparently its splendidly worked guns had shot away much of the Mexican leadership's courage.

The officers, unaccustomed to such general slaughter of their troops, were in no mood to resume the battle. While the enemy officers were waiting grimly for a renewed attack and their own destruction, Santa Anna struck his camp and retreated back toward Potosí.

When Taylor and his officers realized the Mexicans had departed, they embraced each other joyfully. Taylor, logically, declared that he had won a great victory, a claim which was to vault him to the presidency. And in fact he had, even if by default. Santa Anna, on the retreat, raced his coach ahead of the army, hastening to proclaim his own "victory" at México. Behind him, in bitter winter weather, his bloodied army began to dissolve in starvation and desertion. Santa Anna had once again snatched defeat from the very jaws of victory. He had wasted the best army in Mexico for no purpose other than his own political aggrandizement.

At the capital, Santa Anna overjoyed the Creoles with his claims of victory. The local militia regiments, all drawn from upper class youth, were already in rebellion against the vice-president. Now, all the leadership—conservative, *puro*, moderate, monarchist—rushed to congratulate the general. Santa Anna felt strong enough to remove Gómez Farías, and to put a more moderate liberal, Anaya, in as acting-president. Santa Anna then demanded two million pesos from the Church coffers, promising future immunity from demands. He got the money, and began his campaign against Winfield Scott, who had landed near Veracruz and bombarded that city into submission on March 7, 1847.

It is now almost forgotten that when Scott began his march over Cortés' old route from the coast to the Mexican capital, almost all contemporary military opinion regarded him as lost. His ten thousand regulars and volunteers were overwhelmingly outnumbered by Mexicans in the field; the terrain was militarily horrendous, and his logistic problems appeared insurmountable. He was attacking into the heartland of central Mexico, surrounded by millions of enemy nationals. Europe's greatest generals said unhesitantly that his small expeditionary force would be destroyed. General Scott, however, whose innate egotism and love of military pomp made him hated by his unmilitary countrymen, was no fool. He understood the problems perfectly, and his approach was scientific and deliberate. He made much poorer time than Hernán Cortés and his conquistadores had centuries before.

The example of Cortés continually inspired this North American army fighting its way up from fevers into forests and towering, snow-capped mountains, determined to see the "halls of Montezuma." There was a definite analogy, in fact. Again, a smaller, coolly confident, utterly determined, technically superior force was pitted against a crumbling, static, panic-stricken empire of millions, whose leaders and people hated each other more than foreign enemies. But the United States needed only to batter the Mexican empire into recognizing the United States' strategic boundaries and its predominance upon the continent. It never envisioned, as Cortés did, remaking the sovereignty and civilization of Mexico.

In April Santa Anna waited for Scott at Cerro Gordo, where the mountain road rose steeply toward Perote. The Mexican position appeared impregnable; as Santa Anna remarked, a rabbit could not turn his forest-and-ravine-protected flanks. Santa Anna reckoned without West Point engineers, who cut roads and dragged artillery into position on his left. Caught between the cross fires of the superior North American guns, his army was shattered in place. After terrible punishment, and without inflicting damage on Scott, Santa Anna's army broke and ran, streaming in total disorder back toward the capital. Scott marched on and occupied Puebla, whose bishop and Creole council disdained any attempt by Santa Anna to defend them.

By May 1847, the capital was undergoing all the alarms and signs and manifestations that had marked Motecuhzoma's last days. The four great factions, purists, moderates, the clericals, and the monarchists, all blamed each other for the approaching danger. No one trusted Santa Anna: Mexicans had learned of his promises to Polk and half-believed them, and survivors of the battle of Buena Vista, had cast some doubt upon that glorious victory. But there was no one else. Bustamante and Nicolás Bravo were almost in their dotage and themselves suspect; Valencia and Almonte were noted for treachery; Arista had lost two battles; and coxcombs like Lombardini had no field experience. Recognizing the unpalatable fact that Santa Anna's personal interests were now compatible with the nation's, all factions supported him. Santa Anna raised another army, while—incredibly—bilking $10,000 from the invaders at Puebla, by informing a State Department representative with Scott at Puebla that he needed this money to further his plan to sell out Mexico.

By August 1847, as no sellout had proceeded, Scott marched higher into the volcanic strike. The rainy season had flooded Lake Texcoco, so Scott approached the town of Chalco, and from there went south. As the invaders entered the Valley of Mexico, the church bells pealed the alarm, and Santa Anna's warriors prepared to defend the approaches to the great city.

Santa Anna organized forces miraculously, considering his resources, and he encouraged his troops by continually exposing himself to fire. He gathered a host of patriotic young *criollo* and *mestizo* volunteers, the first time such elite volunteers had served in a Mexican army, and these men shocked the North Americans with the sudden improvement in Mexican fighting qualities. The invaders were now superior only in the discipline of their ranks, and in their junior officers, because below Santa Anna the pretorians of Mexico had become a mutinous rabble.

Santa Anna's generalship was good. The conventional Mexican wisdom that blamed him for the disasters of this campaign is not based on military evidence. He knew that if he could deal Scott a single, stunning setback, he could probably bring the invaders to disaster. Scott was fighting in the Valley of Mexico with less than a modern division, supported by a tenuous and difficult supply line, surrounded in hostile territory. But this August and September Santa Anna's lieutenants were touchily jealous and disobedient; each general wanted to fight his own war, and the brave, proud Creole volunteers mistook foolhardy demonstrations for scientific warfare.

At Contreras, the untrustworthy Valencia disobeyed orders to fall back and consolidate with Anaya at Churubusco. Scott defeated him singly, then defeated Anaya, who was short of ammunition. Valencia withdrew all the way to Toluca and in a pronunciamento called for Santa Anna's overthrow. The battered *norteamericanos* fought their way through Molina del Rey and stormed Chapultepec. Old Nicolás Bravo wanted to defend the castle, now a military college but he had only cadets. Here, on September 13, six young cadets died in a futile defense. The officers of the army vanished, and with them all organized resistance. The next day the *ayuntamiento* or city council of the capital ordered a white flag displayed. The invaders broke down undefended gates and walked through deserted plazas while a riotous mob of Mexicans sacked the National Palace.

The city government ordered the halting of sniping or further resistance. The city fathers, after the looting for the palace, were more fearful of the street mobs than the grim *norteamericanos*, who took no insult or resistance, but who did not loot or rape.

Scott's situation was still precarious, even in the capital. Santa Anna knew the invaders were vulnerable to guerrilla warfare, especially directed at their lifeline to Veracruz. The *puros* stood behind him, trying to arouse the national consciousness. By fall 1847, Mexican guerrilleros raided North American convoys and attacked detachments traveling to the capital from the coast. In this kind of warfare, atrocities were freely committed on each side. *Hacendados* and rancheros raised small troops that harassed the occupying forces continually. By winter, Scott was losing one third of his supplies and reinforcements before they reached him.

These tactics could have won the war and forced the invaders out. But Santa Anna lost another battle at Puebla and was now discredited. The *moderados*, who held a majority in the congress, became determined to make peace. Almost all the propertied class in Mexico was deathly afraid of instigating a guerrilla war against the invaders, because this would lead to anarchy. The northern states were again threatening to secede, and in Yucatán the separatist *criollo* government was faced with a racial war, as the Maya Amerindians it had armed turned their guns on the ruling whites.

A hundred thousand Europeans were driven into Mérida and Campeche, clamoring for assistance against the *indios*, while British merchants sold guns to both sides.

Under these circumstances, most conservatives and moderate liberals were eager to end the war, even by a surrender of the distant northern territories. A rump government was established at Querétaro, and the chief justice of the Supreme Court was prevailed upon to take the presidency, which he accepted as a journey "to the grave." Santa Anna figured in these maneuvers, but as the chief justice, Manuel de la Peña y Peña, became president, he was again exiled. He had more credibility with the invaders now than his countrymen. The North Americans gave him safe conduct, guarding him from lynching by irate Texans with the army, and Scott's officers actually wined and dined him before he set out for Jamaica.

Peña y Peña's coalition believed that surrender was the lesser of evils facing Mexico; Scott and Trist, his State Department aide, made rapid progress hammering out a treaty. The United States terms were exactly what they had been when the war began: the permanent cession of Texas, California, and the New Mexico territory, which included the whole Southwest. In return, the United States agreed to cancel the Mexican debt and pay an additional fifteen million dollars. The fact that Mexico had lost the war had not increased the North American demands, but there was still much emotional opposition to signing this treaty among the Mexican leadership. Only the slide toward anarchy, and Scott's threat to resume hostilities finally persuaded the moderate congress at Querétaro to accept it. Documents were signed at Guadalupe Hidalgo in February 1848.

The treaty was forwarded to Washington, where the Senate ratified it immediately, sensibly overriding some opinion to annex all Mexico. The new frontier established between the two republics was realistic, and it was to endure.

The Treaty of Guadalupe Hidalgo took territories that were only nominally Mexican for what at the time was a realistic price; the income or usable resources of Mexico were not reduced. Only a few Mexican citizens in these territories were affected, and the defeated nation was not required to pay the usual indemnities. The terms were not harsh. But they were inexorably decisive; they reduced Mexico permanently to second place upon the continent. This was what was so bitterly felt by the politicized Mexicans, who considered themselves rivals of the North Americans and culturally their superiors. Worse, the Mexicans could take no satisfaction from the fighting, not even the haunted pride derived from a hard struggle well lost. They had not won a single battle. Mexicans could take pride only from such things as Anaya's defiant words upon surrender—"If I still had ammunition, you would not be here"—and the useless but heroic death of the six cadets at Chapultepec.

Thousands of Mexicans had fought stubbornly and died bravely, but few

Mexican generals or political leaders had shown any desire to sacrifice life or property for the country—and this was a record almost too much for intelligent Mexicans to bear. The Intervention ended in a profound sense of loss of dignity and self-respect, laced with fears for the future of the country and a lasting phobia toward all "interventions." The outcome was so decisive there was no hope of a *revanche*. Mexicans became defensive and found solace in outrage, becoming almost neurotically legalistic and moralistic toward the outer world. Yet, there were seeds of hope stemming from the disaster.

The young senator Mariano Otero, who told his wife that he believed the Treaty of Guadalupe Hidalgo was a death warrant for future generations, was driven to ask himself how a handful of invaders could have successfully marched through the most populous regions of Mexico. He found the obvious answer: the Mexicans were not united. The apathy and ineffectiveness of four million *indios* on the haciendas and *ejidos* was understandable; they had no public role nor any stake in *criollo* Mexico. But the three million Hispanic citizens, *criollos* and *mestizos*, had behaved shamefully in crisis. Otero detailed this in a pamphlet brutal in its clarity.

The old Mexican order was dying, he wrote, but the new one had not yet been born. Independence, upon which the upper classes had pinned such hopes, was a false god, because independence solved no problems. Mexicans had attempted none of the changes demanded by the century in which they lived. They had merely played with forms of government, piling disaster upon disaster while the country stagnated under the legacies of colonialism.

Otero saw the evils that undercut all the proud rhetoric of the reformers: the Mexican leadership, traditional or reformist, still prepared its sons for idleness, or for the pretorian army, or for government sinecures. Men taught their sons to serve no master, but also to avoid effort. The arts and crafts upon which the power of Mexico's enemies were based were denigrated and had disappeared. If a Mexican wanted a good carriage, or even a decent pair of shoes, he had to seek out a foreign tradesman. A tiny minority of industrious Mexicans groaningly supported a great mass of privilege: an incompetent army devoid even of honor; religious corporations which produced nothing but held tenaciously to two-thirds of the real wealth; and a horde of ambitious, corrupt, and wasteful bureaucrats.

The classes, *indio, mestizo, criollo*, and the interests, army, church, and bureaucracy, all hated each other too much to unite even in the face of an invader. Otero wrote: "There is no national spirit because we are not a nation."

Soon after publication of his pamphlet the brilliant young statesman died of the cholera. His death marked the end of an era, a custodianship of the *criollos* that had failed.

28

THE REFORM

If the question were only whether or not I should continue in power, the decent thing would be for me to withdraw. This is not the question. The nation is fighting for its fundamental law, as enacted by elected representatives.

Benito Juárez, during the War of the Reform.

By July 1848 the last North American troops had departed from Mexico. The *moderados* who made the peace were not destroyed by it; in fact, José Joaquín de Herrera was rehabilitated by tragic events. He resumed the presidency of a *moderado* government in June 1848, and in the postwar calm, he served out his term and turned the presidency peacefully over to General Mariano Arista, who had also been rehabilitated by other generals' more spectacular defeats.

The Herrera-Arista administrations have been considered the most intelligent and honest up to their time, and together they were a sort of Indian summer of the *criollo* custodianship. The exorbitant military budgets were reduced by more than two-thirds, to three million pesos, and, in their shame, the generals briefly were quiescent. Relations were regularized with European bondholders by assigning them three-fourths of Mexican customs receipts. The indemnity paid by the United States was used to consolidate the internal debt, which the moderates discovered was far greater than the out-of-power politicians had realized.

The same old problems plagued both administrations. The financial burdens of the past generation proved too heavy for the treasury to surmount, and the government still had to live beyond its means. The efforts to enforce discipline on the army and officeholders were fiercely resented;

in fact, the customs service sabotaged financial plans, as corrupt officials in some areas arbitrarily reduced duties or refused to tender them. Under the restored federalist constitution, a few states developed honest and responsible liberal-moderate regimes, but others continued in virtual anarchy.

Yucatán was convulsed in a racial-civil war. The liberal governor of the state offered Yucatán to the sovereignty of Spain, Great Britain, or the United States in 1848—any government which would save the whites from the "Maya savages." In this year the European-whites were almost driven out of the peninsula, and no foreign government would have them. But the Maya serfs, having recovered their lands, as they thought, stopped fighting to cultivate them, and the desperate *blancos* received large shipments of arms from Spain and the United States via Havana and New Orleans. The better armed and organized white minority reconquered and re-enslaved the peninsula once more, in a hideously cruel struggle that continued almost to the end of the century. Half the population reportedly died, as the European-descended planters burned thousands of native villages and drove the Maya remnants deep into the remote rain forests.

Yucatán was not the only region sinking into barbarism. Some of the outlying states, particularly in the north, were ruled by local *caciques* who were no better than bandits; they thrived on anarchy. Sonora and Chihuahua were devastated by Apaches and other wild Amerindian tribes, who grew bolder as they discovered the nineteenth-century republic was even less able to fend them off than the Spanish viceroyalty. The missions and forts were abandoned, and whole settlements of Mexicans were massacred. Large areas of the Pacific coast were impassable for Mexicans, *mestizo* or *criollo*. Even in the northeast, *indios* raided out of the Sierra Gorda, which had been pacified for a hundred years. The Comanches raided from Texas every spring. Filibusteros and bandits from the United States and other nations plundered the borderlands. And in large parts of central Mexico, local bandits made things almost as bad. Haciendas in this era became veritable forts, where *hacendados* and their retainers went armed and sometimes were besieged by brigands for months. Even the suburbs of the capital were not safe.

The Mexican government could not protect diplomats traveling to and from Veracruz, nor foreigners doing business anywhere. Now, in the middle of the century, Mexico had become synonymous with barbarism and banditry throughout the civilized world. The country had good government, but in most areas the government was helpless.

The *criollos* and the clergy began to long more and more for the restoration of a European monarchy. Lucas Alamán and his disciples saw no other hope. But others saw salvation in the subordination of the army and the Catholic hierarchy to the civil government.

Almost unseen beneath the panorama of great events among the Creole gentry at the capital, the second generation of independent Mexico—men who had not been born or conditioned under the colonial regime—was coming of age. These men, mostly from the provinces, absorbed the knowledge and memory of Hidalgo and Morelos from their early years, and a handful of them were securing educations, no longer at the Jesuit colleges, but at the institutes opened by Gómez Farías' purists in the 1830s. These few secular schools and colleges of the arts and sciences could educate only a very few young men out of the great mass; most of the privileged classes still opted for a traditional Hispanic or cleric-administered education or went abroad to Spain or France; and most of the *indios* and working classes received no academic training at all. The majority of the youths trained in local institutes and universities were *mestizos*, a term that now really referred to a Hispanicized Mexican with indigenous blood, or any Spanish-speaking Mexican who lived by Hispanic life styles regardless of his caste or color. In a country like Mexico, where any sort of education was a rarity, any young graduate was automatically a member of an elite. It was not the elitism of the property-owning, nostalgically Hispanic great families; it was a slow but steady expansion of the elites represented by the *castas* who struggled up out of the abyss in colonial Mexico. Only the strongest and most meritorious emerged.

This expanding class of educated *mestizos* added new dimensions to the old strength of liberalism, which was represented on the national level by purist intellectuals steeped in anticlerical, republican ideals and on local levels by ambitious *mestizos* eager for office or *cacique*-bosses wanting freedom from the capital. The orginal liberal intellectuals had never risen from the common people, and they had rarely understood the common people or even sympathized with them, but the emerging, newly-educated elite was much closer in background and feeling to such precursors as Morelos and Hidalgo. Educated in secular institutions dominated by *puros*, they were universally hostile to the Church. They began to provide Mexico with something it had never had, effective politicians. Some *caciques* were politically gifted, but too many were simply ignorant local bosses.

Under the relaxed federalism of the Herrera-Arista administrations, many of these new men were coming to power and prominence in certain state governments. Oaxaca and Michoacán developed excellent home-grown administrations. Melchor Ocampo, the governor of Michoacán, was a Francophile romanticist of the old pattern, influenced by Rousseau, but he was also a trained scientist who combined a search for social justice with practical improvements in agriculture. He attracted other able, honest people, such as Santos Degollado, professor of law, whose purity of motives went far beyond the opportunism of the average socially mobile liberal.

Oaxaca was governed by Benito Juárez, born a Zapotec mountain-

Indian. Juárez had not remained an *indio*, however. With the end of legal, though not social, distinctions in 1821, the question of who or what was an Indian had become increasingly cultural. Those who still used native dialects and lived the old village life styles were *indios*; but even pure-blooded Amerindians who spoke Spanish, wore European clothing, and entered into *mestizo-criollo* affairs were now, in effect, *mestizos*. Orphaned, the young Juárez was brought to the city of Oaxaca as a servant. At the age of twelve his innate intelligence and good character were recognized by a Franciscan lay brother, who sent the boy to a local school. Here Juárez learned Spanish and literacy. He entered a seminary, but soon decided he lacked a vocation. At this time Gómez Farías and his *puros* established secular institutes across Mexico, which were not closed during the conservative reaction, and Juárez was able to study law.

The young lawyer, quiet, reserved, uncharismatic, soon made a reputation for integrity. With his education and abilities, he was one of a handful who could take giant steps upward through the caste and class system at a time when Indians were still considered *sin razón* and Amerindian physical appearances, ugly. He married Doña Margarita Maza, the *criolla* daughter of his first employer. This was not unusual; it is obvious that upwardly mobile *indios* and *mestizos* in this age tended to marry white women. This showed a distinct crumbling of colonial caste barriers—but at the same time revealed their enduring strength, for the upper caste-class tended to coopt able *mestizos* and Indians. The children of such marriages were universally assimilated into the upper class.

Juárez' career has often been compared with Abraham Lincoln's, and there were certain similarities. Both rose from obscure origins, and both shared high qualities and ideals. Juárez was not brilliant, but he had a powerful, logical mind which rejected intolerance and injustice. When he reached high office in a class-conscious society, he kept a common touch. Juárez received *indio* peasants informally, and once disciplined his daughter for demeaning a person of inferior rank. He entered politics, was elected to congress, and after the North American Intervention, became governor of Oaxaca. His administration was famous throughout the country, because he inherited a bankrupt treasury and left it with a fifty thousand peso surplus.

Ocampo, Degollado, and Juárez were outstanding examples of a newer breed of public servant rising in the provinces. The new elite was rising in several fields. At the capital, younger intellectuals trained in the institutes continued Carlos Bustamante's and Quintana Roo's search for an indigenous literature and culture. These new men were nativists profoundly influenced, however, by French Romanticists, for Paris was the cultural center of the entire Latin world by the 1830s. The anarchy and destruction in Mexico did not permit the appearance of a superior native art, and most

Mexican creations were now pale imitations of the French; Ignacio Ramírez, the acid-penned anticlerical, was a second-rate Voltaire. Guillermo
Prieto, however, who chose as his theme the heros of the Insurgency,
stirred deep patriotic emotions with his verse, becoming the Mexican "national" poet.

The younger intellectuals were impatient with the irresolute, stuffy
criollo custodians, whether liberal or conservative, and were all inherent
revolutionaries, young men eager for their day in power. Such men were
inescapably drawn into public life and politics, because there was no private sector to absorb their activities.

Perhaps because of the very degradation from which they emerged, the
new generation possessed an unusual sense of honor and honesty. Despite
the errors they would make, these younger leaders of society had ability;
collectively, this generation was to produce the most honorable and able
figures in Mexican history. Psychologically, the second generation after
independence was less born and raised in ruined houses than its parents,
although it inherited a country the first generation had almost destroyed.
This generation was the first to lay the true foundations of a Mexican
nation.

The young educated elites of the 1840s and 1850s were deeply dismayed with the condition of their country, and understood far better than
the holdovers from colonialism that Mexico was isolated from the progressive nineteenth-century world. They saw the self-inflicted failures of the
recent past. They were still romantics, but not quite so impractical and
irresolute as the old liberal *puros*. This was a generation that laughed
rather than wept at Santa Anna's proclamations of patriotism, and scorned
Gómez Farías' good intentions divorced from realistic actions.

The new leadership was diverse in class, race, and origin, though it was
predominantly *mestizo*. Its great rallying point was an attack on the
wealth, power, and privileges of the Church, which the new men believed
must be destroyed before Mexico could be modernized.

The Church, which was still a Spanish church in Mexico, the reformers'
bête noire, was sunk in medieval torpor, aroused only by Protestantism or
threats of social change. The French Revolution had destroyed certain Catholic movements toward liberalism and collegiality on the European continent. Catholicism became defensive, and the papacy had become
highly reactionary in the nineteenth century. This was reflected in Mexico.
A church-state conflict had emerged in different forms in most Roman
Catholic countries. The Hispanic struggle was not primarily a battle between religion and rationalism—for all their French influences few Hispanic liberals were rationalists or atheists; most died as believing, or at
least, practicing, Catholics. The Hispanic world had woven Catholic
Christianity into its warp and woof.

Whatever the vestiges of surviving paganism among some *indios,* the general Mexican population at independence was more devout and Church-worshipping than that of Spain. Although every Mexican president was and would be a Freemason, each in some respect thought and acted as a Catholic, and even the most anticlerical ones felt uncomfortable among genuine heretics.

The peculiarity of the church-state struggle in Hispanic countries revolved around the former institutional position of this powerful Church. It had been part of government, though subordinate to the crown; crown and Church afforded each other legitimacy. The collapse and disappearance of the Spanish crown created an enormous problem for the Hispanic Church that was frequently not understood in other lands—what was to become of the royal *patronato?* Must the new, republican state continue to uphold the institutional Church, and did the Church now owe the successor republics of the empire the same unquestioning obedience and fealty it had rendered to the crown?

The question in Mexico had been resolved at independence in a most unsatisfactory manner. The *patronato,* or patronage, had devolved back on the Holy See. Therefore the Church came under the direction of the papacy for the first time in centuries—logically enough, had the Mexican Church been truly a private, religious institution. But the new Republic continued all the laws establishing the Catholic monopoly and affording the privileges and immunities of the clergy. Most Mexicans thought this inevitable at the time. But trouble was inherent in this compromise, because the state upheld the privileged position of the clergy and enforced their tithes, while the Church did not reciprocate.

The Catholic hierarchy of the nineteenth century, for all the hundreds of progressive priests, questioned the innate legitimacy and respectability of the republican form of government. The outlook of the higher clergy was nondemocratic and authoritarian and monarchist. To this was added the enormous influence of the papacy, which now appointed all bishops; the popes of this era, like Leo XII, were instinctively hostile toward the rebellious, democratic-leaning Americas.

Owing no allegiance to the Republic, in fact, almost a separate sovereign nation within it, the Church felt free to criticize. Spanish clerics had always engaged in politics; the difference was that now most of them emerged in opposition to rather than in support of the secular government. The hierarchy felt morally bound to interfere again and again in politics. It had denounced and punished insurgency as heresy, and after independence, to the despair of liberals, the Church entered into alliances with the Mexican conservatives-centralists-monarchists. It refused revenues to the Republic that it had traditionally rendered to the crown. This was logical under Catholic rationales, but it enfuriated liberal regimes. Conflict on this ground alone was inevitable.

A complication was the vast, hoarded wealth of the Mexican religious community. It is almost impossible to determine exactly what percentage of the real wealth the hierarchy and the orders controlled; they did not know themselves; but liberal authorities believed this consisted of one-half to two-thirds of all landed property. The true figure was probably nearer to one-fourth or one-third, but since the riches of the Church were highly concentrated in the capital and the major cities, they were highly visible. Whatever the amount, almost all of it was mortmain. The Church lent huge sums at reasonable interest—five percent per annum—but this was almost always in the form of mortgages against *criollo* landed property; the Church rarely supported business ventures. The cash was dissipated frivolously, while more and more dead real estate was acquired, which the clerics managed poorly. In a country where the majority was hungry and diseased, and the government eternally faced financial crisis, the mere existence of this wealth seemed more and more intolerable.

The Mexican Church also continued to collect the high fees established under colonialism, higher than in any European Catholic country, as well as mandatory tithes. Marriage fees, in fact, were so exorbitant that many of the lower classes could not afford them and poor people raised stable families technically in sin, without benefit of clergy. Tithes and fees obviously oppressed the poor most, and meanwhile, as earlier, the enormous clerical income was unevenly distributed. Bishops and some orders had high incomes; some chapter houses and parish priests lived in dire poverty.

The privileges of clergy, meanwhile, became increasingly questionable to the increasing number of Mexicans trained at civil law. A priest, like an army officer, could not be tried in a civil court for a civil crime. He went before an ecclesiastical court even if charged with legal debts. This fact infuriated Mexican jurists, because for sixty years the principle of equality before the law had been established in the advanced nations.

Further, the Church still dominated education, and clerical teachers did their best to inculcate pupils with their own outlooks and beliefs. Despite the few institutes and academies founded by liberals, there was yet no public lower education in Mexico. Juárez had gotten his elementary training in religious schools. This clerical stranglehold on education was the one thing most irritating to liberal intellectuals, because the Church schools fostered enormous superstition and acceptance of the status quo among the *criollos*. While the clergy did provide a few schools for the poor and for the *indios*, to continue the faith, none of the better academies was free.

The Church, in fact, survived the shock of independence better than the state; during the early decades as an institution it towered over the ephemeral governments. It had even gained some reputation, ironically, as a protector of the masses, because men remembered that Morelos and Hidalgo and Matamoros had been priests. But lacking a crown to give it security, the Church had entered into very dangerous politics. The alliances of bishops with conservative politicos and corrupt pretorians were *not* traditional, for up until the War for Independence even the hierarchy had frequently spoken out for oppressed Indians and the poor, and joined the crown in actions protecting *indio* rights. The crown had been eternal, an unassailable symbol; the vested interests which replaced it were neither.

The Church's pervasive internal decay made things worse. Opposed to severance from the crown, independence brought the clergy neither a new spiritual force or mission; it merely made the hierarchy more ferociously determined to defend ancient privileges. The only dynamism in the Church came from those priests more concerned with secular politics than things of the spirit, whether Hidalgos or the bishops opposing them. A basically nonreligious controversy as to the direction of the new nation came to be directed on both sides by clergy. Parish priests roused liberal mobs; canons consorted and conspired with colonels.

Vast numbers of monastics were idle, their missions defunct while the orders still retained large chapter houses and managed large estates. These monastics, probably the most useless and corrupt of Mexican clergy where once they had been the finest, did much to lose the respect of the *criollos*, the Church's most ardent supporters. Holy orders were less and less seen as honorable careers by the upper class; fathers were known to hire whores to tempt teenage sons from contemplated vocations. The ordinary clergy, undisciplined while their superiors engaged in management and politics, grew more ignorant and dissolute, noted for its lack of chastity.

While an enormous reservoir of faith remained among the poor who desperately needed the solace of religion, the upper classes came to see the Church primarily as a supporter of the existing order. Their cynicism gradually seeped downward.

It is hard to argue, in full retrospect, that the Mexican Church did not need drastic reformation. The Spanish-born bishops were totally uncooperative with the struggling state and the aspirations of a growing majority of the people. Their altars were not at stake, as foreigners and non-Catholics sometimes believed; societies which have not experienced clericalism cannot easily understand anticlericalism; but the hierarchy opposed any criticism of the religious corporations as an attack upon religion. This was historically tragic—and the nature of the opposition added to the coming tragedy.

The liberal *reformistas*, like the bishops, had grown up in an ethos in which compromise was akin to emasculation. They demanded more than a mere reform of the Church and its removal from politics—they insisted upon Catholic subservience to the Republic. In their view, the Republic had replaced the crown, and they demanded that the Church now provide the same aura of legitimacy and sanctity. If it never occurred to the bishops to surrender property and privileges in the emulation of Christ, it seems never to have entered the *reformistas'* minds that they had no right to regulate religion. Benito Juárez was almost the only Mexican in this age who perceived a genuine *separation* of Church and state, in which neither interfered with the other. Both sides demanded all, or nothing, laying the basis for a holy war.

If the continuing actions and position of the Church were intolerable, by the 1850s the Mexican reformers fell into a trap: they had come to believe that the Church was the source of all social evil. This view was satisfying, because the Church was visible and easily attacked, but it was intellectually and emotionally sterile. The destruction of the Church could not solve the Mexican malaise, and for this reason, despite all the damage and horrors of the coming Reform, the furor and bloodshed did not bring about a Mexican millennium.

Like all others, the honest, moderate Arista administration had lived on windfalls; when the United States' indemnity for the ceded territories ran out, it ran out of money. The two honest governments of Herrera and Arista solved nothing institutionally; their one great contribution was that they provided a brief period of stability in which popular, progressive local regimes like those in Michoacán and Oaxaca could coalesce and bring good men to prominence. But by 1853, the army was again unpaid; local commandants began to issue ominous pronouncements, and Arista resigned in disgust. The *criollo* moderates, now an anachronism, fell with him.

The immediate heirs were the conservatives, who were equally antiquated and devoid of new ideas. During an interregnum, an *indio* called Quiróz raised a so-called Army of Regeneration and tried to take over idle haciendas in the north. Old Anastasio Bustamante routed this "army" and destroyed the movement, cheering conservative elements, but while the conservatives formed the new government, Bustamante was considered unfit for another try as president. Lucas Alamán, the conservative mentor, also aged and sick, proposed that Santa Anna be brought back to hold the country together for one year, while efforts were made to find a suitable king in Europe. Alamán promised to keep the ex-*caudillo* under control until the new monarch arrived. There were no better ideas; Santa Anna was approached in exile, and accepted with alacrity.

What would have been the relationship between Alamán, who seemingly stood near the realization of his lifelong goals, and the recalled dictator remains unknown, for Alamán died a few weeks later. Santa Anna, installed as president, immediately showed all his old proclivity to destroy himself at the apex of success by taking up all his old habits. He extorted money from fawning clerics and *agiotistas* in return for promises, and his vanity reached new heights. He dreamed up Cossack uniforms for his palace guard, revived the defunct Order of Guadalupe, and assumed the title, Most Serene Highness. He also authorized the sale of Maya captives, taken in the continuing war in Yucatán, as slaves to Cuban planters, taking a fee of twenty-five pesos per head as his share.

None of these expedients paid the army or gave the government contractors what they demanded. Santa Anna survived for seven months through a fortuitous sale, for seven million dollars, of a strip of territory to the United States—the Gadsden Purchase, which was needed for a rail route through New Mexico and Arizona, but which many Mexicans considered a new aggression.

The gaudy *caudillo* had his bloody as well as comic side, as before. Liberal politicians, including Ocampo and Juárez, escaped shooting by fleeing to New Orleans. Ocampo sold pots and pans; Juárez rolled cigars. More important, they and other exiled Mexicans were thrown together, to stimulate each other while waiting for the wheel of fortune to turn.

This time the wheel was put in motion by Juan Álvarez, the sun-wrinkled old ranchero-guerrillero who had never ceased to be the *jefe político* of the sierras above Acapulco no matter who had ruled at the capital. Álvarez joined General Ignacio Comonfort, the *criollo* collector of customs at Acapulco in the Plan of Ayutla, issued in a remote mountain village. This pronouncement had far-reaching repercussions. While it only demanded a new president and the convening of a constitutional convention, nothing more, seven months of Santa Anna had made Mexico rotten for revolution. His Serene Highness' soldiers deserted as soon as the Gadsden Purchase millions ran out, and the northern states all pronounced for Ayutla. The now-philosophic and put-upon savior of his country sensed the game was up, resigned, and sailed for Venezuela. He expected to return, not realizing that what was to come would shake the Mexico he knew to the roots.

The conservatives had been ruined by Santa Anna; now the liberals took over. In a country without firm law or effective citizens, a handful of liberal politicians convened at Cuernavaca and declared Juan Álvarez president. The old Insurgent assumed office, cheered by the fickle capital throng, in November 1854.

Álvarez, for all his folk wisdom and native common sense, was semi-literate, and like his guerrilla-liberal predecessors in the National Palace he suffered from an inferiority complex in *criollo* society. Unlike Guadalupe Victoria and Vicente Guerrero, he was surrounded by a new pool of talent, for he provided an outlet for the energies of the newer *mestizo* generation, which crowded round him.

Benito Juárez, who took ship as soon as he heard of the revolt, became minister of justice. Miguel Lerdo de Tejada took the treasury; Melchor

Ocampo became intellectual in residence at the palace, heading up a horde of new-frontier seekers. The honesty and integrity of the new administration was unique, and these men gave the Álvarez regime vigor and élan. Perhaps unfortunately, however, the old *cacique* felt himself overshadowed, and he resigned the presidency in favor of Comonfort in December 1855.

Comonfort was a man more like the older *criollo* liberals, well-meaning but caught between ideals and friends and family and his own Creole consciousness.

Pending the issuance of a new constitution, the Comonfort regime began to rule by decree. The first issued were explosive. Comonfort signed the *Ley Juárez*, drawn up by his justice minister, which abolished military and religious *fueros*. The *Ley Lerdo* followed, and it was far more radical. Lerdo at the treasury needed money, but the real intent of his reform went deeper. The new men at the palace had agreed upon nothing less than the final destruction of the economic, social, and political powers of the Church. The new law required the Church to sell its landed estates to private buyers, with the state sharing in the proceeds through sales taxes. The law applied to all corporations, and therefore it also affected the Amerindian communal village lands.

This destruction of the *ejidos* was hardly accidental; the reformers had several well-intentioned plans. They expected to destroy the paralyzing political and economic power of the religious corporations and return the dead capital to the economy and production. They included the *ejidos* in the destruction deliberately, because they were expecting to create a new class of Mexican smallholders, men who would buy up the former Church and Indian lands. Economically and socially, the Amerindian communities were dead ends, anachronisms as much as the Church properties in the modern world. Juárez, Ocampo, and Lerdo believed that these properties would come into the hands of small farmers who would be vigorous free citizens—and also remain grateful, politically, to their creators.

The nineteenth-century liberals, despite the fact that so many of them had Amerindian ancestry, saw nothing admirable in contemporary *indios* or Indian culture. They believed, rightly, that the tribal villages where millions pursued an age-old, inefficient, communal agriculture blocked the emergence of a modern, progressive society, for the tradition-cribbed *indios* were not individuals. The Lerdistas hoped to break up the stagnant pattern of this life and forge something on the order of a French peasantry.

The *Leyes* Juárez and Lerdo drew their inspiration almost entirely from similar legislation stemming from the French Revolution, which had created a strong peasantry—in France. The *reformistas* of the 1850s, however, were still better at seizing concepts from abroad than understanding certain underlying Mexican realities. They ignored the fact that Mexico lacked a Western ethos of individual initiative, a native bourgeoisie, and a true peasantry. The *ejido indios* and the hacienda *peones* were not hard-headed French farmers in disguise, but people far more repressed than the French peasantry in 1789. Significantly, not one of the reformers in power had any business experience, or was in any sense an economist or sociologist. They were theoreticians, who forged results entirely divergent from what the destruction of the Old Regime accomplished in Western Europe.

The first effects of the *Ley Lerdo* were disastrous—not because the Church was injured, but because the lands forced on the market were immediately snapped up by rich speculators in large tracts. There was nothing to stop this in the legislation. The communal *indios* and the *peones* and even the rancheros had no money to bid on these lands—they did not even know how to begin the bureaucratic process of acquisition. The government was bankrupt and could not offer loans to buyers or allow them to buy on time—and not even Juárez dared disrupt the entire rural social system by ending debt peonage by edict. The economy was probably slightly invigorated as the Church mortmain and poorly used *indio ejidos* were taken over by adjacent haciendas or put into production by city-based new landlords. But the oppression of the rural masses, both on the *ejidos* and the Church properties, was vastly increased. The stultified Indian villages had at least been free; now bewildered *indio* farmers found their ancestral lands taken from them while they were reduced to peonage. The new owners were eager for revenues to offset the purchase cost. Workers were squeezed, and the whip was used as never before.

A final irony was that the few educational and charitable functions the Church still carried on among the *indios* also ceased. For all its encouragement of superstition and reverence for the existing social order, the religious corporations never, as the liberals came to admit, matched the rapacity and cruelty of the new private owners. The *Ley Lerdo*, in the name of progress, caused a further barbarization of the countryside.

Very little of the proceeds, due to an inefficient collection system, reached Lerdo's treasury.

The secondary effect was equally disastrous. The legal reforms neither destroyed the clergy nor the military while enraging them. Only highly intellectual Hispanic liberals could have believed that entrenched classes could be destroyed by radical pen strokes; the abolition of privilege did not immediately even affect the clerics' or the pretorians' power. Most of the reformers were moved by genuine democratic ideals, but they had no idea how to bring about democracy. They disdained compromise or gradualism, for they lacked pragmatism. They should have understood that their enemies, wiped out by nothing more powerful than a presidential decree issued by a minority in power, would fight.

The old cry, *religión y fueros*, soon went up. There was overt rebellion in the *criollo*-dominated cities, now matched by uneasiness and discontent among the *ejido* Indians. Comonfort at first reacted vigorously, arresting conservatives, banishing resisters, and confiscating property. The bishop of Puebla was exiled for opposition, and the historic convent of San Francisco at the capital was torn down, every stone except the church itself.

Whatever the *reformistas* had expected, ideological warfare was brewing, and Comonfort, although views differ, was not the man to lead it. He was a polished bureaucrat, and a Catholic, whose cabinet pushed him one way while his friends and family—all his womenfolk were under clerical influence—pulled him another. When he punished priests, his mother greeted him with tears and offered up prayers for his soul. These pressures, and his own conscience, made Comonfort temporize and pardon most offenders.

All through 1856, the liberal constitutional convention was paralyzed by the Church-state question. While many Mexicans realized that a new constitution must meet social and political realities better than the tattered charter of 1824, and must strike a balance between a central regime strong enough to govern yet too weak to impose a dictatorship upon the states, no one knew how to accomplish this. A true balance of powers was a concept alien to the Hispanic mentality, as was compromise. The other great problem, how to protect the weak in society against exploitation, was debated and finally avoided. The impassioned plea of Ponciana Arriaga, who had been in exile with Ocampo and Juárez—"How can we have popular government when the people are naked, miserable, and starving?"—could not be answered within the conventional liberal wisdom.

Therefore, the constituent assembly spent almost all its time attacking the Church. After impassioned speeches against "dead hands" and "blood-sucking priests" the proposed constitution incorporated the *Leyes* Lerdo and Juárez, only adding that first choice of sale must go to present tenants, provided they could raise the money.

The whole religious question was agonizing. The majority of the assembly, while liberal in the Hispanic sense, was composed of *criollo* and *mestizo* Catholics who had no desire to attack the Catholic faith. A few agnostics demanded freedom of religion, and were shouted down. The arguments against freedom of worship varied: there was no need, since there were no heretics in Mexico; freedom of religion might encourage the immigration of Protestant *norteamericanos*, as in Texas. One delegate silenced the radicals with the question, did they intend to revive the worship of Huitzilopochtli? The decisive consensus was significant—that Roman Catholicism was part of the national heritage and the one thing that united all Mexicans, even while it seemed to be dividing them. While the new constitution reduced the great powers of the Church, it confirmed its ancient monopoly, with only a limited separation of Church and state.

The new document was submitted in February 1857. Gómez Farías, the old, feeble dean of liberal standard bearers, was the first to kneel before a crucifix and swear to uphold it. He administered a similar oath to the president and deputies—but many delegates refused to sign. They were fortified by the archbishop and the hierarchy acting in a body, who with full papal approval, threatened excommunication for any who ascribed to it, or bought or sold Church property.

The Mexican Church here went too far, emotionally beginning its own destruction, for among other provisions, the clergy refused to accept "impious books" banned by the Index, secular public schools, or diminution of the *fueros*. The hierarchy claimed the canon law transcended any made by modern men, which could not be applied to priests. The clergy refused to absolve, marry, or bury any Mexican who stood for the Constitution of 1857, and in this terrible time more than one liberal, beset by frantic relatives, abjured his oath on his deathbed. In such an atmosphere, the population was polarized, and extremists came to the fore on each side.

The storm broke in March, when it was decreed that all officeholders of the Republic, civil and military, must swear public allegiance and attest by signature. This was an unwise measure, for it put terrible pressure on thousands of clerks and others who needed their jobs but also feared hellfire or the reproaches of their wives and daughters. Honest Mexicans became torn between irreconcilable persuasions.

Comonfort, a decent man, was horrified by the gathering bitterness. Too late, he called for moderation, but the Church was recklessly spending its spiritual capital in a final offensive, while the Ocampos, Prietos, and Ramírezes had taken positions of no return. When he refused to deport the archbishop, complaining that the presidency lacked the power, his cabinet colleagues began to distrust him. Power slipped from his hands, and he was devastated when he was barred from the cathedral at the head of the traditional Holy Week procession of government officials.

The same thing happened to Juárez, when governor in Oaxaca, but Juárez shrugged it off. He was far ahead of his times in his belief that the secular government should not take an official part in religious observances and vice versa.

The situation deteriorated. At the close of 1857, Comonfort lost faith in the Reform. General Félix Zuloaga at Tacubaya issued a pronunciamento calling for the dissolution of congress and repeal of the constitution. Comonfort joined him, thus surrendering whatever place he might have had in the liberal pantheon of heros. Zuloaga seized the presidency. Benito Juárez, now chief justice of the Supreme Court, was arrested and held in the palace, however, Comonfort had him released before fleeing the country, in January 1858.

Under use and wont, Zuloaga was president. But according to the new constitution, Juárez succeeded Comonfort when he abandoned the palace.

Juárez stood fast, arguing for a legal succession for the sake of the nation, and tried to organize a new government at Querétaro. He was forced to flee to Guanajuato to avoid arrest. Soon, Zuluaga, now ensconced in the palace, received an express which stated: "An *indio* is here who says he is president of the Republic." Zuloaga and the capital society laughed, but the War of the Reform had begun.

The governors and *caciques* of the northern states, all liberals, stood behind Juárez, but they refused to surrender their state militias to his control. Therefore, while he found a seat at Guadalajara with Ocampo and Prieto, his irregular forces were no match for Zuloaga's regulars. The professional officers at Guadalajara, who had at first reluctantly recognized his authority, soon abjured their oaths to the constitution and went over to the general.

One of these officers ordered a company of soldiers to seize Juárez and shoot him. Juárez would have died, standing stubbornly in the doorway of the Hall of Justice at Guadalajara, but for Guillermo Prieto. The poet put himself in front of the Indian president and shouted, "Brave men do not assassinate!" The soldiers lowered their muskets, and Juárez was able to flee in a closed carriage.

He went to Manzanillo, sailed to Panama, and from there to Veracruz, where some liberals held an enclave. The pestilent port was both a good and bad capital for Juárez. It was remote, but because of the endemic yellow fever, impregnable to any but acclimatized local troops and though isolated from the main centers of Mexico, it was an opening to the outer world. Juárez could collect some customs duties, and most important, he had communications with the United States, which was to play a decisive role in his career.

By standing on constitutionality, which he called the only guarantee for lasting peace, he had begun a civil war that now transcended all previous conflicts in its intense bitterness. This war had a new dimension. The battle was between *continuistas* and *reformistas*, the eternal lineup of the Hispanic revolution, but new ideological and racial overtones had been added. The emphasis on religion made for an unholy Holy War, and the emergence of the *mestizos*, who now outnumbered both *criollos* and *indios*, behind Juárez's liberals, who more nearly represented *mestizo* aspirations, created something approaching racial conflict.

Inland, the leadership of the liberals fell to Santos Degollado, the myopic lawyer who was liberal minister of war. Degollado recruited thousands of peasants in Jalisco and Michoacán. This was a ragtag army, sneeringly called *chinacos* ("beggars") by its more elegant enemies. The *chinacos* responded by calling the regular forces *mochos*, hypocrites who hid their real intentions behind a facade of religion.

The issue was never clear-cut. Deeply religious members of the elite fought for the constitution and Juárez, while thousands of ragged *indio* soldiers fought against both. Whether the war was between liberals and conservatives, patriots against traitors, rich and poor, civilians and pretorians, the impious and the clergy, the respectable classes versus the demagogues—and it was called all these things—it soon sank into a bloodbath of mutual atrocity. Men fought valiantly on both sides, but on both sides prisoners were shot, hostages were murdered, and partisans massacred, robbed, and vandalized.

The actual path of battle is impossible and fruitless to follow. Every part of Mexico was caught up in a gigantic guerrilla war. In the west Degollado learned to be an effective guerrillero, losing every pitched battle with the regulars but still continuing the war. Harried, he retreated into the tropic wilds that had protected Morelos and Guerrero, only to reemerge again. He became a hero of defeats.

The juaristas had more supporters, but the conservatives had better armies. Three excellent conservative generals—Miguel Miramón, a boy hero of Chapultepec; Leonardo Márques; and Tomás Mejía, a pure *indio*—drove the liberals from all major cities in 1858. The Liberals held out in woods and mountains, however, and in a country that was aflame with fratricidal passions even the suburbs of the capital could not be protected by the army from occasional raids.

Control of territory constantly shifted, and there was also a confusing changing of sides by local chieftains as one force or the other seemed to get the upper hand.

Above all this murderous ideology and Byzantine conflict stood the impassive figure of Benito Juárez. He was "not as smart" as his own cabinet, as a North American envoy said, but he transcended them in firmness and character. Juárez was a sincere patriot who believed his cause was the only just one, who was entirely faithful to his own ideals, and entirely incorruptible. In one sense Juárez was a puritan among men, including his closest associates, who could hardly understand him. An ugly man, he could not dominate a meeting by either rhetoric or charisma, yet amazingly his leadership was never questioned by some of the most brilliant, volatile, and individualistic intellectuals ever produced in Mexico. Juárez in fact held these men together. He did have one fault, and it was a great one, not unusual in his kind of person, or for his background. He could be inhumanly inflexible when a principle was at stake, and he wrapped everything in cold legalism. Thus his great strengths, carried too far, became his weaknesses.

The strengths of the constitutionalists were embodied in Juárez, and in his officers. Melchor Ocampo, Santos Degollado, Miguel and Sebastian Lerdo de Tejada, Manuel Doblado, the poet Prieto, and Ignacio Ramírez —whom the clericals regarded as the antichrist—utterly transcended their rivals on the conservative side. If they were talented but passionate men who made mistakes, the names of their counterparts have not even survived. The conservative intellectuals of this era were so bankrupt that, like Alamán in his declining years, they merely continued to dream of a monarchy and line up behind pretorian generals.

Although by the close of 1858 Juárez seemed to have lost the country, he still had strengths in his men and their ideals and in his recognition as the legal government of Mexico by the United States. The North Americans did not like Juárez particularly; he was not the kind of statesman any ambassador or envoy could like personally. But added to the constitutionality of his office, which was respected by Washington, was the fact that the conservatives had General Juan Nepomuceno Almonte, Santa Anna's old aide, lobbying in Spain. Almonte was in Europe seeking a Bourbon prince, and also a fleet to bombard Juárez out of Veracruz. Juárez interests coincided with those of United States, which was jealous of the reentry of any European power into the Western Hemisphere. He began to receive supplies, including arms, from New Orleans.

In a game of military musical chairs, Miguel Miramón had succeeded Zuloaga in command at México. The young military chief attempted to dislodge Juárez from Veracruz in early 1859 but his highland troops sickened and died. Santos Degollado saw a chance to seize the capital and marched on it out of Michoacán with his *chinacos*. He reached Chapultepec in April.

Here Leonardo Márquez and a small army of regulars utterly routed the juarista army. Miramón, smarting from his lack of success at Veracruz, ordered Márquez to shoot all captured officers. Márquez carried out this order literally, executing even captured medical officers, for which he became known, half satirically, half fearfully, as *El Tigre de* Tacubaya, the suburb where the executions were carried out.

This defeat left Juárez' fortunes at low ebb. The constitutionalists had to have money to buy arms. The United States had a general standing offer to buy more Mexican territory. Since 1848 the dominant Democrats in Washington had never quite lost sight of a desire to spread United States' power and influence deeper into Hispanic America. There had been private filibustering expeditions—one in Sonora—but despite much talk, the United States' government had resisted any temptations to stage another intervention. Conversely, both conservative and liberal Mexican regimes refused to alienate Baja California, Sonora, and Chihuahua, for which various millions were offered. Now, it was possible to sell Lower California, but this was vehemently opposed by a group led by Melchor Ocampo, who the year before had engineered the diplomatic coup that gained the liberals recognition by the United States.

The one remaining source of money, and the favorite target of the

Ocampos and Lerdos, was the Church. With the beginning of hostilities the religious corporations had failed to carry out the provisions of the *Ley Lerdo*, and in fact, the clergy was the principal source of Miramón's funds. The Miramón government was using the old means of forced loans, and against horrified protests by the hierarchy in whose name it fought, was considering mortgaging all Church property to foreign speculators against an advance of cash. Meanwhile, the Church-state controversy had, for the first time in Mexican history, made religious buildings and properties fair game. Most northern *caciques* had already seized Church lands in their states, while the various armies that passed up and down Mexico had taken to stripping altars and convents and melting down Church plate and images—in the name of liberty and the Constitution, or religion and Christ, or that of the local commander, as the case might be. Santos Degollado urged Juárez to confiscate all remaining Church property in the "name of the nation" before it disappeared into some general's bag.

The argument sparked violent debate in the Juárez Cabinet. The lawyers moved Juárez with the legal argument that under ancient Spanish law Church treasures devolved from the crown, and were held in trust for the crown, which had always had the right to use them in times of national peril. The Republic was the successor to the crown, even if the Church did not recognize it as such. Lerdo said that only a confiscation could save the treasury. But Juárez' legal mind balked at confiscations without compensation, whatever the enmity of the Church and the desperation of the hour. Lerdo, impassioned, threatened to resign and carry others with him. Juárez was unable to prevail against his cabinet, and allowed himself to be convinced.

In July 1859, he issued the fateful decree that all possessions administered by the Catholic clergy "have been and are the property of the nation." All such property was expropriated, and the religious corporations were dissolved. The clergy were left their altars; everything else—land, money, candlesticks, and buildings—became the government's. Juárez then followed this decree by a series of executive orders, written mostly by Ocampo, that were clearly more anticlerical than economic. They became known as the Laws of the Reform.

They followed the French pattern. Public officers were to keep registries of births, marriages, and deaths, which previously had been maintained in parish records. Cemeteries were made public, and marriage became a civil rite, thus requiring two ceremonies for most brides. Ocampo wrote the new secular marriage service (which is still used) detailing the civil contract, advising wives not to provoke their husbands with their counsel. The Hispanic passion for regulation went into enormous detail in separating Church and state: besides the making of tithes and contributions voluntary, and the final proclamation of religious liberty, the wearing of clerical vestments, public processions, and even the ringing of church bells were placed under government control.

Confiscations were carried out wherever the liberals held control—or raided, in the middle of a civil war. The damage and destruction of true national treasures has never accurately been calculated, but it was enormous. Most of the colonial art treasures, which like the ancient Amerindian, were religious in nature, were burned, melted down, scattered, or indiscriminately destroyed. Perhaps hundreds of thousands—certainly tens of thousands—of monastic books and manuscripts were scattered or burned in the looting of monastery libraries. Compared to the ephemeral value of the gold and silver ornaments, these were priceless, and irreplaceable. But only in a later century would all Mexicans fully perceive the cultural damage.

The Laws of the Reform marked the turning point in the civil war. Although Ocampo wanted to split up Church estates among small farmers, Lerdo's financial expediency prevailed. Church property had to be sold as quickly as possible to provide money for arms and supplies, and buyers with ready cash had to take preference. Many estates passed into the hands of speculators and foreigners, and not a few into the hands of conservative *hacendados*, some of whom reimbursed the Church, but most of whom eventually conveniently changed their politics.

The clerical forces were thoroughly demoralized by 1860. The Miramón government was running low on both money and arms. Two steamers which Miramón purchased in Cuba, trying to bring munitions to his forces besieging Veracruz, were seized as pirate ships by the United States Navy at Juárez' instigation. Now, the initiative passed to the Liberals.

Degollado agreed to a British-proposed plan that would have removed Juárez as president; he was removed from the military command. However, two far better generals, Jesús González Ortega and Ignacio Zaragoza, had been trained in the fighting to replace him. Armed, equipped, and invigorated, the liberal forces defeated Miramón at Silao and Márquez near Guadalajara, which fell to the juaristas. Then González Ortega routed Miramón in a decisive encounter between Texcoco and Tlaxcala three days before Christmas. Miramón fled to the sanctuary of a Spanish warship and Márquez disappeared into the mountains of Michoacán. Early in 1861, Juárez was able to enter the capital in his small, black carriage. He had won.

This war was the most destructive that had ever been fought in Mexico. It had been far more fiercely ideological and therefore more bitterly waged on both sides, and for the first time great numbers of monuments and genuine cultural and historic treasures had been ruined. But for the first time, hope and vigor emerged among thousands of Mexicans as it progressed. Their triumph and the Constitution of 1857, which was to survive at least in form for sixty years, fundamentally changed Mexican politics. The Mexican Church was disestablished, demoralized, and, as a political force, destroyed. The Church lost, with its property, its predominant economic influence with governments. By 1860 many bishops and priests were in exile. The Church's reactionary hostility to all change curtailed much of its former spiritual power among the people.

The *Ley Lerdo* eventually shattered many of the separate but unequal Amerindian communities that had survived since the sixteenth century by removing these societies from the protection of law. If the short-term effect was tragic, the long-term one was better: the ethnic isolation carefully preserved by the Spaniards was cracked and the way opened for most *indios* to become "*mestizo*."

The war severely damaged the pretorian hierarchy that had inherited independent Mexico. By 1860 the professional generals were scattered, demoralized, or exiled. The new constitution erased the institutional privileges of the military class, if not the actual power of the gun. For the first time, *mestizo* and *indio* militia had defeated the *criollo* professionals and their conscripted *indios*.

A vast shift of power occurred with the discrediting of the *criollo* caste-class that had held a monopoly of politics for a generation. The *criollos* retained great social power in the cities and great economic power in the countryside with their haciendas, but the destruction wreaked on the Hispanic Church and the Hispanic pretorians broke the old pattern. By clinging mindlessly to the past and by their inability to lead decisively, the *criollos* as a class had sacrificed their future.

Now an embryonic Mexican nationality was emerging with the emerging *mestizo* majority and its vigorous leadership. Benito Juárez and his brilliant cabinet formed a rallying point; after them, the *mestizo* majority in Mexico would never willingly or passively accept the reimposition of a European monarchy.

There was still nothing resembling a true citizenry or social justice in mid-century Mexico; the country was still terribly divided in class, caste, culture, and ideology. But things were changed far more than many liberal-minded Mexican historians have cared to admit. The view that the juaristas could have made Mexico into a modern nation is anachronistic. It was far easier to wreck or curb old institutions than to erect new ones. The seeds of further change had been sown.

For his victory proclamation Juárez, known affectionately as "*El indio*," chose the slogan, "Nothing by force, everything through law and reason." Like most slogans, it did not match reality. The law had conquered only with the gun, and there had been precious little reason in what had been a holy war between conservatives and liberals. But, significantly, for the first time in Mexican history, a set of principles had prevailed.

29

POPES AND EMPERORS

We are so superior to the Mexicans in race, organization, morality, and elevated sentiments that I beg Your Excellency to inform the Emperor that at the head of six thousand soldiers I am already master of Mexico.

From General Comte de Lorencez to the French Minister of War,
April, 1862.

Among nations, as among individuals, respect for the rights of others is peace.

Benito Juárez, *Benemerito* of the Americas.

A new Mexican Congress was elected in 1861, which narrowly chose Benito Juárez for president over the liberal military hero, González Ortega. Juárez faced immense problems in the aftermath of civil war. He was firmly in control of the capital, but the outlying regions were as anarchic and separatist under their liberal *caciques* as before. The economy was paralyzed and the country divided. As a first step to restoring full peace, Juárez proclaimed a general amnesty.

This angered Melchor Ocampo, who resigned from the Juárez government and returned to private life in Michoacán. Then, in June 1861, Ocampo was abducted by conservative guerrillas under Leonardo Márquez. Márquez murdered him and left his corpse hanging from a pepper tree for vultures. This act threatened to renew the civil war.

In vengeance, the capital mobs tried to massacre conservatives, who were protected only with difficulty. The congress authorized Santos Degollado to lead a force against Márquez' operations in Michoacán. Degollado was defeated and killed. A second officer, Valle, was also captured and executed. Juárez then mobilized a large army, forcing Márquez to cease operations.

Juárez' crucial problem, however, was not with guerrillas, but with the treasury. All the funds seized from the confiscations of religious property had been spent in the war. Revenues had sunk to nothing in the general devastation, and about eighty percent of the customs duties at Veracruz and Acapulco were already pledged to foreign bondholders and governments. As always, the new president faced demands for money from his followers and worse, there were a host of new claims by foreign citizens arising from the war.

Unpaid debts went back to the Guadalupe Victoria administration. Every Mexican regime robbed Peter to pay Paul, borrowing new monies to pay the interest on old debts. Although the Herrera-Arista governments had worked out arrangements with the British whereby interest rates were reduced and part of the principal cancelled in return for a guarantee of twenty percent of Mexican customs receipts, Mexico had defaulted again under the last Santa Anna dictatorship. Then, during the War of the Reform, British and other foreign property had been plundered freely by both sides.

General Leonardo Márquez robbed an English convoy of six hundred thousand pesos in silver; Santos Degollado snapped up another million (this bothered Degollado's conscience but the money was not returned despite promises of restitution), and finally, General Miramón looted the British Legation of more than half a million that belonged to English bondholders. The British minister to Mexico, Sir Charles Wyke, was personally favorable to the liberals, but his government refused recognition to Juárez until he pledged to make complete reparation.

The French and Spanish governments also had important claims against Mexico. One claim, in particular, was clearly exorbitant. Miramón had succeeded in borrowing seven-hundred-and-fifty thousand pesos from a Swiss banker, Jecker, against a pledge of fifteen million in warrants. The Juárez government correctly ignored Jecker's demand for the full amount. However, the banker had become a French citizen, and the French government pressed this claim.

The United States also had claims, but the United States was temporarily distracted by the outbreak of its own Civil War.

The British government had debated intervention to collect its debts but decided against it as long as Juárez made an effort to pay. The British no longer had any territorial ambitions in America, although their economic penetration was widespread, and above all, Her Majesty's Government had no desire to involve itself in maneuvers that might force a confrontation with the United States.

Juárez wanted to cover these claims. The rights of national sovereignty in this century did not extend to repudiations of national debts, and there was also the matter of maintaining Mexican credit abroad, because no Mexican government could live without such credits. But Juárez in 1861 faced an impossible situation; he was not even receiving enough revenue to maintain his own administration. In July he attempted the only course open to him: he declared a two-year moratorium on all foreign debts.

This created an immediate furor in London, Paris, and Madrid. Representatives of Great Britain, France, and Spain met and decided on a demonstration to force Juárez' hand, by sending a fleet and expeditionary force to Veracruz. This began a chain of events that was to have tragic international consequences.

There was restraint in London, but not in the other capitals. Spain had never willingly relinquished sovereignty over Mexico. Fernando VII's daughter, Queen Isabel II, had continued to dabble in Mexican affairs, seeing deputations of Mexican royalists and passing out Spanish titles freely to Mexican citizens as if they were still her subjects. Nineteenth-century Mexican politics had made these Spanish titles, and also Papal titles, rather commonplace, as queen and pope tried to favor and encourage Mexican conservatives. During the War of the Reform, Spain had made certain agreements with Miramón, who in exile begged for a Spanish uniform. Relations between Spain and Mexico were very volatile, so much so that Juárez expelled the Spanish minister in 1861.

Spain was prepared to intervene unilaterally, and had a small army in Cuba under Juan Prim ready for this purpose.

France, however, was a far more dangerous proposition than Spain. Now, Juárez' default gave the emperor of France, Napoleon III, a long-sought opportunity. When Louis Napoleon Bonaparte had been only an imprisoned adventurer, he had begun to dream of creating a great Latin empire in Middle America which would confound the Anglo-Saxon powers and provide France with a rich protectorate, perhaps a vast economic colony like British India (Napoleon had even considered the digging of an inter-ocean canal across Nicaragua). Even after he had brought about the Second Empire in France, several obstacles remained: a spate of European wars, the problem of making Mexico into a monarchy with a ruler dependent upon France, the obvious hostility to any such scheme, outlined in the Monroe Doctrine, by the United States, and British sea power. By 1861, all these problems disappeared.

The events of 1861 permitted the French emperor to proceed with a fantastic, complicated, and utterly cynical plan: to use a tripartite demonstration against Mexico as the cover for a military penetration, the fomenting of a Mexican revolution, and the placing of a client prince on the Mexican throne. He had already selected the Hapsburg Archduke Ferdinand Maximilian, a younger brother of Emperor Franz Josef of Austria.

The exact motivations, the full activities, and the complete chronology of the events that led various governments and parties to participate in the Maximilian fiasco in Mexico have remained obscure. Mexicans themselves had a large hand in this: an exiled Yucatecán royalist, José María Gutiérrez de Estrada, had lobbied in Europe for twenty years with the pope and Catholic governments, often with the help of Mexican diplomats. There was no secret in Europe that many substantial Mexicans and most of the clergy preferred a monarchy—though the power of this sentiment was overstated, particularly once Mexican nationalism began to coalesce around the Reform. Gutiérrez de Estrada secured the acquiescence of the Austrian court to provide a king, provided Mexicans showed they wanted one and France assisted. Napoleon III, who had a reputation of dishonesty, got the support or at least acquiescence of many important individuals and governments in his schemes. The only possible explanation is rooted in a dream that took hold in nineteenth-century Europe.

Europe, now a brilliant civilization with enormous material advances, was ruled by a series of corrupt, relatively unstable, and cynical courts and ministries, who clung to monarchy and aristocracy while trying to delay or halt the emergence of Western liberalism. The Romantic Movement had somehow also caught up these brittle, gaudy monarchies as much as the liberals; a fervid romanticism permeated waltzing courts where somehow vast dreams of a splendid, imperial future merged with bitter memories of past glories and better days. This was a theatrical, though hardly comical, civilization and milieu.

This was the full tide of European imperial advance across the world, when tiny expeditionary forces and a few gunboats were humbling and overthrowing ancient non-European countries and cultures everywhere. European ironclad warships, explosive shells, money, and telegraph lines and railroad tracks were remaking the earth. The British had the best of it, but others pressed behind. The British had India and other vast domains; it was hardly illogical that France dreamed of an equal empire, Austria and Belgium saw glory in dynasties, and the Holy See envisioned a rebellious America brought back into the Mediterranean-Catholic fold.

Behind every dream was the sure conviction of European superiority. Since European power and technique *was* dominant in this world, the rationale could not be far behind. This was the age of the Comte de Gobineau and Francis Galton, who found men and races inherently unequal, and saw superiority in hereditary merit and human genes. In this world Mexico was seen as a mongrel nation possessed of rich lands and great mineral wealth, inhabited by inferior specimens who could not hope to rule themselves. There were enough Europeans who believed both in the ancient concept of El Dorado and the new mythos of the white man's burden to make a tragedy in Mexico.

By October 1861, Spain, France, and Britain had agreed to send a fleet to Mexico, though upon little else. Napoleon frankly sounded out Lords Palmerston and Russell concerning using the intervention as a pretext for putting Archduke Ferdinand Maximilian on the throne of Mexico. The two Englishmen refused, and in fact, required the other parties to sign a convention in London before they would proceed. The purpose of the expedition was spelled out in the Convention of London: it was to force the Mexicans to honor their debts by seizing strategic sites on the Mexican coast, but "not to seek any acquisitions of territory nor any special advantage," nor "to prejudice the right of the Mexican nation to choose and constitute freely the form of its government."

Her Majesty's Government wanted only the money due British subjects, and Lord Russell now believed he had scotched Napoleon's scheme. But the emperor informed the Austrians and other parties that the British, due to their incomprehensible system of parliamentary debates, merely wanted to make certain the proprieties were observed.

The three-power fleets arrived off Veracruz in December, and put a force ashore unopposed in January 1862. The Spanish contingent was the largest, six thousand men under General Juan Prim. The French had only a brigade under an admiral—though the other allies were startled when an unannounced reinforcement of four thousand regulars arrived under General Comte Charles Ferdinand Latrille de Lorencez. The British force matched British aims: seven hundred Royal Marines, with no supporting shore services.

Ashore, the invaders issued a proclamation that stated they came only to collect just claims that had been presented many times, thus protecting national interests, but also contained the interesting phrase that the expeditionary force would "preside at the grand spectacle of your regeneration." The British expected regeneration, probably, through an honest paying up; the French had something else in mind.

The French and British ministers, Saligny and Wyke, served as commissioners for the expedition; General Prim filled both roles, with historic results. Wyke and the Frenchman detested each other immediately and it was soon obvious that they represented entirely different goals. Wyke, who had not been consulted about the expeditionary force, had never wanted it. Favoring the juaristas, he had worked out a compromise with the Mexican foreign minister earlier, only to have it evaporate in congress, where *hombres de honor* tried to will the debt away, and impugned the British honor for pressing it. But Wyke was still open to any reasonable compromise.

Saligny was not. Saligny demanded the full fifteen millions "owed" Jecker, plus an additional twelve millions in various reparations. Both Wyke and Prim refused to endorse this demand. There was much angry discussion at Veracruz, while the troops, like all aliens on these shores, began to sicken and die of fever.

The key to what now happened was Juan Prim. Prim was a militarist, but he was also two other things, neither of which may have been known to his chief minister in Spain, O'Donnell. Prim was inherently liberal, and had small loyalty to the Bourbons. He got along extremely well with Manuel Doblado, Juárez' chief negotiator, and he had no intention of using his Spanish army to "restore" the corrupt Isabel or any other monarch. Prim negotiated a convention with Doblado whereby the invaders were authorized to leave the coast and occupy Córdoba, Orizaba, and Tehuacán in the highlands, upon a solemn guarantee that they would make no moves against Mexican sovereignty. This satisfied the English, Spanish, and Mexicans, who now agreed to bargain in good faith. It infuriated the French, who had Santa Anna's old aide Almonte in their camp, come along to foment a conservative revolution.

Then, on April 9, 1862, the "allies" fell out completely. Prim and Wyke, acting on their own cognizance, ordered their forces withdrawn from Mexico. Both commissioners were backed by their governments afterward; Prim became almost a hero in Mexico, and partial rapprochement began between Mexico and Spain. Wyke was too insistent upon the mundane matter of owed money, however, for his own brand of liberalism to impress the Mexican mind.

The French army, under Lorencez, remained at Orizaba. The French now broke their covenants signed at two conventions by trying to conquer Mexico, which had been Napoleon III's intention from the first.

The Comte de Lorencez, however, was a poor choice to lead the invading army. Lorencez despised the Mexicans and considered them an inferior, barbarous people in the main, and he believed Almonte's assurances that the "decent" class would welcome the French with a rain of roses. The example of Winfield Scott's passage made the French even more contemptuous, because the French militarists, regarded generally as the world's finest soldiers, had a poor opinion of the United States armed forces, which they considered rank amateurs. Lorencez fully expected to march through the country with his some six thousand regulars. He moved on Puebla in early May.

Ignacio Zaragoza, the Texas-born liberal who had been one of the heros of the War of the Reform, held the passages to Puebla with a ragtag force that included many local *indios* armed only with machetes. Zaragoza, who looked more like a schoolteacher than a general, had only two advantages: he held commanding ground, with two stone-walled forts, Guadalupe and Loreto, and his men were fighting on and for their own soil. He told them: "Your enemies are the first soldiers in the world, but you are the first sons of Mexico. They have come to take your country from you."

Lorencez, arrogantly overconfident, attacked on May 5th. Instead of subjecting Zaragoza's poorly trained troops to a bombardment, he sent his battalions forward with the bayonet, expecting to carry the fortified Mexican positions by sheer élan. This was a rash plan that subjected the veterans of Sebastopol and Solferino to a murderous cross fire from the forts.

The French failed three times to carry Fort Guadalupe. Corpses in bright Zouave uniforms littered the high chaparral as the invaders in reckless assaults wasted a thousand men. Finally, a blinding rainstorm swept in, and Lorencez was forced to retreat back to Orizaba, with Mexican cavalry on his flanks. He sent dispatches to Paris demanding an additional twenty thousand troops.

The battle of Puebla was a small action, but the outcome fired the Mexicans with a sorely needed self-assurance, Zaragoza wired Juárez at the capital: The arms of the nation are covered with glory!" The Cinco de Mayo, the Fifth of May, would ever afterward be an especial holiday, as meaningful to Mexicans as the Alamo was to Texans. And as important as the demonstrated valor of the raw Mexican soldiers under fire was the strategic result of Lorencez' defeat. The French conquest was delayed a full year.

Had Lorencez brushed Zaragoza aside in May 1862, he would certainly have taken the capital, and French forces might well have reached the Rio Bravo this same year, in which the North American Confederates seemed near victory. Napoleon III, already tempted, might have intervened on the Confederate side to assure the cotton supplies needed by continental mills. However, the repulse delayed the French arrival on the border so long that when they at last made contact with the Confederates, the situation had changed, and the emperor was constrained to be more circumspect than he would have been in 1862.

Already committed, Napoleon now ordered a full army corps to Mexico under the command of Elie Forey, a better general.

Meanwhile, the Austrians had become dubious of the whole Mexican venture. The British had backed out; the Mexicans were not welcoming the proposed new king; and the French had not only been caught in lies, they had suffered a defeat, a more damaging consideration. The Austrian emperor's ministers advised Archduke Ferdinand Maximilian to commit himself no more deeply. However, both Kaiser Franz Josef and his ministers reckoned without the archduke's dreams. The young Hapsburg and his ambitious Coburg princess, the daughter of the king of the Belgians, were bored with aristocratic idleness at the Schoenbrunn. They were looking forward eagerly to Mexico; they had spent the winter at their castle, Miramar near Trieste, learning Spanish and Mexican culture.

Ferdinand Maximilian, another Nordic smitten with the charms of the Latin south, had governed Austrian Lombardy briefly before this province had been lost. He wanted another throne. He did not back away despite the news of Puebla. He consulted his brother, the French emperor, the king of the Belgians, and the pope, Pius IX. None of them actively discouraged him. He was also besieged by a train of Mexican royalist exiles and prelates trying to persuade him.

The Mexicans both pleased and bothered him. Gutiérrez de Estrada flattered his ambitions but also advised the recall of Santa Anna. The bishops, who hoped to return behind a French army, insisted upon a total restitution of clerical privileges and property lost in the Reform. These things created doubts, and Ferdinand Maximilian requested further British acquiescence and proof of a genuine invitation from the Mexicans—but in truth, he wanted to be convinced.

Arriving in Mexico, General Forey moved more slowly but much more sensibly than Lorencez. In March 1863, he was ready for the offensive with twenty-four thousand French regulars. Zaragoza having been killed in a skirmish, the thirty thousand Mexicans defending Puebla were now commanded by González Ortega. Against stubborn resistance, Forey mounted a scientific siege, and in two months starved and bombarded the defenders into surrender. A relieving army that arrived under Comonfort was shattered in a set-piece battle. Forey captured González Ortega and hundreds of Mexican officers, including one who would be heard from again—Porfirio Díaz. Before González and Díaz could be shipped to France, however, they escaped into the hills.

The capital was now defenseless. Juárez and the congress decided to remove to San Luis Potosí. On the evening of May 31, 1863, Juárez watched while the flag was lowered at the Zócalo, accepted and kissed the furled banner, and shouted, *"Viva México!"* to the gathered crowds. Then, once more an exile in his own land, he rode north in his small, black carriage.

Forey marched into the city on June 10. Conservative ladies and gentlemen saluted the French colors from their balconies, while the fickle *léperos* cheered lustily. Forey, under instructions from Napoleon III, immediately reordered Mexican politics. He called an assembly of 250 prominent conservatives and constituted them as the government. These men immediately abolished the Republic, declaring Mexico an empire, and voted to offer the throne to Ferdinand Maximilian of Austria. An interim Regency Council, consisting of Archbishop Labastida and Generals Almonte and Salas, sent a deputation to Vienna.

The French army ruled only that part of Mexico where its soldiers stood, so General François Bazaine marched west, occupying city after city, almost without resistance. Understanding the importance of appearances to the proposed Austrian emperor, Bazaine and other French commanders everywhere required acts of obedience, by which citizens signed

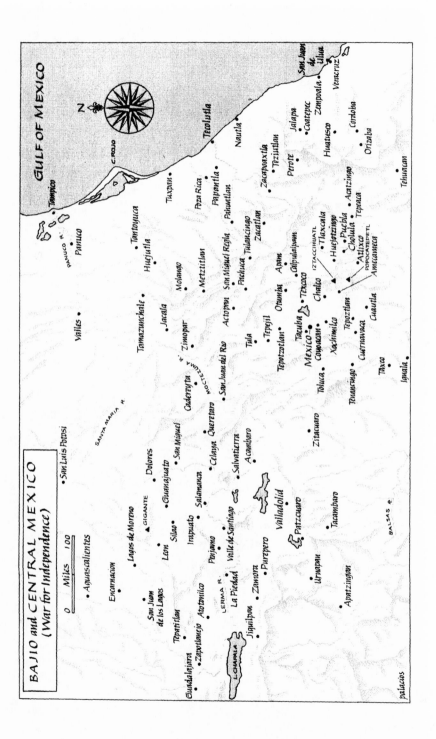

BAJIO and CENTRAL MEXICO
(War for Independence)

0   Miles   100

GULF OF MEXICO

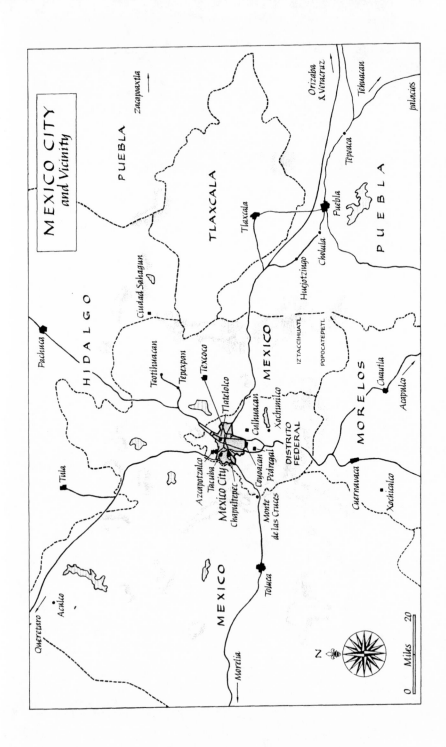

MEXICO CITY
and Vicinity

HIDALGO

PUEBLA

TLAXCALA

Zacapoaxtla

Orizaba
& Veracruz

Tehuacan

palacios

Pachuca

Tula

Acatico

Querétaro

Morelia

Teotihuacan

Tepexpan

Texcoco

Tlatelolco

Azcapotzalco

Tacuba

Mexico City

Chapultepec

Culhuacan

Coyoacan

Pedregal

Monte
de las Cruces

Xochimilco

DISTRITO
FEDERAL

MEXICO

MEXICO

Toluca

Ciudad Sahagun

Tlaxcala

Huejotzingo

Cholula

Puebla

PUEBLA

Tepeaca

IZTACCIHUATL

POPOCATEPETL

MORELOS

Cuautla

Acapulco

Cuernavaca

Xochicalco

N

0   Miles   20

declarations in favor of the empire. Most conservatives signed willingly, but thousands of other signatures were acquired by bayonets; many, probably, were forged. Bazaine was not fooled by the lack of formal resistance; he reported to Napoleon III: "Where we are in occupation, peace reigns and the population declares for us and the monarchy. Everywhere else there is war and a dismaying silence." No town or territory declared for the emperor until it came under French guns.

But if there was no rallying to the monarchy, there was also no gathering around the constitutional president. Juárez and his cabinet fled ahead of French columns, moving farther north in 1863 and 1864. Many liberal leaders felt that Juárez' was a lost cause. At Saltillo, González Ortega and other officers asked for the president's resignation; the liberal state government in Nuevo León refused to turn over custom receipts to the Juárez forces. The northern *caciques* were as independent and anarchic as ever. Juárez' dusty carriage became his traveling seat of government, fleeing from town to town. He seemed powerless—yet, he was becoming a symbol.

Pressure built on Ferdinand Maximilian. Although his brother, the emperor of Austria advised him not to sail without a British guarantee, he encouraged the Mexican deputation sent by the conservatives in October, 1863. The British government persistently refused to approve the venture, so the archduke temporized, asking for further proofs of Mexican loyalty. Napoleon III became impatient, for he needed the Austrian prince to front for what was beginning to appear a blatant French conquest of Mexico. By Christmas, Ferdinand Maximilian realized he had temporized too long to back out now with honor, which was important to him. At last in early 1864 he announced he would go to Mexico if he were convinced the people wanted him, and if the French emperor would guarantee military support for at least six years.

General Bazaine, who now commanded in Mexico, presented him with a purported six and a half million "votes" for the empire, in fact, more signatures than there were literate people in Mexico. Ferdinand Maximilian's tragedy was that now he suddenly ceased to be a free agent; step by step, with the best of intentions, he had not only become a pawn of Napoleon III, but had placed himself entirely in Napoleon's power.

Napoleon promised to furnish twenty thousand troops through 1867—but the financial considerations were crushing, as Napoleon III had no intention of furnishing these soldiers free. The new imperial government was required to pay all the costs of the French intervention through July 1864, and one thousand French francs per annum for every soldier serving on Mexican soil beyond that date. Far worse—and in fact, impossible —were the other French conditions that the archduke agreed to in the so-called Convention of Miramar: the Mexican imperial government was to accept responsibility for the Jecker bonds and the millions in reparations claimed by the French. Napoleon III thus took no financial risks at all, not even guaranteeing the loans of French bankers to the new regime in Mexico. He demanded this, and the archduke accepted, only because the image of El Dorado still lived. Europeans still thought the Mexican mines were inexhaustible treasure troves, if only they could come under efficient management—the illusion that continually floated bonds and drew foreign capital freely into the Mexican financial sinkhole.

One final problem almost dissuaded Maximilian at the last minute. The Austrian Council of Empire demanded that he relinquish all rights to the Austrian throne and his Hapsburg inheritance. This was no easy thing for him to do, but Napoleon extended great pressures, and his father-in-law, the king of the Belgians advised him not to fail the Mexicans. Finally, on April 14, 1864, Ferdinand Maximilian and his wife, Charlotte (now to become Maximiliano and Carlota, as the name Ferdinand or Fernando had unpleasant connotations in Mexico) departed for Veracruz in an Austrian warship. He stopped at Rome for a papal blessing.

The tall, slender, blue-eyed and blond-bearded Maximilian would have made an excellent king of England or a superb constitutional monarch of a Scandinavian state. He was liberal-minded and liberally educated, and interested in the arts and sciences. He had served ably as a royal governor and as ruler of the Imperial Austrian Navy. He was intelligent, honest, conscientious, and hardworking—in fact the epitome of a dutiful mid-Victorian prince. But ironically, those very qualities made him unfit to take a Mexican throne or command the Mexican destiny.

Maximilian was too little the brutal politician with a hard grasp of men and realities. His judgment, tinged with romanticism, was too much influenced by his own concepts of duty and honor and loyalty. He had not been trained to harsh practicalities or to compete in political cesspools with men like Napoleon III or the people he would face in Mexico.

Whether Maximilian understood this or not, he was called to the Mexican throne only by French bayonets, which imposed him on a country whose most energetic and politicized elite—the *mestizo* liberals—would now never accept what he stood for. The royalists, clericals, and various *continuistas* who clamored for him did not represent a driving force in Mexico; they had just lost a disastrous civil war to the liberals. In backing Maximilian, they sought miracles—and as Juárez saw and remarked, the Austrian was no miracle worker.

No one leader could revitalize the Mexican *criollos*, reinvigorate and respiritualize the clergy, or, given Napoleon's crippling financial terms, clean up the chronic fiscal mess. The task was impossible. His empress, Charlotte or Carlota, was never responsible for his failures. Despite legends spawned by modern television serials in Mexico, Mamá Carlota did not dominate him or influence the councils of state, though the proud, pretty Coburg princess created certain problems. Their relationship has always been presented as romantic, but Carlota was unstable, and the husband-wife relationship was not always proper or regular.

Their arrival in Mexico was hardly auspicious. Veracruz, a strong liberal city, greeted them coldly, making Carlota weep. General Almonte's caretaker regime handled arrangements badly—a bad sign, and from the moment he stepped on Mexican soil Maximilian was to be plagued with his supporters' monstrous inefficiency. Things began to look better at Puebla, the ancient center of *criollo* clericalism. Here, *hacendados* and canons came brilliantly-costumed to pay homage, while thousands of dark *indios* gaped as their grandfathers had gaped at arriving viceroys.

The capital that once cheered Juárez met the imperial couple with bells and processions of ancient families—the faithless capital greeted every conqueror with far more empty enthusiasm than Mexican historians care to admit. The *léperos* appreciated any spectacle that relieved the grim barbarity of their lives, and there is no question that the upper classes immediately fell in love with their new emperor and empress. They supplied a lack the would-be aristocracy had felt for fifty years: they were Real Royalty, surrounded by a coterie of genuine, titled European aristocrats, exuding a magic no native upstart could attain. And while this love lasted, the imperial pair afforded the capital a glamor it had never had, and would never have again. It may have been a tawdry, mid-nineteenth-century operatic glitter, but it spoke to the still-colonial soul. A hundred years afterward, there would still be Mexican nostalgics to shed tears for Maximiliano and Carlota. And even those Mexicans who felt only humiliated at the spectacle of the Second Empire found it hard to hate Maximilian, for he was not the author of these miseries but as much their victim as the Mexicans.

Ensconced in the capital, Maximilian continued to misunderstand his true situation. The city was not the country, the discredited elite did not reflect the rising Mexican consciousness. The Imperialists ruled only where the French stood with bared bayonets, and the conquest was far from won—but instead of taking command of the continuing civil war, Maximilian began to operate as though he was a benevolent king on a stable throne.

He spent much time seeing that the National Palace, repeatedly bombarded and ransacked, was restored, at much expense. He made the run-down Chapultepec Castle into a royal residence, and also into a great national monument set among ancient cypress trees, overlooking the shrinking lakes to the white-capped volcanoes. He personally laid out a splendid boulevard to connect the castle with the capital. If the path of mid-century progress displaced or destroyed many *indio* hovels, the grand avenue, later called the Paseo de la Reforma, gave the capital an almost but not quite Parisian splendor.

He commissioned works and statues and ceremonies with imperial extravagance. These follies, however, were dignified and always elegant, for Maximilian fell in love with Mexico. He wanted to refurbish and regenerate. He went deeper than the surface, too, designing legislation to advance the country and demanding from his ministers honest, efficient government. He tried to make an atmosphere for literary, artistic, and scientific revival. He used Spanish only by deliberate choice; he rode around the nearby countryside, relaxing at Cuernavaca like Cortés, and making a pilgrimage to Dolores to honor the memory of Hidalgo, whom he considered a national hero. He wore the clothes of a rich *hacendado* and ate local fare. He took an *india* or *mestiza* mistress. This obvious love of his adopted country won the hearts of many Mexicans.

But this was frittering, because he should have been vigorously crushing opposition and creating a tough, vigorous administration if he intended to remain Emperor of Mexico. The nation was not yet ready for his style of civilization. His power was not consolidated—and soon, the way he tried to consolidate it brought him into angry confrontation with his clerical and reactionary supporters.

When Maximilian received papal blessing for his venture from Pius IX he had made no promises to the Church, but the clergy believed that he would revoke the anticlerical clauses of the Reform. But this went against his nature. Maximilian regarded what he considered the medievalism of the Hispanic-Mexican Church with well-bred horror, and he was encouraged in these views by well-meaning Europeans such as the British minister Wyke and Rodenbeek, the Belgian envoy. Almost all Western governments advised him to avoid the bitter, archreactionary bishops who returned with him to Mexico, and to try to cultivate the *criollo* moderates.

The problem with this was that the moderates were few and wary, while the reactionaries were loud and unremitting in their demands. Archbishop Labastida insisted upon full reparation of all expropriated property. Maximilian, a good Catholic, knew this was both politically and financially impossible. The imperial regime was already groaning under the costs imposed by maintaining the French army; Maximilian was spending more than Santa Anna, though he was getting more for the peso. Also, at least a third of the expropriated property had been acquired by French interests, and much of the rest was now in the hands of conservative landowners who had no mind to return it to the Church.

Maximilian informed the clergy that their demands were irrational, and he sought support from the papal nuncio, offering a typical European compromise, to pay clerical salaries from state revenues. But the papal nuncio returned a papal ultimatum: to restore Church property and to restore the traditional privileges of the clergy as they existed before Reform.

Thrown into an honest rage, Maximilian defied the Holy See and the hierarchy by issuing an edict confirming the Reform. The nuncio was sent home, poisoning relations between Mexico and Rome. Maximilian could have survived this well enough, though most of the clergy now turned neutral, refusing to support him through self-defeating outrage; but the quarrel had larger implications. The Church's final intransigence now fatally strained the old alliance between the clergy and the landowners—most of whom had profited, ironically, from the sales forced by the Reform. Hundreds of rich men became terribly disillusioned with the hierarchy and began to speak of it as "foreign." It is not always understood that in these times Juárez' liberals posed no threat, real or spoken, to the *hacendado* class; all their fulminations were turned against the Church. The great landowners began to believe that their true interests lay with a truly national government, and perhaps a majority now in effect became neutral. They were not ready to fight for Juárez and the constitution—but they were not disposed to fight for Maximilian, either. They withdrew emotionally, prepared to join whichever side won out.

The conservatives whose drives were religious or emotional, meanwhile, also withdrew, raging that the emperor was only another Juárez "with a yellow beard."

Thus, while Bazaine was still chasing Juárez to the outer reaches of northern Mexico (by 1865 and French, Belgian, Austrian, and other imported contingents had reached the Rio Bravo), the underpinnings of the empire were crumbling rapidly. Juárez understood this perfectly. On the run, hiding now in Durango, now in remote Chihuahua, sometimes almost alone—he had sent his family to refuge in New York—Juárez and a few followers held out, serving as a symbol of the nation, fomenting a growing guerrilla war against the invaders.

The thirty-thousand-man foreign army was invincible in open battle, openly arrived at. But the juaristas' tactics spread the conquerors thinly across Mexico. Partisans in the wilds of Jalisco, Tamaulipas, and Coahuila held the hills and staged destructive raids. In Oaxaca a Mixteca-*mestizo* general, the liberal hero Porfirio Díaz, became a growing threat. The French now faced the immense problems the North Americans had avoided by getting out of Mexico rapidly, of an interminable guerrilla campaign that the regular French forces could not lose, but still could never win.

This warfare, by its historic nature, was confused and cruel. It infuriated the French officers, who considered guerrilleros outlaws, which they were under the rules of organized warfare. The Hague Conventions later made all forms of guerrilla warfare war crimes; this was a European concept that ignored the fact that peasants in countries like Mexico had no other way to retaliate and defend their native soil. By Maximilian's orders, the French forces were operating under severe restraints, for the kindly emperor hoped to avoid returning atrocity for atrocity. It was a vain hope in such a situation. Bazaine railed against restraints, arguing that he could never pacify Mexico unless he were allowed to institute a reign of terror.

Bazaine was caught between two masters, for Napoleon III was tired of the Mexican campaign, concerned that the United States, which had won its own civil war and sent twenty-five thousand soldiers to the Rio Grande in May, 1865, would intervene, and alarmed at the rising power of Prussia in Europe. Napoleon ordered Bazaine, who was ostensibly under Maximilian's command, to defeat the northern guerrillas once and for all. Pressed by the French, Maximilian at last signed a decree in October 1865 permitting the execution of any Mexican taken in arms against the imperial regime. Bazaine immediately shot two captured juarista leaders, Salazar and Arteaga.

The policy was a mistake. The *fusilados* made martyrs, causing thousands more Mexicans to take up arms against the empire. In fact, Maximilian had signed his own death warrant.

As the diplomatic and military pressure exerted by the United States on France became too great, Napoleon abruptly broke faith with Maximilian early in 1866. He repudiated the Miramar Convention, ordering out all French troops. The betrayal deeply shocked Maximilian. After protests, he allowed Carlota to sail for Europe, to beg for help from the French emperor, the pope, her father, and the other European royalty which he believed stood behind the Mexican venture.

When Carlota arrived in Europe, she found her father was dead, and her brother Leopold II had no intention of buying Mexican dreams with Belgian blood. Carlota rushed to Paris. The emperor refused to see her. After many days, the Empress Eugenie arranged an interview, and the empress of Mexico passionately but rationally pled Maximilian's case. But the argument hung on Napoleon III's honor, and he had none. When Carlota at last understood that she and Maximilian were betrayed by the cruel exigencies of international politics, her reason began to crack. She fled to Miramar, convinced that Napoleon III was the archfiend, and suffering from a persecution complex. In September 1866 she was granted an audience with the pope, and here, while trying to explain what had happened, she had a complete mental breakdown. Screaming hysterically for someone to save Maximilian in Mexico, meeting only averted eyes and concealed embarrassment, she was brought home to Belgium in the ultimate degradation of a strait jacket. She lived on in an interminable twilight of madness, dying at nearly ninety years of age in 1927.

Maximilian was sick with anxiety for his wife during these events, while all around him his empire cracked and shrank. Bazaine pulled the French regulars from the north, and behind them, everywhere, the imperialists failed to hold. The juarista forces came out of hiding and took over cities and states. The imperialist supporters were now very few. The important landowners, at first neutral, finally began to turn patriot, acknowledging allegiance to Juárez and the Republic. Several Austrian and Belgian regiments, all volunteers, arrived, and Maximilian was encouraged—but these gallants in their fine uniforms soon showed they had no appetite for serious combat. They retreated with the French. Matamoros fell to Juárez, then Tampico and Guadalajara. The north was lost.

By October 1866 Maximilian realized that Carlota was permanently deranged and his empire was finished. He had already considered abdicating, holding fast only because of his wife's appeals to keep faith with "loyal Mexicans." Now, with a fatal irresolution and withdrawal in this bloody crisis, he went to Orizaba, intending to resign. An old friend, the Austrian captain Herzfeld, urged him to leave rather than subject Mexico to a bloodbath. The British, trying to find a rational compromise, advised him to call for elections, then honorably abdicate. This might have averted tragedy, but Maximilian, romantic to the last, listened to the wrong advisors.

The German Jesuit Fischer, an incredibly cynical adventurer, played upon Maximilian's sense of loyalty in a last-ditch effort to salvage the clerical cause. His own mother wrote, saying it was better to die in the ruins of an empire than to retreat ignominiously with the baggage of the French army. And a handful of Mexican conservatives who would rather die than fail again surrounded him. Generals Miramón and Márquez asked for commands, while the honest and loyal Tomás Mejía, a heroic figure for all his political naivete, refused to desert him. Maximilian now disliked and distrusted his conservative adherents, but he resolved to die like a king. He turned his back on those he considered faithless European friends, refusing to grant Bazaine a final audience as the French left Mexico.

By March 1867, the last French had gone, and the liberal forces closed in. Miramón led a desperate cavalry raid against Zacatecas, and almost succeeded in capturing Juárez, but soon afterward was routed. The juaristas, in a deliberate act of terrorism, shot all the prisoners taken in this action, including Miramón's brother.

Only the regions around Puebla, Querétaro, and the capital were in imperial hands. The liberal generals Escobedo and Corona converged on strategic Querétaro with forty thousand men. Maximilian's forces consisted of less than ten thousand. The war was lost, but the imperial forces comprised the last, hard-core resistance, filled with men like Miramón who no longer had anything to lose and with a few utter loyalists like Mejía.

Maximilian decided to die at the head of this army and rode to Querétaro.

The imperialists held out against overwhelming odds for seventy-one days. During the siege, Márquez led a thousand cavalrymen to Puebla seeking help. He found that Porfirio Díaz had captured that city, and his troops began to desert. Márquez, who lacked Miramón's courage, fled to Cuba. Maximilian, Miramón, and Mejía were left at Querétaro with only some five thousand troops.

The imperial generals defeated every attack but wasted their last strength in the efforts. As the exhausted, depleted imperialist ranks fell back into Querétaro under siege, Maximilian was at the front, inspiring the officers and men to prodigious efforts. Escobedo, despite his immense numerical superiority, became afraid to attack. Maximilian, now moving in a sort of irrational exaltation, planned to attack the liberals on May 15, 1867.

The end came, characteristically, through new treachery. An imperialist officer named López defected to Escobedo and showed the liberals how to sneak into the besieged city. Leading the enemy, López ordered his own forces not to fire. The juaristas marched in during the night of May 14 and quickly overran the confused defenders. Miramón fell wounded. Maximilian, his aide, Prince Salm, Mejía and a few others were surrounded after daylight on a small rise called Cerro de las Campanas just outside the town. Maximilian at last gave up, handing his sword to Escobedo, who acted according to the courtesies of war.

The courtesies soon ended. Juárez and Lerdo de Tejada were determined to destroy royalism forever by sentencing Maximilian to death. The president ordered that the ex-emperor be brought before a military court-martial. Juárez was not vengeful, but he believed that killing Maximilian was the only way to assert Mexican sovereignty and shock the outside powers against future interventions. The idea was popular among the liberal elite, who had been humiliated and enraged at the worldwide assumption that Mexicans were fit only to be ruled by a European prince. Thus Maximilian was to be made the unfortunate victim of an object lesson to the world that had not respected Mexican rights.

Maximilian was put on trial, accused of usurping power, serving as the instrument of foreign aggression, and of ordering the execution of prisoners of war. The trial was staged in a theater by seven junior army officers. Maximilian refused to be a spectacle and declined to appear to defend himself. His calmness and dignity, in fact, caused three of the judges to vote against the death penalty, although they had been instructed to return it. The court president broke the tie, four to three. Although Maximilian had believed to the end that he would be allowed to leave the country unharmed, he took the sentence calmly.

An Austrian warship stood off the Mexican coast, but the Austrians did not intervene.

There was a great international clamor for clemency, and many diplomats approached Juárez personally. Juárez was adamant, sternly refusing every initiative. He felt that policy demanded Maximilian be shot, to teach the powers that Mexico was a sovereign nation. The United States government suggested mercy and was spurned—although the United States had been instrumental in forcing the French out and had always backed the liberals, Juárez believed the United States could use a lesson too. Juárez calculatedly denigrated the North American assistance to his cause, because he believed Mexicans must find a sense of pride by thinking they had conquered all alone. He, and most liberals, intended that the shots at Querétaro be heard in Washington.

Maximilian, Miramón, and Mejía were awakened on June 19 to a fanfare of bugles and drums. Maximilian asked Miramón: "Miguel, is this for the execution?"

"I cannot say, Señor," the young general answered, "as I have not been shot before."

The three were taken to Cerro de las Campanas to be killed by fusilade. Maximilian behaved with great bravery, demanding that Miramón take the place of honor in the center. He gave each soldier in the firing party a gold piece and comforted Mejía at the last moment. Maximilian died like Hidalgo, crying *"Viva México!"*

His body, poorly embalmed, the rotted eyes replaced with glass, was finally given back to the Austrians, whose warship waited to bear it home. Maximilian was buried among his illustrious ancestors at Vienna. Later, the Hapsburgs were permitted to erect a pitiful little chapel on the dusty Cerro de las Campanas, but it became a neglected shrine, eventually to be dwarfed by a monstrously ugly statue of Benito Juárez.

Many Mexicans, hating what Maximilian stood for but finding it impossible to hate the man, considered it all a great pity.

30

THE PORFIRIATO

Pan o palo—bread or the stick.
A favorite saying of Porfirio Díaz, president of Mexico.

The era that began in 1867 and ended in 1911, whether presided over by Juárez, Díaz, or Lerdo, was all part of a single period of Mexican development. It corresponded roughly, like other periods, with developments in many Hispanic countries. A generation of liberal-conservative, centralist-federalist warfare in which military men everywhere were at the center of power gave way to a new consolidation. Much of the ancient institutional and political order had been destroyed. There were continuing, but declining, experiments with Anglo-Saxon parliamentary systems, which continued to fail. There was a general disappearance of the old Creole custodians and the emergence of a newer sort of national leadership and also, a newer intellectual elite.

The newer leadership tended to be eminently more practical than the old, more pragmatic and more subtle, less dependent upon sheer fire power but also infinitely more cynical, because this was a postrevolutionary phase. There was less rampant idealism, more attention to practical politics. The Juárezes were finally replaced with Díazes, new men with new ways of exercising power.

It is the conservative view that this era was a necessary one of nation-building, and that only those postcolonial societies in the Hispanic world that went through it showed any promise in the twentieth century. The liberal viewpoint, which in the Hispanic culture has always insisted that the nation was made, needing only social and political changes enforced by fiat, looks back on the phase as horrible. The conservatives have perhaps paid too much attention to the vital laying of rail and telegraph lines, the development of modern industrial and financial systems, and the consolidation of national governments, without sufficient regard for the enormous social cost. The watchword for the whole era could be summed up in the slogan that was applied to the national secular school system inaugurated by Juárez in Mexico—"Order and Progress." Compared to the first half of the century, there was tremendous material progress and enforced order. But the liberals can never forget that progress was achieved in an era of tyranny and injustice, and for that reason have probably denigrated real accomplishments too much.

The age has been criticized for permitting rapacious forms of exploitive foreign capitalism to seize upon the Hispanic-American world. This criticism, which springs from deep-seated emotions more than social or economic theory, ignores the fact that rampant capitalism was the premier power system of the time and that *foreign* capitalism invaded Mexico and the Hispanic world because there was no native entrepreneurism. If Mexicans wanted rails, they had to rely on British companies and engineers; if they wanted new mining techniques, they had to give concessions to North Americans; if they wanted modern banking, they had to do business with the French.

Native labor, resources, and soil were exploited and the native soul further humiliated. But the Hispanic world gained far more than it gave; it acquired rail lines, utilities, and modern organizational systems, and it could have gotten them in no other way. That fact, probably, will never be widely accepted in the Spanish-speaking world, because emotional arguments have always influenced the Hispanic mind far more than coldly practical balance sheets.

The conventional, and predominantly liberal view of the era between 1867 and 1911, and particularly the years between 1876 and 1911, is that it was a time of regression and total frustration, in which a new world was still struggling to break through. The old conservative view, that it was a period of stability, peace, and progress, and that Porfirio Díaz was the best president Mexico ever had, cannot bear full inspection; beneath the surface, this era had too many running human sores. The era was unbalanced; development was all one way, and the reaction, when it came, had to be violent and destructive. The more modern view, with the perspective of elapsed experience and time, is to take the men and the times on their own merits, and to judge both against their circumstance.

When Juárez reentered the capital in 1867, the Church was finished as a partner or an arm in government, and also as a serious political force in Mexico. It still possessed social and spiritual power, because if the majority of Mexican men had now become anticlerical the vast majority of women, of all classes but especially of the upper class, retained their old respect and piety. This was a phenomenon peculiar to most Latin societies, stemming from the position and training of women more than from any deep machinations of the Church. In a Mexico where anticlericalism had now become intellectually and fashionably dominant, and where every president was a Freemason, the Church continued to be given more attention than it perhaps deserved. It was the ancient *bête noire* of the intellectual elite, and a convenient whipping boy. The clergy no longer moved in places of power; the Reform of 1857 stood, and clerics and clericals had to act scrupulously. Unfortunately, the clergy was gripped by a siege mentality (the same mentality gripped Rome) and acted as if the loss of real estate and its educational monopoly had destroyed religion. The clergy aided their historic enemies by acting negatively.

In this century and even later, it was almost impossible for the Catholic clergy to understand that an estrangement of Church and state worked to the benefit of both. Mexico remained Catholic, but it was no longer a Catholic nation.

The Reform and the French Intervention had also given pretorianism its death blow. The professional army had been discredited by the emergence of capable, non-pretorian commanders. The army was still important, and it would always be important in a society as complex and divided as the Mexican, and where government had only a tenuous legitimacy. There was, briefly, a new threat from the liberal armies, which, had they been retained and pampered like the armies of the Trigarante, might easily have become the new pretorians. The liberal warriors expected rewards they failed to get from Juárez, and there was a rash of minor uprisings and pronunciamentos. But Juárez easily won reelection over the soldier hero-candidate, Porfirio Díaz in 1867, and his military chief, Sóstenes Rocha, stamped out rebellion in the army. Juárez then reduced and dismantled the armed forces and made this stick.

Meanwhile, the shooting of Maximilian had served its purpose. Mexican finances were still chaotic and Mexican debts had not disappeared, but foreign gunboats no longer appeared off Veracruz. The powers were now prepared to accept what deals they could make with Juárez. Relieved of foreign threats, relieved of the impossible burden of a huge domestic military force, Matías Romero, a brilliant secretary of the treasury, began to get finances back in order.

The juarista government, for the first time, could attack the problems of the nation without fearing for its very life from the Church, the pretorians, or foreign powers. This was, by any standard, enormous progress for Mexico.

Juárez and the men around him had provided the vital nucleus of a national idea, and Juárez had served as a wonderful symbol of Mexican sovereignty. The juaristas, however, represented only a minority of another minority, the tiny, politicized *criollo-mestizo* educated elite. The concept of *Mexicanidad* hardly went beyond their ranks.

Somewhere between thirty and forty percent of the nearly nine millions in Mexico were still identifiable *indios*. Custom-bound, separate, fearful and resentful of *criollos* and *mestizos*, generally illiterate and unpoliticized, these Amerindians were still caught up in the old Hispanic custodianship. They were still *gente sin razón*, outside of the economy and society, slaves to a debt system no one quite dared to abolish, oppressed, withdrawn, alcoholic, and diseased. The liberals recognized their misery, and Juárez certainly had sympathy for them. But they were also a mass obstruction to the nation. Each of the 153 Mexican Amerindian tribes and cultures struggled separately, blindly, and instinctively to survive, from the mountains of Nayarit to the remote valleys of Oaxaca to the fringes of Yucatán. The long-pacified Amerindians in the core of Mexico still clung stubbornly to their life styles and identity beneath their patina of Hispanicism. In cosmic terms, the desires of the *indios*, either a few miles outside the capital or in the virtually autonomous societies of the Tarahumares and Yaquis in Chihuahua, Durango, and Sonora, were human and admirable. All peoples preferred to live life as they knew it and resisted cultural change. These *indios* did not understand or want freedom within a Mexican nation; they really wanted autonomy and land—liberty to follow ancestral ways and room to plant their cornfields. Ironically, by finally preserving the Indians as Indians, the Spanish Empire had passed on enormous social problems to the Republic, when the Republic sought to become an integrated nation.

Juárez, though an Amerindian, was not an *indio*. He represented a complete adaptation to *mestizo* Mexico, as did Tomás Mejía. The *mestizo* liberals were caught in an anomalous position. They felt deeply, with their indigenous blood, the oppression of the *indios*; they felt a sense of outrage that went back to the Spanish rape and the rejection by their European progenitors. But the nationalistic *mestizos* of the nineteenth century had no real use for Indians, as Indians. Their solution, never completely articulated or rationalized, was for the *indio* to vanish as an *indio*. In truth and fact, no reform government did anything to preserve them as Indians.

Given a desire to forge a Mexican nation, in the pattern of other modern nations, this policy was historically correct. The reformers at first fully expected that to remove the legal and institutional barriers between the *indio* communities and *criollo-mestizo* Mexico would allow the Amerindians to enter the nation as free citizens. They did not foresee the immediate intensified oppression of the Indians, who were not prepared to enter into Mexican life or compete with Mexicans on Mexican terms. The policies initiated by the liberals, such as the *Ley Lerdo*, precipitated a calamity for the surviving *indio* communities, who did not comprehend the complexities of legal titles to land, or the concept of private ownership. The full fruits of this policy have been conveniently blamed on the Díaz dictatorship, but events actually represented a full-scale aggression of *mestizo* Mexico against the tribal Indian, because the liberals, not Díaz, removed the legal protection that surrounded the *ejidos*.

The Hispanic classes and castes also had enormous troubles of their own, without the presence of the Indian. There was yet a distinct bar between the *criollo* and the *mestizo*. The *criollos*, as a group, had been stripped of their monopoly of politics and their dream of a custodianship of the nation under either a republic or a monarchy. New men, mixed-bloods, now dominated the public affairs of Mexico, a position they had earned with valor, patriotism, and energy.

But the *criollos* had not vanished. They retained their virtual monopoly of property ownership, social prestige, and education, and the upper class was still *criollo*. Socially-mobile *mestizos* usually were absorbed into *criollo* ranks, exactly as under the caste system of the empire. Juárez, Díaz, and virtually every other successful *indio* or *mestizo* politician married European women by preference, and their progeny grew progressively "whiter." The caste system had enduring strength, and this was what many *mestizos* complained about when they said plaintively that "nothing had changed in Mexico."

The Reform never attempted to cope with the caste-class system. The liberals misread the social landscape throughout the century because they were intellectuals wrapped up in institutional reform. What they had done by 1857 and reconfirmed in blood by 1867 was to bring about the institutional democratic revolution as it had taken place in France and North America—separating Church and state, abolishing legal class privileges and making men theoretically equal before the law, confiscating religious property, destroying the corporations that supposedly stood between the citizen and the society and state, and permitting the choice of popular government.

This had been a wholesale adoption of the programs of Anglo-Saxon and French liberals. As the antithesis of custodianship by Church, crown, class, or even the state, it threw men back on private institutions. This was deliberate; the Mexican liberals did not believe in strong or activist government, and they were no more hostile to the idea of private wealth or private opportunity than the framers of the United States Constitution, which they had taken as a model. This fact had allowed a mass migration of landowners and rich men into liberal ranks during the French Intervention, when clericalism and monarchy were finally discredited. The social faith and hope of the liberals was in fact rooted in the concept of private property. Its ownership and free use was expected to make the citizen truly free from institutions and confining corporations, and to bring about economic and social progress. But this was an alien ideology, born of alien societies, and it could not work in Mexico as in the United States or even France. The destruction of reactionary institutions did not and could not bring democracy to Mexico.

In Mexico, the throwing of society back on the family or the individual allowed a few great families and a few powerful foreign companies to swallow everything.

Far from destroying the Mexican upper class, the Reform tended to make it more powerful than ever before. Haciendas, stagnant socially and economically since the seventeenth century, in an atmosphere of free enterprise began to gobble up smallholds and *ejidos* as never before, and in the same milieu foreign enterprise could erect powerful economic strangleholds that soon resembled the ancient monopolies. There *was* a growth of small freeholds and of native Mexican businessmen, but this was overshadowed by the enormous expansion of *latifundios* and foreign capitalisms.

Institutional freedom thus backfired in Mexico (as to some extent it backfired in Western Europe and the United States, causing those societies to make adjustments toward the close of the century—which the Mexicans, still running late, did not make in time); it wreaked further destruction on the Amerindians; and it in time created terrible frustrations among the *mestizo* majority. It was another excellent concept that failed to work in practice; it only reinforced the old society.

Perhaps naturally in the Mexican turmoil, the Creoles tended to grow more Europeanized than they had been in 1821. The infatuation with the Amerindian past affected only a handful of intellectuals, though it had become part of the political conventional wisdom of Mexico—men who would not let a contemporary *indio* enter their homes paid lip service to the memory of Cuauhtémoc, and presidents dedicated statues to the last Mexica ruler while they were destroying the last Amerindian tribes. The Creoles, however, found it harder to identify with Spain, which was sunk in the same social problems as Mexico, with prelates and pretorians and bewildering changes of regimes. Their hopes centered on the leader of the Latin, and to some extent the whole cultural world, France.

The French Intervention actually heightened this Latin love affair; old conservatives dropped their Spanish traditions in favor of the things of France. The liberals were already enamored with them. The Mexican upper class read French novels and French philosophers, sent its sons to Paris to learn about the world, and filled its hacienda houses and town palaces with French furniture and artifacts. Unfortunately, the infatuation with French styles came at probably the worst period of French taste, during the Second Empire and Third Republic, and it littered artistic monstrosities across Mexico. The epitome of high fashion was to employ a

French governess/mistress in a French house. This transfer of cultural allegiance was natural, given French prestige and the fact that the cultivated classes could hardly bear the still-barbarous nature of much of Mexico; and it was made easier by the fact that through 1914 the Third Republic represented neither a liberal society nor a genuine political democracy. Rich Mexicans felt at home in Paris, and Frenchmen soon felt comfortable in the City of México.

This Francophilia sprang from the same causes and had almost identical results in Mexico as in another country on the fringes of Western culture, Russia. It further estranged the elite from the masses, and it heightened the xenophobia of the common people, who felt humiliated and culturally betrayed. It banked fires toward an explosion.

The identification with Europe by the *criollos* aggravated the racial problem, because Europeans took their racial superiority over Asians, Africans, and Amerindians for granted; most were also peculiarly intolerant of mixed blood. Science taught that mixed breeds inherited the vices of both races—and most histories of Mexico written in this period at least broached that belief. North Americans, British, French, all gravitated socially to the *criollo*, and the fact that all foreigners placed great weight upon "pure-Spanish" descent colored all their relationships with Mexicans. It also affected Mexican self-esteem. No Mexican of fashion could be proud of his Amerindian ancestry. The standard of physical beauty in Mexico was Nordic or Mediterranean—a standard that only a handful of the population could match. A terrible uneasiness and fury was again aroused in the still-homeless *mestizo* soul. Expected to be vicious, many *mestizos* acted out their stereotype.

These enormous social problems were enough to keep Mexico fragmented through generations whether a succession of Juárezes came or went. And the democratic, republican constitution that was finally enshrined in 1857 made government unworkable. The constitution was federalist, because most liberals still feared a centralized, authoritarian dictatorship. However, the Hispanic mentality did not easily grasp the concept of separation of powers, nor were Mexican minds comfortable with diffusions of powers between the capital and the regions.

Historically, whenever government did not represent some sort of dictatorship it tended to fragment. Given the problems of vast distances, poor communications, and the fact that the *norteños* (inhabitants of the northern provinces) were different in many ways from the *criollo-indio* core, it was almost miraculous that some northern states did not become independent between 1821 and 1867, as they continually threatened to do. Yucatán did its best to separate, and would have succeeded except for two reasons: the racial war, and the fact that no outside power wanted it, throwing the dominant whites back on their need for help from Mexico.

During the period of apparent total incoherency, however, a distinctive Mexican political system was emerging. The states remained part of the Republic, but they were ruled by virtually sovereign political bosses, the *caciques*.

By the 1830s *caciques* really ruled most states and towns. Whether they took power with the ballot or gun, they usually expressed the aspirations of their region. For two generations, while the people who fought over possession of the capital (and theoretically, the Republic) were never able to run their writ beyond the central provinces, *caciques* and their cronies took the place of a bureaucracy in the outlying areas. Locally, the system worked reasonably well; leaders like Juan Álvarez in Guerrero and many of the northern governors ran effective regimes. In national terms, however, they were a disaster.

Whatever his sympathies or politics, every state governor tended to be jealous of the president and his clique, and determined to surrender none of his money, privileges, or power to the central government. Mexico thus devolved into a series of petty, political baronies, which made the nation terribly ineffective during the interventions of the United States and France. Juárez, while accepted everywhere as constitutional president after 1863, got little assistance from local regimes which in effect considered themselves the equals of his government. After 1867, Juárez' prestige gave him the presidency again, but nothing changed; in the face of a horde of local baronies his office was constitutionally almost powerless.

There was a national congress, but it had a long history of worthlessness. The parliamentary system failed to throw up a bar to tyranny or any national leadership. Significantly, no great leaders ever emerged through a congressional career. The congress was an imported Anglo-Saxon idea which few Mexicans understood, and it was unsuited to the Mexican value system. At best, it provided a republican veneer under a strong executive; at worst, it was obstructive and destructive, even of itself. The inability to grease the political process with compromises and to hold personalisms in check made representative government a mockery.

Juárez, though never losing his belief in the democratic process, had to violate it repeatedly in order to govern. As president, he was no democrat, cowing the congress, rigging local elections where he could, and conspiring to put his own men in local state offices whenever he could. He had to. Letting nature take its course under the constitution produced political chaos. Juárez, like every Mexican chief, governed by personality and edict. Unfortunately, he had neither the taste nor the talent for this kind of rule; he believed in legality. He was upright and honest; his concepts were good. He did not grasp, or refused to grasp, the essence of Mexican politics, which had nothing to do with enacted law, but depended upon personal leadership and a balancing of forces.

Juárez never was able to extend his control fully to the northern states, which remained in chaos after 1867. The frontier with the United States was utterly lawless. In national terms, Juárez was to prove a far finer symbol of Mexican sovereignty and rectitude than a great, activist president.

The peace and control he did exercise over the central area allowed the beginning of certain forms of progress. With sovereignty established and finances under control, Juárez could initiate domestic development. The British were authorized to build a railroad between Veracruz and the capital, the start of a great track expansion in railroading's heroic age. The program, however, was flawed from the start; rails were laid with foreign money and skills, and were inevitably planned to support foreign capitalisms rather than to follow a strategic plan or enhance native economic development. The new railroads were designed to provide transportation for the products of foreign-owned plantations and mines to the port cities.

In this age of dominant private capitalism, foreign companies could hardly have been expected to provide lines in accord with long-term Mexican strategic interests, or to invest money to aid the growth of native industries. The rail lines thus grew as a patchwork; they were never designed as strategic national transportation networks, such as those in the United States and Germany. If the liberals had insisted upon such a network, they would have had to supply at least the money.

As far back as the administration of Guadalupe Victoria, Mexico—even after independence was assured—was passing from political colonialism into economic colonialism under foreign interests lacking flag sovereignty. After independence, the Mexican economy continued to require the extraction of fibers and minerals for foreign markets, and the only capital development that went into the country was to assist this process, which was rooted in the past.

The past also hampered Juárez' immediate dream of bringing primary education to every Mexican child. He believed in education with mystic faith; it could make presidents of Indians. By 1867, the former limited educational system was ruined. The Royal and Pontifical University was greatly diminished and only a few provincial colleges remained. Outside the cities there was nothing. The Church schools had been closed to break the clerical monopoly over the Mexican mind; now there were no primary or secondary schools beyond a few private academies.

Juárez' government began a new primary system and sponsored a National Preparatory School aimed at training future professionals. Here the problem was even greater than with railroads, because an educational system required a long-term capital investment with no hope of foreign aid. The difficulties were immense and obvious: vast distances, the remoteness of most of the population in rural Mexico, the shortage of money and teachers, the difficulty of providing the luxury of education to families whose children could not afford the leisure.

Under Juárez, five thousand secular schools were built, providing free education for 150,000 students. Another 150,000 attended private primary schools. Measured against a population of nine million, this was nothing, merely the production of a slightly expanded elite, but measured against the past, the gain was tremendous.

At the preparatory school level, this education system began to face problems common to most traditional societies. The school was attacked by clergy and others for its agnostic faculty, but this was not the real problem. In an unchanged class structure, the few underprivileged students who trickled into the secondary schools by luck or brilliance saw education as a road to public employment. They were less concerned with culture than with jobs; even Mexicans who got no further than the primary schools expected public posts. In a society desperately needing medical doctors and engineers, the vast majority of young scholars insisted upon becoming *licenciados*, the traditional path into the bureaucracy. A few technicians were made, along with thousands of less-needed lawyers. At no level did the Mexican awareness really grasp the principles of economic reality or capital formation. But then no school system could change deep-rooted biases or value systems. The public school system was bent to accommodate dominant attitudes.

By 1871, when Juárez' third term expired, the problem of order was transcending the problems of progress. The triumph of liberalism had caused ideology to lose its fire, and on state and national levels politics was sinking into a question of personalities. Factions gathered around important men and assured them that the country needed them. Most such men required little encouragement. When Juárez stood for reelection to an unprecedented fourth straight term in 1871, there were signs that he was obstructing other men's ambitions. To his surprise, Sebastián Lerdo de Tejada, one of his most loyal followers, also declared, along with the once-defeated Porfirio Díaz, who was still the veterans' candidate.

There was no ideology behind this contest, all three were liberal paladins running on the same program. They divided the liberal support almost equally. However, no incumbent Mexican government ever lost an election, and when the issue went to the congress, it declared Juárez president. Lerdo was mollified with the office of president of the Supreme Court.

At this result, Díaz was thoroughly disgusted. He raised a point: "Indefinite reelection endangers our national institutions," and that "no citizen should perpetuate himself in office." Juárez answered, "To sacrifice law and order for the plans of one man, however deserving, would plunge us into endless anarchy." This exchange was to prove deeply ironic in coming years.

Díaz proclaimed, raising the standard of revolt in Oaxaca.

Only personal ambitions and personalities lay behind this rebellion. The election of Juárez was of course no more honest than any other Mexican election, which was the main reason why defeated candidates rarely accepted willingly the verdict of the polls, but there was no sign that Díaz had any feeling beyond a personal sense of outrage.

Díaz had impeccable liberal credentials. He had joined Juárez as a young, rough-hewn, half-Mixtec, and he had been proscribed in Oaxaca like his chief by Santa Anna. Taking to arms during the War of the Reform, he emerged as a brilliant young officer. Again in arms against the French, he made a romantic escape from Bazaine by climbing down a rope from his cell at Puebla. He had raised an army in Oaxaca, and in 1867 he had doomed Maximilian by seizing first Puebla, then the capital during the siege of Querétaro.

Juárez had treated him coldly, even ungraciously, and sent him back to Oaxaca without reward—where, however, the state government presented Díaz with an hacienda. The two men were estranged from this moment. Díaz never liked Juárez, and it is quite possible that Juárez smelled personal danger in the brilliant young general's obvious ambitions.

Juárez' loyal general, Sóstenes Rocha, smashed Díaz' rebellion easily, forcing the failed rebel to flee into the mountains of Nayarit, where the *indio* Lozada, who like most regional *caciques* had no use for Juárez or the government, protected him from federal troops.

Then, Juárez died at his desk in July 1872 from a massive heart attack. The chief of the Supreme Court, Sebastián Lerdo de Tejada succeeded to the presidency. Holding his own, and Juárez' supporters behind him, Lerdo felt secure enough to declare an amnesty. He allowed Díaz to come down out of the Pacific mountains, and also permitted the aged and half-blind Santa Anna to return to Mexico to die. Santa Anna now dozed and drooled in poverty and obscurity, while his wife mercifully passed out coppers to beggars so that they would come and cheer the fallen Highness' audiences. Díaz, however, was proving himself a far more astute *político*; he learned from experience. He saw that governments no longer fell from a general's mere pronunciamento, and he began to cultivate important army officers, politicians, and *hacendados*.

Lerdo had been an excellent subordinate to Juárez; in power himself he was in many ways a disastrous throwback to Gómez Farías. He was intellectual and cultivated and marred by a cold hauteur; he was honest and meant well but alienated everyone. He forgave enemies, then submitted them to the unforgivable indignity of ignoring them. Once he assumed high office, Lerdo never seems to have tried to keep ties and friendships among the army and leading politicians.

He continued Juárez' policies. He refused, however, to allow railroads to be built toward the north, or to connect with North American tracks beyond the border. "Let there be a desert between strength and weakness," he stated; he feared connecting rail lines might someday serve the *norte-americanos* for a military invasion. The decision angered powerful railroad interests in the United States, and therefore Washington. Washington was also growing irritated over another problem, which Lerdo, unable to cope with it, pretended did not exist. Mexican bandits and Indian tribes with sanctuaries in Mexico had taken to raiding regularly across the frontier. There was a clamor over this in Texas, and this trouble was to lead indirectly to Lerdo's downfall.

Few if any men are willing to surrender power gracefully, and Lerdo proved no exception as Mexican president. Although unpopular, he had been accepted because it was widely believed he would only serve out Juárez' unexpired term. But, persuaded by his friends, he announced for reelection. This caused consternation throughout official Mexico, because no incumbent in power ever lost an election. Díaz, sensing the widespread disappointment, chose this moment to pronounce again.

From the little town of Tuxtepec, his supporters issued a new plan. The Plan of Tuxtepec called for "effective suffrage" and "no reelection"— again with great irony as history was to unfold. This was a strikingly effective slogan that hit home to every educated Mexican—so effective it still appears above the signature block of every official document of the Mexican Republic, although only half the aspiration was to be achieved.

Díaz was in Texas, lining up arms and financial support. Díaz was no lover of Anglo-Saxons, but he was a cold realist. He was prepared to make deals, and he promised potential supporters a more friendly reception than the lerdista assertions of Mexican sovereignty. He got arms and money and recrossed the border. He subverted the Matamoros garrison, but was routed by General Mariano Escobedo, the ex-muleteer hero of Querétaro, short of Monterrey.

Díaz was chased back across the Bravo. He then sailed for Havana and from there to Veracruz, where he came ashore disguised as a workman. He slipped into Oaxaca, and reappeared at the head of a local army of supporters.

Meanwhile Lerdo had pushed through his reelection. But now Iglesias, the new president of the Supreme Court, who had his own hankering to be Chief of State, invalidated the election on the grounds that votes were counted from states that were in technical rebellion. In the general confusion, Díaz marched on the capital, and his little army, aided by horsemen under a Oaxacan compadre, Manuel González, defeated the government forces under Alatorre near Tlaxcala in November 1876.

Lerdo, soon joined in exile by Iglesias, rode for a ship at Acapulco. Díaz, now praised by everyone and most of the generals, entered México in the usual triumph, amid the usual scenes of jubilation by great people and *léperos*—who were now known more delicately as *pelados*, or "skinned ones." The congress immediately declared Díaz provisional president.

All this seemed taken from a familiar script. But things were to be very different this time around, because Porfirio Díaz, as he said himself, was a very different breed of cat from any who had sat in the presidential palace before.

A rather confusing eight years ensued. Díaz took the presidency firmly; when nine men at Veracruz were accused of plotting to restore Lerdo de Tejada, he sent a simple wire: "Kill them on the spot." However, there was no blood bath; this was not the Díaz style. He made no real changes in any policy after 1876; he continued the juárista plan of sober retrenchment, committing none of the follies of the earlier *caudillos*. He committed none of Gómez Farías' or Lerdo's errors, either; he not only appeased most of his natural enemies, but won them over to his side by favors and demonstrated friendship. When the provisional term expired in 1880, he stepped down in obedience to his own dictum of no reelection. He subverted effective suffrage, however, by assuring that his old comrade Manuel González became president.

Whether Díaz planned to use the González presidency as an interlude to assuage public opinion, or as a floater of trial balloons, is not really understood by anyone. What Díaz did was remove himself from the public eye, but stayed close to the center of power, first as governor of his home state, then as chief justice, constitutionally second in line for the high office. It is very likely that he knew what he wanted to do and how he intended to make his era, but preferred to let General González test the wind.

If this was so, González was the perfect tool, loyal but extremely inept, a man calculated to make Díaz look very good in comparison. González, almost certainly with Díaz' approval, if not his instigation, began a series of moves, none of which were new but were now carried to new extremes.

The federal government began selling huge tracts of Mexican soil, which were declared officially "empty," to foreign companies and to native *hacendados*. Almost all this land was actually occupied by various communities of Amerindians, who were displaced under the *Ley Lerdo*. The forms of the law were observed, since the squatters or tenants were allowed to buy the land in many cases, which option, of course, they could not use; some never even learned of the official pronouncement that the tribal *ejidos* were up for sale, or could have read or understood the proclamation had it been presented them.

Railroad and mining concessions were also widely sold, particularly in the northern states. These went to North Americans—a historic change. Díaz was keeping his promises, and also, Díaz believed that if he did not accommodate the United States investors, the railroads and mining concessions would be forced by North American bayonets. The Mexican envoy to Washington so advised the government. In fact, there were twenty-three incursions or violations of the Mexican border between 1874 and 1882 by United States troops or local militias—not, however, to help investors but in pursuit of bandits or savage Amerindians. These incursions made a much deeper impression on the Mexican mind than on the North American. Every Mexican schoolboy could recite them; most United States citizens never heard of them.

The accommodation of North America investors went to extreme lengths in one respect. The ancient Hispanic law had always vested the ownership of subsoil resources in the crown and therefore by extension in the state or nation; miners in Mexico had operating rights but the state owned the mining property. Under Anglo-Saxon law, mineral rights went with land titles unless specially reserved, and it was quite understandable that North American mining companies much preferred to buy mining properties than to negotiate revokable concessions. González rammed a change in the historic law through congress that gave foreign mining companies outright ownership of subsoil resources.

The González administration gained a great deal of revenue from the deals. In one sense, it was "selling" the nation through necessity. The Church had been exhausted as a banker, and so had the old process of selling government bonds abroad. The Mexican government had found a new source of revenues, by making what in effect were alliances with foreign capitalists. However, González and his cronies were so inept and corrupt that the treasury remained bare, and this, not the deals, aroused enormous criticism among the Mexican elite.

In fact, González was so obviously unsuitable and unfit to govern that in 1884 most leading men were pressuring Porfirio Díaz to reassume the presidency. The concept of no reelection was buried in a greater concern for order and stability. When Díaz did reassume the presidency in 1884, promising to restore financial responsibility in government, there was relief throughout the Atlantic trading community and general satisfaction in Mexico.

This was the beginning of the era known in Mexico as the Porfiriato, in which the presidency became Don Porfirio's eternal companion. It lasted until 1911, almost a full generation. It was far more than the perpetual presidency of one man, or a stagnant dictatorship. It marked a new plateau in Mexico, and the era, for good or bad, was a decisive period in Mexico's emergence as a modern nation.

Porfirio Díaz did not somehow change the direction of Mexico; he was not the maker of his times but he was, like Santa Anna, peculiarly representative of them. This is why, probably, both men have been so virulently hated and despised in later times. Each, in his own way, was the symbol of national weaknesses and humiliations, and each was made the scapegoat for the ills of Mexican society and the sins of a whole generation. Both men, truly representative of the malaise of their times, knew how to take advantage of a current vileness in Mexican souls. Díaz, who sprang from the true mixed race of Mexico, was the more representative Mexican and immensely the better man. Most other presidents, had dreamed of perpetual power, but Díaz was canny enough to know how to consolidate it.

A new generation of liberals had emerged since the War of the Reform, and these men were making a newer kind of intellectual establishment. Since virtually all important people had become liberals—Díaz himself was the last political survivor of the old days—there was a marked decrease in emphasis on ideology. The liberal-conservative quarrel had vanished with the conservatives. The younger generation, as always, despised the follies of its elders, and had had a bellyful of their polemics. And turbulence and rhetoric and revolution had brought all the elite, old and new, to a postrevolutionary plateau. The newer intellectuals, who continued to play key roles, were more cool, more rational, and more utilitarian, seeing the salvation of their country less in ideals than through economic development.

The first impulse came from disillusioned intellectuals of the Reform period, who lost faith in visionary democracy. Gabino Barreda, who organized the National Preparatory School for Juárez, and the atheistic poet Ignacio Ramírez, the old anticlerical who was Díaz' first minister of education, now taught disrespect for passionate visions and idealistic reforms. The nation was *not* made, they agreed, and it would never be made by liberal edicts which tried to set aside history with pen strokes. The very people who had sparked the Reform were no longer revolutionary, and held that continuing dreams of more reforms were unpatriotic. What the nation needed now, they thought, was regeneration, which must come from strictly scientific attitudes applied to material progress. First order, then progress, through ruthless economic development under a strong government. Thus the old liberals, though they would have deeply resented the assertion, had in many ways become *continuistas*.

The men, like the brilliant humanist-historian-educator Justo Sierra, who were dominating intellectual life by the 1870s, did not hold to the conservative notions of the past. They believed in the values of early nineteenth-century French and English liberalism. Mexico had completed her own version of the French Revolution only in 1857, confirmed a decade later, and Mexican thought still ran far behind the Western world. Barreda, Ramírez, and Justo Sierra had become positivists; taking their philosophical inspiration from Auguste Compte, the materialistic skeptic, and their economic theories from the Manchester school of English economists. They were inculcating the attitudes of laissez-faire in Mexico when the societies that had developed these notions had already begun to move away from them, through a heightened social consciousness and a gradual implementation of state controls.

Somewhat to the horror of the oldest liberals, the dominant thinkers redefined Mexican liberalism. Sierra's view was in fact much closer to Lucas Alamán (without his Hispanic hangovers of clericalism and romantic ideals of monarchy) than to Gómez Farías or Mora, for like Alamán, Sierra held that history was cyclical and not to be altered by bursts of idealism. Where Alamán believed that Mexico must be ruled with an iron hand while material progress and development was fostered by government, Sierra, who was at heart a democrat, was reluctantly willing to permit authoritarian government until the nation was ready for political democracy. Sierra, as rounded and cultivated as Alamán, followed him as the greatest historian of his age. He was a *continuista* in that he believed Mexican society should be allowed to evolve naturally rather than be torn up by the roots. Significantly, both Alamán and Sierra clearly saw the evils of the regimes they came to support, but clearly considered them necessary evils. Both men based their conclusions on conditions, and they were their respective eras' premier historians because they used facts and figures while other writers limited themselves to ideals and polemics.

Educated Mexicans had come to see the fallacies of Gómez Farías' politics and the weaknesses of the Juárez style of government—but they failed to see the fatal error of Mexican positivism. The flaw was *not* in the politics or the dictatorship of Díaz, both of which were enormously effective, but in the belief that Mexico could be regenerated by an all-out exploitation of the country's material resources and an industrial development carried out by foreign capital, without protecting the weak in society or alleviating the misery of the masses mired in the primitive economy. At bottom, the problem was the old one that caused every importation of Western political and economic theory into Hispanic countries to fail: the lack of a native bourgeoisie.

The old liberalism failed to make a stable peasantry; the new liberalism almost destroyed the rural population and substituted a foreign bourgeoisie for a viable Mexican middle class. The only people who could take advantage of Comptian liberalism in Mexico were the present property holders and incoming foreign investors. The "middle class" that did begin to emerge was overshadowed by great landowning families and invading capitalists; it had raised expectations but was small, alienated, and estranged in its own country. On one level positivism did develop the nation. On another, it primed a social volcano.

The influence of education after the 1870s has often been discounted because of the great weakness in primary education and the lack of schools. However, Mexican secondary and higher education for the small elite that obtained it, was excellent. Most of the better students, admittedly from the privileged classes, passed through Barreda's and Sierra's establishments, learning positivism in the old, ornate, colonial college buildings that had once trained priests. Although their education was not integrated (despite Sierra's efforts to make a true national university) and included too much law and fine arts and too little medicine and engineering and science, it was still extremely effective. It shaped the mind of the elite and the era.

And the era was made for Porfirio Díaz, for the liberal general who had once stood many a clerical and conservative against the wall was now reconciled with most of the upper class. Díaz had no real ideology; he was a superb pragmatist, and at the age of fifty-four still able to learn and change. He had made a fortunate marriage to a much younger wife from an important political family. Doña Carmelita Romero Rubio de Díaz knocked off most of the provincial *mestizo*'s rough edges, teaching him to use gold plate and bread instead of tortillas to scoop his beans; she put him in white tie for ceremonies, and the two lived more regally at Chapultepec than Maximilian and Carlota. Don Porfirio was ready to become the darling of the elite.

His great contribution was that he was the first Mexican president to keep order, with methods that were sometimes callous ("Shoot them on the spot!"), sometimes subtle, usually flexible, and invariably practical. Díaz was the perfect example of the politician who had emerged in the provinces of independent Mexico so many years before and who before his time gave the central governments continual grief, as first one ideology then another tried to run roughshod over the Republic. Díaz was nothing new—a man thrown up out of anarchy, who held power more from personal qualities and capabilities than from any institutional basis. He was a *cacique*, the truly representative Mexican leader-type. But he was the first effective *national cacique*, who in the presidency began to reorder the whole Republic along the lines of a local *cacique*'s domain.

Díaz was not a *caudillo* or a pretorian, despite his apparent military background. For him the professional army was a tool. Nor was he a totalitarian leader, spearheading any ideology or idea, implacably hostile to any faction or group. He had replaced *caudillaje* and custodianship with *caciquismo*; thereafter *every* successful president was a national *cacique* in Díaz' image, though most ascribed to different aspirations and ideals.

His regime was no democracy, but it was hardly the authoritarian tyranny it is sometimes described. Díaz was more a balancer of forces: he balanced the landowners against the peasants, labor against capital, the army against civilian politicos and the mob, foreign investment money against the national deficit. He was the great manipulator with a sure touch.

He was not a reactionary, or even a conservative—though he grew conservative, like most successful men, about his own establishment. He was a *continuista* in the sense that he accepted the Mexican world as it was, and he was conservative in his essentially pessimistic view of human nature.

His *caciquismo* was both essentially Mexican and in the pattern of other Hispanic autocrats emerging in the late nineteenth-century and twentieth-century world. He kept the Constitution of 1857 and even scrupulously followed its forms and provisions—while violating most of them in spirit and fact. Mexico remained a federalist republic, with liberal constitutional guarantees, while Díaz slowly transformed the government into an effective, centralized regime whose writ ran into every nook and corner. Díaz expressed the art of the possible in a distinctly Mexican way.

He perfected a system that was already emerging, by creating a hierarchy of *caciques*. Most presidents had taken control of the federal apparatus, and Díaz did the same: he packed the congress (he called it his *caballado*, or cavvy of broken horses) and he filled every significant post in the Mexican judiciary and bureaucracy with his men. He had an enormous patronage at hand, and, not being bound by ideology or party politics, he could use it judiciously. Lucrative or prestigious offices won over many men who might not otherwise have collaborated in his regime. But command of the federal apparatus in a nation as sprawling and disorganized and separatist as Mexico had never meant full control of the country, and here the genius of Díaz' *caciquismo* emerged.

He erected an imposing political structure in the states and provinces. He devised a system of selecting officeholders by being able to select the candidates. Almost every mayor (now called municipal presidents) was thus a man of his confidence, with a stake in the Díaz system. He appointed between three and four hundred *jefes políticos* himself. These regional *caciques* watched lower officials and saw to it the electoral and other machinery ran smoothly. On the highest provincial level, he also selected and assured the election of state governors. Under the constitution, the governor's office held considerable power, and this meant it was particularly important that each be held by the right man. The governorship was a great plum, and when he had given it to a man, Díaz continued to make his system run smoothly by balancing one governor against another, or against regional military commandants, so that no state governor ever could build up a personal power base. He was master at dividing power and responsibility among several people, so that no rival *cacique* could emerge on the national level. At each level, the *cacique* or chief was responsible and responsive to the national *cacique*. Thus the system ran within and yet without the constitution. It was a total distortion of the purposes of the constitution—yet it worked better than any previous system had ever worked in Mexico.

There was, of course, a great variety in the quality of men who held governorships and political chieftainships. Some were very poor, petty tyrants, corrupt, ignorant, and insufferable. But a very great many were excellent men—progressive and humane executives who kept corruption to a reasonable level. In general, Díaz showed excellent judgment in his appointments and choices. They never endangered the system—which was, at bottom, a system of keeping Don Porfirio in power.

He led the army, always potentially dangerous, equally skillfully. Some generals who appeared too ambitious, greedy, or pretorian were siphoned off into governorships or other prestigious posts where their immediate military contacts and command over troops were broken. Díaz also reduced the regular army to thirty thousand men. He had no intention of fighting a foreign enemy; the only potential enemy was the United States, and in such case no Mexican army would be big enough. Therefore, Díaz prepared a military instrument only powerful enough to fight wild Indians and to keep peace in the provinces, and for his own protection he corrupted it.

He met the generals' monetary demands by assigning them gambling concessions in their garrison areas. Senior commanders found their posts too lucrative to pronounce, and they kept energetic younger officers busy as their bagmen. Díaz made promotion slow and difficult, and when officers were ready for high posts they were usually fat, gray, and corrupt, thoroughly integrated into his system. The army was curbed for the first time since independence.

The peace-keeping functions that had been exercised catastrophically by the army in the past were entrusted to a new-type constabulary, called the "rurales" or rural police. The rurales were a paramilitary organization, riders in handsome, silver-trimmed gray charro uniforms and wide sombreros. They were a decentralized organization, for the use of local officials and political chiefs, but at every level, like civilian officers, they were responsive to the president. The rurales were corrupt and sometimes rode roughshod over the villages they were supposed to protect—but so had the army for fifty years. And the rurales proved vastly more effective in hunting down and killing bandits, possibly because many rurales were ex-bandits themselves.

The rurales worked a rough justice. With Díaz' assent, they employed the so-called *ley de fuga*; more prisoners were shot "trying to escape" than ever saw a Mexican jail. This was nothing new, but Díaz institutionalized it and even rationalized the practice by saying it was necessary to save good blood by shedding bad. The bandit chiefs who had operated fla-grantly throughout most of Mexico since the 1840s were drastically re-duced. Díaz had some shot, others exiled or placed in what was perpetual house arrest far from their old haunts. In this way he cleared up most of the running sores along the U.S.-Mexican border, and became the first Mexican president respected throughout the North American Southwest. Some particularly talented ex-bandits, however, were spared for the rurales or for some other use.

Díaz would have such men brought into his presence, while he calmly loaded a revolver with five bullets. Then, pointing the revolver directly, he would hold out his other hand, offering the prisoner *cinco balasos o cinco dedos*—five bullets, or five fingers in friendship. He recruited some very capable men this way, few of whom ever forgot the lesson.

All of these practices, celebrated, admired, or condemned, restored more peace to the countryside than it had enjoyed for a hundred years. Now travelers were rarely in danger of having their throats cut or their stages shot up in every mountain pass, and the silver trains and merchant caravans proceeded through Mexico with greater safety than at any time since Revillagigedo.

The Díaz regime was peculiarly personal. Díaz had no program except that of holding power; therefore, he was deeply suspicious and wary of any potential rivalry. Always the coiner of maxims, he liked to say, "Two cats cannot live in the same bag." He disposed of governors who grew too independent; he bought generals or posted them to remote deserts or jun-gles; he played off one potential rival against another.

The brutal totalitarianism that characterized later twentieth-century dic-tatorships was absent; Díaz scrupulously observed constitutional forms. There were few overt signs of government oppression. There were police agents, but no secret police; there were no "class enemies" or people who were automatically suspect. While a few newspapermen were jailed—the constitution did not guarantee all civil liberties—there was no terror, few prisoners, and no political executions.

Another of the president's favorite sayings was "*pan o palo*"—("bread or the stick.") The bread was for all who would cooperate; the stick was for outright malcontents or rebels. In these years the regular sale of "vacant" lands, mining, lumbering, railway, and utility concessions, and the rapid accumulation of capital in Mexico produced considerable bread. The rewards for those who served Díaz were considerable. Almost anyone with a rudimentary education who could find a political sponsor got on the public payroll, because "a dog with a bone neither barks nor bites."

The Díaz monopoly, however, lay only in politics. No Mexican who refused to collaborate was persecuted; he simply failed to share in the prosperity. Members of the elite who detested Díaz were free to follow any career they chose outside of politics.

For a dictatorship, the Díaz years produced few martyrs. The old *mestizo cacique* was not paranoid, and the prevailing mood of optimistic positivism did not lend itself to martyrdom. The Mexican conservatives were perfectly satisfied with Díaz and came to consider him the best president Mexico had ever had. Perhaps a majority even of the liberal-minded, accepted him, at least grudgingly because no one had an alternative. Díaz, after all, could not live forever.

The great failure of the Porfiriato was not political or economic. In fact, in this generation, the substructure of a modern economy was laid. Both the framework of Porfirian politics and this industrial framework would survive the regime. Its enormous failure was sociological. Positivism, like its equivalents "free enterprise" and "rugged individualism" created explosive conditions in other Western societies, with industrial slums and ragged farm children, with vast concentrations of economic power and huge disparities of wealth and income. However, the truly Western societies had two things the societies on the fringes of Western civilization lacked: a political structure that could work to ameliorate the condition, and a large, politically dominant middle class that provided islands of stability. Mexico had neither, and thus the collaborators of the Díaz regime unknowingly and unintentionally stoked the fires of a Mexican volcano.

In 1884 Mexico had her present boundaries, but what might be called the Mexican nation hardly extended beyond the civilized areas of the old Spanish viceroyalty. Huge regions of the north and the south were settled only by various communities of Amerindians, some Hispanicized in religion and speech, some still virtually autonomous. These regions, essentially outside the developing Mexican nation and economy, were now brutally reduced under the wholesale application of the *Ley Lerdo* to Indian lands.

In later years, the reduction of the wild and/or autonomous *indios* has been emotionally regarded as a terrible crime of the Díaz government, and not only in an Amerindian-identifying Mexico. The *indios* were treated callously.

In this era, the last nomads and various barbarians were being harassed and destroyed all over the world at the hands of a rapidly expanding world civilization. The Russian Empire destroyed the separate existence of the Central Asian nomads; the Argentines waged a war of extermination against the last wild Amerindians of the pampas; the United States destroyed or displaced the North American Indians. Primitive peoples everywhere were pushed aside or exterminated in the name of progress and empire-or-nation-building. On occasion there was a rough justice, for barbarians had harassed civilization unmercifully in their time.

The destruction of the savage Apaches and certain other tribes, predators who had made a shambles of the Mexican frontier since the late eighteenth century, was necessary. The Díaz regime was the first postviceregal Mexican government strong and secure enough to carry out decisive campaigns. In the 1880s large-scale operations were begun against the raiders of the northern sierras, in cooperation and conjunction with military campaigns of the United States. By 1891, the Apaches of Sonora and Chihuahua were totally destroyed, and Mexican towns and remote ranches in this area were at last freed from constant fear. The Comanche horse-Indians, who had raided from Texas to Guatemala in their heyday, had already been destroyed by North American cavalry.

But as in the United States, the anti-Indian campaigns in Mexico did not stop with purely hostile or predatory tribes. The surviving Tarahumares, who tried to avoid Mexicans, were pushed into the barest and remotest mountains, where only a few skulking savages remained of a once-great tribe. With less reason, Mexico moved against the Yaquis, who were surviving cousins of the Nahua and who now wished only to be left in peace in their northern valleys and meadows. The Yaquis, cruel and implacable as they could be by European standards, were not savages; they were self-governing agricultural communities.

The Yaquis held river lands that were fertile and well-suited to the growing of sugar, cotton, and other valuable crops and that were desired by Mexican speculators and developers. The destruction of the Yaquis— which was never quite entirely carried out—was part of the age-old impingement of a more powerful and dynamic culture upon a weaker and static one, and it was seen as historically necessary.

The Yaqui and other Amerindian territories in the north and northwest Pacific states were officially unowned; the fact that the proprietors had held them for centuries gave them no viable nineteenth-century title. As with the tribal lands in the United States, they were considered the property of the nation, for the government to dispose of as it saw fit. The Mexican government did not move to alienate them all. But under the authority and theory of the *Ley Lerdo*, survey crews soon moved along the Yaqui river bottoms, marking out parcels and plots, reserving some for the government, others for the *indios* in individual lots. Here the modern concept of land ownership came into violent conflict with the age-old

Amerindian system. Even if the division had been entirely fair and generous, which it was not, conflict would have arisen.

The *indios* considered that the water, meadows, and woodlands belonged to tribes and clans in common, and that the Mexicans had no right to apportion any of it. In any case, *indios* could not live with individual titles—they did not fit into the native social system. Also, any *indio* who incurred a debt, however innocently, found his property attached and himself reduced to peonage. Naturally, the arrival of surveying parties in Indian territories caused resentment, dismay, and quickly, bloodshed.

The practice of taking "unused" lands from the Amerindians was fiercely defended by the economists, lawyers, and intellectuals who staffed the Díaz government. Their theory was that Mexico had to follow the lead of the United States, and the opening of new lands would draw a huge immigration of Europeans, such as were now pouring into North America and southern Hispanic-American republics. The elite was entirely European-oriented; it had no faith that the *indios* could be educated or their productivity raised. In the name of this rationale, some fifty million hectares of "national property" were surveyed and sold to private speculators, haciendas, and land companies.

One immediate result was a Yaqui war in the northwest. Under the chiefs Cajeme and Tetabiate, thousands of Yaqui warriors rose in revolt. The federal government had to employ five thousand regular troops in Sonora, and while Cajeme was captured and executed in 1887, sporadic, savage warfare, waged with great cruelty on both sides, continued into the twentieth century. Amerindians who had held off Spanish cavalry in the end were no match for machine guns, and mountain artillery brought into the sierra by new railroads. The Yaquis were crushed; their lands were reduced, and at least eight thousand tribesmen were "resettled" in Yucatán—actually, they were sold to *blanco* planters as slaves. The surviving communities in Chihuahua, Sonora, and neighboring states remained, sullen, depressed, and consumed with an enduring bitterness.

When the Yaquis were pacified, the federal army was used in Yucatán to destroy the last remaining Maya holdouts in the territory of Quintana Roo. Four thousand regulars erased the last Maya autonomy in the peninsula in 1901.

The rationale of providing lands for European immigrants was a valid one among the intellectual elite—though many Mexicans in the countryside simply wanted the *indios* destroyed. But hardy European farmers did not pour into Mexico. Immigrants came, but they were Spaniards, Frenchmen, and others seeking opportunity in the cities. Few if any of these immigrants were farmers, or had any desire to become Mexican peasants or rancheros. These new people did acquire perhaps a third of Mexican soil, and perhaps as much as half the liquid wealth; they were a newer version of the old Spanish emigration during the empire. The Latins and Catholics among these families tended very strongly to absorb the ethos and viewpoints of the Mexican elite by the second generation. They failed to Europeanize Mexico or settle it as similar immigrants were Europeanizing the United States; they became, and were called, the "new *criollos.*"

A large number of Anglo-Saxons entered Mexico, but the cultural distinctions here were too great for these immigrants to become Creoles. The English-speaking foreigners remained a separate community, although they acquired huge interests throughout Mexico. They failed to marry into Mexican families; they stayed foreigners, and they were hated for it.

The alienated national lands fell primarily into the hands of foreign companies and native *hacendados.* The industrializing nations now provided an expanding market for Mexican resources, and they provided new techniques. There was a revival of mining, with new processes for refining silver and gold that were superior to the old patio method. Copper and lead were now extracted for markets abroad. Beef, sugar, coffee, and henequen—used in North American wheat fields to bind sheaves—were increasingly in foreign demand, and this market sparked a great expansion of certain forms of plantation agriculture. Stock raising proliferated in the north, while several kinds of specialized agriculture took hold in the virgin territories of the south. North American capital developed new mines and railroads in the far north and acquired huge cattle ranches; European planters and land companies carved out new tobacco, sugar, fruit, and coffee plantations in the tropic areas.

The central provinces had always been dominated by *latifundios,* but huge holdings had been rare on the frontiers. Now, this changed; the new markets and techniques caused a tremendous expansion of haciendas both in the north and south. The Terrazas clan of Chihuahua came to hold two-and-one-half million hectares (1 hectare = 2.471 acres); the Cedros of Zacatecas owned three quarters of a million hectares in a single hacienda. Further south the estates were smaller, but still averaged in the thousands of hectares. In central Mexico there were a few spectacular haciendas like that of the Escandones, through which a railway train could not pass in a single day.

The north and south had been the home of *mestizo* rancheros, and while there was some expansion of small holdings, these sturdy small operators were completely overshadowed and dominated by the coalescing, sprawling, landed baronies. What was happening in Mexico was akin to the formation of industrial empires in the United States, but in Mexico, the ethos and economics of the times built enormous landed properties along the lines of the old Spanish socio-economic system.

*Hacendado*s grew richer and more powerful as their landholdings engulfed and dominated whole regions and entire states, and the number of peons grew by millions.

In the prevailing ethos and the absence of any governmental control to ameliorate the trend, the fate of the Indian communities was shared by small peasant proprietors and even *mestizo* rancheros. Landowners bought *ejido* property under the law, but in many parts of Mexico, wealthy and powerful families and land companies seized small holdings illegally. They could exercise influence at the capital and with state governments, and they could destroy smaller, poorer farmers with lawsuits. Sometimes such expropriations, whether of peasants or *ejido* Indians, were carried out with extreme callousness, as when a soaring world sugar market made land valuable in the small south-central state of Morelos.

Powerful *hacendados* had boundary markers moved, occupied claimed land, and used their influence at law or with the local governments to stave off the protests of the dispossessed. Thousands of Mexican peasants whose families had farmed the same spot for generations could show no legal title to their ground. During the 1890s sugar boom, some thirty-two families came to own virtually all the croplands in Morelos, with individual holdings as large as sixty thousand acres. Villages were deprived of wells and water rights and common fields, and cane was planted in some village squares. Protests, which were often violent, were squelched by the hard-riding rurales at the beck and call of the local chief politicos.

One *mestizo* peasant in Morelos, Emiliano Zapata, was driven to fury at the injustices and outrages he saw permitted by the authorities. He led a protest, which the government broke up by conscripting him into the army. Díaz did not kill people if he could dispose of them some other way, and it is recorded that he wept at some of the things that happened. Whether he felt any sympathy or not, he never interfered with this Mexican form of manifest destiny.

There were occasional agrarian rebellions among *indios* and peasants but these were scattered and easily crushed by the constabulary or army.

By the end of the century, at least half of the territory of the Republic belonged to a few thousand families and foreign operators. More than half of the cropland was divided between not more than ten thousand haciendas or *latifundios*. It has been estimated that about one million families had been dispossessed of their land and reduced to vagabondage or peonage. Only three percent of the rural families owned any farmland. This occurred over a generation in which the Mexican population grew from nine to fifteen millions, and in which a spotty form of industrialization in no way provided jobs for people forced off the countryside. Millions of Mexicans had nothing to do and nowhere to go. This was in some ways an old situation, but the numbers of miserable *pelados*, constantly swelling, exceeded anything that had existed earlier, and if anything, their living conditions grew steadily worse.

Human labor was so cheap in the oversupply that it cost less to hire a man than rent a mule. Daily wages averaged twenty-five centavos or a quarter of the new decimal dollar or peso, and as the Mexican silver-based currency sank steadily with the depreciation of silver in these years, wages bought less year by year. The standard week's wage of 1.50 pesos equaled the twelve reales paid for incidental labor at the start of the century—but the same money purchased only a fourth as much of the poor man's staple, corn.

The average peon or working man remained eternally in debt, either to his patron or to the hacienda store which supplied him with necessities. Under the law these debts were passed on from father to son. On some estates, especially the foreign-owned plantations, there was a new form of wage: the hacienda ticket or token, exchangeable only at the company store. As long as any worker was in debt, the police would hunt him down if he ran away—unless, as some thousands did, he could escape across the border into the United States, where he might find work in the Southwest at up to $0.50 per day (U.S. money). Peons and *pelados*—who were technically free citizens—were whipped for any infraction by the *mayor-domos*. Petty theft could bring two hundred lashes, which amounted to a death sentence. This was widely justified by the ancient proverb that the *indio* was unteachable except through the lash on his back.

By the twentieth century, concentration of land ownership and a swelling population made labor, and thus human life, cheaper than it had been. Conditions on the ten thousand haciendas which employed the majority of the population differed from estate to estate. On some, owned by absentee landlords, they were horrible; on others, where a conscientious and sometimes quite kindly patron lived and managed affairs conditions were much better. Custom did not allow them to be good anywhere in Mexico.

The quality of life was miserable and hopeless: filthy, overcrowded huts, an unbalanced, monotonous, meager diet, ever-constant death, disability, and disease. The mortality rate was roughly triple that of Western Europe or North America, and the infant mortality exceeded that of Asian countries. Few, if any schools were available to hacienda children, and the survivors of infancy had little to look forward to but their parents' misery. Diversions were also few: dances, festivals on religious holidays, and the ubiquitous pulque, which eased the pain but kept the *pelado* besotted and toxemic from its unbottled, unsanitary, bacterial-culture juice.

Yet the miracle was that the "peeled" Mexican peasant was not a surly dog, an eternally whining *lépero*, or a man choked by an eternal rage. He had a deep and sensuous grasp of life and his humanity, an acceptance of what might be, and a marvelous dignity that let him make music even on his knees. Somehow, the Mexican could not quite be dehumanized. And he survived, and his numbers grew.

Virtually all economic historians agree that the rural standard of living was lower in 1910 than it had been when Hidalgo raised his cry at Dolores a hundred years before. The reason was simple: agriculture, in an overwhelmingly agricultural country, had become totally unbalanced. The social damage and further degradation caused by the disappearance of four-fifths of the villages into enclosures, and the increased population living on the land, was only part of it. Agriculture, never very efficient, had even ceased to produce sufficient food in Mexico.

The newer *latifundios* in the east, the far north, and the far south were organized and managed with considerable efficiency. The baronies of the northern desert produced vast herds of beef, and English, French, and German overseers and managers sent carload after carload of products out of the tropical regions over the new railways. This beef, coffee, sisal, tobacco, fruit, and other produce went abroad to be sold, leaving little for the tables of Mexico. The profits from the sales did not trickle down to the low-paid *pelados*—most profits did not even return to Mexico, and if they did, they remained in the burgeoning city banking system. Thus the new, vast expansion in Mexican agriculture did nothing whatever to ameliorate conditions—at least, not yet—across the countryside.

In the old, historic core of the Republic, haciendas grew larger, but agriculture was no more efficient than it had been two hundred years before. Through the central plateau, many haciendas made no attempt to utilize all their croplands. The owners felt no urge, and there was no real profit in doing so. Millions of hectares of potential corn and wheat fields lay vacant, while millions of the poor struggled against actual starvation. In 1900, when the Mexican population was probably what it had been in Motecuhzoma's empire, Mexico obviously produced far less foodstuffs than the country had four centuries earlier. The foreign exchange produced by exports had to be used to import wheat and maize to feed the urban people—Mexico had begun what was to be a long cycle of having to buy the staple food for her people from the United States. In the terrible imbalance of the development, the city folk were fed (though many starved to death in alleyways every day at México) while few observers worried about the countryside.

The one profitable form of agriculture on the central mesa was a disaster of sorts for Mexico. On once-irrigated slopes where maize had grown, kilometer after arid kilometer was covered with varieties of the blue-green maguey or agave plant. Pulque plantations, interspersed by an occasional shining white hacienda mansion, dotted here and there with dusty, ramshackle clusters of jacales on the hills, ran as far as the eye could see. The *octli* which men had discovered thousands of years before, and which the

Amerindian civilization had decreed must be sparingly used, had become an economic giant in modern Mexico.

Mexican alcoholic consumption, rising steadily over the centuries, in the early twentieth century was probably the highest per capita in the world. Pulque was cheap, cheaper than London gin in the eighteenth century when a penny could get one drunk. The poorest classes consumed more than a liter of pulque daily. They rarely grew roaringly drunk, because pulque usually created stupefaction. It also caused chronic alcoholism and toxemia. The government was aware that up to sixty percent of the inhabitants of both city and rural slums suffered from these effects, and some authorities hoped to substitute bottled beer for the unsanitary native drink. Excellent breweries were established in Mexico by Central European immigrants, but their product was too expensive for the *pelado* class.

Rampant alcoholism, along with the rising use of marijuana and other drugs, was symptomatic of deep social malaise. But this, the widespread illegitimacy, and the endemic venereal disease which Mexicans considered a trivial malady were seen more as moral than social problems by the upper class. The self-destruction of the poor tended to reaffirm the conviction of the white and almost-white *criollos* that the *indios* and mixed bloods were incompetent.

But in the midst of this social and economic agrarian ruin there was enormous change and progress in other areas. The "new *criollos*" threw a new patina of modernization over Mexican cities and industries, very much as the original Spaniards had created islands of European civilization amidst the Amerindian mass. In contrast to the stagnation that had set in with the War for Independence, the Díaz stabilization gave Mexico a new economic vitality in certain fields.

Porfirio Díaz had no training or instinct for business, but he deputized men who were prepared for such roles to regulate Mexican finance. In general his finance ministers were capable, conservative men whose major function was to halt the chronic hemorrhage of the treasury through corruption and mismanagement. Díaz' father-in-law, Matías Romero, who had served Juárez and Lerdo, did well in the first Díaz administration. In 1884 Díaz appointed Manuel Dublán to the post. Dublán worked, with remarkable success, to restore Mexican credit. While no more warships had appeared off Mexico to collect, nothing had been paid on the long-standing British loans since Juárez declared his "two-year moratorium." Dublán first consolidated the internal debt, then was able to negotiate a loan with British bankers to settle the older debts, and also two further sterling loans to finance railroads.

The outstanding financial figure of the Porfiriato, however, was José Yves Limantour, who became secretary of finance in 1893. Limantour, who was to acquire the reputation of an evil genius, was a new man whose outlook was basically internationalist. He took advantage of the mining booms caused by rapid industrialization in the Atlantic world to open Mexico freely to outside investment, abolished the maze of alcabalas and duties surviving from the middle ages, and, through a great expansion of exports and foreign trade, balanced the national budget for the first time since Mexico became an independent nation. From 1894 through 1910 Mexico had balanced budgets and a growing surplus year by year. These reserves opened further credit sources for rapid capital investment. By 1899 Limantour was able to borrow abroad at five percent, and the rate had dropped to four percent in 1910.

Limantour was typical of the new men springing to financial and political prominence in an economy like Mexico's, in which new forms and techniques were being superimposed upon ancient patterns of life. He was a gaudy character of French extraction, a "new *criollo*," in most ways more typical of the industrial societies than Mexico in the 1890s. His outlook was internationalist, and in terms of late nineteenth-century capitalism, utterly orthodox. He thought in terms of investment rather than "sovereignty," and on purely economic grounds it is almost impossible to fault his performance. He brought huge gouts of investment capital into Mexico, primarily from the United States, the United Kingdom, France, and the German Empire.

North American investment began to pour into Mexico. The United States was generating a limitless industrial market that gobbled up raw materials and also producing surplus capital for export. Here began a continuing, permanent pattern: North America provided markets for Mexican beef, lead, copper, precious metals, sisal, and tropical products, and North American capital and expertise helped develop these industries in Mexico. Mexican economic orientation changed from Europe to the United States. In the early Republic, two-thirds of Mexican exports went to Europe; by 1910 seventy-five percent of all Mexican exports were to the United States, and only twenty percent to the other Atlantic trading nations. This trade was favorable to Mexico—though the lasting pattern in which the industrial societies dominated the market and were able to set prices had already begun—because it produced balances which Mexico used to buy European goods and to pay off European loans, both of which Mexicans preferred to North American products and credits. Mexico entered into the United States' economic orbit, like Canada; it could not have been otherwise.

North American investment went primarily into mining, utilities, and construction, heavily concentrated in the north, which began to become somewhat "Americanized." The British entered into these same fields in a major way, generally more to the south. The French, after the Third

Republic and the Porfiriato cemented very cordial relations, tended to dominate banking, textiles, tobacco, and retail trade. The Germans, in this era, showed much interest in developing various agricultural enterprises in the south, with efficient, profitable plantations. They also provided the Mexican army with Maxims and Mausers and modern military techniques.

From 1880 to 1910, European and North American companies and capitalists provided Mexico with the groundwork for a modern economic system. They erected a modern banking structure, a number of industries, utilities, rails, communications systems, and harbors. They provided Mexico with new mining and farming techniques, electric power, and waterworks. Mexicans had neither the finances nor know-how to develop these things for themselves. The exploitation of the Mexican basic resources and burgeoning economy paid for this development. The foreigners received a very heavy share of the profits and kept control of the industries and utilities they founded.

The capital invested was enormous. Exact figures are not available, because modern Mexicans were no more enamoured of statistics than medieval Spaniards, but it was probably very close to 3.5 billion contemporary dollars. These investments built over eleven thousand miles of track, modernized the large cities, raised mineral exports by 650 percent, and stimulated entirely new industries, such as copper, lead, iron, zinc, and coal mines.

A British firm, Pearson, solved (though not permanently) the drainage problem around the capital, modernized the Veracruz harbor, and built a railway across the isthmus of Tehuantepec. Pearson also entered into the infant petroleum business. British and American companies began to compete in a feverish exploration along the Gulf coast that led to an oil boom. Despite the entrance of American capitalists like Edward Doheny and John D. Rockefeller into the field, the British generally had the best of it, with firms like Pearson controlling more than half of all Mexican production.

The mining, petroleum, real estate, and construction booms, even if they were sparked and dominated by foreigners, stoked the native economy and increased domestic capital and trade. Limantour, who not only favored this foreign investment but did everything in his power to foster it, reformed the antiquated, complex, and highly inefficient tax structures. The inherently self-defeating alcabala was finally abolished and customs duties were lowered. There was an explosion of trade. Exports rose from only 40 million pesos in the 1870s to 288 million by 1910. The balance of trade was favorable for the first time in history.

At last a native group of capitalists and businessmen came into being. Most did not begin as Mexicans, but they became Mexican. It was a continual complaint that the country was overrun with foreigners, who were making native Mexicans step-children in their own land. But the French immigrants, who ran banking, textiles, and were prominent in several commercial fields were rapidly assimilated into the middle and upper ranks of society. Levantines and Germans did the same, although the Anglo-Saxons rarely followed this course. Thousands of these foreigners founded respected and extremely useful Mexican firms and families. Even the *gachupines* or Spaniards began to enter Mexico again, never as capitalists, but in their old pursuits of *mayordomos*, grocers, shopkeepers, and plantation owners. This European and Mediterranean immigration was socially valuable; it brought in new ethos and new ideas, though the immigrants became "new *criollos*" and tended far more to reinforce the upper class than to reinvigorate the countryside or create a viable middle class. No European small-farmers or workers ever arrived; there was obviously no opportunity for them in Mexico as in the United States, Argentina, or Brazil. Mexico had empty spaces, but these were jungles or deserts, and the developed areas were overrun with native laborers.

The immense modernizations and improvements, however, did not lead to industrialization between 1880 and 1910. The foreign investors were not interested in trying to erect industrial processes in Mexico; the native businessmen had neither the know-how nor an infrastructure of skills and crafts on which to build. The economic trends of the times worked against Mexican industrialization, in any case. European factories provided a flood of relatively cheap goods in return for either raw materials, agricultural products, or dollars earned by the sale of Mexican metals and beef in the United States. The only native industries of any consequence were cotton mills that turned out cheap prints, tobacco factories, and small pottery works. Actually, under the Porfiriato, it was old colonial economy carried beyond anything the Spanish administrators had achieved. The modernization was paid for by the products of Mexican mines and plantations, worked by cheap labor, capitalized and supervised by Europeans and North Americans. Improved management, newer techniques, and expanding markets extracted more wealth from Mexican soil than ever before.

Except for differences in appearance, costume, and scale, the Mexico of the 1890s was essentially a revival of the Mexico of Revillagigedo. The country was still ruled by a small elite, which traded the sweat of native labor and the riches of Mexican earth for a patina of Europeanization, new electric power for gas lamps. French or Italianate mansions for the classic styles of the late eighteenth century. In the broadest sense, the pattern that had begun in the sixteenth century with the Cortesian kingdoms was still carried on. Modernistic, European towns and cities, keeping at least some pace with newer developments, thrust up out of an extremely primitive countryside. Locomotives chugged between bustling ports with modern docksides to mining camps and remote plantations through country whose culture and social organization had not changed for four hundred years. Outside the cities Mexico was still a culture of the hoe and burro. As in Mendoza's time, there were two economies and two societies, and at least three-quarters of the population, illiterate and hardly ever earning money, remained outside the transplanted one. The basic richness of Mexican mineral earth supported what seemed to be a healthy flush of modernization and improvement, but the modern cities did not spring up native from Mexican earth; they drew everything except their very building stones from abroad—their directing classes, their styles and artifacts, even their ideas.

The development was thus highly unbalanced. The newer *criollos*, like the old, made immense fortunes, but a facade of restless, ruthless, rich modernity covered old sores, which ran deep and were growing worse. Like most colonial societies and economies, Mexico provided splendid opportunities for those who could take advantage of them, an endless frontier where men with energy, ability, and capital could grow rich. For the millions mired in the old society Mexico provided only increasing misery.

Mexico was now being shaped by foreign investment and foreign residents; this was resented, even by the old *criollos*. The natural xenophobia of the *mestizo* classes of course increased; they felt more and more as strangers in their own country. Spanish or French immigrants made social advances in a generation native Mexicans could not achieve in a century, except for the handful successful in the military or in politics. It was widely felt that foreign investors and individuals were favored by the government, and this myth still persists. Actually, foreigners were not favored over native capitalists, managers, and companies; the government simply allowed open competition, and the foreigners were much better equipped to win. If foreign firms paid few or no taxes, neither did most of the Mexican elite. They had the power, influence, or knowledge to avoid taxation while the ranchero and the poorer classes carried a disparate burden.

On purely economic grounds, the leniency of the government toward foreign investment cannot be faulted. If foreigners came to own or operate at least a third of the Mexican economy, they also developed it and made it profitable. The British paid for and built the railroads; North American engineers with new techniques improved the silver-mining industry and developed the untapped resources of copper, lead, and zinc; French and Germans organized a plantation agriculture for foreign markets that the Spaniards and Creoles had ignored for centuries. The tycoons like Pearson, Doheny, and Rockefeller who erected stinking oil field jungles in the states of Tamaulipas and Veracruz provided the expertise, machinery, risk capital, and marketing organization without which there would have been no Mexican petroleum industry. On the whole, all this development was better for the country than if it had never occurred. It provided trading balances, treasury surpluses, vital foreign exchange, and no few jobs.

But no people like to think they, or their soil, is owned or dominated by foreigners. Repatriation of profits also created a capital drain—after a certain point, little was reinvested in Mexico. The Mexican negotiations for railroads, utilities, and the like were generally sensible and fair, because the government retained an interest in these and usually had a say in management. Foreign capital could not be expected to develop Mexico without the expectation of high profits; undeveloped countries, then and later, did not enjoy the whiphand in bargaining. Mistakes *were* made: the alienation of subsoil minerals, contrary to Hispanic law and practice was an emotional and political error, if not an economic one; and the oil industry was virtually granted extraterritoriality between 1900 and 1911, because the Mexican government did not realize either the importance or the ramifications this industry would assume for the development of Mexico. The foreign oil companies began to drain away an irreplaceable resource while they paid no taxes and shared no revenues, and because some of their policies were irresponsible—Standard Oil sold Mexican petroleum at lower prices in the United States than in Mexico—the concessions given foreign oil firms finally became an insult to Mexican pride and sovereignty.

The policy of making Mexico a paradise for foreign investment was an old dream of the *continuistas*, but the Díaz regime, with its unusual stability, was the first Mexican government that created a favorable climate for foreign enterprise. Limantour figured that if Mexico got back only ten centavos on the peso this was still a bargain, because it was ten centavos the treasury otherwise would never see. In fact, Mexico did better than this. While some outside companies made huge profits, creating a capital drain, many others put far more into Mexico than they ever took out. Mining proved very risky throughout. A great many investors never recovered even their initial investment, especially in the turmoil that followed the collapse of the Porfiriato. On sheer balance, all dispassionate observers believe that the foreign flood of investment put far more into Mexico than was ever taken out, even without counting the intangible benefits of the new training, concepts, and ethos that came with foreign capitalists. The basic structures of the modernization, the power systems, the rails, and harbors, could have been brought in no other way. And in the end, almost all this foreign investment, one way or another, came into Mexican hands or under Mexican control.

Although Díaz was never a puppet, and his government never fell under any political domination by Europeans or especially, by the United States, Mexico did become economically dependent upon the United

States. This was geographically and economically unavoidable; it had nothing to do with Díaz' personal wishes. However, there is no evidence that the North American economic penetration profoundly influenced Porfirian strategic policy, which was basically the juarista policy of maintaining the sovereignty and continued existence of the nation. Díaz tried to prevent foreign interventions and intrusions, now a bedrock of Mexican foreign policy. He did this less with pronouncements of sovereignty than by trying to avoid giving foreign powers any reason for reprisals. Díaz summed up Mexico's predicament in his famous plaint, "Poor Mexico, so far from God and so near to the United States." But Washington never was able to dictate to Díaz. At the very time his government made the most lenient concessions on oil, he steadfastly refused to negotiate a United States naval base on Mexican soil.

Díaz' attitude toward the United States was, atypically, more practical than emotional. Díaz did not like North Americans; he remained cool and dispassionate toward them, but he had no illusions of Mexican power vis-à-vis the United States. Díaz knew (though this exasperated many Mexicans) that some nations by circumstance were less sovereign than others, and equality among nations was nothing more than a convenient protocol which carried no weight in actual international politics. He also seems to have understood the true desires of the United States people and government toward Mexico and Hispanic America better than most of his countrymen.

While some North Americans had coveted Mexico at least until the Civil War, the watershed of North American policy had occurred in 1848. In this year the United States achieved its transcendent strategic goals by rounding out its territory and gaining admitted preponderance and ultimate security on the continent. Both the British and the Mexicans, one by tacit admission, the other by war, were removed as rivals. Afterward, American policy wanted only two things from Mexico: the maintenance of order in the neighboring country, and the right to trade on a favorable basis.

While such order was maintained, the terms of trade could be negotiated only according to relative bargaining positions and power.

When Mexican order broke down, and disorder led to outrages against North American citizens, businesses, or investments, Washington moved to interference and/or retaliation. While on many occasions United States citizens pressed Washington cynically for interventions, the actual ones almost always stemmed from a Mexican inability to maintain the responsibilities of a stable nation. It is extremely instructive, perhaps, to compare United States policies vis-à-vis Canada with those toward Hispanic America. Vastly more United States capital and enterprise entered Canada and brought the Canadian economy inevitably into the North American orbit without making Canada in any way a United States political satellite, and there were no reprisals or interventions against Canada because Canada was a stable society where businessmen, investments, or foreign-owned property were never threatened by disorder, nor were foreigners molested without prompt recompense.

There were no troops on the Canadian border because there was never the remotest need for any. But in periods when the Mexican central governments exercised no control over northern *caciques*, could not prevent border raids by Mexican bandits or savage Indians, or could not protect foreign property in Mexico, the United States government could hardly have been expected to consider Mexico equal or inviolable, nor could United States citizens develop any respect for a people who could not achieve stable self-government. In general, the Hispanic pride of Mexicans refused to admit the problem, and this same pride terribly acerbated the situation. Lerdo de Tejada, like Juárez, had virtually no control over the far northern regions, but would never admit the fact, and the reaction of his administration, like most Mexican administrations, to unilateral action on the part of the United States army in raids and reprisals was entirely emotional.

The Mexican insistence was that, no matter if Mexicans could not keep order in their own house, it was still *their* house, and no outsider had the right to interfere. This was a totally unrealistic notion, workable only if the Mexican governments had made Mexico a hermit nation. Mexican autonomy, in the harsh world of *realpolitik*, depended upon the strength and stability of Mexican society and government, not on assertions and wounded pride. Autonomy came with power and respect.

Díaz understood this reality, and he kept order in Mexico splendidly so far as foreigners were concerned. North Americans preferred a liberal government to a tyranny in Mexico—but like the British and others they preferred a stable tyranny to a chaotic government and society, whatever high ideals they expressed, because disorder made stable relations and business impossible. Díaz cleared the border of banditry; he cooperated with the United States Army during the last destruction of the wild Amerindian tribes, and if Mexican nationals robbed or damaged foreign persons or property, his rurales either brought justice or impressive reprisals. This satisfied Washington and Whitehall, and established a lasting reputation among foreigners for Díaz as the best president Mexico had ever had.

After 1848, Washington behaved toward Mexico with enormous restraint, but North Americans neither understood—nor admitted, when they did understand—Mexican sensitivities nor preoccupation with appearances and the deep and ingrained Mexican sense of national humiliation. They were always, in Mexican eyes, adding unbearable insult to minor injuries. Mexicans did not take their inherent pride and dignity from the kind of governments they created, and the North American insistence upon treating Hispanic Americans like irresponsible children was intolerable to Mexican pride.

Because Díaz gave Mexico strong government, his autonomy was never seriously threatened by Washington. He could not exercise complete economic autonomy, however. Mexico was too weak for that, and besides, in his era, theories of economic autonomy were hardly fully developed. The very concept was nonsensical to an internationalist like Limantour. Thus the Díaz regime made concessions that spoiled foreign investors and left them totally unprepared to cope with the virulent nationalism that eventually swept Mexico.

The distaste and even hatred for the Porfiriato, which is very slow to die in modern Mexico, seems to come less from the actual events of the era than from what the ruling cliques believed and represented. Don Porfirio was, from the typical Mexican historical view, the archpriest in a pantheon of cynical and rapacious opportunists who oppressed Mexico. Scapegoats are more palatable, and martyrs are more honorable than the notion that a whole nation or people shared responsibility, or in the scheme of things, could not help themselves. The concept that lands and peoples get the kind of history they deserve will never be popular in Mexico, or for that matter, anywhere in the postcolonial world.

The Porfiriato has retained vestiges of honor mostly among outsiders: the modern Mexican view tends to be narcissistic, a manifestation of the xenophobia that characterized the Mexican revolution. The men who surrounded Díaz and Limantour seem to have been highly educated, reasonably cultivated, capable and patriotic. The intellectuals of the era—almost all of whom supported the regime—were not *vendidos* or sell-outs nor were they all cynics. They represented a continuing tradition in the Hispanic world: men trying to hold onto stability while they remade an intolerable world. They thought they were remaking it rationally.

The great desire of the "Científicos" (as the circle around Limantour and Sierra came to be called—"scientists" because they thought they were applying rational principles of the then-dominant social science in Mexico) was to make a modern, Western nation through the process of capitalism. Their concepts, developed out of the French Comptian and English Manchester-Liberal schools, were intensely progressive, positive, and optimistic, though colored with an inevitable elitism and class interest and some of the social Darwinism that was the rage in many areas of the Atlantic world. They felt they understood the Mexican past, and hated its weaknesses and what they now saw as false ideas and ideals. They saw their country was not a great, or even a very respectable nation, and they pinned their hopes for the future on economic regeneration. Other national economies had been primed and force-fed, and the Científicos believed that a similar process would work for Mexico. The priming could only come from outside capital, at first. It became Científico policy to bring in all the foreign capital available, rather than waiting for generations for domestic capital to be generated, during which Mexico would fall even further behind. The Científicos also had no great faith that Mexico would regenerate on her own; she needed foreign stimulus. Without question, this was a convenient philosophy for certain men who merely hoped to feed off the carcass of a carved-up Mexico, but on the other hand, it was held by academics and others who never expected to profit personally. What all were looking for, profit-seekers and nationalists alike, was that take-off into sustained economic growth that had caught up and transformed England in the reign of George III, and had changed the whole direction of the United States after the Civil War.

Once this was sparked, and the Mexican economy began to grow organically, dependence on foreigners would no longer be required; in the meantime, foreign skills and money remodeled harbors, planted telegraph poles, and lighted cities and created basic structures upon which Mexican capitalists could build. The foreigners also trained Mexicans and helped bring about the emergence of an expanded native industrial elite.

The Científicos thought that most other things must be sacrificed against this capitalist-industrial pump priming: social expenditures, the living standards of the poor, government interference with development, and, once the Porfiriato had stabilized things, even democratic government. Díaz became an acceptable, and in time, almost a necessary cog in this concept of progress. Not that all the elite, or even the ruling clique admired the iron-handed, canny old *mestizo* president or favored dictatorship—they simply believed that once Mexico were regenerated, episodes like the Porfiriato in government would become a thing of the past. Mexico could afford both social investments and democracy when she grew rich enough. It was a pie in the sky concept, faithfully copied from the Anglo-Saxon liberals, with Latin touches. Parliamentary government had not worked in Mexico; therefore, Mexico had to be directed by a strongman and a powerful elite. When order and direction created new wealth, wealth would trickle down; Don Porfirio and personal government would wither away; even the stupid and stubborn *indios* would be caught up in the national momentum.

There was logic in the belief that Mexico was too backward and poor to afford democracy and social legislation; a pie had to be made before it was cut. But there was tragedy in the fact that the Mexican masses were too poor *not* to be allowed some social gains. Mexico was not England or the United States, or even France, where a minor bureaucrat earned no more than a hardworking peasant. In Mexico, a government clerk with a primary education earned twelve times as much as three-quarters of the population. And progress was much too slow. Decade after decade the population swelled, doubling in about thirty years. The economy did not keep pace, especially as in the normal course of things the downward trickle was that and nothing more.

The Científicos were true scientists in their way, for they ignored the human factor. They saw no real danger from the passions and frustrations of the common folk; they believed the masses of Mexico were long-suffering and would bear anything, because they had born much for four hundred years. The Científicos were not rough-hewn entrepreneurs or *caciques* who fought their way to power or even practicing politicians; almost all of them were the products of an elitist education. As an elite, they rejected the notion that change should be forced from below; it had to be directed, in the nation's interest, from above. They were, of course, behind the times, just as the country they wanted to regenerate. For all the vogue of laissez-faire ideas in the Atlantic world between 1890 and 1910, most of the industrial nations had enacted agrarian and some social legislation in the obvious interest of averting their own explosions.

Conditions that were slowly and grudgingly being ameliorated in advanced countries still persisted in Mexican commerce and industry, Mill workers endured a thirteen-hour day, and were subject to fines from their pitifully small wages for countless infractions. Retail clerks put in twelve hours. Peonage applied in mines and factories; Sundays were not automatic holidays; there were no pensions or injury compensations. Labor organizations were outlawed, and strikes were broken—sometimes bloodily, as at Río Blanco by regular troops—and agitators were thrown into prison. These conditions, or something approaching them, were not markedly unusual in the United States, but wages and living conditions were much higher. And Mexican workers had another deep and pervasive irritant: North American and foreign employees in Mexican industry received better wages and favored treatment, sometimes for equal work. North American companies often paid their foreign employees in gold, and Mexican workers in depreciated silver. While Mexican labor suffered much worse at Mexican hands, few things were more likely to arouse a deep and abiding Mexican anger, not only against the foreign firms, but the regime and clique that let this happen.

The enormous failure of the Científicos, however, was in not recognizing the agrarian disaster. Millions of rural families were without land and without steady employment; the luckiest found work on foreign-owned plantations. The *latifundios*, particularly in the inefficient manner in which they were run, had no place in any modern commercial-industrial system. The concentrated ownership of land, and the enormous surplus of labor, was dehumanizing the rural population, which was vastly the majority in

Mexico. Conditions were worse in 1900 than they had been since the worst era of the *encomienda*, primarily because too many peasants could not find even a barren spot of land. John Kenneth Turner, in his book *Barbarous Mexico*, documented the incredible treatment of Yaqui slaves on sisal plantations in Yucatán, where a strong adult hardly lived a year under the lash. But while a million North Americans read Turner's book, it was scoffed at by the elite in Mexico.

The Científicos were hamstrung by the *latifundios*. Gentlemen still desired estates—while at the same time they could not comprehend the peasant's terrible hunger, and his hunger for a piece of soil. The some eight thousand families who owned haciendas also exercised enormous influence—more influence now that the clerics, the royal bureaucracy, and the pretorians had been destroyed. The greatest *hacendados*, such as the Terrazas, dominated their regions, and they had become politically unassailable. The country was quiet, however, if not quiescent, and it can only be recorded that the coming storm took the educated, city-dwelling elite completely by surprise.

This pointed up the fact that many of the elite understood the reality of Mexico no better than the long-dead *criollo* purists. They failed to understand that rampant capitalism and foreign investment was not building a new middle class but was beginning to alienate the small middle class Mexico already had. They failed to see the disastrous social effects of the breaking up of the *ejidos* and the rapid extension of haciendas. They understood very little of the xenophobia and frustrations of Mexican labor in this brave new world. They knew that Mexico had to import food for the first time in history, but they comforted themselves in the growing trade balances and growing respect for the Mexican treasury abroad, and the fact that modernization and order had made life more comfortable and safer for the elite than ever before. There were a million youths in schools, all learning to take their places in the hierarchy, and if some mornings a dozen starved or frozen corpses had to be gathered up in the alleyways of Mexico, these things had always existed. The world in some ways was getting immensely better, though in some ways it seemed to be getting worse. Two currents were running, as always, before a cataclysm.

The newer elite, now joined with the old elite, did not really understand their country; they lived insulated and isolated in their own world. If the Científicos were patriots, they were also people without real roots. Their culture and ideals still came from abroad, where they increasingly sent their sons for educations. Young bankers-to-be trained in Paris, young *hacendados* attended Harvard (if they were from the north, which was becoming more North-Americanized) or mostly, the Sorbonne. Spain had declined from her imperial grandeur; it was no longer particularly fashionable to claim Spanish descent; people hinted at French grandmothers. As the joke went, babies were told they came from Paris, like the draperies or the china, until they were old enough to ask what had happened to the box. Maximilian's old boulevard, now the Paseo de la Reforma, was touted as a second Champs d'Elysee. The elite knew in their hearts that Mexico was not France, but this was the great age of the myth of a "white Mexico."

The fault of this myth was not that Mexico was a nation with a Latin civilization and in which the Europeans were still the only civilizing force. This was true. The fallacy was that for the elite Mexico was a nation of Europeans in which non-Europeans hardly counted, although their numbers were distressingly large. In 1910 there were approximately 1,150,000 people of pure, or nearly-pure European extraction in Mexico. There were 8,000,000 mixed-bloods, and 6,000,000 still considered Amerindians. The whites comprised less than ten percent of the population, although, as the ancient proverb went, since the days of the Spanish Empire, money had usually "whitened" the skin. But this segment, new and old *criollos*, controlled the great majority of the wealth and dominated the professions, and under the Porfiriato, it had come to dominate the government again.

In the apogee of the Porfiriato, the European population came closer than it ever had to emerging as a true aristocracy. With independence, the most energetic military men and politicians had usually been *mestizo*. In the order of the Porfiriato, when economics prevailed above all else and property assumed greater political importance, the European propertied classes reasserted themselves. During peace, and prosperity on the higher levels, there was an inevitable return to social conservatism, whether the men in question were liberals or secret clericals. The older, radical element died off, and an education alone no longer carried bright young men to the pinnacles of society or government. After 1894 the higher posts in the national government went increasingly to inner-circle Científicos and men of ancient, landed families, who could give them dignity. Almost all these men had white faces; the white-haired, brown-skinned old President stood out in his own cabinet. Gradually, more state governors were drawn from the great *hacendados* than the generals, and many were both *hacendados* and generals. Don Olegario Molina, who became minister of internal development, owned several million hectares in Yucatán. The landed classes now exercised genuine power, whether by coincidence or consequence, on the eve of their final destruction.

Many of this class consciously bore the "white man's burden." They would privately if never publicly agree that Mexico *was* barbarous and that the whip was the only language understood by the barbarians. The Díaz regime fitted in with the British Raj in India, the French colonial empire, and other custodianships, and it was widely admired abroad. In 1907 the United States secretary of state, Elihu Root, visited Chapultepec Palace and stated: "I look to Porfirio Díaz as one of the great men to be held up to the hero-worship of mankind." It was believed that the Porfiriato was achieving something the Spaniards had not quite accomplished, the civilizing of Indian Mexico.

In this deepening racial-cultural reaction, the Roman Catholic Church revived. The Vatican had stubbornly kept Monsignor de Labastida in the archepiscopal seat and in the 1870s the demoralized Mexican clergy had been reduced to a few hundred priests. The intellectual liberal establishment remained actively anticlerical, and Mexican education was dominated by anticlericals throughout the Porfiriato. Newspapers, especially, delighted in ferreting out clandestine, illegal clerical operations, such as continuing convents and monasteries or running parochial schools. However, the entire Mexican elite was hardly this anti-Church. Doña Carmen Romero de Díaz was devoted to the Church, as were probably a majority of upper-class women. As the religious controversies of the Reform faded with time, and the liberal establishment grew more conservative socially, the clergy and the federal government became tacitly if not openly reconciled. The Porfiriato did not try to amend the Reform laws—but it tended to overlook their enforcement. Clerics such as the bishop of Oaxaca once again moved freely and effectively in government circles. If a secret nunnery was discovered, the clergy were almost always warned before the police arrived.

Far more important, the government tacitly allowed Catholic schools to begin operations again. The clergy were still small in numbers, about five thousand, but the Church had restored much of its former position in Mexico by 1910.

There were a few prelates, such as José Mora del Rio, who voiced the protests of the rural poor and urban labor and called for social action. Mora, even though he became archbishop, was an anomaly. The Church came back into influence through the doorways of the upper class, and it remained solidly conservative and establishmentarian, quietly if not always openly approving the Porfiriato.

The first decade of the twentieth century appeared to be another of those calm, golden late-afternoons in which history seemed to pause. Díaz was seventy-four when he was reelected in 1904 for a new six-year term, but he seemed able to go on forever. He was still effectively playing off one ambitious subordinate against another, the only cat in the Mexican bag. Riding about the capital in his new Mercedes motor car, he had become a symbol of stability and dignity. He rode over well-paved, well-lighted, and well-drained streets (which did not extend beyond the city's edge) and the *pelados* doffed their hats at his passage, or even the mention of his name, as their ancestors had saluted the Conde de Revillagigedo.

The ferment was among new, secret, radical, left-wing labor groups, and among a newer crop of intellectuals and frustrated politicians. The occasional lightning flashes of unrest—the strikes that flared in 1906 from Veracruz to Jalisco, the shooting by soldiers of two hundred textile workers near Orizaba, the trouble in the Sonoran copper mines—were no more spectacular than similar troubles in the United States and other countries. The rural areas were sullen, but very tranquil; the rurales seemed in full control. There was still more order in Mexico than there had been since independence, and nobody in government, or in society generally, believed that unrest was dangerous, or could in any way destroy the continuing forms of progress.

The era had seen enormous, though still inadequate, advances, particularly in education. More *mestizos* attended schools than ever before—though there was an attempt on the Díaz' government's part to try to hold education in line with development, so as not to overrun Mexico with unemployable *letrados*. Meanwhile, Justo Sierra, as much a symbol as Díaz, had presided over a genuine renascence of the intellectual arts, though little of the prose or music had what could be called a national Mexican style. For these reasons, perhaps, the artistic and intellectual accomplishments of the era have always afterward been somewhat denigrated. The dominant intellectual figures in Porfirian Mexico had not discovered an Indian soul; they would have denied such a thing existed.

From the purview of the imitation-Parisian Jockey Club in Mexico City, it was the best of times, a time of hope and approaching glory. Out in the burning fields of Morelos and Yucatán, for men on their knees with bleeding fingers, and in the dismal mines and shops and airless factories, it was the worst of eras. This was the twentieth century, but millions of Mexicans worked less for money and freedom than in the hope of escaping punishment. Almost in hearing of the capital, *pelados* still screamed and begged under the overseer's lash.

The centenary of the War for Independence was approaching—the 16th September, 1910. Ceremonies and celebrations were planned, for which the government would spend more than it spent in the same year for social services and education. Hidalgo was to be honored as the Father of Mexico, by a society that had never honored his abortive social revolution.

There was still no Mexican nation.

31

THE REVOLUTION

"Who is Francisco I. Madero?"
Who knows, señor? But my captain says he is a powerful saint."
Question and answer by a common soldier in the maderista forces
in Chihuahua, as reported in the foreign press.

For thirty years the Porfirian presidency had been a remarkable tour de force. It was institutionalized only in the person of one man, and, now, as his arteries hardened, the political system atrophied. Don Porfirio was the first Mexican president to achieve perpetual power, but he had not achieved genuine legitimacy. There were no historic institutions, no political parties, no ideology, nor any heirs-apparent to hold the Porfiriato together once the old man was gone.

Like most strongmen, Díaz had deliberately debilitated or destroyed all machinery that might create a smooth succession, out of the simple fear that such succession might come before he wanted it. This—and not the social volcano that had always been inherent in Mexico—made revolution inevitable. Contemporaries, both within and without Mexico, hardly noticed the endemic symptoms of social unrest; Mexico was no more (if no less) ripe for social revolution in 1910 than the country had been in 1810. If the rural misery were greater, the upper classes were more powerful, and the government was better organized to deal with insurrection. The first crisis in the twentieth century was political. Social revolution did *not* erupt spontaneously, or irresistibly. First, the Porfirian political structure collapsed; the collapse led to the anarchy, and in the anarchy at last the long-banked fires of social misery, frustration, and racial tensions broke through.

The long, hideous, bloody Mexican social revolution—*the* Mexican Revolution—might well have taken a less spectacular and damaging course had the leadership of the country been able to keep its vigor, its nerve, and the keen sense of the possible that a younger Don Porfirio had displayed.

Porfirio Díaz refused to fade away gracefully. He understood the imperatives of change, but the old man whose instincts of self-preservation required him to be the only "cat in the bag" simply could not change his ways as he grew senile and his talents failed.

The first cracks in the Porfirian system showed by 1904, when Díaz once more allowed himself to be "persuaded" that he was indispensable to his country. His term was lengthened to six years. However, Díaz would be eighty in 1910, and now concern about the succession was growing acute among Mexican politicians, foreign investors and bankers, and everyone who had a stake in the Porfiriato. The office of vice-president had fallen into disuse prior to Díaz, who had never revised it, since the number-two man in Mexico too often aspired to become Numero Uno. Like the North Americans from whom they copied the office, Mexicans had never known what to do with the vice-presidency, but in the personalized politics of Mexico the problem was much more dangerous. However, having a vice-president would assure the succession—or so it was hoped—and great pressure was put on Díaz by the entire Mexican and foreign power structures to accept one.

There were two obvious candidates. One was General Bernardo Reyes, a powerful, energetic, bearded *cacique*-type of independent character who had served ably as governor of Nuevo León and as minister of war. If the country were to continue Don Porfirio-type government, Reyes was considered the best man. The other possibility was José Yves Limantour, the spokesman and linchpin of the administration, and the acknowledged leader of the Científicos. Limantour, the darling of the upper elite and the international set, would offer a different kind of presidency.

Each man had definite limitations. Reyes lacked Limantour's fiscal finesse and ability to impress international investors; Limantour could never control the turbulent backwater Mexican political scene or master the army. Díaz, seizing avidly on this fact, suggested to Reyes that he preferred Limantour, and he asked the general to serve the Científico politically and militarily in case he became president. When Reyes showed obvious disappointment, he was dropped from the cabinet and relegated back to the provinces as governor of Nuevo León. Meanwhile, Díaz knew that Limantour was not constitutionally eligible to be president of Mexico, because he was born the son of a French national. In 1904 Díaz was determined to play off the two strong men against each other. He refused Limantour's repeated requests to change the law that barred Limantour from the office, and having spurned Reyes, he saw to it that the minister of justice publicized the fact of Limantour's ineligibility. Then, with a truly Machiavellian stroke, he chose as his vice-president Ramón Corral, one of the least fitted and least popular politicians in Mexico.

Corral was an ex-governor of Sonora and a speculator in Yaqui lands. He was too hated, inefficient, and corrupt ever to be accepted by the elite as president. But the nomination amused Díaz vastly. Who, he asked, would dare assassinate or push aside Don Porfirio, realizing that the act would make Corral president? Of course, he did not trust Corral, and kept him under surveillance.

This was all in the ancient *cacique's* character. But then he made an extremely uncharacteristic move, which has never really been explained by historians. He informed a North American journalist, Creelman, in an interview which was reprinted in Mexico in 1908, that he had always intended to prepare Mexico for political democracy, and that he now thought the time had come when Mexico might enjoy a loyal opposition something like the parties out of power in Great Britain and the United States. Díaz suggested that if such an opposition—responsible and loyal, of course—should emerge, he would allow it a share in government. He also hinted, though he did not quite say so, that he was prepared to step down in 1910 and allow a free election to determine the next president. This was peculiar, because Díaz' subsequent actions prove he had no such intention. Díaz must have known the interview would be published in Mexico, because he made no move to prevent it. Whether due to loquacious senility or some special scheme, the Creelman interview was a serious mistake for Díaz. It convinced most of the Mexican political elite that criticism of the regime was in order, and it sparked a new interest in national politics on every side.

General Bernardo Reyes, retired with ambition, began a campaign to take Corral's place. Reyes' son Rodolfo organized a political party called the Democrats. The "reyistas" professed belief in political democracy on the North American order and in generally liberal social principles, and they collected considerable support, particularly in the northern states. They were not extremely active—it was hard to be active politically in Porfirian Mexico where men had already forgotten the old electoral codes —but they wore a red carnation to distinguish themselves from the *corralistas*, who wore white. The *colorados* or reds soon outnumbered the *blancos* or whites, to Díaz' obvious displeasure.

Up to this time the only opposition group was revolutionary and underground; it was called *Regeneración*, from a newspaper published by the three brothers Flores Magón. The Flores family represented what was then an extreme left-wing philosophy, which was actually more Spanish-anarchist than European-socialist and which drew more inspiration from the then-Hispanic syndicalist movements than from Karl Marx. The Flores Magón brothers demanded a total abolition of government and the state, and the control of society through workers' syndics. Since it was absolutely impossible to seed such a movement or philosophy among the illiterate, cowed, rural hacienda masses, the Flores brothers turned to the burgeoning urban proletariat and industries such as tobacco or mining, which concentrated laborers under miserable conditions. Their activities spurred anarchist uprisings and a wave of strikes across Mexico in 1906, from Sonoran copper mines to textile factories in the central states.

The strikes, the Flores brothers, and their newspaper were all suppressed by Díaz. After a sojourn in jail, Ricardo Flores Magón fled to the United States, the historic refuge of all Hispanic American revolutionaries right or left, and in St. Louis, Missouri presided over the Mexican Liberal Party, an exile group which was basically orthodox socialist in rationale. Though the "Party" was outlawed in Mexico, it developed a political program that was to have great influence on Mexican thought. The demands of the new liberals were radical in any developed nation at the time: the eight-hour day, a minimum wage, workmen's compensation, debt abolition, and land reform. Flores Magón, a revolutionary anarchist at heart, might have played a greater role in the death of the Porfiriato if he had been able to refrain from illegal activities in both Mexico and the United States. It was his fate to sit out the decisive events of the revolution in a California jail, and his socialist-anarchist organization was no real threat to Díaz.

The rural three-quarters of Mexico that was *pelado* and illiterate was still splintered into regions and had no real leadership to offset the influence of the *hacendado* class. It was impossible, then or anytime, to form a political party or effective opposition out of such elements, or even to politicize them. The countryside could revolt—but it could play no other role in normal politics.

The reyista faction gave vent to dissatisfied feelings of thousands of politicized Mexicans. The great majority of these dissidents had no drive whatever toward violent revolution or extreme social reform, and their outward goal was an expressed democratization of politics. The Creelman interview had convinced a large middle rank of Mexican professionals and men with democratic or constitutional leanings that the time had come to speak up and for them to strive for a role in public affairs. Díaz was aware that this generation was emerging; in fact, in the Creelman interview he stated the real hope for the future lay with the emerging middle classes of Mexico. The Porfirian school system, inadequate as it was and for all the emotional criticism heaped upon it afterward, had actually helped create a large, literate middle structure. More young men were in school under the Porfiriato than ever before, and despite an historic impression that still lingers, the urban secondary school system was quite good. Díaz had expected that the emerging educated class would become a mainstay of his regime, but by the twentieth century he simply could not furnish enough bones to keep all the growling dogs in Mexico pacified. The economy grew rapidly, but in an unbalanced way, and too much of the growth was due to foreign enterprise. There were jobs for North American and British engineers but not for Mexican, and the de facto alliance between the regime and the very wealthy elite denied the emerging *mestizo* professional majority the status and roles it desired. The newer, educated *mestizos* who aspired to or obtained entrance to the middle ranks of society found their influence and even their status denigrated by the European myths of the upper class.

Despite rhetoric about economic and social reform among the middle ranks, including much socialist rhetoric, the real drive of the educated opposition was for opportunity in their own country. Thousands of Mexicans who bemoaned the lot of labor were at heart intent upon destroying the present power structure so that they might replace it, or at least become honored and rich. In this sense the main opposition to the Porfiriato was nationalist and capitalist. Thousands of Mexicans of the middle social ranks who demanded riddance of French banking structures and foreign oil companies were *not* hostile to such enterprises in themselves; they wanted them to be controlled by Mexicans, and to enjoy a role in them. The foreign capitalists, of course, chose to see this understandable nationalism as a form of Bolshevism, greatly confusing the whole issue and even the image of the revolution as it unfolded.

In the heightened political awareness of educated Mexico after 1904, two writers, Andrés Molina Enríquez and Francisco I. Madero, exerted profound influence. Both wrote for the general literate public rather than the tiny intellectual class, and both reached a wide *mestizo* audience.

Molina Enríquez was the first important apologist for the emerging *mestizo* majority. The earlier *mestizo* intellectuals had always seen themselves as heirs to the European liberal tradition. Up until the twentieth century, the "Aztec" mythology that had caused the Republic to honor Cuauhtémoc and to adopt Mexica symbols for its seals and flag was primarily *criollo*. It was a process somewhat akin to the retention of Amerindian place names and the use of Amerindian symbols on seals and coins by the people of the United States who had displaced the indigenous race. The *criollos* had always lacked identity; they instinctively harkened back to "Aztec" glory while at the same time they oppressed and destroyed the surviving Indians. Molina despised all this mythology of the modern *criollos* as heirs to the Children of the Sun as much as he despised the "white myth" in Mexico. He broached a new, explosive idea: that the *mestizos* were the only true "Mexicans" and the only people around whom a Mexican nation could be built.

Molina showed that the *mestizos*, or mixed-bloods, formed a true national type; they had a similar culture from one end of the Republic to the other. They were *indio* stock enriched by Spanish blood and culture, and in this enrichment they had lost all the ancient Amerindian tribal identities, the separatisms that still divided and hampered the surviving *indios*. From Yucatán to Sonora the *mestizo* Mexican was similar in language, religion, color, and customs, despite his original tribal stock—and therefore actually formed the only homogeneous national type, in a country where the *criollo* emphasized his Europeanness and the *indio* clung stubbornly to his primitive parochialisms.

The *mestizo* tended to look to the future, while both *criollos* and *indios* clung to the past, and unlike the Creoles who looked to Europe for everything, the mixed-blood was proud of his native soil and culture. Molina argued that the *mestizo* was the toughest and most enduring type in Mexico; he had outlived and outbred the *indio* and already vastly outnumbered the weaker *criollos*. (The Mexican population was fifty-three percent *mestizo* in 1910). And the *mestizos* were increasing because they had the capacity to absorb more and more *indios*. They had the virtues of the *indios* in that they could live on tortillas and salt and outwork a horse; they had more energy than the *criollos*, because from the first it had been *mestizo* generals and presidents who had defended and maintained the nation.

Molina's arguments, which were emotionally attractive and in truth almost unassailable, were a direct assault upon the Científico assumption that Mexico must be maintained as a "white" nation. The *mestizo*, despite the fact that Don Porfirio and most of the effective political leaders had always been of mixed ancestry, had always been in an anomalous position, even in his own eyes, because he was always identified as a product of miscegenation. His very name, "mestizo" or "mixed" made him a hybrid, devoid of essential identity. Thus the Molina book was more than an attack upon *criollo* assumptions of superiority; it established a new view of Mexican identity. Molina scoffed at the long-held dominant view that the salvation of Mexico rested upon encouraging European immigration. Mexico already possessed an active, capable population, and all it needed was recognition and a chance to prove what it could do.

Molina's influence was explosive and profound among the ordinary literate people, three-quarters of whom were *mestizos*. They could begin to see themselves as Mexicans, no longer pretending to be descendents of proud Castilian conquistadores or the children of Amerindian lordlings, but as a distinct historical race, as identifiable and as valid as other mixed races such as Spaniards or Japanese.

The other literary bombshell that rocked middle-rank Mexico in 1909 was Francisco I. Madero's attack on the concept of the Porfirian presidency, though not an attack on Don Porfirio. Madero's *The Presidential Succession in 1910* could only have created a sensation in a country where normal political activity had been suspended for a generation, and was suddenly beginning again. It contained nothing new, or even explosive.

Madero wrote that the old Díaz slogan of "No reelection" must be put in practice, and a start must be made toward political democracy, otherwise there would be a return to the old coups and bloodshed when Porfirio Díaz ultimately vanished from the scene. Madero agreed that Don Porfirio should remain in power so long as he lived or retained his senses, but that democratic evolution must be assured by allowing men with democratic principles to assume the vice-presidency, key cabinet posts, and some state governorships. In other words, the Porfiriato should begin to reform itself through free elections. Madero's thesis actually merely expanded on Díaz' own statements in the Creelman article. When it aroused enormous attention, Madero grew bolder, and in subsequent editions urged that all opposition Mexicans from reyistas to anarchists unite in a new "Anti-Reelectionist Party."

The effect of Madero's pen was to push him into prominence ahead of General Reyes' sword. This, however, came mostly from default. Reyes was a vigorous, capable *cacique*-type who might very well have made an excellent Mexican leader, but as a protégé of Díaz, he simply could not bring himself to seek power without Díaz' blessing. He refused to become insubordinate, in his own view, and since Díaz at bottom never had any intention of allowing anyone else into the limelight so long as he lived, Reyes' real position was impossible. Díaz understood Reyes, and forced him into a confrontation, and in the fall of 1909, Reyes, refusing to pronounce or rebel, left for exile in Paris.

Díaz congratulated himself that he had now made the various constitutionalist-democratic-middle-class opposition leaderless, and he expected it to fade away. He failed to see that somehow the ice jam had been cracked, and the ever-present awareness of his great age made it impossible for him to continue ruling Mexico as he had for thirty years.

Madero, meanwhile, had been bitten by the presidential bug; friends and supporters in his native north urged him to seek office; the first was the ill-fated Chihuahua merchant Abraham González. As the reyistas floundered, Madero crossed Mexico on speaking tours, which culminated in the spring of 1910 in the formation of the Anti-Reelectionist Party. Madero was nominated for the presidency, with a reyista, Vásquez Gómez, a former physician to the Díaz family, as his running mate. Since Díaz had always observed constitutional forms while destroying their spirit, this was a legal opposition that under the Constitution of 1857 could not be kept off the ballot. All that was needed was an incorruptible candidate.

Madero, however, was an improbable candidate to upset even an aging dictator.

There was nothing wrong with his credentials. He was thirty-seven, the scion of a rich and important Coahuilan clan. His grandfather, a true Mexican paterfamilias, had been governor of Coahuila under Díaz and had erected a vast family fortune that included cattle and cotton haciendas, wineries, mills, and mines. Don Francisco was one of almost two-score vigorous grandchildren; he had studied first in Paris and then took up agriculture in the United States at the University of California. He developed a great interest in socio-economic affairs, and he had managed a family plantation superbly, and with a rare social consciousness for his class, personally financing educations for the sons of peons. Madero had also learned a love of political democracy as it was practiced in the United States and France. This had led him to try to organize an opposition party in local elections in his home state, despite his grandfather's kindly warning to beware getting "in the way of the horses." He was of course trampled by Díaz' horses; he could not even find local officials who knew there were such things as election laws.

His personal handicaps, however, were enormous. Madero was the antithesis of the *macho* Mexican *hacendado* or *cacique*—a little man barely measuring five feet, bird-like and quivering, with a high-pitched, squeaky voice. Abroad he had become addicted to spiritualism and had become a vegetarian. He was a radiant do-gooder whose honesty and charity were unassailable, but like many men of this type, he could be arrogant, cranky, and unfathomable to the people closest to him. His ideas could set a crowd afire—but Madero unfortunately could not dominate a conference of his peers.

Yet, because of the courage and conviction he symbolized to millions of little men in Mexico, Madero began to draw roaring rallies to his campaign train-stops. His opposition to the regime, and his vague promises to reform society along democratic principles, appealed to the intellectuals, the frustrated merchants and rancheros, and to all the impoverished workers who found the Gilded Age of Don Porfirio intolerable. Above all, he found enthusiasm in the northern states, where *mestizo*-liberalism was as endemic as an ancient hatred of whatever power ruled at the capital. The northern frontier was more populous than ever in the new century, and also more aggrieved, because it had been invaded by *latifundistas* during the Porfiriato. The great cattle baronies were engulfing whole towns and even states; Don Luis Terrazas' domain was as large as the whole state of New Jersey, and from it he ruled Chihuahua almost as a feudal fief.

The situation of the workers and peons in the north was perhaps superior to the older regions—but throughout Sonora, Chihuahua, Coahuila, and Nuevo León there was a far more vigorous, independent, and disgruntled population of rancheros, townspeople, and even smaller *hacendados* who hated the local overlordship of Díaz' magnate-governors, and everything the Gallicized Científicos stood for. Humble workers with whip scars on their backs adored Madero—but tough, pistol-heavy rancheros, self-made school teachers, packtrain operators, and frontier merchants flocked to his cause.

Nothing showed more that Díaz had lost his touch than his fatal denigration of Madero. Díaz saw only the man, never the symbolism. He met with Madero and listened patiently to the little man's pleas for some initiative toward democracy; afterward, he told jokes about this little bird, with his vegetarianism, spiritualism, and God-knew-what other peculiarities who thought he could become president. After meeting with Madero and discounting him, Díaz almost contemptuously announced for reelection, and again chose the hated Ramón Corral for his vice-presidential candidate.

As the July election approached, however, Díaz grew concerned with the almost hysterical reaction produced at Madero rallies. He had no fear of losing—no Mexican government could lose an election; even the concept was foreign to the Mexican mentality. He did fear disorder, because Madero was arousing too much enthusiasm, and had him taken from his campaign train at San Luis Potosí and arrested on a charge of inciting riot. Madero was locked in the local jail, though the campaign and election was allowed to proceed. Don Porfirio, as usual, was authoritarian but never paranoid or murderous; he did not understand that in the new atmosphere in Mexico his old ways would no longer succeed.

Díaz now fell out with Limantour, the one remaining strong man in his administration. Limantour departed on a European tour that was virtually an exile; Don Porfirio, bothered only by rotting teeth, could now live undisturbed, surrounded by fawning foreigners and native sycophants, in his private presidential dreamworld. He was not only living in the past; he was isolated from all reality.

The election was held in July, amid calm but widespread gloom and tension. Millions of Mexicans voted, and millions certainly voted for Francisco I. Madero. The results were to be announced after the government collected all the ballots from the remote areas.

Díaz was only interested in one thing: the celebration of his eightieth birthday, which, because it came one day earlier than the centenary of Mexican independence, the *diez y seis de septiembre* 1910, had been incorporated in a month-long national holiday. All September was given over to fêtes and parties and parades, ostensibly honoring the Insurgency of Padre Hidalgo but actually acclaiming the achievements of the Porfiriato.

The president opened the festivities with the dedication of a new madhouse, which fact appeared symbolic in retrospect, and all month he rode about the capital in his noisy, new Mercedes, surrounded by clattering horse-guards in brilliant uniforms. Díaz was still a royally dignified splendid figure beneath his bemedalled tunic. He rode past the extravagant monuments of his reign with pride: the huge opera house, a melange of Italianate styles, already causing the engineers and architects nightmares as its weight sank into the porous former lakebed; the soaring Column of Independence, capped with a most un-Mexican winged Nike; monstrous statuary of Columbus, Cuauhtémoc, and Juárez positioned on the Paseo. The public and private face of the capital had been transformed from severe Spanish styles to something resembling a *fin-de-siécle* Paris, for the Porfiriato, after a long regression, had been the greatest building age since the days of Revillagigedo.

There were parades, marches, and pageants, in which contingents from all the civilized world participated. One spectacle, viewed by half a million, depicted the great moments of Mexican history as defined under the Porfiriato: the confrontation between Motecuhzoma and Cortés at Xóloco, and the entry of Iturbide and the Trigarante Army into México. Fifty thousand citizens attended a garden party at Chapultepec Park. The climax came on September 15, at a great banquet for two thousand dignitaries at the National Palace, where guests dined from gold plate and consumed ten boxcar-loads of French champagne. The mobs, the elite, the foreigners cheered and praised Don Porfirio, the Civilizer of Mexico; no contemporary seems to have fully understood the rot that pervaded the political structures of all Mexico; its odor was as concealed as the foul breath that emanated from the old dictator's rotten jaws.

On the 16th Don Porfirio, almost casually, announced the election returns: ninety-nine percent in favor of himself and Corral.

This did more than merely make the Mexican regime ridiculous in the eyes of the world; it destroyed the last hope of many Mexicans for peaceful change.

Francisco I. Madero never intended to bring the society of which he was a pillar down in fire and blood. Nor did many of the people who loved him and voted for him really want a violent social revolution; few men in any society ever do. The Madero people included upper-class and middle-class and working-class Mexicans, mostly *mestizo*, but few real radicals. They had the same goals as the Científicos and the handsome, slightly effete would-be aristocracy—to make Mexico into a viable, modern nation. They wanted only to do this in different ways, and under different management.

Madero, and most of his followers, never understood the agrarian disaster, but through blindness, not hard-heartedness. In this they were much more like the Científicos who barred their aspirations than is usually supposed. They went one step beyond the Científicos—they believed that democracy could no longer be eschewed in favor of development, and they believed that democracy in Mexico meant the arrival in power of the native majority.

In jail at Potosí, Madero decided that the democratic revolution could only come by arms, because the old dictator obviously would respond to nothing else. If Madero had understood the volcano upon which Mexican society rested he might have hesitated—then, again, he might not. He was convinced, understandably, that to accept the Díaz verdict and to pass into retirement would be to betray his ideals, his friends, and his country. At Potosí, Madero passed from being an "anti-Reelection" candidate into the standard bearer of what soon came to be called the Revolution. But Madero the Good Citizen was never the man to lead that revolution.

Díaz, meanwhile, still despised Madero too much. After the announcement of his reelection, he let Madero out of jail, though he restricted him to the city of San Luis Potosí, still not comprehending how Madero could be a hero to millions of his countrymen.

On October 6, 1910, Madero was whisked aboard the Laredo Express just outside Potosí by friends, after the local authorities had let him leave the city for a hunting trip. Cheering trainmen—all in on the plot—fired the boilers on an historic passage north. Madero was across the border in Texas before Díaz knew he had escaped.

Madero met in a hotel room at San Antonio with fellow conspirators and issued what he called the Plan of San Luis Potosí, which he had drawn up in prison, calling the recent election fraudulent, claiming himself president, and ordering an uprising against "General Díaz to make him respect the will of the nation" for November 20.

The uprising was idealistic and unplanned, and it failed miserably. Police and a handful of maderistas clashed in Puebla in a four-hour battle in which the gun runner Aquiles Serdán and some companions were killed. Nothing else happened; the people failed to rise; and Madero, who had recrossed the Bravo confidently, had to beat a quick retreat back to Texas.

However, Madero's call had lit a small flame in Chihuahua, where, out of hatred of the ruling Terrazas family and their frustration with local politics, a group of men organized around Abraham González, who proclaimed a maderista revolution.

González was no general, but he quickly found field commanders and a small army among Chihuahuans who resented the federal officials and the cattle barons. González' principal lieutenant was Pascual Orozco, a moody, unprincipled, tough packtrain operator who had a genius for guerrilla warfare in the mountains and desert. Orozco recruited mounted warriors among the *vaqueros*, miners, rancheros, and *indios* of Chihuahua, people who hated the corrupt local government and the society of the Porfiriato in general. Orozco began what was in effect a guerrilla campaign against the federal officials and the Terrazas interests with this irregular revolutionary army. Inevitably, the revolution attracted not only aggrieved citizens but the criminal element, such as the cattle thief and murderer Doroteo Arango, better known to history by his assumed name, Pancho Villa.

The wild country of Chihuahua, vast windblown spaces between the inaccessible sierras dotted with scattered haciendas, mines, and settlements, was made for guerrilla warfare on horseback. Orozco's raiders came down out of the mountains, rode great distances, struck violently, and vanished again in the rugged terrain. They shot up isolated federal garrisons, raided ranches and mining camps, and captured and looted towns. The half-wild, gunslung *vaqueros* of the northern frontier were conditioned and hardened by three centuries of *indio* wars and cruelties; their rebellion was as much anarchistic as an expression of genuine constitutional principles. Yet many of these rough men, even the elemental Pancho Villa, seem to have developed a genuine affection for Francisco I. Madero. They appreciated his courage and understood his essential goodwill toward their kind.

As in all Mexican insurgencies, this developing guerrilla warfare could hardly be distinguished from banditry, and the rebel leaders acted like bandits. But in an oppressive society where there was no rule of law and where the vested interests relied on force, such banditry was almost sanctified by purpose and ideology. Don Abraham González did not plan a racial and class war, but this was what Orozco and his hard-riding captains waged: a campaign of terror by the dark, poor, and dispossessed against the white, privileged, and rich. In such a war, criminality was almost impossible to define, because the ends justified the means on both sides.

The governor of the state and the local federal authorities were almost helpless against this ferocity. Don Luis Terrazas tried to recruit his own *vaqueros* into an army, offering them two pesos a day to fight the rebels, only to find that the common people would not fight against the revolution. The regular army was particularly ineffective. The khaki-clad soldiers had not waged a real war for twenty years, and their aging officers were far more accustomed to the gaming table than the saddle. Orozco, and particularly Villa, soon displayed talent at defeating the regulars in small actions. Villa was already revealing those qualities as a junior officer that he would later show as a general: personal valor, a grasp of maneuver over vast spaces, the ability to make correct decisions in the saddle based on an uncanny knowledge of the psychology of friend and foe, and that personal charisma that appealed hugely to the soul of the rough cowboys of the north. Villa was cruel and anarchistic, a part-Indian, illiterate *pelado*, but he possessed enormous qualities of leadership and command, above all on his home ground. After several defeats, the *federalistas* barricaded themselves in their garrisons; the guerrilleros rampaged, and the economy of Chihuahua was paralyzed.

Trains stopped running or were in the hands of the rebels; haciendas were occupied by raiders, and towns and mines were under siege.

Madero and his brother, Gustavo, who served as an effective chief of staff, made their way to Chihuahua. However, the Maderos soon found these initial successes had finite limits. The maderistas had no money beyond the personal fortunes of the Madero brothers; they needed modern weapons to match the Mausers and machine guns of the federales; and a rebel army paid only through its looting was extremely difficult to hold intact. By spring, 1911, the maderista revolution had disrupted Chihuahua but could not advance beyond the deserts and sierras.

For Díaz, the maderistas were only a flash on the distant horizon. The key central states remained quiet, and very probably, Madero would have failed and been forced to flee again had not the Porfiriato suddenly come under siege from a different, closer quarter.

In the sugar state of Morelos, the thirty families who had dispossessed the *indio* communities of their common lands during the sugar boom now began to reap the whirlwind. The *indios* had acquired a leader in the valiant, implacable *mestizo*, Emiliano Zapata, a small farmer who had opposed their oppressions all his life. Zapata organized the Liberating Army of the South—a horde of Morelos peasants, sugar workers, and Indians—and began to tear up the social order by the roots.

This was a spontaneous agrarian revolt, greater and better led and organized than anything that had occurred before. Zapata had only the most tenuous connections with Madero; the Morelos uprising was *sui generis*; it had nothing to do with constitutionalism and everything to do with the Amerindian peasants' hunger for land. The zapatista aims were simple, expressed in the slogan of the Army of the South: *land and liberty.*

The zapatistas emerged from the forests and mountains, small, dark men with brush knives and with icons of the Virgin of Guadalupe pinned to their large, conical *indio* straw sombreros. They swarmed through Morelos like soldier ants, killing overseers and driving off landlords, burning down mills and hacienda houses, seizing and dividing the great estates on the spot. The rich sugar belt was soon in flames, and by Holy Week 1911, frightened citizens in the capital city could see the fires of burning mansions across the lava flow.

Emiliano Zapata was as uncomplicated as his horde—and therefore was always to be almost unfathomable to the various power structures of

Mexico. His aims were pure, but also implacable: land for the poor, and the right to be left alone. Zapata was the one revolutionary hero who proved to be incorruptible, because he wanted nothing for himself, not even power. His name aroused reverence among the poor *indios*, and ultimate horror among the landed class, and extreme annoyance to whatever power was dominant in México City. Zapata was to become a symbol, and his memory would remain green as long as any poor agrarians remained in Mexico.

His revolt in Morelos was then and later of utmost importance, not in itself, but because it created a diversion almost at the gates of the capital. Rich refugees and influential landowners poured into the city, pressuring the government, diverting arms and attention from Madero. The newspapers, all conservative under the Porfiriato, hysterically demanded action. Regular forces that might have destroyed Madero's Constitutionalist Revolution had to be deployed to the south, in a chase of the will-o'-the-wisp zapatistas that invariably met frustration.

The zapatistas fought much like the guerrilleros of Padre Morelos a hundred years before. They sacked haciendas and faded away into the forests and mountains before the advance of federal troops; they derailed troop trains and slaughtered small detachments, gathering arms. This kind of guerrilla war, in this kind of rugged country, was always hard for regular soldiers to stamp out. But to Don Porfirio's expressed bewilderment, his army could not cope with Zapata at all.

As in Chihuahua, the Mexican federal army under the Porfiriato had become more ornate than efficient. Díaz had caused this deliberately—to protect himself from vigorous, ambitious generals, he had allowed a situation in which most high commanders were his own contemporaries. He had generals of eighty, majors of seventy, and even lieutenants in their sixties. He had systematically weeded out most officers of ambition and ability and filled the officers' corps with corrupt timeservers. These leaders were no danger to Don Porfirio—but they were not the kind to protect him, or the social order of Mexico.

Díaz was now also reaping another harvest; he had destroyed all initiative among the federal and state officialdom throughout the Republic. The old man, unable to direct or take the field, remained in the palace, firing off angry telegrams, while all of official Mexico did nothing. Officialdom did not take the maderistas and zapatistas very seriously, but it did believe the old *cacique's* days were numbered, and politicians everywhere were worried most of all by the succession. As weeks went by, it at last became evident even to Don Porfirio that he could no longer command.

Reluctantly, he recalled Limantour from Europe to try to save the regime.

Limantour returned, stopping off at New York to meet with Gustavo

Madero, who was in the United States trying to procure arms. He parleyed with Madero and Dr. Vásques Gómez; the maderista revolution was still an affair that might be compromised between gentlemen. Gustavo Madero and Dr. Vásquez assured Limantour that there was no need for a war to the knife. All the maderistas wanted was the assurance that Díaz would allow a democratically-elected government to come to power.

Limantour entered the City of México in March 1911, and in effect took control of the government. He dismissed the unpopular Corral, he cabled General Bernardo Reyes to come home at once to take command of the army, and he sent emissaries to try to hammer out a workable compromise with the Maderos. Representatives from each faction met at Ciudad Juárez, across from El Paso on the Chihuahua-Texas border.

What went on here is not clear. The Madero clan put pressure on the brothers to be reasonable; other supporters, such as Don Venustiano Carranza, a fellow *hacendado*, told the Maderos that a revolution compromised was a revolution lost. Ciudad Juárez was held by the federals, and Madero apparently was afraid to engage in battle there, because of the town's proximity to the border. He feared a border incident might provoke United States intervention; Madero, like most of his class, was extremely hostile to North Americans, but also very much afraid of North American power. The reyista faction within the maderistas, represented by Dr. Vásquez Gómez, claimed that Madero had lost his nerve and was prepared to sell out. Finally, while the turbulent rebel forces and the federal garrison faced each other at Juarez, Madero presented his terms. They were hardly a sellout, or even a compromise. They required the resignation of Díaz, the expulsion of all Científicos from government, the cession of a majority of state governorships to the maderistas, and the payment of all prior maderista expenses by the federal treasury. Limantour rejected them.

What Madero might have done is unknown, because at this point the impatient Generals Orozco and Pancho Villa disobeyed orders and attacked Ciudad Juárez. While thousands of people in El Paso climbed on rooftops to watch the show, the rebels poured into Ciudad Juárez and destroyed the federal garrison in a bloody battle. This was a minor victory in one sense, but in two others it was tremendously important. The capture of Juárez was a psychological blow against the regime, and it gave the rebels a port of entry to acquire arms and supplies from the United States.

Two days later Zapata overran Cuautla. Limantour was a banker, not a soldier; he did not know how to react. The army was intact, if so far ineffective; there was no groundswell of revolution outside Chihuahua and the small area of Morelos; there was not even a real civil war. But Limantour faced the same problem Díaz could not surmount. Everyone was convinced the government must change, and both the army and civil officialdom would do nothing, waiting for a coup. At last Limantour stated that he had no idea what the people of Mexico wanted, but that it obviously was no longer Don Porfirio and himself. He offered to secure Díaz' resignation, resign himself, and accept Francisco de la Barra, then ambassador to Washington, as an interim president pending a new election. The Maderos and the reyistas agreed to this, and a convention was signed at Ciudad Juárez on May 21, 1911.

There was distaste for Madero in the circles of the government and the elite, but Madero was considered infinitely better than the horror of the zapatista rebellion, which perhaps frightened the capital more than it should have.

Limantour did not find it easy to get rid of Díaz, despite his promises. The old dictator refused to listen, to sign papers, or to discuss anything except the agony of a bad tooth. Díaz would not believe that the same people who had cheered him the past year had now turned against him. When a great mob gathered outside the palace on the Zócalo, shouting for his resignation, he ordered the presidential guard to open fire. Machine gunners killed two hundred demonstrators before Limantour at last forced Díaz to sign the resignation.

On May 26, Díaz, half delirious from pain, was hustled to the train station, sent under guard to Veracruz, and put on a ship bound for France. Here he and Limantour passed out of history, the old man at least convinced that he had served his country to the last. What was to happen in Mexico in the four remaining years before his death perhaps convinced him more so, and comforted him to the end.

But as Díaz departed, most Mexicans believed the democratic revolution had triumphed, without real bloodshed. Few men, certainly not the Madero brothers, understood that the triumph had come much too late.

32

FIRE AND BLOOD

If they are going to kill me tomorrow,
I'd much rather they killed me today.
From the carranzista marching song, *La Valentina.*

The Porfiriato had ended in a whimper. Somehow, it dimmed the glory of the new day.

Madero entered the City of México to a roaring welcome, perhaps the warmest given any leader since Juárez, but it was as meaningless as all past ovations from the time of the viceroys. Nothing had been decided; the remnants of Porfirio Díaz' power structure struggled for power with the new men coming into government.

The interim, while elections were held, was stormy and perilous. Madero, obviously destined to win the presidential election in 1911, did not have the heart of the whole country. The majority of the *criollo* elite, and the whole foreign investment community, either feared or despised him. Madero's personal foibles, above all in an Hispanic country where so much historic emphasis was put on appearances and on virile manhood, kept his credibility at low ebb. Madero was a saint to many of the common people. He was and remained a sort of queer duck to the people in inner circles who met him daily; he failed to command respect.

While the election was arranged and carried out, the actual government of the country had fallen to a set of amateurs who replaced the Científicos and Díaz' appointees. They were generally what might be called middle-rank democrats. But they had no unity: there were liberals of the old school, who believed government had no right to initiate social reform; there were reyistas who wanted their champion to take control; and there was a faction of reforming left-wingers who demanded incisive change throughout society. Most of these men were well-meaning, but like the old *puros*, they tended to be more theoretical than practical. Amid these lawyers, doctors, and other middle-class new men, de la Barra only presided over government; he did not rule. For five months, in effect, no one ruled Mexico.

This hiatus allowed factions to coalesce around different leaders and different ideologies, all vying for power. There was agreement only on one thing: that the revolutionary armed forces must be disbanded before they grew too powerful. The Orozcos, Villas, and Zapatas had been useful in destroying the Porfiriato, but the people who had done the actual fighting were not considered fit for a role in government.

The new democratic groups did not have enough talent to staff the entire bureaucracy, and except at the very top the de la Barra government kept most of the old officeholders in service. These officials had not been willing to fight for Díaz—but few of them had any allegiance to the revolution, either. The effect was paralyzing.

Some forms of the new freedom proved immediately disastrous. A cardinal principle of the democrats was the free press, which Mexico had not enjoyed for a generation. But the freed newspapers were conservative and venal, and collectively the Mexican press behaved with utmost irresponsibility, irrespectively of ideology, carping, satirizing Francisco I. Madero's peculiarities, and damaging Madero's prestige among large segments of the population during and after the presidential election.

The greatest problem for the interim regime was Emiliano Zapata. While Orozco and Villa, the heroes of the north, stood on their arms, Zapata refused to lay his down. Madero had made only the vaguest references to land reform in his revolution; he was an *hacendado*, and above all, he was no expropriationist. Madero had a real love for the oppressed, though he hardly understood their real condition, but his love for legality and constitutional forms was greater. Zapata wished Madero well—but refused to disband his army, or even give up the territory he had seized in Morelos, until the new government assured him his peasants would get their lands. Zapata believed his demands were reasonable, and could not understand the de la Barra government's reluctance to grant them. Actually, the new men who came to power with Madero's revolution had in no way agreed among themselves that land reform was even necessary. The northern políticos like Venustiano Carranza and Abraham González had no sympathy for Zapata's Indian uprising; the urban middle-class professionals were distrustful of it. Zapata's concept of the revolution was land for the peasants; Madero's was constitutionality.

Zapata's people went on seizing sugar plantations and burning sugar mills. President de la Barra ordered new army operations against them, now commanded by General Victoriano Huerta, who was considered Mexico's toughest soldier. Madero, distressed, arranged a meeting with Zapata at Cuernavaca, and though Madero did his best to convince the peasant leader of his own good intentions, Zapata was adamant. His *pelados* and *indios* had had a bellyful of good intentions by rich men. Zapata insisted that all the *ejido* lands sequestered under the *Ley Lerdo* be returned to the Amerindian villages by decree. Madero argued that he could not do this, even after he became president; reform must come by "lawful means."

Then, a brief truce was snapped when Huerta's soldiery took to looting *indio* villages in Morelos, and when they could not catch armed agrarians, hanged no few peaceful ones. The Morelos insurrection was still flaming when Madero was elected president and replaced de la Barra in the National Palace on November 11, 1911.

Few important men at the capital believed Madero could rule Mexico, and he soon proved them right. Though he meant well, Madero could not really understand Zapata or the zapatistas, and he did not basically understand the condition of Mexico. He had arrived in power because he had come to symbolize the aspirations of the urban professionals and a large number of the northern common people, but the evidence is overwhelming that Madero never understood those aspirations. He thought his election *was* the revolution, and his concepts of democracy, learned in France and the United States, followed the forms of very gradual evolution. For example, he stated that the best means of bettering the lot of the Mexican laboring class was by creating trade schools, establishing retirement pensions, and campaigning against drinking and gambling. He was in favor of small landholdings in general, but he did not conceive of the magnitude of the agrarian problem or understand the dispossessed peasantry's deep hunger for soil. When a newspaper printed that he intended to "share the lands of the rich with the proletariat," Madero indignantly denied that he would ever "deprive any large landholder of his property." When a deputy, Luis Cabrera, insisted upon introducing a moderate program of land reform in congress, he was appalled and refused to act upon it.

Madero's whole revolutionary program, as history revealed it, was simply one of effective suffrage and no reelection. He was no revolutionary, but a good-hearted nineteenth-century liberal filled with the old optimism of the juarista years, believing all would work out with time and moderation. He urged compromise and reconciliation between all parties, insisting over and over that all change must come through a legal process. To prove his own faith in compromise, he appointed a few porfiristas to his cabinet along with reyistas, and of course alienated his more ardent reforming democrats. He appointed commissions to study things. Francisco Madero might have made a passable president of an Anglo-Saxon nation or presided over a Western democracy in a placid era. In Mexico he had to command a volatile, deteriorating situation that could only have been controlled with the strongest leadership. When it became more and more evident he could not or would not command it—despite his brother Gustavo's pleas he allowed the press to run wild with irresponsibility—he lost prestige daily, both with his friends and foes.

Zapata in Morelos grew exasperated with waiting. He issued his own pronunciamento for land reform, the Plan of Ayala, drafted for him by a Cuautla school teacher. The plan demanded the distribution of enclosed hacienda lands to the peasants and instructed them to fight for the woods, waters, and fields that were theirs by right. Zapata strengthened his position with this pronouncement, and weakened Madero's, both with the *hacendado* class and the poor.

The Zapata movement should have served notice on the capital that true peace in Mexico was going to be hard to come by without some effort toward land reform. Zapata himself was becoming a new saint to the thousands of soft-spoken, small peons who had doffed their hats for centuries to their landlords, but who had now somehow formed effective armies and performed military prodigies. The federal soldiers more and more resorted to atrocities against the Morelos *indios*, and the Zapata country endured a plague of burnings, reprisals, and mass executions on each side. In all fairness to Madero, however, Zapata still represented something no government of a modern state could accept, and since Madero insisted that Zapata quit fighting, the war went on.

When, by early 1912, it was clear that Madero could not command even his cabinet, a rash of attempted coups and revolts began. Bernardo Reyes pronounced in the old-fashioned manner at Nuevo León, but he had misjudged the people and the army, neither of which was yet as disillusioned with Madero as the inner circle, and was jailed. Madero did not believe in shooting enemies, always trusting they could be salvaged.

In February Pascual Orozco rose in Chihuahua. General Orozco—every revolutionary leader in the north from Abraham González to Pancho Villa had become a general—was a bandit by nature and his rebellion was personal; he felt denigrated by his rewards from Madero. Orozco showed his true colors in 1912 by accepting money from the Terrazas interests, which were blindly ensuring their own destruction by trying to bring Madero down—but significantly, Orozco issued proclamations based on the demands of the Flores-worker movement, and stated his rebellion was against the slow pace of revolutionary reform.

This northern uprising pulled General Huerta away from Morelos in time to save his military reputation. Fortunately for the government, Orozco split the old maderistas; González the governor and General Pancho Villa remained loyal to the president. With their assistance, Huerta quickly crushed Orozco.

Huerta was a brutal, bullet-headed professional officer. His military reputation had come from his campaigns against the Maya in Quintana Roo, and now he gained new luster by scattering Orozco's wild *vaqueros*. Huerta was, however, perhaps the ablest of all the Mexican professional soldiers in this era, but under a rough, somewhat impressive presence he was drunken, immoral, and devoid of loyalty and honor.

Huerta quickly quarreled with Villa in Chihuahua and intended to shoot him for insubordination. Madero, however, intervened and lodged Villa in the capital prison, which was rapidly filling with various dissident generals. Here a zapatista "general" taught Pancho Villa to read and write, and soon had him struggling through the old Spanish of Cervantes' *Don Quijote*, which may or may not have helped convince him that the world was mad.

The triumphant military hero Huerta immediately fell from grace when it was discovered after the Chihuahua campaign that some one million pesos in military funds had unaccountably vanished. Madero dismissed him from the army, though he did not consign him to the "generals' jail" at México.

Madero had survived a series of threats, including a hopeless effort by Porfirio Díaz' nephew, Félix, to pronounce at Veracruz. The challenges actually pointed up the precariousness of his regime. Madero failed to inspire respect or loyalty—except among the common folk of the north—and he was limited by his democratic, liberal ideals, which did not permit him to destroy his enemies, or the enemies of constitutional government. Madero preferred moderate counsel. More and more, he came to rely on his brother Gustavo and certain relatives he installed in government. They were loyal, but they also unfortunately cut him off from reality and the dangerous national ferments. In full retrospect, only one thing might have saved the Madero Presidency or directed Mexico toward a peaceful revolution, and that was the influence and goodwill of the United States.

By 1912 the United States was no longer just an enormously powerful neighbor vis-à-vis Mexico; the northern nation had emerged as a great world power, predominant throughout the Western Hemisphere. The United States, after the defeat of Spain in 1898, did not always play this role with judgment or restraint, although the basic aims—order and trade on good terms—had not changed. The great expansion of the North American economy during and into the Porfiriato had inserted a newer factor into Mexican life and politics. Mexico had become an economic satellite of the United States. United States citizens and corporations held huge investments, and three-quarters of Mexico's foreign trade—the trade on which the higher Mexican economy lived—was with the United States. Washington was thus deeply concerned with the course of Mexican politics, particularly politics leading to disorder, disruption, or destruction of property;

besides, the United States had become the principal, and often the only source of arms available to Mexican governments as well as rebel movements. Public opinion generally in the United States was largely sympathetic to Madero's democratic revolution. President Taft recognized Madero immediately in 1911 and even discreetly tried to give his government assistance while maintaining official neutrality. Taft wanted Madero and democracy to succeed.

But Madero was vociferously nationalist and rhetorically hostile to North American economic interests in Mexico; the Mexican middle class and budding businessmen felt threatened by North American economic dominance. While Madero's opposition was largely verbal, it aroused fears among foreign capitalists and investors. Another problem was the obvious fact that all foreigners in Mexico, including the North American, had become utterly spoiled by their favorable treatment under the Díaz regime. To attract them, Díaz had offered extraterritoriality, gradually arousing a deep nativist response, while many foreign companies, especially in oil, had learned to act irresponsibly. Oil paid no taxes and the great petroleum corporations believed they could get away with never paying Mexican taxes. North American petroleum and mining interests refused to make compromises with any new Mexican government, and they could and did exert considerable pressures on any administration in Washington to support them in every controversy. Foreign companies were contemptuous of Mexican sovereignty, and all educated Mexicans resented this deeply; the United States, tended to be paternalistic and even arrogant in its goodwill. Recognition by Washington had become vital to any Mexican government—and this was a heavy cross for both Mexicans and North Americans to bear.

Madero in 1911 and 1912 insisted upon attacking North American capitalism with fierce rhetoric. He also proposed a three-centavo-per-barrel tax on crude oil extracted in Mexico. This sum (1.5 U.S. cents) was less than any United States company paid on domestic production in any state, but the mere idea that a Mexican government might impose taxes seemed to infuriate most investors. The contempt for Mexico that consciously or unconsciously pervaded most North Americans, including those who hoped for the best for that country, made the powerful United States companies intransigent; they hoped to see Madero succeeded by a more "reasonable" man. Tragically, these economic interests found sympathy and support in United States Ambassador Henry Lane Wilson.

Wilson, sent abroad to lie for his country, ended by lying to everyone, including his own country. Without actual instruction from his government, Henry L. Wilson considered the North American billion-dollar investment in Mexico his paramount concern; his instinctive leanings were toward the foreign capitalists with interests in Mexico. He was the first great practitioner of what came to be reviled on both sides of the Rio Bravo as "dollar diplomacy."

Wilson was also a cold, unemotional Anglo-Saxon who was exasperated with the visionary, impractical Madero and his high-pitched orations. Wilson planned to influence Madero's policies, and when he could not, the natural antipathy both men felt turned to actual hatred. In 1912 Madero informed the president-elect of the United States, Woodrow Wilson, that he would prefer a new envoy—strong diplomatic language. The extent of Henry Wilson's dislike is shown by the fact that he publicly stated that the president of Mexico should be locked in a madhouse.

Taft instructed him to maintain good relations with Madero, but Wilson deliberately gave Madero the idea that Washington was hostile to him. Meanwhile, Wilson reported nothing good of Madero to Washington, detailing his patent dislike of United States capitalism, his supposed addiction to radicalism and magnified all of Madero's personal failings and weaknesses. Wilson did his best to make Madero appear a communist, and, incredibly, he exaggerated the destruction of foreign property in Mexico, and in 1912 falsely reported that every North American citizen's life and property was in jeopardy.

Wilson's machinations soured much opinion in the United States toward the Madero government. Worse, as the North American press quoted Wilson's assertions that Mexico was in anarchy and that Madero was a madman, it created a dangerous instability between the two governments. Although it is evident that the United States government did not credit everything Wilson said, domestic opinion forced Washington to strengthen army garrisons along the border. The maderistas now believed the United States had turned against them, and their enemies believed that the United States government would welcome anyone who pulled Madero down. The abortive revolt of General Félix Díaz in October, 1912, seems to have stemmed almost entirely from his expectation of United States support; Díaz only landed in the "generals' jail."

Unfortunately, Madero's prisons were becoming the principal centers of political activity by the close of 1912. Mexican jails and prisons, then as now, were far more open places than the grim bastions in the United States. For political prisoners, or people with money, prison life was made quite comfortable, with unlimited visitation rights and free access. Generals Díaz and Reyes in fact found their cells at the capital excellent headquarters; whole delegations of Mexican colonels and general officers visited them regularly. No high officers visited Pancho Villa, but he took advantage of Madero's loose security to walk out of prison early in 1913 and escape to Texas.

Reyes and Díaz entered into a plot. Most Mexican historians, probably rightly, believed that Ambassador Wilson was at least privy to it. A coup was set for Sunday, February 9, 1913.

On this date Reyes and Díaz were released from their cells by army officers. They took command of a small group of rebellious soldiery in the capital garrison and marched on the National Palace. Here began the fortnight Mexicans call "The Tragic Ten Days."

Madero was alerted; his presidential guard was loyal, and when the conspirators arrived at the palace, the troops protecting the president fired on them. In a sudden, blazing fire-fight, civilians coming out of the cathedral from Mass were killed by machine-gun bullets while Reyes rode his horse forward, against the advice of his companions, who feared he would be shot. Reyes shouted he would at least not be shot in the back, and fell dead.

Félix Díaz, of lesser courage, retreated quickly back to the Ciudadela, which his fellow conspirators held with machine guns. Here the rebels were isolated and surrounded by local troops.

Madero emerged from the palace and rode down the Avenida Juárez to the Reforma amid cheering crowds. At this point, the coup had failed and he was in command—but Madero had been badly shaken. He recalled General Huerta and gave him command of the federal army. It never occurred to Madero that Huerta hated him, or that the general would put anything before his country.

In the state of armed emergency, Huerta pushed Madero out of the way, effectively taking over the army and government. Then, while the rebels in the Citadel and the loyalists outside and in the palace bombarded each other, killing mostly bystanders, Huerta began to negotiate a deal with Félix Díaz.

Huerta did order several attacks on the Ciudadela, which were bloodily repulsed. But he made no all-out effort, keeping in reserve large contingents of reinforcements which were pouring into the capital by rail. Huerta was merely keeping the emergency going until he could arrive at certain understandings with General Díaz—who had been prepared to surrender on demand.

During the stand-off Ambassador Wilson suggested Madero resign, and when Madero angrily rejected this interference, arranged a truce between Díaz and Huerta—ostensibly so that civilians could be removed from the line of fire, but actually so that Díaz and Huerta could meet. The two quickly concluded a pact, on February 17, a cynical and unstable alliance of convenience by two men eager for power. Huerta agreed to assume control of the Mexican government, remove the Madero brothers, and hold the palace until an "election" might ratify General Díaz as president.

Now, in the confused and murderous milieu of a capital under siege, where sandbagged machine guns guarded every corner and gunshots resounded day and night, the tragedy ran its course. Huerta lured Gustavo Madero, who was stronger than his brother, out of the palace to a meeting in a restaurant. While Gustavo was thus delayed, Huerta's trusted officers burst into the palace and arrested Madero and his vice-president, José María Pino Suárez. Once the president was in custody, a group of General Díaz' minions, drunk and dangerous, disarmed Gustavo Madero and rushed him off to the Citadel. As soon as Victoriano Huerta knew both Maderos were in his power, he appeared on the balcony of the National Palace and announced that peace and order had been restored to Mexico.

No one lifted a finger to aid the Maderos. When Huerta, however, refused to hand Francisco Madero over to the Díaz group, Díaz' officers tortured Gustavo savagely before shooting him, in a drunken orgy. In a week, Mexico seemed to have regressed to barbarism comparable to the brutalities of the pretorians.

That same night, February 18, Generals Huerta and Díaz met at a reception given by Ambassador Wilson in his embassy. Wilson announced the Díaz-Huerta pact to the diplomatic corps and offered a toast: "Long live General Díaz, the savior of Mexico."

The horrible game continued. Huerta asked Francisco Madero and Pino Suárez to resign, offering them safe-conduct to the coast. Madero refused. But he was then persuaded by the foreign minister, Lascourain, whose role in these events was very ambiguous. The foreign minister offered to serve as provisional president, and to withhold the resignations from Huerta until the two were safely at sea. It is said that Huerta swore an oath to Lascourain over the medallion of the Virgin of Guadalupe that like most Mexicans he wore around his neck, to respect Madero's and Pino Suárez' lives. At any rate, the foreign minister said as much to Madero, who finally turned over the resignations, signed in secret.

Within the hour Lascourain gave them to Huerta. He appointed Huerta foreign minister and resigned himself, letting Huerta succeed "constitutionally" to the presidency.

Madero was now in deadly danger. He failed to see it, telling a visitor that if he ever came to rule Mexico again, he would surely look for better men to serve him. Madero's family, after Gustavo's fate, were terrified of the callous Huerta. They approached Ambassador Wilson and begged him to throw his protection over the ex-president. Wilson coldly told Señora Madero that her husband's problems stemmed entirely from his refusal to listen to his own advice, and that it was impossible in any event for him to interfere in Mexican affairs.

Then, Wilson intimated to Huerta that the United States would approve any course of action he saw fit to take in the best interests of Mexico.

There was one more act. The next evening, while Huerta attended a Washington's Birthday gala at the embassy, two motorcars manned by men in grey rurales' uniforms pulled up at the National Palace. The rurales came out with Madero and Pino Suárez and drove off. The president and vice-president were not seen alive again. Their bullet-riddled bodies were found at the rear of the federal penitentiary.

Huerta claimed that the two had been killed trying to escape, and when this announcement met total unbelief he then blamed the whole affair on Díaz, who he drove from the government. He was now in full power in Mexico.

This was the law of the gun, however, and in 1913 the world was not prepared for this new kind of twentieth-century politics. Most foreigners professed profound shock, and if the capital was silent, thousands of Mexicans were wild with rage. Huerta's murders were a classic case of the blunder transcending the crime. The murders of Madero and Pino Suárez destroyed any chance Huerta had of being recognized by the United States government, or ruling legitimately in Mexico.

The Taft administration flately denied Ambassador Wilson's requests that Huerta be recognized. President-elect Woodrow Wilson was horrified, and became determined to remove Huerta from office if it were in his power. And in fact, several North American newspapers were savagely critical of Henry L. Wilson's hand in the whole affair.

In Mexico, Huerta had made the tragic, well-meaning little Madero into that most beloved of Mexican saints, the bloodstained martyr-hero. In death, Madero became the first Hero of the Revolution.

Huerta's blunders were not at first apparent. The capital remained silent under martial law. The Mexican congress, although elected with Madero and containing a maderista majority, ratified Huerta without resistance. The one senator who spoke out was shot to death by Huerta's assassins.

Huerta quickly showed his regime had a brutality and cynicism that Don Porfirio's had never possessed in its worst years. Drunk half the time, Huerta ran the country from a bar, surrounded by cronies and military appointees of the lowest sort. He dismissed all the maderista and reyista elements along with the Díaz faction. But in a real sense Huerta's regime was a continuation of the Porfiriato; it showed what the Porfiriato had become at last.

The army saluted him; the Church blessed him; the elite congratulated him; and the foreign community praised him. The British government, thinking of its majority interest in the oil fields at Tampico, recognized him as a necessary evil. Huerta was called the Restorer of Mexico.

The capital was not the country. When Madero died, the hopes of millions died. Then the despair was drowned in rage, especially among the young, who for a generation had been living amid rising expectations.

By 1913 Mexico was experiencing the phenomenon that was to be a feature of most underdeveloped nations in this century: an exploding population that created a high proportion of young people. There had been great advances during the modernizations of the Porfiriato, mainly in the towns, with a great decline in the death rate, and especially in infant mortality. If this was still greater than in Europe, it was lower than it had ever been in colonial times. Mexico was filled with volatile teen-agers, and hundreds of thousands of them were better educated than any *mestizo* generation in history.

Thousands of such young people were politicized. They had waited impatiently for Don Porfirio to die. Now, they were ready to kill Huerta. *Muera Huerta* was their slogan. Ironically, General Huerta had destroyed that very authority among the young people of Mexico that the older elite and the foreign community had hoped he might restore. It was Huerta rather than the "radical" Madero who destroyed at last all the symbols of authority and legitimacy; his coup was a crack that opened Mexico to the core. Through the crack ancient class, ideological, and racial hatreds poured out unrestrained, proclaimed most stridently by the young.

Again, the northern frontier, the birthplace of the true Mexican race, played the dominant role. But now, the northern states had both the population and the leadership to make their weight felt. The north was Madero country, had always joined all liberal revolutions since 1810, and now, would lead the revolution.

The political leadership of the northern states was maderista. The first leader to declare against Huerta was Don Venustiano Carranza, now governor of Coahuila. Carranza was a white-whiskered *hacendado* of fifty-three, aging but hard in the saddle, a tough and often pompous man who wore blue-tinted spectacles. He had served in Don Porfirio's *caballado* as a senator, but he was a northern separatist and constitutionalist, disliking the suave "foreigners" at the capital. He may have been an opportunist—or he may sensibly have realized that his days were numbered if Huerta consolidated his power. Carranza issued his Plan of Guadalupe, which called for Huerta's resignation and the restoration of constitutionality. He ordered Coahuila into rebellion against the federal government, and styled himself First Chief of the Constitutionalist Army of the North.

The governor of Chihuahua, Abraham González, recognizing the first chief's lead, proclaimed next. To the west, the enormous state of Sonora, half-North Americanized like its neighbors, also rebelled. Here the state legislature acclaimed Carranza's Constitutionalist Revolution without support from the governor.

The first flare of the revolution was indecisive. The regular army garrisons remained loyal to Huerta. Carranza was soon forced to flee Coahuila, though his military chief, Pablo González, held enclaves in the east. The federalistas captured the governor of Chihuahua and executed him by hurling him under the wheels of a moving train.

In Sonora a handful of younger, effective leaders secured the border town of Nogales and formed a Sonoran Constitutionalist army which acknowledged Carranza's leadership and gave him a secure base. They included new names: Álvaro Obregón, ex-worker, ex-school teacher, a ranchero-type with ancient roots in the frontier; Adolfo de la Huerta; and Plutarco Elías Calles, a man of obscure origins with enormous ability. Obregón was their paramount general, and Obregón was to become the best military leader produced in four centuries in Mexico. He started with a force of Yaquis with bows and arrows; with his lieutenants he raised, trained, and armed the most cohesive, responsive, and disciplined army of the Mexican Revolution.

These leaders, like most of their rank and file, were men of the frontier, whose historic roots were Mexican rather than European or Amerindian. They surged to prominence as the end product of the long *mestizo* Mexicanization of the north. They had few of the outlooks and few of the conceits of the southern *criollos*; they lacked all sense of being Indian. Whether all-European or almost all-European in blood like Obregón, or descended from several races like Calles, they were "muy Mexicano," as men said of them; they were "la raza," the Mexican race, of varying hues and backgrounds but of one culture. They were to be the cutting edge of the Mexican Revolution.

The Sonoran Constitutionalists soon secured their state from Huerta's federalistas and formed the hard core for the revolution in the north. When the Constitutionalists had created firm bases and were fighting in Sonora, Coahuila, Tamaulipas, and Nuevo León, hundreds of young Mexicans began to pour into the north from all parts of the Republic to join the first chief and his generals. These teen-age warriors, often led by commanders in their twenties, were inspired by more than a hatred of Huerta; they were consciously fighting for reform of the whole society.

After the Constitutionalists captured the city of Matamoros in Tamaulipas, the very young general Lucio Blanco distributed an estate belonging to Félix Díaz among its peons. When Jefe Primero Carranza remonstrated against Blanco, warning that if the revolution were to be directed against landowners it would delay its triumph for years, another young general, Francisco J. Múgica answered brashly that the young radicals were ready to fight five years or ten, whatever was required, Múgica, Blanco's elder, was twenty-eight.

The younger revolutionaries made Carranza, whose aims for the revolution did not go beyond Madero's, reluctantly face the fact that the rank and file of the Constitutionalist armies were fighting and dying for more than the mere demise of Huerta. He admitted as much in a speech at

Hermosillo in Sonora, by saying that "like it or not" once the armed struggle was over there was going to be a social struggle to "change everything."

The carranzistas or Constitutionalists began to advance inexorably out of the high northwest while they secured some gains in the northeast. Obregón's military genius, and the skills of his lieutenants de la Huerta and Calles, forged the best military force in Mexico, including the regulars. Obregón swept the federalistas out of Sonora and marched into Sinaloa and Jalisco in a campaign aimed at the capital. His disciplined Constitutionalist army was the main force of the revolution. Yet, somewhat ironically, the attention of most outsiders, especially North Americans, was seized by the explosion that reerupted in Chihuahua.

Here the peon born in 1880 as Doroteo Arango had at last found his métier in social revolution.

Pancho Villa was one of those historic men who could never be seen unemotionally and who must inevitably pass into myth. In March 1913, Villa rode back across the Rio Bravo from Texas, calling for vengeance against the murderers of Madero and Abraham González. What neither Madero nor González had been able to do he did superbly: he raised a people's army and a people's revolution out of the dregs of the northern population.

Villa was wild and elemental, a man of undisciplined emotions rather than intellect, but also a leader of energy and valor, with that especial machismo that appealed strongly to the northern Mexican race. He called on *la raza* to rebel against Huerta, against ancient oppression, against the rich. He caught the imagination of the poor and dispossessed: *vaqueros* deserted their haciendas to ride beside him; miners came up out of their pits; trainmen captured their locomotives and puffed cheering into his camp. He had fewer tough rancheros in his growing army than Obregón and fewer men of the middle ranks, but he had enormous success in recruiting regiments of grim Yaqui warriors from the sierra, implacable fighters who had an ancestral hate of the federal uniform. Villa called the *indios* his "race brothers" and they responded to his call by thousands.

Villa's force was mounted, and the defection of the railway workers to his cause added a new dimension to his warfare. Rails extended his operations indefinitely. Villa formed his Division of the North along the railroad tracks; his soldiers lived in battered boxcars. They were a colorful and tumultuous band of revolutionary brothers who came with horses, goats, cooking pots, and "soldaderas," the women, wives, sweethearts, and camp followers who lived in the midst of this people's army. The soldaderas did the cooking and laundry and sometimes they picked up guns and proved they could fight as fiercely as the men.

Villa's Division of the North knew very little about Constitutionalist principles. Its warriors were motivated by old hatreds against rich men and their lackeys, the soldiers and rurales, and by a hunger to own their own fields and farms. The songs of this army, whether the sad, haunting "La Valentina" with its awareness of ever-present death, or the catchy "La Cucaracha," a meaningless tune about the perambulations of a cockroach, had little if any socio-political content. Although Pancho Villa made reformist proclamations and tried to assign revolutionary families portions of hacienda lands, his rationale and "government" were more nihilist than reformist. Villa's real pattern of "social reform" was to seize haciendas and drive off their livestock, which he sold in Texas to pay for arms and ammunition to expand his operations.

Villa was the epitome of the Hispanic *bandido en héroe*, called forth by the social sores and eruptions of his times.

The Division of the North traveled along the tracks, capturing mining camps and towns, slaughtering federal garrisons wherever it went. The huertista army was still ineffective against this kind of warfare, and the regulars no longer were safe even in the cities. Villa drove a freight train filled with armed men into Ciudad Juárez in the night, surprising the garrison and seizing the important border city. The coup added immensely to his fame. Equally important, he looted three hundred thousand pesos from the whorehouses and gambling halls operated by the politicians, which bought him a great store of military hardware in Texas. With the fall of Juárez, Pancho Villa and his cockroach army began to steal the Mexican scene.

Villa did possess definite genius for understanding the federales' weaknesses. He outfoxed and outfought the regulars at Tierra Blanca, here seizing a large store of Mausers, ammunition, and artillery pieces. Just as he had grasped the principle of using railroads in this vast country, Villa understood the importance of artillery, and he incorporated the field guns into his army.

By the fall of 1913 Villa's explosion had paralyzed all Chihuahua and was threatening the borders of Coahuila and Durango. His troops took the rich town of Torreón in the Laguna cotton-raising oasis, but could not hold Torreón at this time.

Villa had ten thousand irregulars in the field in Chihuahua, and he was now a force to be feared. His relationship with the revolution, and the Constitutionalist camp in Sonora, however, was quite vague. Like virtually all rebel generals operating in the hinterlands of Mexico, Villa paid lip service to the Jefe Primero, but in effect his was an independent campaign. Carranza did not control him; no one controlled him; he was an elemental force loosed on Mexico. He stole the thunder of the revolution from Obregón's disciplined rancheros, because he and his army were colorful, and journalists flocked to him. But while Obregón was organizing a Constitutionalist regime in Carranza's name in the wake of his army, Villa was releasing the whirlwind between the cordilleras.

The villistas, leader and men, had no firm policies. As they poured over the countryside, they looted some haciendas and mines and towns; they ransomed others; and sometimes, virtually on a whim of Villa or one of his lieutenants, they spared them altogether. Villa might befriend even a rich *hacendado* of kindly reputation; on the other hand, his followers often massacred hapless peons in drunken orgies and carried off the wives and daughters of poor men for rape. The fact that there was no policy made the villista depredations peculiarly terrible—no one knew what to expect from a villista visit. It might be amicable, with courtesies exchanged; if the riders were drunk on tequila, or surly from a brush with regulars, it might turn into a massacre. Villa personally had a rough generosity, although he had his hatreds—women of the upper class, and foreigners, especially Chinese. Villa usually murdered any Orientals he found working at North American-owned mines or cattle haciendas indiscriminately, and his rapes ran into the hundreds. And Pancho Villa himself was a paragon of virtue compared to some of his lieutenants. Rodolfo Fierro and Tomás Urbina (who in the end was faithless even to his chief) were two of the vilest men who ever rode in Mexico. They shot helpless prisoners wantonly and they practiced the incredible tortures Mexicans had learned from the desert *indios*, staking men out on anthills to be eaten alive.

But Villa received a good press, especially from North American correspondents. The villistas received virtually all their arms and ammunition, beyond what they took from the federals, from agents in the United States. Villa did steal and sell beef from the ranching interests owned by the press magnate William Randolph Hearst, but otherwise in this period he was scrupulous not to injure North American lives or property. He robbed Mexican *hacendados* and *políticos*; he found a ready market for his loot in Texas; and the press made him into an Hispanic Robin Hood.

There is no denying that there was more to Villa's insurgency than rape, robbery, and massacre. The fury of his soldiers and soldaderas stemmed from class and racial grievances that had built for generations. The order of the Porfiriato, particularly, had ridden roughshod over the small people of the north and the tribal *indios*, enclosing and sequestering their lands, while the rurales and the *hacendado*-políticos had systematically robbed them. Blood debts, and insults that grated against the Hispanic soul, were paid in full. And despite his acceptance of human beasts like Urbina and Fierro, Villa's magnetism and vague ideals drew decent revolutionaries to his camp from all parts of Mexico.

These high-minded recruits staffed his headquarters, organized his supply lines, and trained his artillerymen. Many genuinely liberal Mexicans saw Villa as a passing phenomenon, a cruel but necessary leader whom in fact they preferred to the opportunistic Venustiano Carranza, who was obviously not committed to a genuine social revolution. If Villa could be unpredictable, he was uncomplicated and sincere in both his hatreds and his friendships. He attracted and held the loyalty of Felipe Ángeles, a professional soldier born into one of the great landowning families. General Ángeles, Mexico's premier artillerist, blasted Villa's path into the heart of Mexico with his efficient guns. Ángeles, whom all contemporaries considered an inherently decent man, believed that Villa was necessary to bring a Mexican rebirth, and to erase the evils of the past.

By the first months of 1914, the north was in full-scale rebellion against Huerta. Villa was stalled but deadly outside Torreón; Pablo González owned the high northeast; Obregón was systematically mopping up the northwest along the Pacific. In the south, the stubborn Zapata still played his secondary but decisive role by holding down a federal army on the outskirts of the capital. Zapata, simplistic and direct, attracted few of the urban idealists or the militant workers and he continued to be detested and feared by most city dwellers. Yet Zapata, from first to last, embodied the one thing that probably most motivated all the actual fighters in this revolution: the hunger of the rural poor for land and bread.

Zapata desired neither titles nor pesos nor power; he was perhaps the purest revolutionary who ever lived. This gave him one kind of power, but robbed him of all effectiveness in the reality of Mexican politics. His services to the revolution in 1914 were two: he revealed the extent of the agrarian problem; and he fatally distracted General Huerta from the decisive campaigns in the north.

However, in early 1914 the Huerta government had the allegiance of the regular army, which was improving, and the support of the power structures and the social elite. Holding the ports and major cities, he could import modern Mausers and machine guns that were superior to the miscellany of frontier weapons used by the armies of the north. Huerta's regime, unlike Díaz', was not rotting away from inertia in 1914, and a very large part in his downfall was played not by revolutionaries but by the government of the United States.

Woodrow Wilson had arrived in office with a deep distaste for Huerta, which developed into a determination to destroy the Mexican militarist. Wilson was the kind of president, in the kind of age, when such goals came naturally. Wilson had a rigid morality and a pervasive liberal instinct which made him sympathize with the Mexican Revolution and drove him to help bring about a democratic order south of the Bravo.

When Wilson took office in March 1913, the Mexican situation had become the United States' most pressing foreign policy problem. Taft bequeathed the Huerta-recognition question unresolved. The problems of protecting North American private investments in Mexico, protocol, ideology, and instinct all pulled the Wilson administration in several ways. Above all, Wilson believed in a "Large Policy," envisioning the United States as a self-imposed protector and democratizer of the Hispanic republics in the Western Hemisphere. More often than not policy implementation met with unexpected and even disastrous results.

Like most North American liberals, for Wilson it was an article of faith that human beings were very much alike everywhere, and he tended to see Mexicans as "Anglo-Saxons who happened to have brown skins." This was of course false; there were cultural differences between the Anglo-Saxon and the Hispanic world that transcended even the differences between North Americans and Japanese. Wilson's honest statement in 1913—"I am going to teach the South American republics to elect good men"—was unconsciously patronizing. Wilson and the men around him did not comprehend how agonizing the concept behind such statements was to Mexican pride. The politicized Mexicans knew well enough the tendency of Hispanic societies during their time of troubles to throw up vile leaders; being reminded of it only prodded the deepest, suppurating sores of the Mexican consciousness of national humiliation. Wilson believed that most Mexicans would be grateful for his help in destroying Huerta. But Mexicans resented any kind of foreign interference, saying that while many Mexicans wanted Huerta dead, no Mexican believed that any North American had any sort of right to carry a candle at his funeral.

Woodrow Wilson informed the Huerta regime that the Mexican government would be recognized only if Huerta ceased to be a part of it. He offered to mediate between Huerta and Carranza. To put pressure on both sides—for most of all Washington wanted the civil war ended—Wilson recalled the American ambassador and placed an arms embargo on all Mexico. The moves were ineffective. All Mexicans were glad to get rid of Henry Lane Wilson; Huerta was buying arms in Germany; and Villa and Carranza found a presidential arms embargo no bar to their buying weapons from private interests in the United States. Wilson then sent a mediator, John Lind, to the Mexican capital, who threatened Huerta with recognition of the Carranza faction unless he cooperated. Huerta was logically intransigent, although he grudgingly promised to hold elections in October 1913.

Then Villa captured Torreón for the first time, and although he was forced north again, this victory sent shock waves through the Huerta government. Huerta reacted violently to congressional criticism by dissolving the congress and arresting more than one hundred deputies. He packed the halls with military cronies, and as soon as the October election was held, he invalidated it. This infuriated the United States president, who attacked Huerta in the harshest possible diplomatic terms and confided to intimates that he intended to destroy Huerta by every means short of actual invasion.

Wilson's moves against Huerta were misunderstood in Mexico, where they dredged up the old fear of a North American conquest and annexation; Mexicans simply could not comprehend a person of Wilson's morality and mentality, or the North American compulsion to force democracy on other countries. Wilson's pressures actually drove support to General Huerta rather than away from him.

Wilson was surprised, even hurt, by Carranza's reaction. Carranza became totally enraged by the fact that Wilson's inept interferences were giving Huerta some popularity. To ensure his own popularity with a basically anti-*yanqui* people, he blasted Wilson's attacks on Huerta as interventions. Carranza was intelligent enough to see, while Wilson could not, that while the revolution needed U.S. support, no Mexican government dared seem to come to power through the good offices of the United States.

Wilson finally decided that despite Carranza's noises, he hated Huerta more. Therefore, in 1914 he authorized the sale of arms to the Constitutionalists without dropping the embargo against the huertistas.

The act logically won no friends in Mexico. But this was the beginning of the end for Huerta, because now North American aid poured openly across the border to the northern rebels. Villa smashed his way into Torreón, this time permanently, in April; Pablo González moved toward the great oil fields around Tampico.

This last military operation created a very dangerous international situation. The Tampico oil was mostly British-owned, and the Royal Navy was dependent upon Mexican sources in 1914. The British government had recognized Huerta primarily because he controlled Tampico. Now, a British fleet, joined with several other European contingents, stood off Tampico ready to intervene. In deference to the Monroe Doctrine, the British and other warships were placed under the operational command of the U.S. admiral whose own forces waited out in the Gulf.

The problem was the old one: the nature of Mexican disorders was such that no government could protect private property during a revolution, leading to the fact that no foreign government respected Mexican sovereignty entirely. In 1914 both the contempt in which Mexicans were held by foreigners and Mexican sensitivities to this caused a minor tragedy on the Gulf coast. The various foreign warships patrolling Mexican shores from time to time put in for leave or supplies, and in April some United States sailors inadvertently entered a restricted area while on shore leave at Veracruz. The local authorities arrested them, but afterward, quickly released the sailors with apologies. The matter would normally have gone no further between nations with normal relations. But in the tension between

Wilson and Huerta, the United States chose to make something of the incident. The North American admiral, Mayo, insisted that a Mexican public apology include a ceremonial salute to the United States flag, the so-called *desagravio a la bandera*. This was the kind of ceremony that offered freely, won hearts, but demanded by force, caused wars.

The evidence is that Wilson was trying to humiliate Huerta and destroy his regime but not to start a war witht Mexico, which, of course, the United States could have forced at any time in these years. When Huerta denied the *desagravio* or apology, Wilson concentrated the United States Atlantic Fleet off Veracruz, and Admiral Mayo was ordered to intercept arms shipments bound for Mexico.

This order presented Mayo with a considerable problem. A large shipment was known to be arriving on a German freighter, the *Ypiranga*, but to interfere with this on the high seas was to risk war with Imperial Germany, to say nothing of violating historic United States policy and international law. Mayo's solution was fantastic, but showed the utter contempt North Americans had for Huerta and the sovereignty of his regime. The United States squadron landed bluejackets to seize the port area and custom house at Veracruz, so as to confiscate the German arms on Mexican soil.

Resistance was unexpected but it was spontaneous. Mexican soldiers, some cadets from the local naval academy, and civilians opened fire on the landing party. The offshore fleet responded with a bombardment that destroyed the naval academy and killed some hundreds of Mexican civilians. Ironically, in the confusion the German freighter captain slipped his vessel out of port and landed his cargo at another harbor on the Mexican coast. Then, United States naval forces occupied Veracruz, amid a certain number of atrocities not forgotten by Mexicans, but rarely mentioned in North American history books.

President Wilson was in fact horrified by this outcome. He had not expected fighting; he believed that Huerta had little support, and totally misunderstood the Mexican reaction to the intervention. While thousands of young Mexicans demonstrated to be allowed to fight at Veracruz (few actually entered the army) Huerta protested vigorously. Not to be outdone, Carranza protested even more indignantly, terming the landing an offense against Mexican dignity and a threat against independence. Pancho Villa alone kept silent, because at this time he was Wilson's favorite Mexican general and his camp was the terminal of a United States arms pipeline.

There could easily have been war at this point. However, Argentina, Brazil, and Chile offered a face-saving plan of arbitration, which in fact was rather gratefully accepted by both sides. Meanwhile, the United States landing force held Veracruz, cutting off Huerta's supply line and customs revenues and seriously weakening his power and prestige. The arbitration finally rendered a fair decision for Mexico, but this result came only after Huerta had fallen and the recommendations were ignored. The North American action damaged Huerta gravely—but it also seriously damaged Mexican feelings toward the United States for many years.

However, while the Veracruz incident went on, matters began to move toward crisis in the civil war. Villa and Obregón had again taken the offensive while Huerta was engaged at Veracruz. Villa, traveling down the rail lines from the north, moved spectacularly and rapidly with an army grown to some twenty-two thousand men. To operate beyond the rails, he had organized a colorful cavalry, the "Dorados" or golden ones, brown-skinned raiders in golden-hued uniforms and the northern, or Texas-style hats, who rode and raided demonically. This was the *vaquero* army that in most foreign eyes epitomized the Mexican Revolution—dashing, reckless, bandoleered horsemen, who like the zapatistas in their white cotton pants and huge, cartwheel sombreros, were far more colorful than Obregón's khaki-clad ranks. Huerta massed an important segment of his forces at Zacatecas to halt Villa's mad advance.

The ancient mining town seemed impregnable, a high eagle's nest among the encircling mountains of the grim central bowl of Mexico.

Obregón's forces were marching through Jalisco when Villa arrived at Zacatecas. By this time, a deep rivalry had grown between the Division of the North and the main Constitutionalist Army. Carranza, determined that Villa must not gain the prestige of overthrowing the regulars, ordered him to halt at Zacatecas, and forbade him to assault the city.

There was never any possibility that Carranza and Villa, would be compatible. Villa, the *pelado*, was elemental and careless of consequences, whether in seizing a town or a woman; Carranza, the *hacendado*, was vain, didactic, and enormously jealous of his position as Jefe Primero. Villa responded to Carranza's wired instructions with an emotional scene, swearing he would capture Zacatecas with or without the license of the "old goat whiskers" Carranza. His subordinates supported his decision; the battle began late in June.

General Felipe Ángeles kept the troop and ammunition trains rolling down from Laredo and Ciudad Juárez and marshalled the villista artillery.

Pistol in hand, screaming, shouting threats and encouragement, Villa drove his warriors up sheer mountainsides under sleeting fire. They dragged field pieces up slopes to outflank the federal forts. Villistas climbed the horrendous rock of La Bufa, the historic silver mountain, and drove the huertistas out of their eagles' nests. By will, passion, courage, and a storm of fire, Pancho Villa shot his way into Zacatecas, and on that day he carried the revolution.

Although in these same days Obregón was capturing Guadalajara and

Querétaro and moving into the Bajío, Villa had emerged as a legendary hero. The genteel people of Mexico would never forgive him, not then, not later, but by now the myth, secured by Villa's genuine achievements at Zacatecas, was obscuring the man.

The North American press had made him a hero; only one North American journalist wrote that Villa was a "peon who thought like a peon." President Wilson's agents in Villa's camp were impressed by his refusal to smoke and drink, or to gamble—except occasionally on a cockfight. These reports impressed the puritan in the White House; but there were other, more pragmatic considerations. Pancho Villa was not given to mouthing anti-*yanqui* slogans like almost all Mexican intellectuals; he did not lecture every visiting North American, like Carranza and Madero before him, on Mexican dignity and sovereignty. While Carranza's rhetoric was mostly for Mexican consumption (as his general Calles freely admitted) it could not help but chill relations between Wilson and the first chief. Villa seemed far more "flexible"; he became Wilson's first choice for president of Mexico.

The psychological blow of Zacatecas, and Obregón's steady march into the Bajío, crumbled Huerta's last supports. The federal army was refusing to give battle; Obregón issued an order disbanding it in Carranza's name. And Carranza at last stopped Villa by cutting off his coal supply and immobilizing his locomotives at Zacatecas while the Sonoran army reached the capital.

Obregón took the city without bloodshed in August 1914. Huerta fled to the *Ypiranga*, the same German ship that precipitated the affair at Veracruz. This ended the military phase of the Mexican Revolution—for what came afterward was no part of the Constitutional revolution, but a bloody quarrel between triumphal revolutionaries.

Villa was furious at what he considered a betrayal by Carranza, to cut him off from the power and the glory of having saved Mexico. Carranza and his generals were distrustful of Villa, whom they considered a wild man on horseback at the head of a dangerous force. As the Huerta regime now fell quietly, the federal soldiers vanishing or laying down their arms, the heros of the revolution themselves were poised on the brink of a murderous, fratricidal war, which was to do more damage to the body and soul of Mexico than the revolution.

The three revolutionary forces, Constitutionalists, villistas, and zapatistas, had fought in isolation from each other, and with only one common goal, the downfall of Huerta. In the victory, Villa was alienated and enraged. Zapata, from bitter experience, trusted no one in power at the capital. Carranza was pompous and determined not to let a real social revolution succeed. Obregón, who held the balance of power with his Sonoran army, was the only leader who could prevent a new explosion.

Álvaro Obregón, a stocky, moustached, pragmatic, half North-Americanized frontiersman, sincerely wanted peace. At the risk of his life he went to Villa's headquarters and arranged a truce between the villistas and carranzistas. He agreed with Villa that the revolution had to be a struggle of poor Mexicans against the elites, going beyond Carranza's dicta. He further agreed to convene an assembly or convention at Aguas Calientes, neutral territory, to try to bring order and form to revolutionary principles, and to invite the zapatistas to this. The basis of representation was practical: one delegate to be allotted to each leader for every one thousand soldiers in his army.

Meanwhile, the Sonorans held the capital. Obregón's wild Yaquis frightened the citizenry with war cries and drums, but he held the army under disciplined control; there was more order in the city than during Huerta's barroom regime. And Obregón, with an eye to the future, seized the federal armories and incorporated the best of the old regular army into his own.

Obregón and the Sonorans held the people of the capital in quiet contempt, because few of them had done anything in or for the revolution. Once, at a ceremony held at Madero's grave, he handed his pistol to a school teacher, María Arias, with the remark she was more fit to keep it for him than men who had not defended their president. As María Pistolas," she became a legend of the revolution, but nothing more clearly revealed the feelings of the northerners toward the passive populations of the great cities.

Though in various places certain military commanders had cancelled debts, raised workers' wages, and parcelled out some land, no revolutionary program had been established or agreed upon when the convention met in October 1914. The meeting was a confused and highly emotional scene, armed men cheering as Obregón and Villa exchanged *abrazos*, weeping with Villa when he wept trying to make a speech. All of the delegates had been fighters, and for the most part they were the youngest and most valiant rebels, chosen by the armies themselves. They tended to represent the young, the idealistic, and the poor. The small, polite zapatistas gained great attention describing how they were dividing up the estates of sugar barons among the *indios*, and it was soon apparent that a majority of the other delegations were in sympathy with them. But this did not necessarily represent the true power structure of the revolution, and certainly not Obregón's or Carranza's views.

When the convention quickly incorporated Zapata's Plan of Ayala into a proposed program, demanding immediate confiscation of haciendas, Carranza denounced the move. The young delegates retaliated by voting his removal as Jefe Primero—however, this was beyond their powers, for instant democracy had not arrived in Mexico. Carranza ordered his officers to ignore the convention and to return to their posts. All obeyed, though Obregón, hoping for compromise, showed some hesitation.

The rump convention continued for five weeks without coming up with any concrete plan. Even the most generous and idealistic among the delegates lacked common goals and experience with public affairs, for which they substituted rhetoric and principles. In the absence of the carranzistas, Pancho Villa took over, making Eulalio Gutiérrez, a respected but conveniently army-less general provisional president, and reserving real power for himself as secretary of war.

This new regime then marched on the capital. Carranza and Obregón were not ready for war. Obregón moved the Sonorans out to the east, to Veracruz, which the United States Navy finally evacuated. Ostensibly, the convention was now the government of Mexico, with Villa the power behind the throne. In fact, there were three governments in Mexico: Villa and his Dorados; Zapata in Morelos; and Carranza, who, through Obregón, controlled by far the most territory.

The capital awaited Villa and Zapata in dread. For years the capital had been informed of zapatista depredations by the conservative press, and their ominous fires had been seen across the lava flow. But when the small, white-clad figures wearing huge sombreros and carrying heavy rifles and cheap prints of the Virgin of Guadalupe entered the city, they stole nothing and raped no one. In fact, lost in the great city, they soon went door to door begging for provisions—which infuriated the new workers' press. Anarchist writers denounced the "stupidity" of peasants with rifles on the shoulders begging favors of the "bourgeoisie."

The various urban labor movements had taken no organized part in the revolution. The urban workers tended to be supercilious toward the campesinos or peasantry in Mexico and could find little common ground with the armed agrarians. The problem was that the leadership of the small but growing labor organizations was dominated by anarchist-syndicalist ideology that was much too radical for a Mexico that was still fundamentally conservative. Carranza in 1914 denounced trade unionism as "atheistic and hostile to the fatherland"; the labor leaders recognized no deity or the concept of national government. In return, urban labor remained neutral; labor leaders described the revolution as a war between two camps of "capitalists"; they were vocal but eschewed effective politics. When the convention, and the armies of Villa and Zapata took over the capital it was immediately apparent that the agrarians of both the north and south and the city proletariat lived in disparate cultures.

The villistas rolled into the capital on rails—men, women, and horses packed in bullet-riddled boxcars, roaring their ranchero ballads and firing their weapons into the air. The wild northern cowboys liberated all the liquor they could find and chased women. Villa himself created an international incident by forcing his attentions on a Frenchwoman. The villista army was much more dangerous to the citizenry than the zapatistas. The gunslung *vaqueros* answered any implied "slur on the revolutionary uniform" with a bullet. Villa, surly and unpredictable, had his firing squads exterminate suspected counterrevolutionaries, including carranzista spies.

The period came to be called the "day of the peon." The lowest classes from the countryside controlled the capital with guns, while those of the elite and bourgeoisie who had not fled locked their doors and prayed and were forced to sell their belongings for food. The anarchy of December 1914, was the beginning of bloody, hungry times. The day of the peon paralyzed government and the economy. Militant workers took over the Jockey Club and issued manifestos while little work of any kind got done. Trains ran only when it pleased Pancho Villa; food was scarce; and money became worthless, as the paper peso issued by the convention government drove gold and silver out of circulation.

Both the former rich and the always poor suffered enormously in the total paralysis of life in the center of Mexico. Thousands of refugees, rich and poor, had already left the country. During the Revolutionary years, 264,000 Mexicans emigrated to Texas, seeking work on ranches and farms, as servants, or as low-paid laborers in the towns. This was the beginning of an historic emigration that at last populated the regions above the Bravo with Hispanic people. Some 25,000 members of the elite gathered and lived in relative comfort in San Antonio alone—wiser, or luckier, they had gotten their money out of Mexico.

Two things were soon obvious in this day of the conquest of the peon. Although Villa and Zapata embraced at Xochimilco, which was then a muddy village south of the capital, their two armies did not mingle. It was also soon apparent that neither Villa nor Zapata had a program to reorganize Mexico. Zapata had no interest in the capital, or power, or government; he only wanted to assure some means of his people getting lands. He was pessimistic, because while he continually spoke of his peasants' love for the land, he feared the *hacendados* loved their estates too much to ever willingly give them up. Villa's rhetoric was characteristically expansive, bullying, and nihilistic in its way: "With the help of God, the men of the south, and my forty thousand Mausers and sixteen million cartridges, there will be a new day." But Villa could no more define his new day, or bring it about, than the purer Zapata.

Pancho Villa held the real power in the capital. Psychologically unfit to organize a national government, he disregarded advice from the former bureaucracy, bankers, and businessmen; he berated the middle class for "sleeping on silken pillows" while his horny-handed Dorados had died for the revolution. Villa soon drove most of the members of the revolutionary middle class out of government. Significantly, after a few weeks of this, the provisional president General Gutiérrez escaped from the capital and begged for refuge with Carranza at Veracruz.

Villa and Zapata had already made their contribution to the Mexican Revolution, one by dramatizing the need for land reform, the other by his smashing victory at Zacatecas, and had nothing more to offer Mexico. Armed mobs were bringing Mexican civilization to complete collapse. The *pelados* of the north and south, and the urban workers found no solidarity despite their common grievances, and while the convention aroused expectations with its rhetoric, the inability of the armed peasantry to govern threw the initiative back to Carranza's moderate Constitutionalists.

Carranza had withdrawn the moderate and more conservative elements with him when he broke with the convention. The Carranza faction consisted of *reformistas*; few were wild-eyed revolutionaries or nihilists. The events of 1914, and the obvious popular enthusiasm for the programs demanded by the radical convention—the destruction of *latifundios*, the return of public lands and waters to the *indios*, the establishment of agricultural schools, the expropriation of private property to feed the poor, the recognition of trade unions by the state and labor legislation, divorce laws and the legalization of bastardy, and restrictions on the operations of foreign capitalism—finally convinced the conservative democrats and moderates that the Constitutionalist revolution had to incorporate social reform. The villistas and zapatistas could not form governments, but they kept the masses demonstrating in the streets and encouraged armed peasants to seize haciendas.

Carranza was extremely reluctant to espouse class conflict, but he had had to recognize the reformist and class-struggle nature of the revolution even before he had marched beyond Sonora in 1913 ("whether we like it or not a social struggle will follow the armed struggle"). Carranza was more an opportunist than an ideologue, however, and the actions of the convention in "deposing" him as first chief and the fact that the peons were springing to arms all over Mexico caused him, unlike Madero, to pay heed to those Constitutionalists about him who insisted that he must take command of a genuine social revolution. Carranza's moderates wanted to prove that they were both revolutionaries *and* statesmen, and they pressured Carranza to coopt the social revolution, first by proclaiming himself the true government of Mexico, secondly by issuing "additions" to his Plan of Guadalupe, which had only demanded the destruction of the Huerta regime.

Carranza proclaimed himself president, and on January 6, 1915 issued a decree called the "Law of Restoration and Donation of Ejidos," copied directly from Zapata's Plan of Ayala. This pledged the return of common lands and waters taken from the villages under the *Ley Lerdo* and further, to provide lands for the landless from *latifundios* "if the need arose." This far-reaching commitment, drawn up by Luis Cabrera and reluctantly signed by Carranza, was the first step toward the legal expropriations of haciendas, and it became the fundamental law every following president implemented to some degree.

To attract the urban proletariat, Carranza also promised labor reforms and a new constitution. The Constitutionalists, basically a moderate, middle-class, *mestizo* faction, had begun to coopt the causes that roused so much of the population to arms.

However, it was Álvaro Obregón, the Sonoran ex-school teacher, who held the center and saved the sum of things. General Obregón was intelligent, pragmatic, and moderate, and sympathetic to the aspirations of peasants and workers though in no sense a radical reformer. Above all, he commanded the best army in Mexico and he understood modern military techniques. He now had access to machine guns and technical advisors who had absorbed the tactical lessons on Europe's bloody Western Front. He had started in Sonora with a "people's army" using bows and six-shooters, but by 1915 he had incorporated the regular army into his forces and was training his battalions to dig trenches, implace barbed wire, and to cover fortifications with interlocking fields of fire. He had learned what Villa never grasped: that one automatic weapon was worth a hundred brave men on horseback.

Obregón, nominally under Carranza's authority but very much his own general, waited until the zapatista and villista hordes had eaten the capital bare. Zapata was soon forced to withdraw to Morelos, while Villa sought forage in the nearby Bajío. In January, 1915, Obregón quietly reoccupied the capital, thus splitting Zapata's and Villa's forces. He wooed the workers, encouraging them to form unions and enlisting many into his army. These workers formed the famous "Red Battalions," which were more colorful and attention-drawing, however, than decisive in the coming conflict.

He followed Villa into the Bajío. Villa did not recognize "Old Goat Whiskers" as president and was in a surly temper. Obregón's men dug trenches and strung wire in the wheat fields surrounding the lovely colonial town of Celaya and commanded the approaches with machine guns.

In April, the Centaur of the North's temper snapped. Impatient, angry, frustrated with the logistic problems of holding a large force together without action, Villa decided to destroy the Constitutionalist army by direct attack. Unfortunately for him, General Felipe Ángeles was absent from his headquarters.

Villa's men and horses rode forth bravely. Now, in the spring of 1915, fifty thousand revolutionary soldiers met each other in a bloody fratricidal war. Mass assaults littered the wheat stubble with the Dorados' blood and bone; they died screaming on the cruel wire, chopped down by chattering machine guns. Thousands were killed and wounded on each side, for Villa's field pieces took their toll; Obregón himself lost his right arm to a shell fragment. The Red Battalions adopted a picture of Obregón's severed hand, preserved in a pickle jar, as their icon. But Villa was decisively beaten at Celaya and in a series of engagements, and pushed rapidly out of the Bajío back along the route he had come the previous year.

This was the most destructive warfare Mexico had seen since the siege of Tenochtitlan four hundred years before. Villa's charisma and personal leadership held his army together for a time under tremendous punishment, but Villa could not cope with the Sonoran's modern arms and disciplined battalions. The villistas fell apart. Tomás Urbina deserted with the war chest. Felipe Ángeles went to New York to beg for money and weapons, but by summer, Villa was a spent force, driven back to his old haunts in Chihuahua.

These were terrible times for Mexico and Mexicans. Though the core of Obregón's army remained reasonably under control, the Constitutionalists had auxiliaries and allies who were no better than the most depraved of Villa's officers. These, and Villa's remnants, ravaged over the countryside. Wherever armies went, or wherever various "revolutionary" generals appeared, haciendas were sacked, villages and towns looted, and rich citizens of any persuasion were held for ransom. The armies drained every peso at pistol point. The Catholic Church and clergy paid a high price for their support of General Huerta. Priests were killed and churches ransacked for ornaments—though there is evidence that the hierarchy deliberately exaggerated the atrocities, even inventing certain supposed mass rapings of nuns in an effort to inflame foreign opinion against the revolution.

This was the "poor, bleeding Mexico" described by countless correspondents—a country torn by mindless struggles between emerging rival warlords for power. In the towns and cities men went armed, and Constitutionalist deputies carried pistols into the halls of congress. Some authorities estimated the anarchy and warfare killed as many as two million Mexicans. Whatever the cause, the net population dropped by several hundred thousands between 1910 and 1920.

The stubborn campesinos endured these calamities as only a Mexican peasantry could. The great institution of the extended family helped society to survive. The Mexican view of these times is perhaps the sanest: the death and destruction was evil, but also destroyed ancient evils as nothing else could have done. Even Villa served a purpose, because he and every bandido general forced the Constitutionalist moderates and conservatives to raise their promises to the people in order to win support, and from all the horror at last came significant reform.

In 1914 North American policy primarily was concerned with protecting the investments of United States citizens in Mexico. The problem was that villista territory contained North American-owned cattle ranches and mines, while carranzista domains held oil fields and utilities. Washington thus favored neither side in the fratricidal war, wanting to restore order at any cost. Unfortunately for Woodrow Wilson's diplomacy, the United States retained little leverage or good will after the debacle at Veracruz.

Wilson preferred Villa's "flexibility" to Carranza's polemics, but Villa lost the civil war. Despite Wilson's personal distaste and exasperation with Carranza's poses, Washington was forced to recognize that Carranza was in control by October 1915. Wilson withdrew all support from the villistas.

Villa took this as betrayal and reacted murderously. Some observers explain all Villa's subsequent actions in terms of *la venganza*, the personal vengeance for injuries that was imbedded in the rough codes of the northern frontier. Others claim that all the supposed atrocities attributed to Villa were inventions of Wilson, who was looking for an excuse to invade Mexico. Mexican history and North American actions had given Mexicans a certain excuse for paranoia, but there was more to Villa's plans than that.

As one Hispanic American observer wrote, the tragic fact was that sometimes interventions were deliberately provoked by the vileness of leaders who hoped to profit from the intervention. Villa was never the man to consider consequences when he was angry, but he believed he could accomplish certain things by turning against North Americans. One was surely revenge—but Villa also hoped to rally the nation behind himself in hatred against the gringos, and he figured that if he could provoke a reprisal, he might even engage Carranza in war with the United States. If the United States destroyed the Carranza regime, Villa believed he might again emerge on top.

Villa cold-bloodedly declared open season on United States citizens living or working in Mexico. In January 1916, villistas murdered a number of men and looted scattered properties. Then, in March, Villa, hoping to provoke a reprisal that would destroy Carranza in the process, led a raid on Columbus, New Mexico. People were killed and property destroyed.

Wilson, running for reelection, was forced by popular opinion to take a hard line with the Mexican government over bandit depredations. Carranza, who had his own popular opinion to assuage, offered nothing substantial except a defense of Mexican sovereignty. Wilson requested that Carranza, since he obviously could not control Villa, permit the entry of a United States punitive expedition into Chihuahua. The concept was practical, and it was to the advantage of both governments to destroy Pancho Villa. But cooperation was virtually impossible in the inflamed atmosphere in Mexico. Fortunately, President Wilson refused to send troops into Mexico without Carranza's permission.

And Carranza skillfully made Villa's scheme backfire in the end, by finally admitting the North American troops, but with so many restrictions and such a show of protest that he convinced all Mexicans he was actually defending the nation against North American aggression. The restrictions made it impossible for General John J. Pershing, the expeditionary commander, to operate effectively against Villa, and Carranza's policy was so cynical that some of his own lieutenants, such as Calles, remarked on it—though Calles well noted its effectiveness and would remember this in time. The carranzistas did little to catch Villa, but gained a great reputation as "defenders of Mexican sovereignty." All this was a game that derived from a century of Mexican frustration and fear; vis-à-vis the United States, Mexicans were no longer rational.

It was a very dangerous game, because it raised tempers on both sides of the Rio Grande. Mexicans who despised Villa cheered when Villa eluded Pershing; North American opinion could not understand the lack of cooperation in running down a mad dog—after all, the Porfiriato had joined the United States in the destruction of the wild Amerindians. United States soldiers accidentally brushed with carranzistas at Parral, killing forty Mexican soldiers. Carranza demanded a United States withdrawal; when Wilson refused, Constitutionalist officers in Chihuahua killed some of Pershing's troops and took others prisoners.

Wilson mobilized the National Guard and sent a large force to the border. Had he wanted war, he could have had it, with the majority of the people supporting him. But Wilson preferred to avoid war, for by now, 1916, he believed the European situation far more compelling and dangerous for the United States than the tiff with Mexico. Wilson acted toughly but calmly, giving Carranza time to realize that in the end nothing but disaster could be milked from a Mexican-North American confrontation. Carranza freed the prisoners and agreed to refer the whole dispute to a mixed U.S.-Mexican commission, and he cooled the incessant propaganda that manipulated Mexican fears and hatreds.

The commission reached no agreement, but now Wilson decided to withdraw Pershing unilaterally. United States relations with Imperial Germany were deteriorating so rapidly that Wilson could not afford a continued Mexican adventure, and in January 1917, the last United States cavalry recrossed the border. Pershing had not caught or destroyed Pancho Villa, but indirectly he had carried out his mission. He had driven Villa into hiding, while the carranzistas had seized effective control of all Chihuahua. Further, Villa had destroyed himself by killing North Americans; afterward his agents above the border were never able to sell looted property or buy more weapons. The border was closed to him, making effective guerrilla operations impossible. He remained a minor nuisance, nothing more, by 1917.

He continued in sporadic banditry until a later Mexican government, unwilling to mount an expensive campaign in the north, in a cynical but brilliant turn-about bribed him with amnesty and a cattle hacienda. The former peon ended his days as a *latifundista*, surrounded by servants.

By early 1917 the German Empire was locked in its final death struggle with the European Allies. The United States government was determinedly neutral against Germany, and Berlin, perhaps more realistically than Washington at the time, saw that war between the two powers was inevitable. Zimmermann, the German foreign secretary, hoped to create a diversion for the United States in Mexico.

He sent the Carranza government a secret note, the gist of which was to offer Mexico assistance in recovering the lands lost in 1848 in return for an alliance, effective if the United States went to war with Germany. The Germans were popular in Mexico, as in all Hispanic countries where the Prussians were admired for building themselves up from nothing. The historic foe of the Hispanic world was the Anglo-Saxon powers, and in the current war Mexicans, at least emotionally, preferred Germany over the English and certainly over the closer monster to the north. However, the offer came too late, after Pershing's troops had gone, and after tempers had cooled on both sides. Carranza knew the Treaty of Guadalupe Hidalgo could not be overturned and rejected the German offer.

The Zimmermann note had far greater repercussions in the United States than in Mexico. British intelligence intercepted and decoded the message, turning it over to President Wilson, who published it on March 1, 1917. The note boomeranged against the German government, by becoming a major contribution to the United States' declaration of war in April.

When the United States entered the European war, the "Mexican problem" ceased to be the United States' most pressing foreign policy question. The "North American question" had been and was destined to be Mexicans' overriding external problem, and when the United States turned outward on the world, the predominant feeling was always relief in Mexico.

33

THE CONSTITUTION

The consequence of the latifundist regime is the division of society into a dominant minority, ready to commit any crime to keep its domination, and a dominated majority, usually on the point of rebellion. The aristocratic latifundism that predominates in Mexico is fatal. But the experience of the Reform showed that land cannot be turned over to any except those capable of using it. The ejido cannot, therefore be seen as anything but a transitional solution for a backward people. Mexican land tenure is incompatible with the higher types of civilization, and it has been the basic cause of all Mexican ills; and the Revolution itself came directly from this imperfect distribution of soil. It would be an act of folly, however, to pretend to encourage widespread state ownership according to Marxist doctrine—just as any industrial development would have to be forgotten if any attempt were made to nationalize industry, for all such steps can only be taken when enterprise has reached full development.

From Fernando González Roa, theorist of the Mexican Revolution, summing up succinctly the guiding rationales of the Constitutionalists.

After two full generations, some see the Mexican Revolution as a revolution that made a modern miracle; some see only the destruction and death and the regressions of the aftermath; some, an increasingly large body in younger Mexico, see it as a revolution betrayed. The revolution that began in 1910 and in many ways has not yet ended was an important, but not a world-shaking or trend-setting event. Mexico was and is a secondary nation in the hierarchy of states, and its revolution was peculiarly parochial. It also tended to be lost in the crescendo of the much vaster events of the First World War, which began an age in which societies and governments toppled all over the world, from Central Europe to China, and in which empires disappeared with bewildering rapidity.

In its beginnings the Mexican Revolution resembled most of the periodic Hispanic upheavals of the twentieth century: a middle-class revolt against ancient, clinging governmental and socio-economic institutions, characteristically devolving into guerrilla warfare and local anarchies. Pretorianism occurred, but proved to be a passing phase. This distinguished Mexico from Hispanic America and Spain. The enormous and singular success of the Mexican Revolution was that it broke the bonds of the past at last and actually permitted institutional change.

The early leaders of the revolution, the maderistas, sprang from groups and classes who were following in the footsteps of the nineteenth-century liberals from Morelos to Juárez. Their intention was not to destroy society but to democratize it. The democratization was of course synonymous with the emergence into power of the middle ranks, because the struggle for "equality" usually cannot be separated from a battle for predominance. The Mexican Revolution is almost always seen as a form of agrarian uprising, which is a distortion of fact. While it is true that most of the men whose blood sealed the victory fought at least in some sense for land, the mainstream leaders and most effective men of the revolution were neither peasants nor agrarian reformers. The middle-class elements in Mexico who ended the Porfiriato and destroyed the Huerta regime only gradually came to understand and represent the anguished aspirations of the dark, suppressed masses as they erupted in bloody anarchy. In the end, the revolution did not produce the kind of democracy the maderistas had envisioned but it created a new society which they found eminently satisfactory.

Mexicans finally began to derive institutions and laws from their own experience and culture rather than importing ideals and inspirations wholesale from alien societies. If the Mexican Revolution has usually confused outsiders, this is probably because they insist upon defining it in foreign terms, from French liberalism to Marxism to Spanish syndicalism. All of these concepts played a part more rhetorical than actual.

In the Mexican conventional perspective the revolution was a culmination of the frustrated aspirations of Hidalgo, Morelos, and Benito Juárez —which admittedly were not yet wholly achieved even by the events of 1910 to 1920—and was and is a necessary phase of nation-building, part of a continuing Mexican search for national identity. The revolution was both an event and a continuing process based on a continuing ideal. This view is functional and it is far from being wrong, though Mexicans tend to state it too neatly.

"Revolution" thus came to mean something different in Mexico than in most other nations. The term became virtually synonymous with "progress." While to outsiders the word still inspires visions of thundering, bandoleered Dorados, chattering machine guns, murders and *cuartelazos*, and wholesale confiscations of property, to Mexicans "the Revolution" was something that quickly passed beyond all that, into an institutionalized drive toward dynamism and socio-economic opportunity. The revolution created a new Establishment, whose goals were not very different from the goals of the Porfiriato, or from those of the *continuista* Lucas Alamán. The bloody phase of the revolution *was* necessary, judging from the failures in the same century in the Hispanic world from Spain to Argentina, because the horrors of 1913–1917 finally cut the decaying albatross of ancient institutions from around the necks of both *continuistas* and reformers.

In any period of rapid development, some sectors prosper more than others, under any system of society or government. Anthropologists, Mexican and foreign, have paid too much attention to a factor that at last was ceasing to be socially important: the Amerindian. And constitutionalists have continued to confuse the Constitution of 1917 with law and fact, when many of its provisions in effect expressed ideals. Most Mexicans, when asked about the condition of Mexican education, would instantly state that the constitution required six years of primary education for all citizens—an ideal far from realized sixty years after the clause was written into fundamental law, and perhaps not realizable in an undeveloped nation with an exploding population.

Historians, when their view is untrammeled by social, economic, and anthropological theories have developed perhaps the most serene and logical viewpoint of all toward Mexico: the modern nation has proven that a land and people can endure an incredible amount of ruin, degradation, and suffering, and yet survive.

Venustiano Carranza's name is inscribed in golden letters in the Mexican Chamber of Deputies as a Hero of the Revolution, beside the names of other chieftains who were his mortal enemies. But Carranza's image is clouded with his opportunism, his vanities and pompousness, and his obvious reluctance to preside over the kind of Mexican Revolution that evolved. Carranza's virtue did not lie in being heroic or with his ideals, two things beloved by Mexicans, but with the dominant influence of his Constitutionalists on events. Carranza and his lieutenants held the revolutionary center; their victory was a triumph of moderates, and it was the carranzistas who eventually institutionalized the revolution.

The first chief had won recognition as the head of government and state, but by 1916 he ruled over a smoking ruin. The great world war had created high prices for Mexican raw materials, but the Mexican economy was too shattered to take advantage of conditions. The entire financial and banking structure had crumbled as the revolutionary presses poured out bales of worthless paper money. Production had ceased at mines and haciendas; much of the managing class had fled. The foreign-owned companies were in little better shape. Oil, still pumped from around Tampico, paid no taxes and it went abroad, doing the local economy little good. All production was down; real wages severely depressed; and a deep economic regression was taking hold in many of the sectors that had been prosperous earlier.

Worst of all, Carranza was not fully in control of Mexico politically or militarily. Villa and Zapata, though contained, were still at large in the north and south. More important, a score of lesser dissidents operated throughout the Mexican states, running a political gamut from the right-wing partisans of General Félix Díaz to local armed agrarian reformers who seized property and estates. And most important of all, Carranza had neither the personality nor authority to discipline and control the score of revolutionary captains who had come to power in the several states. These men, all ostensibly Constitutionalists and carranzistas, did what they pleased without heeding instructions from the capital. Out of the turmoil and agony of Mexico, the Constitutionalists had become a sort of revolutionary Mafia, a fragmented "family" that governed the country without any real cohesion or any overall policy.

The governors were new men, usually risen in the revolution from obscure origins, but in effect they were new models of the old *caciques*. They were mostly citizens who had become generals in the civil wars. While most of them held revolutionary ideals there was no real pattern. General Cándido Aguilar in Veracruz promulgated labor reforms, such as the nine-hour day; General Salvador Alvarado in Yucatán sponsored agricultural workers' cooperatives and paid for social reforms out of the high prices received from abroad for henequen or sisal. Some governors distributed hacienda lands to peons. But still others protected the great estates from agrarian reformers; the governor in the Tampico oil region was in the pay of the oil companies and suppressed local labor movements; and too many local *caciques* were merely corrupt.

Carranza lacked Benito Juárez' personal prestige and the younger Don Porfirio's skills at taming local bosses. There was nothing the federal apparatus which Carranza controlled could do immediately to reconstruct the country. By 1916, power had passed from the hands of "the people" —if it could be considered to have been theirs at the apogee of the *peón* uprisings—into the hands of this "revolutionary family." The fact disturbed the intellectuals around Carranza, especially Luis Cabrera, the secretary of the treasury, who was probably the most capable man in the federal government. Cabrera believed strongly that the revolution must be given form and unity, and that it must come under some kind of central direction if it were to succeed—and also if the Constitutionalists were to retain power. He urged Carranza to convene a constituent assembly, which might formalize the revolution in a new Mexican constitution.

Carranza convened a congress at Querétaro in November 1916, and this act was to be his greatest contribution to the revolution.

The delegates to the convention of Querétaro seem to have been elected without any undue pressures from the first chief. They proved to be broadly representative of the "Revolutionary family," though no zapatistas or villistas were included, and members of the old convention of Aguas Calientes were not yet fully accepted into the new fold.

The newer constitution-writers were very different men from the various clerics, *criollos*, and highly-cultivated lawyers who had written earlier Mexican documents. The old dominant elite of Creole professionals, great landowners, and monopolistic businessmen had been discredited. The present delegates were newer men, though not a new class, for their roots went back to the Virreinato, and they represented a caste and class that had been emerging strongly since the 1840s: the middle-rank *mestizo*. On the whole, the constituents were less polished, less intellectual, and less ideological than their predecessors; they consisted of school teachers, country lawyers, petty bureaucrats, engineers, druggists, and journalists. Many had risen from very humble origins to high rank in the Constitutionalist armies. But as a whole they were very much an elite, especially in a country where sixty-five percent of the population were *peones* and three-quarters were illiterate. The triumphant faction of the revolution was not a purely popular party; it represented most clearly the minority of literate *mestizos*. Ironically, these men were products of the Porfiriato, whose greatest failure perhaps had been that it provided an energetic and opportunistic emerging class too few "bones."

The Constitutionalists did not, however, represent a true "middle class," though they are almost always mistakenly described by this term. They were not the independent professionals, merchants, manufacturers, *rentiers*, and prosperous farmers who composed the bourgeoisie of Western nations; they were instead that middle rank often confused with the middle class in Hispanic societies, men whose status came not from property but from education or employment. Their ethos and outlook was not radical (except defined against Hispanic tradition) but it was far less bourgeois than bureaucratic. They were the sort of men who had staffed Hispanic bureaucracies since the days of Fernando and Isabel; for good or bad, they represented the active core that had held Hispanic government together for centuries. The viewpoints of such men were instinctively tutelary; in their way they saw themselves as much "guardians of the nation" as the old custodians.

For all their inherent elitism, they came from a class and caste that had always been denied equality and full opportunity and they tended to be insecure. As a group, they had always been inherently aggressive and self-seeking—they had to be, to survive. Their ethos is sometimes mistakenly called entrepreneurial; it actually was opportunistic, which in no sense could be a bad term in Mexico. Passive men died, or were downtrodden; the Mexican *mestizo*, the truest "Mexican" of all, had not only survived but prevailed, though he could not help but carry enormous psychic problems forward with his victory. Out of their *mestizo* background, the Constitutionalists did desire a more egalitarian society—but out of their Hispanic heritage, they could not help but worry about how to hold the sum of things together. They were not, and could not be, in the Anglo-Saxon sense, libertarian. A spirit of tutelary regulation had been handed down to them with their whole civilization, stretching back to Rome.

Thus the new power structure emerging in Revolutionary Mexico was both radical and at the same time essentially conservative. Both radicalism and conservatism had to be measured against purely Hispanic-Mexican standards. The revolutionaries were hostile to latifundism, scientism, peonage, social injustice, dependence upon foreigners, clericalism, and dictatorship. Their hatred of a society in which a few thousand families owned all the arable land and a few hundred foreign companies exploited all the physical resources and a Spanish-dominated Church attempted to continue the ethos of the middle ages could hardly be equated with bolshevism, though of course it was by Mexican *hacendados*, foreign oil magnates, and high clerics, who convinced no few outsiders. On the other hand, the revolutionaries were in no sense hostile to the concept of private property, government, or religion. They were essentially capitalist, believing only, and then often only theoretically, that there should be a balance between capital and labor. They had no intention of destroying private property, the state, the family, or religion. They wanted to make it possible to destroy the growths they saw as inherently evil and detrimental to the emergence of Mexico as a nation: *latifundia*, a reactionary Church, bossism without legitimacy, mass servitude, and foreign ownership of Mexican resources.

Cabrera felt that only the disappearance of these evils, and certain other reforms, would allow Mexico to emerge as a more homogeneous country and to form a genuine Mexican nation, a *mestizo* nation, not a nation of backward *indios* or a would-be white aristocracy.

The revolution was not a full stop or major turning point, it was a great breakthrough on a continuing road. The goal of independent Mexico had been expressed in the words of the Trigarantine Pact: ". . . that all the inhabitants of New Spain, without any distinction between Europeans, Africans, or Indians, are citizens . . . with the option of choosing any

employment according to their merits and virtues." However, the various
democratic and liberal principles expressed throughout the nineteenth century invariably broke against the reality of the colonial society, wherein,
giving the Indian the vote and the *mestizo* theoretical opportunity was
largely meaningless. Only after the Porfiriato (for all its bad memory) had
allowed a much larger *mestizo* middle rank to evolve, and the old structures had been cracked by popular revolt could there be any marked
progress toward nation-making. Cabrera, Molina Enríquez, and other cen-
trist intellectuals of the revolution saw the clear opportunity for the nation
in the debris of the revolution's smoke and blood.

The emerging *mestizo* middle rank was more practical and less caught
up in theory than their forebears. They had a century of Mexican experience and were no longer suffused with the deep hatred for all things
Mexican that had colored the *criollos* and made them think French. The
twentieth-century Mexicans no longer suffered from the delusion that they
had only to adopt the forms and notions of other nations in order to enjoy
those nations' socio-economic success; it was extremely clear to them, for
example, that alien institutions could not easily be applied, whether positivism, Marxism or other nonindigenous doctrines. Nor did the new intellectuals have enough education to think in English, French, or Russian;
they were therefore thrown back on their immediate heritage.

This, more than anything else, made the constitution that was adopted
at Querétaro the only viable charter the long Hispanic Revolution had yet
produced. Any workable fundamental law had to incorporate the past
rather than merely flee from it; it had to accept the present, and allow for
the future. It had to be both liberal and conservative, because all men
combine both tendencies; its aspirations must be ultramodern yet its realism as old as human nature. The constituent assembly of 1916 seemed to
understand clearly the Mexican art of the possible, and also those things
over which they intended to stand guard.

The conservatism of this middle-rank, *mestizo* congress was shown by
the fact that Luis Cabrera presented a draft based largely on the Constitution of 1857, and the new constitution in the end incorporated two-thirds
of the old text. However, even before the vital questions of codifying social
and economic reforms were taken up, certain changes were made that
reflected Mexican experience with government.

The Constitutionalists have often been accused of wanting to secure
their own power in the codification, but beyond this they wanted to
achieve a government that could actually work within its legal principles.
Out of bitter experience their leading men no longer had any belief in
direct or participatory democracy, or in the North-American concept of a
separation of powers. Neither had worked in a country in which the vast
majority were not prepared for full citizenship.

The idea of direct democracy was so attractive to the revolutionaries however that the Constitutionalists did not dare attack it head-on. The carranzista spokesman Félix Palavicini, an engineer who was close to the first chief, expressed the disillusionment in a series of published articles rather than in direct debate. Palavicini branded the old notions of the *puros* as "dogmatic lies," an "ever-lasting leprosy" whose "consecration" had repeatedly been an "abdication of good judgment." The *puro* concept that the "people" was somehow infallible was no longer credible to Palavicini. He did not deny that the "people" had rights, but a "people" that was two-thirds peons and three-fourths illiterate was not apt to express excellent initiatives at the polls or anywhere else. Of course, the people had just expressed such initiatives in arms, but Palavicini argued that what the people really wanted was a broad-based oligarchy that could represent the needs and aspirations of all classes to govern it, and to preside over an orderly progress. Thus the mainstream of Constitutionalist thought was much closer to the old concepts of the *continuista* intellectuals such as Alamán than to the expressed ideals of the early *reformistas*. Palavicini and Cabrera and even Molina Enríquez were at heart Custodians; the only difference was that they envisioned a custodianship of the *mestizo* middle classes rather than an oligarchy of landlords, pretorians, and aristocratic Creoles. Palavicini drew on history, by demonstrating that all Mexican initiatives and revolutions had really come from the intellectual middle class. If the Republic had a minority of citizens, then that minority would have to maintain it.

This idea was widely accepted, and it formed the theoretical framework of the emerging Constitution.

The earlier constitutions had all relied on the basic structure of government of the United States: a federal system separated into three independent branches of government, with a further separation into sovereign states. The problem was that while this worked in the north, it did not work at all in Mexico. The tendency of the Hispanic Mexicans was not to unity but to anarchy in the absence of all-powerful government. Hispanic Mexican intellectuals had been fascinated by the principle of separation of powers, but the Hispanic Mexican soul simply could not make any such system workable. So long as Mexico had been governed constitutionally under the charters of 1824 and 1857 the central governments had been ineffective, even paralyzed. The outlying states were constantly in rebellion not only against dictators but such honest executives as Herrera and Juárez, and all effective Mexican presidents had had to subvert or violate the constitution to rule. The separation of powers between states and federal government had not prevented tyranny under powerful, authoritarian leaders—it had in fact encouraged it. In 1916 Carranza was constitutionally virtually helpless to rule over state governors determined to go their own way, fragmenting both the revolution and the nation. The constitution-writers were determined to end this impasse.

Further, the independent congress and judiciary had acted as irresponsibly toward the national good as ambitious state governments. Both had impeded and harassed chief executives who had tried to behave legally, though once again neither branch had thrown up the slightest defense against tyranny. Mexican congresses had proved peculiarly ineffective. They split into quarreling caucuses; the innate separatism of the Spanish-speaking soul would not let the body cooperate even within itself. The Constitutionalists had no faith in independent congresses, and they agreed that both the legislative and judicial branches must be made subservient to the Mexican executive.

The Mexican mind could not cope with a true separation of powers, but it did understand hierarchy. The Constitutionalists kept the form of the federal government—three branches and states each with their own divided governments—but utterly violated the spirit of a true federal system, by enormously increasing the powers of the presidency. Under the form and spirit of what was evolved at Querétaro, the Mexican president became the chief hierarch of an imposing system, who could enforce his will on the judiciary, the congress, the state governments, and even the municipalities.

The role of the Mexican Congress, the Senate and the House of Deputies, was reduced to one of ratification. The legislature was deprived both of initiative and veto. Whatever the emerging concept of government might be called, it was not and could not be called parliamentary democracy.

This enhancement of presidential power, immediately following the bitter experiences of the Porfirian dictatorship, puzzled some outsiders, who thought the Mexicans would have been constrained to try to whittle away the all-powerful executive. Mexicans saw things differently, then and later, because they had no faith in a congress, a judicial branch, the several states, or constitutional prohibitions to limit a powerful president. Díaz had subverted the constitution effectively but he had had to fall back on intimidation and corruption. The dominant Mexican viewpoint was that a country as loosely knit and unformed as Mexico required a very powerful hand at the helm, who could operate legally. Thus the lessons of the Porfiriato led them to codify a national *caciquismo*. They hoped to avoid the disasters of the Porfiriato by writing the principle of "no reelection" into the national fundamental law; the term of the president was fixed at four years, and neither he nor any other elected executive was permitted to stand for reelection.

The Mexican Constitutionalists had fallen back on fundamental forms and premises of their society and civilization. They did not restore the Porfiriato; they went deeper, and restored the crown. The presidency under the constitution was clothed in sovereignty and legitimacy; it became possible to complain against the ministries, laws, and acts of government, but never to attack the image or the person of the president. The North Americans had also given their presidency the powers of a constitutional king, but having a government of laws, they had not had to wrap his office and person in such legitimacy and sovereignty.

What the Mexicans made in 1916–1917 was a recreation more in the spirit of Hispanic society and civilization than all the alien notions imported since the North American and French Revolutions. Nothing was paradoxical if approached from the ideas, experiences, and aspirations of the men who made it.

The greatest task, and the greatest success of the Querétaro convention was to stabilize government and give it legitimacy. Stabilization was impossible without an incorporation of the social reforms so many fought for in the revolution, and they were included in two articles which had nothing whatever to do with the form of Mexican government but which finally embodied the aspirations of a majority of the population. These were the famous Articles 27 and 123, and while it is not correct to define the entire Constitution of 1917 by them, they were fundamental to the kind of Mexico that emerged from Querétaro and the revolution.

The men who were establishing the Constitutionalist custodianship were far from unified. Carranza, Cabrera, and Palavicini represented a conservative wing or faction. Carranza still was unenthusiastic about land reform that in any way included confiscations, and he was positively antagonistic toward organized labor. A few months before the convention met, he had branded illegal a strike against the foreign-owned utility company in the capital, chiding the workers and asserting that their needs did not give them a right to infringe on the rights of other classes. This faction would have been content with the first draft presented by Cabrera—but Querétaro was representative of the revolutionary family, and there was a large number of independent intellectuals, agrarian reformers, and labor union members in attendance. These men demanded more, and they stood on the blood shed in the revolution.

A "radical" faction, generally influenced by Molina Enríquez, formed around General Francisco Múgica, who at thirty-one was still a firebrand. Múgica got the chair of the main committee, and from this post he and his followers, more nationalistic and more reformist than the older intellectuals, managed to carry most of the crucial votes that determined the constitution. Significantly, Múgica did not dispute Cabrera's nature or form of government, but he insisted that reforms and aspirations be codified into any new charter—even if these were understood to be not immediately achievable. Múgica had the backing of Generals Obregón and

Calles, and Obregón's influence, although he had ostensibly retired to private life, was profound, for he was probably the most admired man in Mexico. Still, the essential social conservatism of the mass of delegates delayed the issue to the last.

Even the most reluctant middle-rank bureaucrat realized that the Constitutionalists could not hope to rule without adopting some social and economic reform; the debate was primarily over form and detail. Labor leaders wanted all workers' rights to be spelled out, even if the final form of such labor legislation was detailed and awkward.

The debates clearly showed that the delegates were determined to try to strike a balance of power between employers and labor. The result was a logical compromise that guaranteed labor the right to organize and strike, but which required each interest to defer to the "nation in particular." Thus the government was given the right to intervene in economic questions, and specifically to protect labor through a regulation of hours and wages. The union members were also able to insert a clause that acknowledged labor was entitled to more than wages, and therefore a share in profits. Despite the evident anarchist-syndicalist tendencies of Mexican labor, Article 123 was not intended to give labor any sort of control over industry or management; it was to permit the government to rebalance any enormous inequities. This clause was not particularly effective. It was not to be implemented at all until the 1960s, and then imperfectly. Another clause which the laborers demanded and got—and which through 1972 had never been implemented by the government—was the guarantee of a sort of headright in housing and savings for workers' families.

Other clauses in Article 123 included spelled-out rights and benefits for workers such as social security, medical care, schooling, and housing, pensions, and severance pay. These were specified as rights in addition to whatever guaranteed wage was paid. The constitution also abolished child labor, night work for women, and set minimum wages and maximum working hours on the national level.

So much attention has been paid to these extraordinary clauses—radical in their time and context—that the thrust of Article 123 is often overlooked. It reserved the real power to the federal government. The government, that is, the presidency, held the right to compel compulsory arbitration in disputes and also to regulate all activities of labor unions. Thus Mexican workers got far more than labor in most countries, but in another sense, far less. They did not escape bureaucratic custodianship, which inevitably would be articulated by the middle classes of society.

By any standard of 1916–1917 or even much later, the labor legislation incorporated in the Querétaro Constitution was extremely progressive—actually, an anomaly in an undeveloped country with a miniscule labor movement. Because of this very fact, very little of the legislation could

realistically be implemented. These clauses of the constitution were then
and later very loosely applied—such things as a ban on child labor in a
society where most children were forced by economics to go to work at the
age of nine or ten were totally unrealizable, and even the stated minimum
wage could be and was widely ignored. But this pointed up two essential
tenets of the constitution: it gave government a big stick to reward or
punish either capital or labor depending upon the need and circumstance;
and it codified aspirations which could always be implemented when and if
they became feasible politically and economically.

This codification of future hopes in detailed legislation which men
clearly knew could not be enforced was peculiar to the Mexican Revolution. There is little evidence that it was done cynically, and the effect was
in the long run excellent. It satisfied the Hispanic Mexican passion for
detailed regulation; it gave the workers hope, even if deferred; and it
allowed labor and capital to get on with nation-building. There was no
realistic hope that everything spelled out in the constitution in Article 123
could come to pass, even in several generations, in a society not yet
emerged from hacienda-feudalism. There was realistic hope that the legislation would spur progress, and the Constitutionalists above all wanted to
avoid the errors of the Porfirian positivists, who helped build a nation but
failed to understand the sensitivities of the masses.

Article 123 might be seen as a bonus won by Obregón's Red Battalions.
Actually, these reforms did not coopt the labor movement or bring it into
responsive and responsible national activity so much as certain clauses in
Article 27, which was only passed in the last session at Querétaro.

If the labor clauses were in some sense concessions to "decent opinion"
there was little question that the constitution must embody land reform.
And this required an examination of the entire matter of property rights.
The great problem was how to do away with the semifeudal *latifundios*
which were clearly a socio-economic incubus on Mexican society while
preserving the inherent rights of Mexicans to hold private property. Here
some principle had to be violated, either the rights of the ten thousand
hacendados or the aspirations to property of the three million male *peones*.

The problem was handed to Andrés Molina Enríquez, who was determined to find a basis in legality, that incorporated both the Mexican
indio's deep hunger for his own fields and the Hispanic respect for landed
property. Molina delved back deeply into his Hispanic heritage, finding his
rationales in the laws and concepts of the Spanish Virreinato. Molina
found that all title lay with the state or nation, and that society had merely
recognized and granted the rights of private ownership to meet social
needs. One set of needs had demanded the *encomienda* and the hacienda;
now a newer requirement demanded fields for the peasantry. Molina followed in the exact track of Spanish-colonial law, which always stated that

private ownership must be socially-oriented—though obviously, the Mexican people were now changing the basic orientation.

Molina argued that private property could and must be expropriated by the state (crown) when the dominant national interests decreed. But to preserve the principle of private right, such expropriations must be paid for. The convention agreed with this principle in Article 27—but the delegates refused to include a requirement for payment prior to expropriation. Again, as with certain labor legislation, it was obvious that prior payment would be impossible in an impoverished society. The constitution therefore established the right of the government (president) to expropriate landed property when and if the social needs of the nation demanded, and avoided the question of when and how the payment must be made. What the crown had given, the crown/presidency could take away, for the same reasons.

This was a violation of private right as it had been established in Anglo-Saxon law, which required prepayment, but under Mexican circumstances it is hard to perceive how any land reform, respecting the principle of private ownership, could otherwise have been achieved.

Molina's dredging also revived other old concepts of Hispanic crown law: the inviolable retention of subsoil rights by the sovereignty. The Porfiriato had violated this ancient principle by selling mines and oilfields outright, and nothing the Porfiriato had done had come under such compelling criticism in Mexico—not just because of ancient Spanish laws, but because of virulent nationalism among the educated classes. A clause in Article 27 restated the principle that the Mexican subsoil was the inalienable property of the nation, which could only concede its exploitation to private individuals or companies, as the crown had once granted mining concessions. This clause, of course, was bound to cause trouble, especially if the Mexican government ever chose to implement it retroactively against the foreign mining and petroleum interests.

Having declared that the state could seize hacienda properties, the Constitutionalists were faced with how to return fields and water to the dispossessed peasantry and Indians. They knew, from the *Ley Lerdo*, that lands simply could not be put up for sale; no peasant could buy them—or, if granted them outright, the *indio* communities and the peonage were in no position to put them to economic use. It was now accepted that a mere law could not make peons into effective smallholders overnight. Therefore, the Constitutionalists agreed on what was seen as an interim measure: the return of *ejidos* under strict government supervision. The delegates did not believe in anything resembling communal farms; their dream was the old one of a rural society composed of each small farmer owning his own land. The government-owned *ejidos*, which would make lands available as gifts, were to be interim and tutelary, where peasants could learn to be independent farmers, and their allotments could be revoked if misused. Whatever this ideal of small farms symbolized socially, in economic terms it was actually a regression in twentieth-century agriculture, for everywhere, though over enormous social opposition, modern farming was tending toward some form of plantation organization, with large, highly productive units and full mechanization.

The final draft of Article 27 stated that no one person could own more than so much land, but left the determination of the acreage to the several states depending upon crops, climate, and conditions. Obviously, a rancho devoted to bull-raising in Chihuahua could not be limited to 250 hectares, and in parts of Sonora 40 hectares might be required to graze a single head of beef.

The heart of Article 27 was the assertion that all soil belonged to the sovereignty, which might grant or revoke it according to the national need. This was a return to Hispanic medievalism that would permit the expropriation of both haciendas and oil fields, and it legalized those confiscations already carried out. In consonance with the other "radical" clauses, it was adopted in the belief that it would not be implemented immediately.

The constitution was finally approved on February 5, 1917, and therefore became the Constitution of 1917. It was to be amended frequently, but none of its fundamental concepts have ever been changed. It has been seen as radical, progressive, conservative, and sometimes, even cynical, depending upon the times and the biases of the viewer. All these definitions miss the point. The Constitution of 1917 was, above all else, nationalist.

34

CHIEFTAINS

To an observer, the Mexican government (under Obregón) appeared then no different from that of the Díaz period, with its politicians, demagogues, ambitious generals, big landowners (albeit new, uniformed owners who, as a rule, had seized their lands during the Revolution), small groups who disputed the executive power, and fraudulent elections. All this was too deeply imbedded in Mexico by thirty years of the Porfiriate to be conjured away in an instant. Nevertheless, the observer could note that young intellectuals filled some of the cabinet posts, there was great activity in the field of public education, and, above all, land was being distributed. Furthermore, the tone, even the physical appearance of those wielding power had changed; the new men were not the distinguished Europeanized white men of the Porfiriate, but men of the people, mestizos . . .

Victor Alba, *The Mexicans: The Making of a Nation.*

For a hundred years, the more Mexico changed, the more the country remained the same. No matter who ruled at the capital, the dead weight of *latifundios* had governed the countryside. The *latifundistas* had never created a genuine ruling class, at least not before the apogee of the Porfiriato. But the existence of their holdings, and the social concepts behind them, effectively barred most progress in Mexico.

Zapatista and villista agrarian reformers blasted most of this historic facade away. The revolution did not, however, immediately destroy *latifundios*—in fact, many great estates continued and continue to this day, despite the constitution. What the revolution destroyed was the social and political power of the *hacendado* class along with its rationales. By 1917, the leading *latifundistas* were living in exile in Europe or the United States; in Mexico, whether they still held property or had been dispossessed, the nostalgic old landed class gathered in cafes or family groups, haranguing sympathetic foreigners with denunciations of the godless barbarians who had seized their country. They had cast their lot with Huerta, and as a class they were defeated and demoralized, the good and decent families with the bad and arrogant.

The professional politicians of the Porfirian era were also submerged or gone, along with the foreign businessmen who had been their clients. New men, of a new class, had replaced the Europeanized gentlemen of the porfirista oligarchy at the apex of society and in the halls of power, and with the change the old social fabric was damaged beyond repair.

What was then and later confusing to outsiders, particularly those who did not know the country and only read the revolutionary rhetoric or studied the enacted laws, was that the life patterns of most Mexicans had not changed at all. Most rural peasants still lived in poverty. Few estates fell into disuse. The urban proletariat still worked for low wages under miserable conditions, for domestic and foreign capitalists. What had changed was the texture, rather than the patterns of life. Peons were no longer whipped and made to feel like dogs; peonage was ended in the shops and factories. The caste system that had made most Mexicans strangers in their own land was gone. On the surface life was very much the same, but as the old colonial elite vanished from public life and influence, something was lifted from the soul of Mexico.

The caste system crumbled after a hundred years of independence. The class system, however, remained, dividing the middle-rank professional sharply from the urban worker, and the skilled laborer from the rural *pelado*. Too much could not be expected from any revolution. With the destruction of the upper class, the middle ranks were freed from social and psychic oppression and these were willing to share some—but not all—of their new opportunities with the masses. The revolution confused many foreigners as to its true nature, and they remained confused by the class system, because old prejudices among foreigners were too strong. Few if any recognized the emerging *mestizo* middle classes as an elite. Measured against the former top ranks of society, who had always siphoned off the would-be bourgeosie into the upper class, the elitism of the *mestizo* middle ranks seemed pale. Measured against the bottom of Mexican society, this elitism showed through starkly.

The class feeling of the middle ranks was strong, though its members felt insecure vis-à-vis the bourgeois world outside Mexico. They shared blood and the mystic experience of the revolution with the masses, but beyond this, human nature imposed on them the rationales of all people who hold, or have the opportunity to hold power. The revolutionary family believed it should rule Mexico.

The "family," a sprawling, amorphous alliance, had two main groups: the *mestizo* medical doctors, lawyers, engineers, and teachers who were the intellectuals of the revolution; and the peasants, Amerindians, and workers who had risen to high rank in local armies or local regimes during the bloodshed. These groups were mixed, for some intellectuals had become generals and some *indios* intellectuals, and they worked together quite effectively. The first group had a genuine sense of class and social mission; the second was more opportunist, but respected the reformists' goals. They needed each other. The intellectuals had to have the generals' guns, and looked upon the self-aggrandizement and sometimes childlike greed of these upstarts tolerantly. The violent military *caciques* deferred to the intellectuals in the historic way of the Hispanic world. The result was a genuine social revolution that made incisive reforms amid radical rhetoric while at the same time it permitted a horde of soldiers to seize cattle *estancias* and haciendas and grow very rich. Most of the old haciendas were now owned by new, brown-faced men in uniform, but there had been a break with the past and the soldier part of the alliance did not become oligarchs on the land.

The broad spectrum of the revolutionary family gave it strength, and it was very much united by a common desire to hold power. Whatever shared mystique derived from the anti-Huerta days, both intellectuals and generals wished to make Mexico a viable nation under themselves, and therefore, the new power structure was determined to make the constitution it had written work. If the revolution faded, so would the men brought to power by it.

Venustiano Carranza, by now an aging nineteenth-century liberal like Madero, fitted poorly into this new world. Inaugurated as constitutional president in March 1917, he believed in good government but had no heart for activist politics. He accepted the constitution because he had no choice, and he was becoming more and more obstinate against the dominant social and political trends. He disagreed violently with views like those of González Roa, who insisted that only men who satisfied the peasants' and workers' demands could govern Mexico; he wanted to halt all further revolution until good administration provided stability.

Carranza was rapidly ceasing to be a hero to the revolutionary family determined to ride with the masses' aspirations in order to keep power. But he was hardly alone. Thousands of the professionals, smallholders, and businessmen who had fought for the revolution had returned to old careers; they wanted nothing further from government beyond a normalization of politics. This conservative core did not disbelieve in the radical aspirations, but believed in gradualism. The continuing revolution now became a tug-of-war between the moderates who wanted to proceed slowly, and the zealot intellectuals consumed with social missions allied with soldiers and politicians eager to promote their own welfare together with that of the people in a never-ending revolution.

The division was inevitable; doctors tended to go back to practice and tradesmen to their trades—but school teachers who had become governors and peasants who were generals did not find it easy to give up heady new careers. The army tended to be the same problem in 1921 it had been in 1821; it refused voluntarily to disappear. However, this time the army tended to be allied with revolutionary aspirations rather than reaction, and the enormous inequities and sheer continuing misery of Mexico gave the radicals and reformers great leverage, then and for at least another decade.

In the best of situations the Carranza government would have faced almost insurmountable problems. The economy was wrecked; paper money had depreciated, destroying real wages; organization had broken down. The outlands were far from pacified—Zapata was still in control of Morelos, Villa at large in the northern desert, and Félix Díaz pronouncing from Oaxaca. The male population went armed; no prominent person appeared without his *pistoleros* or bodyguard. Sandbagged machine guns guarded city squares, and some men even were married with weapons inside their waistbands.

Carranza did not have the personality to enforce his power; the various revolutionary *caciques* continued to run Mexico. One of them, his old general Pablo González, did rid him of the Zapata problem.

González aspired to be the next president but knew he was overshadowed by the greater hero Álvaro Obregón. González determined to become known as the "Pacifier of Mexico" by erasing the zapatistas, who never trusted the revolutionary family and who refused to lay down arms. The *indios* and peasants were fearful that the alien city government would again take away their lands, although Carranza had decreed that public lands taken away during the Díaz years were to be returned to the state. The fears were justified, for Carranza's land reform program proceeded very slowly.

Pablo González' army had no more success with Zapata's guerrilleros than its predecessors, despite a terror campaign. The federals burned every building in Morelos state and sacked every hamlet and town, but the peasants plowed their fields with rifles on their backs and held out into 1919. Finally, González fell back on the old ploy that had ended most Mexican civil wars, treachery. His plot was incredibly brutal and cold-blooded. He had one of his colonels, Jesús Guajardo, pretend to defect to Zapata, and in order to allay the suspicious peasant leader's doubts, he arranged for Guajardo to attack another unsuspecting government detachment and slaughter fifty-nine government soldiers. This act convinced

Zapata as nothing else could that Guajardo had indeed changed sides. He came to a meeting with Guajardo, riding on his sorrel horse with a small bodyguard—into six hundred government rifles. He died instantly in the fusillade, and while his memory would live on throughout all the Americas, his movement collapsed. Colonel Guajardo was promoted and awarded fifty thousand pesos.

Carranza also had problems in the cities and towns. At a convention at Tampico in 1917 workers' organizations formed a new national federation called CROM, from the acronym for *Confederación Regional Obrera Mexicana*. This labor congress was historic, for it marked a divergence of the labor movement from anarchist to a more nationalist line, allowing labor a greater part in the revolution. But under either anarchist or nationalist leadership, labor was suffering from the inflation and called a general strike in the City of México. Carranza reacted characteristically; he closed the Workers' House and arrested labor leaders. Luis Morones, who was emerging as a labor chieftain, was sentenced to death, but the sentence was commuted to imprisonment through the intervention of General Obregón. In Tampico, another labor leader who tried to organize oil-field workers was shot by army officers.

Over three years, Carranza's pace of social and economic reform was tortoise-like. In fact, most of his acts contravened the spirit of the Constitutional law. Carranza organized a national agrarian commission to distribute the former public lands retaken by the state, and gave this commission full powers. The commission, however, moved glacially, issuing plots to only forty-eight thousand family heads—it was a ploy to take more active land reform measures from the hands of activist governors. In the same way, following the same philosophy, the justices Carranza had appointed to the Supreme Court nullified the states' powers to appoint labor-dispute arbitration boards under Article 123 of the constitution.

Despite a worldwide influenza epidemic, which hit particularly hard in Mexico, Carranza brought considerable order to the economy and government finance. The peso was restabilized at half its old value, about one quarter of a United States dollar. Gold and good silver coins on the .720 standard came into circulation; after the experience of the blizzards of paper pesos issued by the federal and state governments, it would be a generation before the campesinos again willingly accepted paper currency. Meanwhile, production of all kinds rose steadily during the period from 1918 to 1920, but the revolution exacted its inevitable toll: real wages in terms of a constant peso were lower than they had been under the Porfiriato.

Carranza would have been allowed to serve out his term despite his failures if he had retired and turned the government over to Álvaro Obregón. Obregón had "retired" to Sonora, where his comrades-in-arms Adolfo de la Huerta and General Plutarco Elías Calles as governor and chief of the armed forces controlled the state. The revolutionary family believed Obregón should be president; the nation expected it; and Obregón himself merited it, with his services, his strength, and his pragmatic grasp of popular sentiments and needs. But Carranza, who realized that he could not set aside the constitution, tried to bar Obregón's way and to throw the office to a nonentity, Ignacio Bonillas, Mexican ambassador to Washington. Whatever purpose Carranza had in mind, his standing in Obregón's way was a fatal error.

Since Mexican elections by their very nature were fraudulent, it was obvious that Carranza could sponsor Bonillas to office. Obregón and his friends decided not to wait, and Carranza rather stupidly played into their hands by sending the hated federal troops into Sonora to break a strike by railway workers. Governor de la Huerta proclaimed Sonoran independence on grounds of illegal federal intervention; he and General Calles issued the Plan of Agua Prieta, calling for Carranza's resignation. Meanwhile, Obregón evaded Carranza's police and joined Calles.

The Sonorans marched south again in a replay of the events of 1914. Calles took city after city, collecting more arms and volunteers. General González deserted Carranza, and no capable officer would oppose the popular hero, Obregón. Left with only a few cronies, Carranza decided to flee. Seizing bags of gold coins from the national treasury, his party boarded a special train for Veracruz, where Carranza hoped to hold a base. But en route, he learned that the governor of Veracruz state had joined the rebels. Leaving the train, Carranza and his friends took to the hills on horseback, dropping a stream of gold coins behind them in their haste.

They hoped now only to ride through the mountains and reach the sea. But the pervasive cynicism, treachery, and brutality that protracted warfare had again sowed in Mexico ordained the outcome. A local military *cacique*, Herrera, pretended to aid Carranza, then while the exhausted presidential party were sleeping in a hut where they had taken refuge from the wind and rain, he sent soldiers to surround them. Carranza and his friends were slain by a sudden fusillade, and Herrera announced that the president had committed suicide.

The Sonorans entered the capital peacefully, acclaimed by the ruling groups. Adolfo de la Huerta became provisional president, until a special election replaced him with Obregón in November 1920. De la Huerta is remembered mainly for three things. He legalized all on-the-spot land confiscations that had taken place, which Carranza refused to do, thus satisfying all the new-rich generals who held new haciendas and inducing Zapata's warriors at last to lay down their arms. He exiled Pablo González, Zapata's nemesis, and had Zapata's executioner, Jesús Guajardo, shot. Finally, he bought off Pancho Villa with amnesty and a huge cattle property in Chihuahua-Durango states.

The new *hacendado* of the north did not live long to enjoy his rewards. In 1923, Villa and his *pistoleros* were gunned down while traveling in an automobile to his town house in Parral. The shooting was not political, rather a rough justice meted out by friends and families of men and women Villa had killed and humiliated. Not until forty-four years afterward, after a generation of movie-makers and folklorists had mythologized his memory beyond recognition, was his name entered beside Zapata's and Madero's in the Hall of Congress, as a Hero of the Revolution.

Álvaro Obregón was a man of and for his times, the sort of chieftain Mexico needed to emerge from postrevolutionary anarchy. Most of the myths, especially among foreigners, that surrounded him have blown away with time. Amid incessant brutality and violence, shot through with rhetoric from firebrands wanting far more "revolution," it was popular in 1920 to see Mexico as a country run by Bolsheviks. Because the Sonoran allied himself with workers' unions, he was identified as an emerging communist. But when the myths and prejudices are placed in retrospect against Obregón's actions, he comes through as what he was—a tough, pragmatic leader who laid the foundations for late-twentieth-century Mexico.

Obregón was a hardheaded realist who concealed a ruthless ambition beneath an air of modesty and affability. He was a dictator; a democratic administration could not have survived the pressures of the period. Obregón's great contribution as president was his understanding that Mexico must be modernized before its patterns of life could change, and that no social gains could be made or consolidated without order and security. The turmoil that had broken the old society had lowered the entire nation's living standards, a fact that ardent revolutionaries usually tried to conceal. Obregón's dominant policy was to allow Mexico only the Revolution he believed the society could afford.

Obregón was leftist only in comparison with the Mexican right, whose viewpoint was still almost feudal. In Marxist terms, he was a bourgeois reactionary: he believed in private ownership of the means of production, and the dominance of the middle class. His courtship of the Mexican labor movement through CROM and the Action Group was political. He sympathized with the workers and believed that labor must acquire rights and privileges common in the advanced countries as part of the Mexican modernization, but he utterly rejected the notion that labor should have a dominant influence in society.

Obregón's statism was natural to any Hispanic society, and statism came naturally to the Mexican middle class, whose major source of opportunity had always been the state. The only possible initiative toward building a modern nation and society had to come from the state; any form of laissez faire or positivism in Mexico would only erect a newer Porfiriato. Thus Obregón, involved the state in huge programs of public education and capitalization whose purpose was never to enhance the state but to direct Mexico toward a basically capitalist society.

Interestingly, at the same time that much North American opinion considered Obregón communistic he was ruthlessly deporting communist agitators, most of whom originated in the United States. North Americans tended to confuse nationalist revolutions with communism, beginning with the Mexican Revolution.

The question of whether Obregón's fundamental leanings toward capitalism and the middle class was fortunate or unfortunate must rest on purely subjective judgments and the prejudices of the observer. The question of his dictatorship amid the confusion, corruption, and violence of the 1920s must be seen against the incredible pressure of Mexican problems. To assert the power of the central government against a score of local power centers thrown up by the revolution, Obregón had to act far more brutally than Díaz. He faced more brutal, cynical, and violent men. In buying some of them—he made a famous statement that "no general can withstand a cannonade of one hundred thousand pesos"—and shooting or exiling others he practiced the only art of the possible that was possible in Mexico. After the eruptions of 1910 to 1920, Mexican order could not be restored except through more violence. Obregón was not quite all-powerful, despite the constitution and his control of the army. Foreign property interests, and therefore foreign governments, viewed him with hostility and suspicion because these interests were inherently hostile to the nationalistic trends of the revolution. The Mexican Church and Mexican conservatives, scattered and spent nationally but still retaining strong local influence, hated him bitterly. The press, which he left free in all respects, was owned by conservative interests and attacked him regularly. A horde of opportunistic revolutionary generals, every one a potential rival, remained dangerous and difficult to control. Finally, his own revolutionary intellectuals and the more radical elements in the revolutionary family were disappointed with his deliberate pace and antagonized by his efforts to win back international respectability. Whatever glory accrued to Obregón was fastened to his memory. Only later was it understood that Obregón employed the fine art of the *caudillo* to destroy *caudillaje*.

That his regime accomplished anything is miraculous. Obregón inherited a ruined economy, a bankrupt treasury, and hundreds of voracious military politicians who were enriching themselves, building grotesque villas at Cuernavaca, and opposing all efforts to impose either order or democracy. He also inherited a Mexican population poorer than under the Porfiriato but enflamed with rising expectations and always capable of again taking up arms; a turbulent labor movement; and an intellectual elite that was irrational in both its domestic and international policy demands. Finally, he inherited serious trouble with the United States.

Obregón's first great problem was in foreign relations. World War I had ended, and the powers could concern themselves with Mexico. All the old problems and controversies remained. Relations with the United States were poor. The U.S. consul at Puebla had been abducted in 1919 by a band of maverick revolutionaries, almost causing a new intervention. The Democratic Wilson administration in 1920 refused to recognize Obregón due to the circumstances surrounding Carranza's ouster and murder. This was a serious matter for Obregón, who understood clearly that in a still-unstable Mexico he could be brought down by a North American policy that encouraged and supplied arms to any of his rivals.

Fortunately for him, Harding's administration, replacing the Democrats in 1921, was more pragmatic than Wilson's. The new administration did not busy itself with the quality of Mexican democracy; it was more concerned with property. Washington informed Obregón that recognition was possible, but depended on three things: resumption of service on Mexican debts; settlement of the huge reservoir of claims arising from the revolution; and clarification of the oil companies rights of ownership under Article 27 of the new constitution.

These demands were logical, but they presented Obregón with ticklish situations. Almost all the modern parts of the Mexican economy were still foreign-owned, from utilities to oil—a fact that no revolutionary could accept with equanimity. But what Limantour and Díaz had built, no Mexican could immediately destroy. The mines, oil fields, electric power systems, rails, banks, and most of the productive plantations represented foreign capitalisms; when the dust of the revolution settled they were again operating as before. The former relationship between foreign shareholders and managers and the Díaz regime, however, had become a morass of hostility and distrust. The outside investors *had* to be hostile to the revolution because it threatened their interests and what they had come to consider their rights. The revolution *had* to be hostile to foreign capitalism out of its drive for opportunity for the Mexican middle class and the rising xenophobia of all classes toward foreign ownership of Mexican soil. The problem was both economic and political, because the theorists of the revolution agreed that foreign capitalism endangered Mexican sovereignty.

The question of sovereignty appeared emotional, theoretical, and actually irrelevant to foreign governments. Of course, it was the mark of a people deeply unsure of themselves, either in normal diplomatic exchanges or in economic competition, but the Mexicans had some reason on their side. They and their governments were weak, and outside investment had always brought terrible pressures upon them while they struggled to re-order their own house.

The whole house that Díaz and Limantour had built made for a dirty business on both sides. Given the world for the asking, the investors be-lieved they held immutable title to it no matter who came to power in Mexico; they regarded all attempts to renegotiate suspiciously, branded them as bolshevism, and used money influence on their own governments, especially in oil, to bring pressures on the Mexican regime. The petroleum industry employed any and all means: bribery, coercion, the hiring of goons in Mexico, though in all fairness they usually had to protect their interests against officials little better than gangsters and labor leaders who were anarchists. Meanwhile, Mexican labor and intellectuals and in fact most of the opportunity-seeking middle classes denounced all attempts of their own government to find reasonable solutions and to negotiate a grad-ual Mexicanization of foreign interests, as treason to the fatherland. A vociferous public opinion gave Obregón more trouble than foreign pres-sures, and Mexican officials who harassed or seized foreign concessions in the name of sovereignty, but actually for advantage or political profit played as fully dirty a game as the great oil companies. Obregón had to negotiate skillfully between very narrow limits. He did not dare sabotage the economy by seizures because in 1920 Mexicans lacked the capital, expertise, and experience to run their own economy and there was a real danger of North American intervention, and he had to allay both rabid domestic and suspicious foreign opinion.

Obregón walked his tightrope brilliantly. He refused to nationalize the oil fields under Article 27, which Mexican opinion demanded, and his Supreme Court upheld the continuation of contracts granted prior to 1917, but he placed a small tax on oil extraction. The oil companies immediately protested this to Washington, where the State Department took their side. Obregón's finance minister, however, had meanwhile made a deal with United States' banking interests by which the oil taxes were assigned to pay off the Mexican debt. He was able to divide, and if he did not quite conquer, he survived because he blunted Washington's pressures in a domestic North American conflict of interest. Washington insisted that Obregón's promise not to apply Article 27 retroactively be solemnized in a treaty, but Obregón could not agree to this without committing political suicide. Like all Mexican-North American controversies, this one was marked by a continual North American failure to understand the extreme importance to Mexicans of appearances. Obregón knew he had to deal and was prepared to deal—but he could not do so openly or act as if he were making concessions. Finally, when Obregón was understood on a personal level by United States diplomats, Washington agreed to informal guarantees that concessions granted between 1876 and 1917 would stand despite Article 27. The air cleared, and recognition was proffered in August 1923.

At Obregón's suggestion, mixed commissions were appointed to try to settle the question of damage claims on the same informal basis, one to handle claims going back fifty years, the other those of the revolutionary period. Soon, similar committees took up the same questions with European nationals. Negotiations continued for ten years, and the Mexican foreign ministry used the tactics of delay, obfuscation, and exhaustion with great success, eventually settling most claims on a basis of three centavos on the peso. But the negotiations themselves marked an historic change. The North American and foreign governments were growing disillusioned with battling Mexican governments over claims. In the 1920s, United States public opinion did not fully support the demands of oil companies or the claims of expropriated landowners, marking a growing maturity toward the perils of outside investment.

Obregón walked another tightrope with agrarianism and labor. His policy toward land reform was simple. He decided to implement the revolutionary demands of peasants, but never at the risk of damaging agricultural production. Further, as a northerner, he had the usual dislike for Amerindian *ejidos* and preferred private holdings by a ranchero class. He saw nothing wrong with large estates so long as their ownership was divorced from direct political power. He was utterly adamant against destroying estates or landowners for ideological reasons, unless it was certain that such destruction would increase the supply of food and fibers. Obregón understood the desires of the peasantry to obtain land, but he was painfully aware that Mexico, an agrarian country, was still importing food, and the most productive farms were not *ejido* plots, but well-run haciendas. Ironically, the greatest pressures on him to distribute land came from intellectuals and theorists—few of whom were farmers—who in the 1920s seized upon the programs and ideology of the Russian Revolution. The theory of collectivization became popular with such groups in Mexico, though it had been and remained alien to the mainstream of the revolutionary family. At the same time, he had a few problems with the remaining *hacendados* of the old school, whose estates yet employed a million peons; some of this class tried to coopt revolutionary generals who had joined them as owners, against Obregón.

Given his views, Obregón's course was pragmatic in this, as in everything. He pretended to continue land reform, while deliberately delaying transfer through bureaucratic procedures, which, as he said, came naturally to all Mexicans. Initiatives for land reform had to be begun locally by villagers, who must prove that confiscations would not cut production. Full investigations took ten years, while landowners fought desperate legal battles in the courts, often paralyzing the whole process. Obregón's regime distributed 3,000,000 acres to 600-odd villages, only one percent of existing hacienda holdings, leaving 320,000,000 acres still in large estates. Obregón was satisfied that the greatest menace to the revolution, the political power of the great *latifundistas*, was broken, and he set a pattern that delayed wholesale land reform for years.

Likewise, while he favored CROM, the labor movement which had supported his candidacy, against employers and rival labor groups, he had no intention of allowing workers' organizations to overturn the capitalistic structure of the new society. Under the law the government must recognize a strike to make it legal, and under Obregón the government regulators refused to recognize wildcat walkouts, or those called by radical unions. His compulsory arbitration boards granted wage increases, but slowly. The policy was to prevent labor from paying the total cost of capitalization through starvation wages, but also to prevent any distortions or disruptions that might damage industrial growth or production.

Obregón actually succeeded in coopting the labor movement by bringing its leadership into the centers of power and in effect making them part of the government bureaucracy—again, something that was not easily seen or understood while it was happening. By 1924, labor leaders were saying that there was no longer a question of destroying capital (the original, traditional, and almost mystic goal of the earliest labor movements) but rather one of bringing capital and labor into "harmonious merger" for the benefit of workers. Labor leaders also stoutly defended compulsory arbitration, because they "trusted the government" of which they formed a part. The cooption of the leadership alienated a horde of lesser leaders and extreme leftist groups and led to tremendous internal dissension and even gun battles in labor ranks. All this was vastly more spectacular than effective, and various radical organizations and leaders came and went. The effect was that the labor movement, as a movement, became disoriented under Obregón, as most workers became disillusioned with both CROM and its anarchistic rivals, such as CGT (*Confederación General de Trabajo*, or General Federation of Labor). The workers made slow gains, but they were no threat to revolutionary government.

Obregón had pacified the United States and gained a measure of international respectability none too soon, because in December 1923, the Mexican pot again boiled over. A very mixed crew rose in rebellion against the Obregón regime in various parts of Mexico. The rebels had little in common. Some were opportunists; some were counterrevolutionaries; and some were Obregón's own friends, disappointed for various reasons. Collectively, they almost overturned the regime.

The immediate cause of the rebellion was Obregón's designation of General Plutarco Elías Calles, his minister of the interior, as his successor in the National Palace. Calles was the kind of man who made enemies. Intellectuals, correctly, recognized his unsavory traits; military men felt a keen rivalry; and conservatives took advantage of the internecine revolutionary strife. When Calles was tapped, insuring his election, many deputies, some members of the cabinet, British oil companies, labor unions outside CROM, and many military chieftains were prepared to make trouble.

José Vasconcelos, the brilliant minister of education, resigned in disgust. The secretary of the treasury, Adolfo de la Huerta, broke with Obregón, because de la Huerta believed he should have been chosen. The army commandants in Jalisco, Oaxaca, and Veracruz states, who were simply opportunists in the old pattern, proclaimed. De la Huerta joined them. The uprising took on counterrevolutionary tendencies as Generals Estrada and Sánchez returned land to *hacendados*, and in Yucatán the popular Socialist governor, Felipe Carrillo Puerto, was killed by armed conservatives. Rebel forces marched on the capital, and it appeared that Obregón might suffer the same fate he had meted out to Carranza.

The common people of the northern states stood by him, however, and he now received help from an unexpected source, Washington. The United States government had little love for his dictatorship, but it had come to working agreements with Obregón, and above all, it wanted no return to anarchy below the border. The United States government furnished Obregón with enormous shipments of arms and ammunition, including aircraft. With these weapons, and northern soldiers, he and his loyal General Calles destroyed the rebellions in ninety days.

Obregón was now ruthless, sending rebel generals before firing squads in a reign of military counter-terror. He let de la Huerta escape to live by giving singing lessons in California. In the end, the revolt strengthened both Obregón and the revolution, because it allowed him to destroy large parts of the army. He had had to incorporate all the irregular forces of 1913–1917 into the federal army in order to satisfy and control the soldiery, which had forced the government to support a largely useless force of eighty thousand men. Half this force joined the revolt, and when Obregón won, he shot or got rid of these men. Most of the revolting leaders had been "finger generals"—so called because it was said they had been designated by a pointed finger and the accolade "You, be general" during the revolution. These officers were replaced with younger professionals graduated from the new national military academy, where they had learned loyalty to the government rather than to some mystique of the revolution.

This purge was perhaps the greatest of Obregón's accomplishments, because here he began the professionalization of the military and its subordination to civil government.

With Obregón fully in command, Plutarco Elías Calles was easily installed in 1924. The new administration is sometimes known as the Obregón-Calles government, because Álvaro Obregón remained a one-armed eminence, and Calles continued his basic policies in every respect. In Mexico an inherently anarchic society was held together at the private level through a vast web of personal relationships—kinship, friendship, and *compadrazgo*, the godparenthood taken very seriously throughout the country. The Hispanic nature was one of intense personalism, and personal relationships inevitably suffused government. Whether in business, pleasure, or in ruling a country Mexicans instinctively surrounded themselves with people they knew or with whom they had some tie; all Mexican organization from colonial times tended to revolve about the great, extended family which might contain as many as several hundred persons. The revolutionaries followed a family organization more than anything else, and it was inevitable that Obregón would begin a Sonoran dynasty. The practice of forming governments and cabinets in the United States with men from different regions who had never met was unthinkable in Mexico. As Mexicans saw it, this went against human nature; it was cold and depersonalized. Therefore, the only question had been which Sonoran Obregón would tap.

His choice of Calles was bitterly criticized, because Calles had great faults. In retrospect, however, the times made it impossible to select a civilian president, an intellectual, or a true democrat. Obregón chose well, because he picked Calles for his ruthlessness, his military leadership, and his keen political instinct.

Calles had all of Obregón's ambition and ruthless strength without Obregón's redeeming qualities of openness, good temper, and easy affability. Like Obregón, he was no demagogue—but he was a scowling man, merciless to real and supposed enemies, dirty in his personal habits, gross in his appetites, corrupt, greedy, and utterly lacking in education or refinement. He was a former elementary teacher of part-Levantine ancestry, from an era when any literate Mexican could teach school. Calles the man appalled genteel Mexico and the foreign diplomatic corps. What was far more important was that Calles the president was a dictator who could carry Mexico one step farther up her spiral road. His personality was sour and Stalin-like; he committed crimes against humanity—but so had all the previous more attractive Mexican heros.

Calles came in during a turbulent era, which became more turbulent as the revolutionary central regime increased its power and control and continued to implement the revolution against regrouping resistance. Calles never hesitated to use police and soldiers against his opposition. He employed the *ley de fuga* in a way that would have impressed old Don Porfirio, and with a new twist—political prisoners began to "commit suicide" in increasing numbers. The Calles presidency was, as Mexicans said, very severe.

It was also very progressive. By 1924 the Sonoran dynasty was agreed that the government needed to lay broader foundations to assure its continued power and also that Mexico could now afford more reforms. Without exception the communities granted lands had stood by the regime during the finger generals' insurrections; therefore it behooved the regime to distribute more fields. The worldwide prosperity of the 1920s increased demand for Mexican raw materials; the Tampico oil fields, opened early, were producing a quarter of the global petroleum. Obregón's policies of keeping order and restraint in factories and on plantations bore splendid fruit in increasing revenues; the bloodshed in Mexico was now largely between rival political and labor factions, rarely between employers and employees. Calles therefore could accelerate the pace of reform and pay for it.

The army still had to be stood off with peso cannonades: a full quarter of the federal budget. But now there was something left over for roads and dams, for health services, and especially for education. The Calles government initiated the first steps of a planned, large-scale modernization.

Land was seized and distributed more rapidly, eight million acres to some fifteen hundred communities in four years. This was still an infant program, but it was enough to allay complaints. With that passion to reform reforms that was a continuous process in Mexico, the government also tried to improve the program. The peasants farming *ejido* lands had come under the mercies of the federal bureaucrat or local political *cacique* running the land programs. To strengthen the *ejidatarios'* sense of private ownership, Calles enacted the law of *Patrimonio Ejidal*, which prevented the sale of granted plots, or the expulsion of peasants from *ejidos*. To encourage the development of farms outside the *ejidos*, he established farm credit banks.

Calles had proclaimed himself a socialist while he was fighting in Sonora and his critics never forgot it. However, his form of socialism did not encompass state ownership of the means of production, either agricultural or industrial, and it did not prevent men from trying to get rich in finance or industry. He instituted the Bank of Mexico, a private organization, to regulate the national money supply. His adoption of a miniscule income tax was, like his building of roads to carry automobiles to remote areas, a modernization following the path of capitalistic societies. Calles built dams and irrigation projects by government because no other agency could. The great push toward public education, which began under his dictatorship, brought primary schools to the sierras and remote valleys for the first time since the missionary friars. The new teachers went out using much socialistic rhetoric, but their efforts to impart literacy were no different, only later and more dramatic, than programs begun in older nations earlier.

Calles actually fostered the growth of native capitalism in two major ways. One was through corruption. His cronies grew very rich out of government favors, and were encouraged to invest in the new Mexican consumer-goods industries, oiling the wheels of industrialization with a capital that once went abroad or into inefficient landholding. These new industries were also adding a new ingredient to the revolutionary family, by creating a rising, richer, hopeful middle class of minor and larger capitalists. And the accelerated land confiscations also encouraged the trend toward industry, by ricochet.

Expropriations were paid for in treasury bonds, which were not redeemable for twenty years and non-negotiable except to pay taxes. Mexican landlords had little faith in the treasury, and had become disillusioned with land investments. While thousands of the old upper class had been impoverished, many thousands had far from been wiped out; they still had money or resources. An amnesty had been declared for all ordinary refugees, and during the 1920s most of the fugitive upper classes returned. Since the government did not persecute any form of enterprise except large landholding, the rich began to get out of land and to reinvest their capital in banks and industries. The memory of the turmoil and inflation hampered capital formation, because almost all the wealthy kept some money outside the country, damaging an economy that needed capital badly, but a marked switch by the rich from baronial estates to industrial shares and bank stock began to create a new native business and financial class.

Most of the new *criollos*, French, German, English, or Levantines, had carried on business throughout the revolution without being destroyed by politics; and the trends of the twenties, reinforced in the 1930s, added many of the old *criollos* to the business classes. The faces in the army, and in government from village presidents to the National Palace had become bronze, but in one field, the ranks of the modern capitalists, the Europeanized Mexicans made a strong comeback. The business owners for the most part in Mexico remained or became white. Thus a "European" society was not totally destroyed, though it was disassociated from public life or politics.

Calles did not permit the labor unions to harass this incipient capitalistic development. He tightened the government's hold on *Grupo Acción*, the ruling circle of CROM, and made CROM a virtual labor movement monopoly. CROM claimed control over a million unionized workers and five hundred thousand organized peasants, or all the organized labor in Mexico. The federation had less than twenty thousand dues-paying members in reality. Its power came from the alliance between the dictator and Luis Morones, the once-sincere, now flashy, diamond-encrusted labor chief who had become a *mestizo* millionaire. Morones moved into the cabinet as minister of commerce and industry (which ministry controlled labor affairs). CROM achieved small wage gains for its workers from the government, never enough to prevent the capitalization of new industry from being wrested from their sweat, but enough to keep the rank and file mollified. A dozen splinter groups, including the communists, engaged in agitation and some violence, but they remained totally ineffective to change the course of events. The labor movement had ceased to exist in Mexico as a movement; it had been incorporated into the bureaucracy.

The principal tragedy of the Calles era was not the frequent political repressions and assassinations but the bloody conflict that erupted between state and Church. This was the last act of a facet of the Hispanic revolution that had been developing for a hundred years.

In 1914 the Mexican Church, largely composed of Spanish clerics of the old school, had learned nothing from the days of Archbishop Labastida. The clergy continued to emphasize ritual and dogma, ignore ethic, and preach resignation and submission in the face of hunger and pestilence and brutal landlords. The clerics' affinity for the conservative wing of Mexican politics was profound, although many parish curates did serve the revolution. The great strength of the Mexican Catholic Church was the enduring mysticism and superstition of the Amerindian masses, which had hardly changed since the sixteenth century. The great weakness of the Church was that its social policies and politics had cost it most of the intellectuals (though by no means all of the whiter, wealthier class) and it lacked prestigious, and even intelligent leadership. A little good sense among the hierarchy would have avoided trouble in the twentieth century, but the Church lacked the vision to try to stand above the bloodshed of the revolution. The bishops issued an anathema against all agrarian reformists, praised Huerta, and even refused to condemn the murder of Madero. It was barely comfortable even with Carranza.

Although most Mexicans in 1917 were still deeply religious, and Catholic peasants and workers made endless pilgrimages, approaching the shrine of Guadalupe on bleeding knees, and some Mexicans still flagellated themselves during Holy Week, the Constitutionalists who met at Querétaro were understandably in a hostile mood toward the Church. The new constitution confirmed all the anticlerical clauses of 1857 and also added insult to injury. Now, the temples themselves were seized by the state (though the clergy continued to use them); the chalices and altars were nationalized; and the priests permitted in the churches only as guests of the state. Religious processions were banned, and priests barred from appearing in public in clerical garb. The Spanish nature of the Church, which the Holy See seems to have preserved throughout Spanish America for the excess production of peninsular priests, was attacked through a law requiring the sacraments to be administered by Mexican citizens. The worst blow of all to the clerics, however, was the insertion in the constitution of a clause requiring six years of *socialist* education for every child. Almost all Mexicans, who scarcely knew what "socialist" meant, interpreted this to mean *secular* education, but in any event to the Hispanic Church the terms socialist and secular were equally anathema. The Reform of 1857 had not destroyed the virtual Church monopoly of elementary education, but now most priests believed this clause would destroy religion itself.

Thus the whole body of the clergy, including many priests who supported the social aims of the revolution, were thrown into opposition to the Constitution of 1917. For ten years, however, the new laws were loosely implemented, where they were applied at all. In some areas local *caciques* persecuted priests, but the death sentence—as the Church considered it—was stayed and things continued very much as under the Porfiriato.

The hierarchy mounted futile counter-attacks. The Church branded membership in CROM a mortal sin and organized Catholic labor unions in 1921. However, unions founded by priests who neither implemented nor even approved the concepts of social justice expressed in *Rerum novarum* recruited few members. Catholic workers went to Mass, closed their ears to sermons delivered against the "godless" government, and demonstrated in the streets with CGT and CROM—whose leaders in fact detested *all* organized religion. To the intense annoyance of the leadership on both sides, the Church could not influence the politics of the faithful Catholics, while Marxist labor leaders could not shake loyal unionists' religion.

Underneath the apparent stand-off, however, there was a deepening crisis. The Church was no longer powerful politically or economically, but it remained the one institution that the revolutionary family had not controlled, cowed, or coopted. The Hispanic mentality of the rulers was, as always, disturbed by such independence. And the Church used its independence to criticize the government and to call certain revolutionary principles into question in the minds of the very young. When Calles became president, many intellectuals began to support the Church's accusations against his brutalities, and this quickly became intolerable to the regime.

The new secular school program precipitated the crisis. The schoolteachers who were sent into rural areas in 1924 to teach the peasants and *indios* to read and write tended to be very young, very secular, and very reformist, impatient with the past and the status quo, determined to break the superstitions which the clergy permitted and even fostered among the ignorant. They immediately engaged in spiritual and psychological warfare with the priests as part of the struggle to destroy the patterns that had existed for four centuries. Sordid measures were resorted to on both sides.

Priests defeated some educators with superstition, linking a local epidemic or crop failure to the wrath of God, and even inspiring the murder of a few teachers by fearful peasants. The schoolmasters destroyed some priests by exposing their sexual immorality—rural priests had fathered illegitimate children widely since the days of the Virreinato—and the exorbitant fees that were a peculiar feature of the Mexican Church. The attacks from both sides were frequently bitter and passionate; they polarized opinion and led to violence.

Overall, the schoolmasters were remarkably effective, because they were dedicated and they were better able to catch the aspirations of the poor people than the clergy. The priests, opposing the constitution, found themselves in opposition to legitimate hopes for education and progress. Secular education was winning across the countryside, and would have triumphed without serious bloodshed, except that Calles was a ruler of Stalinist temper who brooked opposition badly, and other men in government circles used the obstructionism of the padres to excuse certain of their own failures in bringing the millennium.

When a conservative newspaper published a long-hidden declaration of opposition to the anticlerical clauses of the constitution by the clergy—at the request of Archbishop Moya, who thought the arguments would have weight—Calles took this as a declaration of war. The president and his circle also saw a chance to break the clergy at last and bring it under government domination. He ordered immediate implementation of all the punitive articles applying to religion, and went much further, deporting all foreign priests by decree and requiring that the appointment of all native-born clergy be subject to government registration.

The Church had to resist this last order, because it passed the inherent control over religious appointments to the state. The archbishop declared noncompliance and sought and received Papal permission to conduct the world's first "religious strike." Mexican priests were ordered to abandon their altars and to refuse to administer sacraments until the government backed down. The hierarchy believed that in so Catholic a country popular indignation would be roused against Calles—but this was a bad miscalculation, because the bishops did not really understand the nature of Catholic faith in Mexico.

The interdict oppressed only the thinking Catholics in the towns, a small minority. To the clergy's amazement, most of the common people continued to pass into the open churches, light their candles, say their prayers, and continue their pilgrimages as if nothing had happened. The government owned the church buildings and shrines and kept them open and did not interfere with worship. What had happened was simple, if startling: over centuries the Mexican Church had inculcated a religion of formalism and observance that did not require a Catholic clergy, for few of the uneducated faithful even understood the theology of the Mass. The churches remained without clergy for three years, but without any popular protest from the lower classes.

The people who came to the clergy's defense were those same white, affluent, Hispanic elements who had already been discredited by the revolution. When the Vatican supported the strike and branded Calles publicly as the antichrist, groups of fanatic young laymen organized and battled police. There were also many people who, whatever their religion, hated what the revolution had wrought. These elements were especially strong in Jalisco and Michoacán, where the ancient cities were heavily *criollo*, and here they began a new guerrilla war—incongruously waged not by peasants, but by journalists, traditionalists, and young aristocrats, joined by many fervently religious middle-class rancheros.

These guerrilleros called themselves *cristeros*, from their war cry *Viva Cristo Rey!*—Long Live Christ the King! They waged war against the rural schoolmasters, burning down schools, hanging teachers, and in some cases, cutting off teachers' ears and tongues. The horror of this campaign waged in Christ's name was emphasized when the hierarchy disavowed any connection with them, but refused to condemn the *cristeros* or command them to halt their depredations. A party of *cristeros* led by a priest dynamited a passenger train, killing a hundred men, women, and children. Caught up in inchoate rage, the young rebels engaged in senseless destruction.

The regime retaliated with abominations of its own, which were fully reported in the worldwide Catholic press. Bishops were deported, and the army was sent against the *cristeros*. Calles gave command to the most anticlerical and antireligious generals, who not only enjoyed suppressing Catholics but found opportunities for private gain. The army decorated telegraph poles with the bodies of people whose only crime was that they were known to be devout Catholics and shot or plundered other families who took no part in the insurrection. Neutral observers soon reported that the generals seemed in no hurry to defeat the rebels in the hills, who never once seriously threatened Calles' government, but were retaliating against the upper classes in the towns. Colima, Jalisco, and Michoacán came under the rule of Calles' warlords, with the *cristero* movement providing an excuse for plunder.

The rebel chief, the journalist René Capistrán Garza, bitterly realized that his movement was actually strengthening the regime. He was an intelligent man who tried to throw off the counterrevolutionary image but without success. The warfare began to alienate the passive Catholics both from its indiscriminate violence and the fact that all Catholics were punished for it. This last weakened the bishops' stand.

By 1928, the hierarchy tried to seek an accommodation with Calles.

However, too much passion had been unleashed, and the clergy could not halt the bloodshed. In Jalisco, the government military chief moved whole populations, sixty thousand peasants in one case, to isolate them from the guerrilleros. This created so-called "rebel zones"—in effect, free-fire zones in which everyone found was considered an insurgent. The measures were bloodily effective, and the *cristero* rebellion withered, though persecution of Catholics set off by the warfare continued.

The capital meanwhile turned to the gripping question of Calles' successor. Calles was a dictator in everything but name, and few Mexican politicians thought he would relinquish power, constitution or no constitution. But they reckoned without Obregón, who had made Calles president, and who still controlled a powerful faction within the revolutionary family. Obregón was unwilling to let Calles succeed himself. Neither of the two strongmen was powerful enough to defy the other without causing a civil war. Both understood this, and both believed that there was no other general or politician strong enough to guide Mexico. Therefore, the two leaders hammered out an uneasy compromise by which Obregón would return to office for a new six-year term. To do this, Calles had to pressure the congress into amending the Constitution, to the effect that a term following a break in office did not constitute reelection. This change, and the extending of the presidential term from four to six years caused consternation among rivals and democrats, because it was assumed that this would open a game of musical chairs in which either Obregón or Calles would always hold the presidency.

Two army leaders protested; the ruthlessness of the regime was shown by the fact that Calles had both arrested and executed. It was also significant that the two generals received no support from the officer corps, which stood by the government however constituted. In 1928, Álvaro Obregón was the only candidate on the ballot. Luis Morones, who had had aspirations, refused to support him but did not obstruct. Obregón was ratified in July.

Whatever damage this might have done to the constitutional process was saved by an accident. On July 17, 1928, Obregón was shot to death by a young newspaper artist pretending to sketch him. The assassin was killed on the spot, but he was branded as a Catholic fanatic, and this remains the official version in Mexico—but many of the inner circle believed privately that the murder was instigated by Morones and CROM, or even by Calles himself.

Mexican Catholics, however, were made the sacrificial victims of official retribution. The priesthood was driven underground by what can only be called an official antireligious terror campaign. A priest and nun were accused of having plotted the assassination, and the priest was publicly executed at the capital in a scene reminiscent of the earlier autos-da-fé. A powerful international reaction surprised and shocked the regime; foreign embassies protested vigorously behind the scenes, and the new United States ambassador, Dwight Morrow, intervened quietly in the trouble between the government and the Church. Tempers cooled, and Morrow was able to mediate an agreement that officially let the clergy to come out of hiding and return to its altars in 1929.

The state, however, continued a policy of official hostility and strict enforcement of the anticlerical clauses. This policy encouraged officials in some states to give vent to their anticlerical and antireligious biases without restraint. The governor of Tabasco tried to uproot the Church entirely in his state; he organized the so-called "Red Shirts" who demolished churches and machine-gunned Catholics en route to Mass. Similar forms of "Red terror" took place in many parts of Mexico through 1934; they were not carried out by the national government—but they were not restrained by government. The entire clergy of the country was reduced to less than a hundred priests, and in most areas the priests had to operate clandestinely. These years were the nadir of the Mexican Catholic Church.

Whoever was behind the killing of Obregón, his death left the political scene dangerously muddled. Calles was a brutal man with a naked power drive, but having just changed the constitution to permit Obregón's presidency, he could not now technically succeed Obregón without the utmost cynicism. There never was any evidence that he was behind Obregón's assassination, but ironically the fact that so many Mexicans suspected it not only caused him to persecute Catholics as scapegoats, but also to move circumspectly. The revolutionary power structure was also extremely sensitive to appearances, and another Calles dictatorship would do vast damage to revolutionary mythology. Calles realized that he could not risk seizing the presidency, but he was not quite ready to give up power.

On September 3, 1928 he called all the important members of the revolutionary family into a private session at the capital. The assembled generals, governors, *caciques*, and deputies were read a prepared statement. Let Obregón, Calles told them, be the last *caudillo*; henceforth no man, not even one so indispensable as Calles himself, should be allowed to shoot his way to power or become a perpetual president. The hour had come for the democratic ideals of the revolution to be institutionalized. Like many Calles statements, this speech was enigmatic in parts, and it left some listeners feeling "defrauded," as one said. But the public showed only relief at the news Calles would step down, and the congress roared enthusiastic approval.

The constitution provided that congress select a provisional replacement pending new elections if a president died during his first two years in office. The congress was not overcome with boldness now, for it carefully chose a chief approved by both Calles and the adherents of Obregón. Emilio Portes

Gil, a lawyer who had served as governor of Tamaulipas, was knowingly selected to be a figurehead. He called himself a socialist, but his ideology was exactly that of Calles and Obregón. He might actually have made an excellent chief executive but he was not to be given a chance—he came into office with General Calles standing at his elbow.

The six years of Obregón's unexpired term were a continuation of what Mexicans now called the Calles-Obregón era under a series of puppet presidents. Calles held the real machinery of government, through the army and the fact that most officials were his appointees. Portes Gil was only a provisional president so there was no possibility of his taking command, and Calles carefully arranged the new order of things during this interim.

Calles deliberately took a new title, *Jefe Máximo*, or "Maximum Chief," to let the nation know who really held power. He made policy decisions, dictated appointments, and sent his wishes to congress from his villa at Cuernavaca, which now was the capital for the new-rich revolutionary elite. Calles ran the country amid drinking and poker sessions with his cronies. The street where his and other new, sprawling pink palaces rose was dubbed the "Street of the Forty Thieves."

The poorly-hidden cynicism and naked corruption of this regime did not prevent Mexico from enjoying reasonably good government. The foreign press, which hailed his step-down as evidence of democratic sentiments, was overoptimistic, but foreign governments sensed that Calles had gained maturity. He had most of the vices of the Mexican military *cacique*, but despite his unattractive qualities and a certain Stalinesque frame of mind, he was shrewd, capable of changing his opinion, and quite free of megalomania. He was and had to be a controversial figure, hated both by the communists and Catholics he persecuted equally, but from the historical view he was no national disaster. He solved some problems, and kept the machinery of government going.

One major accomplishment was his personal improvement of relations with the United States.

In 1926 nationalistic pressures and popular rhetoric had pushed a law through congress that required the holders of oil-bearing deposits to exchange their land titles for fifty-year concessions, to date from the original acquisition. The application of this law would have destroyed some major foreign oil operators, because the titles they had obtained from the Porfiriato were dubious, or did not exist—some oil companies had simply staked out claims, driven or bought off proprietors, and begun drilling without any legal sanction other than the benign approval of corrupt officials. These companies ignored the new law, and the United States government, sensitive to major petroleum interests, branded the legislation a breach of the informal guarantees given by Obregón in 1922 and 1923. The Hearst newspapers, hostile to the revolution since the early expropriations of their owner's cattle ranches, blasted Calles and called for North American intervention in Mexico. The U.S. Senate, however, was isolationist in mood, and the administration was determined to improve United States-Mexican relations despite the demands of certain North American millionaires. Washington understood that Calles, like his mentor Carranza, was playing an old game of *yanqui*-baiting for popular support, and that his regime had no intention of bolshevizing foreign oil holdings.

One of the ablest envoys in hemispheric history, Dwight Morrow, the father-in-law of the hero aviator Charles Lindbergh, was accredited to Mexico with instructions to keep things cool on both sides.

Morrow arrived in 1927, and he was the first North American ambassador to achieve popularity in Mexico. He showed no signs of prejudice or paternalism and went out of his way to respect Mexican sensitivities about "sovereignty." He soon made friends in government circles and became one of Calles' cronies, and his poker playing, both for table and diplomatic stakes, was entirely successful. Ironically, it was actually easier for the United States to deal with a powerful behind the scenes dictator in Mexico than with a popular demagogue. Calles' congress had passed the oil-lands legislation to assuage a popular outcry; now, Calles' Supreme Court, subservient to the executive, declared the law unconstitutional, requiring only that owners of oil-bearing properties must develop them or lose them. This game exasperated many North American businessmen, who too often failed to realize that it was desperately necessary for governments in weak, backward, but enormously sensitive nations whose very lack of the means to enforce sovereignty heightened their insistence upon it. Calles was prepared to make deals, provided he was permitted to observe "appearances."

Morrow, with the same cool hand, helped both Calles and the Church emerge from their impasse by de facto, rather than de jure agreements. The hierarchy acceded to the registration law, after Morrow passed on sub rosa assurances that the government would never use it to alter the spiritual independence of the clergy. While Garrido Canabal and several other state governors violated this agreement, Masses and confirmations began again in the cathedral on St. Peter's Day, 1929.

Morrow again played a vital role in the confusion that surrounded Obregón's assassination. He undoubtedly advised Calles in his actions, and strengthened the general's hand by showing that he had the confidence of Washington. Now, however, the cordial relations between the ambassador and Jefe Máximo began to arouse criticism in Mexico, especially from the highly intellectual, more radical, and *yanqui*-hating ranks. Calles was ac-

cused of selling out to *yanqui* oil interests and turning reactionary under
Morrow's influence.

The agrarian problem, the fundamental problem of Mexican society in
the twentieth century, was not as easily smoothed over as the foreign
relations controversies. The coterie of northerners who ran the government
during the Portes Gil and two following presidencies shared the Obregón-
Calles distaste for confiscations and the breaking up of large estates for
theoretical purposes. Almost all the northerners felt alien to the peasant
masses who dotted the mountains and valleys of central Mexico; their own
concept of agriculture and stock-raising ran much closer to the practices in
vogue in the United States, where the trend was to farms and ranches large
enough for economic efficiency. Calles' experience confirmed that confiscations of producing *latifundios* and the division of their lands among
peasants, each family with a tiny holding, cut production sharply. This
kind of subsistence farming produced no surpluses to feed the growing
urban population, and it reduced production in the kind of crops that were
sold abroad for foreign exchange. The economics of the twentieth century
ran counter to the deep land hungers of the Amerindian peasantry; the
agrarian aspirations of the revolution were opposed to the equally desired
modernization of Mexico into a twentieth-century nation state. Splitting up
estates into nonproductive plots cut the revenues needed for dams, roads,
and schools and industrialization. This was a core problem for every undeveloped society in this century, and one for which there was no easy
solution. It was also corroded by theories and ideologies ranging from the
old dream of a nation of small farmers to newer collectivist fancies. The
strong belief in the principle of private property that pervaded most revolutionaries prevented state ownership of the soil along the lines of a Russian Marxist approach, but neither collectivist nor bourgeois theories
offered a clear path to the transformation of impoverished peons into
citizens able to support the apparatus of a modern state. Men in power
quickly saw the dichotomy of the agrarian revolution. Too many theorists,
Marxist and otherwise, continually did not. They saw only the needs of the
peasantry and tended to romanticize an agrarian reaction.

The government had to balance demands and needs. There was always
a full understanding that future zapatista or villista-type risings were probable if the government became too unresponsive to rural demands for land.
The guns in Mexico had not been destroyed; they had only been put away
in countless peasant huts. The government continued to meet the desires of
intellectual reformers and peasants by a hesitant program of land reform
under Calles, but Calles himself soon became disgusted with the eternal
problem of the campesinos. Like the *indios*—and no revolutionary regime
did anything for the *indios* as *indios*—the mass peasantry was a stone
around every Mexican government's neck. *Indios* and peasants had little or

no functional use in society—unless Mexico was to be a society of Indians and peasants eschewing all efforts to modernize herself. Therefore, the land program became one of starts and stops, and continual reforms of reforms, as the ensuing regimes struggled to find a reasonable way out of the morasses created by the society of the past.

Calles, through Portes Gil, distributed an additional 2.5 million acres through 1929. One reason for this acceleration was the fact that many of the new-rich revolutionary generals were acquiring haciendas owned by enemies of the revolution, and while Calles was not really fearful of a newer landed aristocracy, he preferred the revolutionary capital to be invested in industry. Calles, and a very important segment of the ruling family, had begun to see an eventual salvation for the country through industrialization—the old goal of the best of the *continuistas*.

Calles had tried to assure the means to farm to smallholders and *ejidatarios* through the creation of credit banks. Unfortunately, official corruption sucked the funds made available into other channels, and agricultural production sank steadily in proportion to confiscations and redistributions. The onset of the worldwide economic depression in 1929 caused a crisis in the land program. Demand declined, prices for Mexican products fell; and only the best-run, well-capitalized plantations could turn profits. By 1930 the average Mexican campesino was only earning forty-four centavos daily. This, equal to eleven cents in U.S. money, was half of what he had lived on under Don Porfirio.

Deteriorating conditions changed Calles' mind decisively. He announced that land reform must end; many states now put time limits for future expropriations; and distributions had ceased by 1932. Calles was bitterly attacked as a counterrevolutionary in some quarters, and it was widely said that Ambassador Morrow had influenced him to try to turn Mexico into an industrial society on the capitalist order of the United States.

The agrarian problem was fundamental, but organized labor presented government with another problem. It was more concentrated and therefore more vocal. The labor unions had already come under the control of government, but they made a great deal of sound and fury, enough often to convince foreigners that Mexico had become a socialist state. Calles, like Obregón, continued close relations with labor leaders for political support. But by 1928 he and his coterie of northerners had become angered by some labor leaders' insistence that the revolution lead to socialism, and Calles had become distrustful of Morones because of that leader's obvious political ambitions. Calles had no more intention of letting organized labor exist as an unruly, independent force than the Church, and he determined to teach trade unionism a lesson.

He destroyed CROM by the simple expedient of ordering the bureaucracy to declare every CROM-instigated strike illegal. He could do this because CROM's leadership had grown so corrupt that it had lost influence with the rank and file of labor. The organization sank rapidly, until by 1932 it controlled only a few unions in the textile industry. This splintered the trade union movement. New unions did rise, such as the CGOC organization under Lombardo Toledano, and a number of regional organizations, some of which were communist. None of these were effective on the national level.

Calles made his greatest contribution to Mexico after he left office, during the six years he remained behind the scenes but still the most powerful individual in the country. Under Carranza the revolution had been institutionalized; Obregón had enforced order; but Calles normalized political life for the first time in independent Mexico. His motives in this normalization are not entirely clear. Many apologists have held that Calles was a whole-hearted revolutionary; others have attributed his actions to a continuing determination to hold power. Unlike Carranza's and Obregón's, however, Calles' effect upon Mexican government was decisive. What he built was not easily overturned.

The events of 1928 had made it clear to Calles that the condition of government was chaotic. Although one dominant revolutionary outlook ran through the whole revolutionary family, the stability of the nation and the revolution itself had been continually threatened by personal rivalries. Carranza's refusal to stand aside for Obregón, and de la Huerta's for Calles, had led to bloodshed. Civil war in 1928 was again only narrowly averted, because the revolution had come to depend on the rule of a single strongman. The principle of No Reelection was so powerfully and emotionally established that each strongman was forced to step down after his term, and this meant that the close of every presidential term must lead to power struggles between rival factions. In 1923 the whole structure of Revolutionary Mexico was almost undermined over the question of the succession. The president was becoming an institutional monarch, but the means of selecting a president was far from institutionalized or normalized. Further, the plateau of order and relative efficiency brought about by Obregón rested entirely on the power and personality of one man.

The weakness ran through the whole governmental hierarchy. Like most governments, the Mexican ran on favoritism and patronage. Patronage and favor descended through a series of *caciques* from the National Palace. Governors on good terms with the capital received funds for roads, schools, irrigation projects, and clinics; they were supported through any troubles by the president. They could pass these favors down through regional bosses and municipal presidents. The system was effective in a raw sort of way; control was maintained by patronage. If a governor or local político fell out with the national regime, it was immediately apparent, at least to the politicized, for his public works stopped and he ran out of funds. If this happened, there was almost always a local power struggle, because rival men or elements in better favor put themselves forward. The ouster of a local government, however, was rarely peaceful; there were shoot-outs in state houses and bloody clashes between rival partisans.

Calles' historical greatness rests on the fact that he was able to seize on newer forms. Through 1928 it had been accepted in Mexico that only the revolutionary family had any right to political activity, to contracts or concessions, or in effect even to the protection of the laws. Calles understood—when many of the older generals and políticos did not—that this was too small an institutional base for a continuing revolution. A new Mexican generation that had been too young to fight in the revolution was already coming on. Calles made it clear that he believed the family could not remain entirely a closed club and that the political base must be considerably broadened. For this he was again described as a counterrevolutionary, but he was not stayed. Calles had determined that Mexico required a newer political party, a broad-based organization that could not only unite all the diverse and rival elements of the family but could eventually offer a means of expression to people now outside the family.

Since independence, Mexican political parties had remained more factions than true parties, usually revolving around some strong personality. Calles, on a post-presidential trip through Europe, was greatly impressed with the British Labour Party and the German Socialists. These organizations, representing national constituencies, seemed to provide unity, hierarchy, discipline, and continuing direction toward long-range goals. Calles became convinced that the revolution needed a great political party to carry it forward—a party that would incorporate all the ineffective splinter parties and factions such as the Agrarians, the Mexican Labor Party, the Liberal Constitutionalists, the National Cooperatists, and the several varieties of socialists. None of these parties had shown themselves capable of forming a national government, but Calles saw that the European parties effectively brought various wings and interest groups within a single organization that could attract outside support at the same time it gave thrust and unity.

Back in Mexico, the Jefe Máximo urged the formation of the *Partido Nacional Revolucionario*, or PNR. Calles seized upon radio broadcasting to popularize the idea. The PNR was immediately formed in 1929, and the government of Portes Gil threw its entire power and patronage behind it. It must be understood that the PNR was never intended to be a democratic political party in the Anglo-Saxon sense, nor was it supposed to operate within a democratic political arena. The PNR was not made to compete but to control. It continued the whole Mexican middle-rank concept of a national guardianship. To start, every member of the revolutionary family was considered ipso facto to be a member of the PNR. Portes Gil required that everyone of rank in government—senators, deputies, governors, generals, judges—become official members, and further, that every government employe contribute a portion of his salary to the party treasury. The rationale behind this was not the enforced exactions that had always been a feature of Mexican political life but a stated belief that anyone who had been admitted to the bureaucracy had joined the revolutionary family and was enjoying its benefits—the same rationale as that behind the union dues check-off in certain North American states. The Mexican government had become a "party shop."

The PNR, never a political alliance to win votes in fair competition, was to be the guiding and controlling organization behind the state—the state, in fact, was to be its instrumentality. Thus its true status as a political party was much closer to that of the Communist Party in Russia or the Fascist Party in Italy than to the ideological political parties in democratic nations. The PNR began with special privileges which no other party could receive; it was not subject to the state or to constitutional responsibilities. Like the Communist Party, the PNR was formed as a bureaucratic hierarchy descending from the maximum chief. But the resemblance ended with form, because the ideology and ethos of the Mexican Revolution was very different from that of the various communist and fascist monoliths. The PNR was middle-class, and tutelary rather than totalitarian.

The PNR created an institution in which the diverse and rival elements of the revolutionary family from businessmen to agrarians could and did hammer out a basic harmony while maintaining custody of the revolution. It could not end *caciquismo*, which was peculiarly and indelibly Mexican, but it brought *caciques* under some control. Obregón and Calles had been dictators; the party could work out group solutions. The party obviously would be under the direct influence of whoever was the national *cacique*, but it created an instrumentality in which the national chieftain could be selected and brought to power without plunging the country into civil war. Obviously, the PNR gave Calles, who held no office, a splendid means to control the whole government from the sidelines, and it became an immediate octopus that devoured the revolution as well as potential rivals. But the evidence is overwhelming that Calles brought much vision to the formation of PNR and was thinking beyond his own power and prestige, and toward a national government imbued with the ideals of the revolution, and in which the revolution could stand for something beyond a process of change forced by armed strongmen in an atmosphere of continual rivalry and turmoil. There might be a certain tyranny of the party, but this was preferable to the unstable tyranny of a Calles or an Obregón. Whatever Calles intended ultimately, the results were decisive. The PNR began as Calles' tool; it quickly became a mechanism that normalized the presidential succession, and with it, the political life of the emerging nation.

The PNR held its first convention in 1929 to select the official candidate for president. Nothing was immediately changed, for Calles had only institutionalized the old process by which Mexican chiefs dominated government. Calles blocked CROM from influence in the party and undermined the influence of outstanding agrarian leaders like Soto y Gama, whose view was restricted to the land. The delegates obviously preferred Aaron Saénz, a callista who had become Mexico's largest sugar producer under the dispensation of the revolution, but Saénz was too strong a personality for the Jefe Máximo. Calles chose Pascual Ortiz Rubio, a colorless political nonentity and rammed him down the party's collective throat.

It was inevitable that some kind of revolt would erupt in the turbulent revolutionary family. It took three forms, each unrelated.

In Sonora, the old "finger general" Gonzalo Escobar tried to rally the army behind a traditional pronunciamento. But only a quarter of the remaining political generals rose, and something very untraditional happened. The army itself, supported by worker and peasant groups, put down the military insurrection. The reforms initiated by Obregón in 1923 and carried on by Joaquín Amaro—who was an Amerindian and a finger general but also a Mexican and true professional—had changed the entire infrastructure of the officers' corps. As war minister under Calles, Amaro had professionalized the military by regularly raising educational requirements for appointment and promotion. Many of the old generals survived and were ostensibly in command, but they were surrounded by newer field officers, graduates of staff colleges, who were very different men. The new officers now came from the less affluent middle ranks of society, and they were careerists instead of *políticos* in uniform. Obregón, the last *caudillo*, and Amaro the *indio* general, had done something that proved impossible in other Hispanic nations: they tamed the pretorians and made a truly national army.

Amaro was almost unknown outside of Mexico, and the transformation was complete before it was noted anywhere. When Calles replaced Amaro as war minister in the Portes Gil administration, the political generals were isolated. The Escobar rebellion allowed Calles to complete the job. He reduced the army to fifty thousand and cut its budget by half, since much of the money went to support political generals who were now summarily shot, dismissed, or retired. The Mexican army did not disappear—it had become an extremely powerful pillar of the state. Díaz had corrupted the army in order to control it, but by doing so rendered it useless for his own protection. Obregón and Calles disciplined the army and made it an effective tool of government.

Extreme left-wing elements made trouble, also, and Calles moved against these as ruthlessly as against the pretorians. José Guadalupe Rodríquez, who tried to organize "soldier soviets" on the Russian model, was shot along with some of his soldiers. A peasant and labor bloc of the

Communist International that had formed under the artist Diego Rivera was disbanded, and many leftists ended up in the Marías Islands penal colony.

The third form of dissidence was less tumultuous and bloody than military or communist uprisings but equally abortive. Calles' blatant manipulation of the party convention offended many younger intellectuals, who formed around José Vasconcelos, the country's leading intellectual figure and Obregón's secretary of education. Vasconcelos was a stubborn nonconformist who had rendered prodigal services in organizing the new school system from the rural districts to the university. He was universally admired in revolutionary ranks, but he had blasted away at the corruption and brutality of the Calles regime since 1924. Now, he tried to organize a political opposition by democratic methods, but against Calles' iron control of the government machinery he had no chance. The announced result of the 1929 election was one million to twenty thousand in favor of the official party candidate, Ortiz Rubio.

Vasconcelos charged fraud and fled to the United States like Madero. He believed the country would support him—but Mexico had again entered into a weary, disillusioned, postrevolutionary era. Vasconcelos busied himself with a book on aesthetics and when the call did not come, eventually returned to the capital, where he remained an ornamental but uninfluential critic of what he considered wrong with Mexico.

During the postrevolutionary pause from 1929 through 1932, little happened. Economic misery deepened from the depression, but actually the world depression did not have the disastrous social and psychic effects in Mexico that it caused in the industrial nations. The government was not a democracy; therefore it could not retrogress or fall as certain democratic regimes did in parts of South America under economic pressures. Calles, playing golf at Cuernavaca, continued in full control. His almost total control of Ortiz Rubio's administration made that president something of a laughing stock.

In September 1932, Ortiz attempted to assert some independence by dismissing Calles' cronies from his cabinet. The popular version of the outcome is probably true: when informed of Ortiz' moves, Calles announced to the press that the president had resigned. When the press informed Ortiz Rubio of this statement, he immediately wrote out his letter of resignation.

The congress chose a callista financier, Abelardo Rodríguez, to fill out the term. Rodríguez was a northwestern businessman, a revolutionary conservative opposed to reform for the sake of reform. No more land was redistributed. Rodríguez symbolized the emergence of a powerful set of self-satisfied revolutionary parvenus who had created a new Establishment, and many observers in Mexico and abroad believed the revolution had clearly lost its steam. However, the callistas, in retrospect, were far more consolidators than reactionaries. They were establishing the *mestizo* revolution, not recreating the days of Don Porfirio. Ideology within the revolutionary family, now operating through the PNR tended to fluctuate somewhat, and between 1928 and 1934 capitalist sentiments were clearly in the ascendancy.

If Mexico temporarily seemed to stagnate politically and economically, the decade had been one of enormous, fundamental change. In retrospect, the historian has to assess the accomplishments of the Obregón-Calles years against what had been before, and against what was possible in these years.

The strongmen generals had tamed the army. They were creating a national tool that could eventually be used by a nonmilitary man. They shot dissident soldiers and unruly *políticos*—but the crimes seemed less when weighed against the nature and the desires of those who were assassinated or stood before the wall, almost all of whom represented further anarchy or a worse tyranny.

The dictators, even the suspicious Calles, had never succumbed to paranoia. Opposition and criticism by influential citizens such as Vasconcelos was never suppressed; the strongmen reserved their furies for acts resembling plots or pronunciamentos. The press was free, and for fourteen years it continued to be mainly hostile to the Obregón-Calles regimes. The average Mexican was in no danger from the government; historic and bitter enemies of the revolution returned under amnesty and prospered from business and investment. The landowners were not persecuted as a class; there were no marked "class enemies" in Mexico as in the Russian and Chinese Revolutions. Both the congress and the courts were corrupt, but both branches of government contained honest men with widespread respect and prestige. A peculiarity of the Obregón-Calles years was that corrupt officials were tolerated to a great extent, but both regimes regularly appointed their Vasconcelos and Amaros to key posts in government. Calles improved the judiciary even while he dominated law and politics.

Few things aroused so much hatred of Calles as the persecution of the Church. Yet, the old Hispanic Mexican Church had to be destroyed root and branch before a newer or better organization might take its place; the Church's whole philosophy had to change if the old religion based on dogma, rituals, and empty observances were to ever improve in Mexico. The old Church fought for its life, and in the process destroyed itself. But religion was far from destroyed in Mexico; it was finally divorced from public life and politics. It was impossible for the old Church in its despair to understand that Christianity would emerge far stronger and fresher from the ordeal.

Through 1933, four thousand Mexican communities totalling about 750,000 families had received 19,000,000 acres in returned lands. There were still 300,000,000 acres enclosed in *latifundios*, and some two million families without land. But while the land program in many ways had been less than successful, the Obregón-Calles era confirmed the abandonment of the ancient *latifundista* social system. There were still haciendas, but they were enterprises rather than social systems. The power of land ownership over society had been broken like the power of the Hispanic Church. The newer *hacendados*, like the newer bishops, were very different kinds of men.

The strongman era between 1920 and 1934 did not begin to solve all the social, economic, and psychic problems; a decade could not undo four centuries. However, fundamental breakthroughs had been made. The dictators presided over the destruction of the unholy trinity of institutions that had always prevented Mexico from emerging as a modern society: the pretorian army, the *latifundistas*, and the clerics with seventeenth-century minds.

The writers and the press of the times reported mostly calamities; these were more newsworthy than the steady normalizations going on in life and politics. Most of the Mexicans and institutions destroyed by the dictators—the vicious generaldom, the reactionary Catholics, the anarchic trade unions, and the communist ideologues—actually stood in the way of order and modernization. By 1934 Mexico, though still violent, was far from anarchic or lawless.

And the new order was not quite oligarchic, a mere changing of the guard. The parvenu generals, financiers, politicians, and industrialists who made up the ruling order might appear to be a *mestizo* oligarchy, but unlike the porfiristas they were basically bourgeois in outlook. And the creation of the party kept the ruling structures fluid, by blending aggressive businessmen with rustic agrarians, and forcing men who became rich through revolution to associate and deal with unionists. The party structures could not form a true "ruling class." There had been a subtle but enormous change in social hierarchy.

Mexicans grew wealthy from being part of government, where previously the rich had dominated government. The new class tended to pass from government, once wealthy, to careers in private industry, farming, or finance. For the first time, the economy was creating alternatives to feeding at the public trough. Some of the more energetic *mestizos* had become entrepreneurial, and thus were forming a true middle class.

The strongmen were hated most of all by outsiders for their nationalism. Almost all foreign investors and concessionaires, conditioned by a century, viewed Mexico's emergence as a truly sovereign, independent nation as a calamity to their interests. This was shortsighted, and it created a definite dichotomy in the 1920s between North American investors and the United States government. Washington preferred a powerful, order-keeping regime in Mexico, while North American oil, mining, and ranching concerns preferred a loose, essentially weak, oligarchically-controlled territorial agglomeration like the Mexico of the Porfiriato, which they might manipulate. While Obregón and Calles never lost their own cool heads, Mexico was becoming emotional and xenophobic in demanding her sovereignty, whether prepared to exercise it or not. The dictators had to make concessions to the popular feeling, while this violent surge of nationalism caused many foreigners to confuse a bourgeois revolution with bolshevism. The greatest thrusts for nationalizations were coming from Mexican industrialists fearful of outside competition by the 1920s rather than from leftist intellectuals or trade unions. Of course, foreign investment might initially suffer as much from bourgeois nationalism as from Marxist confiscations —but the effects in terms of international relations and hopes of future business was quite different. The Mexican revolutionaries were not demanding that foreign investment end, only that the terms be renegotiated. Washington seemed to understand this between 1920 and 1934, and the United States governments, whether Democratic or Republican, in effect granted Mexican sovereignty precedence over the claims of domestic claimants. This was a vast watershed, laying the basis for future harmony.

Neither Calles nor Obregón fitted the romantic pattern of high-minded, poetic martyr-hero that dominated so much of the Hispanic revolution. Obregón's assassination could not be construed as martyrdom; Calles' ponderous regime seemed the antithesis of idealism. The dictators were not articulate or attractive, and human nature often prefers high-minded futility to cold, effective politics. Calles and Obregón had their share of ambition, and they often operated from ruthless instinct to seize and hold power. They were not democrats in practice or theory. The great problem in assigning these members of the Sonoran dynasty their proper niche in history is that they were not the kind of men or symbols to which later generations raise statues.

But judged against their time they take on impressive stature. The era of the Sonorans was a chaotic, brutal, postrevolutionary phase, when there could be nothing resembling democracy in Mexico. Mexicans were disillusioned, exhausted, and deeply brutalized. Too many revolutionaries achieved their personal aspirations in the upheaval and never thought beyond these. But in the light of what Álvaro Obregón and Plutarco Elías Calles built, and what came after them, the charge that they did not keep a basic faith with the revolution seems false and specious.

In 1920 Mexico had to emerge from a brutalized, backward, ruined, and exhausted society, and if leaders had not risen who could bring form and order and institutionalization, the past would have had to be repeated all over again.

Whatever else they were, the Sonorans were chieftains who laid the bedrock for the modern Mexican nation.

35

TRANSITIONS

We are Indian, blood and soil; the language and civilization are Spanish.

José Vasconcelos.

While Álvaro Obregón and Plutarco Elías Calles were presiding over the making of a nation, history in another form had reemerged again to haunt modern Mexico. Mexicans' central problem, that of identity, began with the Spanish Conquest, and it remained, because the Conquest was and still is the supreme fact of Mexican history.

The conquest of Mexico destroyed all continuity with the Amerindian past, but left the vast majority of the Mexican population Amerindian at least in part, differentiated from the conquerors in color and appearance. This was not the source of the problem, for Irish and Norwegians have had identity problems in the twentieth century as they emerged as independent nations. But racism muddied the waters. The Spanish destroyed the Amerindian consciousness, made Mexico into an Hispanic country, but for centuries barred most doors to men with Amerindian blood. The effects of the Spanish centuries were incalculable; they are still sensed emotionally by every child born in late-twentieth-century Mexico.

The blood and soul of the people of Mexico may have remained Amerindian, but by the sixteenth century, the Amerindian civilization vanished. Indigenous blood, words, techniques, foods, garments, and certain family relationships—all the survivals beloved by North American anthropologists and Mexican demagogues—by the twentieth century were exactly that: survivals, not of a great civilization, but of a primitive indigenous culture whose head was severed. These primitive remnants had little meaning, and no real place, in a modern world. The entire cosmos of the Amerindians was shattered under the Conquest. The pyramids of Mexico once symbolized something vital to a civilization. They became like the pyramids of Egypt, valuable tourist attractions, but otherwise meaningless. Like modern Egyptians, Mexicans no longer speak the language or even comprehend the thought processes of their remote racial ancestors. They were both enveloped by vast cultural diffusions. But while the Nilotic Egyptians came to consider themselves Arabs, the racial attitudes of the Western world made it very difficult for Mexicans to see themselves as Europeans.

The very primitive tribes and clans that remained outside the Amerindian civilization in Motecuhzoma's time still exist. They were never part of that civilization; today, they do not know of its existence. Ironically, since late colonial times only the most educated, most modern Mexicans have been aware of their ancient past. This awareness, rising mainly among Mexican mixed-bloods, was unsettling. It gave the Mexican with Amerindian ancestry something to feel pride in—but it was also something to which he could hardly relate. From the late eighteenth century the educated Mexican, whether *mestizo* or *criollo*, found his history increasingly unpalatable. The past prior to 1521 therefore became enormously important to him, not economically, politically, or even culturally, but emotionally and psychologically. In 1821 the pure-blood Creoles felt a strong urge to identify with the conquering Mexica, and to bolster their own rule of Mexico with Mexica symbols. By 1921, this old drive had focussed an unusual degree of emotion on the vanished past, which many Mexicans tried to treat as if it had some connection with the present. While, ironically, the initial discoveries and reconstructions of the Amerindian civilization were made by North American and European scholars and scientists, Mexicans soon seized upon them. The men of the Porfiriato, with their European genes and myths of a white Mexico were vaguely embarrassed by Amerindian Mexico. The generation of the revolution, with its nativism and awareness of its indigenous origins, grasped all things Amerindian. In revolutionary Mexico, archeological discoveries and controversies were paraded and debated in the popular media as current events, usually with more bias than perspective. Old prejudices remained and still exist.

While the revolution opened all doors to all men without regard to race, Mexican *continuistas*, the historic conservatives, instinctively exalted all things Hispanic or European and denigrated the Amerindians as barbarians. The much larger, heterogeneous Left meanwhile created a cult of the indigenous, to the extent of sometimes erroneously describing Mexico as an "Indian nation." Elements of this cult are not entirely rational. The term *indio* was made pejorative under the Spaniards (which is why most

Mexicans use "indígena" for "Amerindian") and most Mexicans resent the implication of the word—that the original Americans derived from the Orient. The concept of the indígena, while popular and powerful in modern Mexico in political, cultural, and intellectual life, is wonderfully unreal. Mexica motifs on public murals do not constitute a usable past. The cult of the indigenous has created new psychic problems. Because the *indio* became a symbol of oppression in Mexico, it keeps alive the Mexican awareness of having been oppressed. And the basic problem is that the indigene or *indio*, as an Indian, can live no more effectively in modern Mexico than he could under the Viceroyalty. The Mexican present and future centers around business suits and machines, cement, electric power, tractors, and chemical plants, rather than Amerindian outlooks and crumbling pyramids.

If some part of the Mexican soul is Amerindian (and most Mexican intellectuals insist it is) then only more bifurcation lies in store, because the Mexican cannot live in an Amerindian world. He has never had a choice since 1521 but to emerge as part of a greater Western, Latin, Hispanic civilization. The Mexican has no choice but to speak an Indo-European language, live under Roman law, operate within a European-derived money economy, and accept or reject a totally nonindigenous Judaeo-Christian religion. From the sidewalks of the Paseo in the capital to the bustling factories built by the border industrialization program in the north, Mexican civilization provides no place for the Amerindian. The cult of the indigene is based on a vast hypocrisy, because the destruction of the *indio* was accelerated by the revolution. Roads, dams, and automobiles, new schools and school teachers, began to impinge everywhere upon the *indio*, swallowing him in *mestizo* culture. The intellectuals of the revolution, most of whom praised Indians, did more to destroy the *indio* through Mexicanization than all the viceroys. In 1910 about thirty-nine percent of the Mexican population were considered identifiable Indians. In 1972 the proportion could not be more than ten percent. The Mexicanization of the *indio* was and is absolutely essential to the formation of a true Mexican nation, and no amount of rhetoric or lamentations has stayed history.

Since the Conquest, no Mexican has ever been effective except by ceasing to be an Indian, whether President Benito Juárez or General Joaquín Amaro. The question is not one of blood, because blood has never been a determinant of civilization—but centuries of racist colonialism made this hard for Mexicans to understand. Nor does the present entirely clear the way. Mexico is caught up in a Western culture in which the dominant standards of physical beauty are Italianate or Anglo-Saxon—ideals which only a minority of Mexicans can meet. Mexicans falsify their pictorial advertising with European types—and most are acutely conscious that the various Westerners they do business with seem to prefer lighter skins.

The Conquest did not mean that Mexico became another Spain, anymore than North America became another England or Northern Europe. But Mexico became an Hispanic country, in the same sense that the United States, Australia, and Canada form parts of a larger, English-speaking culture. Mexico, which emerged in the century as the largest Spanish-speaking nation, surpassing Argentina and the Peninsula, is an integral, and probably now the leading nation in the Hispanic branch of Western culture. All Mexican artists and intellectuals, like Mexican soldiers and diplomats and businessmen, operate within that world; their market does not consist of Amerindians.

Mexican writers are published as a matter of course in Argentina, and they are regularly inspired and fertilized out of Peru. And the Hispanic world does not exist only on higher cultural planes. The comic Cantínflas is as great a folk hero in Spain as he is in Mexico. When the Spaniard Manolete was gored to death in the bullring, corridas lamented the event from Mexico to Madrid. Mexican history, and progress, is in fact only meaningful when Mexico is placed in full perspective with the whole Hispanic world. The triumphs and failures of the Mexican people cannot be measured against the French or Russians; they become clearer seen against the rise and fall of Colombians and Bolivians.

It is of course perfectly possible for a modern Mexican to refuse to be a Roman Catholic, to reject his Spanish cultural heritage as his Spanish rapist-father once rejected him, and to lament the Conquest and despise the aftermath. However, it is not always seen that the most xenophobic brown-skinned muralist must do all these things in terms of Catholic-Christian reference and in thought processes actually formed by the Spanish tongue. The angriest Diego Rivera cannot go home again (which may be why Rivera looked to foreign doctrines); the anthill utopias of Amerindian Mexico are forever gone. The modern Mexican who considers himself Amerindian can only survive by living in a capitalist society as a thorough individualist—not an Amerindian trait. Even his nostalgia is more a Latin than an Amerindian trait, and in truth, more Mexican intellectuals are nostalgic for the never-was of a Latin-speaking nation of two hundred million souls, which might have embraced the North American continent, than for Motecuhzoma's mud-bottomed empire. If there is a cultural tragedy in modern Mexico, an emerging nation, it is that a people whose greatness lies in the future cannot quite escape the past.

The tides and passions of the Mexican Revolution released enormous cultural energies. Since the revolution was statist but never totalitarian, these energies had free expression—they were often encouraged by a government that had no confidence in the artists. The Mexican intellectual and artistic revival, though parochial, crested a splendid era of genuine native achievement. Obregón's regime culturally and intellectually ranks as one of the definitive periods of Mexican development, comparable to the early flowering of Spanish letters and the great era of church-building. Like all important artistic periods, the revolutionary era created its own styles.

The War for Independence and the separation from Spain produced no cultural revival in Mexico. The sterile nineteenth century is usually blamed on the state of Mexican society and politics. However, rulers from Santa Anna through Díaz spent huge sums on art and monuments. The problem probably lay with the spirit. Dominant rationales in intellectual circles despised most things Mexican, and with the exception of the painter Velasco, Mexican artists copied foreign styles and produced hybrid monstrosities from French and Italian themes. The artistic explosion that came with the revolution was part of it—a desperate search for nativism that was a normal reaction and long overdue.

Mestizo creativity drew consciously and heavily on its own heritage for the first time, and the result was a sudden splendor of a peculiarly Mexican art, expressed in mural painting following the manner of the ancient Amerindian civilization. Its practitioners became world famous: Clemente Orozco, Diego Rivera, David Alfaro Siqueiros, and afterwards Rufino Tamayo and a host of successors comprised a school of Mexican muralists. The initiative was consciously Amerindian, so much so that some went to extreme lengths. Gaitia was interested only in *indios*; Gerardo Murillo changed his name to Atl (Nahuatl: "water") and Carmen Mondragón became Nahui Olin.

It was difficult for Mexican artists and intellectuals of the period to keep their balance in the collapse of the hated, Europeanophile Porfiriato and its decadent Latinity. The first perspective lost, in the sharply-divided, European-Amerindian south, was Molina Enríquez' view of the *mestizo* or mixed-bloods as a distinct people, without emphasizing either the *mestizo*'s European or Indian origins. The concept of la raza was primarily a northern view, and the northerners were too busy fighting the revolution and assuming its direction to become caught up in intellectualism or art. The deep hatred of the white men of the Porfiriato and their styles led some Mexicans to overemphasize the Indian nature of Mexico. In reverse, this was as bad a hybridization as the artistic monstrosities of the past age.

The mainstream of Mexican art, however, was dynamic and it drew its themes, spirit, and rationales from the aspirations of the revolution—the people's desire for essential dignity and freedom and a piece of their own land. These themes gave Mexican mural art its genius and stark vitality, expressing idealism in brilliant warmth and color. The very form as well as themes derived from the revolution: Diego Rivera despised easel painting as a prostitution for the rich, choosing to daub broad murals in public places as "art for the people." The enemies the artists attacked on walls were the enemies of the revolution—clericalism and militarism and arrogant landlords.

Very few of the best artists were satisfied with the course of the postrevolutionary years, and their enthusiasms sometimes became an embarrassment. A revolutionary Establishment that was essentially middle class did not always approve of the bourgeois-hating Rivera, who with Siqueiros joined the Mexican Communist Party when that organization was introduced in the 1920s by various foreigners. Siqueiros and Rivera insisted upon carrying the revolution against the whole middle rank, and were not above affronting most opinion with nasty little digs, painting legends such as "Dios no existe" ("God does not exist") into murals commissioned for public buildings. Clemente Orozco was less political; he tended to see Mexican suffering as a human tragedy more than as an avoidable sociopolitical disaster. But while Orozco's paintings depicting the finely-kept white fingers of a priest accepting the *óbolo* of a ragged, horny-handed peasant were applauded generally, his portrayal of the "betrayers of the revolution"—generals who destroyed the old elite only to put on fat diamond rings and toast their whores in imported champagne—made most of the Obregón-Calles Establishment flush and squirm. Other artists like Cabral and Covarrubias drew caricatures only, though their caricatures were vigorous and true. To its everlasting credit, the revolution tolerated all these men.

In fact, the cultural explosion probably would have been much less except for the Obregón administration and its principal intellectual figure, José Vasconcelos. Vasconcelos was the third in the trinity of outstanding Mexican intellectuals that included Justo Sierra and Lucas Alamán. Like his predecessors, he was contradictory, splendidly nonconformist, and brilliantly intelligent, skillful in several fields. He was an old maderista who had spent a while with Pancho Villa, and he was not yet forty when Obregón appointed him minister of education. Like Alamán and Sierra, Vasconcelos was more than a leading intellect; he dominated and shaped his whole times. Like theirs, his politics failed miserably, and the fact that Mexico's three leading intellectuals were or became cultural *continuistas*, clinging to the Hispanic heritage, has always made the holders of the conventional Mexican wisdom uneasy in their deepest souls. Vasconcelos was a brilliant writer, an excellent administrator, especially in inspiring men, a pro-Spanish Mexican whose deepest cultural hatreds were reserved for North Americans. He was, or became, a devout Roman Catholic, and in the end he turned against the revolution—or rather, what he believed the Mexican Revolution had become.

Vasconcelos' arrival in government was an explosion in itself. At a time when the workers were restive, the peasants hungry, and every general had his hand out, Vasconcelos convinced Obregón to make the education budget the largest single item in the federal outlay—a prominence and position the educational budget ever afterward retained. Obregón cheerfully allowed him a free hand. Vasconcelos saw that one thousand new rural schools were built; he made these buildings into true cultural centers in the backwoods; and somehow he inspired Mexican schoolmasters to serve indefinitely in rural exile and to risk torture and death to carry Mexicanization, literacy, and hope to the *indio*-peasant masses. At least eighteen of Vasconcelos' young men were killed at schoolhouse doors. The others were able to pass Vasconcelos' own inspiration on, and to kindle that desire for education that became a hallmark of the continuing revolution. Such an effort was almost incredible in the times of Obregón, and the results had much to do with the eventual course of postrevolutionary Mexico.

Vasconcelos commissioned Rivera to paint the walls of the Ministry of Education Building and the National Palace. His commissions gave a host of artists their first chance, and his influence in spreading their fame was profound. As minister of education Vasconcelos acted as a sort of cultural czar. He appointed and dispatched cultural missions to other countries; he brought important cultural figures into Mexico from throughout the Hispanic world. Gabriela Mistral, Valle Inclán, and Henríquez Ureña fertilized the Mexican literary scene while Mexicans carried their own story abroad.

In this era Antonio Caso began to teach at the revived University of Mexico; Mexican archeologists like his brother Alfonso Caso were starting important excavations in which the ancient center of Monte Albán was unearthed in Oaxaca; poets were publishing everywhere. Much of the activity was second-rate. Some of the energy and enthusiasm, particularly of younger artists, was continually siphoned off into protest and politics, but this was endemic in the Hispanic milieu. It did not interfere with art, but it did interfere considerably with higher education, as universities became more centers of agitation than of genuine research or scholarly endeavor. This was perhaps inevitable in Mexico as in other nations, since the government affirmed the principle of autonomy in the university.

Cultural advances did not extend much beyond the fields of mural painting and secular education. "Corridos," or popular songs, continued to carry much of the national culture in the absence of literacy. Music, whether ranchero or Amerindian in inspiration, such as the Yucatec song "Las Golondrinas," was lively and folkloric, but hardly high art. The revolution and Mexican nativism found no expression, then or later, through the written word. Mexican literature and poetry was Spanish in language and Hispanic in content. Mexicans novels were indistinguishable, except for setting, from similar works in a dozen Hispanic nations.

Vasconcelos resigned from the government in opposition to Obregón's selection of Calles as his successor. By 1924 his administrative work could be carried on by lesser men, and the fame of Mexican muralists was already established. Vasconcelos, who was always deeply involved in esthetics, continued to grow more and more appalled at the excesses of the Revolutionary parvenus who surrounded Calles, and this led him into full-scale opposition in 1929. Perhaps fortunately for Mexico, he did not become a typical, ephemeral Hispanic poet-president, and ended his days as a librarian, writing his memoirs.

The elusive spirit he had given Mexican culture faded, except in education. Vasconcelos attacked the Mexican problem of identity, by identifying the emerging *mestizo* as a new, "cosmic race"—part of a *mestizo* America that ran from the Rio Bravo to the tip of South America. He wrote the motto for the National University: "Through my race the spirit will speak." But somehow, the Amerindian spirit failed to speak through the Hispanic written word, and the new cosmic race had small impact on the world. The concept itself was a sort of failed racism, and as he grew older Vasconcelos retreated more and more into Hispanic culture and civilization, finding comfort in sources beyond the myths of racial origin. Widely quoted, he left the Mexican soul still bifurcated, and not quite sure whether its Amerindian blood, or its Spanish language and civilization were dominant.

The Mexican muralists had their days of glory in the 1920s; they expressed a national feeling no other media could. However, the inevitable in art soon happened: mural painting stultified. The fury and idealism of the founders could not be sustained across a generation, and technically superior imitators were unable to catch the spirit of the revolution. Within a few years the Mexican muralists were no longer a movement but a sort of establishment.

Like the ancient Amerindian sculptors who copied stagnant forms, the muralists that followed began endlessly repeating folk murals that more and more resembled the last stages of Mexic friezework on temple walls. Their work had form and color but had lost its meaning.

By 1933 both the cultural renascence and the ideals of the revolution seemed to be faltering. There was not so much a failure of nerve as a weariness and self-satisfaction in the revolutionary generation. The leadership of the revolution, those that survived the internecine wars, had secured most of their personal aspirations: wealth, respect, and power. Here the revolution might have stagnated completely, had not the Obregón-

Calles years, proceeding very slowly, given the revolution an institutional form.

By 1933 the revolution had mainly benefitted the revolutionary family. As a society Mexico was still backward and impoverished and brutalized. The peasants earned almost no money wages, and two million rural families yet lacked land. The urban workers had made very few real gains. The bureaucracy, and especially the missionary schoolteachers, were miserably paid. Illiteracy, while declining, was a high fifty-nine percent. The old society had been uprooted, but the new one had not yet come about. The revolution had not translated its new institutions into broad social gains. Between 1920 and 1934 stability was maintained only by the willingness of an exhausted people to bear suffering and the determination of the rulers to keep order.

However, by the 1930s a newer generation was coming into the bureaucracy and government via the schools. These were men who barely remembered the revolution, and they tended to see the events of 1910 to 1917 as only a first step, not a culmination. They were poor and powerless; they had grown up with the problems of society and were deeply impatient and dissatisfied with everything done to date. They had enjoyed more fundamental freedoms than any Mexican generation; they were not, like the older veterans of bad times, largely desensitized. They did not look on violence and arbitrary police power as normal, or the corruption of government as ineradicable in the scheme of things. Much of this younger group felt an immense urge to revitalize the government, and to press on with the goals of the revolution, especially land reform.

Because the younger generation had been better educated than the revolutionaries of 1917 in Vasconcelos' schools, it tended to be more susceptible to ideas and ideologies. Marxism, which before 1920 had only a foreign following in Mexico, was very much in vogue in these years; while few of the newer lawyers, doctors, and engineers were communist-oriented, most were influenced by Marxist economics, and many by Spanish Republican ideas. Thus as a group the younger men were more dogmatic and doctrinaire than their elders, and more statist and collectivist in their outlooks. They were also more optimistic. Some carried optimism too far: there were intellectuals who believed that with literacy the Mexican masses would become a reading public, though this had not happened anywhere in the world. The strength of this generation came from its youth, idealism, and energy; its weakness was a frequent reliance on foreign ideas. Peculiarly, the same men who were most offended by foreign economic influence in Mexico were often those most susceptible to foreign notions.

In broadening the base of the revolutionary family through the party Calles had opened the revolutionary ranks to upcoming men who had played no part before 1920. As young engineers and lawyers came into the bureaucracy they entered the ruling party, and their ferments could not help but be felt. Calles, the real ruler of Mexico in 1933, was a keen politician as well as a brutal dictator. He sensed the deepening dissatisfaction in the PNR; he knew it could be transmitted to the masses; and he realized that at least an appearance must be made that the country was still on the march.

Calles called a major conference and delivered a monologue to the men regulating Mexico. Like most of his speeches, it was deliberately enigmatic, but he left a deep impression that the Jefe Máximo was personally disappointed in what was being done. He demanded fresh approaches, and suggested that the PNR, at its 1933 convention, explore the possibilities of adopting a Six-Year Plan. The suggestion pleased the younger leaders who had become fascinated with the five-year plans of Soviet Russia; it did not alarm the older satraps who suspected this was just another popular gambit of the Jefe Máximo. Here the conservatives among the revolutionary family badly miscalculated—but so did Calles himself.

The Six-Year Plan was drawn up at the party congress that met in December, 1933 to nominate the official candidate for president. It proved to be a worthless mishmash—but other results of this convention marked a major turning point for the revolution. Calles dictated the man to be tapped for the highest office: General Lázaro Cárdenas, a young austere, and tight-lipped *mestizo* from Michoacán.

Cárdenas had qualities to please all camps. He had joined the old revolution at the age of twenty in 1915; he had had an impeccable military career; and he had served ably as governor of his state. He was also one of the rarest birds of the revolution, a puritanical, dourly honest Tarasca weaver's grandson who refused to use office to get rich. Sent to the Tampico oil fields to restore order during a tumultuous strike, Cárdenas had sent back the customary bribe from the oil companies, in this case a Packard motor car. He created legends by driving a Dodge, which he paid for on time at one hundred pesos per month. In the oil fields General Cárdenas was deeply affronted by the squalor of the workers, and especially by the contrast between the living standards of foreign managers and technicians and Mexican employees, between families in neat bungalows surrounded by servants and roustabouts in waterless shacks. He had expressed reformist sympathies which made him popular with the PNR's younger left wing. But he also owed much to Calles, and Calles fully believed that Cárdenas would make an excellent figurehead for another six years of the old politics.

Two candidates ran against Cárdenas and PNR in 1934, one an anticallista, the other a communist. Neither had any chance. Cárdenas, however, aroused much comment by touring Mexico as though he were engaged in a bitter contest. He traveled twenty-five thousand kilometers, some sixteen thousand miles on every means of transportation from horse to airplane. Few people actually understood that Cárdenas was actually forming a power base. He went everywhere, talked to important and little men, found out what was on their minds, and made them promises.

He took office in November 1934. He said nothing when he found his cabinet had already been selected by Calles; it included the notorious Governor Garrido Canabal of Tabasco state, a debauchee as different from Lázaro Cárdenas as could be found among the revolutionary family. In office, Cárdenas continued to move about the country, listening gravely and politely to peasants and workers, who were tremendously impressed with his humble manner; it was traditional for Mexican presidents, like Mexican bishops, to carry themselves aloof. He offered seeds and clinics to the peasantry, public works to the local officials. He explained his trips by the need to know the people's problems. The secretariat at the National Palace postponed official engagements by saying that "el Presidente is off teaching the Indians how to grow lettuce." The president was actually finding new allies.

His first moves in office reflected his temperament more than his politics. Cárdenas moved out of the Chapultepec Palace, the seat of Mexico's rulers since Maximilian, and made the castle over into the present museum of Mexican history. He did not smoke, drink, or gamble, and he closed down gambling hells and whorehouses, many of which belonged to Calles' cronies. This amused Calles, who expected this sort of thing. He was not amused, however, when the new president spoke out forcefully on the side of workers during a strike—accusing the employers and the unions of corruption and collusion against the workers' interests, and promising government intervention, and also promising to resume the wholesale distribution of hacienda lands.

Cárdenas became a consummate politician, who understood the postrevolutionary generation far better than men who had grown to maturity under Díaz. He was the first president to sense the profound changes in Mexican thinking that had come about toward the close of the 1920s, and to grasp the real meaning of Obregón's and Calles' normalizations. He understood the full institutional powers of the party and the presidency in a way that even their founders never did. After Obregón and Calles had destroyed the political power of the Church and the military, and brought the agrarians and socialists into the revolutionary party, it was no longer necessary for Mexico to have a dictator. The president was made allpowerful institutionally by the constitution, and could begin to act as a king. Cárdenas was the first Mexican president of whom it could be said his office transformed him. The great change was not so much in the office, or in Cárdenas, as in Mexico. Like Franklin D. Roosevelt, Lázaro Cárdenas was able to enact sweeping changes by strictly legal means, without resort to police power, chicanery, or corruption. Calles, perhaps unwittingly as many historians assert, had supplied him the tools.

Cárdenas, an enormously controversial figure, was more leftist and statist than his predecessors, out of necessity. He also took friends where he was most liable to find them, among the more leftist and statist younger generation. Because of Cárdenas' agrarian program and his affinity for labor, Calles accused him of being a communist. However, he marked the fall of one Establishment and the rise of another, without violent revolution, and the evidence is that he was neither truly a leftist nor a revolutionary. He was fundamentally conservative in that he wanted to preserve and consolidate the 1917 revolution.

Calles, the Jefe Máximo, warned Cárdenas by stating to the press that Cárdenas' policies permitted too many strikes. The president replied that while labor troubles might cause temporary drops in production, they built a stronger society in the long run by assuring a fairer distribution of wealth. While the press battle absorbed capital comment, Cárdenas quietly checked on the loyalties of army commanders. He used his constitutional powers to remove, isolate, or demote any who appeared to be Calles' creatures. He organized huge cardenista rallies among workers and rural peasants. His complete control of the army officers corps and his mass support among the people quickly cowed the Mexican Congress. Calles had packed it and allowed it to operate as a free forum of debate, while essentially ignoring it. Cárdenas now began to manipulate it. When Calles went so far as to hint that the new President was treading the path of Ortiz Rubio, Cárdenas not only failed to resign, he dismissed all of Calles' cronies from his administration and appointed new men who were confirmed by the congress.

Calles was furious but helpless. The generals who might have helped him were supplanted by younger officers, graduates of the Colegio Militar loyal not to chiefs but to the government. Senators and deputies Calles had made shied away from him, seeking the side of power. Cárdenas made a great point of dismissing his secretary of agriculture, the ex-governor Garrido, the persecutor of Catholics, and dissolved his "Red Shirts." Cárdenas ended the unofficial persecution of the Church, replacing hostility with cool neutrality, and gained the support at one swoop of many Mexican Catholics.

The president brought back Portes Gil and charged him with purging the PNR of overt callistas. Other callistas were frozen out of governorships.

While politicians and the public waited for Calles to make trouble, the Jefe Máximo realized ruefully that he had been hoist by his own petard. He cried: "I am a slave to my own device: institutional government!"

Finally, in April 1936, Cárdenas deported Calles to Texas, where he died nine years later. Cárdenas also sent Luis Morones packing.

Cárdenas was now undisputed national *cacique*, and more, for he wielded constitutional, institutional, and political power for the first time in presidential history.

Cárdenas explained to the public that the revolution's loss of momentum had come from the failure of the ruling family and their intellectuals to keep in constant touch with the Mexican masses. It was well and good to have a tutelary regime, but the masses needed participation, and they expected continual processes of reform. He would retain the party, but it needed to be reorganized on even a broader basis than before. Therefore, the party would be reshaped into four "sectors": the army, the peasants, the industrial workers, and the bureaucracy, in which definition Cárdenas included much of the white-collar middle ranks engaged in private enterprise. These sectors or groupings most accurately represented the aspirations of the majority of Mexicans, according to the president, and they would dominate the revolutionary party, and through it, the government. The sectors, collectively, would select Mexican leadership, and such an alliance would be powerful enough to withstand all counterrevolutionary forces.

The landowner and the capitalist were pointedly excluded from a power base within the party.

To consolidate the agrarian or peasant sector of the party, Cárdenas organized the *Confederación Nacional de Campesinos*, whose power revived the agrarian movement. To give thrust and cohesion to the workers's sector, Cárdenas favored a labor organization that had given him stellar support during his ouster of the callistas: the *Confederación de Trabajadores Mexicanos*, the Federation of Mexican Workers, or CTM. It was headed by Vicente Lombardo Toledano, a Marxist of Italian extraction, who like most Mexican labor chieftains was an intellectual rather than a worker. The CNC and CTM were mass organizations whose membership was solidly behind Cárdenas emotionally and politically, and they formed the major part of his constituency.

Cárdenas, a son of the south, possessed a strong mystique for soil and peasants. A Sonoran *mestizo* could not identify with Indians, but a president with Tarasca blood could. The dominant theory in Mexican political circles was changing with the generations, and distaste and despair for the *indio* had been replaced with a belief that the solution to the agrarian problem lay in collective farming, which was nothing more than a return to the old *ejidos* in modern guise. Cárdenas' education and circle of friends turned him strongly toward collectivism in agriculture.

He led a new attack on the remaining haciendas with a massive program of legal expropriations, diametrically changing the policy of the 1920s. He brought the CNC into the process of land seizure and redistribution, whicn created chaotic conditions in the rural areas. Hordes of landless campesinos joined with agrarian leaders, political agitators, and government officials in arbitrarily seizing large properties.

The agrarians naturally went for the best fields and the improved, irrigated, and productive farms. Despite the law which stated a landowner retained the right to select which property, within limits, he wanted to keep, many haciendas were stripped of everything. In some localities, agrarian officials waited until the landowner's crops were ready to harvest, then seized the fields. Cárdenas had intended a sort of participatory democracy in bringing the peasants themselves into the act of land reform, but he very nearly created chaos in the countryside. However, in some regions landowners were able to postpone seizures indefinitely through bribery of officials or legal maneuvers, and in a few places *hacendados* organized armed "White Guards" to battle the "Red" agrarian leaders and government land agents. In general, despite a continuing myth fostered by the Mexican government that the better lands were successfully reserved by the owners, the 1930s expropriations took mostly improved properties that were easy to cultivate and which were expected to show an immediate profit. The fact that agriculture was paralyzed and production dropped showed that something was wrong with either the theory or the application.

Cárdenas' program especially wreaked havoc on the henequen haciendas of Yucatán, the rice fields of Michoacán, the coffee plantations of Chiapas, and the sugar estates in Sinaloa. While there was little enthusiasm for cutting up the huge cattle *estancias* of the northern states—there were few peasants or *indios* in the deserts—the important cotton-growing complex around Torreón was also selected for government experimentation. A basic fallacy lay behind the seizure of large-scale plantations producing valuable export crops; the reformers confused these with the old, inefficient hacienda and its hordes of peons, each of whom worked an assigned plot of land. The Hispanic hacienda could be turned rather easily into an *ejido*, which was nothing more than a village surrounded by small family plots on which peasants grew their subsistence corn. But the *indio ejido* form of organization could not possibly be used for the production of sugar or cotton or coffee, or Yucatán's main source of revenue, sisal. While the large acreages devoted to these cash crops for export were called "haciendas" they were really large-scale plantations, whose operations were more an industrial process than farming as it was understood by the average peasant. The operations required planning, expertise, constant management, marketing connections, and much capital. The finished product, whether a ton of sugar or a cotton bale, represented a much greater investment than the worker's sweat that went into it. Actually, the Sinaloa sugar plantations and the Laguna district cotton farms and the southern coffee-growing operations were not seventeenth-century survivals; they were modern businesses, most of which had been built up by European immigrants in modern times. But the theory of the urban intellectuals who combined with the landless peasantry in an assault on these businesses was that the large property per se was an evil on the land. They were seized, and mills and machinery taken over with the soil.

This ran counter to all modern economics. It *was* seen that if plantation agriculture were destroyed for social purposes, there had to be some alternative form of organization to keep the exports flowing and the money returning, and this provided the great push toward cooperative or collective farming. The seized plantations were reorganized into government collectives in 1936, with the bureaucracy now providing the capital, planning, and management for their complex operations. This experimentation was forced by the more radical wing of the party. The CNC and CTM leadership did not regard collectivization as an experiment, however, but as a permanent solution to rural problems. Collectives in 1936 were intellectually very much in fashion.

Using a strike by the cotton plantation employees in the Laguna region of Torreón as an excuse, Cárdenas' government confiscated six hundred thousand acres from landowners and organized a federal cooperative or collective farm. This was a very different kind of *ejido*. The peasant here was not given a *patrimonio*; the government retained the land, while the peasant became a worker who was expected to share in the common labor, decisions, and profits.

This was carried out at a time when the government already had accurate statistics supporting the Sonorans' biases against *ejidos*. By the mid-1930s, the earlier-established *ejidos* were in serious trouble, for demographic growth was making a mockery of progress. Families on the *ejidos* grew against a fixed amount of soil, constantly reducing the amount of land that could be allotted to each farmer. The average *ejido* family now got less than ten acres. Only a few *ejidatarios* had more than twenty-five acres, and thirteen percent worked barely more than two acres—hardly enough for mere subsistence under the primitive methods used. The basic problem was insoluble, for the rural population in the twentieth century grew faster than *ejidos* could be expanded. Many men in government, dragging their feet on expropriations and the formation of new *ejidos*, recognized the basic trouble—only about seven percent of Mexican soil was arable as it stood, and if every hectare in the Republic were confiscated and redistributed, there would still be more people than the land could absorb.

While the elements that Cárdenas raised to dominance in government rejected these facts as negativism, there was considerable, vocal resistance to the massive confiscations and reorganizations into collectives, now not from *hacendados* but from the rancheros, the small independent farmers and their spokesmen. Luis Cabrera, author of the first land reform law, cried out that the regime was undermining everything the original agrarians had fought for in the revolution—especially the ideal of dignity for the peasant on his own soil. He stated that instead of making the peasant a free man on his own farm, the government cooperatives or collectives were merely creating a new class of peons, bossed by the bureaucracy and the Ejidal Bank in place of the old *hacendados* and *mayordomos*. Prominent cardenistas such as Florencio Palomo Valencia, the governor of Yucatán, also began to have grave doubts about collectives, saying that the campesino wanted land, but the reorganization of the plantations in his region did not give him any sense of ownership. On the newer *ejidos* the peasant was assigned land which he could not bequeath or sell, and he could not even leave it until he had repaid his loan to the Ejidal Bank, which in practice he never did. The *ejidatarios* were thus becoming government serfs.

Cárdenas was *not* a confirmed Marxist, but he was subject to enormous political pressures by his supporters, who were determined to take over the profitable plantations. The millions of unemployed, underemployed, and landless rural people, whose hopes and aspirations had been delayed so long, created danger for the party. The Marxist-influenced intellectual leadership insisted on confiscations and collectivizations as articles of faith. There is evidence that Cárdenas did not quite share this faith, but he continued land reform for political, rather than economic or social reasons.

Between 1934 and 1940 the Cárdenas government expropriated and distributed forty-five million acres among 750,000 rural families. Out of some eighteen thousand *ejidos* formed, five hundred were organized as collectives. This turned over about one-fifth of the arable land in Mexico to *ejidos*, though it left two-fifths still in the hands of large owners, and the remainder to smallholders. The large plantation in this period lost even the protection of the laws, but in spite of this, and despite popular opinion, many survived.

The *ejidos*, whether old-style *indio* communities or new collectives, proved to be a triumph of ideology and political pressure over experience and reality. The peasantry and the collective workers could not capitalize or manage their properties. The government tried to offset this through the Ejidal Bank, which made federal loans, and a rapidly expanding *ejidal* bureaucracy, which included local farm managers and a bewildering maze of technical experts such as agricultural and hydraulic engineers, agronomists, and financial and marketing executives. The trouble was that the new agrarian bureaucracy knew very little about profitable farming or marketing. The whole process became fantastically bureaucratized and soon developed a stifling hierarchy, which was supposed to help the peasant or worker, but in reality boxed him in and ruled his life as he had never been regulated before.

The "comisarios" or local managers, appointed by the federal government, became petty *caciques* who told the workers what to do daily. The technical experts wrapped them up in complex, grandiose plans. The bank functionaries turned into genuine petty tyrants from Torreón to Yucatán; since they controlled the flow of capital, they told the *ejidos* what and when to plant, and they set the prices and profits the *ejidatarios* received. The class system in the countryside did not disappear in a society of free peasants: white-collar bureaucrats from the Mexican middle class merely took over the tutelage of the *indios* and *peones.*

This enormous bureaucratization, so normal to the Mexican ethos, both increased inefficiency and made the *ejidal* system impervious to effective reform. The agrarian bureaucracy quickly formed a special interest group and like all bureaucracies it was determined to perpetuate itself. It was a central part of government, entrenched in the ruling party, and it now met any suggestions for reform of itself with loud and, in Mexico, paralyzing accusations that the reformers showed reactionary or counterrevolutionary tendencies. By 1940, all objective evidence showed the system was not working—but it had become a sacred cow in governmental and intellectual circles.

The economic failure of the *ejidal* system is revealed by the best available statistics for 1940. One quarter of the population, five million Mexicans, lived on *ejidos,* planting forty-seven percent of the croplands and using twenty-four percent of the pasturage. The *ejido* population comprised forty-two percent of all Mexicans employed in agriculture. But the *ejidatarios* produced only nineteen percent—at best—of the cattle, fowl, and honey, and their relative production of staple crops like corn and above all, cash crops for export, was so disastrously low that Cárdenas' administration deliberately concealed the figures by refusing to calculate them. Four-fifths of all agricultural production came from private farms and ranches. The plantations still produced almost all valuable crops for export, and Mexico was actually being fed by that forgotten hero, the small independent operator or ranchero.

Cárdenas' land reforms were an economic failure, and these early statistics—understood if not released—soured future regimes against further confiscations. But the program aroused vast political enthusiasm and must be accounted a political success. It may even have prevented violence, because even in 1940 half of the rural population was still employed as day laborers, owning no soil. The realists in government knew that the *ejidos* were self-defeating, because their formation cut production, but they had to balance this against the fact that they were immensely popular politically. The *ejido* had already become a permanent, crippling feature of the agrarian scene. On the old *ejidos* peasants struggled with small plots, harassed by visiting bureaucrats who lived off them, rarely rising above the subsistence level anywhere.

The great collective experiments failed. The huge cotton cooperative at Torreón and the sisal plantations in Yucatán slowly but surely collapsed from a combination of managerial inefficiency and falling commodity prices. Unlike private businesses, the sociology of collectives could not be readjusted to changing market conditions. In the south the peasantry became mired in serfdom to the federal bankers, while in the north the *ejidatarios* gradually gave up and moved away. In the 1960s the government finally ended the experiment at Torreón, transporting the survivors on the land to the far south to pursue a newer dream: the settlement of virgin tropic territories. The inspiration for this move, which aroused new enthusiasm in the bureaucracy, came like the old ideas, from abroad.

None of the dominant cardenistas were farmers, but their mystique of soil and peasants had made them dogmatic on the agrarian question. The same intellectuals and politicians knew even less about business and industry, but fortunately for the development of Mexico they were far less sure of themselves in these areas, and they avoided permanent disaster.

Under Limantour the government had begun to buy control of the foreign-owned rail system, but during the revolution payments stopped and the system had slowly degenerated into obsolescence, while claims and counterclaims plagued every administration. In June 1937, Cárdenas nationalized the major rail lines and consolidated their debts into the national debt, turning the management of the lines over to government officials.

Unlike the *ejidatarios*, the rail unions were organized and vocal, and thus they could put up a concentrated opposition to the bureaucracy. By 1938 unions and management were completely at odds. Facing a breakdown, Cárdenas experimented according to the prevailing prejudices of his worker-oriented administration: he turned the running of the railroads over to a board composed of seven union leaders.

This gave the union management immense problems which nobody had foreseen. First, there was the problem of bringing order and efficiency to a decaying industry by a board which was split by personal rivalries. Worse, the labor leaders were caught up in problems of rationale and doctrinal position, because as "management," they had to take a broader view than merely representing the rail workers' desires and positions. These were peculiarly acute, because the workers, led by Lombardo Toledano, were Marxist-oriented. Lombardo Toledano realized that the lines were bankrupt and had to be restored by revenues, and therefore all new revenues could not go to meeting workers' demands for wages. If he behaved irresponsibly—that is, did not follow the laws of bourgeois economy—he might ruin the lines and hurt the workers themselves as well as the nation. Lombardo and his communists could not solve this basic problem of image and rationale. They rejected Trotsky's advice that they use the railroads as a base to seize national power, because Lombardo and the Communist Party knew they were not ready to assume power.

Another labor leader, Rodrigo García Treviño, wrote that since Mexico was basically a capitalist society, even an industry run by Marxists had to follow the basic laws of that society—in other words, a union management had to behave like any other management, disciplining workers and assuring profits, though he hoped it could be sympathetic both to workers and the public interest.

However, the union leaders were paralyzed by their responsibilities; they neither improved service nor met workers' increased expectations. Cárdenas soon realized that his progressive industrial experiment had failed. It was even a political failure, and when he turned the roads back to a government corporation even the unions were glad to be rid of their role. The unions retained only a minor consultant role in the new management. Cárdenas did not believe in the principle of either state or labor control of industries, though he was a nationalist with advanced leanings toward social justice; he had experimented and learned from experience.

The rails were reorganized on a purely commercial basis, which eventually allowed the lines to modernize, pay off all debts, and finally return a profit to the national treasury. The new state railways corporation did not represent any known theories of socialism, but it was a peculiarly Mexican form of state capitalism, which operated vis-à-vis workers and the public almost exactly like a private industrial bureaucracy.

The lesson learned through the railroad experiment and through several other nationalizations carried out at the same time was extremely valuable. Cárdenas saw that nationalization alone could not guarantee the vast social programs promised under Article 23 and for which many Mexicans kept clamoring. In every case where an industry had been turned over to worker management, the results were disastrous. The union chiefs were psychologically incapable of management, for they could not accept the fact that profits were necessary for recapitalization, and that only small portions of profits could be used to meet current pay demands. By 1938 Cárdenas was listening only to the orthodox economic advisors in the Mexican government, and there were no more nationalizations or experiments for the sake of social goals alone.

The nationalization for which Cárdenas will always be remembered, the seizure of the oil industry, came about almost by accident.

From his experiences as garrison commander at Tampico, Cárdenas had remained hostile to the British and North American oil interests, for he believed their existence and policies demeaned Mexican workers and the Mexican nation. But he had no expectation of forcing these companies from Mexico, and he did not want trouble with foreign governments. Mexican-United States relations had steadily improved, for the Morrow era of de facto non-intervention in Mexico was followed by the Roosevelt Administration's promulgation of the noninterventionist Good Neighbor Policy. Cárdenas approved the trend and did not want to disturb things. Despite continual agitation by his leftist advisors, he made no move to upset the sub rosa agreements made by Obregón and Calles with the North American oil companies and the British Royal Dutch Shell.

However, a crisis was precipitated by labor troubles in the oil fields. In 1936 the Petroleum Workers Syndicate, affiliated to Lombardo Toledano's Marxist CTM made demands on the companies which included the social benefits guaranteed by the Mexican Constitution as well as higher pay. The companies were willing to negotiate, but a sticking point was the union's demand for access to the companies' confidential books. In May 1937, negotiations were deadlocked, and the Syndicate struck the fields.

The law and the principles under which the Mexican government ran required federal intervention. Cárdenas therefore officially declared the strike an "economic conflict" as defined in the constitution and invoked compulsory arbitration. The clause had never before been applied to disputes involving foreign companies; both Obregón and Calles had felt it wiser simply to break up labor troubles in the oil fields with federal troops. Cárdenas appointed the court, and not surprisingly the commissioners' report heavily favored the Syndicate. Two parts of the report revealed facts that had long been obvious, but which were explosive when first brought to the attention of educated Mexicans: the foreign companies made higher profits in Mexico than anywhere else in the world, and they paid Mexican workers far less than workers in their own countries. Significantly, all shades of Mexican opinion ranging from radical to conservative, and including the opinion of native employers who paid their own workers far less than in the oil fields, strongly backed the arbiters' recommendations that union demands be met. The dispute had taken on nationalistic overtones.

The oil companies were ordered to raise workers' pay by twenty-seven percent and meet other conditions. They appealed to the Supreme Court, arguing that the raises were too expensive and that the intrusion of unions into management affairs was intolerable. The whole question rapidly became a cause célèbre throughout politicized Mexico, for the Cárdenas regime followed the old carranzista policy of *yanqui*-baiting in public pronouncements to the press. Under extreme pressure, and also under Article

23, the Court had no choice but to find against the companies. They handed down the decision March 1, 1938, giving the oil interests one week to comply.

Beaten, the companies agreed among themselves to compromise. The settlement was unpalatable psychologically, but there was no question that they could live profitably with it. In discussions with Cárdenas' representatives the companies accepted virtually all the arbiter's orders on condition that they were guaranteed that the Syndicate would not be allowed to be so encouraged by success that it would make new demands. Cárdenas had won a victory, both for his government and for Mexicans, and he was ready to give the same private, binding assurances that former presidents had given. But now, the corporate management of the oil interests, who had learned absolutely nothing about how delicately political deals had to be made in Mexico, made an incredible blunder, by demanding that Cárdenas put the deal in writing.

This was politically impossible, and Cárdenas also took it as a personal insult from obtuse Anglo-Saxons. From being prepared to bludgeon CTM and the Syndicate into the compromise, he exploded full circle into wounded dignity and fury. When the whole story leaked out, all official Mexico reacted the same way. The regime was divided between progressives and conservatives where social and economic policy was concerned, but all the men in the halls of power now showed the reaction of people who could brook no more lacerations, even unintentional, of their long-battered sense of pride and national dignity.

On March 15 Cárdenas broadcast to the nation that he had nationalized all foreign oil industries on the grounds of flagrant disrespect for Mexican law.

This was an act of almost desperate improvisation by a politician whose official family had been infuriated. It was a dangerous step, for no one had thought of the reaction of the British and North American governments, or even if the Mexicans could operate the oil fields.

The companies believed this was a bluff, because management agreed that it would be impossible for Mexicans to operate the industry and especially, sell the oil abroad in a largely-controlled market. They also firmly believed that their governments would intervene, putting intolerable pressure on Mexico. Regarding the presidential decree a mere move in a poker game, they countered by announcing readiness to pay the wage increases. But Cárdenas, backed into a cul-de-sac by Mexican emotion, signed the expropriation decree on March 18, 1938—an unprecedented move then anywhere in the world, where great powers and their overseas interests were concerned.

Cárdenas explained to the people that nothing less than national sovereignty was now at stake: either the president of the Republic ruled, or he did not. He enflamed public opinion effectively, as only the opinion of an unsure and long-humiliated people could be aroused, by reiterating the history of exemptions and privileges long granted foreigners, the selfishness of the oil companies in refusing to reinvest profits in Mexico; their use of bribery, violence, and crime in controlling local government and labor in the oil fields; and especially the companies' humiliating discrimination between their own nationals and Mexicans in pay, benefits, and promotions. In complete fairness, the oil companies had generally operated only as most industries had operated for a hundred years in Mexico, including domestic concerns. The great difference, which the oil managers did not realize, was that the world and Mexico had changed with this generation, and things would never be the same.

The companies were thrown back on their home governments. They immediately began a campaign to vilify Cárdenas personally and Mexicans generally as incapable, communistic, and untrustworthy. They made marketing agreements that boycotted Mexican oil. Unhappily for them, however, in the world of 1938 the United States and British governments were not prepared to commit themselves to a united front. The British were for a hard line. Washington, caught up in the much-declared Good Neighbor Policy, mainly sought a peaceful way out of the eternal oil dilemma. Mexican oil production was no longer vital to the world, because vast new reserves had been founded and exploited elsewhere; the policy of the North American government was to accept Mexico's right to nationalize, so long as payment was made for expropriation. The value of Mexican reserves held under concession was excluded from any future settlement.

In the controversy, the directors of Royal Dutch Shell had invariably been the most intransigent, and their feelings were reflected at Whitehall. The British diplomatic note to Mexico accepted the right of Mexico to nationalize, but impugned the entire process of Mexican justice and law—which was of course completely impugnable under Anglo-Saxon concepts and principles. The British demanded immediate restitution. The tone of the note was acid and contemptuous. It backed the Mexicans into a new corner: Eduardo Hay, the Anglophile Mexican foreign minister, who was himself of English descent, was forced to sever diplomatic relations.

What might have happened to Cárdenas if the United States had taken the same line and been prepared to retaliate with full economic pressure against Mexico is moot; Washington was not ready to do so. Indignation and bad relations and feelings ran high on each side, and the Mexicans were in fact extremely apprehensive at high levels. However, Washington failed to retaliate at all, only entering negotiations on the question of compensation. This guaranteed that the conflict would eventually be resolved in Mexico's favor, though the process took years. In 1942, under

Ávila Camacho, Mexico agreed to pay the North American oil interests twenty-four million dollars, plus interest, which amounted to a settlement of about ten centavos on the peso. One company, Sinclair, settled privately for eight and one-half million. The British-Dutch interests came out better, due primarily to the stern line taken by government. Relations were not resumed until 1941, and after the conclusion of the second World War Mexico paid the British more than eighty million dollars.

The rights and wrongs in this whole, dirty business are like the rights and wrongs that cause most international conflicts; they are hard to grasp without the confusions of nationalism, emotion, or ideology. Cárdenas' position was grounded in Mexican law and social policy. It was blackened by Mexican xenophobia and a type of political expediency on his part that amounted to blackmail. Once his government came in on the side of the unions, there was no hope for an impartial review or settlement; sociopolitical arguments had to prevail. But the companies were guilty of contempt for Mexico and Mexicans, of careless exploitation, and of indifference to the poverty of Mexican employees. They were stupid in their negotiations, and the stupidity was punished. If there was any lesson, it was that the nineteenth century era of exploitation of Mexican resources was finally dead.

The oil controversy and its outcome was an unmitigated triumph for Lazaro Cárdenas and for Mexico. Cárdenas had turned a labor dispute into a test of national sovereignty, and the Mexican response was overwhelming. Mexicans considered the expropriations a new declaration of independence, this time economically. Men and women marched past the National Palace for hours, saluting the president who stood beneath the church bell of Dolores, a newer Hidalgo. When Cárdenas called for contributions to help pay off the compensation to the oil companies, old porfiristas donated pesos and gold rings; peasants tried to present chickens; even the Mexican Church donated some of its hidden religious treasures. All this, much remarked in Mexico, provided none of the millions needed; the congress had to pick up the debt, and ironically, no little of it was paid off through generous North American credits and loans. But the country had found an emotional unity as never before, and Lázaro Cárdenas had established for all time the image of a great president.

This unity and power aided Cárdenas tremendously in what had become very difficult times. The depression lingered; agriculture was failing; labor was restive everywhere, partly because of the encouraging policies of the government. Cárdenas reorganized the PNR in 1938, renaming it the *Partido de la Revolución Mexicana,* or PRM. The army, the agrarians, the workers were retained as sectors, but the role of the middle ranks was increased. The role of the army was declining, but the army was still considered to be a threat unless it were favored and mollified. How small a threat it actually was was shown in May 1938, when the right-wing general Saturnino Cedillo revolted at San Luis Potósi.

None of the professional military joined Cedillo; even the Church had learned its lesson and avoided him, though he professed to defend Catholic rights. Cedillo was executed. His pronunciamento was notable for only one fact—it was to be the last coup attempted by a military man in modern Mexico. The army now obeyed the president, whoever he might be or however his regime might be constituted.

The situation of the newly acquired oil industry was precarious. Mexico had neither technicians nor tankers; there was an international boycott instigated by the great companies, and legal action was threatened against Mexican oil imports in areas where Royal Dutch Shell and the North American combines operated. Cárdenas organized a new autonomous company or government corporation, called *Petróleos Mexicanos*, along the lines used in the railway industry. Here experience prevailed; there was no question of turning the oil industry over to the workers.

The early record of PEMEX was far from brilliant. The nationalized industry was plagued by a lack of management skills, markets, transportation, inevitable political bureaucracy, and the irresponsibility of the Syndicate which had precipitated the expropriation, which encouraged worker incompetence and waste. For eight years, production did not regain the level of 1937. PEMEX did succeed in renting tankers and selling oil in the few markets beyond the reach of the great international oil corporations, principally Fascist Italy and Nazi Germany. The pragmatism, and desperation, of Cárdenas was shown by the fact that while he supplied the Spanish Republicans with arms during their civil war and allowed fifty thousand Republican refugees to enter Mexico, he furnished Fascist forces petroleum to fuel the planes that bombed Guernica. The outbreak of the Second World War ended the international pressures and boycotts against PEMEX. The Allies needed petroleum where they could get it, and the United States government particularly wanted to secure Mexico as a source of raw materials. The United States actively assisted in making PEMEX successful in the war years, with parts, advice, and technical assistance as well as credits to the Mexican government. By the war's end there was little question that PEMEX was to be a resounding success. In the 1950s the organization grew into a giant power complex that supplied modern Mexico with nine-tenths of all her natural gas, electric power, gasolines, and diesel fuel, supplying cities, factories, transportation nets, and farms at a reasonable rate, capitalizing itself for constant expansion, and still providing surpluses for the treasury. PEMEX was not the most efficient corporation in the world; as a government organization it was plagued by bureaucracy and featherbedding among its sixty thousand employees, but it was also far from the worst.

Perhaps as important in the long run as PEMEX's fueling of the Mexican economy was the corporation's service as a training ground for Mexican executives and technicians. PEMEX was the first large-scale employer of native engineers, technicians, white-collar workers, and industrial executives. PEMEX, like the rail corporation, served splendidly as a training ground for government, and also newer industry. The psychological lift was incalculable; Mexicans proved that an historically backward people could rapidly develop skills and expertise under favorable conditions. The "springs of the Devil," as one Mexican poet had called the oil fields, became springs of pride in accomplishment.

There was a final irony, also. The oil workers' Syndicate took credit for the nationalization. The Syndicate was Marxist-dominated, and for eight years after the nationalization the unions made the management task of the government corporation extremely difficult. Wages were quadrupled while productivity fell, and the union leadership could not refrain from applying political pressures. But it was one thing to enlist the government in a struggle against foreign management and quite another to hamstring the Mexican government itself. Eventually, under Miguel Alemán, politically-motivated strikes were declared illegal and the Marxist labor leaders were jailed. Gradually, Marxist influence was eradicated from the union leadership. PEMEX was born of ideology and politics but it soon became a business managed with relative efficiency as a business.

The Cárdenas era seemed revolutionary in many respects. Actually, it was a transitional age, in which the groundwork of the earlier chiefs had created opportunities for problem-solving on an institutional basis. Cárdenas' sweeping acts were all experiments, and whatever their successes and failures, they were valuable as historic guides.

It was shown that trade union leaders could not be trusted to run basic industries; the management role was inherently hostile to the labor-leadership role as both had developed in a fundamentally capitalistic ethos. The hasty farm collectivization proved that *ejidos* were not the answer to the agrarian problem. The ruling party learned a great deal from Cárdenas' failures, and the lessons were reflected in succeeding administrations.

In retrospect, it has been accepted that Cárdenas' nationalizations of rails and oil, the creation of a federal electric power commission, and the implementation of a social security system within the government corporations laid the basis for rapid industrialization. Statist measures were necessary; there was no private sector capable of taking over the railroads and refineries. Mexico's peculiar form of statist capitalism was correct for the situation and the times, however difficult it was to define. Mexico was experimenting, and in some ways even anticipating capitalist trends in more advanced nations.

Cárdenas was the only modern president genuinely committed to agrarian reform, but ironically his agrarian failures speeded up industrialization. The master plan of his administration was to turn Mexico into a nation of prosperous peasants and *ejidatarios*; instead, his agricultural failures and his unpremeditated thrust of the state into basic enterprise turned Mexico strongly toward industrial organization.

During this transition the old ghosts of militarism, latifundism, and dictatorship were fading from the Mexican scene. The new specter, agrarianism, was not exorcised completely, but it was halted by the cold light of statistical analysis. And the spirit of Mexico—for all Cárdenas' mystique of Amerindian blood and soil and all José Vasconcelos' return to the glories of Hispanic culture—was ceasing to speak through race and in the terms of the Spanish-Indian past. A new spirit was rising and finding expression in shining refineries, humming rails, and quiet discussions in paneled board rooms.

36

THE MAN
IN THE HIGH PALACE

*We leave the museum but not history, because history lives on
and through us. Our country endures, and we are the architects of
its grandeur. In the lessons of the past, we find strength to deal with
the present and reason to hope for the future. Let us meet whatever
responsibilities freedom puts upon us so that we may always deserve
the honor of being Mexicans.*
From an inscription at the exit of the National Museum of History
in Chapultepec Castle.

The quality that made the Mexican Revolution so different from others,
and so confusing, was its lack of dogmatism. The revolutionary constitution laid out broad social goals, and the Mexicans never diverged from
these fundamentally—but they pursued them in many different ways. Unlike the liberals of the nineteenth century or the twentieth-century Stalin-
ists, the Mexican revolutionaries refused to be bound by doctrine. The
governing groups might be said to have ruled more through sheer instinct
than clear planning. The revolution was never captured by its intellectuals;
it was inconsistent from decade to decade in minor things, in what became
almost a natural rhythm of surge and consolidation. For a people trained
in centuries of dogmatism, the twentieth-century Mexican elite was surprisingly pragmatic. Their goals of social justice, modernization, and nation-
building remained constant, but each succeeding government was able to
change emphasis and directions to meet changing needs or conditions.

The institutionalization of the revolution in a broad-spectrum political party and the principle of No Reelection permitted this natural rhythm full play. No Mexican president—and the president with his awesome powers was the heart of government—now could outlive his age. No ruler could fasten a lasting pattern on society or state in just six years, and since he had to surrender office he could not influence the governing elite beyond a short span. The ruling party, now the Party of the Mexican Revolution, or PRM, was proving a marvelous institution, for the first time providing an arena where crucial decisions could be made without recourse to enflaming public opinion and chancing blood in the streets.

The 1930s had been an era of predominant leftist sentiment, when intellectuals were Marxist-oriented, biased toward trade unionism, land confiscations, collectivism, and nationalizations, a time when the president sought the support of the masses and consorted with avowed communists. In 1940 the basic direction of the cardenistas had not changed. But when Cárdenas in 1938 opened up greater opportunities to the middle ranks in PRM, dominant opinion within the party changed. Power shifted behind the scenes to the business/bureaucratic sector, away from intellectuals, agrarians, and labor leaders. The rising forces were not reactionary, but they wanted a period of consolidation and social stabilization, a turn away from the tumults of the thirties.

Lázaro Cárdenas preferred a successor in his own image and pushed Francisco Múgica for the presidency. But a majority of the ranking bureaucrats, state governors, military chiefs, and representatives of the middle classes feared the radical Múgica would sacrifice economic progress to social reform, and that in the worsening international situation in 1940, he was not the man to lead Mexico.

They had strong arguments. The European war had caused serious economic repercussions, cutting off Mexican markets. Domestic ferment was also rising. Spanish Republican refugees agitated for anti-Fascist policies, while a smaller but very influential body of Germans, Italians, and Franco agents fomented the reverse. A new rightist movement had emerged in the old *cristero* strongholds in 1937. This was "sinarquismo" ("without anarchy"), a peculiarly Hispanic philosophy that was hostile to the concepts of the revolution and which espoused authoritarian Catholicism to an extent that embarrassed the now-neutral Church. The sinarquistas were strong in Guanajuato and the Bajío, and their spirit was perhaps best revealed by their doffing of hats at the invoking of Porfirio Díaz' name. They were not yet dangerous, but very disturbing to the new middle classes, who feared that a further push leftward would push the discredited Right to renewed violence.

Also, the more pragmatic Mexicans believed that in the war situation the nation should draw closer to the United States. The Franklin Roosevelt administration, and the 1938 oil crisis, had laid most of the old fears of intervention. The left wing of PRM, led by intellectuals and labor leaders like Lombardo Toledano, remained very hostile to the United States on ideological and emotional grounds; the more conservative elements tended to be pro-Axis. The moderate majority, however, saw either course as impractical, and in 1940 the moderates were in control of PRM, marking the maturing of a newer political generation.

The moderate majority was so evident at the party convention that Cárdenas reluctantly dropped his backing of Múgica in deference to party unity, and accepted his war minister, General Manuel Ávila Camacho, an officer from Puebla with a known Catholic background, as the official candidate. Cárdenas had prevailed over Calles in a personal power struggle by invoking popular and party support. This was different; the party now prevailed over a sitting president. Cárdenas accepted defeat, although he was still the single most influential individual in Mexico, and took on a new role graciously—that of making the party's choice acceptable if not entirely palatable to the agrarian groups and urban workers. Cárdenas also had immense prestige with the newly professional military. This was important, for the army now backed the party candidate over one of its own heros.

The agrarian and union leaders disliked Ávila Camacho, but they did not obstruct, partly from respect for Cárdenas, partly from realization that serious party strife might weaken PRM's custodianship of the country. Even losing factions within the party remained part of the national leadership, with all the advantages and perquisites of power.

A diverse but active opposition sprang up outside the party around a colorful general, Miguel Andrew Almazán, a revolutionary of the old school who had become a multimillionaire through public works contracts. Almazán drew conservatives, provincials, and many intellectuals and young people who believed that the destiny of Mexico should not be left to the dictates of party bosses. His supporters did not hope to win; they did hope to enflame the election to the point where the winning PRM candidate would not be able to govern.

The Party-government machine carried Ávila Camacho over Almazán in the election of 1940 by 2,265,199 to 128,574.

This was obvious fraud, because Almazán attracted far more than a hundred thousand supporters. When the results were announced, a huge crowd protested at the capital, and Almazán made vague hints of violence. However, Cárdenas faced the roaring crowds, alone and unarmed, and his cool dignity quieted the disorders. The presidency had become unassailable. Throughout Mexico, there was only sporadic unrest and shootings, while Almazán discreetly departed for Texas. Although marked by minor bloodshed, to date this was the most orderly and peaceful national election.

Abroad, it was publicized as a coming of age for Mexican political democracy. However, in Mexico it brought profound political disillusionment, particularly to the younger intelligentsia and the more left-leaning elements. It was widely understood that PRM would not surrender power through an honest election; it could only be overthrown by an armed insurrection that the army would oppose and the people generally would not support. 1940 was in fact a great watershed for political thought. Thousands of the educated, formerly wrapped up in political ideas and ideals, turned away from politics to cultural and economic activities, following the lead of José Vasconcelos earlier. The extreme Left continued a noisy but ineffective opposition, but the citizenry as a whole abandoned government to the party professionals.

Whatever damage this did to democratic ideals or concepts, it did permit the stability most Mexicans craved. And in the coming decades it allowed the government of a developing nation to carry out policies and programs that probably never could have been adopted in a highly-charged, emotional atmosphere of free political competition and effective challenge and debate.

Ávila Camacho's arrival at power did not cause a basic change in the policies of the revolution, but it brought about a shift in emphasis and style. Ávila had been a general, but with so low a profile he was jokingly called the "Unknown Soldier," a quiet, heavy-set military executive without charisma, a person of excellent, sober judgment rather than a crowd-pleaser. Born in 1897, he and especially the people he attracted around him represented the second revolutionary Establishment—not the old finger generals who enriched themselves with haciendas, or the missionary teachers and agrarianists, but soft-spoken, career-minded *mestizos* in business suits. Ávila Camacho was essentially a successful bureaucrat, and he was not peculiarly Mexican or *mestizo*. He was in the mainstream of that new class that defied description in nineteenth-century terms but was emerging to run the private and public bureaucracies in much of the modern Western world. His type could be found now in the upper echelons of General Foods and General Motors and in great law firms, where it had replaced old-style capitalists; such men staffed modern military machines and most modern governments. Whether these men were career soldiers, politicians, or business executives, they were rarely ideological. Their suite was expertise; they were technicians, or technocrats.

Mexicans were surprised when Ávila, influenced but never controlled by Cárdenas, took firm control—but the times were ripe for him. The government had been thoroughly bureaucratized; it had reached a stable plateau above anarchic *caciquismo*. The presidency under Cárdenas had become a newer crown, with the symbol outweighing the incumbent. Rule was articulated through a hierarchy of offices rather than by personalities. The ruler no longer had to be colorful, pistol-packing, or macho.

The new administration marked the final end of *norteño* dominance, as Ávila Camacho replaced the older politicians with a newer set of men from the cities of the central *meseta* or plateau. These men, the president's friends, relatives, associates, and compadres, tended to be less earthy, less "Mexican," more Catholic, and more bureaucratic. They were more statist than truly bourgeois, more pragmatic than ideologue. They were urban types, including few *indios*, peasants, or rancheros. At last two of these associates were outstanding executives: Ezequiel Padilla, who took the foreign ministry, and Miguel Alemán, minister of the interior. These two gave Mexico the most progressive foreign policy and the most orderly internal government in the nation's history.

Like its postrevolutionary predecessors, the new regime did not stand still; it made new breakthroughs while reforming old reforms. The cultural passion of Mexicans for regulation was now more a help than a hindrance, because in an era of experimentation and advance, policies had to be regularly amended or discarded. The Mexican government, which operated on a regulatory rather than a legislative basis, in fact could more easily change directions than that of the United States to fit changing times.

The policies and directions that emerged between 1940 and 1946 were to be the dominant guidelines for post-Cárdenas Mexico. No succeeding administration changed them in anything but degree.

In 1940 Mexico was threatened by a dangerous international situation; however, the internal government was stronger than it had ever been since independence. Ávila Camacho's administration moved rapidly to shore up relations with the United States. The old, almost hysterical fortress mentality was replaced by something resembling a responsible junior partnership. By 1941 Ávila Camacho and Padilla had settled all the pending, troublesome claims stemming from the revolution and expropriations, concluded an excellent commercial treaty, pegged the peso to the dollar, and secured generous credits for industrial development through the Export-Import Bank. The benefits went both ways, for the United States government was on the brink of war and was anxious to secure the Mexican front diplomatically. Further, the war made a vast demand on Mexican metals and petroleum.

Though probably most Mexican opinion favored remaining neutral after Pearl Harbor the government steered steadily toward a declaration of war against the Axis. This was a coolly pragmatic decision, made in an absence of patriotic enthusiasm or popular belligerency; even after two Mexican tankers were sunk by German submarines in the Gulf with loss of life, Ávila Camacho proceeded cautiously. There was no hatred of Germans or Italians in Mexico; in fact, the two small colonies were much admired; and few Mexicans could side emotionally in any foreign war with the "imperialist Anglo-Saxons." The May 14, 1942 declaration was an historic milestone, ending a century of Mexican isolation. An even more significant one, perhaps, was the visit of the president of the United States to Monterrey in April 1943—the first entry of a North American president on Mexican soil.

The war was overall of enormous benefit to Mexico. Prices for Mexican commodities boomed, and the absence of foreign imports allowed many small domestic consumer industries to be established. There was never any intention of sending the Mexican army of fifty-two thousand men overseas; only a volunteer air squadron went to the Pacific. However, the Mexican military was refurbished under United States Lend-Lease. In order to stimulate production for the war effort, the United States assisted Mexico with gouts of capital and thousands of technicians, spare parts, and technical expertise. Overall, Mexicans gained valuable knowledge from a leading technical society, and North American money fueled a rapid industrial boom.

This forced draft, of course, caused its own problems. Prices and profiteering rose sharply; Mexican manufacturers took advantage of war conditions to flood markets with shoddy products while shortages of food developed. The regime fought stolidly and overall, sensibly against conditions no government could handle anywhere. It reduced the money flow by paying off some of the national debt. It created the *Nacional Financiera* to control investment policy, and while the cost of living tripled, the inflation was beneficial to most classes except the agrarians. The urban industrial proletariat grew in numbers, and so did the middle classes; the percentage of Mexicans in the money economy swelled rapidly. At the end of the war, Mexico in one sense was filled with shoddy goods and corruption; in another, the economy and finances were healthier than they had ever been, as in the United States.

Mexico's World War II was fought entirely on the economic front; for the first time thousands of the educated elite took an interest in technics and economics. Men who would have taken up law and entered politics or the bureaucracy studied to become marketing experts or engineers. Even the press reflected the subtle change in national attitude, by recording various economic breakthroughs ahead of political events.

On the political front, wartime controls tended to consolidate the government's power to follow the agrarian policies it preferred. Ávila Camacho redistributed only seven million acres before halting the agrarian program, under a valid rationale of increasing the national food supply. The government, reading the statistics, now recognized that the private farm was vital. Medium-sized estates were guaranteed against future expropriation by being granted government titles, and it was these properties, operated by skilled farmers rather than primitive peasants, which were to provide virtually all the future advances in Mexican agriculture. New *ejidos* were authorized only if it could be proven they would immediately be productive. Emphasis was changed from giving peasants land to supplying private farms with irrigation and other techniques and services.

Miguel Alemán, the interior minister, had internal problems with sinarquistas in the Bajío and with some clergy, who did not attack the government but openly sympathized with the Axis enemy. The regime countered Catholic opposition by a repeal of the irritating clause under Article 3 of the constitution which specified "socialist education." To win rural support, new schools were erected everywhere, and in 1943 a social security system was promulgated to pacify the proletarians. Because of a lack of funds, however, the program was delayed until the 1950s.

The government had its greatest internal problems with organized labor. Under Cárdenas the unions had ridden high, and much of the leadership was communist. By 1940 Lombardo Toledano, the chief of CTM, was at the height of his power—but just as ideology had always hamstrung Lombardo's effective use of his power, ideology now destroyed him. During the 1939–1941 era of the Nazi-Soviet Non-Aggression Pact, the communist unions fought the government's anti-Axis policies and its efforts to draw closer to the United States. This was intolerable to the regime, and it also discredited the labor leaders' rationales when they abruptly changed after Germany invaded the USSR, because it showed them subservient to Russian influence. Lombardo Toledano lost all influence in the PRM, and was removed from the secretary-generalship of CTM. With his fall, the communist elements lost their leverage. Although the reopening of the Soviet embassy in 1942 provided a center for leftists of all persuasions, Marxist influence declined. The government, out of historic antipathy to all forms of intervention in Mexican affairs, kept Soviet activities under strict surveillance then and later.

The main thrust of Ávila Camacho's administration was toward conciliation and stability; therefore, it never used severe measures against the turbulent unions despite disturbances in the rail and petroleum industries during the war. However, Ávila Camacho tried to strike a balance; if he tolerated the Left, he conciliated the Right. He publicly declared himself "a believer" and removed overt anti-Catholicism from government circles. Certain educational doctrines stressing anticlericalism and socialism inserted by Cárdenas' education minister were expunged from the school books. The new minister, Torres Bodet, emphasized scholarship rather than doctrine. There was less fervor in the schools, but conversely a far better record against illiteracy was made than under Cárdenas. The government did not take the side of religion, business, or conservatism generally; the policy was one of strict neutrality.

Therefore, there were no startling innovations, but also no major national controversies or confrontations. The revolution was learning to self-adjust. Even the army was handled with exquisite skill. With the technical and material assistance of the United States, the army was thoroughly modernized and received new weapons—but it was not allowed to enlarge itself or increase its budget because there was a war.

The new atmosphere of conciliation and stability allowed the unthinkable to become normal in this new Mexico. Old enemies learned to tolerate each other, if not quite lie down in friendship. On the 16th September, 1942, Independence Day, Ávila Camacho appeared on the balcony of the National Palace with all six living former presidents. Before a cheering crowd that filled the gigantic Zócalo, the dictator Calles stood shoulder to shoulder with Adolfo de la Huerta, with whom he had been at pistol-point, and beside Lázaro Cárdenas, now commanding the army, who had exiled him. The badly-used Ortiz Rubio, Abelardo Rodríguez, and Portes Gil wept together as the current president of the Republic gave out the traditional grito: "*¡Mexicanos! Viva México!*"

The old, violent men were vanishing; a generation that never fought had moved to power. Prominent men were now well-educated people from middle-rank *mestizo* backgrounds. They had been reared in the principles of the Revolution, but they were far less nationalistic and ideological than the leaders of the 1930s. Markedly, the great interest of the new generation was in economics. The average educated Mexican now distrusted revolution for the sake of revolution and hated turmoil, because he had no old scores to settle, and the future was full of opportunities.

Foreign relations were newly stable, for no power threatened national sovereignty, and meanwhile, men in government had learned during the war that tremendous benefits accrued from keeping trust and confidence abroad, and above all, from cooperating with the United States.

All these things led to a stabilization and liberalization of politics beyond what had already been achieved. A new electoral law was enacted in 1945. It was not designed to loosen the hold of the ruling party, but it was hoped that it would increase the confidence of both Mexicans and foreigners in the government. Mexico now officially professed to be a democracy—a measure begun in the war years—and there had to be some improvement in the national political image.

The party was again reorganized and given a new name: *Partido Revolucionario Institucional*, the Party of the Institutional Revolution, or PRI. The military sector was dissolved (though this did not mean that the army lost all influence) and there were now three recognized sectors: the peasant-campesino groups, the urban workers, and the bureaucracy/middle class. It was made easier for citizens to vote and take part in party affairs

—but decisions were still worked out between the leaders of the sectors, in meetings between farm collective managers, rural politicians, union leaders, government executives, and businessmen, then submitted to the voters for ratification. This was not democracy. But it was an increasingly liberal form of authoritarianism. Dissent was tolerated both within and without the party, and on most issues the decision was only made after a genuine consensus had been arrived at. Critics of the party rule sometimes overlooked this, and the fact that the sector leadership was representative of the major interests of the total population. PRI shaped public opinion, but also followed it; otherwise, no dominant political party could have continued to direct the nation exclusively in almost a complete absence of serious protest.

Cárdenas was still very prominent in party ranks. He continued his role, patriotically dissuading restive generals and local politicos from obstructing government, and using his immense prestige with the common people to bolster the party's choices. Cárdenas was less and less in step with the age, and he disapproved of many party decisions, but his loyalty showed the strength of the consensus.

Stability was now being guaranteed by the fact that continuity in government was training leadership. It was now impossible, under party guidance, for an inexperienced man to arrive at high office in Mexico. The historic radical and violent character of the changes in governments had always prevented the establishment of a hierarchy of service. For a century soldiers had become generals overnight, and generals presidents. Men totally lacking executive experience had been thrown up as heads of government, disastrous in a country where there was no stable governmental infrastructure. By 1940 this had changed. The party controlled all important offices, and this was exerting a tremendous training and disciplining influence. All ambitious politicians in Mexico now had to work up through party ranks. And the party, from bitter experience, was suspicious of rampant ambition, violent personalisms, empire building, and demagoguery.

By 1946 it had been established that the top job, the presidency, must be filled by a screening process. The man who was tapped must have proven his worth and ability over a number of years in high-level, responsible assignments where his activities had been closely observed by the party hierarchy. Equally important, he had to represent a compromise between the dominant factions, ideologies, and personalities within the leadership. Only then could he be put before the people, to be ratified as ruler of the country.

The president was a monarch; his powers vastly exceeded those of the leaders of democratic societies, or those like the Anglo-Saxon, with traditions of the rule of law. His congress was like the old Spanish parliament;

it found ways and means to provide what the sovereign desired. The congress had no powers to oppose or impede the president. The judiciary lacked a power of review, both of legislation or acts of the executive. The president was the source of all power and legitimacy throughout the entire hierarchy, like the former crown. His ministers were personal appointees, not subject to congressional confirmation or questioning. He was chief of the party, and as the party nominated all elected officials down through municipal president; therefore every important official in Mexico was the president's man. He made the law and was above the law, except in three things: no president could alienate Mexican soil, take land away from Indians or *ejidos*, or succeed himself.

The Mexicans in 1917 considered such powers necessary, and history justified the opinion. The Hispanic-Mexican personality was anarchic and ill-disciplined, the society without traditions of viable local government, separation of powers, or the rule of law. They replaced the vanished crown with a newer symbol of the nation, and made a new legitimacy. The party, the ministers and their policies, the congress, the judiciary, any government officer could be criticized and even ridiculed in this new Mexico—except the president. Custom did not allow either the office or man to be impugned.

Other Hispanic countries came to admire this Mexican institution. No other nation was able to duplicate it, for they lacked the unique experience of the Mexican Revolution and the Revolutionary Party, which produced a series of stable, seasoned, disciplined six-year autarchs. And the Mexican president could only be king because he embodied and remained sensitive to, the aspirations of the institutional revolution. There was one great difference between the power of the Mexican president and the tyranny of the party and other authoritarianisms. The Mexican custodianship represented all major interests and had popular goals, and so long as the rulers pursued those goals the people permitted them, and even took satisfaction in their power. And so long as the power was used with restraint, there was little need for repression of any kind.

The principal thrust of the revolution as defined in 1917 was toward material progress in which all classes would share. The president was the supreme arbiter and driving force behind this thrust. Therefore his quirks, personality, and circle of companions were of immense importance. The hardest task for the party, and the system, was in choosing the right personality and viewpoint for the times. After Cárdenas, the choice was always made by consensus and compromise, influenced but never dictated by the incumbent president. The success of the system rested upon pragmatic choices, showing a decent respect for, but no slavish obedience to a sometimes emotional popular opinion. The evidence is that between 1940 and 1970 the Mexican system worked as well as any two-party political system, and better than most democratic multi-party structures. The Mexican government rested also, like that of the United States, upon its spirit as much as its institutions. From 1940 onward, the spirit was remarkably free.

By 1946 two men had proven their right to be considered as Ávila's successor: Foreign Minister Padilla and Interior Minister Alemán. Padilla was better known abroad and was considered the more democratically-inclined. However, he was unpopular with the left wing of the party because of his pro-United States policies. Alemán was considered the stronger man and was passed on in backroom conferences for the job.

Padilla ran as an independent candidate. He was defeated by the concentrated might of officialdom, 1,786, 901 to 443,537, but the election was orderly, and the size of the opposition vote showed an increasing maturity on the part of government. Padilla did not have to leave for exile, for Mexico was becoming a free, if still not democratic country.

Miguel Alemán, a lawyer from Veracruz whose father had been killed fighting for the revolution, was not expected to make sweeping changes. He continued the dominance of the business-oriented *mestizo* Establishment of the south-central states, bringing in an enthusiastic official family of "veracruzanos," men from a region long excluded from power or prominence. The veracruzanos were ambitious and eager to wield power, and their mystique, so far as they had one, centered on public works to encourage industrial enterprise, and also in securing new sources of capital for development.

Alemán, a dominant personality but flexible and tolerant with an excellent sense of humor, had suffered severe annoyances from labor during Ávila Camacho's regime of conciliation. The three great national corporations, PEMEX, the railways, and the Federal Electric Commission, had fallen into considerable disarray due to political hacks and union obstructionism. Alemán appointed tough, pragmatic, competent executives to head these corporations, then moved against the entrenched, still ideological labor leadership. He deliberated courting the labor rank and file, trying to hold its confidence while he removed the Marxist union bosses. He purged the board of CTM of communists, replacing them with five unionists who became known as the Five Little Pigs because of their common corpulence. The new leaders were dedicated labor leaders who believed in getting benefits for the workers, but without pursuing political goals or socialistic theories. The Lombardo faction was expelled from CTM; it split off in the extreme-leftist CTAL. The Mexican trade union organization now began to resemble that of the United States, with a tough-minded leadership that was devoted to economic gains without class warfare, or strikes waged for purely political goals.

When the Marxist leadership in the PEMEX union struck against the government, Alemán jailed the leaders and replaced them with new men. In all these battles, the majority of workers stood behind the president, because he convinced the rank and file that it would share in gains won through more efficient management. Social services and wages for urban labor did continuously improve.

Old business out of the way, Alemán's people drew up plans for large public works projects, rural dams and irrigation networks to bring power and water to the depressed countryside. The Papaloapan Dam Project was similar to the Tennessee Valley Authority in the United States. Alemán did not allow sacred cows to stand in the way of these projects; he did not hesitate to resettle Amerindian communities when it was necessary to assist the productive farmers.

The thrust was statist, but not socialist, because the goal of every federal project was to increase production by private enterprise. The government became highly involved in an indirect pushing and control of industrialization. While purely private enterprise was encouraged, the government financed a series of semipublic industries, usually retaining a minority interest in these. Certain industries were given tax breaks to assist rapid growth. Such policies promoted quick industrialization. The result was not so much government control or direct management of industry as a government direction of industrial goals. The spirit of government investment and development was essentially capitalistic, a fact that confused both the Right and Left, neither of which had terms to define the government policies. The Alemán administration desired rapid industrial growth, and did not care whether this was carried out by public or private concerns; it favored either as the situation seemed to require. The state entered into enterprise, acquiring interests in hundreds of new industries, but without any rationale of eventual state ownership. The Alemán administrators were uninterested in rationales. They were problem solvers by instinct and training, who understood that Mexico was at least a century behind the industrial world in organization and technology, and they sought any means to correct that situation.

Alemán had inherited a healthy treasury with a large dollar surplus. The high prices earned by Mexican raw materials during the war paid off most pressing national debts. As a postwar boom developed, however, the economy was threatened with a foreign-exchange hemorrhage. Mexico had to acquire tools and machinery for industrial projects abroad—but there was a rising, newly prosperous industrial and business class clamoring, after years of austerity, for new luxury goods from the United States. Alemán handled the balance of payments problem technically and with considerable success by devaluing the Mexican peso. This made it harder for rich Mexicans to buy Cadillacs and also slowed the growing consumerism of the middle class, which raised its living standards mainly with imported goods, but made Mexican raw materials competitive abroad and brought in more exchange. This discipline, which was not harsh enough to alienate the money-rich new class, paid off handsomely by providing capital for the tractors and industrial machinery Mexico needed more than Chryslers and consumer goods.

The thrust of government into industrial development inevitably increased corruption. The government had credits, tax breaks, licenses, and contracts to hand out in a period of headlong, chaotic development. Cabinet ministers, and the friends and associates of ministers and the regime grew very rich. Official corruption, always part of Mexican life, was in one sense becoming healthier, however, because this was not quite the former feeding from diverted public revenues. Corruption did not damage development and may have aided it, because corruption money capitalized some new industry. While officials absorbed some of the increasing revenue and more often, took a piece of new industries they helped create, they almost always reinvested in Mexican enterprise. And while few important enterprises could operate in Mexico without some official sharing in the pie, taxes were very low; Mexican businessmen paid government less overall than in most developed nations. The Mexican forms of corruption in high places were rarely hypocritical, much less so than the influence-peddling in Washington which was disguised as law practice.

The beneficiaries of corruption were primarily sharing in a new pie their policies helped make, and there is no evidence that the practice hindered development, the growth of the middle class, or lowered the living standards of the poorer classes. However, it was potentially dangerous unless kept under control, and the free and easy atmosphere of this new Mauve Decade south of the Bravo began to worry many Mexicans who could not correlate it with the ideals of the revolution.

With rapid industrial growth, profits spurted in relation to the whole economy. Profits always grew rapidly in times of expansion, in developed economies as well as Mexico. The government made no effort to control profits; this was contrary to its rationales which centered on continuous growth. Profits rose from 26 percent of the total national income in 1939 to almost 42 percent of all wages and income in 1952. This seemed to show that labor was not sharing proportionately in the boom, but in reality it reflected the fact that sectors beyond the reach of the new industrialization were falling far behind. The newer profit ratio was very close to the true scales in countries like Great Britain and the United States, allowing continuous recapitalization.

The total national product rose sharply after 1946, and wages rose with production. There was a corresponding rise in living standards for the urban population. The entrepreneurs and the middle class benefitted most, but if "labor" were defined as the urban, unionized proletariat, including organized workers from factories, shops, and restaurants, Mexican labor kept pace with the other sectors. Every city showed visible improvement, with new shops and automobiles and fewer miserable beggars; people no longer starved to death in the alleyways of the capital. But beyond the cities and regions where the industrial programs and the irrigation projects had not reached, gains were negligible.

There were social and political dangers in this imbalance, as in the pervasive corruption in high places. But noticeably there were few complaints from the politicized urban populations, which could see visible improvements in conditions. The strident complaints came mostly from a small group of intellectuals and ideologues, and from the Marxist Left, which primarily resented not the development, but its direction.

The postwar regime also proceeded rapidly toward the eventual solution of a problem that had existed since Guadalupe Victoria—the question of foreign capital in Mexico. The Mexico of the 1950s needed new capital from outside as badly as the old, perhaps more so, since expectations were rising. But old nationalist specters, and the very real antagonism toward foreign competition from the growing group of Mexican entrepreneurs, required that capital be barred from entry under the old terms. The government must avoid new petroleum-industry controversies. The pragmatic application of a law requiring that the ownership of Mexican enterprises must be at least 51 percent Mexican proved to be a workable solution. All new enterprises had to be organized under domestic majority ownership; this was the price of a foreign capitalism's entry into the growing native marketplace. The law was flexibly applied. Already-established industries were required to divest slowly, the pace usually depending on the availability of Mexican capital to buy up the majority control. In some cases, the Mexican government acquired the interest, then resold this to private parties as they appeared. The market was strong for investment in consumer industries, where huge profits were quickly made; Mexican investors were much more reluctant to acquire shares in mining interests or utilities, where capitalization was large and returns came slowly. For example, the Anaconda Cananea copper mine in Sonora which had figured so prominently and so bloodily in the labor conflicts early in the century, found no takers until 1971, when the government finally announced a nationalization agreement by which a Mexican board would take control.

Many North Americans saw these nationalizations as communistic expropriations, not recognizing that the Mexican government usually had no interest in assuming ownership or management, or that the majority interest was almost always acquired by private parties. Foreign companies could still make excellent profits, and a flood of new foreign concerns entered Mexico. The laws were pragmatically applied to subsidiaries of great North American corporations, particularly where they offered employment and savings in foreign exchange by making or assembling needed products that otherwise had to be imported. The stability of government and the peso, and an expanding market, made it possible for hundreds of large companies to enter Mexico, finance industry, build plants, and even train a purely Mexican labor and management force. Spectacular gains came from this quarter. The entry of North American companies was the largest factor in the steady rise in living standards and a strong growth among the white-collar and technical classes. Foreign subsidiaries, branches and franchises trained thousands of skilled workers, provided opportunities for the educated middle ranks and began freeing the Mexican economy from a total dependence upon imported products. It was still impossible to create many Mexican industries without North American money, equipment, and expertise. The new airlines had to be financed through California banks. The Alemán regime was flexible; it made deals with foreign banks and companies. The deals were usually equitable, and Mexicans and foreigners shared far more fairly than during the Porfiriato.

The government tried to balance enterprise between light and heavy industries and those producing consumer goods through credit policies. This annoyed most Mexican manufacturers, who clung to consumer goods. They also protested the government's investments in mechanized agriculture. Ironically, Alemán often found it easier to deal with foreign companies than with Mexican industrialists, because of the Mexican insistence upon quick profits and a very high rate of return. In any case, the government kept taxes low for all enterprise and permitted large profits to spur development. The average Mexican industry paid about twelve percent in total taxes—far less than the rates exacted in more developed countries.

While the first results of industrialization appeared to be successful, the results of the government's investments in agriculture were more mixed. No agrarian law was changed; this area was too sensitive politically; however, the implemented policy was now to favor relatively small, self-sufficient holdings. The *ejido* structures, ferociously defended by an entrenched bureaucracy, could not be dismantled, but the government avoided creating new *ejidos*. Although distributions could never entirely be stopped—any president could win a roaring ovation in congress and instant popularity across the nation by merely announcing new distributions in deference to the mythology of the revolution—land was now normally given only to those individuals who proved they could make productive use of it. These new recipients were given clear titles, and to the intense annoyance of the *ejidal* bureaucracy, removed from its smothering incubus.

Laws and myths were ignored or evaded, to take advantage of mechanization and new techniques imported from the United States. Modern technology demanded large farms; private and corporate owners began to lay out new plantations that were *latifundios* in everything but name. These grew rapidly in the north, where land was reclaimed by irrigation from the desert, and in rich Michoacán. These farms strongly resembled the California corporate farm; they represented the most viable form of twentieth-century agriculture. In Sinaloa and surrounding states huge tracts were almost indistinguishable from agricultural operations in California and Texas. Many of the new enterprises were segments of diversified economic empires which included marketing and banking; others were owned by a new class of Mexican entrepreneurs with no interest in land other than to make money. Smaller, but still profitable farms were operated by an expanding class of rancheros, sometimes called "nylon farmers." The nylon farmer, like the "drugstore farmer" in the United States, had the capital or credit to plant many acres, and to hire peasants to do his work.

Much of the capital as well as the techniques for this new farming came from the United States. Foreigners were not allowed to buy land, but there were ways of evading any Mexican law. However, the usual form of North American investment in the huge new northern and northwestern plantation operations was in furnishing credits, expertise, and marketing connections. Growers and shippers, many of whom moved out of similar operations in California or the southwestern United States because of rising land pressures, costs, or labor problems, transferred their activities to Mexico, working through and with Mexican landowners or corporations. By the 1960s at least a third of the tomatoes and certain other fresh produce consumed in the United States came from these operations in Mexico, and trends indicated the proportion would increase rapidly.

These vast new agricultural enterprises were in the same pattern as the coffee, pineapple, and other plantations that European companies had established in the previous century. They provided employment for the teeming peasantry; unfortunately, with their neat new row houses for workers, they also began to reestablish the old hacienda in a newer form. Whatever their social implications, they were important to the economy, providing exports for foreign exchange. Government officials fostered them, and assisted profitable operations with new federal irrigation and drainage projects. Some officials also clandestinely shared in ownership and profits.

With an expanding domestic urban market, and new markets in the United States, almost all forms of efficient farming had become profitable in Mexico.

On the *ejidos*, and the small, unmechanized hoe plots that covered central Mexico like a tattered green blanket, what progress there was seemed to be a mixed blessing. The half of the Mexican population still confined to *ejidos* and peasant holdings grew enough to eat, but not enough to raise their comfort level. Meanwhile, a rising population depressed the future. One form of modernization that had entered the country was modern medicine; the government provided clinics, medicines,

sanitation instruction, and nurses. Peasant children were no longer weaned
on chiles or carried off by epidemics. The human balance in rural Mexico
had been maintained for centuries by an infant mortality rate of 50%,
with only a handful of people reaching genuine old age. By the 1940s the
death rate was falling spectacularly, creating an exploding rural population.

The *ejidal* and family plots, too small to begin with to support profitable
farming, had to be divided and redivided. Huge numbers of campesinos
were day laborers, and usually underemployed. While this supply of cheap
labor provided the nylon farmers and plantations with opportunities, the
human social damage was immense.

Unhappily, in the very years that the modernizations of the revolution
took hold firmly in the countryside, with expanded medical services and
schools, the indirect effects of these services threatened to overload and
swamp them. Illiteracy fell rapidly for some years, to about 25 percent—
then, the ratio held steady despite the huge increase in schools. Now,
illiteracy began to rise again. Even with one fourth its budget devoted to
education, the government could not provide the country with enough
schools.

In the 1940s the rural misery was increased in the central states by an outbreak of the dread hoof and mouth disease that killed all animals with cleft
hooves. The United States government, hoping to confine the outbreak
below the Bravo, provided the Mexican government large credits to pay
for the destruction of infected stock. Many violent and sometimes bloody
confrontations occurred between uncomprehending campesinos and soldiers who came to shoot cattle. A final tragedy was that very little, if any,
of the millions provided by the United States ever found its way to the
peasants.

The unemployed peasantry found an old escape route, walking north to
seek work in the United States. This trek had begun again during the war,
when Washington pragmatically ignored its immigration laws to provide
labor for Southwestern farms. Now, in the late 1940s and early 1950s
hundreds of thousands of Mexican migrants swam or waded the Bravo,
becoming *mojados* or "wetbacks," or slipped across the wire into California or Arizona, becoming *alambristas* or "wire-crossers." Whole peasant
families, and sometimes entire clans, went in a body. Many were cruelly
exploited—but at twenty U.S. cents an hour, stoop labor for a ten-hour
day, a family could make more cash in a month than the same labor
earned all year in the arid, maguey-dotted valleys of central Mexico. The
mass migration was finally halted toward the close of Alemán's term by a
combination of North American labor protests and a pricked Mexican
pride—only to begin once again on a mass scale in the early 1970s. In the
first year of that decade, 320,000 Mexican illegal aliens were deported

from the United States, undoubtedly a tiny fraction of those who went to find any work they could. Meanwhile, 50,000 Mexicans emigrated legally per year, some finding opportunity, most adding to the accumulated social and cultural problems of the Southwestern United States.

The peasantry provided the ruling circles with a monstrous dilemma. Like the *indios*, they were not really needed anywhere. It was increasingly impossible for them to live contentedly as they had for generations; roads and schools and clinics had destroyed that. Millions of them poured into the Mexican cities and towns. Metropolitan centers overflowed with ragged, uneducated agrarian workers, almost totally unprepared for modern urban living or employment. They clung to life in horrendous slums, selling lottery tickets or chewing gum. Their children went uneducated; their child mortality rate was again rising. This was again not a purely Mexican problem—but it was an acute one that the Mexican society and government failed to solve, and in fact, no government anywhere had a workable solution.

The Alemán leadership clung to two great hopes in their effort to modernize Mexico and solve the tremendous socio-economic problems the society faced. The first was the fashionable one of its time, that lavish developments in industry, electrification, irrigation, and education could quickly provide the jobs to absorb the rural population. The bureaucracy fed native and foreign capital into Mexican development at forced draft, accepting maximized profits and corruption as a price of rapid progress. The programs seemed grandiose by Mexican standards, and they were criticized on the grounds that they were too expensive and that they were open-ended—Alemán began huge projects that would have to be carried on by later administrations. The great university complex on the lava flow south of the capital was a typical project; it seemed visionary and ambitious because it was designed for thirty thousand students who did not yet exist. But Alemán's people saw no other way to try to meet the demands of a rising population, and there was no other way within the conventional wisdom.

The other hope was that the population would suffer the pain of imbalances caused by rapid industrial expansion and the delay of immediate social benefits. This was not a visionary trust; the Mexican people were used to enduring conditions that more advanced societies would no longer tolerate. The party leadership believed that the majority had confidence in its ability to meet Mexican aspirations, knowing, however, that this was a trust that could not be banked long without a continuous flow of dividends.

In six years, the administration achieved Mexican miracles, considering the base from which it began. The gross national product nearly doubled; real income almost kept pace. Consumption rose sharply. A hundred thou-

sand new jobs were created between 1940 and 1952, out of an economy
that had been stagnant for decades. By any standard, there was enormous
progress.

However, the population explosion continued, an ominous specter beyond the stage where the economic battles were waged. The university
designed for thirty thousand students would have to enroll a hundred
thousand, and the time was approaching when the economy would have to
create four hundred thousand new jobs each year just to absorb the increase. Rising numbers, as the population grew from twenty to fifty
million in the coming decades, made Alemán's grandiose projects of the
1940s seem small and inadequate, and the soaring expectations of these
new citizens made the victories won at such great cost seem increasingly
hollow.

Alemán's domestic needs shaped Mexico's foreign relations.

The Mexican development programs had to have money from the World
and Inter-American Development Banks, and the Mexican economy
needed huge infusions of private capital and industrial techniques. The
Mexican economy in 1946 did not make even such prosaic mass-produced
items as can openers, hairpins, or a decent cotton shirt. The prices of all
Mexican-manufactured products were higher than North American or European goods, while the quality was markedly inferior. The foreign exchange earned by sugar, cotton, oil, and metals no longer had to be used
for food, but it flowed out of the country for consumer goods demanded by
the middle class. Mexico needed the capital and skills provided by General
Motors and General Electric, and also the expertise of Sears Roebuck.
Alemán's pragmatic approach to Mexicanization made Mexico a happy
hunting ground for outside business, especially for those businesses that
produced a local product that reduced the need for imports. It was no
accident that Mexico became flooded with North American goods made in
Mexico, and the Mexican landscape with North American corporate brand
names. The prosperous new class began to drink Coca Cola and drive
Detroit-designed cars, all of which marked a great modernization, but all
of which inevitably began to shape the culture of this class.

The Alemán policy was one of pragmatic self-interest, but dependence
upon the United States, despite the terms and appearances, was still dependence. Alemán and Company, under different conditions and better
terms, reaffirmed the old policies of the Porfiriato. They looked outside for
help. The result was a new, massive diffusion of outside civilization, and
one that in its way was as profound and historically unsettling as the
Spanish Conquest of Amerindian Mexico.

There was a grave question whether Mexicans could cope with this
diffusion and infusion that began to change the face of their land and every

aspect of the lives of the urban masses. It was not a question of learning to keep ancient automobiles running or managing PEMEX or French-built subway systems. The creativity from which all these artifacts and systems came represented a different world view from the Hispanic Mexican, and the systems themselves demanded a different range of human relationships. A man on an assembly line was no less a man than one in the saddle, but his place in the world, and his relationship with other men, subtly changed. A great part of the material success of the Anglo-Saxon, Germanic, and Russian worlds came from the ability of their peoples to accept a dehumanizing organization and self-discipline, submerging individual personalities in collective goals. The effective Russian, German, Japanese, or North American was not and could not be an individualist—in fact, in all those languages, the meaning of the term differed from the Spanish definition.

Under the new dispensation, Mexico retained a more and more meaningless territorial sovereignty, but if Mexicans were to make this new world work, they had to develop a newer personality. There was little room for the *culto* or machismo, or for the contemplation of things, or even the constant awareness of tragedy in an era when the gross national product was supreme. There were still men and women making music in the fields, living on islands of elaborate, sensual courtesy, but all of them were essentially meaningless against the changing reality of a modernizing Mexico.

Against the actuality of what was taking place in Mexico, the visible relationship with the United States, though continually pointed out, had little importance. After Roosevelt, every North American president made a point of meeting amicably with the president of Mexico, releasing press notices of eternal friendship; Truman would lay a wreath on the monument to the Niños Heroes of the Intervention; John F. Kennedy would be greeted by a cheering million in the City of México. Mexico generally followed the United States line in the United Nations; most Mexicans believed that the United States had conquered the world in 1945, and they adjusted to it. Meanwhile, Mexico was permitted her historic defense of sovereignty and her religion of nonintervention: she opposed North American machinations in Guatemala or in Cuba; she recognized all governments except that of the Spanish Caudillo Franco, thus proving the rule. *In extremis*, against outside powers, Mexico had little choice except to side with the United States. Thus, the government backed Washington in the Cuban missile crisis of 1962.

In foreign affairs, Mexico was not a puppet, though self-interest and common interests caused her generally to follow North American initiatives. Her real stance was more one of self-imposed emasculation. Mexicans, asserting that every nation, however constituted, must be sovereign and must not be interfered with, simply could take no real initiatives in international relations.

The trends that the Alemán presidency solidified in institutional cement aroused their own opposition.

The Mexican Left, consisting of a series of splinter groups of differing Marxists, remained bitter that the revolution had not gone down the path of socialism. The extreme Left, frozen out of the PRI, coalesced around the *Partido Popular*, or People's Party, headed by Vicente Lombardo Toledano. This Left was vocal and *anti-yanqui*, but extremely ineffective in halting any trend. The Left had grown up ensconced in the labor movements, and when it ceased to lead labor, Marxist intellectuals and anarchist organizers never found another popular home. Mexican communists and assorted Marxists were peculiarly theoreticians from middle-rank backgrounds, with a deep, urban, class suspicion of the candle-lighting peasantry. The Left lost the labor unions and never found a rural constituency, and by 1952 had no audience.

A more important, though still not very effective opposition came from the Mexican Right, which was no longer composed of priests, pretorians, and sulking profiristas but of the rising business entrepreneurs. It was a small, but quite wealthy and influential class, whose views were like those of conservative Republicans in the United States. The Right opposed governmental entry into and influence over the economy. It financed the *Partido de Acción Nacional*, whose origins were Synarchist, and whose acronym spelled PAN, or bread. PAN dominated the halls of the Confederation of Mexican Chambers of Commerce, but had little opportunity at the polls. Ironically, however, PAN drew more support in the provinces and in the impoverished rural areas than the Partido Popular; its organizers respected religion and talked in terms the campesinos might not agree with but could at least understand. In higher circles, PAN was very fashionable, particularly among the thousands of Mexican businessmen of second- or third-generation European background, who formed the backbone of the entrepreneurial class. Against PAN in business circles the government supported the Chamber of Manufacturing Industries, which was composed of the managers and directors of the *mestizo* new class from the partially nationalized concerns.

No opposition had any chance of unseating PRI, even in an honest election. Further, Alemán's people left the Right and Left to bombard the population with rationales while with unerring instinct they seized upon the real means of power in modern Mexico. They ran the major banks, the great governmental corporations, and they held interests in many of the great industries. They controlled the flow of money, both from the government and from outside. They dispensed contracts and licenses and shares;

they could make their friends rich and make life difficult for their enemies. Many of them owned or shared in haciendas, but they operated them sub rosa, through agents. They sat on the boards of the new, "Mexicanized" North American corporations whose plants were beginning to blacken the blue skies of the Valley of Mexico; while most foreigners preferred PAN members socially, they had to deal with the friends of Alemán. The alemanistas, intelligent if not always honest, possessed a keen sense of what most Mexicans wanted and tried to give it to them. With the disappearance of Church and army influence, and the cooption and quiescence of the proletariat and peasantry, the new class held most of the power in society. Restive generals and pistol-packing *caciques* had some power in the hinterlands but now came to the palace hat in hand rather than pronouncing. Generals and *caciques*, when cooperative, got their shares.

The power was used with great restraint. By 1952, Mexico was not a democracy, but it was a very free society. The press was free, the universities unfettered; any Mexican could chose any career within the range of his capabilities and education. The economic pie was still very small, and the class system had not disappeared—but these restrictions upon freedom had nothing to do with government. Every Mexican, out of his past, was highly sensitive to race, but no doors were closed to anyone. It was better socially to be white, and necessary politically to be *mestizo*; and cooption was the price of entry into PRI. The ruling clique had one major purpose behind its retention of power, and this was to force the pace of economic development. The alemanistas believed in this with religious fervor, and the enrichment of many of them in these programs was only a by-product.

The alemanistas were fearful in 1952 that a new administration might change the directions they had set. They launched a few trial balloons to test national sentiment toward amending the constitution so that Alemán might succeed himself. The effort was quickly abandoned, because it became apparent that any attempt by Alemán to hold power would bring Cárdenas out of retirement in full cry, unsettle the army, and probably cost the presidency the aura of legitimacy it had acquired. Therefore, the alemanistas, cardenistas, and other factions had to hammer out the usual compromise, choosing an elderly bureaucrat, Adolfo Ruiz Cortines, as the next president.

The self-correcting mechanism of the party was at work. The cardenistas were angry over the pervasive corruption seeping down through the regime; more conservative elements were concerned with the side-products of headlong development, such as inflation, inefficiency, and waste. Ruiz Cortines was an anomaly, a scrupulously honest civil servant who had handled millions in contracts and never grown rich. The cardenistas considered such a symbol of probity was needed, and there was a pervasive feeling in the party leadership that Alemán was going too far, too fast. The choice of Ruiz, therefore, was expected to serve two purposes—to restore public confidence through honesty at the top, and to consolidate the gains already made, marking time until the economy was ready for another dynamist. Ruiz was an instinctively cautious bureaucrat, who would administer well but not initiate.

He was colorless, but the PRI organization carried him to the usual victory over a general, PAN, and a coalition on the Left.

The only change Ruiz made was to grant female suffrage for the first time. He did not cause a housecleaning in government, but he put a chill on official corruption. He managed the power apparatus—the Nacional Financiera, the social security system, and the national corporations—extremely well, as he had been expected to do. He carried through uncompleted programs, such as the Ciudad Universitaria but started no new ones. Development was slowed.

The agrarians, feeling population pressure, clamored for an enlargement of the *ejidos*. However, in the regions where most *ejidos* were located, all the large haciendas had disappeared, and any enlargement would now gobble up small, highly productive farms. Ruiz wanted to amortize the old *ejidos*. Meanwhile, he effectively halted their enlargement by granting certificates of "inaffectability" to surrounding small landholders, which guaranteed them against future expropriation under the agrarian law.

Ruiz again devalued the peso, to a firm basis of 12.50 to the dollar, and enforced austerity in import policies. The national product continued to rise. Ruiz did not choke off the growth by any means, but his measures did take some steam from the headlong, chaotic boom-times of the Alemán years. Between 1952 and 1958 this was a normalization that was probably needed.

But it created immediate problems. The labor force was now growing faster than the jobs being created in industry and through public works. To ease this, Ruiz Cortines ordered one step that was purely regressive: hand labor was substituted for machinery on public projects, even if this meant that there were delays and machines stood idle.

Although the Mexican credit situation improved, and the national debt was reduced to a manageable proportion of the national revenues, and PEMEX enjoyed a splendid era of capitalization and expansion, opening new fields at Tehuantepec, building refineries, and developing gas wells, pipelines, and a sulfur industry at reduced interest rates, Ruiz' cooling of the economy was enormously unpopular. He was strengthening the Mexican economy fundamentally, balancing the uneven growth, halting corruption, improving credit, and providing efficient management, but many Mexicans felt the administration was a disaster. The urban population, labor, the middle-rank bureaucracies, and the ebullient new class of businessmen, had had their expectations raised enormously during Alemán's flush times. They had all become accustomed to making constant and visible gains through a forced flow of government money and contracts; they demanded these gains, whether the economy was sound or unsound. And in fact, it was becoming evident that governments enjoyed little time to consolidate in Mexico; they had to rush merely to stay abreast of population increase.

The labor unions again became restive. Ruiz Cortines, through his capable and popular labor secretary, Adolfo López Mateos, convinced the labor leadership to support his policies, but at the price of communist resurgence in the unions. The leadership was accused of making immoral deals with government at the expense of workers. A campaign by radical elements led to the election of communists as heads of the PEMEX, National Railways, and schoolteachers' unions.

By 1957 most of the PRI leadership recognized these dangerous pressures and agreed that government must again turn to rapid development policies, huge and expensive public works, and the diversion of more capital into social services. While the debate was going on, the economy fell into a definite recession: this was one price of the presidency's awesome powers over the economy. Not knowing who the new ruler would be or what policies he would follow, businessmen and bureaucrats hesitated to make plans or investments. Since the presidency would set the new policies for six years through the Financiera, public works expenditures, and wage and price controls in basic industry, there was a certain drift until the old king was dead and the new one crowned.

In 1958 the cardenistas and alemanistas were united, demanding a president who would both stimulate the economy and be more responsive to the Left. Despite much mythology, it was not possible for a candidate to politick for president except through disciplined service and demonstrated capability. The choice was made by many men, who balanced their prejudices against what seemed to be the necessities of the times, if PRI were to continue to wield undisputed power. While many flamboyant men were suggested, the PRI leadership would not accept a maverick or truly independent man, and further, the choice had to be at least acceptable to the outgoing president. All factions compromised on the labor secretary, Adolfo López Mateos, who appealed to the masses because of a progressive image and his wife's services to the poor, but who was also a disciplined party man who would carry out mandates. It was expected that the communist-led unions would create great problems for government, and López Mateos was considered the man to handle them.

In the summer of 1958 he was ratified, 6,767,754 to 705,303 over the candidate from PAN. The only noticeable effect of female suffrage was to swell the total vote. He took office in December with promises to expand social security, to regulate prices to offset the effects of inflation on the poorest class, to redistribute land, and to launch a series of ambitious programs ranging from new nationalizations to a renewed campaign against illiteracy.

The communist labor chieftains apparently had learned little during their decade out of power. They returned to office supported by the legitimate grievances of the rank and file and workers disappointed in the slow progress under Ruiz Cortines. But now, as a progressive and even vaguely leftist president took power, they instigated a massive wave of strikes in PEMEX, among teachers, and the railways. The strikes were political, not economic in basis, for the Marxists believed they had to destroy the incoming, more liberal regime before it satisfied the workers.

The strikes paralyzed the economy and threatened the authority of the government. No president, of any ideology, could have tolerated this. When it became obvious that the leadership of the unions would not compromise and were bent on bringing down the government, López Mateos revealed a steel will beneath his genial exterior. He broke the strikes with federal troops, sending in soldiers to seize the union chiefs. They were brought to trial on charges of "social dissolution." Several of these men received sentences of up to eight years. The muralist David Siqueiros, who had previously been jailed for his activities in efforts to assassinate Leon Trotsky in 1940, was also convicted under this charge. The Left considered the imprisoned to be political prisoners, but the strikes were broken and government authority restored.

López Mateos emerged more popular nationally from this crisis, because he carefully disassociated the communist labor leaders from the workers and took no reprisals against labor. He expanded the social security system to more industries and created jobs with public works, and invoked the constitutional clause that gave workers a share of profits in certain enterprises. White-collar workers received new benefits, along with the federal bureaucracy, in social security and housing programs. The teachers were pacified by the recall of the scholar Torres Bodet to supervise a massive new school-building program. There were plums for both the private and the public bureaucracies, for López completed the nationalization of basic industries by acquiring the foreign-owned utilities, and through a purchase of the telephone company by private interests, providing new jobs and managerial posts for Mexicans.

Non-Marxist leadership revived in the unions, vigorously trying to offset the communist accusations of toadyism by winning gains for labor. The PRI labor chiefs appointed by Alemán were now aging men who clung to their positions with the stubbornness of petty Don Porfirios, but as they asserted themselves under a sympathetic president, they at last created a responsible labor movement. They made gains by hard bargaining, but stayed aloof from politics.

The old Alemán program of rapid investment and development was renewed. New industries were sought outside. While sixty percent of these continued to be North American, now Japanese, Swiss, German, and French films also entered Mexico heavily. The normal form of investment was now for foreign corporations to build Mexican assembly plants for their products, and gradually to produce even their component parts in Mexico. Ford, General Motors, and Volkswagen built automobiles in Mexico along with smaller firms, and also autobusses, tractors, trucks, and diesel engines were assembled or produced. In one sense this was Mexican industry; in the most fundamental sense it was not. While Mexicans capitalized most of these plants eventually, worked in them, and gradually came to manage them, they did not represent a true take-off into sustained economic activity, in which capital, invention, research, and marketing fed upon themselves. The Mexicans were still almost totally dependent upon technological advances from outside. When they began to build their own automobiles at Monterrey, it was in a Borgward plant shipped in from Germany.

López Mateos' government tried to scatter some of this new industry through the Republic; the earlier investment had created an enormous concentration in the environs of the capital, which was causing the City of México to grow at an unsupportable pace. The capital had become one of the great cities of the Western Hemisphere, and of the world—but the concentration of at least one in six Mexicans in a capital where services could not keep pace made for hideous slums and enormous pollution problems in the suburbs.

López Mateos' renewed development schemes were made easier because of Ruiz Cortines' retrenchment; it had become possible to float Mexican bonds in New York for the first time since 1910. The temptation to borrow heavily abroad was irresistible. López financed his projects through massive government loans, although some Mexicans remembered this had been a pathway to fiscal disaster in the past because of the inherent Hispanic-Mexican resistance to financial discipline. The López regime however was optimistic that heavy interest payments would be carried by expanding growth.

The agrarian problem could not be eased by either foreign money or new investments. Political pressures demanded action, and López Mateos received the expected ovation in congress and the press by announcing a new program of expropriations. This, however, was a very careful and selective redistribution. The government did not dare disturb the 15 percent of Mexican landowners who produced 75 percent of all marketed crops, for the *ejidos'* production was still completely disappointing. Despite continual agrarian pressures, the government resisted creating new *ejidos* in the largely arid, over-populated central plateau. Instead, it began a politically motivated and politically popular program of expropriating huge tracts in both the far north and far south. Most of this land had belonged to failed foreign land companies or developers and had never been put into use or production. The government offered small freeholds to families willing to migrate from the teeming central states. This program, and an amortization of the *ejidos* faced insuperable problems in the resistence of the *ejidal* bureaucracy to any change or reform. Former President Cárdenas brought all his vast influence to bear on the side of the agrarian bureaucracy whenever this vested interest was threatened in any way. Some millions of hectares of actually vacant lands were expropriated in the 1960s; little came of this except perhaps a lessening of agrarian tensions from an illusion that something was being done—for which purpose the program was designed.

The aging Cárdenas, who swung further to the left as he grew older, grew more and more opposed to the newer generation who had inherited his Mexico. He was perhaps reliving old revolutions, but he was enshrined in the national consciousness as a dynamic president and his personal influence with army leaders and labor and agrarians had remained strong. Cárdenas now agitated for a much more far-reaching agrarian revolution, annoying a government whose major interest was in fostering industry. He might even have forced a new program of land distributions, had he not made mistakes in the early 1960s that seriously discredited him.

Cárdenas misjudged the Castroite revolution in Cuba between 1959 and 1961, believing that it was following the course of the Mexican Revolution. He became vocal in support of Castro. His son headed a so-called National Liberation Movement, comprised mostly of fidelista intellectuals. Becoming more and more leftist, Cárdenas accepted a Stalin Peace Prize, and during the Bay of Pigs affair in 1961, he offered to go to Cuba to fight "*yanqui* imperialism." His statements and activities embarrassed the Mexican government, which believed in nonintervention but was also determined to keep good relations with the United States. The Mexican view of the Cuban revolution was slightly schizoid. While the government refused to break relations with Havana like other American states and maintained air service to Cuba, the administration was extremely suspicious of Castro's efforts to export his revolution. Agents enveloped every Castroite who arrived in Mexico, and the country was extremely hostile to fidelista activities even while its spokesmen chastised the United States for the Bay of Pigs.

Cárdenas' pro-Cuban statements won some popularity at first. But after the Bay of Pigs, when Castro declared himself a "Marxist-Leninist" and made war on the entire Cuban middle class, then took Cuba out of the

North American orbit into a new dependency on Soviet Russia, pro-Cuban sentiment in Mexico dropped sharply. The government and most Mexicans held that the entry of Russian missiles into Cuba in 1962 was "intervention" and stood behind the United States in the missile confrontation. Cárdenas now lost virtually all his influence in the army and among the middle-income groups, both as a statesman and a symbol.

Mexico was perhaps the only Hispanic country where a fidelista revolution was unthinkable. The middle classes and urban labor were making steady gains and were again reasonably satisfied. The regime was vaguely leftist, hardly a corrupt dictatorship. Rural conditions were bad, but the rural people were enduring them. Most Mexicans still took pride in their own national revolution, believed in its eventual triumph, and were xenophobically suspicious of other revolutions.

Major protest in the 1960s was noticeably confined to a small circle of leftist intellectuals and a growing body of university students. These groups attacked both the government and the middle classes for their indifference to continuing poverty in Mexico. These dissidents were very prone to get caught up in extraneous causes and foreign controversies— the hallmark of alienated intellectuals everywhere. The Castro revolution enflamed the imagination of the Mexican Left, which hoped a similar revolt in Mexico might bring its members to power. The Left posed no real political threat to PRI, and the tiny, proto-revolutionary groups such as the National Liberation Movement supported by certain cardenistas were ineffective. But the Left was extremely vocal and able to express its ideas, and it began to create an image of Mexico abroad that by 1962 was having a stunning effect on both the Mexican wealthy and foreign investment.

That year, 1,500,000,000 pesos were drained from the economy by anxious entrepreneurs and sent abroad—a serious blow to a nation that needed investment capital above all else. The drain continued, as more rich Mexicans developed an illusion that the country was poised on the brink of a Castroite revolution. Cárdenas was politically discredited in Mexico, but his mounting attacks on United States "imperialism," which received wide notice in the press, paralyzed North American investment, and worse, began to destroy the tourist trade, which López Mateos had fostered as Mexico's most important source of foreign exchange.

The government, now extremely dependent upon foreign loans, investment, and tourist dollars to feed its domestic developments, could not afford a weakening of confidence in the stability of the country. López Mateos worked strenuously to offset any impression that Mexico was unstable or that PRI might lose control.

The Left had lost face by siding with Russia during the Cuban missile crisis, offending majority opinion, but López tried to mollify the incessant attacks on his administration by freeing Siqueiros from prison. The artist had become the object of a worldwide, communist-directed sympathy campaign. This was an embarrassment, and having mollified the conservatives by standing firmly with the United States on the missile question, López could rid himself of accusations of political persecution. He also made foreign tours to project an image of calm, and invited major heads of government, such as President Kennedy and Charles de Gaulle to visit Mexico. The warm reception given Kennedy at the capital, which agreeably surprised even the government, did much to offset the illusion that Mexico was about to proceed on an anti-*yanqui* course.

Enough damage was done, however, to affect seriously the choosing of a new president. It was now established that the cabinet was the training ground for future presidents. In 1964, the inner circle tapped the most conservative and pro-North American cabinet minister, Gustavo Díaz Ordaz. The choice reflected both the party's belief as to what kind of man was needed at the helm, and the deepening conservatism of the leadership under vocal leftist attack.

Democratization stood lower on PRI priority list than development, but democratization of politics had continued since 1946. As the party grew more confident, it also became more concerned with things that had earlier been considered luxuries, such as image. The opposition had never drawn more than a quarter of the official vote, and PRI was institutionalized into the very fabric of the nation. Believing itself secure, the PRI leaders had become more tolerant of opposition. López Mateos expressed himself that a legitimate opposition was necessary for Mexican political health—and for PRI's health, too. By the 1960s the most overt abuses of the electoral process that had been commonplace—the intimidation of voters, stuffing of ballot boxes, destruction of opposing ballots, and blatant miscounts— were going out of official fashion, though these had been by no means eliminated. There was still regional violence during elections, but clashes such as occurred in 1946 between federal troops and sinarquistas in the Bajío were rare. Gradually, PRI had allowed its opposition to operate with almost complete freedom. The whole weight of official Mexico stood behind PRI, but active repression was vanishing. The government even secretly subsidized *El Popular*, a leftist opposition newspaper.

López Mateos liberalized the election codes further, giving opposition parties a certain amount of proportional representation in the congress. Neither the Left nor Right had ever been able to elect candidates outright; the new law reserved fifteen seats in the Chamber of Deputies for the opposition, to be divided according to the percentage of votes they received. In 1964 under this arrangement, PAN secured ten seats, the various leftists, five.

The Left, despite its influence in the universities and intellectual circles, was too splintered among dissident brands of Marxists to carry weight at the polls. The Partido de Acción Nacional was slightly more credible, for two reasons. PAN had become more respectable, and its leadership was more ideologically flexible than that of the Marxists.

PAN moved away from its dubious origins in sinarquismo, a past redolent of hooded penitents and arch-reaction, and avoided becoming merely a hobby for Mexican millionaires. The party's anti-Revolutionary leanings were a great handicap to winning mass support, or even the acceptance of the *nouveaux riches* who owed much to PRI. However, PAN tended to move toward the center, while PRI and the Revolution moved slowly to the right. By the 1960s both professed Catholicism and a defense of private enterprise had become entirely respectable in political circles; the middle classes no longer indulged in anticlericalism and "socialist" rhetoric. PAN won adherents among the second and third generation businessmen who now formed the bulk of the Mexican bourgeoisie. The party was hardly any more subversive of the revolution than the comparable Republican Party in the United States was of the New Deal. PAN leaders like Adolfo Christlieb merely waited for the day when PAN might inherit power out of a PRI disintegration under the weight of its own contradictions.

PAN now occasionally won local elections, largely on local issues, startling only because this was unprecedented.

PRI had always represented a mass of contradictions, as a party of ragged agrarians, restless unionists, government bureaucrats, and new millionaires. It was always hard to keep the contradictions submerged. The party under its changing names had always coopted the entire political spectrum between PAN's affluent "new criollos" and the communists. PRI welcomed all opinion from the far left to the moderate right. For decades this inclusiveness was far more a strength than weakness, because PRI was not organized or managed democratically. Men more liberal, or more conservative than the dominant faction came into the party with the clear understanding that their careers depended on going along—following party discipline. It was impressed on all that the tutelary or guardian principles upon which PRI's rule was based precluded any splintering for ideological reasons. Ambitious people had to accept this, because there were no viable political channels outside the party. However, by 1964 a large faction inside PRI believed the time had come to democratize the party and to allow all shades of opinion open debate. The conservatives quashed this and chose and elected Díaz Ordaz, but only at a cost of bringing party quarrels into the open. The contradictions suddenly became more visible in 1964.

The policies of the new administration were predictable; Díaz Ordaz did exactly what had been expected of him. His election reassured foreign investors and foreign embassies. He came in calling for peace and unity, but advising that discipline was the price of further social gains. Labor did not choose to test him. Díaz was a highly efficient, rather sour executive on the pattern of Ruiz Cortines who lacked López Mateos' affability. He assembled the most efficient and talented cabinet that had so far directed the nation. These men, divided between newcomers and holdovers as was now done to assure continuity, were essentially conservative-minded technocrats who moved the thrust of government from López Mateos' vague progressivism to slightly right of center. They initiated some financial entrenchment and looked for ways to integrate Mexico economically with other Hispanic nations.

However, the new regime spent heavily to encourage private industry. It built splendid new highways and opened new air routes, all leading to new factories and tourist hotels that were rising everywhere. Millions of North American tourists poured through Mexico, whose scenic beauty, climate, and thousands of historic curiosities made the country a tourist paradise. Díaz also kept Mexico a shoppers' paradise, by holding down basic prices and wages. This gained much dollar exchange, but meanwhile the spiraling inflation in consumer goods—which tourists did not buy—hurt the poorer classes badly. The government made every effort to assist industrial investment and tourism. While the rule requiring 51 percent native ownership of industry remained, all rules were interpreted flexibly. It was again possible to make deals, and Mexico again became an investment paradise.

Luxury hotels sprang up along the Pacific shores of Acapulco against a backdrop of festering agrarian misery in Guerrero, Mexico's poorest state. Tourists who rarely left the bright cities or clean new highways seldom saw the poverty or the backwardness of the impoverished *meseta*. North American industry poured into the far north under the so-called Border Industrialization Program. By agreement between the governments, the border regions were made into something resembling "free zones." Here expatriate United States industries could establish factories, creating countless jobs in a depressed area, and making products either for use in the Mexican market or for export. Many such products were returned to the United States in unfinished form, thus subject to minor duties. The arrangement held advantages for both sides. The stagnant border regions were revitalized; North American companies found an endless supply of industrial labor at wage rates, including fringe benefits, of about $3.00 per day.

There was no change in foreign policy. Mexico followed the "Estrada Doctrine," named for the foreign minister who articulated it. This held that every nation was sovereign, with the right to organize its internal government any way it chose, and that diplomatic relations between Mexico and other nations depended upon Mexican national interests rather than the ideologies of those nations. Under such a rationale policy was flexible: Mexico participated in the Organization of American States, the

Alliance for Progress, and in hemispheric defense treaties sponsored by the United States, but also maintained correct if suspicious relations with communist Cuba and condemned the North American intervention in the Dominican Republic in 1965. The government did not recognize the Franco regime in Spain—but traded with it freely. It also traded freely with the communist powers, while government officers regularly arrested and deported suspected foreign communist agents. The Estrada Doctrine gave Mexicans a sense of independence, and it was fully tolerated by the United States; relations with Washington improved steadily.

When Díaz Ordaz and President Lyndon B. Johnson met in the customary abrazo, however, there almost seemed to be an historic reversal of old roles. Johnson proclaimed lofty goals for the hemisphere in impassioned rhetoric, while the Mexican president confined himself to a few remarks concerning current business—a stance that amused official Mexico.

The Díaz government had not forgotten the agrarian problem, but no one yet knew how to handle it. Díaz dared not say officially everything had been a failure, but he did state that the agrarian situation had to be adapted to newer realities. The president made a point of never mentioning the word "ejido." His approach was follow the López Mateos pattern of land distribution, parceling unused tracts out to individual families, nine million hectares in three years. Díaz Ordaz disliked cooperatives, and began a subtle assault on the existing ones, by redistributing land within existing *ejidos* to individual smallholders. This destroyed any potential benefit the *ejidatario* might have gained through cooperative organization —but the evidence was clear from decades of experience that the *ejidal* bureaucracy simply could not efficiently manage the *ejidos*. Díaz Ordaz would have destroyed this bureaucracy had it been politically feasible; his policies marked a return to the original concepts of the revolution: that the *ejido* was to be a transitional training ground to make private small holders, not a permanent fixture on the land.

But between 1964 and 1970, nothing was solved. Given his own plot, the Mexican peasant clung to his ancient, unproductive methods. He could not afford the seeds, fertilizers, and machinery required for commercial agriculture, and even if credit had been available, he was still a poor risk. Noticeably, neither the government nor even the Ejidal Bank, specifically set up for the purpose, was willing to loan money to peasants. Private banks were even more uninterested. Capital was scarce in Mexico, and interests rates ran as high as six percent per month. The campesino continued to grow his few bushels of corn, raise a few goats and chickens, or tap a few hundred maguey plants for pulque. The billions of pesos invested in rural irrigation, electrification, and transportation programs, and the fertilizer plants developed by PEMEX, benefitted only the large or medium-sized commercial farmer, who in Mexico did make an excellent living on the land.

Despite the image of conservative calm that Díaz Ordaz threw over Mexico, there was much ferment under the surface in thought and politics. Younger members of the ruling elite, now maturing with more faith in democratic processes than a veneration for the custodianship of the party, were increasingly impatient with "ancient" history—the tales of the revolutionary struggles—and with an aging leadership which had generally come to power in 1946. The younger men were concerned with newer, popular issues and their own careers, and both were often paralyzed by the older political and economic Establishment. Some of the men now rising through the ranks refused to bow automatically to the wishes of whoever was dominant in PRI.

The president found himself increasingly engaged in intra-party conflicts. Some of these revolved around personalities, but most of them revealed a growing liberal-conservative split in party ranks. The older and younger generations did not always communicate. Díaz Ordaz, understanding there was a problem, appointed a young former state governor, Carlos Madrazo, to head PRI, with orders to revitalize the party structures. Madrazo took his mandate to be one of democratization. He began to oust the older, standpat leaders and party hacks in favor of more dynamic men, meanwhile accusing the leadership in the provinces of denying advancement to qualified newcomers, hostility toward reforms, and brutal indifference to democratic principles within and without PRI. Madrazo created such an uproar that it shook the presidential palace, and Díaz removed him.

Madrazo refused to quit PRI, or to be coopted or silenced. Even out of office, he gathered a considerable body of opinion behind him and began an unprecedented campaign of sniping at the party and the government from the sidelines, though polity did not permit any Mexican to criticize the president himself.

In another political battle, Díaz replaced the municipal president of the capital, a long-term incumbent, with an appointee more in sympathy with the presidential viewpoint. In still another move that shocked inner circles, he sacked the rector of the National University, the distinguished physicist, Ignacio Chávez, apparently for being too permissive to radical students—who were beginning to create a very visible problem for the Establishment. The president remained in complete control, for no Mexican official of any rank could win a struggle with the presidency, but the depth of the ferment was revealed by the openness of the conflicts.

The most serious incident, one which caught up the whole tenor of the emerging dissidence, was the university riots of 1968.

From the time of Alemán, every regime had gone to great expense to foster higher education, for while Mexico needed literacy and rural schools, a developing nation also needed hundreds of thousands of trained professionals and technicians. The fourth of the national budget that had erected primary schools at a rate of one classroom per hour and sent out cultural missions to schoolless areas composed of medical doctors, nurses, agricultural engineers and arts and science teachers had forged an educational revolution over the years. Illiteracy was—perhaps—reduced to the official claim of twenty-five percent in the late 1960s. Meanwhile, private secondary schools and colleges had proliferated, such as the excellent Technological Institute at Monterrey. From all these programs, hordes of eager students had poured into the newly expanded university system. In 1910, only a few thousand Mexicans were studying at the college level; in 1968, there were a hundred thousand in the National University at the capital alone.

Mexicans had taken pride in this remarkable expansion of education, without realizing its attendant problems. A mass student body had been made, which felt the frustrations such new masses of students felt all over the world. Despite immense budgets, it was impossible for the federal government to provide new facilities fast enough to meet the needs of a radically increasing college-level population. The children who still went unschooled often tragically went unseen. Those who reached the university, and found overcrowded conditions, a harassed faculty that had no time for them as individuals, and the vast impersonalism that the mere existence of thousands of young people crowded into one institution brought about, developed an explosive frame of mind. Probably, the frustrations of Mexican university students did not have a political origin, for most of them arrived unpoliticized. But here they quickly became enflamed into political activity by leaders who used legitimate grievances and needs that were not being met to stage huge mass protests. Students grew impatient with all authority asking them to be patient; frustration in their daily lives was easily translated into anger at the government, and even society. They became rebellious and adopted romantic, exotic causes. In a country like Mexico, also, they could be shrewdly exploited by the Left.

Ironically, the development of such a student body and student problems could be considered the mark of an advanced society. Student radicalism and unrest was a worldwide phenomenon in industrialized nations from the United States to France to Japan—it was perhaps a sign that the Mexican Revolution had fostered a modern society at least among her educated elite.

The Mexican government, however, was far less tolerant of student disturbances than the older societies—or weaker governments—might have been. Mexico's image of political stability was too new and precious for the Establishment to be amused by student marches and rhetoric demanding its destruction and a truly "just" society. Precisely because they were the grievances of an elite, the government had given the students' complaints low priority. In Mexico, students were not destined to become part of the elite, they were already an elite. Díaz Ordaz's circles were exasperated by what were considered radical and irresponsible demands. Above everything, the regime was hostile to the students' romanticizing of foreignisms like fidelismo and vocal support for North Vietnam's Ho Chi Minh and China's Chairman Mao. The leadership of a country like France could take such things in far better humor than leaders who were still quite sensitive about their nation's essential sovereignty, vis-à-vis *yanqui* imperialism, communism, Fidelism, or *any* foreignism.

Out of Hispanic tradition and Mexican policy, the universities were entirely free. Students were permitted to indulge in any fantasies they liked—so long as these were confined to campus. The unwritten rule was that the campuses were off-limits to police, but the greater arena was also off-limits to student politics. The students began to violate this in 1968, by staging protest marches and mass rallies in the City of México. The students' reasons were logical. In Mexico the press was also free, and a largely conservative press refused to print news of student demands or activities. The students felt they were completely powerless to get attention, or to bring about any of the things they wanted, without confronting society and government in the streets of Mexico. This reasoning was also very dangerous.

Mass demonstrations began at the capital in 1968, on the eve of the Olympic Games. Despite much criticism by students and others of its priorities, the Mexican regime had taken great pride in being awarded the site of the 1968 Olympic Games and planned to use the Games as an excuse to show the new, postrevolutionary Mexico to the world. A vast drive, headed by ex-President López Mateos, was begun to bring in tourists for the Games; the famous architect Ramírez Vásquez was commissioned to spend hundreds of millions in erecting new sports stadia and a communications complex to support the athletics contests. Hotels, roads, and other tourist facilities were improved or expanded. The Mexican government had taken the award of the Olympics as a sign that Mexico was accepted as a modern nation rather than a poor, backward country that could not support such events, and as host the Mexican government—and most Mexicans, generally—wanted to make the event a landmark of Mexican planning, hospitality, and technical efficiency, a glorification of what the revolution had brought about. Whether the student uproar was only a passing phase, or representative of a deeper social malaise, it was intolerable to the government. It seemed to make a mockery out of Mexico's claims to be a stable "democracy."

When the student leadership threatened openly to disrupt the Games, confrontation was inevitable. The form of the confrontation revealed how deeply and bitterly the government, many Mexicans, and the student elite had become polarized. On October 2, 1968, army troops and security forces opened fire on a mass rally of students staged in the Tlatelolco section of the city, near the foreign ministry. Infuriated by student violence and defiance of orders to disperse, the security forces themselves ran amok in a night of screams, beatings, and gunfire. At least two hundred students were killed as they were driven back to the university complex, though the official government version admitted only forty-nine. This was a terrible massacre, staged before the eyes of a gathering world press, and it produced shock. But in retrospect, the students had failed to understand one thing: the government would not have accepted such mass demonstrations from either the Right or Left, and it would not accept the overt defiance of what many Mexicans considered a new privileged elite.

While stability was preserved—the student movement collapsed utterly after the bloodshed; the Olympics were held and were praised by all as a tremendous success—the widely accepted concept that Mexico was rapidly evolving toward full democracy was badly scarred. Student leaders were rounded up by security forces in moves comparable to the worst practices of outright police states. Actions were taken that were impossible under the judicial systems of the United States. Students, charged with conspiring to bring down the government in conjunction with Cuban revolutionaries, were lodged in the Lecumberri Prison, the infamous "preventive prison" known as the Black Palace. They were held without bail, and very slowly brought to trial—in 1970 the majority were still jailed, waiting for trial. And the charges they were being brought up on ranged from kidnapping to murder to the destruction of government property—a very serious offense in Mexico.

Some parents whose student son or daughter disappeared in October 1968 never received any word of what had happened to the missing persons. Government agencies revealed extreme hostility toward the students, and utter indifference to their fate. Wounds were made that would not soon heal. Insistence that civil liberties were fully respected in modern Mexico seemed very dubious.

None of this presaged immediate trouble or social unrest. The students were peculiarly isolated. As in many other countries, the mass of people failed to support them. How deep the social cleavage could be was shown by the attitude of "regular" or nonpolitical prisoners at Lecumberri. On one occasion the criminal element staged a riot and severely beat the politicals, probably with the full approval of the authorities.

The bloody incident at Tlatelolco faded from the news, though not entirely from the Mexican consciousness. The students had raised too many questions that could not be silenced by bullets—why, after two revolutionary generations, at least a quarter of the population was still illiterate, and at least a quarter of the children were not in schools; why half the rural people were underfed, why 80 percent of the houses had two rooms or less, why 71 percent of them had no sanitation, 79 percent had no bathroom, 68 percent had no water, and half of them were in urgent need of repair.

The power of the president had not been undermined. The ruling group in Mexico was still a a tight circle of neo-conservative economic techno-crats, men well satisfied with the courses of the Revolution, social conser-vatives who detested anything resembling the youth movements or youth culture in other lands and were determined not to let any such culture flower in Mexico. Yet thousands of the educated younger generation were becoming alienated from the conventional revolution of the Gilded Age. Future Mexican governments, obviously, would have to contend with a restless, restive younger generation increasingly unwilling to accept the present guardians of the Republic and the revolution on present terms.

In 1970 there came the usual changing of the guard, which was now more a changing of faces than of government. The hardliner minister of the interior, Luis Echevarría Álvarez, who had played a major role in suppressing the student riots, was tapped for president. The forty-nine-year-old, bespectacled Echevarría was the fifth *mestizo* civilian in succession to enter the National Palace as chief of state.

During his candidacy he toured the country vigorously arousing the usual bemused curiosity of outsiders, who did not understand that this was not campaigning but an inspection of the future kingdom, to see problems firsthand, and to make strategic alliances with diverse groups. The view from the high balcony was far different than through the win-dows of a ministry; the presidency had come to have an enormous sober-ing effect on its incumbent.

Echevarría Álvarez was ratified with 85 percent of the vote in July, 1970. He took office in December, promising to carry the revolution on-ward and upward to new plateaus.

Over twenty-five years, the structure of politics had subtly changed. PRI was still the warp and woof of government, the army, a small and now wholly volunteer force, was still pampered but subservient; from a con-stant threat it had been turned into a major asset of the regime. The government, however, no longer rested on armed force; it had acquired a vital legitimacy that no one, not even the opposition, questioned. And the rulers of the party, the men who actually controlled the machinery of government, ruled through their control of the economy.

Through their hands poured the pesos of the public works, the Nacional Financiera, and the development agencies; they headed the great bureaucracies centralized and decentralized, with their thousands of well-paid jobs; they managed the social security system, with the clinics, hospitals, allotments, and pensions that were so peculiarly important in an underdeveloped nation where five-sixths of the population belonged to the working class. They controlled loans and licenses and prices, and all these things were the sources of their power.

Because the power of the ruling circles was mainly economic, the condition of the Mexican economy was vital to them. Any collapse of the economy that had been built up since the days of Alemán would almost certainly entail a collapse of government. This created peculiar pressures in some ways: the succeeding regimes had been able to slough off the problems of the agrarians, once the richer minority had assured the basic food supply, because the peasants were not part of the money economy. Their misery did not impinge directly on the cities or the industries or the financial structures that formed the true pyramid of power. In a genuine democracy, where peasant votes would have been organized effectively rather than diluted within PRI, the rural poverty would quickly have influenced government priorities away from industrial development into rural investments. The government was relatively free from such pressures. However, other pressures were quite acute. These came from the constant need to expand the economy to provide new jobs for a work force increasing by almost 400,000 per year, to provide schools and other social services to exploding urban areas, and from an increasingly serious problem with foreign exchange and the foreign debt.

By 1970, the glittering economic structure which, perhaps, both Mexicans and foreigners had praised too much, seemed only a worm-eaten facade. Progress in some fields had been enormous, as statistics showed: the national income had increased sixfold; the gross national product had reached 375 billion pesos ($30 U.S. billions); the number of hectares under irrigation had leaped from a few hundred thousand to many millions; steel production had gone from nothing to more than a million tons; electric power had been vastly expanded; a road network of some four thousand kilometers (1 km = .6 U.S. miles) had been lengthened into sixty thousand. The death rate had dropped almost in half against a rising birth rate. Despite this, consumption of necessities had jumped by 31 percent, and the production of capital goods had risen by 156 percent. The signs of change were everywhere highly visible. New factories, new power lines, new dams with impounded waters and hydroelectric plants, and new high-rise structures dotted the land. A pall of industrial pollution hung over the Valley of Mexico; the highways and city streets were jammed with PEMEX-fueled autobusses and private cars. Everywhere were new playgrounds, hospitals, towering office buildings and apartments, and roadside hotels. The urban cafes were jammed with cheerful people in modern clothes; the urban shops were choked with luxury goods; in the Lomas de Chapultepec and across the lava flow at the capital, two-million-peso ($160,000) mansions had become commonplace.

However, by the 1970s it had become clear that much of this great modernization and industrialization had been erected on very shaky foundations. What had been considered temporary distortions and imbalances, necessary in an age of headlong development from nothing, had somehow become permanent.

The alemanistas had begun with an economic structure basically unchanged since the Porfiriato. Their spirit was new and different from the Científicos, but almost unwittingly the alemanistas had in some ways only brought the Porfiriato up to date, under revolutionary management. They had made a newer Gilded Age.

Alemán had efficiently organized the three great "decentralized agencies" of government, PEMEX, the railways, and the Electric Power Commission. The effect of these agencies, once run efficiently, was profound— but they were essentially supporting agencies, and to capitalize them, Alemán had gone outside. In fact, beginning with Ávila Camacho and gaining tempo with Alemán, the Mexicans had looked for all the capital they poured into public works and so-called national developments and social investments, outside the Mexican economy. After 1946, almost all the money that allowed the alemanistas to seize firm control of the power structure poured in from abroad: $347 U.S. millions from the Export-Import Bank; $120 U.S. millions from various international agencies. The World Bank provided $30 U.S. millions to modernize the creaking railroads, and another $130 U.S. millions for electrification. The roads and splendid public projects that kept regional bosses and governors wedded to the regime mostly were funded with foreign loans. Through Ruiz Cortines' term, these loans were carefully amortized. Then, under López Mateos, brimming confidence and a leftward thrust toward faster development and social gains—without any concurrent steps to pay for them—had caused a deterioration in Mexican financial discipline. Under López Mateos, the foreign debt rose steeply.

As Echevarría took office, the foreign debt had become a "time bomb sitting under successive governments," as one Mexican economist said. This debt came to $3.5 U.S. billions. The federal budget amounted to only eighty billion pesos—$6.4 U.S. billions—and it could not easily be raised against an annual product of goods and services of $30 U.S. billions. The foreign debt equaled more than ten percent of the economy, and its service consumed a full quarter of all Mexican foreign exchange. The debt and interest could not be written off or paid in paper pesos; it was required to be serviced with dollars or other accepted international exchange.

The revolution had not changed the facts of international finance; they were as simple, and as brutal, as in Benito Juárez' day. Successive governments that had taken the easy way, borrowing abroad for long-term development, were running out of credit.

The rapid industrialization had not, as López Mateos' planners hoped, ameliorated the eternal problem of earning foreign exchange. Despite government entry into steel and a host of minor industries, most Mexican industrialization was private, whether capitalized by foreign companies or domestic entrepreneurs. Two huge structures had grown up side by side, a government development program financed by grants and loans, and a large domestic consumer goods industry—this was Mexican "industrialization." The government push had been to create new jobs in private enterprise, and also toward what was called "import substitution"—the production of goods that relieved the economy from importing them. Under this policy hundreds of North American and other foreign firms established franchises and assembly plants, side by side with native industries devoted to the same goal. The thrust in the early years had been to raise the domestic standard of living without draining scarce foreign credits, and almost all goods qualified as "import substitutes" because Mexico lacked every kind of manufactured goods. But the policy never changed. Understandably, both foreign and native industrialists chose to invest in making cheap consumer products, for which there was an expanding peso market, and which returned an immediate profit on investment. Above all, native entrepreneurs had gone for the quick peso. They had no real interest in making quality products, or engaging in any sort of international competition.

To foster and protect these " import substitution" industries, the government erected high tariff walls, barring foreign competition. The government's policies also aided rapid development in various ways: wages were controlled to rise much more slowly than profits, and inflation was managed so that it damaged mainly the poorest classes and those outside the new economy. Taxes on industry were held low. The Mexican basic income tax rate was kept at 3 percent (where it had stood in the United States in the 1930s) and total taxes on industry rarely rose above 10 to 12 percent. Thus consumer industries were encouraged to expand with policies far more favorable to business and industry than existed in any other industrial society. The early results were good: profits soared, allowing an enormous reinvestment in domestic industry. The volume of Mexican domestic credit doubled each four years—a fantastic growth rate. Thousands of new industrial jobs were made, and the Mexican technical, professional, and salaried white-collar classes expanded rapidly. Unionized labor entered, in Mexican terms of reference, the middle-income class, because unlike the rural masses or those not regularly employed, it shared in rising wages and consumption. There was a continual peso inflation remarked by all economists—but the terrible effects of this, which lowered real income for the majority of the working class, were felt mainly beyond the favored industries—in the city slums and on the *ejidos* and hard-scrabble peasant farms, among that sixty percent of the population which remained effectively outside the new industrial society.

The great problem was that at least sixty percent of the people did remain outside the industrial development, and its terrible imbalances began to stabilize by 1949. In that year, profits comprised fully 49 percent of the total national income, which was not large by any standard. Over the next twenty years, profits stabilized at 41 percent, while total wages, earned by forty million of forty-eight million Mexicans, never rose above 25 percent of the national income. A tiny class of ultra-rich entrepreneurs was created along with a larger but relatively small new class of salaried managers, technicians, and skilled workers, a number of prosperous larger farmers who could take advantage of expanding credit and modernizations but who never amounted to more than fifteen percent of all independent agriculturists, and a thousand extremely profitable foreign "Mexicanized" enterprises. This, the new revolutionary class whose demands and aspirations came to dominate PRI and government after 1946, rose against the background of sixty percent of the population who remained on the very borderline of subsistence, and ninety percent of the population who by any modern standard remained extremely poor. Less than one percent of the people became rich, and no more than five percent fully entered into the enjoyments of an affluent society. The imbalance in incomes was shown clearly by one statistic: while the rise in overall consumption was only 31 percent in twenty-five years, the consumption of luxuries rose by 68 percent.

The average Mexican did eat better than ever before, though the diet of the poorer two-thirds was still extremely deficient in the animal proteins found in eggs, fish, meat, or milk. Most of the population still ate only tortillas and beans. They lived in one-room shacks without water or sanitation, and entered the work force in some manner at about the age of ten. The per capita income in 1970 stood at 6,250 pesos or $500 U.S. per year, but the imbalances between profits, technical salaries, union wages, and the huge majority of underemployed peasants and "transitionals"— the men and women existing in the slums looking for a job—made this figure meaningless. A wage earner in Mexico who gained the industrial minimum wage of less than $3 U.S., or a table waiter who drew $2 U.S. per day at a luxury hotel, was an envied and respected member of the Mexican "middle class."

In relative terms, Mexicans who earned 50,000 pesos annually in the 1960s were considered to be members of the "upper class," and those who drew 250,000 pesos ($20,000) U.S. were astronomically rich. The latter, which included the tiny class of multimillionaires, made up no more than one percent of the entire population. The proportion of rich and unrich was not strikingly different from those in advanced or industrial economies. What was different was that the base of the Mexican poor remained so low. Between the affluent classes in the cities, living in huge, modern houses, overrun with servants, and the poor campesino was a consumption and cultural gulf fully as great as the one that had yawned between the nineteenth-century *hacendado* and his *peones*.

None of this was planned; it happened. The alemanistas planned to encourage and foster capitalism in Mexico; after the breakup of the semi-feudal society this was to be the next, decisive step toward the total fulfillment of the nation. What they created was capitalism with a vengeance, a structure that not even the most die-hard believers in untrammeled enterprise in the United States could quite defend. The custodians of the Mexican Revolution were in no sense evil, or even callous men—but then, neither had the Porfirians been essentially evil men. Neither had solved Mexican social problems, with their theories of modernization and industrialization.

The new custodians, however, had created newer fiscal problems and acute problems of foreign exchange; they had failed to throw up a Limantour. The turn of the Mexican industrialist toward fast profits had resulted in an industrial complex that spewed out relatively high-priced, shoddy consumer goods. Behind government protectionism, these goods sold splendidly in the hungry Mexican market. They could not and did not compete abroad, with far superior, relatively lower-priced North American, European, or Japanese industrial products. Mexican industry sold very little in foreign markets. In 1970 the bulk of all foreign credits was earned from the traditional sources, the plantations and mines which provided raw materials and food products for the highly industrialized economies. Ironically, almost all the mines were still in foreign hands, because few Mexican capitalists wanted such high-cost, heavily capitalized, and slow-return investments; the Mexican economy was still "colonial."

But the industrialization that had occurred had worsened Mexico's colonial position. Most of the "Mexicanized" industries erected with foreign help repatriated millions of their government-assured fast profits, thus making a steady drain on foreign exchange. The new class that had become affluent in them and in native enterprise had rising expectations; it demanded more and better goods, which Mexican industry simply did not make. Affluent Mexicans spent hugely for foreign consumer goods, from cars to fancy clothes. By 1968, hundreds of thousands of Mexican tourists were going north of the Bravo, and each one was spending an average of a thousand United States dollars, bringing home the fruits of a foreign industrial society legally or illegally.

The products that Mexico did sell abroad, other than raw materials and minerals, were tourist-oriented gewgaws. Straw hats, guitars, zarapes, leather goods, and imitation Amerindian artifacts did not pay for the diesel locomotives, cars, machine tools, and electric generators that the Mexican industrial facade had to have. Although a small true industrial complex had emerged at Monterrey, making steel and glass, the so-called Mexican industry poured out soap and beer, refrigerators, television sets, washing machines and cases of Coca Cola; it acquired patents, tools, and even plants abroad. By 1970 the Mexican trade deficit had reached the astronomical figure of nine hundred million United States dollars.

Mexicans had not built any self-sustaining industry. They probably could not have, without a ruthless policy of Stalinization. Unfortunately, the sweat and suffering of the Mexican poor at whose expense the consumer complex had been built had gone for very little in the cosmic scheme of things. When Luis Echevarría began to blast Mexican businessmen and industrialists for their failure to seek markets abroad and operate their enterprises competitively, he was only attacking what the Mexican Establishment had earlier encouraged. Mexico had reached an economic plateau, its consumer goods meeting the needs of only the better-paid minority, but the high-profit, controlled-cost operations of Mexican industrialists had been normalized. And any move to change conditions and directions was bound to be resisted bitterly by the economic power structure built up over a full generation.

The whole government-industrial complex was kept solvent and viable by only one phenomenon: the Mexican tourist industry. The millions of North American tourists who poured annually across Mexico did not enrich the public, though they provided employment in services. Too many of them left their money with North-American-operated travel agencies, flew on North-American owned or capitalized airlines, and slept at North-American-owned hotels, many of which were held illegally on the seashore through Mexican fronts. But the tourists provided the national economy with foreign exchange, which the much-vaunted industrialization did not. The tourist dollars offset the trade deficits.

More and more foreigners took advantage of the low prices and cheap labor costs, stunning scenery, and the thousands of magnificent Amerindian and Spanish-colonial monuments. Yet for Mexicans tourism was a new form of dependency in some ways as humiliating as the old. While all Mexicans took pride in the ancient relics of civilization on their land, there were social dangers that the glittering resorts erected on the edge of horrendous barrio slums and miserable *indio* villages might in time produce a violent, hostile reaction against foreigners, whose display of wealth and leisure was strikingly cruel against the backdrop of Mexican poverty. The government, however, had no choice except to foster tourism feverishly, planning new Caribbean resorts and opening up better communications to hidden scenic treasures.

Ironically, the president who now ruled over a nation whose sovereignty was no longer questioned from the North was now far more dependent upon North Americans than had been Madero. Seventy percent of Mexican trade still went north of the Bravo, and seventy percent of Mexico's modernization returned the same route. A regime whose power rested upon its control of economics was uniquely dependent upon the United States. If a serious quarrel developed, the United States would not have to intervene with troops—a mere closing of the border, a minor nuisance to North Americans, would wreak economic disaster upon Mexico. Economic recessions in the North or a swing toward economic nationalism could do damage to Mexican stability, and hints of both in the early 1970s were chilling omens.

Echevarría, who probably owed his office to his tough stand against rioting students, had far greater problems than student unrest, which was again submerged. Like his predecessors, he was a hard-minded realist who understood the necessary rhythms of what Mexicans still called the Revolution. His actions reflected less his personal ideologies than the ruling circles' understanding of the deep caverns now revealed underneath the prosperous facade, and the necessity of buttressing the pillars of their custodial power. It was again necessary, by 1970, to divert more capital to social investment to appease the increasing expectations of the poor, and there had to be at least a psychological appeasement of the onrushing generation. The Echevarría regime recognized the necessity of some redistributions, now not of land but of income and capital.

Its actions were all consistent in the light of these pressures and necessities. Echevarría understood that protectionism no longer served a useful purpose; Mexican industry needed to be made competitive and to seek world markets. He attacked the complacency and relative inefficiency of native Mexican entrepreneurs. The government began to direct a dispersal of industry from the congested urban areas favored by earlier regimes to rural areas, near the sources of raw materials and major ports. Echevarría struck down the last bureaucratic delays holding back the Border Industrialization Program, permitting scores of United States corporations to begin operations near the Arizona boundary and south of the Rio Grande, providing mass employment in the north and earning new gouts of foreign exchange. To foster even more tourism, he amended the law that barred foreigners from holding coastal properties, so that foreign hoteliers and developers would be encouraged to invest in seashore resorts. The government no longer allowed old phobias to stand in the way of the dollar flow—though, as always, appearances were maintained by apparently contradictory statements.

To encourage austerity at home, the regime raised taxes ten percent on luxuries and clamped down on imports. Prices for basic commodities were rigidly controlled while the prices of imported luxury goods were raised, to relieve the inflationary pressures on the poor. The government practiced new economies. The overall effect was to slow a headlong growth that had benefitted only part of the population, while channeling investment into more solid, long-term structures to provide economic stability.

To lessen the tensions with the Left, Echevarría dismissed a conservative municipal president of the capital and his rigid police chief, who had stood by while right-wing groups assaulted student demonstrators. Touring the United States, he lectured the congress in diplomatically discourteous terms and expressed support for the Mexican minority north of the Bravo. These stands won much favor in Mexico, but Echevarría had to move cautiously—any apparent swing leftward, or too much vocal anti-*yanqui* rhetoric could cut off the vital flow of North America investment.

The regime faced a central political problem. Dissent could not be put off forever with restated ideals; industry had to be disciplined; and austerities, redistributions, and new taxes were necessary to provide capital for social investments which could no longer be financed from abroad. But unlike the former redistribution of land, a redistribution of capital and income had to be taken primarily out of the hides of the revolutionary classes—the very power structure of the regime. The new policies were a cold bath for the new-rich and were bitterly resented. By late 1971 many domestic consumer industries were suffering because of government policies: forty textile plants had closed, and the native automobile industry was in serious financial trouble. Businessmen in Mexico began to issue unprecedented criticisms of the presidential policies. Democratizations that pleased the young enfuriated the old party bosses. The regime, by 1973, had taken only the smallest steps and made only a few small advances along the endless, spiral road.

These themes continued to be played out over the next decade. The Echevarría regime followed the then-fashionable theories of statist economic management, borrowing foreign money when possible, using both rhetoric and judicious social spending to maintain domestic social peace. No basic structural problems were solved. The population continued to grow, outstripping development.

Now began a pattern in which successive presidents, elected by the overwhelming patronage and power of the Institutional Revolutionary Party (PRI) machine against token opposition, entered office each six years attended by hope and popular adulation but left it arguably the most hated men in Mexico.

Echevarría's verbal attacks on Mexican industrial inefficiency, aimed at the private sector, created more rancor than results. No reforms were urged or made in the bloated governmental bureaucracies and myriad agencies. The more entrepreneurial, prosperous, and U.S.-influenced culture of the northern states turned toward PAN, which gained adherents among businessmen and city-dwellers. An inevitable devaluation of the peso drained more confidence from the ruling faction.

Echevarría flirted with Third World dreams and rhetoric, which made Mexico neither a leader of the developing nations nor more popular with Americans.

Finally, as the traditional dramatic act while leaving office, Echevarría revived land redistributions. Estates in the prosperous northwest Pacific region, some belonging to heirs of revolutionary generals, were confiscated, arousing enormous shock waves and tensions. This act did nothing to ease the agrarian problem—which was beyond solving with any "forty acres and a burro" solution—but it marked the last flailing effort of the old *cardenista* dream.

José López Portillo, more poet and scholar than technician, followed Echevarría in 1976. His administration proved to be both a normal progression and an aberration. The same policies were followed, but now everything was deranged by the oil boom.

Mexico characteristically did not join OPEC, the Organization of Petroleum Exporting Countries, but it benefitted from its embargoes and price hikes. And when vast new petroleum reserves were discovered in southern Mexico in the 1970s, Mexicans dreamed of becoming a major oil power. Many became intoxicated with the prospect of unimaginable wealth. Meanwhile foreign bankers, dazzled by seemingly inexhaustible collateral, lavished credits upon both public and private sectors. The external debt skyrocketed overnight.

This new-found wealth might have refurbished Mexican industry and infrastructure. However, the billions no more served Mexico than the gold and silver from the Indies had served Spain. While port facilities and transport were recklessly neglected and the 1960s highway system crumbled, billions were either sent abroad or spent on consumption. While a dangerously polluted industrial landscape ran short of water, two-thirds of new luxury condominiums in San Antonio and Houston, Texas were sold to Mexican nationals. Union bosses frequented northern hotspots like Las Vegas, and the spending of the Mexican elite, both private and official, became legendary.

The malfunctioning economic structure could not have handled the inflow well in any case. The new money benefitted primarily those who had access to it. The well-connected grew richer: Some Mexican families now had fortunes of $100 U.S. millions or more. The poor gained only from an expansion of government employment, both in the bureaucracies and state-subsidized industries, together with subsidized food prices and a proliferation of pick-and-shovel payrolls.

Much was also stolen. Because of the system of no-reelection, Mexican administrations had a short time in which to steal. López Portillo's made the most of it; his own family was reputed to have seized the equivalent of $3 U.S. billions. This was not the most corrupt government in Mexican history, but it had more to loot. Mexico had always known amiable official corruption; now opportunity gave it a hard-edged greed. It suffused through society; even the judicial police took to beating and robbing hapless *mojados* returning with full pockets from the North.

Both bankers and the regime were slow to see the coming bubble-burst. Signs were everywhere—by 1981 the budget for PEMEX, the giant state petroleum monopoly, was almost double total oil revenues. In 1982 PEMEX alone spent $32 U.S. billions, while oil prices were sinking.

Despite López Portillo's emotional vows to defend the peso "like a dog," the whole financial system teetered toward collapse. The currency could no longer be maintained artificially against the dollar. Fuming against profiteers and "traitors," López Portillo lashed out at Mexican bankers, and as his last act in office he nationalized—without meaningful compensation—all private banks.

This, like Echevarría's confiscations, may have placated the Left but it created financial chaos. The business community lost all confidence in government. More money fled abroad. Worse, because of bank holdings some sixty percent of all Mexican enterprise was now owned or managed by increasingly inept government agencies.

Widely despised, López Portillo handed the wreckage to his successor, Miguel de la Madrid, in December 1982. This was the beginning of incisive change in both the government and economy of Mexico.

De la Madrid and the coterie he brought to power were of the new generation of *técnicos*, mostly men who had earned doctorates in economics or technology at prestigious American universities. Unlike many of their colleagues in richer nations, they had no faith in statist methods or state management of economies: They had seen the results at first hand. Submerged during the oil-mad years, they were in fact free-marketers, before that philosophy became fashionable in the Hispanic world. They began a slow and painful process of turning things around.

By 1982 Mexico was suffering from a rampant case of "Brazilian disease"—escalating inflation, gross official mismanagement, widespread corruption, stagnant industry, and fleeing capital. The foreign debt had reached $80 U.S. billions. Oil prices were collapsing; there was no succor from that sector. The government survived only by printing more money than its total revenues, which sent the peso into free-fall against hard currencies. The peso, 4:1 to the dollar in 1946, sank to 1000:1, 2000:1, and lower. The country's infrastructure and industry could not operate without imported technology and equipment, but credit was exhausted.

However, de la Madrid also inherited important strengths and assets. First was the immense power of the ruling party, controlling not only patronage but most of the economy. Second was the enormous power this gave the presidency, dominating the Congress, all state governments, and the municipal presidencies of all important towns. No one reached important office without PRI and the direct approval of the president. There was the historic tendency of the Mexican population, especially the poor, to suffer hardship stoically. Finally, there was the utter lack of a core ideology within PRI, which represented every spectrum from professional to peasant and from Left to Center-Right.

All these afforded the new regime powers that few other ruling circles enjoyed. They allowed de la Madrid and his successor to carry out reforms successfully where in other parts of the world, notably the Soviet Union, they failed.

As the "technicians" emerged and took control, there was always an uneasy alliance between them and the *políticos*, the politicians who ran the electoral machines. However, union chiefs and party bosses had one thing in common with doctorates from M.I.T. and Yale; they all desired to hold power. The politicians, organized down to the last remote *ejido* and fetid, overcrowded barrio, could maintain the technocrats in power while they tried to save the nation.

The progress was slow and painful, incremental in fact. However, the results were swift and severe. The external debt had to be managed, some credit flow maintained. The regime accomplished this with some adroitness and more pain. Default was unthinkable. The pressures of external debt were now more acute than of old; foreigners no longer sent invasion fleets, but they could cut off further credit. Now, both private bankers and foreign governments helped avoid a crisis. The debt was managed, while rising to $100 U.S. billions.

The price was austerity. Currency restrictions were imposed, dollar accounts impounded, hard currency paid out only under strict licence. Public spending was reduced, not all at once, but gradually. Price controls were relaxed and subsidies, which had made a shambles of the marketplace, reduced. The effect of this medicine was that initially prices, especially for subsistence, rose; imports halted; industry stagnated, crippled for parts; and the standard of living, inflated during the boom years, fell as much as fifty percent.

The very rich, who had sequestered funds abroad, survived. The newly affluent middle classes were devastated, both financially and psychologically. In many cases, their lifestyles were destroyed. They could take no trips, buy no imported luxuries, nor send their children abroad for education. Many had to sacrifice property bought abroad on credit. The poor, the majority of Mexicans, endured.

The Mexican middle classes were enraged but hardly revolutionary. Their reactions were more rhetorical than rebellious. They had never been organized politically along class interests, though now many voted for PAN, which was a revolutionary party only in the electoral sense. There were several reasons. Most middle-class Mexicans believed going to the barricades was futile—the now thoroughly professional army, entirely loyal to the government, would probably exterminate them as successfully as it did the various guerrilla bands that popped up here and there. In Mexico hundreds of dissidents and journalists were killed or disappeared each year. But even more important, revolutionary ardor was dulled in the white-collar classes by the knowledge that uprisings against authoritarian regimes from Cuba to Iran had backfired tragically against the middle class.

The Mexico they represented was a small if vocal minority; they were in no position to assume custodianship of the country.

De la Madrid's presidency was in some ways analogous to Franklin Roosevelt's New Deal in the Depression-torn United States, though it had different impetus and goals. It did not solve the pressing economic problems, but it stabilized the situation, and things began to improve.

The Mexican Left, however, especially the large segment within the ruling party, was dismayed by the regime's acceptance of capitalist realities and subservience to foreign bankers. When it became clear that de la Madrid intended to reform the economy completely—standing much of the revolution on its head—through the choice of his successor, the acrimony within PRI became rebellion. The natural rhythm of the revolution called now for a relaxation of austerity, more social spending, some pampering of the Left. When Carlos Salinas de Gotari, a Yale-trained *técnico*, was anointed as PRI's candidate for 1988, the party itself exploded.

The Left-Center split off, creating a separate party led by Cuauhtémoc Cárdenas, son of the legendary president. The new PRD, or Democratic Revolutionary Party, took many workers, peasants, and no few of the *políticos* with it.

With the far-Left weak and fragmented, the Right mainly of local importance in the north, this made the election of 1988 an intramural power struggle, at least at first. Running with an immense tide of popular protest against both de la Madrid's policies and the "undemocratic" method of choosing his successor, many people believed that PRI, the longest-ruling political party then outside the USSR, would founder. But the government held the political machinery with all its state powers and patronage. Most of the bosses, though disliking Salinas, stayed loyal. This proved decisive in the end.

After an acrimonious campaign marred both by violence and widespread irregularities, the official results—announced after suspicious delays by the government—gave Salinas a majority by less than one percent. Many if not most observers believed the election was stolen by fraud, that Cárdenas won but was counted out.

The immense stability of the Mexican Republic was shown by the fact that while there were large demonstrations in the capital and elsewhere, no revolutionary shout was raised. Cárdenas cried fraud but did not lead his party to the barricades. Salinas assumed the presidency without serious incident on December 1, 1988.

Salinas, a slight, balding, almost unimpressive technocrat in a culture that prized charisma and machismo, seemed to have the shakiest of mandates. The nation was divided; his own party was uneasily separated into reformers and the old bosses, now know as "dinosaurs"; most Mexicans, including many of his supporters, believed he had won power fraudulently.

Salinas, however, turned out to be the most skillful politician to reach the presidency of Mexico in decades. He quickly performed the now-ritual act of proving he was in charge by removing or jailing certain ponderous PRI dinosaurs. Political recalcitrants were no longer shot; they were fired or brought up on charges of corruption. Using the still-undamaged powers of his office he pressed through what was in historical terms a radical reversal of policy.

The overarching philosophy of the Salinas regime was simple in outline, complex in implementation. The vision might be described as this: to pursue the *alemanista* goal of making Mexico a modern nation, raising the standard of living, and providing work for all within the structure. The philosophy stemmed from the fact that Salinas and his cabinet observed that all of the richer nations of the world were market economies and democracies, whichever came first.

If Mexico were ever to enter the First World, it must emulate such principles, even if this meant dismantling not the revolution itself but its countless encrustations. This vision was not peculiar to Mexico. In the 1980s it was sweeping the world, even into Hispanic America, the stronghold of statist-mercantilism where market capitalism, like democracy, had never had much chance. Both democracy and free markets, of course, were horror-visions to political dinosaurs of the older school. In either case they threatened to destroy PRI's eternal hold on power. And they were enormous gambles for a society such as Mexico's.

With control of the legislature as firm as Augustus Caesar's of the Roman Senate—the president moved, Congress acted—Salinas quickly dismantled the prevailing autarky. The laws hindering foreign investment and ownership were repealed, even if it meant amending the Constitution. High Mexican tariffs were unilaterally lowered. State spending was reduced, mainly through attrition of the public workforce. The banks were reprivatized, along with scores of former government monopolies, nearly all of which had been losing money. With inflation lowered, the peso was stabilized against the dollar at a new rate of 3:1, the highest value it had held since the beginning of the century. Foreign investment poured in; the Mexican Bolsa or stock market soared, though it remained nervous as all such markets, and trade with the United States increased four-fold.

Mexican economists were painfully aware that despite every hindrance, the nation's percentage of trade with the United States had risen from about 60% to 70% in recent times. This led to a more radical notion—why not bring Mexico within the North American market area completely, letting nature take its course?

Ironically, the greater push for NAFTA, the North American Free Trade Agreement ratified by both countries in 1993, came from Mexico, where Salinas staked his prestige upon it. This was not an easy decision, given that the productivity of Mexican labor was one-sixth that of North Americans, or $4,000 to $24,000 per capita.

These and other economic reforms were still simpler to bring about than the movement toward democracy. With reluctance even in his inner circle, Salinas sanctioned an independent electoral institute, removing control of balloting from PRI. Voting and registration laws were amended to make outright fraud more difficult. In the most acerbic confrontation of all, Salinas forced the PRI organization in three states to accept the election of opposition candidates, two for PAN in the north, one for PRD in the impoverished center.

This did not bring Mexico to full democracy. The PRI, still the party of "pork, patronage, and power," had enormous advantages over the poorly organized opposition parties, which had little but protest to offer. And PRI, in a process closed to the public, still chose all major candidates, whose anointment was tantamount to election. The press was only partially free, the judicial process far from incorruptible. More was promised, in good time.

The results of reform were mixed, as always. The northern and Pacific states enjoyed rising standards of living, but the Gulf regions and southern states from Guerrero to Chiapas had steady or falling incomes. Eighty percent of Mexican farms comprised less than 25 acres, forty percent held less than 2.5 acres. Some thirty percent of all Mexicans had no formal employment in 1993.

The top twenty percent of families earned 54.2 percent of the national income, the bottom 80 percent received only 45.8 percent, a much greater spread than in most rich nations. Privatization also erected vast new Mexican fortunes for those positioned to take advantage of opportunity. By

1993 there were more than a dozen dollar-billionaires, ranking the country in that respect only behind the United States, Japan, and Germany.

The federal debt was halved in terms of Gross Domestic Product; manufactured goods rose to 88 percent of all exports. Economic growth faltered, however, and the trade deficit worsened. Some industries thrived, while countless small, inefficient enterprises foundered. The gross, costly state monopolies and industries suffered heavily. PEMEX shed 90,000 employees, and textiles, steel, and mining all took large losses. In some cases government ministries downsized by as much as 50 percent. These had all been overstaffed, but the changes were painful.

The real income of Mexicans rose from 62 percent of the 1980 level, before economic reform began, to only 73 percent by 1993. Mexico was closer to the United States, but still far from prosperity.

Realistically, the nation could not expect to enter the charmed circle of rich nations for at least thirty years, if ever. This was Salinas' gamble, that given hope, the masses might endure. He had increased social spending, from 6.6 percent of the national product to 10.2 percent. He also directed this spending through a new agency, Solidarity, which, significantly, he removed from party control, placing it directly under the president. However, against a sea of Mexican poverty, this was the proverbial drop in the bucket.

Unlike his immediate predecessors, Salinas approached the end of his term not universally loved but almost universally respected. Whatever the value of his programs, from relations with the North to reform of the economy, he had carried them off majestically.

The great issue of the 1994 changing of the guard was, would this course be continued or would there be a change of direction? Some reform would certainly stand; both PAN and PRD, the opposition parties, had accepted NAFTA. However, PRD had moved significantly leftward, while PAN, though not quite co-opted, approved of almost everything that had been done except for the lack of protection of some Mexican industry and the continuing lack of open democracy.

The crucial election year began with sound and fury, though in the end this seemed to signify little. The armed uprising in Chiapas, seemingly designed to be more a media event than a real revolution, succeeded in that instance. It caught both the government and the world by surprise. In an era before Cable News Network, probably the Mexican army would have pursued and smashed the *indio* rebels with much bloodshed; after all, small wars were continually being waged between dissidents and authorities in many areas. But this would have embarrassed the regime before the world, and the uprising stalemated into negotiations.

Rarely noted by the visiting media, however, was that while the appearance of armed descendants of the Mayas and their mysterious spokesman, Subcomandante Marcos, energized the Left, it also marginalized it. Most Mexicans sympathized with the Indians of Chiapas, but not to the point of desiring more dead bodies in the streets. A Zapata-style revolution held few charms for millions of modern Mexicans. In the same way the shocking assassination in March of the chosen PRI candidate, Luis Donaldo Colosio, did not destabilize the government or nation. Whoever engineered the killing—the Left, the PRD, or disgruntled elements within the ruling party—it was done probably because Colosio, a charismatic figure who promised far greater movement toward democracy and inspired confidence, was certain to win.

How this changed history can never be determined. Salinas quickly chose another *técnico*, the Yale-educated and quite uncharismatic Ernesto Zedillo, who had played a major role in the reforms. And PRI, battered, surly, and shorn of much patronage and power, still could fashion one more hurrah in the face of invited foreign observers by the score and the cleanest election ever held in Mexico.

There were certainly irregularities in many places, but neither foreigners nor Mexicans had much doubt that PRI and Zedillo won. He polled 50.1 percent, with only a plurality needed, to an attractive PAN candidate's 26.69, and Cárdenas' 17.08. He had, perhaps, not got quite the majority overall—local ballot boxes could still be stuffed—but there was little question that the opposition lost. PAN would acquiesce, counting now on an opening process to bring it eventually to power. The PRD would demonstrate half-heartedly, but was shattered by its repudiation at the polls. As Salinas said, Mexicans did not want to destroy what had been built, but they did want it improved.

When Zedillo took office, 92 million Mexicans needed 800,000 new jobs a year; they were creating 400,000.

The revolution was far from finished.

Mexico was still the most fundamentally stable of the Hispanic countries, if not yet a democracy. The revolution had provided society and government with legitimacy for a while; future legitimacy probably depended upon movement toward full democratic institutions. Mexico had seemed stable under her older dispensations, the Spanish crown and the interminable twilight of the Porfiriato. For the man in the high palace there were flashes of distant lightning and thunder on the wind. For thirty years guerrilla groups had operated in various regions. Urban *guerrilleros* calling themselves *zapatistas* kidnapped officials in the capital. In the sweltering lunar landscapes that rose above Acapulco, where Morelos and Alvarez had ruled, schoolteachers led bands that robbed and killed rich landowners. Remote Chiapas remained in a state of civil war. In Morelos, Zapata's old warriors were dead, but their heirs were still poor and landless. Until the 1990s the army and the national judicial police, who stood firm behind the regime, hunted down and exterminated such bands and dissidents one by one.

Under the international spotlight thrown over Mexico by the success of *Salinastroika*, such killings had become impossible. Negotiations with *guerrilleros* were now in order. However, as in Chiapas, there was very little to negotiate. The *zapatista* dream, if not the *zapatista* rebelliousness, was dead.

Yet the spirit of a hundred violent ghosts, not co-opted by the rewards of the revolution or imprisoned within the grotesque statues that celebrated Mexican martyrs from Zapata to Hidalgo, walked the land, seeking embodiment in new generations.

Mexico became a nation in the twentieth century. This was the great contribution of the revolution. The days when people knew themselves as *indios* or *criollos* and not as Mexicans, or believed that there was a taint to blood and that European ancestry was proof of inherent superiority, were gone. The *meztizo*, the true Mexican, whether almost white or almost Indian, had engulfed both the people and the culture; he had made his own establishment. The new Mexican had found pride—though pride sometimes confused his priorities—in new political and technical achievements. There was still a certain confusion about what comprised a Mexican, shown when the *mestizo* establishment spent millions of a poor country's revenues on the anthropological museum at the capital in 1964. The finest institution of its kind in the world, it glorified the Amerindian past—an exercise Mexicans could hardly afford, but believed in their souls they must.

Despite this esoteric seeking of the past and the naming of children after ancient Nahua warriors, the Mexican was rapidly ceasing to be Amerindian. By 1970 no more than ten percent of all Mexicans could be identified as *indios*. And while the numbers rose with reductions in the death rate, such percentages held. The *indios* were in transition, like the millions of *mestizo* peasants, leaving ancestral plots and villages. They were still submerged in hamlet and slum, but no longer the "worms in the Mexican grass" one of their number had described them. Except in the remotest regions, *indios* were becoming acculturated, learning to speak Spanish while Spanish-speaking anthropologists mourned their passing. Their blood and heart and soul would not disappear, any more than the blood and soul of Rome disappeared in holocaust and assimilation. The *indios*, and all people with Amerindian blood, were becoming members of a newer Mexic civilization. Within that civilization the remnants of the Tarahumares, Lacondones, and Mayas would either acculturate or remain pitiful, primitive vestiges. In the world of motor cars, refineries, dams, factories, and computers, the knowledge in men's minds had far more meaning for the future than whatever blood coursed in their veins.

The revolution made an imperfect nation. The nation did not yet include all of Mexico's nearly 100 millions. At least sixty percent of the people within the Republic's borders were not yet citizens of a modern state; they were still dispossessed, living more or less as the dispossessed had lived for four centuries. The cities the revolution allowed to flourish on the plateaus were still much like the white cities the Spanish built in a strange land with and upon the backs of Indians; they were huge but still something of anomalies rising in an ancient country. There was almost as great a cultural gulf between the *mestizo* who wore a business suit, went to his office, and wrote the title *Licenciado* or *Ingeniero* before his name and the *campesino* who could barely carve out his own signature as between the Spanish master and Indian serf.

There were still three distinct Mexicos.

One was the Mexico of the submerged *indios* and agrarian *mestizos*, many trying to make a living upon a hectare or two, now becoming indistinguishable except in the far south—poor, remote, apathetic people who expected very little and received it, humble as only the Mexican poor could be, but people with enormous strength to endure. Ironically, they would endure if all the Mexicos above them collapsed or disappeared. Their numbers swelling dramatically, they formed the Mexico that created enormous problems for the regime.

A second Mexico was the one now in transition. This was comprised of the people who moved culturally from *indio* to *mestizo* and from *jacales* on arid, maguey-strewn hillsides to the burgeoning towns. They found what work they could, and their joys in gregariousness and garrulousness. Their spiritual ancestors had endured being outcasts for centuries, and those who had gone before them had emerged as the Mexican nation. Like the submerged mass from which they sprang, they were tough, enduring, and now, increasingly aware. They lived in a world of petty *caciques* and day labor and neighborhood stores, a world now crumbling under the pressures of *Salinastroika*. Their aims and ambitions were immediate: work, food, a place to sleep, a few pesos. They were less humble than the country folk, for they had found hope even in the teeming slums surrounding Mexican cities. Most were aware of *el norte*, the glittering Colossus of the North. Many went there; many stayed home and bettered themselves.

The third Mexico existed only in the great cities and on a few prosperous farms. This was the world of bureaucrats and businessmen, professionals, intellectuals, and technicians, supported by all the trained supporting classes of modern society. They were the only Mexicans who understood the world beyond the immediate neighborhood, or cared or worried about who or what they were. In 1970 there were only two million Mexicans who read newspapers, and no more than five percent read periodicals and books twenty years later. They were informed and proud of it, knowing that they formed the Mexican nation. They ruled the other two Mexicos. A country with a tiny daily press run, however noisy, where forty percent were barely employed and sixty percent mired in a struggle for mere existence and took little part in organized economic or political life, except to vote as directed, was unready as yet to dispense entirely with custodians. This upper, visible, self-aware Mexico ran the nation; it *was* the nation, as classes before it had formed and directed the Mexico since civilization first sprouted on the land.

This rule had been inevitable; it was good or evil depending upon the spirit of the guardians and their goals. There was a vast difference in spirit and goals between the custodians in the high palace in the 1990s and the Científicos, though both were modernizers; between the Científicos and the conquerors who came on cockleshell ships with Cortés; and between the Spaniards and the ancient lords who expended the blood and sweat of Mexico on pyramids. In this was hope.

Like all custodians, the new class shared dangers with the old. They were prey to arrogance, as are all men who rule. Because of their diverse origins, the new custodians had an identity crisis and were driven to adopt extraneous cultures and ideas. The *criollos* had fled from their Hispanic heritage to disaster in the bosom of French thought. The revolutionary establishment, the new class, in the twentieth century became Americanized by their northern educations and technology, while some were drawn irresistibly by other, Marxist, foreignisms. People who adopt the artifacts and organizational forms of a diffused civilization cannot avoid being influenced by the thought patterns, habits, and manners of the diffusors. Three generations of the new elite had completed education in an industrial society, and they were deeply imbued with its thrust and power. They increasingly lived the lifestyles and patterns of U.S. Americans, though in Latin color schemes. The new class drove to offices in cars; they observed the cocktail hour; their women thought nothing of short skirts and entering bars. Their vast, warm, extended families were cracking under the strain of concepts of social mobility and constant career pressures. They were hesitantly forming a meritocracy from the presidency down, in a society where historically merit played little part. They had cracked one class system but were creating another.

If the new class grew estranged and apart from the Mexico of its origins, it would embark on the perilous course and inherit the sterile futility of the Científicos. This concern lay at the heart of Mexican politics, more than ideology or economic tinkering. Large numbers of the younger elite were radicalized, demanding democracy whatever the consequences. And they argued, logically, that without movement toward democracy, all the other progress of Salinas' reforms were doomed. Yet democracy itself, like market economies in worldwide fashion, remained something of an exotic plant in Mexico. It flowered under the shadow of the volcano.

Put in proper perspective, Mexico was still a nation struggling to emerge from centuries of colonialism under a backward empire. Modern Mexico began with the Spanish conquest and the bloody diffusion of Hispanic civilization. A Mexican nation began only with the twentieth-century revolution, which was both forward and backward-looking. The nation of the twenty-first century would be partly the creation of that revolution, partly the result of a newer diffusion of culture fostered by a new custodianship, which turned toward American and European financial and industrial systems. The changes of the twentieth century rivalled the changes wrought by Spanish swords. Both destroyed old worlds that had outlived their usefulness, but without freeing Mexicans completely from the past or thrusting them fully into the brave new world.

Mexican history, like all human history, is a succession of racial and cultural waves breaking over ancient lands. Each era makes its own glories and horrors, both out of necessity and circumstance. The tragedy of Mexican history is that Mexicans, more than many other peoples, could never escape their past. They came burdened into the twentieth century, and would go burdened into the next; problems the Porfiriato could not solve remained unsolved. The hundred million Mexicans who would inhabit the 2000s were already inexorably shaped, from Chapultepec to Chiapas.

Mexico and Mexicans in their emergence had little effect on the greater world. Their struggles were parochial—yet there was and is a universal element in Mexican history from which every people might learn. The past is not frozen in stone monuments or buried with old bones and artifacts. It lives on in each new generation.

Enfolded more than ever before within a larger North American civilization, a larger Mexico was already having a greater effect upon the outer world. Unless things went very wrong, Mexico would take a greater place within that world.

The lesson is that people endure, and enduring, may yet hope to prevail.

SELECTED
BIBLIOGRAPHY

MAJOR SOURCES:

Alamán, Lucas. *Disertaciones Sobre la Historia de la República Mexicana desde la Época de la Conquista*, 3 vols. Mexico, 1844–1849.
————. *Historia de Méjico*, 5 vols. Mexico, 1849–1852.
Alcáraz, R. et al. *Apuntes para la Historia de la Guerra entre Mexico y Los Estados Unidos.* Mexico, 1848.
Altamira y Crevea, Rafael. *Historia de España y de la Civilización Española*, 4 vols. Barcelona, 1900–1911.
Bancroft, Hubert Howe. *History of Mexico*, 6 vols. San Francisco, 1881–1889.
Barca, Madame Calderón de la. *Life in Mexico.* London, 1844.
Benavente, Toribio de (Motolinia). *Historia de los Indios de la Nueva España.* Mexico, 1941.
Benítez, Fernando. *Century After Cortes.* Chicago, 1963.
Blom, Frans. *Tribes and Temples.* New Orleans, 1927.
Bravo Ugarte, José. *Historia de México*, 4 vols. Mexico, 1941–1944.
Brenner, Anita, and Leighton, George. *The Wind That Swept Mexico.* New York, 1943.
Bulnes, Francisco. *El Verdadero Juárez.* Mexico, 1904.
————. *Las Grandes Mentiras de Nuestra Historia.* Mexico, 1904.
Bustamante, Carlos Mariá de. *Cuadro Historico de la Revolución de la America Mexicana*, 6 vols. Mexico, 1823–1832.
Cabrera, Luis. *Obras Políticas*, Mexico, 1921.
Callcott, Wilfrid H. *Church and State in Mexico, 1822–1857.* Durham, N. C., 1926.
Cameron, Roderick. *The Viceroyalties of the West.* Boston, 1968.
Caso, Antonio. *El Problema de México y la Ideología Nacional.* Mexico, 1924.
Chapman, Charles E. *A History of Spain.* New York, 1918.
Cháves Orozco, Luis. *Historia de México.* Mexico, 1934.
Clavijero, Francisco J. *Historia Antigua de México.* Mexico, 1945.
Cline, Howard F. *Mexico: Revolution to Evolution, 1940–1960.* Oxford, 1962.
Colección de Documentos Inéditos del Archivo de Indias, 57 vols. Madrid, 1969.
Cortés, Hernán. *Cartas de Relación de la Conquista de Méjico.* Mexico, 1946.
Cuevas, Mariano. *Historia de la Iglesia en Mexico*, 5 vols. Mexico, 1921–1928.

Díaz del Castillo, Bernal. *The True History of the Conquest of New Spain,* 5 vols. London, 1908–.

Durán, Diego. *Historia de las Indias de Nueva España* . . . Mexico, 1951.

Fernández de Lizardi, José J. *El Periquillo Sarmiento,* 2 vols. Mexico, 1816.

Fonseca, Fabián de, y Urrutia, Carlos de. *Historia General de Real Hacienda,* 6 vols. Mexico, 1845.

Gage, Thomas. *New Survey of the West Indies.* London, 1928.

Gamio, Manuel, ed. *La Población del Valle de Teotihuacán.* Mexico, 1922.

Gamio, Manuel. *Forjando Patria.* Mexico, 1916.

García, Genero, ed. *Carácter de Conquista Española* . . . Mexico, 1901.

García, Genero. *La Inquisición en México.* Mexico, 1916.

Garibay, Angel María. *Visión de los Vencidos.* Mexico, 1959.

Gómara, Francisco López de. *Historia General de las Indias.* Zaragoza, 1952.

González Pena, Carlos. *History of Mexican Literature.* Dallas, 1943.

Gruening, Ernest. *Mexico and Its Heritage.* New York, 1942.

Guerra, José (Fr. Servando de Teresa y Mier). *Historia de la Revolución de Nueva España, Antiguamente Anáhuac,* 2 vols. London, 1813.

Guzmán, Martín Luis. *El Águila y la Serpiente.* Mexico, 1928.

Herrera, Antonio de. *Historia General de los Hechos de los Castellanos* . . . , 2 vols. Madrid, 1730.

Humboldt, Alexander von. *Essai Politique Sur le Royaume de la Nouvelle Espagne.* Paris, 1811.

Hume, Martin A. S. *Spain, Its Greatness and Decay.* Cambridge, 1899.

Hyde, H. Montgomery. *The Mexican Empire.* New York, 1946.

Indigenous Sources: *Anales de México y Tlatelolco; Cantares Mexicanos; Códices Aubin, de Duran, Florentino, Ramirez, etc.*

Instrucciones Reservadas Que los Vireyes de Nueva España Dejaron . . . Mexico, 1967.

Ixtlilxóchitl, Fernando de Alva. *Obras Históricas.* Mexico, 1952.

Landa, Diego de. *Relación de las Cosas de Yucatán.* Cambridge, 1941.

Las Casas, Bartolomé de. *Breve Relación de la Destrucción de las Indias Occidentales.* Seville, 1821.

Leonard, Irving A. *Baroque Times in Old Mexico.* Ann Arbor, Mich., 1959.

Lewis, Oscar. *The Children of Sanchez.* New York, 1961.

Márquez Sterling, M. *Los Últimos Días del Presidente Madero.* Havana, 1917.

Mendieta, Gerónimo de. *Historia Eclesiástica Indiana.* Mexico, 1945.

Molina Enríquez, Andrés. *Los Grandes Problemas Nacionales.* Mexico, 1909.

Mora, José María Luis. *Obras Sueltas,* 2 vols. Paris, 1847.

Muñoz Camargo, Diego. *Historia de Tlaxcala.* Mexico, 1947.

Nicholson, Irene. *The X in Mexico.* New York, 1965.

Ocampo, Melchor. *Obras Completas,* 4 vols. Mexico, 1872.

Palavicini, Félix F. *México, Historia de su Evolución Constructiva,* 4 vols. Mexico, 1945.

Parkes, Henry Bamford. *A History of Mexico.* Boston, 1960.

Paz, Octavio. *The Labyrinth of Solitude.* New York, 1961.

Pereyra, Carlos. *Historia del Pueblo Mejicano.* Mexico, 1909.

———. *El Orba de España en América.* Mexico, 1925.

Peterson, Frederick A. *Ancient Mexico*. New York, 1962.
Prescott, William A. *The History of the Conquest of Mexico*. New York, 1844.
Prieto, Guillermo. *Memorias de Mis Tiempos*, 2 vols. Mexico, 1886.
Recopilación de Leyes de los Reinos de las Indias, 4 vols. Madrid, 1841.
Ricard, Robert. *The Spiritual Conquest of Mexico*. Berkeley, 1966.
Riva Palacio, Vicente, ed. *México á Través de los Siglos*, 5 vols. Barcelona, 1889.
Romero de Terreros, M. *Historia Sintética del Arte Colonial*. Mexico, 1922.
Sahagún, Bernardino de. *Historia General de las Cosas de la Nueva España*. Mexico, 1956.
Sierra, Justo, ed. *México, Su Evolución Social*, 3 vols. Mexico, 1900–
Sierra, Justo. *Juárez, Su Obra y Su Tiempo*. Mexico, 1905–1906.
Simpson, Eyler N. *The Ejido, Mexico's Way Out*. Chapel Hill, N.C., 1937.
Simpson, Lesley B. *The Encomienda in New Spain*. Berkeley, 1950.
Soustelle, Jacques. *La Vie Quotidienne des Azteques*. Paris, 1955.
Spinden, Herbert. *Ancient Civilizations of Mexico and Central America*. New York, 1928.
Tannenbaum, Frank. *Mexico, The Struggle for Peace and Bread*. New York, 1950.
Tezozómoc, Hernando Alvarado. *Crónica Mexicana*. Mexico, 1944.
Torquemada, Juan de. *Los Veinte i un Libros . . .* Madrid, 1723.
Turner, J. K. *Barbarous Mexico*. Chicago, 1911.
Vaillant, George C. *Aztecs of Mexico*. New York, 1941.
Vasconcelos, José. *Indología*. Mexico, 1926.
———. *Ulises Criollo*. Mexico, 1935.
Vasconcelos, José, y Gamio, Manuel. *Aspects of Mexican Civilization*. New York, 1926.
Zavala, Lorenzo de. *Ensayo Histórico de las Revoluciones de Mexico Desde 1808. Hasta 1830*, 2 vols. Mexico, 1845.

INDEX

Abad y Queipo, Bishop, 285–286, 299, 324, 346
Academy of San Carlos, 287
Acamapichtli, 59–61
Acolhua, 50
Acolnahuacatzin, 50, 56
Action Group (*Grupo Acción*), 548, 557
Age of the First Builders, *see* Preclassical era
Age of the First Priests, *see* Preclassical era
Agrarianism
and Cortés, 190–191
development of, 11–17, 23
economy, breakdown of, 224
famines, 36–37, 48, 74–75, 102
and foreign investment, 591, 616–617, 633–634
and mechanization, 616–619, 625–626, 633–634, 639, 642–643
migrant labor, 618–619
milpas (cornfields), 12–13, 19, 23, 29, 35
Morelos revolt, 464, 494–496, 500, 529
and Obregón, 552–553
peasant population, 465–466, 477–478, 616–619, 633, 642–643
during Porfiriato era, 463, 465–467, 477–478
pulque plantations, 466–467
reforms of Tlacaélel, 66–67
and religion, 14–17, 22–23, 26, 36–37, 48, 74–75, 102

see also Landholdings; Land reform; Slavery
Agua Prieta, Plan of, 547
Aguilar, Cándido, 531
Aguilar, Jerónimo de, 120–121, 123, 158
Agustin I, Emperor, *see* Iturbide, Agustin de
Ahuízotl, 78–81, 83, 85, 108, 154
Alamán, Lucas, 306, 323–324, 354–355, 367, 370, 381, 393, 404, 411, 455, 581
Alamo, the, 383
Alarcón, 248, 261
Alatorre, 452
Aldama, Juan de, 315, 317, 321, 326, 328, 331–332
Alderete, 184
Alemán, Miguel, 600, 606, 608, 612–623
Alemán, administration ("Mauve Decade")
accomplishments, 619–620
agrarianism, 616–618
education, 618
foreign relations, 620–623
industrialization, 612–616, 619, 640
opposition to, 622–623
peasant population, 618–619
public works, 613, 619
Alfonso, X, 171
Alhóndiga de Granaditas, 323, 329, 332
Allende, Capitán Ignacio, 315–318, 321–324, 326–328, 330–332, 345
Almanza, Enríquez de, 251

Index   679

Index

683

), 56.